LA
DUCHESSE

LA
DUCHESSE

The Life of Marie de Vignerot

Cardinal Richelieu's Forgotten Heiress
Who Shaped the Fate of France

Bronwen McShea

PEGASUS BOOKS
NEW YORK LONDON

LA DUCHESSE

Pegasus Books, Ltd.
148 West 37th Street, 13th Floor
New York, NY 10018

First Pegasus Books cloth edition March 2023

Interior design by Maria Fernandez

Front cover image: Pierre Mignard, *Portrait of a Lady, Said to be the Duchess of Aiguillon*, latter half of the 17th century. Oil on canvas, 119.2 x 94.5 cm. Bequest of Grenville L. Winthrop, 1943.1349, Harvard Art Museums/Fogg Museum, Cambridge, Massachusetts, USA.

Library of Congress Cataloging-in-Publication Data is available.

ISBN: 978-1-63936-347-6

10 9 8 7 6 5 4 3 2 1

Printed in the United States of America
Distributed by Simon & Schuster
www.pegasusbooks.com

For Patricia Siedlecki Zinsser

Contents

Part Two—Pair de France

Prologue

B efore dawn on Wednesday, December 3, 1642, the most feared and hated man in France received Last Rites from a fellow priest of the Catholic Church. His Eminence Armand-Jean du Plessis, the Cardinal-Duc de Richelieu et Fronsac and the First Minister of State to King Louis XIII, had been bedridden since the weekend. Suffering a fever and sharp pains in his side, he struggled to breathe and periodically coughed up blood.

The King and many other dignitaries visited and prayed with the fifty-seven-year-old Cardinal-Minister at his deathbed. Among them was one of the only people alive who truly loved him, despite all he had made her endure, beginning with that marriage he had pushed her into when she was just a child . . .

Thirty-eight-year-old Marie-Madeleine de Vignerot du Pont Courlay, titled the Duchesse d'Aiguillon and a Peer of France since 1638, had learned of her uncle's worsening condition on Sunday. She had rushed across the Pont-Neuf in Paris from her stately home on the Rue de Vaugirard to stay with him at his colossal palace near the Louvre. Ever since, she had been storming Heaven with prayers, begging for the restoration of his health.

As Wednesday drew on, the Cardinal's decline appeared to reverse course. By dawn on Thursday, the word on the street was that the true ruler of France, the King's controlling *Éminence Rouge*, would live after all. But by late morning, it was clear to his intimates that his time was approaching.

Marie by this point was so distraught that Richelieu asked her to leave his bedchamber, the better for him to concentrate on his final spiritual exertions. Overcome by tears, she ran out of the room, never to see him alive again. But before this, the Cardinal had whispered secret instructions to her, kissed her hands, and told her that he loved her more than anyone else in the world.

Marie would go on to mourn Richelieu more intensely than she had her own father, a courtly military officer who had died eighteen years earlier. She also prayed more urgently for her uncle's soul, recruiting countless others to do the same in churches across France, Italy, and faraway mission lands. His Eminence had been far more powerful than her father. His sins were numerous and had affected the lives of so many. There were, for example, those ruthless banishments and executions of people whom Marie had first known as friends . . .

Signaling his complete confidence in Marie—and cutting out her brother François in the process—Richelieu made her the major heiress and administrator of his staggering fortune. While his male protégés such as Cardinal Jules Mazarin would succeed him in high office, Richelieu ignored ancient French norms by giving far more to his niece than to his nearest male relatives, all of whom because of their sex had had far more advantages than Marie from the moment of birth. These men included not just her brother, who was then serving as a royal governor in Normandy, but also her other ambitious uncle, Urbain de Maillé-Brézé, who was a highly decorated commander and diplomat.

Indeed, Richelieu entrusted Marie not just with one of the largest fortunes in Europe but also with titles, offices, vast lands and palaces envied by royalty, and patronage powers exercised by few men at the time, let alone other women. He knew that Marie would work better than anyone else to preserve and enhance his legacy in ways that would serve France, the Catholic religion, and the honor of the Richelieu name.

What Marie would do with the power put in her hands would shape the course of French history, the history of many other countries, and the history of the worldwide Catholic Church. It would also influence how Richelieu himself, and other prominent men of the age, would be remembered.

Yet *her* name and achievements are all but forgotten today. Perhaps because Marie was a woman, and a laywoman at that, too few noticed or cared as she was slowly written out of both European and Church history over time. This was in spite of the fact that in her own time, she was known, respected, and sometimes feared by monarchs, popes, scholars, and saints.

She also had famous enemies, including Medicis, Bourbons, Habsburgs, and members of her own powerful clan. During the height of the French civil war known as the Fronde, Cardinal Mazarin, her uncle's successor as prime minister, confided to his inner circle that Marie was his most dangerous and irreconcilable opponent in French politics. Some of the duchess's enemies so effectively dragged her name into the mud, exploiting the burgeoning popular press of the time, that no less a novelist than Alexandre Dumas, two centuries later, was able to plausibly caricature her as the slutty slave of Richelieu's every whim who hypocritically behaved in public like a nun.

Marie faced down her detractors with steadiness and grace. Literary lights of the age said of her that she possessed "the courage of a king" and that her eyes, although enchantingly beautiful, could "make even the most resolute eagles" lower theirs with their intensity. She was adept at courtly intrigue in an era when political missteps could be deadly, and more than once she proved herself capable of the sort of ruthlessness that made her uncle Richelieu legendary. But she often used her power for unexpected causes, for example to champion other women—poor and rich, living and already in history books—who were misunderstood, mistreated, and, above all, underestimated. All the while, she played critical roles in the social and intellectual life of Golden Age France and in the ongoing reform and expansion of the Church and disciplining of its clergy. Even more than this, she was an early prototype of the modern entrepreneur, philanthropist, and global businesswoman as she built up a veritable empire of religious and cultural institutions, business ventures, and social charities that stretched into Asia, Africa, and the Americas.

One of the most independent and energetic women of her age, Marie nevertheless lived a life that is incomprehensible apart from her uncle's. Much of her career can be seen as the natural fruit of her unusual relationship with one of history's most renowned and controversial clergymen. Her stage for action and her accomplishments owed much to the unconventional decisions that the great, political churchman, long regarded as a misogynist, made in her favor. Furthermore, Marie's life may be interpreted, in part, as an epic attempt to make reparations to God for countless offenses her uncle, with her assistance, had committed against his own countrymen and against an already disintegrating Christendom—the latter of which he had left war-torn, divided over faith, and dominated by new sorts of nationalistic rivalries.

But it is also true that Richelieu's story, although it has been told many times over the last four centuries, has never been complete while that of his beloved niece and heiress has been neglected.

Marie de Vignerot's story is that of a scared, sheltered girl who rose to the challenge—beyond even her uncle's expectations—of shouldering an unprecedented role that was thrust upon her amid dangerous and turbulent circumstances. It is one, too, of a woman whose ambitions changed over time as she became one of the most influential leaders of her age. Subject to all the temptations that come with great wealth and power, she held exceptionally true to her deepest convictions and her evolving sense of her unique purpose in the lives of her family, friends, and dependents, her Church that was expanding globally, and her country, which was wracked by a succession of crises at the very same time that it was emerging as Europe's cultural standard-bearer.

Tenacious and creative, fierce in her loves and loyalties, and as enigmatic and captivating as any of the well-remembered personalities of France's Golden Age, Vignerot is a figure without whom the times she lived through cannot be fully understood.

PART ONE

Princesse Nièce

1

A Long Journey

In mid-November 1620, a motherless, aristocratic French girl of sixteen found herself in a stately horse-drawn carriage, traveling to Paris from her family's estates in the Loire Valley. Taking several days, the trip was unpleasant at times due to the wet, cold weather of the season and the changing moods of the adults traveling with her.

This was a momentous journey. Not only was this girl about to see a city many times larger than any other she had known, but she was also to be presented at the great Palais du Louvre to young King Louis XIII and the rest of the royal family. She would then marry a twenty-three-year-old nobleman she barely knew and did not love. He had been chosen for her by one of her uncles in a high-level political negotiation.

As the carriage rolled along, jerking awkwardly at times, the girl had to wonder what this man would be like once they were alone. Would he be kind or ungenerous? Would they enjoy each other's company? She was increasingly praised as a beauty—especially for her bright brown eyes, her chestnut hair, and her exceptional singing voice. But her fiancé, whom she had met only briefly in summer, was used to elegant and experienced women. Did he think she was too tall? Not pretty enough? Laughably naïve?

She had reason not only to fear her wedding night but also to wonder whether it would be a kind of betrayal. Because she cared for someone else: a lovely boy of seventeen whom her uncle, just months before, had given false hope when he had asked to court her. [1]

Whatever feelings plagued this girl on that long road to Paris, there were happy things to think about, too. What an honor it would be to visit with the

King and his family! And marvelous sights, sounds, and tastes awaited her in the great capital—not just the Louvre but also beautiful Notre Dame Cathedral, countless shopkeepers hawking their wares, and of course scrumptious dishes and desserts like nothing she had known before.

Nothing would be the same after this trip. But this sensitive, sheltered girl could not have fathomed, then, that it was the relationship already developing between her and her *uncle* who had arranged the journey, not her impending marriage or encounters with the royal family, that would most imprint her life. This man would eventually give her, against the wishes of other men in their family, tremendous wealth and powers that she would exercise with exceptional strength and independence, putting her on a par with princes. At the same time, he would push her onto center stage in a drama he intended would climax with Catholic France—and with it one of their family names, *Richelieu*—standing supreme in Europe and, in that increasingly imperialistic age, across the world.

Young Marie could not even guess at any of that in late 1620. She had more than enough occupying her mind and heart then, especially trepidation as her marriage to a stranger loomed ever nearer with each passing hour.

2

Glénay

T hroughout a life that unfolded from 1604 to 1675, the girl we have just
met would go by many names. From her mid-thirties onward, she would
be greeted with low bows and curtsies as *Madame la Duchesse d'Aiguillon,
Comtesse d'Agenois et de Condomois*. She would also be saluted by soldiers as
La Gouvernante du Havre-de-Grâce, or the royal governor of a fortress city in
Normandy that was of strategic importance during the era of the Fronde civil
war and the drawn-out Franco-Spanish War. In that same period, statesmen
and churchmen who collaborated with her on projects in Europe and overseas
would refer to her simply as *La Duchesse*, knowing her identity was clear.

Before that, from the moment she was rushed into marriage at sixteen, she
would be known primarily as *Madame la Marquise de Combalet*. The name *Combalet* would stay with her for eighteen years, even though the marriage would
last only two.

In letters and contracts she usually signed off as *Marie de Vignerot*. Occasionally
she used the surname *Du Pont*. Marie was the first part of her given name, *Marie-
Madeleine*. *Vignerot* and *Du Pont* were surnames passed down from her father.

René de Vignerot du Pont Courlay was a nobleman who lived from 1561 to
1624. He possessed considerable land and properties in Poitou, one of the western
provinces of pre-revolutionary France. His Vignerot forebears had become established as a noble family in the mid-1400s at the end of the Hundred Years' War.
That was the same drawn-out conflict between French and English forces in
which the teenaged Saint Joan of Arc famously led troops into battle—spending
time in Poitou at one point—before being burned at the stake in 1431.[1]

It was a generation after Joan's time that René's half-English great-grandfather, Jean, became the first Vignerot to hold the ancient title of *Seigneur du Pont Courlay*. This gave him feudal lordship over a domain near the Sèvres Forest, which was about a day's journey to the Atlantic coast.

Until René's time, Marie's paternal ancestors lived modestly, even though as nobles they were elevated in rank above nearly 99 percent of French people. Preoccupied mostly with farming and village affairs, their way of life did not differ markedly from those of the wealthier peasants and townspeople in their midst who looked to them for leadership. Because of this, Marie throughout her life was subjected to snobbish gossip that her grandfather, François de Vignerot, was no nobleman at all, because he had dirtied his hands with husbandry, spending most of his life in rural obscurity. However, he had dutifully fulfilled the traditional function of the local nobility: military service to a higher-ranking feudal lord. Indeed, generations of Vignerot men had served similarly, as men-at-arms and archers.[2]

What set Marie's father apart from his forebears was that he was elevated as a young man to service at the royal court. Although he was a sword-bearing noble of the traditional sort, trained for hand-to-hand combat, the hunting of game, and sports such as jousting, he was also a new-styled gentleman of the King's chambers. This required refined manners and conversation and attentiveness to dress. The one surviving portrait of him, a statue for his tomb commissioned long after his death, depicts him with hair past his ears and a style of moustache and goatee that was fashionable at the turn of the seventeenth century.[3]

Royal service came with financial rewards and a range of responsibilities, including a willingness to go to war for the King or travel for other reasons at a moment's notice. René's increasing wealth and status, in short, joined him to an elite minority even among French nobles—courtly, rich aristocrats who were expected to possess several country estates and townhouses, move about continuously, and socialize with the leading families of the realm. Only one of every four hundred French persons belonged to this upper echelon of the nobility.[4]

René was known at court as the Baron du Pont Courlay. He developed a reputation as a good storyteller, singer, and lute player. He was also well-liked by King Henry IV, himself known for his humor, generosity, and philandering. It helped that René had been one of the King's first Catholic supporters: Henry was a Protestant when he acceded to the throne in 1589, and this caused serious conflict. Indeed, at twenty-eight, René fought bravely for Henry against the forces of the Catholic League, an alliance among Spain, the Papal States, and some French forces seeking Henry's removal and the eradication of Protestantism in France. At the Battle of Arques, René survived hand-to-hand combat after his horse was stabbed by multiple lances beneath him.[5] His mettle helped to secure Henry's forces the advantage as the devastating Wars of Religion that pitted French Christians against one another for more than a generation were drawing to a close.

It was at court that René met Marie's mother, Françoise du Plessis de Richelieu. The two married on August 23, 1603, in the presence of the King, who gave René as a wedding gift the lucrative position of captain of his royal guard. René was forty-two. Françoise was almost twenty years younger but had been married earlier to a nobleman named Jean de Beauveau de Pimpeau who had died within months of their wedding.[6] We know little about Françoise's appearance, but her funerary statue in Glénay, commissioned decades after her death, depicts her with a full face and a high-waisted, ample dress with fashionable puffed sleeves and a ruffed, gadrooned collar.[7]

Françoise was a native Parisian. She had grown up at the court of the previous king, Henry III, because her parents, Suzanne de La Porte and François III du Plessis de Richelieu, were prominent courtiers when she was born around 1578. Marriage to her thus confirmed René's climb into the upper ranks of the French nobility.

However, by the time René and Françoise married, the latter's family was no longer based at court but in the Loire Valley, its ancestral region. The newlyweds decided, therefore, to base their primary household close to there and also an easy distance to the *seigneurie* of Pont Courlay. They chose Glénay, a hamlet then part of a barony under the feudal protection of an independent-minded widow, Charlotte Brabantina of Nassau, an ancestor of Winston Churchill. With her approval, the couple purchased a château from a cash-strapped, older noble family of the region.[8]

Situated prettily along the Thouaret River, the stately Château de Glénay was a productive agricultural, aristocratic seat. It had foundations that dated from the early twelfth century but had been remodeled and expanded considerably since that time. It had strong defenses, high and thick walls, and large turrets with round, pointed roofs. On the sides that faced its farm fields, orchards, pasture lands, and a *vivier* (water reserve) that supplied fresh fish, it had deep ditches, a watchtower, and a number of outbuildings that served as fortifications—defenses that had been necessary during recent periods of warfare in the region. The oldest main building, with four stories of rooms for servants and family members, had Italian elements in its façade, with a Gothic-style chapel attached to it that was dedicated to Saint Margaret of Antioch, a virgin and martyr of the fourth century.[9] The château was separated from the hamlet of Glénay by a large park. All of this distinguished it from the kind of manor home typical of the middling and lower nobility in which René had grown up. With its multiple buildings, the château was large enough not only for a growing family and staff to live comfortably, but also to accommodate rounds of visitors, including hunting parties that would stay for days at a time.[10]

Marie, the couple's first child, was born in 1604. Her precise birth date is indeterminable from existing records. But sometime in July is a possibility, because she was christened *Marie-Madeleine*. The feast day of that sainted companion of Christ and the Twelve Apostles has long been celebrated on July 22 by Catholics.[11]

It is also probable that Marie was born in a bedchamber of the château in Glénay. Members of René's family had already been inhabiting this château, but not as its owners, for two generations.[12] And although René did not have legal claim on paper to all the lands traditionally attached to the *seigneurie* of Glénay until the spring of 1607, he had been purchasing the land rights piecemeal before that and was receiving homage as the local lord within a few months of Marie's birth.[13]

Local tradition has it that Marie was baptized down the road at Glénay's parish church of Saint-Martin, a stout, Romanesque structure that still stands and dates to the eleventh century. This event would have drawn in villagers who paid respects to the leading family of the district and offered prayers as a priest proceeded with the rite. It is also traditionally believed that the honor of sacramentally incorporating the infant into the body of the Catholic faithful fell to a great-uncle on her father's side who was curate of the parish.[14]

Happy as the occasion was, the birth and baptism five years later of Marie's brother, François, were treated with much more fanfare. As René's firstborn son, François was privileged under French law as the primary heir to the family's lands, wealth, and titles. His safe delivery was all the more joyous as his parents had suffered the death of a second daughter when Marie was a toddler.[15]

Little François's baptism was celebrated with several days of feasting. Representatives of Poitou's great families traveled in to Glénay, and members of

Françoise's courtly family were present, too. Among the latter was Françoise's younger brother, Armand-Jean du Plessis de Richelieu, the twenty-four-year-old Bishop of Luçon and the future Cardinal-Duc de Richelieu et Fronsac.[16] This young churchman performed the baptismal rite for his new nephew. Intoned in Latin, it included an exorcism of the infant—*Exorcizo te, omnis spiritus immunde . . . in nomine Iesu Christi . . . Domini et Iudicis nostri* ("I exorcise thee, every unclean spirit . . . in the name of Jesus Christ . . . our Lord and Judge")—as well as the pouring of water over the baby's head at the church's stone font. *Ego te baptizo in nomine Patris, et Filii, et Spiritus Sancti . . .*

It is easy to imagine five-year-old Marie, barely visible among the billowing skirts of the women of her family, looking on as her tiny brother was anointed and blessed by this uncle. The young bishop's thick embroidered vestments would have glistened with candlelight with each choreographed movement of the ancient rite.

Little Marie was taught at moments like this that while some men like her father were soldiers, servants of the King, and husbands with children, others were priests who served God in special ways, such as performing the sacred rites of the Church. Indeed, by this point, three of Marie's closest relatives were clergymen: her father's uncle in Glénay, her young uncle Armand, and another of her mother's brothers, Alphonse-Louis, who lived far away in the mountains. In 1606, Uncle Alphonse had abandoned worldly society and his family's plan for *him* to become a bishop to instead join the Carthusians, an order of monks who wore white robes and spent all their time praying and studying in silence. Uncle Armand, in fact, had been training for life as a soldier and courtier in Paris when he received the unsettling news about this. Since his older brother had departed for the solitude of the Grande Chartreuse monastery in the Alps, Armand would have to lay down his sword and any hopes for marriage, enter the priesthood, and himself become the Bishop of Luçon—an ecclesiastical position gifted to his family by the Crown.

By the time Marie saw Uncle Armand baptize her brother, the clergyman, despite his youth, had already lived through a great deal. His father, the Seigneur de Richelieu, had died years before in 1590, leaving his wife and five children in debt and disarray—an embarrassment that later fueled his youngest son's insatiable ambition. As a child, both before and after his father's death, Armand moved back and forth several times from Paris to the Richelieu family seat in the Loire Valley. The future cardinal-statesman also suffered migraines and severe melancholy as a boy. While still quite young, he was sent from home to be educated by Benedictine monks at the Abbey of Saint-Florent de Saumur, but by the age of ten he was attending a secondary school in Paris where he was expected to speak Latin every day. At sixteen he moved up to a finishing school for young noblemen who were marked out for courtly and military careers. There he learned fencing, horsemanship, courtly manners, and music, as well as mathematical and engineering knowledge for service as a military officer. He was preoccupied with such training until he was twenty-one.

Armand in this period is believed also to have learned sexual arts from at least two Parisian women. However, when his family asked him to change career tracks in 1606, he was required to embrace celibacy as part of the deal. Without much complaint, he abandoned the glittery side of the Parisian world he was getting to know to prepare for holy orders. He quickly excelled in philosophy and theology courses at the University of Paris. His ordination to the priesthood then took place in Rome on April 16, 1607, because a dispensation from the Pope was needed to ordain someone younger than twenty-five. During the same visit, he was consecrated as the Bishop of Luçon by Pope Paul V, who was impressed with his bearing and intelligence.[17]

A year and half later, Armand was installed as bishop in the cathedral church at Luçon, a city near the Bay of Biscay about half a day's journey to Glénay. Young as he was, he proved himself capable in high ecclesiastical office. He oversaw a large diocese that had been ravaged by the recent Wars of Religion. Negotiating with resistant local clergy and lay elites, he took initiative—as few French churchmen then were willing to do—to institute reforms that had been ordered by the Pope more than forty years earlier at the Council of Trent.

These reforms included the moral disciplining of the clergy and their improved, more formalized education.[18] For many generations it had been common in Catholic Europe for priests to be living with concubines or violating their vows in other ways and to be seen drinking, gambling, and generally living like laymen except when saying Mass or performing other priestly functions such as baptisms. This became increasingly unacceptable after Trent, but the French bishops—despite seeing droves of their countrymen defect to Protestantism—had resisted the Council's reforms into the seventeenth century. The establishment of seminaries for training future priests was also not the norm in Christendom until leading churchmen began promoting the idea at the time of Trent. The young and untested Bishop of Luçon variously surprised, impressed, and angered his fellow French clergymen when he began to locally enforce the Council's program with a firm hand.

Early in life, Marie interacted infrequently with this strong-willed uncle and churchman who would later become a father figure and mentor to her. Although Uncle Armand occasionally visited Glénay, he was a distant figure to Marie as she spent her childhood in relative seclusion with her mother, little brother, and a governess who minded the children while Françoise managed her large household and staff.[19]

Marie's mother preferred country life to the busyness of Paris. While rearing her children, she rarely joined René at court or when he was away on other business. This put her frequently in the position of standing in for René in village affairs—for example helping to mediate local disputes and performing ceremonial duties during festivals. Françoise also shared with René the management of their increasingly complex family finances.[20] Marie thus saw her father intermittently while having always before her, as her first model of womanhood, a mother independently busy with many things.[21]

At a time when formal schooling for most boys, let alone for any girls, was still not the norm in Europe, Marie's education was a priority for her parents. Marie spent many days learning to read and write as well as the principles and practices of the Catholic faith. She also learned needlework and other domestic arts. Furthermore, taking after her father, she demonstrated a talent for singing, which was nurtured from a young age.

Many days, however, Marie and her brother were free to play out of doors on the extensive grounds of their château, which included barns, stables, a bakery with great stone ovens that could service as many as two hundred people, and other outbuildings. Their *pigeonnier*, shaped like a silo, was one of the largest in the kingdom and was full of birds, raised for their eggs and eventually to be eaten themselves, that offered the children hours of entertainment. The family castle overlooked a bend of the Thouaret River and a small valley that changed colors during the year along with its seasonal flowers and foliage. The children therefore learned from men and women in service to their parents the names of many kinds of fish, birds, game, and other living things that filled this scene. The animals they saw—trout, wild boar, chickens—not rarely ended up on their table inside the château.

The children were taught furthermore that invisible beings were present among them—God the Father, Son, and Holy Spirit; the Blessed Virgin and other saints; angels and demons; even the souls of the dead who had lived in Poitou before them—looking on close by in Heaven, Hell, and Purgatory. These realms were mysteriously interconnected with everything that could be seen, heard, touched, smelled, and tasted. They were told stories, for example, about Glénay's fourth-century patron saint, Martin of Tours, who had helped convert their once-pagan region to Christianity, and about the virgin-martyr Margaret, to whom the family chapel was dedicated. More than this, they were urged to ask these saints for favors, by lighting candles and quietly talking to them in the family chapel or in the nearby parish church.[22]

Late in 1615, Marie found herself in dire need of help from Saints Martin and Margaret and from other holy beings to whom she was taught to pray. Her mother had fallen ill, and it was unclear whether she would survive the calendar year.

3

Richelieu

F rançoise's death at only thirty-seven shattered the idyllic world that her children were getting to know in their family's corner of rural Poitou.[1] Devastated by this sudden loss, eleven-year-old Marie and her six-year-old brother spent little time in its aftermath grieving alongside their father. René was busy, as usual, before and after his wife's decline. He was overseeing his domains at Pont Courlay and serving in a new royal assignment: monitoring Protestant activities in Poitou for the widow of King Henry IV, the Queen Regent Marie de' Medici. After burying Françoise, the baron removed his children from Glénay and put them in the care of his mother-in-law, Suzanne de La Porte, who was keenly mourning the loss of her beloved eldest child.[2]

Marie's grandmother was a formidable woman in her mid-fifties who, following a fashion from the late sixteenth century, at times donned a wide, stiff, and round lace collar atop her black, farthingaled widow's gowns. She lived a day's journey east of Glénay at Richelieu in the Loire Valley. Richelieu was a modest aristocratic seat not unlike Glénay, set in a quiet, unexceptionally beautiful landscape with farm fields, forests, small hills and valleys, and a river running past it called the Mable.[3]

The Richelieu château that became Marie's new home was a modest hunting lodge compared to the magnificent palace that the future Cardinal Richelieu would transform it into years later. And for some time it had been dominated by strong women, Suzanne foremost among them. Marie's grandfather, François III du Plessis de Richelieu, had been a respected figure at the royal court, serving the Crown capably as a military leader and negotiator during the Wars of Religion. But after dying prematurely in 1590, he had bequeathed to Suzanne and their children substantial debts, not just lands and titles, having lost money in risky commercial ventures and having borrowed and lent too much during his years at court. Suzanne, while in the thick of raising a brood of children aged three to twelve at the time, had been burdened with picking up the pieces of his remaining legacy and setting her children upon steadier paths.[4]

Ironically, much of the squandered wealth had come into Suzanne's marriage as part of her dowry. She was the daughter of a wealthy lawyer and member of the Parlement de Paris, which was the chief judicial court in France, and she also descended from successful businessmen of non-noble status. Although she had served as a lady-in-waiting at court due to her husband's position, she was blessed with a bourgeois capacity to prioritize thrift over aristocratic pride. This led her at the time of her husband's death to sell the family's townhouse in Paris so she could save the family's estates in Richelieu. She was aided by several other independent-minded women. These included her iron-willed mother-in-law, the widowed Françoise de Rochechouart, as well as a widowed sister-in-law, Françoise de Marçonnay.[5]

By the time Marie and her brother were in Suzanne's care, the women of the stabilized Richelieu household included an unmarried, high-strung aunt in her late twenties named Nicole. From the age of eleven to thirteen, Marie was party first to Nicole's dramatic expressions of anxiety that she would die a spinster and then to a remarkable turn of events. In November 1617, Nicole contracted a brilliant marriage with the young, talented Urbain de Maillé, the Marquis de Brézé. This man outshone his grateful bride, as he was only nineteen at the time and dashingly handsome.

Maillé-Brézé, as he was known for short, had already been acquainted with Nicole's brother Armand, the Bishop of Luçon, who by this point was already making a name for himself in the kingdom's halls of power. Raising eyebrows among peers who thought little at the time of such a match, Maillé-Brézé perspicaciously suspected that an alliance with the Richelieu family would accelerate his own rise to power. Indeed, due to the influence of his brother-in-law, he would later serve as an ambassador to Sweden and as a military commander.

Although Marie was only thirteen at the time, it was she, not Nicole, whom Maillé-Brézé first was after. But the family—especially Armand, who enticed him with cash—put the older spinster in his path. Not unrelated to this, Maillé-Brézé in later years would become an enemy to Marie, embittered over what she, rather than his children by Nicole, would inherit from Cardinal Richelieu.[6]

But none of this was foreseen when the family celebrated Nicole's marriage. And Marie's attentions then, when not engaged with great events such as weddings, deaths, and visits by important relatives, were still focused on her education.

Nurtured especially in this regard by the women at Richelieu while her father largely remained absent from her life, Marie continued with the exceptional education that she had begun in Glénay. Unusually for the time given prejudices about women and book learning, Marie's education was taken almost as seriously as her brother's, partly because she showed considerable intellectual promise.[7]

Marie exhibited talents especially for music and foreign languages. She learned to sing beautifully in Italian and Spanish as well as in French and in the ecclesiastical Latin that reigned supreme in Catholic hymnody in that era. She may also have received lessons in literature during visits by the Prior of Saint-Florent de Saumur—the Benedictine monastery where her uncle Armand had once been a student.[8] At a time when the great majority of French people—including the majority of men—could barely sign their names, these beginnings grounded what would grow into Marie's lifelong passions for reading, poetry, drama, and patronizing authors and artists.[9]

At the Richelieu château, Marie and François were educated in another way: about French politics and the great families of the kingdom, especially through stories about their own relatives. Stories about their deceased grandfather reinforced pride in their noble lineage, which stretched back to the tenth century, as well as the principle of loyal service to the Crown. When the Protestant Henry IV had acceded to the throne, Marie's maternal grandfather, like her father René, had been among his first Catholic supporters while other nobles joined in with the militant Catholic League against him. Marie was urged to revere this grandfather, despite his financial failings, as a great man who had sacrificed himself honorably for the King, insofar as he had perished—albeit from a fever—amidst a failed siege of Paris in 1590, when the royal forces were attempting to retake the capital from the Catholic militants who had held it for a time.[10]

Another figure Marie grew up respecting was her uncle Henry, who was the Marquis de Richelieu and Armand's eldest brother. Against his mother's wishes, he had decided in 1598, at nineteen, to renounce his inheritance. He had also received permission from the King to act in his own name—even though the age of majority in France was twenty-five—as he began to recover his family's honor, wealth, and estates in his own way. The King then appointed him to a lucrative court position and commissioned him as a military officer. Henry soon was able to buy back lands and properties that his mother had sold or relinquished to creditors since the time of his father's death.[11]

Indeed, Henry, with Armand's support, began to act coldly as a creditor to his deceased father's estate. By the time Marie was living with his mother, he had succeeded in buying back, bit by bit, considerable tracts of his family's lost or endangered domains. The major exception was Richelieu itself, which remained in Suzanne's hands and eventually passed to Armand. In addition, he was able to add new territories to his estates, in part by marrying a wealthy widow, Marguerite Guyot, who came with a handsome dowry.[12]

Unsurprisingly, Henry's mode of recovering status and stability for his family did not endear him to all who shared his surnames. Suzanne, in particular, was humiliated when he pressured her to hand over lands and possessions that she was at risk of losing to other creditors. In short, in the period when Marie and her brother lived with their maternal relatives at Richelieu, emotions often ran high over financial matters and disagreements about them.

At the same time, as a bright and perceptive girl, Marie quietly absorbed lessons from her uncles Henry and Armand about economy, enterprise, and independent judgment. These were not lessons that most young French noblewomen were learning from a culture in which ancient traditions, aristocratic pride, and pressures from political events and powerful patrons freighted decision-making at every turn.

4

Uncle Armand's Fortunes

Although they did not realize it at the time, the most significant events for all of Marie's family members in the 1610s occurred in Paris, almost two hundred miles northeast of Richelieu. There, young Armand began laying the foundations for a stunning rise to power—something that in time would alter European and world history.

During the period when Armand, as the Bishop of Luçon, was reforming his diocese, France suffered a trauma that almost plunged it into renewed civil war. On May 14, 1610, Henry IV was stabbed to death by the Catholic militant François Ravaillac. As Henry had been the first member of the Bourbon family to sit on the throne, the succession of his eight-year-old son Louis XIII was more fraught with danger than a royal minority would normally be. The boy's half-Italian mother, Marie de' Medici, was a German Habsburg on her maternal side and leaned politically toward the militant, international Catholic cause that was bound up then with support of Habsburg Spain and the Holy Roman Empire. Many French nobles who commanded armies thus opposed her assertion of regency powers on behalf of her son after her husband's assassination.

The rebels were led by the King's cousin, Henry II de Bourbon, the Prince de Condé, who was second in line to the throne. Although Condé failed to take control of the royal council, he continued to stir up unrest. Widespread opposition to the regency, coupled with financial dilemmas facing the Crown and ongoing hostilities between Protestants and Catholics in the kingdom, led the Queen Regent to call together an Estates General. [1]

The Estates General was an exceptional gathering in Paris of representatives of the kingdom's "three estates," or major social-political groupings: the privileged First and Second Estates, or the clergy and the nobility respectively, and the heavily taxed Third Estate, or the common people. The last time an Estates General had been convened was in 1588, amid the Wars of Religion. The Queen hoped that her legitimacy would be confirmed if she provided an opportunity for leaders of the three estates to petition the government and iron out various differences. At the same time, this unscrupulous daughter of the despotic Grand Duke Francesco I de' Medici mounted a campaign of bribery, printed propaganda, and visits with her son to different parts of the kingdom to ensure that representatives of the three estates who were friendlier to Condé were chosen to travel to Paris that fall.

This great political gathering convened on October 1, 1614, and proved to be Armand's chance for new, national recognition. His growing reputation for effective Church reform had led to his election by the clergy of Poitou as one of their representatives. Once in Paris, the young bishop enjoyed the patronage of a senior churchman, Cardinal de Sourdis of Bordeaux, and he impressed other First Estate representatives with his charisma, deft negotiations on their behalf, and refusal to side with any one faction among them.[2]

Still only twenty-nine, the future Cardinal Richelieu had a gravitas that men twice his age found magnetic. He was also tactful and charming in situations that tested others' good graces. This helps to explain why, like a meteor rising, he was selected by all the First Estate representatives to give an extended address on their behalf to the King, Queen Regent, and everyone else gathered for the Estates General. Determined not to squander the opportunity, he put a great deal of effort into a speech he delivered at the closing session of February 23, 1615. The setting was the great hall of the Petit-Bourbon, one of the royal family's grand homes in Paris.

The Bishop of Luçon made a powerful impression with his speech. In it, he defended the rights and liberties of the clergy in France, especially those of reform-minded bishops who faced conservative opposition from local elites while trying to implement the decrees of Trent. He also appealed to the early centuries of French history, when monarchs such as Charlemagne consulted prelates on matters of state, including about when to go to war. And he argued, with his own future in mind, that the monarch of his own time should appoint churchmen to the royal council who possessed virtues such as probity and prudence that were developed in ecclesiastical office and who displayed a firm commitment to both God and the well-being of France.[3]

The silver-tongued clergyman also appealed to the Queen Regent in his speech. She was already impressed by him at this point, as he had found other ways to get into her good graces while the Estates General was underway. But his performance at the Petit-Bourbon confirmed his reputation to her and her chief advisor, Concino Concini, the Marquis d'Ancre—a Florentine who commanded his own army and a thick network of agents, including spies—as someone who should be given an important political position.[4]

Partly to shore up this success and to drum up public interest in his career, Armand arranged to have his remarks published by an up-and-coming printer in Paris, Sébastien Cramoisy, whose family were clients of his own and whose star in time would rise dramatically with the young churchman's. (Cramoisy would one day run one of the most internationally recognized publishing firms in Europe.) Not long after this, Marie de' Medici appointed Armand as chaplain for her young daughter-in-law, Anne of Austria, who had recently married Louis XIII when they were both only fourteen. Then, in November 1616, she appointed him to the royal council as a secretary of state with a focus on foreign affairs. In this position, Armand adopted the pro-Habsburg position of his patroness, which put him in an awkward position given how divided the leading men of France were over international alliances. However, his opinions began to shift as he watched a small war play out in Europe, the Uskok War, which resulted in territorial gains by the Holy Roman Empire. He began to wonder whether France should begin intervening in such conflicts in the future—even at the risk of allying with Protestant states against Catholic ones—to contain the power of the Habsburgs, who already controlled much of Europe and a growing world empire.

In the meantime, a dramatic change of fortune came for the Queen Regent's councilors on April 24, 1617. That day, the now fifteen-year-old King Louis, acting under the influence of a favored advisor, Charles d'Albert, the Duc de Luynes, had Concini murdered. Additionally, he had Concini's wife, Leonora Galigaï, who was also close to the King's mother, arrested and burned at the stake after being convicted of witchcraft and "Judaizing" those under her spell.[5]

Luynes had achieved a palace coup. This nobleman, who had formerly served Henry IV as a falconer, had encouraged young Louis to assert independence from his mother and, once Concini was removed from the scene, to appoint him as First Minister, the highest position in the royal council.

The violence of April 24 almost engulfed Armand. After Concini was shot in the head by a Luynes loyalist on a bridge near the Louvre, his corpse was mutilated by a mob that had been stirred up by propagandists working for Luynes. Louis, once he received confirmation of the assassination, shouted from a window at the Louvre to a swelling crowd, "Thank you! I really am King now!" Soon after, Marie de' Medici was forced to remove herself and her favorites to the city of Blois so the royal council could be remade in Luynes's image. Amid the spreading chaos, the Bishop of Luçon was stopped in his carriage by another crowd of inflamed Parisians. Had things gone differently in the moment, he, too, might have been killed in cold blood and his body dragged through the streets.[6]

As it happened, he only lost his seat on the royal council and was ordered by the teenaged king to retire to his faraway diocese. Throwing himself back into ecclesiastical duties and a theological writing project he had in mind, the young bishop thought it would be possible to lie low while charting a path back to court. He thus spent almost a year splitting time between Luçon and a manor he owned in Poitou. He also was sure to visit with his niece Marie and other family members at Richelieu, who by this point were mourning with him the loss of their matriarch, Suzanne.

Marie had lost her grandmother and guardian in December 1616, less than two years after her mother had died. A solemn funeral had been held at Richelieu, and Suzanne's body was entombed in the family's chapel there.[7] Although Marie saw her uncle Armand only occasionally in this period, the two bonded in their mutual grief. As a sensitive girl, thirteen-year-old Marie may have absorbed some of the acute melancholy the bishop is known to have suffered over his mother's death in the months before Luynes's coup and while he was away from court beginning in the summer of 1617.[8]

Even short visits with this simultaneously depressive and charming uncle made deep impressions on Marie at this stage of her life. Uncle Armand was not only a bishop of the Church in an era when bishops outranked most members of the nobility. He also had exceptional presence and charisma for a man in his early thirties. He commanded the attention—if not always the fond feelings—of the other adults in Marie's life with his strange mix of humor, intellectual force, and vacillations between intense anger, sorrow, and chilly detachment. He was tall and thin, with dark eyes, dark hair, and high cheekbones. He had stories for Marie about her deceased mother and grandmother, both of whom he loved and mourned with feeling. At the same time, the young churchman was drawn to his niece, because she reminded him of his beloved older sister. He did not express affection readily, even to close family members. But he found it easy to do so to this sweet, bright girl.[9]

Marie noticed in this period that her father was showing more interest in Uncle Armand's affairs. It came as a special shock in April 1618 when René and Uncle Henry were ordered by the King to follow Armand into exile—in Avignon, a territory owned by the Pope that was faraway to the southeast, near the Mediterranean Sea. This harsh directive from Louis XIII was the doing of Luynes, who did not want either of the ambitious Richelieu brothers or their brother-in-law anywhere near the royal family as he replaced men loyal to his mother with his own friends and clients.

From Avignon, Armand, Henry, and René rented a house and plotted a return to the French court. Demonstrating his seriousness about Church reform, but also to distract himself during bouts of melancholy, Armand also labored intensively over a Catholic catechism to ground and fortify the faith of the clergy of Luçon. It would be published in 1621 under the title *Instruction du Chrestien* and reissued in various editions thereafter.

Henry's exile in Avignon, meanwhile, was marked by tragedy. In the autumn he learned that his young wife, Marguerite, had died while giving birth to a son and would-be heir to the recuperated Richelieu legacy. Devastated and unable to be present for the burials, he fell into hopelessness. He expressed this by drawing up a will stipulating that most of his fortune and properties, upon his death, would go to several religious orders. This was a strange thing to do, as he was young and easily could have remarried. This will, had it gone into effect, would have deprived his natural heirs—who included Armand, his sister Nicole, and Marie and François—of any expected inheritance in the event he died without issue.[10]

It is unknown how René spent his time in Avignon. Any correspondence he may have had with his children at the time has not survived. Regardless, Marie and François were used to their father's absence. At the time of their grandmother's death, their care had been entrusted to their aunt Nicole before she left for Paris with Maillé-Brézé. Although François around this time left for boarding school, Marie remained at Richelieu with Henry's young wife. Thus at fourteen she was at hand when Marguerite and her infant died. A bittersweet reunion with her father and Uncle Henry then occurred at Christmastime, when the two men were called out of exile without Uncle Armand.[11]

For good reason, the ambitious bishop was deemed more of a threat to the status quo at court, and so he remained in Avignon a bit longer by himself.

However, his moment came early in 1619 when the King suddenly faced a contingent of rebellious princes who had rallied this time around his mother, attempting to give her back control of the royal administration. The kingdom was now beset by a small civil war between the opposing armies of mother and son. As the conflict drew on, young Louis called the Bishop of Luçon back to court and appointed him again to his mother's household, hoping he would serve as a mediating figure. Indeed, by April 30, the future Cardinal Richelieu had deftly engineered the Treaty of Angoulême, which formalized a reconciliation between the King and Marie de' Medici, who was now called the Queen Mother.

This restoration of the young churchman's position of influence at court led to events that dramatically changed the lives of his relatives—especially Marie, who, at fifteen, was now unquestionably on the aristocratic marriage market.

5

A Political Marriage

O nce he was back at court, Armand was determined that his whole family would rise to power along with him. Most notably, he secured his brother Henry's appointment as the governor of the western city of Angers. However, this provoked resentment in the family of another nobleman who had been under consideration for the post. Charles de Lauzières, the brother of the bypassed candidate, drew his sword against Henry during a casual meeting on a street in Paris. Marie's uncle Henry died on July 8.[1]

Armand was suddenly the head of his family, even though he was a celibate bishop. It was thus only at this point that he began to be called *Richelieu*, as he inherited his brother's titles and estates. But he did not rejoice over this. Henry's death hit him terribly. In his *Mémoires*, he later wrote, "I cannot represent the state this event threw me in, and the extreme sorrow it caused. . . . My quill won't describe it." He threw himself into his work for the Queen Mother partly to save himself from a permanent downward spiral.[2]

Henry's death also signaled, alarmingly, that the noble, male Richelieu line—which extended back six centuries—was now extinguished. The only way to recover it would be for either Armand or his Carthusian brother, Alphonse, to sire a son, either illegitimately while still in holy orders or legitimately after leaving the ecclesiastical state.

Neither clergyman was willing to take either step. Instead, Richelieu looked to his dead sister's children as the next-best hope for their family. Young François could one day inherit the Richelieu title and legacy. And Marie could play an important role by marrying well and producing additional heirs as security.

This is why suddenly, in 1620, Richelieu's machinations included close involvement in Marie's life.

According to well-established customs among European nobles at the time, Marie was marked out for an early marriage, preferably in her teens, to a man from a wealthy family with courtly ties. This was a destiny she had been raised to desire and dutifully accept. Although she might hope to fall in love with a suitable match, emotional preferences were beside the point. Marie's charge was to devote herself to a man approved by her family—a family that at this point no longer included the mother, grandmother, aunt, infant cousin, or uncle she had come to love and had seen buried in quick succession from the time she was eleven.

Thus Marie found herself in the autumn of 1620 ordered to travel to Paris to marry a nobleman military officer she hardly knew. His name was Antoine de Grimoard de Beauvoir du Roure, and he was titled the Marquis de Combalet. He was twenty, and he had been chosen for Marie by her uncle Armand.

Coincidentally, this young marquis had been ordered to marry Marie by his own powerful uncle: the same Duc de Luynes who had recently orchestrated the murder of one of the Queen Mother's councilors and been an enemy to Richelieu. Antoine was dependent upon Luynes's good graces for his career, as his own father had left him with little but their ancient lineage and a title that referred to a strip of useless, rocky terrain in the Ardèche region of France. It was Antoine's relationship to Luynes and other courtly connections on his mother's side that made him a valuable piece in the rival uncles' real-life chess game.[3]

In the summer of 1620, another small war had broken out between the King and his mother. Richelieu had sided with the latter without the eighteen-year-old Louis's knowledge. Men serving both royal personages met one another in battle on August 7 at Les Ponts-de-Cé near Angers, not far from the Château de Richelieu, where Marie was still living. The Queen Mother's forces were defeated, but in the negotiations that unfolded thereafter, Richelieu helped again to bring about a reconciliation, much to his own advantage. Louis and Luynes made concessions, including on a point upon which Marie de' Medici insisted: Richelieu would be made a cardinal of the Church. This would give him princely status at court.

As a sign of his trustworthiness, Richelieu agreed that Luynes's nephew could marry his niece Marie. The Queen Mother and the King approved of the match as a fine symbol of their reconciliation.[4]

Richelieu later wrote only one cold line about the marriage in his *Mémoires*: "It was hoped that the bond between these two people would create more trust between the uncles."[5] Privately, Richelieu was, in his way, demonstrating confidence in his niece, of whom he was fond. He was, after all, plucking her up from the simple, rural life she had known and placing her close to Luynes, of whom he remained distrustful, to serve as an agent of her family's interests. At the same time, the numbness of heart required of Richelieu to throw innocent Marie into the wolves' lair that was the court of France was underlined by the additional fact that, at this point, he knew full well that she already cared for someone else.

Earlier in the year, Marie had befriended and become smitten with a young nobleman—a boy, rather, as he was just a year older than she was. His name was Hippolyte de Béthune and he was the son of the French ambassador to the Papal States and the nephew of the celebrated chief minister to Henry IV known as Sully. Hippolyte had been born in Rome, where Pope Clement VIII had stood up as his godfather. He had spent part of his childhood in Italy, as well as in Paris and at various estates of his father's, including Selles-sur-Cher in the Loire Valley, not far from the Richelieu château.

Marie had met Hippolyte in Angers at the time the young man was introduced to Richelieu while the Queen Mother's court was temporarily based in that city. The young people were quickly taken with each other. Hippolyte was given reason to hope that René de Vignerot might approve of him as a potential son-in-law. Richelieu expressed his own positive view of the idea to Hippolyte's father, Philippe, while indicating that René, of course, would have the last say about Marie's future.[6]

In the end, political exigencies and Richelieu's changing views on the matter outweighed other considerations. Within months, the match with Antoine was arranged, and there was no question it would help Richelieu more readily than a match with Hippolyte in the chess game he was playing at court. The Béthunes were already loyal to the Queen Mother and needed no extra incentive, such as the dowry and connections of the daughter of the Baron du Pont Courlay, to serve her interests. Furthermore, Philippe was healthy and not about to leave titles and properties to Hippolyte any time soon.

René agreed that an alliance with Luynes's family would come with immediate rewards and should therefore be pursued. Soon after the Treaty of Les Ponts-de-Cé was signed, Marie learned from the men who controlled her destiny that she would be marrying a stranger before the year was out.

It was determined that the marriage would take place in the presence of the royal family in late November. Marie and Antoine became minimally acquainted at Angers in late summer before the court relocated back to Paris.[7] Marie thus had three months to say goodbye to her quiet life and her girlhood in the Loire Valley and to prepare for her long, fateful journey to the ancient capital of France. There, she would spend a few days with her father, uncle, brother, and other relatives before the wedding festivities at the Louvre.

6

Paris

The sight of Paris in mid-November 1620 would have overwhelmed Marie as her carriage approached the city from the southwest and rolled through one of its medieval stone gateways. So many church spires, monastic buildings, shops, marketplaces, and palatial and humble dwellings alike were clustered together and stretched as far as the eye could see. The streets teemed with people, some of them shouting in accents and languages Marie had never heard, and on a scale unlike anything she had known. Indeed, Paris at this time was inhabited by nearly 400,000 people, many of them from all over France and countries across Europe. Marie also would have seen more foreign-looking people than ever before out the carriage windows—merchants and other migrants from places beyond the Mediterranean. The contrast with a provincial capital such as Angers, which then had a population of about 30,000, was dramatic.

There were new smells, too. The mud of Paris was already legendary by that time because of the magnitude of human and animal waste that piled up and drained through a city initially built up during ancient Roman times. But the food of Paris was also already famous by the early seventeenth century, so there were wonderful aromas, too. The smells of breads, sweet and savory pies, sausages, and meats roasting over open fires and glazed in ways unfamiliar to provincial visitors wafted from shops with open doors and from some of the first restaurants in Europe, the family-style *tables d'hôte* that were becoming commonplace in the French capital at that time.[1]

Marie spent a little over a week in this city full of wonders before her wedding day. And among the wonders was Uncle Armand's new home, a townhouse that was located in the Place Royale (today called the Place des Vosges), which was an urban renewal project of the previous king. This square had recently become the social center of the already fashionable Marais district of Paris that was home to many of the highest-ranking nobles. It consisted, as can be seen today, of many townhouses with identical façades of stone and red brick, designed in a new but understated, Baroque-era mode different from the generally traditional styles Marie knew in the Loire Valley and Poitou.[2]

The marriage was celebrated at the Louvre on November 26, 1620. The Louvre then was smaller than it is today, but it had already transformed considerably under Henry IV and the previous Queen Mother, Catherine de' Medici, into something close to the Italian-palazzo-style building of the present from its beginnings as a medieval fortress and Gothic-style royal residence. Its Grande Galerie stretched imposingly along the Seine River on the southern side of its grounds and made the Louvre, by far, the largest building in Paris. The Grande Galerie also connected the Louvre to the Tuileries, a beautiful palace that centuries later would be destroyed by Communist arsonists.

Her own wedding festivities were grander than anything Marie had yet experienced. First, she was presented to the young King, his wife Anne of Austria, and the Queen Mother. Princes and princesses of the realm, other high-ranking courtiers, and members of the adjoining families then witnessed the signing of the marriage contract. The array of witness signatures on the contract, which is today preserved in the Archives Nationales de France, includes, alongside illustrious others, those of her father, brother, uncle Armand, aunt Nicole, and uncle Maillé-Brézé, the latter of whom was now the captain of the Queen Mother's guards, thanks to Richelieu's influence.[3]

Marie was dressed richly and adorned with jewels gifted from both queens. Her dress would have been in the latest silhouette favored at the French court—low-necked, high-waisted, with ballooning mutton sleeves and a wide skirt that was open in the front, revealing a rich underskirt beneath it. In a pale shade if not in white, the garment would likely have been embroidered with expensive metallic threads, made of the richest, shimmering silk satins, and embellished generously with the finest lace and ribbons, pearls, or gems. Antoine would have been as richly attired—in some ways outdoing his bride in splendor—with a brocade doublet, debonair cape draped behind one shoulder, and britches reaching to the top of his heeled and spurred boots. He also would have donned a finely crafted sword: the mark of his noble status. Both young people would have had artificially curled hair that framed their faces on either side. Antoine's would have appeared longer than Marie's, as part of hers would likely have been braided and wound into a chignon.[4]

The nuptial Mass took place in the younger queen's chapel. The priest who blessed the union was François de La Rochefoucauld, a cardinal and leading reformer of the Church in France who would soon be appointed as the president of the young King Louis's council. Marie vowed before this bearded, old churchman in red robes to love, honor, and obey Antoine until death. A wedding ball then took place in the Grande Galerie, with Marie and Antoine under scrutiny by the experienced courtiers as they danced in some of the complex, late-Renaissance group dances of the period.[5]

Toward the end of the evening, the newlyweds were ushered into a palace bedchamber that had been specially prepared for them.

Marie then found herself alone with Antoine, who was still a stranger to her, in a somber, candlelit room with dark wooden furnishings. The only physical description we have of him—the man who was now by law Marie's lord and master—is a verbal one. A writer of the era said that the marquis was, on the one hand, "badly built and red-faced" and, on the other, "the best equipped man at court" in the region of his loins.[6]

7

Antoine

M arriage brought more pain than joy into Marie's already sorrow-filled life. The young Marquis and Marquise de Combalet did not get on especially well from the moment they are supposed to have consummated their union in the Louvre. Antoine left Marie for long stretches while serving the Crown as a military officer. If these absences led to any newfound fondness for the other in either of their hearts, any hope that their marriage eventually could be a happy one would be lost within two years of the wedding.

Six months into the marriage, Antoine was called to serve as the captain of a royal regiment based in Normandy. Soon after, he was called to lead troops from Navarre. Most of his duties thereafter were in Languedoc in southern France—a region in which tensions still ran high between Catholics and *Huguenots*, as Protestants had come to be called in French. Marie in the meantime stayed with the Queen Mother at court, serving as a junior lady-in-waiting.[1]

The first major campaign in which Antoine took part was the Siege of Montauban, an effort by some twenty-five thousand of the King's men to take a Huguenot stronghold about thirty miles north of Toulouse. Running from August to October 1621, the siege did not result in the capture of the city but did check Huguenot rebelliousness for a time. Antoine made it through unscathed. While living apart from him most of that time, Marie would have spent time with him nonetheless, as the entire royal court relocated temporarily to the region before the siege.[2]

The young couple then spent the Christmas season together in Paris after the court returned there for the winter. However, it was not a social expectation among the upper nobility of the time that a husband and wife, especially if the former were a military officer and the latter serving a queen, sleep often in the same house let alone the same bedchamber.

Military duties again preoccupied Antoine for much of the first half of 1622. By the summer, the young marquis was among the officers leading thousands of men in preparations for a great siege of Montpellier—a center of Huguenot resistance to royal control located halfway along the French Mediterranean coastline.

Antoine was struck down from his horse in a charge outside the city in early September, only days after the start of the siege. He was then killed, although reports differed as to whether he was dispatched swiftly in the place where he had fallen or, more agonizingly, days later inside the city walls after being dragged there by the Huguenots. There was speculation, too, that he perished partly as a result of a youthful excess of valor.[3] What is undisputed is that he fought valiantly and did not live to see the disappointing outcome of the royal forces' efforts—a stalemate by early October—for which he had given his life at only twenty-five.[4]

From a young age, Marie was exceptionally discreet about her feelings and private affairs. Thus, she rarely commented on her short-lived marriage with Antoine, even though it was the subject of speculation throughout her life. Some believed she had suffered a broken heart over Hippolyte de Béthune, the young man she would have preferred to marry. Others presumed more simply that she maintained an aversion toward Antoine—or at least toward sexual congress with him. Rumors even circulated that she never gave up her virginity to him. At the same time, some contemporaries believed either that Antoine did not find *her* appealing in the bedroom or, much the reverse, that he developed tender feelings for her that were all for naught, given his untimely demise. The fact that no pregnancy resulted from the marriage of course fueled the gossip that the two had been sexually incompatible. A poet named Dulot who was Marie's contemporary circulated the line "Marie de Vignerod, vierge de ton mary" ("Marie de Vignerot, virgin to your husband").[5]

All the same, Marie sincerely mourned Antoine and became closer to his grieving sisters, Anne and Marie. And in that era, when men of substance engaged competitively in martial exploits for the honor of God as well as for King and Country, she derived satisfaction in becoming the widow of one of the Catholic heroes of Montpellier.

Nevertheless, Marie at eighteen was, on the whole, relieved to be freed from what had been a politically determined union. Ironically, the marriage had not secured in a timely way the prize for which it was exchanged at Les Ponts-de-Cé.

Uncle Armand did not receive his red cardinal's hat until after both Antoine and the Duc de Luynes had died. The latter, who had purposely stalled Richelieu's elevation to the cardinalate, had fallen ill and died several months before his nephew.

Marie herself got more from the marriage when it was over than at its inception. As the widow of a war hero and of Luynes's nephew, she acquired honor and a degree of independence rare for a woman so young. That independence derived especially from the wealth now in her hands. Already at the time of her marriage she had received 60,000 livres and some 12,000 écus worth of jewelry from the Queen Mother, as well as 50,000 livres and a host of jewels, rings, and fine furniture from her uncle Armand. When Antoine died, she acquired another 150,000 livres that had been promised to him by the King. Accounting for inflation, the total value of all of this according to a simple gold-standard estimate would be at least 10.6 million U.S. dollars.[6] But accounting for many other economic factors such as purchasing power and the exceptional degree of social power such wealth brought with it, the equivalent monetary value today would be far greater.

In addition, Marie maintained rights to some of her deceased uncle Henry's legacy. With a standing welcome at court, and elevated in her status, too, as Richelieu's star continued to rise, she was suddenly, in her own right, firmly in the upper echelon of the nobility that her aging father had labored to join.

Both René and Richelieu hoped this would enable Marie to marry well and usefully again within a few years. But the girl asserted her newfound independence in a way that neither man expected.

8

Carmel de l'Incarnation

M ourning customs were strict in Marie's time. In France when a woman
lost her husband she was required to wear black from head to foot, with
the most modest of necklines and no jewelry, for a year. Most young widows
with hopes of remarrying tended to welcome the end of this period, when they
could once again wear favorite colors and more provocative cuts.

After her own mourning period was over, the widowed Marquise de Combalet
moved into a cell inside a cloistered convent of nuns in Paris on the opposite
side of the Seine River from the Louvre. These nuns wore sandals on their feet
and ample, long, brown and white habits that completely covered their hair and
womanly shapes.

They were Discalced Carmelites, belonging to a reformed branch of a religious
order founded in the Holy Land during the Crusades. They looked to a Spanish
mystic who had been heavily scrutinized by the Inquisition, Teresa of Avila,
as their spiritual mother.[1] Although she had died relatively recently, in 1582,
Teresa had just in March 1622 been canonized as a saint by Pope Gregory XV.

The convent was called Carmel de l'Incarnation. It was located along a major
artery of the Left Bank, the Rue Saint-Jacques, close to today's Val-de-Grâce
military hospital. Under the leadership of Spanish nuns who had known Teresa,
the reformed Carmelites had established a community there in 1604, the year
of Marie's birth.[2]

Even before she was a widow, Marie had developed an interest in the Discalced Carmelites when one of Antoine's sisters entered another of their convents,
in Amiens, in May of 1622. Additionally, Marie was encouraged to spend time
with the nuns by the Queen Mother and her senior ladies-in-waiting, who

regularly visited the convent on the Rue Saint-Jacques for spiritual nourishment. They had known the original Spanish sisters of the community and the French-woman most responsible for bringing them to France. That was Barbe Avrillot d'Acarie, who was venerated as saintly after her death in 1618.[3]

Some months after Antoine's death, Marie informed René and Richelieu that she would be making a retreat at Carmel de l'Incarnation. The assumption was that she would visit the convent for a short period—several weeks at most. But then months went by. Indeed, Marie ended up taking the brown habit and white veil and wimple of a novice, aspiring to stay inside the convent's walls for the rest of her life.

She took this step under the guidance of a priest in his forties named Pierre de Bérulle. He was well known in courtly circles and he had become a spiritual father to many of the Carmelite women in Paris. As it happens, he would become famous as one of the great mystics and spiritual writers of the French Catholic Reformation, credited even with inspiring an entire "French School" of spirituality that influenced Catholicism worldwide into the twentieth century.

In his preaching and in counseling sessions with Marie and other women in the convent, Bérulle encouraged intensive devotion to the fully divine and fully human person of Jesus Christ. He also stressed imitation of Christ's constant prayer and sacrificial self-giving to God the Father.

From Bérulle and from experienced nuns in the convent, Marie also received strong messages about the spiritual value of denying one's fleshly appetites and of cultivating detachment with respect to wealth, prestige, and the fleeting pleasures that life in this fallen, sin-weary world offered. In one of his spiritual treatises of the time, Bérulle said of Christ: "He is our all; and our happiness is to be in Him." Elsewhere he said that an excellent spiritual life demands that one "renounce oneself and all actions and thoughts which are not the fruit of obedience, or of charity, or of necessity, and then allow Jesus Christ to take possession of our soul."[4]

While reflecting on such messages, Marie spent days in the convent that were structured by the Divine Office, or the chanting of the Psalms and other prayers at set times of the day while sitting in choir with the nuns. She also attended Mass and confessed her sins regularly to a priest. The aim was not simply to cleanse her soul from the stains of wrongdoing but also to allow God to perfect her being into something ever more holy.

Marie furthermore spent many hours in front of the Blessed Sacrament—unleavened bread, shaped into a thin disc, which had been consecrated by a priest and was reserved in a tabernacle. Sometimes it was displayed on chapel altars in a monstrance. She had been taught from childhood to revere this Eucharistic Host as truly Christ Himself, who was miraculously present in it. Bérulle and other mentors in the convent encouraged an intimate relationship with Christ through a posture of silent spiritual receptivity before this holy food.

Marie learned the *Lectio Divina* from the nuns. This entailed the reading of biblical passages followed by prayer and contemplation. She also ate meals in common with the sisters, typically in silence as edifying passages from spiritual texts, including some by Saint Teresa, were recited. She had opportunities to engage in other reading, too, of approved books.[5]

Given the strictness of the Discalced Carmelites' rule of life, Marie only rarely received guests. One such moment came in mid-March 1624. Her father had just died, at the age of sixty-three, and Richelieu visited Marie to express his intention of serving as her guardian in his place. He also made it clear that he did not approve of a religious vocation for her.[6]

Despite her wealth and relative independence as a widow, Marie at the age of nineteen found it difficult to refuse Uncle Armand, especially as he was replacing her father in a society that insisted that all women be governed by men. She also received little help from Bérulle or the convent's leading nuns in resisting Richelieu's wishes. Indeed, they helped him to dissuade her from seeking full profession of vows as a Carmelite.[7]

So, late in the spring of 1624, just as she had done four years earlier when she had agreed to marry Antoine, Marie complied with Richelieu's wishes at the price of her own desires. She abandoned Carmel de l'Incarnation and returned to French high society—not only as the rich, attractive, and widowed Madame de Combalet but now also as the favored niece of the increasingly powerful *Éminence Rouge*.

9

The Young Cardinal's Ward

According to poets and artists of her day, Madame de Combalet was tall and graceful, with curly, chestnut-brown hair, clear-brown eyes, and a lovely oval-shaped face. One poet drew special attention to the brightness of her eyes and to her lips, which formed "the most beautiful mouth in the world."[1] She was shapely and wore the low-cut, wide-hipped, and bell-sleeved dresses that were in style at the court of France in the late 1620s and the 1630s. When not in mourning, colors she wore—blues, reds, silvery gray, and golden yellow—shimmered on rich fabrics adorned with lace, linen, ribbons, pearls, and flowers and complemented the milky tones of her shoulders, forearms, and décolletage.[2]

Observers also remarked on her wit and intelligence, which shone through her expression, and on the exceptional beauty of her voice, both when speaking and singing. Furthermore, as she grew confident in herself and in her elevated position in life, she carried herself with a dignity that men and women alike found formidable.

It took time, of course, for Marie to become this woman, especially after she had spent the better part of a year shrouded in a convent with her head bent in contemplation of the Last Things: death, judgment, Heaven, and Hell.

When she left Carmel, she could not rejoin worldly society altogether, anyway, because she was mourning her father's death. In the Ancien Régime, a six-month mourning period was the norm when one lost a parent. Until late in the year, then, Marie again wore black down to her shoes. Even for a time thereafter, somber colors such as dark gray and brown were considered appropriate, especially for a woman who was also a widow.[3]

Although Richelieu planned for his niece to serve the Queen Mother at the royal court, he first welcomed her into his home in the Place Royale, today's 21 Place des Vosges in the Marais district of Paris. Her brother François, now fifteen, was also there while completing his education and training in soldiery. Richelieu, serving as his guardian, too, was administering his modest fortune as René's heir and assisting him with his obligations as the new Sieur de Vignerot and Baron du Pont Courlay.[4]

Since Marie had first seen Richelieu's townhouse in 1620, its owner's wealth had increased considerably. So she was welcomed into a home full of some of the finest furniture and decorative works available from European artisans, sculptors, and painters. Richelieu in fact was Europe's first major private art collector. In time his collection would rival those of many monarchs.[5] Already by 1624 his collection was known outside of France, as it included a number of fine paintings by Italian Renaissance masters.[6] We can thus imagine the pleasure the churchman began to take in sharing his love of art and discussing his latest acquisitions with his perceptive niece once she was ensconced in his home.

Richelieu's time for such things was limited, however. His home was a busy power center. By 1624 he was building up a large personal and political staff. He was waited on by many servants, assisted by several secretaries and clerks, and advised by trusted clergymen he kept close at hand.[7]

Among the men most often in Richelieu's company was a priest in his late forties named François Leclerc du Tremblay. Known better by his religious name, *Père Joseph*, he was a Capuchin friar who empathized in ways Richelieu did not with Marie's interest in a religious vocation, which persisted in her heart after she was forced to leave the convent. Père Joseph had himself renounced a courtly nobleman's life at the age of twenty-one to join the Capuchins, a reformed branch of the Franciscan order. But, while zealous about prayer and about the reform of Catholic institutions and moral life in France, he had also been drawn by circumstances into political life, first as a papal envoy and eventually by Richelieu, who valued his judgment. He was the original *Éminence Grise*. Over time he became Richelieu's dear friend and trusted advisor.[8]

In Richelieu's home, Marie also encountered visitors of different ranks whom the Cardinal received on an ever more frequent basis. Many tried to impress him in the hopes of gaining positions in royal service, in his household, or even in his family as prospective spouses for his relatives. Some of these visitors piqued the young woman's curiosity in a special way: diplomats and other travelers who had gotten to know distant countries and who often bore intriguing gifts for her uncle. Richelieu especially enjoyed conversing with such men as he wished to become better informed about the wider world, partly to facilitate new French commercial activity abroad.[9]

In this period of adjustment, Marie also got to know her uncle better. Thinner, taller, and younger than most churchmen of high status, he was at thirty-nine an imposing, dynamic figure. Even contemporaries who disliked him admitted how magnetic he was. Nicolas Goulas, a nobleman in service to the King's brother Gaston, wrote, "He carried himself with high poise and in the manner of a grand sire, he spoke agreeably . . . his mind was focused and worked with subtle ease, his general manner was noble, his ability to handle business inconceivably adroit, and finally he put a grace in what he did and said that ravished everyone."[10]

While impressed and intimidated by such an uncle, Marie also found Richelieu to be more lenient than stern with her. Unlike other reform-minded churchmen of his day, he was not a moral rigorist and indeed encouraged Marie, who exhibited some self-punishing tendencies after emerging from the convent, to become more comfortable with an ordinary, worldly life.[11] Although she resisted this for a time, she also learned a great deal from her uncle, absorbed some of his studied, elegant mannerisms and speech patterns, and came to depend on his caring attitude toward her. But she was also affected by his ever-changing moods. She saw sides of him that few others did, including his swings into melancholy and anger as well as his kind, tender moments. She probably saw him in tears on occasion and fighting back tears while he felt emasculated by the experience. He was affectionate toward her—something he demonstrated through gifts such as floral bouquets. He also shared with her his fondness for pets, especially an increasing number of cats that he kept at home.

Richelieu instructed his niece on how to behave in courtly company, warning her about deceptions, bribes, and sycophancy. She learned to withhold her trust from acquaintances who seemed winsome at first. Especially as his star was rising, the Cardinal wished for Marie to be under no illusion that she herself, because of her connection to him as well as her own wealth and noble status, would not become a target of manipulation by those seeking access.

Marie had joined Richelieu in Paris during a critical period in his rise to power. By 1624 he controlled the Queen Mother's private affairs and some of her political business in his dual capacity as superintendent of her household and president of her council. While separate from the King's, Marie de' Medici's court was a true power center. Richelieu had access to the Queen Mother's extensive network of secretaries and others in her service. He won over the loyalty of many of them, who began to serve his interests quietly on the side. When there were openings in the Queen Mother's household, Richelieu was able to place men and women from his own network in them.[12]

Richelieu also in April 1624 was readmitted to the King's council after a seven-year hiatus. This was welcome news, initially, to both major political factions at court, the Dévots and the Bons François. The Dévots were militantly anti-Protestant Catholics who generally favored Habsburg Spain and the Holy Roman Empire in international affairs. The Bons François (or "Good Frenchmen") were a national-minded party that favored *rapprochement* with Protestant powers such as England and the Dutch Republic as a way of checking the Habsburgs' imperial influence, which then stretched across Europe, the Americas, and even parts of Asia and Africa. They were devoutly Catholic, too, but had a narrower view than the Dévots of both the papacy's and theologians' competencies to weigh in on French political affairs.[13] At this early stage of his career, Richelieu was seen as both a loyal representative of the Church and as a true servant of French national interests. Members of both parties therefore saw him as an ally.[14]

The Dévots were especially hopeful while a rivalry played out between Richelieu and the King's most trusted councilor at the time, Charles de La Vieuville, a leader among the Bons François. Richelieu exposed La Vieuville as dishonest and financially corrupt. By mid-August La Vieuville was fleeing to the Netherlands to escape execution.[15]

From this point forward, Richelieu was the de facto prime minister of France.[16] Nevertheless, it was not a given in 1624, despite several precedents in France and other countries, that a churchman could fully participate in all the decision-making required of the head of a royal council, especially where wars and capital crimes were concerned.[17] Richelieu therefore secured permission from Pope Urban VIII to silence the naysayers.

Ironically, this papal blessing, together with his own cardinal's robes, gave Richelieu more cover among pious French Catholics than the layman La Vieuville had enjoyed to maneuver militarily against Spain and even against the Papal States in a northern Italian region called the Valtellina. Richelieu also led France into new partnerships with the Dutch and the English and helped finalize a marriage alliance between Louis XIII's Catholic sister Henriette-Marie and the new, young Stuart monarch Charles I, who was an Anglican.[18] Richelieu thus began to make enemies among the Dévots close to the Queen Mother.

While preoccupied with such matters, Richelieu ensured that his own family members were given lucrative positions at court. Among these was the Cardinal's young first cousin, Charles de La Porte, the Marquis de La Meilleraye, who had earlier served Richelieu as a squire. A Protestant convert to Catholicism, he was appointed by Richelieu as a lieutenant in the Queen Mother's armed guards.[19] In that role, he joined Richelieu's brother-in-law, Maillé-Brézé, who had been commanding the guards since 1620.

For Marie, Richelieu had a special position in mind—one that would enable her to keep an eye and ear out for valuable information she might glean among the highest-ranking women of France. At Christmastime in 1624, the Cardinal secured his niece's appointment as the Queen Mother's *dame d'atour*, or second-highest-ranking lady-in-waiting. Marie replaced her aunt Nicole, who was by this point approaching forty and raising a son, Jean-Armand, the first of her eventual two children.[20]

Although it was not an unexpected role for Marie to take on, becoming a high-ranking lady-in-waiting to a queen was in that era one of the greatest honors to which a noblewoman of any age, let alone one so young, could aspire. Furthermore, that Marie was made *dame d'atour* at only twenty demonstrates the degree of trust the Cardinal already had in her.

The honor of Marie's appointment was formalized with a beautifully penned invitation from the King. Louis signed it on December 29, 1624. It was sealed with a large disc of red wax impressed with an image of the Bourbon coat of arms. Marie received it from a palace courier that same day and had to move to court by New Year's Day.[21]

10

Serving Marie de' Medici

W hen Marie took up her high position in the Queen Mother's household, she made an unusual impression on many seasoned courtiers. Although she was not obligated to do so, given the time that had passed since her husband's and father's deaths, she wore somber, dark mourning dresses made of worsted wool and muslin, leaving her hair unadorned except on occasion with black ribbons. A contemporary quipped that, at twenty, Madame de Combalet "dressed as modestly as a fifty-year-old Dévote."[1] The term *Dévote*, in the feminine, referred to an especially pious Catholic woman preoccupied with prayer, penances, and charitable activity. There was some overlap between such women and the Dévot political faction.

Ironically, Marie's primary duty as *dame d'atour* was to supervise Her Majesty's *garde-robe*, or a great, locked wardrobe room where numerous gowns, hats and veils, jewelry, and other finery were kept. This task, however frivolous it must have seemed to a young woman with tastes that ran to reading, music, and the rigors of a nunnery, was aesthetically educational. It familiarized Marie with rich materials and the latest fashions from across France and from abroad.[2]

Exposure to the Queen Mother's wardrobe eventually made an impression on the widow Combalet. In time she discarded her mourning clothes and extremely modest style and began to dress more sumptuously and youthfully than was even customary for courtly young widows at the time. She began to wear all sorts of colors and to decorate her hair and her more exposed décolletage with flowers and jewels. Other widows began to imitate her in these respects.[3]

There were periods, too, when supervision of the *garde-robe* was exciting, such as the spring of 1625, when there were balls and other festivities in honor of the marriage of Princesse Henriette-Marie to the King of England. Marie was expected to attend such events, dressed beautifully, but relatively simply, according to the Queen Mother's tastes for her ladies. She was also encouraged to dance, sometimes by prospective suitors. Courtly dances of the time included the *pavane*, a slow couples dance in which men and women lined up opposite one another, held hands, moved in circles, and in the case of the men took turns strutting like peacocks for their dance partners.[4]

The position of *dame d'atour* involved a range of other duties, some of them crucial to the management of a royal household that employed hundreds at a time. Marie supervised all the *femmes de chambre* (serving maids). She also stood in for the highest-ranking lady-in-waiting, the *première dame d'honneur*, whenever the latter was absent at court. That role was filled throughout Marie's time at court by the beautiful, pious Antoinette de Pons-Ribérac, the Marquise de Guercheville.

Sixty-four at the time that Marie joined the Queen Mother's ladies, Antoinette was a grandmotherly presence to Richelieu's niece as she took her under her wing. She trained Marie to take over for her whenever she was called away from court, especially with regard to purchasing and budgeting duties for the royal household. At these times, Marie also safeguarded the keys to the queen's chambers, supervised the household's entire female staff, and served as the queen's chief companion in the morning, at bedtime, at meals, and at promenades and formal audiences with an array of dignitaries and petitioners for royal favors. These responsibilities gave Marie valuable experience with courtly etiquette, interpersonal diplomacy, and leadership.[5]

As *dame d'atour*, Marie also of course got to know the Queen Mother well. The two had become acquainted at the time of Marie's wedding. They had also spent time in each other's company in the early 1620s, when Marie was at court often while her husband Antoine was still alive. Now they interacted frequently, including in times of religious observance in royal chapels and in the intimate hours of the queen's dressing, bathing, and lounging in her nightdress.[6]

Approaching fifty in early 1625, Marie de' Medici was robust and matronly. Her light brown hair, which she often wore piled up dramatically and bejeweled to distract from her high forehead, had grayed considerably. Her light brown eyes often flashed with fire, as she had a tremendous temper—something of which her son the King lived in constant fear.[7] She was a controlling, jealous woman, and she resented efforts by Louis and his bride, Anne, to assert independence. She employed a vast network of spies and alienated many in France with her militant Catholicism. The latter was often more political in tone—favoring especially the interests of her maternal Habsburg relatives in Europe—than spiritually elevated.

In her position at court, Marie heard stories from the queen—some of them bloodcurdling—about the Medicis, Borgias, and other ruling families in Renaissance Italy. She was further nurtured, too, in her growing love for Italian art and music, which Richelieu also encouraged. And she learned details about the Queen Mother's strange journey to the French court and marriage with the late King Henry.

Somehow, when growing up amid the splendors of the Medici court as the half-Habsburg daughter of Grand Duke Francesco I of Tuscany, the future queen had escaped being married off in her teens as Italian girls of her station tended to be. Indeed, by her early twenties she feared she might remain a spinster. But unexpectedly, in 1596, agents of the already married King of France inquired about her hand and her fabulous dowry. By that time, Henry had determined to have his first marriage with Marguerite de Valois annulled. Marguerite by her mid-forties had borne Henry no children. She also betrayed the marriage over the years—something that was excused in kings in those days, but not in queens. Because of this double standard, Henry was able to persuade Pope Clement VIII to grant the annulment. Then he married his Florentine heiress by proxy in October 1600.[8]

Once beside Henry in France, Marie de' Medici made up for lost time and bore the King six children within nine years. After it became clear, however, that Henry was chronically unfaithful to her, she determined to take revenge. But rather than take up with lovers, too, she shocked the polite French courtiers with barbed, Italian-accented language against Henry's women. She feuded openly with his leading mistress, Catherine de Balzac d'Entragues. When Henry failed to side with his wife in these catfights, Marie de' Medici retaliated further by showing favor to the spurned Marguerite de Valois. She even made Henry, to his embarrassment, restore his ex-wife to an honored position in courtly society.

These dramas were long in the past, of course, when Richelieu's niece took up her post in the Queen Mother's chambers. Nevertheless, stories about them and her mistress's bitterness over them contributed to an already precocious cynicism in the young widow's psyche about marriage and sexual politics generally.

In her early days as *dame d'atour*, Marie focused on her budding friendships with women, not on attracting suitors. One of her new friends was Madeleine de Silly, eventually the Comtesse du Fargis, who had also spent time in a convent—but as punishment for coquettish behavior when she was a girl. Madeleine had a salty tongue, which amused the guarded and pious Marie. The two became close enough that Richelieu, partly as a favor to his niece, secured Madeleine the position of *dame d'atour* to the young Queen Regnant, Anne. This made the young women peers at court and also created a ready line of communication between the two queens' households, which was useful to Richelieu.[9]

Marie also befriended the first prominent *salon* hostesses of Paris, the cultured, Italian-born Catherine de Vivonne, the Marquise de Rambouillet, and her beautiful and quick-witted daughter, Julie-Lucine d'Angennes. Through them, she began to meet poets, playwrights, and other authors and artists who depended upon aristocratic patronage. She began to exercise patronage powers herself, taught by these women as she was also being taught by Richelieu and at court. Patronage in the early modern sense, which is crucial to understanding Marie's story and the power she would eventually wield, has been defined by one scholar as "a form of social relation where the patron possessed resources in the form of power, wealth, influence, and . . . connections and offered those to clients, who offered in return their loyalty and, in some cases, even their own networks."[10] Friendship and patron-client relationships sometimes overlapped and were symbiotic. They were so normative in Marie's time that most people did not think about them analytically: they were too inside these relationships, so to speak.[11]

Marie also became close to other noblewomen who enjoyed conversations about literature and other elevated topics. Eminent among them was Charlotte-Marguerite de Montmorency, the Princesse de Condé, who was ten years older than her and whose life was full of drama. At fourteen she had been subjected to King Henry IV's unwelcome efforts—when he was in his mid-fifties—to make her one of his mistresses. Shortly before her fifteenth birthday, Henry forced her to marry his twenty-year-old, cash-poor cousin Henry II de Bourbon, the Prince de Condé, with the expectation that the two men would share the bride sexually. Condé, however, escaped with Charlotte to Brussels and, as he was second in line to the throne, joined in with the Catholic League's effort against Henry. Several years later, he joined in with the rebellion against Marie de' Medici's regency, only to be captured and sent to the dungeon of the Château de Vincennes east of Paris. Condé and Charlotte were not in love, but it was said that Charlotte voluntarily spent several years with her husband in this prison where their first living child, Anne-Geneviève—the future famous and rebellious Duchesse de Longueville—was conceived and safely delivered.[12]

Charlotte was regarded as one of the most beautiful princesses in Europe with her golden hair, alabaster complexion, and striking blue eyes. She was also rumored by the mid-1620s to have had several extramarital affairs—including with the charismatic young Louis de Nogaret, the Cardinal de La Valette, who had been forced into an ecclesiastical career as a boy.[13] Through Charlotte and her other friends, Marie became acquainted with this flirtatious, reluctant churchman. She could not have predicted at the time how much she would come to care for him herself in subsequent years.

Richelieu was happy for Marie to widen her social set with such people. It enabled him to further cultivate his own network of trusted contacts and to stay informed about the kinds of conversations taking place among influential women. He also hoped that some of Marie's new friends might assist him with the goal of seeing her married again.

Indeed, from the moment the Cardinal had brought Marie into his home in 1624, he had hoped that she would soon join into a new marriage with a great nobleman or even a prince of the realm. But by early 1626, after Marie had spent a year in service to the Queen Mother and encountered at court some of the most eligible bachelors of the kingdom, Richelieu noted that there had been no promising developments in this regard. Marie behaved as if she were uninterested in the prospect, to the point of engaging in private "austerities" she had learned in the convent and which the Cardinal believed were unhealthy and contrary to the will of God. What these mortifications were, precisely, we cannot know. Richelieu referred cryptically to them in one of his surviving letters to Marie.[14] It is possible that she may have been disrupting her sleep to pray the Divine Office on a rigorous, conventual schedule. Or perhaps she was whipping herself or fasting in extreme ways.

At the same time, Richelieu was frustrated by the reappearance of Hippolyte de Béthune, Marie's first suitor from the period before her marriage to Combalet. Hippolyte had remained unmarried since he had first sought Marie's hand six years earlier. When he renewed his suit, this time for the more experienced widow Combalet, Richelieu regarded him as insufficiently established for Marie. Béthune's father, a count still preoccupied with ambassadorial duties in Rome, was in good health and still unlikely to pass down titles and properties to his son any time soon.

Poor Hippolyte was turned away once again, but this time by Marie herself.[15] Unfortunately, it is unclear from the few sources in Marie's hand from the period how she regarded the young man. Did she not wish to disappoint her uncle? Was she simply uninterested now in the prospect of marriage with Hippolyte, whatever she may have felt toward him at sixteen? Had she determined never to marry *anyone* again after her experience with Combalet?

It has long been believed that Marie in 1624 had privately determined to remain faithful to an initial vow of chastity—and therefore to remain celibate the rest of her life—which she had made during her stay at Carmel de l'Incarnation. However, the only surviving statement from Marie herself that sheds any light on the matter is a frustratingly brief remark in her will, written half a century after the time in question, that she had desired to live among the Carmelites in her youth.[16] Furthermore, even had she committed herself privately to celibacy, it would not have been binding under Church law in the way that a permanent religious vow, professed solemnly in a convent, would have been.

Whatever was the case, around the time she turned away the heartbroken Hippolyte, Marie received permission from the Queen Mother to leave court temporarily to make another retreat with the nuns. Richelieu reluctantly gave his blessing to this.

11

A Pivotal Year

Marie's second long stay with the Carmelites occurred in the second half of 1626, which was an eventful year for her family. First, Marie's brother François was ushered by Richelieu into a marriage with a young woman who, although she was the daughter of an executed criminal, stood to inherit a fortune from a childless aunt.

Second, Marie late in the spring learned in no uncertain terms that men and women close by her at court wanted her uncle dead. A conspiracy was discovered that involved key members of young Queen Anne's inner circle—two of whom were bedding each other—and which almost resulted in Richelieu's murder at a dinner party.

Third, one of Marie's Combalet sisters-in-law, Anne, decided to go on a long retreat with the nuns in Paris. This provided Marie with an excuse to take a holiday from her *dame d'atour* duties. The Queen Mother approved of periodic religious retreats for her ladies, which made it easy for Marie to join Anne inside the order's newer convent situated on the Rue Chapon in the Marais district.[1]

These events in 1626 would prove highly consequential to Marie over the longer term. To begin with, her brother's marriage would in time result in five children, including a niece named Marie-Madeleine-Thérèse, whom Marie would later come to treat like a daughter, and a nephew named Armand-Jean, who would become a thorn in her side for many decades. Furthermore, later in Marie's life, political enemies would circulate the foul rumor that some of these nephews and nieces were secretly her own children, fathered incestuously by her uncle Richelieu.

All of that was far in the future when, in early 1626, Richelieu learned of the rank and financial prospects of a girl from Brittany in northwestern France named Marie-Françoise de Guémadeuc. She was close in age to his nephew François, who was nearing his seventeenth birthday. Marie's brother had assumed his deceased father's titles and legacy two years earlier and he was old enough, in the Cardinal's view, to marry and become useful in his expanding network of loyal political officials. Richelieu had in mind at the time for François the French ambassadorship in Istanbul, but this scheme did not move forward.[2] Instead, François within two years would succeed his cousin La Meilleraye as the royal governor of the port city of Havre-de-Grâce in Normandy.

Marie-Françoise was the daughter of Thomas II de Guémadeuc, the royal governor of the fortress town of Fougères in Brittany, whose medieval castle stands to this day and remains one of the most impressive in France. However, Thomas had been condemned as a criminal and beheaded in Paris in September 1617 for his role in a local rebellion against royal authority.[3]

Marie-Françoise was a little girl at the time and grew up enveloped by her family's shame. Her disgraced mother, Jeanne Ruellan, abandoned her to hide away in a Discalced Carmelite cloister, in which she would remain for the rest of her life.[4] But Marie-Françoise was also the favorite relative of a wealthy noblewoman, her aunt Hélène de Beaumanoir, the Vicomtesse du Besso. Without children of her own, the vicomtesse by the spring of 1626 had made it clear that her cheating rapscallion of a husband—who was attempting to get rid of her and marry one of his mistresses in high style—would not get the fortune he was trying to steal. Instead, her niece would get most of it once she died.

Learning of this, Richelieu urged François to pursue the heiress. (He also made sure that the vicomtesse's husband, Charles de Cossé, the Marquis d'Acigné, was arrested and banished from the kingdom for his attempted crimes against his wife.) The two young people married on June 29, 1626. The newly-weds eventually settled in Le Havre, where their first child would be born. But they also set up a household in Paris, close to the Louvre. Furthermore, thanks to a combination of persuasion by Marie-Françoise and pressure by Richelieu, the Vicomtesse du Besso relinquished her fortune to the couple while still years away from dying.[5]

Marie did not attend her brother's wedding. Instead she was settling into her retreat with the Carmelites in late June 1626.[6] The match was arranged so neatly for the teenaged boy, and without any pretense that it was not primarily a business arrangement, that its announcement could hardly have engendered happy feelings in the young widow. How soon would it be, she had reason to wonder, before a new candidate for her hand, approved by her uncle, would appear and the same thing would happen again to her? However, if she were safely ensconced in a convent, she could escape this fate . . .

By the time of François's wedding, Marie had something else to be anxious about: Uncle Armand was now the target of serious assassination plots involving eminent figures at court with whom she socialized.

The first major conspiracy against Richelieu arose in reaction to the Cardinal's influence on the Queen Mother with respect to her younger son's prospective marriage. Prince Gaston, called simply *Monsieur* but also known in time as the Duc d'Orléans, turned eighteen in April of 1626. He was handsome, blue-eyed, confident, athletic, quick-witted, erudite, cheerful, popular . . . everything his brother Louis was not, some whispered. He was also single and far too trusting of his hangers-on. All of this made Gaston not just the most eligible bachelor in France but also the focus of anxiety and plotting at court. In addition, the King had not yet fathered an heir, despite having been married for a decade. Gaston therefore became a magnet for opportunists who were conscious of the rising odds that, should he marry and have sons, he and his bride would form the real power center at court.[7]

The King was therefore not eager for his little brother to get married. But their mother had different ideas. Marie de' Medici had long desired that when Gaston came of age he should marry a high-ranking young noblewoman named Marie de Bourbon, the Duchesse de Montpensier. One of the wealthiest heiresses in France, the duchess was also closely related to the Guises, a militantly Catholic family favored by the Queen Mother because they had been especially active against the Protestants during the Wars of Religion. Indeed, the powerful Guises were behind the infamous Saint Bartholomew's Day Massacre of 1572 that had left some three thousand Protestants dead in Paris alone.

While the Queen Mother had emotional reasons for favoring the flower of such a family as her prospective daughter-in-law, her primary advisor Richelieu became convinced that a marriage between Gaston and Montpensier would favor stability in the French state. So, with the Queen Mother's warm approval, he helped to persuade Louis to support the union.[8]

At this point a young noblewoman close to Queen Anne began a whisper campaign against Gaston's planned marriage in the hopes that, should it come to be disfavored by other influential courtiers and never take place, Richelieu would be dismissed from court for his ineffectiveness. This was the beautiful, scheming, twenty-five-year-old widow of the Duc de Luynes, Marie-Aimée de Rohan-Montbazon, the Duchesse de Chevreuse, about whom Louis XIII later said, "This woman is the very devil!"[9]

By marriage Chevreuse was the deceased Marquis de Combalet's aunt, and so she was well known to Marie as an in-law. Since 1619 she had been serving Anne of Austria as her highest-ranking lady-in-waiting. She had attended Marie's wedding in 1620. Since early 1625, Marie and this attractive duchess had interacted frequently at court.

Chevreuse managed to convince Anne that if the King's brother married Montpensier, she would lose some of her real power. It is supposed, too, that she whispered to Anne an even more enticing reason to oppose the marriage. Should (God forbid!) Louis himself die unexpectedly without issue, Anne herself might get to marry handsome Gaston and remain the Queen! Gaston, after all, was not immune to the charms of his sister-in-law. The two kept up a courtly flirtation whenever in each other's company.[10]

The two women set about convincing Gaston to reject a marriage with Montpensier. They began by luring into their conspiracy a usually serious and distinguished—but also ugly and easy to charm—colonel who served as Gaston's tutor, Jean-Baptiste d'Ornano. Ornano now encouraged Gaston to demand from Louis and the Queen Mother that he have a say in affairs of state, including with respect to his own marriage.[11]

Richelieu responded with unexpected severity to all this. Demonstrating more rawly than ever before the power that he and his network of loyalists wielded, the Cardinal on May 6 had Ornano arrested and imprisoned at the Bastille. In the meantime, plans for a summertime wedding for Gaston proceeded apace.

But this only galvanized Chevreuse and a growing circle of conspirators close to the King's brother. This group now determined upon Richelieu's assassination.[12]

Chevreuse, who was vivacious, golden-haired, and slim with blue eyes and full lips, had in the meantime seduced a handsome and gullible young nobleman who was also well-known to Marie. This was Henry de Talleyrand-Périgord, the Comte de Chalais. Chalais fell passionately in love with Chevreuse, which made it easy for her to employ him as a pawn in a conspiracy to kill Richelieu in a way made to look like an accident. Chevreuse convinced Chalais that the Cardinal had made sexual advances toward her (something for which there is no evidence). Enraged—and with Gaston's full knowledge—Chalais planned to retaliate by making a surprise visit with friends to one of Richelieu's residences, a mansion close to the royal palace at Fontainebleau southeast of Paris. Upon arriving, they were to ask to stay the night and help Richelieu welcome Gaston himself the next day, who wished as a courtesy (they would say) to drop in, too. Then they were to stage a drink-induced fight in the evening, during which Richelieu would be "accidentally" stabbed with one of the visitor's swords.[13]

Unfortunately for Chalais, a relative who learned of the scheme informed on him to Richelieu. With this intelligence on the plot in hand, Richelieu then permitted events to unfold more or less as planned up to the "surprise" dinner.

On May 10, nine men from Gaston's entourage were welcomed into Richelieu's home but then were astonished when the Cardinal abandoned them toward evening. In the morning, Gaston, upon waking at Fontainebleau, was stunned to be greeted not by an attendant informing him of Richelieu's assassination but rather by the Cardinal himself, who stood quietly at his bedside. Richelieu then handed the prince his shirt and, in the politest of tones, suggested to Gaston that he would prefer if, next time, he and his men would provide more advanced notice about any visits, so that they might be received with all the pomp and circumstance owed to men of their rank.[14]

Richelieu after this began to employ a personal armed guard. Authorized by the King, it consisted at first of four cavaliers on horseback and twelve captains on foot. For Marie, the presence of this guard added to otherwise ordinary visits with her uncle a new component of drama while heightening her sense of alarm about the Cardinal's safety.

Almost as unsettling to Marie as the conspiracy itself was her uncle's response to it after it was foiled. Initially falling into extreme melancholy, Richelieu suggested to the Queen Mother that he should resign his position at court. But the King then reiterated his unswerving support and had his own half brothers arrested. These two men were the sons of Henry IV and one of his mistresses. Titled the Duc de Vendôme and the Chevalier de Vendôme, they were carted off to the Château de Vincennes prison for partaking in the plot against Richelieu.

With Richelieu again pulling strings at court, the King also had Chalais imprisoned in the city of Nantes. After confessing his crimes, blaming Chevreuse, and begging for mercy, Chalais on August 18 was pronounced guilty of high treason and sentenced to death. Because of his status, he was promised a relatively painless death by a professional executioner who would behead him with one swift movement of his sword. However, after some of Chalais's friends attempted stupidly to kidnap the executioner, hoping this would save his life, the affronted judges simply asked a local shoemaker with an unsharpened sword to do the deed. After multiple ineffective blows that caused Chalais tremendous pain and blood loss, the shoemaker was offered a small hatchet by another commoner in the crowd. Chalais, who kept crying out to Jesus and the Blessed Mother until he no longer could, was decapitated only after nineteen more attempts by his hapless executioner.[15]

Richelieu was blamed by many for the horrid way in which Chalais died. He was accused of unnatural cruelty. He was also feared in a new way, because the plotters around the King's brother were all subdued and punished—except for Chevreuse, who managed to flee to the then-sovereign Duchy of Lorraine, where she was protected by the ruling duke there who, too, fell sway to her charms.[16]

Even Gaston demonstrated remorse and submitted to the marriage with Montpensier. This made Richelieu's dominant position at court, if anyone still doubted it, crystal clear.

It was some weeks before Chalais's execution that Marie had left court for her retreat with the nuns. She already by that point feared for her uncle and was troubled by the behavior of Chevreuse and others she knew socially. Especially in such circumstances, her thought of accompanying her sister-in-law for a time at the convent on the Rue Chapon was hardly an unreasonable one. Despite Richelieu's qualms about Marie's return to the sisters, the Cardinal agreed that a cloister was the safest place for his niece during this fraught time.

It was during the climactic period of arrests of the various plotters that Richelieu grew concerned that Marie was staying longer than expected in the convent. In early July he communicated with Marguerite du Saint-Sacrement, an official of the community on the Rue Chapon, inquiring whether his niece would soon be rejoining him in the world. She assured him that Marie planned to return in the near future and that, in the meantime, the nuns were taking good care of his beloved niece.[17]

But Richelieu's weeks of waiting for Marie turned into months. By late summer, it was clear that she was hoping once again to profess vows with the sisters.

The Cardinal resorted to extreme measures to prevent this from taking place. He recruited Bérulle, who had been given authority by Pope Urban VIII over the Discalced Carmelite communities in France, to help him again to force Marie out of the cloister. He also inquired with Denis-Simon de Marquemont, the Cardinal-Archbishop of Lyon, about the possibility of obtaining a papal brief that would forbid Marie from taking religious vows with *any* community, Carmelite or otherwise.

However, Marquemont died in mid-September, requiring Richelieu to make additional inquiries in Rome. A brief from Urban was subsequently promised to him but never materialized. So, toward the end of October, Richelieu wrote to the French ambassador in Rome, Philippe de Béthune—the father of the twice-spurned Hippolyte—to request his help in obtaining the brief from the Pope. On the very same day, October 22, Richelieu wrote to Urban to name Bérulle as his preferred candidate for succeeding Marquemont as cardinal. Richelieu was on the one hand rewarding Bérulle for his help with respect to his niece and other matters and, on the other, attempting to secure his fellow churchman's loyalty in the future. [18]

A myth was perpetuated by Marie's nineteenth-century biographer, Alfred Bonneau-Avenant, that both the Queen Mother and Pope Urban VIII intervened on Richelieu's side and forbade the young *dame d'atour* from taking permanent vows with the Carmelites. It is possible that some informal, strongly worded recommendations were made to Marie by such authoritative figures. But a definitive prohibition, binding under ecclesiastical or French law, was never issued. [19] Quite the contrary, Richelieu in subsequent years remained worried that his niece might still go her own way and become a nun. [20]

What is certain is that Marie dutifully left the convent on the Rue Chapon near the end of 1626. She then resumed her post as the Queen Mother's *dame d'atour*.

Richelieu had no serious regrets about his decision for Marie. Just as before when he had arranged her marriage to Combalet, he was unhesitating in his interference with her periods of discernment regarding a religious vocation. The young woman's desires in the moment were of low priority compared to his political and dynastic goals.

The Cardinal was, indeed, increasingly convinced that the well-being of France was closely bound up with his own position at court and that of his most talented family members and protégés. Young as she was, Marie's intelligence, perspicacity, and indeed stubborn will—perhaps most of all when it was in tension with his own—impressed him greatly compared to what he saw in other family members. His nephew François was not as bright as Marie. His sister Nicole was temperamental and jealous. His brother-in-law Maillé-Brézé was capable and ambitious, but would he prove loyal over time? Marie's capabilities and virtues, in the meantime, were proving useful at court, even apart from her attractiveness to potential suitors more powerful than Combalet.

Richelieu had a growing list of enemies, too, as we have seen. And as a churchman who appears to have taken his vow of celibacy seriously (despite slanders to the contrary), he had no wife, mistress, or daughter who could serve as a loyal pair of eyes and ears for him among the women of the court. Marie could serve his interests in this way and become a great lady herself while firming up their family's legacy. That Marie seemed indifferent to such goals—that she preferred life within a cloister—was yet another reason, in Richelieu's view, why she would prove to be a trustworthy assistant to his ambitions both for France and for the House of Richelieu.

It was not that Richelieu was unsympathetic. Much the reverse, he had developed a tender affection for Marie—something he allowed himself to feel toward a rare few. He also recalled with feeling how his own youthful plans had been swiftly clipped when he was directed to prepare for the priesthood and the diocese at Luçon. So he was determined to shepherd Marie in her courtly, worldly life with fatherly care. But he would learn soon enough that—short of allowing her to enter into religious life, after all—he could protect his niece only so much from the multiplying slings and arrows coming his direction as he continued to tighten his grip on the French state.

12

The Blue Room

N ot long after she left the convent on the Rue Chapon in late 1626, Marie found another welcoming space in which her desire to focus on transcendent realities was appreciated. This was the *Chambre Bleue*, or "Blue Room," inside a mansion close to the Louvre that was owned by Charles d'Angennes, the Marquis de Rambouillet. A mature man of fifty, the marquis had served in the King's household and had an impressive record of military and diplomatic service.

The Blue Room was his wife's domain. Catherine de Vivonne, the Marquise de Rambouillet, is remembered as the first great *salon* hostess of pre-Enlightenment Paris. Born in Rome in 1588, she had married Charles when she was only twelve and he twenty-three. Unlike so many aristocratic marriages of this kind, theirs grew to be loving and strong. It helped that Charles approved of his wife's talents and allowed her to drastically remodel their Parisian townhouse and turn it into a gathering place for poets, other authors and artists, and the most intellectually engaged aristocrats of the day.[1] Her receptions commenced around 1618. By that point Catherine was also busy with motherhood. She and Charles had seven children. The eldest, Julie, was born in 1607.[2]

After Charles brought her to France, Catherine found her new country's courtly culture to be coarser than what she remembered of the social scene in elite Italian homes. She was witty and beautiful—dark haired, dark eyed, with an ample bustline she was not shy about displaying—and could have been a celebrated woman at court, at which she spent considerable time in her youth. But she chose instead to socialize on a small scale, with people she genuinely liked, in the comfort of her own home.[3]

Inspired by her Italian memories, Catherine turned one of the rooms of the renovated Hôtel de Rambouillet into an attractive setting for this purpose. Eschewing the reds, browns, and golds that predominated in French palaces and mansions then, she employed blue curtains, blue brocade wall coverings interlaced with metallic threads, and jewellike lamps unlike those seen elsewhere in Paris.[4]

Young Marie was struck by the exceptional quality of the Rambouillet's home, even after many days in the Louvre, other grand palaces, and her uncle's townhouse in the Marais. Even discriminating observers of the time stressed its inviting spaciousness, which was made possible by an architectural scheme upon which Catherine had insisted: putting staircases to the side of the building, something rarely done at the time. This had allowed for large suites of rooms and the greater flowing of air, light, and traffic through wide windows and doorways. The Blue Room, in particular, was also perfumed by fresh, seasonal flowers displayed in baskets.[5]

It was of course not simply the aesthetic of the Hôtel de Rambouillet but Catherine herself and the attendees of the *salon* that captivated Marie. In her late thirties when Marie met her, Catherine was strikingly different from the other Italian woman prominent in her life. The Queen Mother could be ostentatiously pious, jealous, mercurial, and overbearingly focused on projecting images of herself as a dutiful wife and mother and as a great ruler. Catherine by contrast was genuinely close to her family but also plagued by sad moods that she counteracted with her gatherings and a studied buoyancy. She loved sharing jokes and surprises with her friends. She was also exceptionally erudite and deeply committed to virtue and the Catholic faith. But she did not like to be showy about such things.[6]

Marie at twenty-two found a remarkable role model—and new mother figure—in Catherine. But what began as admiration for the marquise would in time mature into a fond, lasting friendship.

Other women who attended the Blue Room gatherings became important friends to Marie. Among them was Madeleine de Souvré, the Marquise de Sablé, who would eventually establish her own *salon* and engage in serious writing projects. She was five years older than Marie, had already borne many children, and was unhappily married and known to be engaging in extramarital romances.[7]

There was also the petite Anne de Neufbourg du Vigean, also a young mother at the time and unhappily married. She spent much of her time apart from her husband, a Protestant nobleman named François Poussard, the Baron du Vigean and eventually the Marquis de Fors. She was quite taken with Marie, who was four years her junior—to the point that rumors eventually began to circulate that she was in love with her friend.[8]

The Blue Room attendee most familiar at first to Marie was the stunning, blond Charlotte-Marguerite de Montmorency, the Princesse de Condé. The two knew each other from court. Charlotte behaved extremely proudly in courtly contexts. But she left her forbidding haughtiness at the door of the Hôtel de Rambouillet, helping Catherine to create an atmosphere in which highborn and lowborn guests alike could mingle and liberally debate ideas.[9]

In her early thirties in 1627, Princess Charlotte was also a young mother with an unhappy marriage. Indeed, she cultivated friendship with Marie partly to secure Richelieu's protection, because her husband at times attempted to lock her away in their château in Bourges. The Prince de Condé believed that his wife had cheated on him with several men. When Marie began visiting the Blue Room, Charlotte was linked to the dark and rugged Cardinal La Valette. He was jokingly called Charlotte's "little husband" by his friends, and he was also nicknamed *L'Africain* because of his tan skin, thick black hair, prominent lips, and robust physique. These were all unusual traits for an aristocrat, so La Valette was considered ugly by many in high society—but not by the women of the Blue Room.[10]

La Valette came regularly to the Blue Room, too. So Marie got to observe him and the effect his charms had on many of the women there. She learned his story and, judging from the secretive friendship she would later develop with him, she came to sympathize with him. Eleven years her senior, he had been forced into the ecclesiastical estate as a child, despite the fact that Church reformers following the program of Trent had been trying to stop this age-old practice of many Catholic noble families. His desire had always been to serve the King as a soldier—something for which he trained on his own time, and something Richelieu soon would help him do. He was also good with Catherine's children at the *salon*, playing games with them and winning over the women partly by this means. It was poignantly apparent that he wished he had his own family, even as he was loath to give up the prestige, incomes, and influence at court that his princely, ecclesiastical status afforded him.[11]

Another woman with a perfume of scandal about her whom Marie got to know in the Blue Room was Angélique Paulet. She was a red-haired lute player and singer with whom Marie at times performed duets, given her own love of music and talent for singing. Angélique was a former mistress of King Henry IV and of many other men. In the early 1620s, when she was about thirty, she decided to change her life. Catherine liked her and did not appreciate how many in courtly society at the time condemned her in ways they never did unchaste men. Catherine helped restore Angélique to respectability and encouraged her in a converted life of chastity and prayer. At the same time, she urged her to sing and to play her instrument at the *salon*, and thereby to charm the men who attended the Blue Room gatherings in a more wholesome way than had once been her custom.[12]

Last but not least among the women regularly in the Blue Room was Julie d'Angennes, Catherine's eldest daughter. She and Marie became fast friends. Julie was nineteen at this time, had dark hair and eyes like her mother, and was both vivacious and exceptionally intelligent. Men found her to be exceedingly attractive and she enjoyed making emotional conquests—without committing herself to anyone or losing her virginity. In fact, she was ambivalent for many years about giving herself sexually to a man. She would remain stubbornly unmarried until finally accepting a proposal in her late thirties.[13]

The Blue Room gatherings were, of course, not simply informal get-togethers for Catherine's family and friends. They drew Marie into new worlds of ideas, literary conversation, artistic production, publishing, patronage of the arts and letters, and specifically feminine intellectual achievement and empowerment. Regular attendees of the *salon* included some of the great French poets, dramatists, prose authors, and artists of the era—among them Pierre Corneille, François de Malherbe, Jean-Louis Guez de Balzac, Vincent Voiture, and of course the Marquise de Sablé and another great woman of letters, Madeleine de Scudéry, who would join the group in later years.

Even the younger and most fashionable women of the Blue Room shared Marie's fondness for reading and were determined to take advantage, in a nontraditional way, of the great city in which they lived. Paris by this time had become one of the publishing capitals of the world, producing books on all manner of subjects, from classical poetry and expositions on medieval theology to newsy *relations* from abroad and the latest plays being performed for courtly audiences. Books were available often at affordable prices in shops and street stalls throughout the central *quartiers* of the city. Paris, in short, afforded exceptional opportunities for the era to women as well as men who desired to read, to be entertained as well as educated in the privacy of their homes, and to become better informed both about events affecting their lives and about worlds, past and present, different from their own.

With the encouragement of the Blue Room set, Marie would eventually develop her own ideas about what kinds of books, as well as artistic projects, she could help bring to life as a patron. But in these early days when she was young and busy with her duties as a *dame d'atour,* she was simply grateful for the new, stimulating friendships and the respite from court that the Blue Room provided.

At the same time, Marie could not enjoy these things in a simple way. Because she was Richelieu's niece, her presence occasionally cast a chill over the Blue Room. All were aware that she would not be participating if her uncle did not approve it for his own reasons. He expected his niece to keep him informed about what was said, who attended, and what projects were favored. Marie indeed was put in an awkward position early on when Richelieu urged Catherine to report on aspects of her guests' private lives. Catherine politely refused. [14]

But Marie was also welcomed into the circle *because* of her connection to Richelieu. Everyone hoped that friendship with her would guarantee them protection. Catherine herself was not shy about requesting favors through Marie. [15] So, while still quite young and sensitive, and discerning whether her new Blue Room friendships differed from the transactional, often insincere connections cultivated at court, Marie experienced pangs of disillusionment even in the charmed atmosphere of the Hôtel de Rambouillet. And the life with the Discalced nuns that she had twice been forced to abandon still beckoned warmly as a result.

13

Uncle Armand's Triumph

I n the late 1620s, Marie could not attend the Blue Room gatherings as regularly as she wished because she was often on the move as the Queen Mother's *dame d'atour*. The court relocated frequently depending on the season or on royal family members' changing moods or preoccupations. There were several royal residences in Paris, others not far from the city in places such as Fontainebleau, Saint-Germain-en-Laye, and Versailles, and still more in cities and country retreats across France.

As mistress of the Queen Mother's *garde-robe*, which was based primarily at the Louvre, Marie arrived at an encyclopedic knowledge of the numerous dresses, undergarments, capes, furs, hats, shoes, and adornments that were preferred at different locations. She oversaw, as well, the careful packing of the same into chests that would be transported by carriages sometimes over hundreds of miles, other times down a few Parisian thoroughfares.

All the same, Marie's friendships with the Rambouillets, Anne du Vigean, and others developed because the Queen Mother's favorite palace in this period was a new one just minutes away from the Blue Room. The Palais de Luxembourg, which opened its doors in 1625, had been the queen's pet project for a decade. Located in the Saint-Germain district of Paris, it was modeled after the Medicis' Palazzo Pitti in Florence.

The Luxembourg, which today is the seat of the French Senate, was a veritable shrine to the Queen Mother. It featured Italian styles and flourishes that made her nostalgic for her youth. But it also incorporated design elements—such as high and wide doors and windows placed opposite one another—that she envied in the homes of others in Paris, especially the Rambouillets.[1] Most notable of all was a cycle of twenty-four paintings by the Flemish master Peter Paul Rubens, which the Queen Mother had commissioned for the interior. Dramatizing scenes from her life on a heroic scale, they employed both Christian imagery and pagan Greek and Roman motifs. They depicted her as a dutiful, truth-seeking woman and anointed queen as she interacted not only with her deceased husband, Henry IV, her children, cardinals, and other historical figures, but also with gods such as Mercury and Juno.

The intended effect was for viewers to regard their royal mistress as a kind of goddess herself. But the reality everyone whispered about was that the Queen Mother's grip on her son's government, and even on her own household, was weakening in inverse proportion to Richelieu's.

After he had defeated the Duchesse de Chevreuse and the others planning his assassination in 1626, Richelieu assumed additional government posts that added to his incomes and control of the state. In October 1626, he was appointed Surintendant Général de la Navigation et du Commerce, which gave him authority over French trade and colonial expansion.[2] He was also given the governorship of Le Havre, the navally strategic port city in Normandy. In February 1627, he became the Governor of Brouage, an Atlantic port city near Luçon. And in March he obtained a privilege that allowed him to voice opinions at the Parlement de Paris, the preeminent judicial body in the kingdom. This put a chill over the institution's proceedings, as many *parlementaires* felt pressured to support the Cardinal's preferred policies and case outcomes.

Most remarkably, Richelieu on February 4, 1628, was appointed as Lieuténant-Géneral of the royal armies stationed in the western provinces of Poitou, Saintonge, and Angoumois—all near a major Huguenot stronghold called La Rochelle.

A war had broken out in that region. Early the previous summer, King Charles I of England, despite having married Louis XIII's sister, had stirred up a revolt against the French Crown by the Protestant Huguenots of La Rochelle. After several months of difficult naval and ground combat, the English had admitted defeat.

However, the Huguenots kept fighting, so the English aided them from the background. In response, King Louis ordered the famous Siege of La Rochelle, which commenced on September 10, 1627, and would last until October of the following year.[3]

La Rochelle was the most well-fortified city in France. Despite its proximity to the coast it was not easily accessed by seacraft, and during the earlier Wars of Religion it had not fallen despite similar efforts. However, its inhabitants' resistance during the epic siege would prove to be the last major stand against the French Catholic state by Huguenot forces. And the leadership of Richelieu, who took charge in the middle of the siege, would be credited with the Crown's ultimately decisive victory over them.[4]

Marie observed the exhilaration with which her frequently melancholy guardian took up his new role. At forty-two, he was suddenly able to dress like a knight, not a churchman—something that satisfied a longing to serve France militarily that he had harbored since boyhood.

As the Queen Mother's *dame d'atour*, and through her own communications with Richelieu and his secretaries, Marie received word sooner than most about each of her uncle's accomplishments in the field. Most impressive of all—and something hailed by other commanders at the time and long after—was his orchestration of the construction by some four thousand laborers of a great seawall almost a mile in length. It prevented the English from resupplying the Huguenots by sea.

With such engineering feats and Richelieu's effective siege tactics, too, the King's victory was all but assured except that the will of La Rochelle's inhabitants was difficult to break. Loss of life on their side was tremendous, yet they continued to resist. By October 1628, while few troops under Richelieu's command perished, La Rochelle lost some fourteen thousand men, women, and children—well over half the city's population—to starvation, battle wounds, and disease.

News of such loss of life and of the tenacity of the Protestants in the west stunned Marie and her friends at court and in the Blue Room. Yet there was great rejoicing after the siege concluded on October 29, 1628. That day, a delegation from La Rochelle surrendered unconditionally to Richelieu, who stood in for the King.

Humiliated, the Huguenots of La Rochelle were granted basic toleration of their faith. This meant that they could believe and congregate as they wished without fear of arrest. However, they had to watch without incident as Catholicism was reestablished as the official faith of their city. La Rochelle was also subjected to new degrees of centralized royal control over its affairs, which cut against the traditional power and independence that local elites had previously enjoyed.[5]

Back in Paris the subduing of La Rochelle was celebrated not simply as a royal and Catholic victory, but also as a political victory for the pro-Habsburg Dévots. With a mix of pride and concern, Marie received compliments on her uncle's heroism from Dévot friends who believed that the successful siege, and the terms Richelieu had imposed on La Rochelle, signaled the defeat of the Bons François, who in prior years had favored generous concessions to French Protestants.[6]

Ever the calculating strategist, Richelieu allowed his name to be associated with the Dévot cause as he traveled deliberately slowly back to Paris. Along the way, crowds hailed him as a new Alexander the Great. The Pope sent him compliments, and the King gave him more governorships: Aunis, the Île de Ré, and La Rochelle itself.[7] The Cardinal welcomed all of this not only as an affirmation of his indispensability to the Crown and of his commitment to the Catholic Church, but also as political capital to bank for use at another time when the Queen Mother and the Dévots might be less pleased with him.

That time was just around the corner.

14

The Cardinal-Minister's Reluctant Aide

"He is utterly depressed when fortune is contrary to him," Marie de' Medici said once of Richelieu. "But when the wind is in his sails, he is worse than a dragon."[1] This dragon was in so many ways the Queen Mother's creation. The heights to which he had risen were due considerably to her patronage. In the period of the great siege, she had even rewarded him with a new Parisian residence right next door to her new Palais de Luxembourg and nicknamed, therefore, the Petit Luxembourg. But in the wake of the siege, it became clear that the dragon was uncaged and no longer controlled by his mistress.

As soon as he was ensconced again in his ordinary duties, Richelieu began to energetically favor an anti-Habsburg position in the larger European war that had been raging since 1618. France had remained neutral since the conflict had first erupted in Prague. The Queen Mother and the Dévot party assumed that if and when the French ever entered the war, they would naturally do so on the side of Spain, the Holy Roman Empire, and other Catholic powers. Unlike the Dévots, however, Richelieu did not regard the cancellation of the Huguenot threat in western France as part of a larger, domestic and international war against Protestantism per se. The strength of Catholic France, he calculated, would depend on the weakening of the Habsburg powers and a willingness to partner with Europe's emerging Protestant nation states.

Even before La Rochelle's fall, the Cardinal had quietly opened talks about an alliance with the Lutheran monarch of Sweden, King Gustavus Adolphus. Then, toward the end of 1628, Richelieu openly broke with the Dévots and convinced Louis to build up a French military presence in northern Italy in order to prevent two small states, Savoy and Venice, from falling under the sway of the Holy Roman Empire.

The Queen Mother was horrified that her son was preferring this foreign policy when it was so opposed to her own. She newly cast Richelieu as disloyal and began to favor the counsel of two leading Dévots who favored *rapprochement* with the Catholic Habsburgs. One was Cardinal Bérulle—the same who had been Marie's spiritual advisor. He was proving disloyal to Richelieu, who had secured him his cardinal's hat. The second was Michel de Marillac, the Ministre de Justice and Garde de Scéaux (Keeper of the Seals).[2] These councilors were frustrated to see Louis and Richelieu by March 1629 leading an army into the Alps toward Savoy, signaling that the French were willing to go to war to preserve alliances with small principalities in the region and thereby check the Habsburgs' imperial power.

This movement of troops signified more specifically France's entry into the War of the Mantuan Succession. At issue were the claims of a French prince, Charles Gonzague, the Duc de Nevers, to the thrones of Mantua and Montferrat, two northern Italian states. The Habsburgs hoped to topple Nevers and then reward Montferrat and Mantua respectively to an Italian nobleman named Ferrante II of Guastalla and to the Duke of Savoy, Charles-Emmanuel I, in order to seal alliances with them against the French. The arrival of the French, however, prevented this from occurring. Instead, the Duke of Savoy stood down as the French pushed back Spanish troops in the region, gained access to other parts of Italy, and secured Nevers's rule.

Back in France, Richelieu was once again hailed as a conqueror. But he remained away from court long enough after this war that he was shocked by what awaited him once he returned in late summer. During his absence, the Queen Mother and the Dévot councilors had campaigned against his general strategy, weakening the King's resolve to stand by it. When Richelieu finally rejoined the royal family on September 14, the Queen Mother registered displeasure with him and, to the shock of everyone present, dismissed young Marie from her position as *dame d'atour*.[3]

The next day, Richelieu offered to retire from governmental service, hoping the King would not accept this. To his relief, Louis broke down into tears over the break between his mother and his most trusted advisor. Within days, the King achieved a reconciliation.

Marie thus remained a *dame d'atour*. But this did not overjoy her. She was rightly concerned that her relationship with her mistress would remain strained. Indeed, as an omnipresent reminder of Richelieu's ascendancy, Marie was now a thorn in the Queen Mother's side.

This was truer after November 21, when Louis formalized the Cardinal's role with the title *Principle Ministre d'État* (First Minister of State). Richelieu was now officially the prime minister, and courtiers began referring to him—with new notes of respect, fear, and in some cases thinly veiled hatred—as *Le Cardinal-Ministre*.

Other marks of favor from the King were forthcoming, such as another governorship for Richelieu, this time over the island of Oléron close to La Rochelle. Furthermore, Richelieu's brother, Alphonse the Carthusian monk, was elevated as a cardinal after taking up the prestigious post of Archbishop of Lyon. (Ironically, the man who had punted his teenaged brother years before into an undesired ecclesiastical career with his decision to hide away in the Alps was now obligated to take up generally unwanted, high-profile, public duties for the Church.) Finally, on Christmas Eve—in a blatant show of disharmony with his mother—the King made Richelieu the commander of his forces in Italy. This was because the Habsburgs had renewed their efforts to topple Nevers in Mantua, and fickle Savoy was enabling them. Richelieu was determined to maintain a pro-French balance of power in the region and even to invade Savoy to check Habsburg aggression. The King approved of this plan and wanted Richelieu to see it through to completion.

That same day, while thrilled to be headed toward the Alps again for more military campaigning, Richelieu focused his attentions on Marie. Not only would he miss her while he was away from court for another long, indeterminate period, but he insisted that her communications would be ever more crucial for helping him to keep track of the Queen Mother's dispositions during this sensitive period of Dévot opposition to his administration. He arranged that his niece would remain in regular contact with him and with a trustworthy secretary of state, Claude Bouthillier, the Sieur de Fouilletourte. Before joining his troops, he asked Bouthillier not only to look in often on Marie, but also to do whatever he could to prevent her from rejoining the Carmelites should she attempt it.[4]

It is striking that Richelieu was still worried about this possibility four years into Marie's time as *dame d'atour*, three years after she had dutifully left the convent a second time, and when she was, at twenty-five, finally coming into her own as a hostess, woman of fashion, and friend to some of the most fascinating and influential people in high society. Indeed, just before his departure, Richelieu had cohosted with Marie a great banquet and a series of ballets and other entertainments for the royal family and most of the court. This was just the beginning of Marie's career as one of the great French hostesses of the age. She played her role well, and Richelieu communicated his approval at a farewell luncheon with her.[5] Yet she still at times pined for life in a nunnery.

Part of the problem, in Richelieu's view, was the influence of a particular Carmelite on Marie. This was Mother Madeleine de Saint-Joseph du Bois de Fontaines. Parisian by birth and the daughter of a former ambassador to the Low Countries, Madeleine had been influenced by Bérulle to join the reformed Carmelites and was eventually appointed prioress of Carmel de l'Incarnation on the Rue Saint-Jacques.[6] She then moved to the convent on the Rue Chapon shortly before Marie stayed there in 1626. Regarded by many as a holy mystic, she was also a published writer—something rare for a woman of the time—and exchanged letters with all sorts of priests, religious, and laypeople such as Marie who sought her spiritual counsel.[7]

Mother Madeleine was the same age that Marie's long-deceased mother, Françoise, would have been. She was gentle and sweet in disposition but also unfrivolous and capable of sternness where situations demanded it. For example, she urged spiritual advisees "to lift themselves to God in silence and humility" when tempted to engaged in chatty oversharing about their feelings and their interior experiences while praying.[8]

Marie and Mother Madeleine corresponded regularly. Marie confided all sorts of worries and facts about her relationships. She also visited the nun regularly when in Paris for sessions of spiritual direction.

Around the time Richelieu was worried Marie might attempt to rejoin the Carmelites, Mother Madeleine was counseling her in terms such as these:

> You must keep your spirit elevated above human things and look at them only as shadows, as things that exist only for a moment. . . . [You must] conform yourself to the privation that God makes you bear. Because, since it comes from Him, it is necessary as an act of homage to the divine will that you do not receive within yourself any created thing whatsoever, that you instead remain simple, suffering, and dependent upon Him to whom you belong.[9]

The "privation" to which the nun referred was almost certainly Marie's not becoming a Carmelite herself. Mother Madeleine was encouraging the young woman to live as much like a nun as possible in her worldly circumstances, focused on Eternity and choosing suffering over the satisfaction of ordinary human appetites.

Mother Madeleine's counsel conflicted with Richelieu's continued hope for Marie at this time: that she would remarry, bear heirs, and do all she could to assist their family's further social and political ascent. It worried him that he would be unable to closely monitor and guide her behavior while on this new campaign.

Richelieu's mode of departing Paris at Christmastime was a striking illustration of the irony then dominating Marie's life: her priestly uncle, who had devoted serious time to Church reform and spiritual affairs in earlier years, was now the second-most-powerful man in France, the embodiment of worldly ambition and glory, and the biggest roadblock to her pursuit of a religious vocation. He normally wore clerical attire and regularly prayed Mass and the Divine Office. But as he rode off at the close of 1629, he was again dressed in armor and donned a hat, similar to a cavalier's, with a large feather. Hundreds of knightly officers accompanied him on horseback along with several pages. Rendezvousing with his army outside the capital, he and his men then headed southeast to Lyon.[10]

There, representatives of Savoy attempted to negotiate with the French before they marched into the Alps. But Richelieu realized they were bluffing, hoping additional Habsburg forces would reach Italy during the talks. He then led his forces into Italy, forcing the Savoyards to retreat from their positions near Turin and Pinerolo, the latter of which the French took at the end of March in 1630. Not long after, Richelieu and the King began to plan for the invasion of Savoy.

Amid all this the Cardinal was in touch with Marie. In late January, he sent her an item he called "a piece of the true cross," which he asked her to gift to the Queen Mother. He also asked Marie to tactfully petition the Queen Mother to write to him while he was away. Despite the formal reconciliation the previous autumn, Richelieu could feel coldness from the Queen Mother while he was abroad. He was counting on his niece to help melt the ice.[11]

Richelieu also confided to Marie his concern that the Queen Mother was unrealistic in her expectation that he could secure a quick peace with the Habsburgs while abroad. In his view they were unwilling to take the necessary steps toward that end. "God, perhaps, will arrange things for the better," he added, concluding, "I see nothing that . . . promises peace. Whatever may come, patience is needed."[12]

Marie knew that her uncle's carefully chosen words signaled a dark view of the situation—and dismay over the Queen Mother's preference for harmony with Spain and the Empire at the probable cost of greater French power and influence in Europe. She understood, too, that Richelieu expected her to diplomatically represent his outlook to others in her conversations at court.

This was not easy for her, as she had friends on both sides of the French political divide. The Queen Mother's pro-Habsburg councilor, Bérulle, had died unexpectedly in October the previous year, sparking rumors that Richelieu had had him poisoned. A cult developed around his memory, remains, and viewpoints—something Marie had facilitated, with her gift of a reliquary for his heart to the Carmelites in Paris. And Marillac's position at court had only strengthened since then. Marillac firmly opposed Richelieu's Italian strategy, believing it was worsening divisions that should not have existed in the first place among Catholic powers in the post-Reformation context. He was winning over more courtiers to this view in Richelieu's absence. Marie's spiritual counselor, Mother Madeleine, as well as other friends such as the Princesse de Condé, shared this Dévot outlook.[13]

In the meantime, the French forces under Richelieu's command overpowered Savoy in May and eventually achieved a peace with the Habsburgs in the autumn that was favorable to French interests. Somehow, despite several lackluster military performances throughout the campaign, the French—and especially Richelieu, the mastermind—came out looking like victors against the Habsburgs when the Treaty of Regensburg was signed in mid-October 1630.

Throughout this period, Richelieu came to value Marie's judgment and abilities even more. He trusted her to ensure that expensive gifts he commissioned at a distance, which were important in his diplomatic dealings with various foreign dignitaries during wartime, were executed by Parisian artisans with the finest craftsmanship.[14] He also had Marie vet new appointments to the Queen Mother's household, guaranteeing their loyalty to him.[15]

Above all, he depended on the intelligence his niece supplied to him. Most notably, Marie reported in late July that a new plot was developing at court to remove him from power. The ringleader was Charles I, the Duc de Guise. Proudly related to the ruling family of the sovereign Duchy of Lorraine, Guise was resentful that Richelieu had not appointed him to a high office. Marie relayed that Guise was speaking ill of Richelieu to members of other great families that increasingly resented not just the power he wielded, despite his less exalted lineage, but the ways he was augmenting the powers of often lower-born royal officials generally at the expense of the traditional independence of the upper nobility of France.[16]

Marie would have preferred not to be engaging in such activities for her uncle. She was also uncomfortable in her role as the increasingly hostile Queen Mother's *dame d'atour*. Nevertheless, she did not attempt a third time to rejoin the Carmelites during Richelieu's long absence from court.

15

The Coup d'État

M arie's increasing value to her powerful uncle notwithstanding, the year
1630 was a difficult one for the young *dame d'atour*. For one thing, the
Queen Mother's increasing impatience with Richelieu was often aimed at his
niece during his absence. Marie was reproached as ungrateful, too loyal to her
uncle, and derelict in her palace duties. The last charge was not entirely unjust,
as she was spending considerable time outside of court with the Rambouillets
and other friends.[1]

On another front, because of hardening opinions against her uncle, Marie
was more the object of envy and gossip than in prior years. Among the rumors
circulating at this time was that she and her uncle were scheming for her to
marry the King's second cousin, Louis de Bourbon, the Comte de Soissons.[2]

The truth was more complicated than this. The count's mother, the dowager
Duchesse de Soissons, liked Marie and wanted her son to marry her. Richelieu,
however, was unsure Soissons was trustworthy. This was because, several years
earlier, he had taken part in the failed Chevreuse-Chalais plot.[3]

Marie, for her part, could not have helped being momentarily open to the
possibility of marrying Soissons.[4] Light-haired, exceptionally handsome, in his
mid-twenties, and something of a daredevil, he was as a prince of the royal blood
one of the most eligible bachelors in France. The problem was, however, that
Soissons himself was uninspired by the idea. While a match with Richelieu's
pretty, rich, but also very pious niece offered advantages, the count wished to
keep his options open.

Attractive as Soissons was, and as approving a mother-in-law the dowager
duchess might have been, Marie as a point of pride, given the young man's

reluctance, did not press for the match. Furthermore, Mother Madeleine was encouraging her, amid a temporary weakening of her resolve, to remain privately committed to celibacy.

Nevertheless, embarrassing rumors continued to swirl that Marie and her uncle together had set their caps at Soissons. Additionally, the prospect of a second marriage to *someone* remained real, whatever Marie's private preferences. Indeed, the matter was becoming tied into the military campaigns Richelieu was pursuing.

Most remarkably in this vein, Marie in 1630 received a marriage proposal from a young cardinal of the Church. Richelieu toward the end of February was handed a letter from the younger son of the Duke of Savoy, the thirty-seven-year-old Cardinal-Prince Maurice, who was the Bishop of Verceil. Like Richelieu himself, he had been pushed into the ecclesiastical estate by his family when young. Unlike Richelieu, he was itching to be released from his clerical obligations, including the requirement to remain celibate. Although he had never met Marie, he had heard of her beauty, piety, and money and her close relationship to the most important man in Louis XIII's government. He thought she would make an excellent bride and, as she was already accustomed to the ways of churchmen, help ease him into a lay existence.

Richelieu understood immediately that the proposal was first and foremost intended as a political carrot by Duke Charles-Emmanuel, Maurice's father. The duke was still at that point hoping to negotiate the French away from their anti-Habsburg strategy.

In private Richelieu laughed away the proposal as "ridiculous." Nevertheless, for strategic reasons, he pretended he was honored by Maurice's interest in Marie. He even promised to seek Louis XIII's permission to accept the extraordinary offer—and to do what he could to facilitate the dispensation from the Pope that Maurice would need to be laicized. But he had no intention of doing either.[5]

The Cardinal-Prince thus remained hopeful for some time about a conjugal future with Marie. But in time, when no word ever came back from France on the matter, he refocused on his ecclesiastical duties. Years later, however, at the age of forty-nine, he would receive a dispensation from Pope Urban VIII not only to renounce his clerical offices but also to marry his own niece, Luisa, who was only thirteen at the time.

Marie did not have an opportunity to discuss this stranger-than-fiction proposal with her uncle until he returned to court. That was in the autumn of 1630. The two warmly reunited and caught up on many matters, personal and political.

Most pressing was the continued plotting against Richelieu by a growing list of enemies. Dévots such as Marillac were especially concerned that the Cardinal's anti-Habsburg strategy was still only in an early, developing stage. They feared, rightly, that Richelieu planned to convince the King to assist Sweden and other Protestant powers more vigorously against Spain and the Empire in the ongoing continental war.

Matters came to a head in November. Uncle and niece learned that the Queen Mother had turned completely against Richelieu and was encouraging Louis to give command of the forces in Italy to Marillac. By November 10 she was even attempting to convince Louis that Richelieu was plotting to overthrow him.

In a meeting with Louis at the Palais de Luxembourg that was supposed to be private, the Queen Mother was counseling Louis in this direction when suddenly the Cardinal burst into the room unannounced, hoping to redirect the conversation. Richelieu had learned of the meeting from a spy (probably Marie or a lady loyal to her) or by seeing it begin through a window, as the Petit Luxembourg was close enough for that to have happened. And he had arrived through a secret passageway to which he had special access, thanks to a chambermaid, Claire Bricet, who had been hired by Marie.[6] Attempting to plead his case, he only stunned the Queen Mother by his intrusion. Making matters worse, Marie also entered the room a little while after her uncle.[7]

Enraged, the Queen Mother put before her son a stark choice: either dismiss the prime minister or dismiss his own mother from court!

To demonstrate that she was not bluffing, she accused Richelieu of treason and again dismissed Marie from her position in her household. She also dismissed Marie's cousin La Meilleraye and other Richelieu associates.[8]

Richelieu fell to his knees and asked for pardon. But he and Marie were sent away, unforgiven. They left the palace quickly for the Petit Luxembourg next-door. Mortified by what felt to him like the greatest miscalculation of his career, Richelieu could not believe the Queen Mother's vehemence toward him and he feared what the King was thinking.

Marie remained with her uncle during an emergency meeting with Bouthillier and other secretaries. The main questions at hand were whether the Cardinal's career was over and what, if anything, could be done over the next twenty-four hours to prevent that from being the case.[9]

This fateful day became known as the Day of the Dupes. This was because, once news of the palace incident had gotten out, nearly everyone in courtly society believed—wrongly, it turned out—that the Cardinal would be disgraced and possibly even executed. As a result, even close friends of Richelieu and members of his family were afraid to express any support.

One notable exception, to the surprise of both Richelieu and Marie, was young Cardinal La Valette, whom Marie knew from the Blue Room gatherings. Three years earlier, Richelieu had taken La Valette under his wing and had allowed him to participate as a military officer in the long Siege of La Rochelle. The two soldier-cardinals got to know each other well during that campaign. Richelieu's fondness for La Valette was sincere, and the younger cardinal responded with true loyalty at this crucial moment. Hopeful that the King had not turned against his prime minister, he tried to buck up Richelieu's courage.

Louis, they had learned in the meantime, had quickly departed Paris for Versailles twenty miles to the southwest. In this relatively secluded spot, where there was a royal hunting lodge and not yet the great palace his son Louis XIV would build and make famous, the King deliberated for hours about what to do with his audacious first minister and his raging mother. He then sent for Richelieu.

When Richelieu received this summons, he hesitated to go. But La Valette convinced him to brave the journey, offering even to accompany him.[10] With La Valette at his side, Richelieu left his niece and his staff in a spirit of trepidation the next day. To his astonishment, Louis greeted him warmly at Versailles and assured him that he could keep his eminent position in the government. The next morning, Richelieu dispatched La Valette back to Paris to tell Marie the good news in person. The young churchman found her among her favorite nuns at Carmel de l'Incarnation. She was praying with them for a favorable outcome to the political crisis.[11]

Although he did not know it at the time, Richelieu on the Day of the Dupes had achieved a *coup d'état*. His bold appearance from a hidden passageway at the Luxembourg had actually impressed the King. By contrast, the Queen Mother's outburst, and the revelation of her true feelings toward Richelieu, had alarmed her son. To the great surprise of everyone at court and in the government—including Richelieu himself—the King soon sidelined both the Queen Mother and Marillac. Indeed, Marillac found himself beset by royal guards who took away his seals of office and put him under house arrest. Eventually he was imprisoned in a medieval castle at Châteaudun in the Loire Valley. He would die there in the summer of 1632.[12]

Because of her royal status, the Queen Mother remained at court longer than Marillac. Louis indeed attempted to reconcile her to Richelieu, as he had been able to do in the past. But tensions boiled over once the court moved from Paris northward to Compiègne. On February 22, 1631, Louis boldly before his full council assured Richelieu of his confidence in him and ordered his mother to the provincial city of Moulins, where she had a château. She refused to obey. She then found herself veritably imprisoned at Compiègne, where she would remain until mid-July. At that point, a network of supporters helped her flee the country. She made Brussels her base in what would prove, in time, to be a permanent exile. From there she worked to stir up international opposition to Richelieu.[13]

While all this was playing out, Marie had remained in Paris. It had been deemed prudent that she would not put salt on the Queen Mother's wounds by returning to her duties as *dame d'atour*. This was a relief, as it allowed her to spend quality time at the Hôtel de Rambouillet and to engage in intensified conversation with Mother Madeleine. However, a new note of politics entered into these communications. Mother Madeleine pressed Marie to intervene with Richelieu so that he might show leniency to Marillac.[14] It is unclear if Marie agreed to this request, but a follow-up letter that survives from Mother Madeleine—counseling that God sends suffering to those whom He loves, and that this life properly "is only tribulation and affliction"—suggests that young Marie was anguished to find herself in the middle of sharply divided family members and friends.[15]

Marie was also in steady communication with her uncle. One letter, penned by Richelieu in late February the day before the King ordered his mother to Moulins, is revealing:

> My niece . . . I pray that you continue to have a care for your health and that you do not engage in any of the austerities that are so detrimental to you, since this is not what God asks from us. . . .
>
> I have been told that some individuals do what they can to make others believe that . . . I had refused to humble myself before the queen or demonstrate to her every imaginable sign of respect, and that I wish that everyone connected to me such as yourself be re-established in her household against her will. I do not fear these artifices; they are too weak to make any kind of impression on the minds of those who wish to open their eyes. There is no form of humility or reverence that I have not rendered to the queen in the King's presence. . . .

I desire passionately for . . . the queen to receive me back into her benevolence. I have done everything that I can do to bring about this happiness. But my displeasure is simply that this has not advanced things in any way and that, instead . . . many intrigues are underway. . . . I am apprehensive that, if this present state of affairs continues, we [the French] will in the end fall into evils from which it will be difficult to recover, considering that they will require a royal authority not vitiated by division.

I ask you to please recommend this matter to God and to the prayers of your good Carmelites, whom I love as dearly as you do.[16]

There are obvious notes here of solicitude for a daughterly interlocutor. Most striking is the reference at the beginning to some sort of harsh ascetic practices in which Richelieu knew Marie engaged—perhaps having to do with a rigorous prayer schedule, or even self-flagellation, extreme fasting, or some other mortification of the flesh. Uncle and niece clearly disagreed about what God wanted from the latter. The way in which Richelieu closed, insisting that he also cared for the Carmelites, betrays some doubt that he was getting through to his niece.

At the same time, the prime minister confided to Marie sensitive news from court and his anxieties about the harm that continued factional division would do to France over the long term. He also defended his behavior to his niece with respect to the Queen Mother. Was he concerned that his fall from the queen's good graces had disappointed Marie? Due to the influence of Mother Madeleine, the Princesse de Condé, and the late Bérulle, was Marie herself sympathetic with the Dévots? Was he trying to save face with her, or to win her fully to his position?

Less defensively, Richelieu was also providing his niece—who was practiced with this by now—verbal formulations she could deploy should anyone important in Paris ask her for an update about the Cardinal-Minister, his present outlook, and the fortunes of his family and other associates in the wake of the Day of the Dupes.

His worries notwithstanding, Richelieu was decisive in this period. He had already by February moved forward with his anti-Habsburg strategy. On January 23, 1631, a Franco-Swedish alliance was sealed with the Treaty of Bärwald. Without yet formally entering the war as a belligerent, France began to assist the Swedes, who went on to achieve important victories against the imperial forces.

Furthermore, to the alarm of many great nobles of the realm, Richelieu acquired even more powers and titles from the King once the Queen Mother was in exile. Louis gave him the governorship of Brittany and made him the Duc de Richelieu as well as a *Pair de France* ("Peer of France"). The French peerage dated back to the twelfth century. Only a select few nobles, including some of royal blood and the highest-ranking churchmen, held the title *Pair* at any one time. Its holder had the special privilege of engaging with the monarch and the other leading royals as an equal in certain contexts. In other words, Richelieu now had to answer to no one in France—however higher-born—save the King.

16

An Abduction Plot

R ichelieu's further ascent of course elevated Marie. To underscore this, Richelieu set her up with her own grand household in a mansion on the Rue de Vaugirard. This home neighbored the Petit Luxembourg, where he was primarily residing. From this base of her own, Marie continued to attend court regularly—but no longer with laborious duties there—as well as parties and *salons* at others' homes. She also came fully into her own as a hostess. A contemporary described her in this period as similar to a "brilliant star" that had arisen and as a grand young lady who outshone many princesses of the realm.[1]

Unsurprisingly, Marie was confronted to a new degree with the challenge of prominent personalities attempting to leverage whatever connection they had with her. Soon after the Day of the Dupes, Françoise de Lorraine, the Duchesse de Vendôme, played up her friendship with Marie while begging for her husband's release from prison. César de Bourbon, the Duc de Vendôme and the illegitimate half brother of King Louis, had been involved in the Chevreuse-Chalais conspiracy against the Cardinal in 1626. He had been languishing at the Château de Vincennes ever since, leaving his wife and three children to grieve over his absence.[2]

The duchess's approach worked with Richelieu. Vendôme was released the following month. But in July 1631, the wife of the disgraced Michel de Marillac was unsuccessful with the same tactic. Writing from northern France, she highlighted a recent friendly interaction with Marie while requesting that her husband be fed sufficiently and treated respectfully while incarcerated at Châteaudun. Marillac would go on to languish there for a year, dying in August 1632.[3]

Marie unsurprisingly lost friends during the period of Richelieu's break with the Queen Mother. Among them was the pert Madame de Fargis, her fellow *dame d'atour*, who in the end had refused to be loyal to the Cardinal despite his patronage of her career. At the end of 1630, Richelieu banished her from court.[4]

The loss of the Queen Mother's friendship caused special difficulties for Marie. Shortly before she had left the country, Marie de' Medici began to speak spitefully ill of her former *dame d'atour*, claiming that she was impudent and even loose in her morals. Once she was in exile, the Queen Mother had her partisans in and outside of France spread all kinds of rumors about Marie as well as her uncle. Among them was that niece and uncle were scheming to trap the King's handsome and once again eligible brother into a marriage alliance with their family.[5]

Gaston d'Orléans had become a widower in 1627 after just one year of marriage. The Duchesse de Montpensier had died shortly after giving birth to a daughter. Several years later, twenty-two-year-old Gaston fell in love with Marguerite de Lorraine, the fifteen-year-old sister of Charles IV, the Duc de Lorraine, who—amid the larger European conflict at the time—was an unreliable friend to France. Eventually, in 1631, Gaston married Marguerite in secret.

Word of the union reached the King and Richelieu several months later from Henry II de Montmorency, the Governor of Languedoc in southern France. Montmorency was the brother of Marie's friend from the Blue Room, Charlotte, the Princesse de Condé. Subsequently, Gaston joined forces with his mother and encouraged Montmorency to lead in the summer of 1632 what proved to be a disastrous rebellion against Richelieu's government. This led to Montmorency's arrest on September 1 and his execution on October 30.[6] This of course put a strain on Marie's friendship with the princess, who felt newly alienated from Richelieu and his entire circle of loyalists, including her rumored paramour, Cardinal La Valette.

This arrest occasioned a dramatic turn of events for Marie. In early September, less than a week after Montmorency's capture, the commander at the Bastille prison in Paris learned from a priest named Dolé that a plot was underway to kidnap Richelieu's niece. This officer, Laurent Testu, was a kind of chief of police decades before a formal police force was established in Paris. He informed Marie about the danger she was in but initially was unsure who was behind the plot.[7]

Testu next suggested hesitantly to Marie and Richelieu that, with Dolé's assistance, it might be possible to find out more by letting the plot move forward without making hasty arrests. Marie readily agreed. Richelieu also found the plan acceptable, despite the danger in which it required his niece to remain.[8]

Over the next few weeks, Marie and her uncle learned from Testu that the plotters were supporters of the exiled Queen Mother. The goal was to hold Marie hostage in Brussels until Richelieu agreed to several demands. These included welcoming the Queen Mother back to a respected position at court in France, ceasing any attempts to wed Marie to one of the great princes of the realm, and freeing Montmorency.[9] When King Louis was informed of some of these details, he assured Richelieu that should the nefarious plot succeed, he would personally go in search of Madame de Combalet with an army of 1,500 men.[10]

The plot's ringleader was a priest. Father Jacques d'Apchon de Chanteloube was fiercely loyal to Marie de' Medici. He had followed her to Brussels to escape arrest after writing against Richelieu in a way that was deemed treasonous. From abroad Chanteloube began serving the Queen Mother as one of many scribblers flooding France with anti-Richelieu propaganda.[11]

The more Marie learned about the plot, the more she impressed Testu with her determination to let it unfold further so that as many perpetrators as possible could be brought to justice. Testu expressed his admiration to Richelieu in a letter dated October 25. Marie, he reported, had received the fuller story of what her enemies were planning "with great constancy and resolution." He related further that Marie insisted on taking part in difficult conversations with his lieutenants and other agents of her uncle as they pieced together more details about the plot. Other young ladies of her station, Testu suggested, might have become too distraught in such a situation or felt compelled by the norms of propriety to leave such things entirely in the hands of male protectors. But Marie went so far as to encourage Testu not to arrest one of Chanteloube's positively identified coconspirators so that even more could be learned about the principals involved, their whereabouts, and their large support network.[12]

More than two weeks later, Testu still had little more information about the kidnapping plot to send to Richelieu. In the meantime, Montmorency's execution had gone forward, to the shock of many in and outside of France. Demonstrating his ruthlessness, Richelieu exchanged clemency toward Montmorency's family members for two sculptures by Michelangelo that he had been coveting in the duke's collection. These were, rather symbolically, *The Dying Slave* and *The Rebellious Slave* that are today displayed prominently at the Louvre Museum.[13]

In early December, Richelieu and his agents remained concerned that Marie's abduction was still planned—now as retribution for Montmorency. At that time, then, Bouthillier wrote to the Cardinal to assure him that Marie was safe and, indeed, staying with him and his wife in their home. He wouldn't let her return to her own house until she received instructions from her uncle.[14]

Marie was never kidnapped. The plot was foiled by Richelieu's agents, although Chanteloube and the others involved escaped punishment while in exile and then were granted clemency by the King within a few years. Although she was physically secure in Paris, Marie suffered emotional blows as new details about the unsuccessful plot came to light. According to an account provided by an informant, the Queen Mother herself had come up with the idea of kidnapping Marie. The informant claimed further that the Queen Mother attempted to resurrect the plot early in 1633, even after Montmorency's execution, and that she wished this time to see Marie *killed*, preferably by stabbing. The conspirators were ultimately planning to assassinate the Cardinal-Minister. Furthermore, the Queen Mother's rage toward both uncle and niece had been fanned by a false rumor: that Richelieu was maneuvering for the annulment of Louis XIII's marriage to Anne—so that Marie could be crowned Queen of France![15]

More persistent and damaging to Marie's reputation was the rumor that Richelieu hoped his niece might marry Gaston d'Orléans. In the coming years, it would occasion vicious propaganda, some of it produced by an ex-Jesuit serving the Queen Mother named Mathieu de Morgues. In addition to suggesting that Marie was much less devout a Catholic than she pretended to be, the catty Morgues, who was more than twice Marie's age, broadcast far and wide the view that she was getting too old—that she was "hardly a damsel" and already "the widow of a gentleman"—for Richelieu to be holding her up as a prospective bride for any Bourbon princes.[16]

Such comments were mild compared to the rumors Richelieu's enemies would spread through the streets and *salons* of Paris as Marie's star continued to rise in the 1630s.

17

"Demi-Vierge"

As Marie neared thirty, her fabulously wealthy uncle became more powerful than any figure in French political memory. Richelieu was even whispered to be the real ruler of the kingdom. But this meant that he was constantly busy with state matters, many of which took him regularly away from Paris and the royal court. More than ever, the celibate, childless Cardinal-Minister needed Marie to serve as a kind of first lady for him—before such a role was defined in Western politics.

She accepted this and made no more attempts to become a nun. She turned out to be excellent in the role, prudently mediating between her uncle and all manner of people who sought access and favors. And she came into her own as a lady of fashion. The phrase *à la Combalet* came into use in reference to various things, such as necklines on dresses and Marie's favorite citrus pie recipe.[1]

Marie was even nicknamed "La Princesse Nièce" because of the star power she enjoyed as Richelieu's right hand.[2] The most privileged members of French society watched with both envy and admiration as she hosted with her uncle the grandest dinners and entertainments for dignitaries including the King, Queen, and representatives of foreign powers.

At the same time, Marie took new advantage of the independence that her widowhood, wealth, and increasing power afforded her. She attended court on her own time, no longer at the beck and call of a temperamental royal mistress. Frequenting the homes of Catherine de Rambouillet and her other close friends, she also hosted her own *salons* and house parties. Indeed, a kind of court developed around her, as she was attended to by an expanding number of servants, stewards, guards, gentlemen, and ladies-in-waiting of her own, such as her friend Anne du Vigean.

Marie and her entourage sometimes spent leisurely weeks at her friends' country estates and in the grand palaces that Richelieu had been adding to his family's massive portfolio of properties. These included the dramatically renovated Château de Richelieu in the Loire Valley, where Marie had spent part of her childhood during the château's humbler days, and the sprawling Château de Rueil west of Paris, which the architect Jacques Lemercier was remodeling and enlarging. Lemercier was designing gardens for it, too, that would become the envy of royalty.

In such settings and at her primary residence in the fashionable Saint-Germain neighborhood of Paris, Marie received the attentions of prospective suitors. She also enjoyed balls, festive meals, and theatricals in the company of eligible men. Yet she would not remarry, despite Richelieu's hopes for a brilliant match for her. She took more interest, instead, in facilitating matches for others and in patronizing up-and-coming writers, artists, and poets—including those who dared to portray women as the moral and intellectual equals of men.

All of this gave Marie pleasure and a sense of independent purpose even as she devoted a lot of energy to her uncle's interests. But in her era, an aristocratic woman of childbearing age who pursued a path other than marriage or vowed religious life inevitably courted gossip.

Marie endured slanderous accusations with stoicism. She rejected several eligible suitors and clung to her singleness in the brightening spotlight of Richelieu's polarizing career. Some antagonists, who exploited the rumor that her early marriage had never been consummated, called her a *demi-vierge*—a woman who appears to be sexually available and who is suggestive about it but who, in the end, privately safeguards her virginity.[3]

In this vein, the ex-Jesuit Mathieu de Morgues faulted Marie in print for wearing makeup, displaying her décolletage at parties, and "having invented new fashions nicknamed *à la Combalet*." In a pamphlet hawked in the streets, he complained that she was often seen "laden with feathers, covered with ermines," and "amid the liberties of comedies, the gallantry of balls, and the coquetry of the Tuileries."[4]

Morgues furthermore accused Marie of betraying God's will for her:

> She is a liar, having broken faith with God. She had promised Him that she would spend the rest of her days among the Carmelites,

that she would never again wear pearls or diamonds, nor expensive dresses. She promised she would never wear makeup . . . or show off her neck and bosom. . . . She is a crafty woman, and an adroit courtesan, having taken care of jewels and embroidery.[5]

Morgues's pamphlet, *La Vérité Défendue* ("Truth Defended"), was one of many that appeared in the French streets written by paid propagandists for the exiled Queen Mother. Now Richelieu's implacable enemy, the Queen Mother wished to lay ground for her return to power in France and for the Cardinal's banishment. Sullying the reputation of Marie and others close to Richelieu was integral to this strategy. Morgues, who in the 1620s had been staunchly loyal to Richelieu but who now offered himself fully to the Queen Mother, was happy to help.[6]

Marie in time would become hardened to the attacks she increasingly had to endure as Richelieu's most trusted relative. But Morgues's words were stinging. The ex-Jesuit even suggested that she posed as a woman devoted to prayer and penance while secretly enjoying "ravishments" at every turn in the royal palace.[7]

It was doubly stinging that the Queen Mother was encouraging such slander when she knew, full well, that her former *dame d'atour*'s life was more like the inverse of Morgues's portrait. During her years at court, Marie had learned to play the part of a great lady who enjoyed finery and entertainments. But her desires to leave worldly society for life as a nun had been real, intermittently strong, and fiercely opposed by Richelieu, who stood in authority over her and whom she loved and wished to please. Had she been engaged in secret practices, they generally would have been ascetic and self-punishing in nature, not hedonistic.

Furthermore, while serving at court, Marie had often sought escape from what the palace offered. By 1627 she was regularly attending the *salons* of the Marquise de Rambouillet—intellectually stimulating gatherings at which deeds and speech of an erotic nature were explicitly forbidden by their hostess.[8] Indeed, one of the Queen Mother's first outbursts against Marie had stemmed from annoyance that she was not always at the palace when expected but was getting away with it because she was Richelieu's niece.[9]

The most malicious rumors spread about Marie during the Queen Mother's years of exile were about her relationship with her uncle. The Cardinal's enemies—including not a few Dévots who regarded themselves as some of the most righteous Catholic elites of Europe—spread far and wide the heinous charge of incest.

Marie faced down all the gossip with grit. She began to find ways of fighting back, too. But given the way she veiled from public consideration her most private thoughts throughout her life, she did not leave posterity definitive answers as to why she chose never to remarry.

However, surviving documents hint that, eventually, it indeed had something to do with a hidden relationship with a churchman—just not the one Marie's detractors had in mind.

18

A Budding Friendship

The dark, athletic, and soldierly Louis de Nogaret de La Valette was only reluctantly a cardinal of the Church. He had been too young to challenge his powerful father, the Duc d'Épernon and an Admiral of France, when at age six he was given the first of his many ecclesiastical benefices. By twenty-one he had been appointed as the honorary, not acting, Archbishop of Toulouse, drawing in incomes without having to shepherd souls. And by twenty-seven he had been given a red cardinal's hat by Pope Paul V.

Eminent churchman though he was, La Valette somehow stubbornly avoided ordination even to the diaconate, let alone to the priesthood or episcopate. He was an anomaly: a cleric not in sacred orders who was also a prince of the Church.[1]

When Marie first got to know La Valette in the Rambouillet's Blue Room, La Valette was living in a strange sort of limbo that was, in a way, the reverse of her own. She, in those days, wanted to be a cloistered nun but was forced to live a worldly life at court. La Valette, by contrast, was a non-ordained cleric, not solemnly vowed to celibacy but required by the position his family put him in to renounce things he greatly desired: marriage, family life, and service to France on the battlefield.[2]

The tragedy of the attractive young cardinal's situation endeared him to Richelieu as well as Marie. So did his rank, his haughty but also warm and generous nature, his serious interest in the arts and sciences, and his unshakable loyalty—seen especially on that fateful Day of the Dupes.[3] By the early 1630s, as he approached forty, La Valette was firmly in Richelieu's inner circle. Thus Marie, in her late twenties, came to see him more often than did her Blue Room friends. This was true even of La Valette's rumored mistress of past years, the Princesse de Condé, who was increasingly preoccupied with her growing children and who could not forgive Richelieu for the execution of her brother Montmorency.

Marie became familiar with the ups and downs of La Valette's career. She observed, for example, how Richelieu gifted him the coveted priory of Saint-Martin-des-Champs in Paris early in 1633. Second only in prestige to the Abbey of Cluny in France, it had become very lax despite its great spiritual legacy dating back to the early Middle Ages. Marie saw and sympathized as the younger cardinal tried to reform the institution but then faced so much resistance that he gave up, returning the benefice to Richelieu within a year.[4] She was aware, as well, of La Valette's ongoing conversation with Richelieu about how he might serve the King militarily again after getting to do so at La Rochelle.

La Valette got to know Marie better, too. Eleven years her senior, he observed the once shy young woman blossom into not only a confident lady of fashion but also a capable and courageous right hand to one of the most powerful statesmen in Europe. More fascinating still, this charming, wealthy widow, although good with children, continued to eschew the very thing denied to him and the very thing, too, that was most expected of her by her formidable uncle and a highly judgmental French high society.

Most of French high society expected a woman in Marie's position to remarry, that is—but not the part of it that mattered most to her. The women of the Blue Room put far less pressure on her to take a second husband than a similar collection of courtly noblewomen even just a generation before would have done. They preferred to discuss relations between men and women in philosophic ways. And they did not busy themselves as much as other women did with matchmaking and gossip about love affairs.

Even where these women did attempt to facilitate love matches for the unmarried in their circle, their efforts at times went awry. This was the case, for example, when they encouraged Charles de Sainte-Maure, a kind and serious young nobleman and military officer, to court the beautiful and vivacious Julie d'Angennes.

From a distinguished Protestant family, Charles became the Baron de Montausier upon the death of his older brother in 1635 and in time would be elevated as a marquis. After meeting Julie, he quickly fell in love with her. But while Julie enjoyed his attentions, she treated him—for many years—with mild disdain while flirting just enough here and there to keep his hopes alive. He participated often in the Blue Room conversations about poetry and theater, but primarily to be near Julie, despite her cruelty. For this he endured merciless teasing from the poet Vincent Voiture and from Julie's boorish, hunchbacked brother, Léon-Pompée, the Marquis de Pisani.[5]

In the meantime, virginal but coquettish Julie was herself the butt of jokes in the Blue Room. Somehow, she had developed romantic feelings for King Gustavus Adolphus of Sweden—a man she had never met and who was married to a German princess. Julie had developed this strange, vocal passion after learning of the Swedish monarch's military exploits in the continental war, in which France was still officially neutral at that point. She went so far as to hang a portrait of him in her bedroom. The Blue Room set had a great laugh at her expense when Voiture sent Julie a clever, fake love letter from her extremely unavailable hero.[6]

In short, Julie's romantic business, not Marie's, was most under the microscope at the Rambouillet *salon*. The young woman's behavior toward Charles, especially, helped to distract from Marie's situation, as the older women were often frustrated on Charles's behalf.

In the meantime, Cardinal La Valette, given his closeness to Richelieu, would have taken note—with a mix of surprise, amusement, and perhaps growing personal interest—of the sort of men who were surfacing as suitors for Marie's hand. Perhaps because she was like a daughter to Richelieu and by 1629 had another uncle, Alphonse, made a cardinal—perhaps, in short, because her family was in the same business, so to speak—Marie by 1633 had received proposals from not one but *two* unenthusiastically celibate cardinals of the Church.

Incredibly, not long after she had disappointed the eager young Cardinal-Prince Maurice of Savoy, Marie received an offer of marriage from Nicolas-François de Lorraine, the Coadjutor Bishop of Toul who was, like La Valette, a cardinal who had never become a priest. This was in August 1633. Had she accepted the proposal, she would have become the Duchesse de Lorraine, joining her and her kin to the ranks of Europe's ruling dynasties.

At this time, France and Lorraine were in negotiations regarding the latter's traditional sovereignty and freedom to deal with the Holy Roman Empire without French interference. Toward the end of the summer, in a bargaining session at Pont-à-Mousson in the French province of Champagne, Marie's name was brought up as a potential bride by the Cardinal de Lorraine himself. He was the brother of Charles IV, the reigning Duc de Lorraine, and of Marguerite de Lorraine, Gaston d'Orléans's wife.

Like La Valette, this twenty-two-year-old churchman was in a highly unusual ecclesiastical position, having been forced into the clerical estate by his family when just a boy and risen to become a prince of the Church without ever having been ordained or properly consecrated to his bishopric. Although unhappy about this, the Cardinal de Lorraine proposed to Marie for respectably political, not merely personal, motives. Having demonstrated docility to France at the beginning of what would prove to be a long French occupation of his country, he was about to replace his brother as the reigning duke, as Charles was being forced to abdicate. In this new role, he was expected to have a consort, father heirs, and therefore retire his miter and red robes.

Richelieu was open to this prospect for his niece and considered giving the Cardinal de Lorraine the Duchy of Bar in France were the marriage to go forward. Marie was resistant, however, and unfortunately for this young cardinal, Richelieu's goals for Lorraine were far more ambitious than strengthening its ties with France by means of a marriage that was not, in truth, necessary to achieve them.[7] Richelieu believed that France should annex Lorraine and cut all its ties with the Holy Roman Empire. So, while a marriage with Nicolas-François would have greatly elevated Marie's status, Richelieu declined the proposal.[8] By September 20, the French occupation of Lorraine was formally imposed by the Treaty of Charmes.

However, even after he became the Duc de Lorraine, Nicolas-François remained convinced that he should marry Richelieu's desirable niece. He proposed again—by post this time, and communicating directly with Marie. Marie politely declined the offer. Resigning himself to a different fate, Nicolas-François received permission from the Pope to marry his twenty-one-year-old cousin, Claude, who would go on to bear him two children with very concentrated Gonzaga and Medici bloodlines.[9]

Back in France, word got out that Richelieu and Marie were turning away such princely suitors as the cardinals of Lorraine and Savoy. It also became known to some at court that Marie had earlier declined Hippolyte de Béthune, who stood to inherit a great deal from his father, as well as the attractive young widower, François de Bonne-de-Créqui, who would eventually succeed his extremely wealthy father, the Duc de Lesdiguières and a Peer of France.[10]

All of this became fodder for the partisans of the exiled Queen Mother and for other opponents of Richelieu's administration. La Valette and other friends watched with dismay as Marie was increasingly targeted by pamphleteers and street entertainers who exploited the growing common knowledge of both true and invented tales about her and her string of disappointed suitors. One street song claimed that the aging Duke of Mantua and Nevers, who had been widowed decades earlier, had expressed interest in Marie but was rebuffed.[11]

Much more damaging was a long satirical poem that began circulating in the streets in 1633. Its anonymous producers claimed to have printed it in Hell. It primarily targeted Richelieu, of course, whom it described as a strange new Saint Francis of Assisi who "protects the Swedes" against the Catholic states of Europe and who "labors for the heretic." But it also defamed Marie. Her uncle, its anonymous author claimed, had perverse wishes:

> To mingle with the blood of France,
> The vile blood of his Eminence,
> To make a queen of Combalet,
> The widow of a poor cavalryman,
> The descendant of a notary,
> The voluntary hermaphrodite,
> The female and male beloved of Vigean,
> The princess with the saffron complexion.[12]

In other words, Richelieu and his niece were turning away excellent suitors because they secretly planned for Marie to marry into the House of Bourbon. Richelieu was, in fact, working to have Gaston d'Orléans's marriage to Marguerite de Lorraine annulled, as he deemed it a threat to French political stability. It was not a great leap to imagine he wished to replace Marguerite with Marie. But some even whispered that Richelieu was looking for ways to remove Queen Anne so that Marie might marry the King![13]

In the versifier's eyes, either possibility was grotesque, because the Cardinal's niece was too low-born to marry anyone in the royal family. The reference to her skin tone, likening it to saffron, was not a literal remark about her coloring, but a reference to her obscure origins in rural Poitou, where saffron was a staple crop cultivated by the peasants and local nobility. The poem insinuated further that she was sullied in other ways, for instance because she kept close company with the baroness Anne du Vigean, who was alleged by some to be a lesbian.[14]

Questioning Marie's relationship with Anne du Vigean was an effective strategy for undermining Richelieu and his associates. It could hardly be denied that Marie and Anne were a bit unconventional. One willfully remained unmarried, and the other made little effort to reconcile with an estranged husband. And both of them were known for a more intensive commitment to Catholic piety than was the norm even in their deeply Catholic society. What better way to tarnish their reputations than to hint that they were hypocrites and that at least one of them was in love with the other?

Such gossip belied what were the unremarkable basic facts about the women's relationship. Anne was a relatively cash-poor noblewoman, and it was not unusual in the period for such women to leave their homes, without their husbands, to enter into prestigious forms of household service to female friends and patronesses of greater rank and fortune.[15] Marie by 1633 had known Anne for almost a decade. It actually would have been strange, given the customs of the time, for Richelieu's "Princesse Nièce" *not* to have invited such a friend to spend long weeks as a houseguest and even to join her household.

Even were she to remarry, Marie, given her rank and responsibilities, would have required a trusted, aristocratic, and educated woman to serve as a personal attendant. Anne du Vigean was best suited to this role among Marie's closest friends. But this did not stop Richelieu's enemies from alleging what they wished.

19

A New Kind of Literary Patroness

Measured and wise beyond her years, Marie did not dignify the gossip about her with direct responses. But neither did she suffer it passively. She had access to her uncle's deep and wide network, including his contacts in the exploding Parisian publishing sector of the time. And she took a cue from Richelieu, who was utilizing the printed word to shape public perceptions as no French prime minister had ever done. She began to assert herself as the patroness of writers and artists who had things to say that she wished to see amplified across France.

Some of the works she patronized were about women and the ways they were underestimated by more than a few moralists and preachers of the time.

Around the time of her foiled kidnapping by the Queen Mother's henchmen in 1632—something she had faced with a courage that had shocked the men around her—Marie lent support to an aspiring book author named Jacques du Bosc. He was a young Franciscan friar who had much to say about the dignity and moral and intellectual capacities of women, whom he believed were the equals of men in numerous respects.

Du Bosc had written a manuscript on the subject that dared to argue that women were as capable as men of demonstrating courage in the most difficult of situations. They were also capable of great achievements in the arts and sciences even as they were shut out of institutions of higher learning and prevented from developing in such ways.

Bold as he was with his pen in private, the friar was afraid to publish the book under his own name. When his book appeared in print with the title *L'Honneste Femme*, Marie's name appeared on it instead, as the anonymous author's protectress. After Du Bosc had shown the manuscript to Marie, she had financed its publication by Pierre Billaine, an established Parisian printer.

Du Bosc said of Marie in the book's dedicatory epistle that *L'Honneste Femme* was "a portrait made in [her] likeness" and an "effort to bestow upon [her] virtue the recognition it deserves."[1] The book went on to portray a woman who was pious, chaste, guarded in her speech, capable of regulating her emotions, but also lively and engaging in her conversation with men on an array of topics. She was able to enjoy herself at dinners and other festive gatherings without endangering her virtue, whatever naysayers and gossips might say. And she was able—at least when permitted by men to develop her character and her mind—to serve higher causes such as political justice and to study and deliberate over things that traditional moralists, Christian and pagan alike, regarded as the purview of men alone.

While controversial, *L'Honneste Femme* was an immediate success. In 1633, Du Bosc came out of hiding and worked with Marie and Billaine to produce an expanded second edition. In it, the friar praised Marie more emphatically: "If all women could contemplate your actions, reading this book would not be necessary at all; they would know without additional lessons that it is not necessary to be unsociable in order to be virtuous, and that devotion and civility are not contrary to one another."[2] Du Bosc would go on to expand the book again, see it republished several more times, and produce additional works on the theme of women's capabilities, education, and equality with men. By 1645, he was emboldened—this time with Queen Anne of Austria's protection, which Marie secured for him—to produce a work entitled *La Femme Héroïque*, which featured a quote by Plutarch on its frontispiece declaring, "The virtues of man and woman are but one and the same."

Fresh off the success of *L'Honneste Femme*, Marie threw her support behind another controversial work. It was a French translation of an unusual work of theological poetry, *De Partu Virginis* by Jacopo Sannazaro, a Neopolitan humanist who had been active a century earlier. The translator, Guillaume Colletet, was a Parisian of humble birth whose linguistic talents had won him the attention of the Blue Room regulars. His work of translation of 1634, *Les Couches Sacrées de la Vierge*, was, as a result of Marie's patronage, published by Jean Camusat, an up-and-coming printer who would soon be made the official publisher of her uncle's new Académie Française.

Les Couches Sacrées de la Vierge treated in accessible, fashionable Parisian French a perennially awkward question in the Catholic tradition that Sannazaro had taken on in scholarly Latin—a language that even highly educated women were discouraged from studying. That question was about how, precisely, the Blessed Virgin Mary had come to be pregnant with the Second Person of the divine Trinity on the evening of the Annunciation while still remaining completely virginal, as the Church taught.

Most provocative was the work's bold suggestion that despite the truly miraculous conception of the Christ Child through the action of the Holy Spirit, His mother had experienced on that pivotal night a fear similar to that of a woman who was about to be raped by pirates.

Marie, in other words, patronized a book that dared to consider the mystery of God's Incarnation from the perspective of the young woman at its center—a woman portrayed in a real and very human way. What is more, *Les Couches Sacrées de la Vierge* also depicted Mary of Nazareth as so heroically committed to her own chastity—as a prerequisite for her *Fiat mihi* and acceptance of the unimaginable divine plan for her womb—that she forced the angel who announced the plan into a sort of bargaining session. Indeed, Mary argued with the angel until she was satisfied that the Lord of all Creation was not going to violate her.[3]

Colletet also helped Marie to redefine her own public image while it was under attack. In his published letter of dedication to his patroness, he underscored Marie's own purity of spirit, which he likened to that of angels, and not just her beauty and generosity. He rendered her special homage by saying, furthermore, "Your power of judgment is without equal . . . your soul's goodness, is without example."[4] Although his inflated praise was a bit embarrassing where it likened Marie to saints already in Heaven, it was a useful counterweight—in that era when printed words had an almost magical power among populations still getting used to them—to things Richelieu's enemies were saying.

By mid-1634, Marie was also assisting the late-blossoming writing career of a remarkable woman named Marie Le Jars de Gournay. Approaching seventy, Gournay as a girl had taught herself Latin and other humanistic subjects at a time when such endeavors were forbidden to most women. By chance, she had befriended early in life the great essayist and philosopher Michel de Montaigne, whose work she would edit and help bring to further renown.

In 1622, Gournay had published a treatise arguing for women's moral and intellectual equality with men and advocating for women's access to higher learning. This work, *Égalité des Hommes et des Femmes*, had achieved some recognition when first in print, but it was given new life more than a decade later after Marie convinced Richelieu to take an interest in its author. Marie recruited into this effort the Cardinal's literary secretary, François Le Métel de Boisrobert, a witty and charming man of known homosexual tendencies whom Richelieu liked and nicknamed *Le Bois* ("Wood"). (Boisrobert's less affectionate nickname, given by others, was *Bourgmestre de Sodom*.)

Hoping to appeal to Richelieu's patriotism, Marie and Boisrobert presented him with a quatrain that Gournay had composed about the medieval soldier maiden, Joan of Arc:

> Can you properly reconcile, Virgin so dear to Heaven,
> The sweetness of your eyes with that angry sword?
> The sweetness of my eyes caresses my country,
> And this raging sword gives it back its freedom.[5]

Richelieu liked these verses and showed favor to their elderly, female author. Gournay had never married and she lived modestly in Paris. Now, suddenly, she was offered a handsome pension and unexpected recognition late in life for her talents and life's work.[6]

Indeed, in 1634 the firm of Toussaint du Bray in Paris published a voluminous edition of Gournay's essays, poems, and stories. At a time when it was rare for women who wrote to see their work published at all, let alone under their own names, Gournay went on to see second and third editions of her collected works published before she was eighty.[7] Furthermore, when Boisrobert put together several great volumes of propagandistic odes on the King's and Richelieu's military exploits, Gournay was the only female poet featured in them.[8]

Marie's activities were pioneering—and only just beginning—on behalf of authors and literary works that encouraged both men and women not to underestimate the fairer sex. However, they and the dedicatory letters to her now appearing in print did not protect her from attacks on her character. Morgues, for one—the exiled Marie de' Medici's bulldog—openly accused her of debauchery in 1635. He called Marie an "adroit courtesan" who "plays the Queen" in Richelieu's home.[9]

To undermine Richelieu's regime—and perhaps also to try to put an increasingly powerful, independent-minded, and spirited young woman in her place—some even began to advance the rumor that the Cardinal-Minister's affection for Marie was anything but avuncular.

One dirty street song in this vein maligned not only Richelieu and Marie but also their friends the Princesse de Condé and Cardinal La Valette, who was now belittled with the nickname *cardinal valet* because of his loyalty to Richelieu:

> The Combalet woman and the Princess
> Do not think to do any evil
> And do not go to confession
> About having, each of them, a cardinal;
> Because when they let their chemises go up
> And give their bodies to abandon,
> It is only the Church to whom they submit,
> Which, in any case, can grant them absolution.[10]

As far as the historical record can reveal, the truth of Marie's private life with her uncle and others was far less sensational—and far more complicated—than such slanders remotely accounted for. For one thing, Marie's communications with Richelieu in this period were affectionate, direct, and respectful, with no hints of any underlying emotional turmoil suggestive of a relationship other than that of a niece and uncle who had come to relate to each other more the way a daughter and father would.

If anything, because of Richelieu's travels for the King and his intense focus on preparing France to enter into the Thirty Years' War, Marie was at times frustrated by his periodic inaccessibility and his continued insistence that her primary task was to secure a worthy husband even after she had proven herself time and again to be a capable assistant in his career. She increasingly utilized intermediaries to communicate with him, such as his secretary Claude Bouthillier. At one point, after communicating through Bouthillier her concerns about political whisperings she was hearing at court, Richelieu dismissed her in chauvinistic terms: "Just as women have no voice in the Church, I am of the opinion, shared by ancient and modern philosophers, that they should not have any in political life."[11]

That was in the spring of 1633. It is possible, indeed, that Marie's choice of writers and poets to patronize—underscoring women's intelligence, points of view, and capabilities for public service—were partly intended to teach her uncle some lessons.

In the meantime, Marie's brother François was rewarded and raised up by Richelieu. While Marie's general resistance to remarrying was annoying her uncle, François and his wife were, in the early 1630s, pleasing the Cardinal with what they were doing for his dynastic goals. By this point they were raising two little boys—future heirs to the Richelieu legacy—named Armand-Jean and Jean-Baptiste-Amador. Another son and several daughters were still to come.

Presuming that François would make a worthy primary heir to the family legacy he was building, Richelieu found ways to elevate his nephew among the nobles of France. Having already given the young man the governorship of Le Havre several years earlier, he arranged with the King to put François in charge of the French galley fleet based at Marseilles. As the Général des Galères, François was now in charge of French naval operations in the Mediterranean. He was also to supervise French trade throughout the region, especially with merchants of the Ottoman Empire.[12]

Furthermore, within two weeks of dismissing Marie's warning to Bouthillier, the Cardinal in mid-May 1633 secured François's induction into the prestigious knightly Order of the Holy Spirit. Richelieu's father had once been given this honor by Henry III, who had established the order during the Wars of Religion. As a mark of his new status, Marie's brother was given a new coat of arms by Louis XIII, which featured three boars in the upper left, representing his Vignerot and Pont Courlay forebears, the three red chevrons of his Richelieu ancestors in the upper right, and birds and a lion below these.[13]

Richelieu brought other men from the family into the Order of the Holy Spirit that spring. Also made knights of the order were Marie's capable cousin, Charles de La Porte de La Meilleraye, and another cousin named Charles du Cambout, who was the Marquis de Coislin. La Meilleraye was a favorite of Richelieu; he had distinguished himself as a young commander at La Rochelle and, after getting into a duel with another French officer, was let off lightly by Richelieu, who otherwise favored harsh punishments for dueling.[14] And then of course there was Marie's uncle-in-law, Urbain de Maillé-Brézé, the talented and ambitious young husband of Richelieu's sister Nicole.[15] He received his regalia as a new knight of the prestigious order with a sense of entitlement, as he was proud by nature and also by this point a Marshal of France, the Governor of Calais, and the French ambassador to Sweden.

Maillé-Brézé's relationship with Marie was another complication in the young woman's life that the vicious gossips overlooked. If Marie was receiving uncomfortable kinds of attention from an uncle in this period, it was not from Richelieu but rather from this haughty, womanizing uncle by marriage.

Maillé-Brézé, many years before, had hoped to marry Marie at the time that the Richelieu family presented her much older aunt to him instead.[16] Renewed thoughts about a financially and politically favorable match with the young and attractive widow entered his mind in this period after his wife had been quietly removed from courtly society by Richelieu. While Maillé-Brézé was typically in Paris, Nicole was now in the care of the Bouthilliers at the Château des Caves near Nogent-sur-Seine. Her mental health, which had always been fragile, had deteriorated. "At one time," a contemporary wrote, "the poor woman imagined that she was made of glass, and never sat down except with infinite precautions; at another, she thought that her hands and feet had turned to ice, and was continually warming them, even in the hottest weather."[17]

Marie was required to see a lot of Maillé-Brézé in this period. Their lives in Paris were increasingly intertwined. Maillé-Brézé and his three children spent a lot of time visiting with Marie. Marie and this uncle were also asked several times in 1634 to stand up as godparents for the same individuals, including a Jewish convert to the Catholic faith who had befriended them, a young Venetian named Raphaël-Marc-Arman Abinun.[18] One of Marie's ladies, Isabelle de Pena, was also a tutor to Maillé-Brézé's son, and this young woman asked her mistress and Maillé-Brézé to serve as godparents to her daughter, Marie-Madeleine Pioche de La Vergne, the future Comtesse de Lafayette and novelist.[19]

Maillé-Brézé was free to pay court to Marie when Nicole died faraway in Saumur, at the age of forty-eight, in August 1635. Ten years Nicole's junior, Maillé-Brézé was suddenly an eligible, attractive widower with a teenaged son and two young daughters to raise. But although Marie was as obliging as possible as a mature cousin to these children, she had no wish to become their stepmother.

Some contemporaries believed that it was from bitterness over rejection by Marie that Maillé-Brézé—who would never remarry—began to fan the flames of gossip about her and Richelieu that the Cardinal's enemies were circulating.[20]

Ironically, Maillé-Brézé and other gossipmongers did not realize that by making ugly suggestions about Marie and Richelieu, they were overlooking something that was quietly developing in the young woman's life that could have caused a legitimate scandal. If Marie was inspiring unchaste thoughts in a churchman in this period, historical records point not to the punctilious Richelieu but to the adventurous Cardinal La Valette, whom misinformed taletellers were still linking to the Princesse de Condé.

20

Falling in Love

Late in the spring of 1634, Marie spent many days inside the cloister at Carmel de l'Incarnation, but this time as a patient in the convent's infirmary.[1] It is unclear why, but the shame, paranoia, and anger that the devout and sensitive young woman surely endured over the public attacks on her character may have had something to do with it. What is more, her suffering was compounded in this period by embarrassment over Richelieu's rumored machinations to arrange a match between her and Gaston d'Orléans.

In May, the King's brother caused great offense at the French court by signing his own personal treaty with Spain, at a time when it was an open secret that both Louis and Richelieu opposed the Habsburg powers in the continental war. Rethinking his rash move, Gaston within a few months signaled through his agents that he regretted his decision and hoped to reconcile with his brother and the prime minister. This was in September after Habsburg forces had soundly defeated the Swedes and German Protestants at Nördlingen in Bavaria, something that constituted a major setback for Louis and Richelieu, who now had to plan France's entrance into the war and drop any pretense that they did not favor the Protestant powers. When Marie de' Medici and her supporters in Brussels celebrated the Habsburg victory, Gaston realized that his love for France was stronger than his loyalty to his Habsburg relatives. It was time for him to return home.[2]

But Gaston knew that one thing, especially, stood in the way of the reconciliation. Awkwardly for the prince, both Louis and Richelieu expected him to cut ties with his beloved wife, Marguerite de Lorraine. To make this clear to him, they secured a declaration in September by the Parlement de Paris that the couple's marriage was null and void. This was in spite of a firm protest by Pope Urban VIII that the marriage was valid and indissoluble.

It was now more loudly said at court, in the streets, and even outside of France—especially in Spain and the Low Countries—that Richelieu hoped this would free Gaston for a marriage with Marie.[3] The plausibility of such a marriage increased when, after a complicated series of negotiations, Gaston returned to France, after almost four years in exile, without Marguerite at his side. On October 21, he was received warmly and with great ceremony by Louis at the Château de Saint-Germain-en-Laye in front of a crowd of amazed courtiers.

He greeted Richelieu a few hours later, and the leading nobles and officials of the kingdom joined the Cardinal and the royal brothers in a feast. Furthermore, to demonstrate his cordial reconciliation with the prime minister, Gaston visited the Château de Rueil the next day. With Marie at his side, Richelieu hosted a party for the prince that was even more magnificent than the one at the royal palace.[4]

Amid the scripted formalities of Gaston's return to court, the response of the prince's now seven-year-old daughter by his first wife was most telling—and a cause of pain for Marie. Overjoyed to see her father again, Anne-Marie-Louise, known by the nickname *La Grande Mademoiselle*, was also anxious for him. Her entourage had persuaded her that Richelieu was working to make his niece the girl's stepmother. Young as she was, La Grande Mademoiselle was horrified by the thought that her father, a Bourbon and the next in line to the throne so long as her uncle remained childless, might marry someone of such low birth as Madame de Combalet. She got her point across by singing some of the bawdy street songs about Richelieu and his niece, feigning naïveté about their meaning.[5]

Marie's literary patronage, her visits to the Carmelites, and her hours with the Blue Room set—sometimes at country estates, far from Paris—were welcome distractions from such embarrassments. But in this same season, Marie also began to experience a new sort of joy amid her difficulties, and from an unexpected quarter: her blossoming friendship with Cardinal La Valette.

The two were thrown together more than ever in late 1634 when their families united in a marriage. La Valette's older brother, Bernard, the Duc de La Valette, married a cousin of Marie's and Richelieu's, Marie du Cambout.

That marriage, along with two others, occasioned one of the grandest parties in Paris that year. Indeed, on the same afternoon of November 28, and in the same chapel at the Petit Luxembourg, three of Marie's cousins on the Richelieu side—Cambout, her younger sister Marguerite, and Françoise du Plessis de Chivré—married great noblemen of the realm in a single ceremony. Marguerite married Antoine l'Âge, who was made the Duc de Puylaurens as a reward for helping Richelieu negotiate Gaston d'Orléans's return to France. And Françoise married Antoine III de Gramont, the Comte de Guiche—a talented military man seen by some as more loyal to Richelieu than to the King.

Cardinal La Valette enjoyed parties. At these festivities, he was one of the most honored guests, as the brother of one of the grooms and as a prince of the Church. So he watched at close range as his once shy friend Marie helped Richelieu host, first, the intimate gathering at the Petit Luxembourg and then, on her own, a spectacular wedding feast for almost two hundred courtiers at L'Arsenal in the Marais district. L'Arsenal, called such because it was a former arms depository, was a grand residence reserved for the Grand-Maître de l'Artillerie, who was at that time Marie's recently widowed cousin, the Marquis de La Meilleraye.[6]

The events were featured a few days later in *La Gazette*, the first weekly magazine in France. The beauty of L'Arsenal's main hall was "without comparison," with its "rich tapestries," great buffets of ciselé silver and gold vermeil, "so many other exquisite things," and the magnificent light—from a hundred crystal candelabras with eight white wax candles each—that caused the women's jewels to glisten marvelously. Each woman of the court was escorted through this hall into a grand ballroom by a gentleman paired with her for the honor.[7]

Abraham Bosse's etching *The Ball* from 1634 gives us some idea of the latest Parisian silhouettes Marie and most of the wedding guests would have cut amid the splendor. While La Valette, like Richelieu, would have donned his richest red robes for such an occasion, Marie would have worn a high-waisted, low-cut dress of shimmering silk or another fine fabric, with an underskirt of a complementary color showing in the front, and with its ballooning sleeves and bodice adorned with trimmings of lace, ribbon, and fresh flowers. They both had dark hair. La Valette's was thick and grown out to his shoulders and complemented by a fashionable moustache and goatee. Marie's would have been done up with a braided chignon in the back and billows of curls framing each side of her face, which was also framed with one of her most expensive necklaces—likely her famous string of pearls, which was envied by many at the time.[8]

Marie was tall and moved with a dignified, noble air. Dressed as she was while greeting the numerous high-ranking guests who arrived at L'Arsenal, she could not have failed to capture some approving glances from La Valette, who, whatever his ecclesiastical status, was not a man to hide his appreciation of female beauty.

Given the intense scrutiny she was under by so many of the guests, Marie was all the more impressive as she welcomed Queen Anne in a grand fashion about an hour into the party. While acting friendly in courtly settings, the blond, green-eyed queen was among those who fanned the rumors about Marie, Richelieu, and Gaston.[9] Yet Marie greeted her in L'Arsenal's courtyard with formidable graciousness—and to the sound of three cannons and hundreds of muskets. Marie also honored the Queen's arrival with a light show. It involved five hundred multicolored Roman candles and a great machine with eight rotating wheels that pyrotechnically shot off colored lights, too.[10]

The insert in *La Gazette* went on to describe the rest of the evening Marie had helped to arrange. The acting troupe of the great Mondory presented several short comedies and a farce. One comedy featured musical interludes by twenty violinists. The farce featured a Spanish *sarabande* performed by sixteen lute players and ended with a timed, second salute of musket fire and cannon shots outside in the courtyard. This signaled that dinner was ready.[11]

The ladies, starting with Queen Anne, were then escorted again by the gentlemen through more stunning rooms and hallways toward six long dining tables with about thirty place settings apiece. The Queen sat in one great room with her ladies-in-waiting and several princesses of the realm. Marie sat in a neighboring room called the *petit pavillon* with the newlywed couples, some of the younger ladies-in-waiting of the Queen, and various princes and dukes. La Valette and Richelieu sat close by, in the *grand pavillon*, with a group of noblemen and foreign dignitaries. After a dinner with several meat courses, everyone returned to the ballroom and there was music and dancing until two in the morning, when there was a final salute to the Queen by the guards in the courtyard.[12]

In the weeks following this utter social triumph, Marie and La Valette saw more of each other. La Valette not only continued to attend the Blue Room gatherings and other smaller gatherings where Marie was present but also was regularly in Richelieu's company, preparing for a military commission.

On the eve of France's entry into the Thirty Years' War, La Valette was high among the trusted men to whom Richelieu gave strategic political posts with military responsibilities attached to them. In mid-March, he was made the Governor of Metz, a well-fortified former city-state in Alsace. Traditionally known as the Messin Republic, it had come under the protection of the

French Crown in the mid-sixteenth century but was also claimed by the Holy Roman Empire.

Richelieu also gave La Valette command of the French forces in the German lands that were soon to face combat.[13] The King authorized this decision toward the end of June 1635, several weeks after France had formally declared war on Spain and its allies. Before deploying for this command, La Valette traveled back to court to receive his orders directly from the King. He brought with him a capable officer from Scotland, Colonel John Hepburn, who was serving as his *maréchal de camp*.[14]

Hepburn caused a stir when La Valette introduced him to the Blue Room set, as Marie and the other women found him to be quite attractive. After the cardinal-commander had departed Paris, the poet Voiture teased him about his being eclipsed in the women's affections by such handsome officers of new acquaintance because of the war.[15]

By October, however, Voiture was consoling La Valette that the news of his successful military exploits in the Rhineland was helping him make new "conquests" within the same group of ladies, and ones "more to be desired than all of those that [he] could make along the Rhine." La Valette might want to hasten back to Paris, the poet urged, to collect such spoils.[16]

Marie's heart was foremost among them. La Valette was corresponding with the young widow by the time he was commanding soldiers in the French-German borderlands. By late 1635, these communications were facilitated by the young Léon Bouthillier, the Comte de Chavigny, the son of Richelieu's secretary Bouthillier and himself a secretary of state in regular contact with La Valette about state and military business. Chavigny became a confidant of both Marie and La Valette about the evolved nature of their friendship.[17]

Marie eventually burned La Valette's letters to her, and only a few of hers to him survive, all from 1637. But references to their earlier communications appear in Chavigny's correspondence. Also, the poet Voiture left clues to posterity about their relationship. Indeed Voiture, who was especially loyal to La Valette over time, acted as Cupid for the pair while La Valette was abroad.

Although he had known Marie for years, Voiture suddenly began composing poems of a romantic nature for her in this period, including three *rondeaux* on the theme of her "beautiful eyes." In one, Voiture described her eyes as so "consuming" in beauty that "nothing so charming" throughout "the entire universe" could be discovered.[18] In another, he playfully described fights breaking out in

Heaven over Marie's beautiful eyes, to the point that Venus started choking on her own jealous anger.[19] Other new lines by Voiture portrayed Marie as both physically appealing and of strong character and intelligence:

> The beautiful Combalet
> Has the mouth of a carnation,
> The eyes of a lively flame,
> The courage of a king. . . .
> Her generosity equals her beauty,
> She is good and intelligent.[20]

Voiture was newly in Marie's debt, as she had secured a handsomely paid place for him in the household of Gaston d'Orléans's wife, Marguerite de Lorraine, so the existence of such verses is partly explained by that.[21] But it is also possible that Voiture was helping the busy—and less poetic—cardinal-commander to compliment Marie, because La Valette had developed feelings for her prior to the summer of 1636. The feelings were mutual, according to a letter Voiture sent to La Valette in August and in which the poet referred to a friend from the Blue Room, in code, as the churchman's "wife."[22] That woman was almost certainly Marie, as Voiture also sought to alleviate La Valette's worries over new rumors going around that a powerful rival for the woman's affections—probably Gaston d'Orléans, who was still the heir-apparent to the throne and who many believed was considering renouncing his wife and marrying Marie, after all:

> I would like to talk to you about "your wife," *Monseigneur*. . . .
> What you have seen in her that is lovely, admirable, and charming
> has only increased, hour by hour. And every day we discover in her
> new treasures of beauty, generosity, and wit. Besides, I can swear
> to you that in your absence she has behaved in all the ways you
> would wish her to. I know there are some rumors out there which,
> no doubt, have made you a bit suspicious of her conduct. . . . And it
> is true, there is a *gallant* from a good household, and who one day
> will possess a great deal, who visits her quite willingly. But I assure
> you, that amid all that, she has all the feelings that a wise and very
> careful woman should have, and that you yourself have inspired. . . .
> So hasten your return.[23]

Marie's and La Valette's regard for each other had been able to bloom into something romantic when La Valette had returned to court early in 1636. In late January and early February, he had performed admirably as a military commander for France, helping to save the towns of Colmar and Haguenau from falling to the imperial forces. This was after a long campaign in which he and his men had helped to lift a siege of the city of Mainz and to capture the town of Zweibrücken in the Rheinland. He did so while serving alongside a German Protestant prince named Bernhard of Saxe-Weimar, whose formal alliance with the French La Valette he had helped to achieve by late 1635.[24]

Thus, when Marie saw him in Paris in late February, La Valette was being welcomed home by her uncle and others as a fine soldier, tactician, and leader of men.[25] At the same time, Marie found him to be enthusiastically loyal when he returned to find her, Chavigny, and others close to Richelieu veritably at war with Maillé-Brézé and his coterie. La Valette quickly became linked to "le parti de Combalet" in this conflict, which was tied to Richelieu's eventual dismissal of his Secretary of State for War, Abel Servien, who was loyal to Maillé-Brézé.[26]

Amid all this, Saxe-Weimar also journeyed to Paris. He was welcomed to court in March and fêted as a great friend to France. It very soon occurred to some at court, including Richelieu, that Saxe-Weimar and Marie might make a good match and strengthen a strategic alliance. Richelieu went so far as to suggest the possibility to Saxe-Weimar, but the ungainly and corpulent German prince balked at the idea. "Madame de Combalet possesses every quality that I should want in a *mistress*," he remarked ungallantly at the time, "but hardly one that I should expect in a *wife*." His primary objection was that she was too lowborn to become his consort, her far greater wealth and other charms notwithstanding.[27]

While this momentarily affronted Richelieu, Marie likely shed no tears over the stout and staunchly Protestant Saxe-Weimar, especially while regularly enjoying the company of La Valette that spring. How much time she spent with him, and how she spent it, is untraceable. But Marie and La Valette were both frequently with Richelieu and seen at the same courtly functions and other gatherings. In early April they were linked publicly, but perfectly respectably, in an announcement in the *Gazette* about the baptism of Chavigny's two daughters. Chavigny asked the two to stand up together as godmother and godfather to his eldest, Louise-Françoise.[28]

Given the terms in which Voiture was able to speak to La Valette about Marie after the churchman's return to the front in May, there must have been private moments in which at least emotional bonds were sealed. The weight of historical evidence suggests that Marie had more scruples than La Valette about sexual relations outside of marriage. But private encounters would have been easy enough to arrange by the pair, given La Valette's firm place in Richelieu and Marie's inner circle—even to the point of having a room always ready for him at the Château de Rueil.[29]

Whatever transpired between them, Marie's and La Valette's displays of familiarity that spring had been enough that by later in 1636, rumors were circulating (along with the others about Marie) that Richelieu was considering La Valette for his niece. Indeed, no less a figure than Hugo Grotius, the great Dutch humanist and ambassador to France for Sweden from 1634 to 1644, referred several times in his official and personal correspondence to a planned wedding between Marie and La Valette—one that Richelieu favored, hence the younger cardinal's new military charges and other secular rather than ecclesiastical preferments on the horizon for him. This was in the second half of 1636, when Grotius spent considerable time in the presence of Marie and other French courtly elites. He told the Swedish chancellor, Count Axel Oxenstierna, that there was reason to believe that La Valette was the reason why Marie would never marry anyone else, despite various eligible prospects for her. He even reported that Marie herself joked to Grotius's wife, in front of a group courtiers, that perhaps Grotius could soon be made a cardinal, going from the married to the ecclesiastical estate.[30]

Rumors of impending nuptials between La Valette to Marie were hardly far-fetched. After all, he was at least as good a match as the Cardinal-Prince Maurice of Savoy or the Cardinal de Lorraine. He was a never-ordained prince of the Church from an exalted family who could potentially arrange with the Pope to be freed from his ecclesiastical charges. Besides this, he was unflaggingly loyal to the French Crown, even to the point of taking up arms for his country and upsetting Pope Urban VIII in the process.[31] Richelieu, it was whispered, had arranged to give La Valette governorships and military commands to pave the way for a new, fully lay role in the world—as a new, beloved member of the Richelieu family.[32]

More such gossip swirled in 1637. After more months of combat, La Valette returned to Paris in January. Following close behind was Saxe-Weimar. After formal audiences with the King and Queen, La Valette and the German prince were fêted again for many weeks in Paris and in châteaus outside the capital. This festive season would last for La Valette until mid-May, when the King would give the warrior-churchman a new command.

That winter and spring of 1637, Marie and La Valette had numerous opportunities to enjoy each other's company at theatricals, balls, and more intimate settings. Beginning immediately in January, their behavior toward each other and speculation about it was noteworthy enough that, far beyond Paris, even an aging astronomer, Nicolas-Claude de Peiresc, a Richelieu loyalist, expressed concern about it. He wrote from Aix-en-Provence to the equally serious brothers Jacques and Pierre Du Puy, who were in charge of the King's library: "We do not know how to shut the mouths of those chatterers who have already married off Monsieur the Cardinal de La Valette to Madame de Combalet."[33]

21

La Valette

I n this period of her intensifying relationship with La Valette, Marie became
further emboldened as a patroness of arts and letters that veered from some
of the conservative, French aristocratic conventions and tastes of the era.

When La Valette returned from the war in January 1637, there was a playwright everyone was talking about in Paris. His name was Pierre Corneille, and
he was Marie's protégé. A play he had written, *Le Cid*, had caused a stir,
and Marie was standing by it even at the risk of alienating the members of a new
institution her uncle had just founded, the Académie Française. Devoted to the
perfection of the French language, the Académie's primary task was to produce a
dictionary that would standardize the language across the country. But the men
Richelieu appointed to it quickly got into judging the aesthetic merits and sub-
jective content of new literary works.

Corneille was among the most talented up-and-coming dramatists of the
age. Two years younger than Marie and from a respectable bourgeois family in
Rouen, he had been known to her, La Valette, and their Blue Room friends since
1630, when a lighthearted comedy he had written was a success in Paris and
brought him out of provincial obscurity. By the mid-1630s, he had seen more
success in Paris with his plays, including *La Veuve*—a comedy about a widow in
a messy love quadrangle that was first performed at La Sphère, the seventeenth-
century equivalent of a seamy nightclub. By this point, he was a regular at the
Rambouillet salon.

Marie often got to critique Corneille's works in progress, as he regularly tried
out verses and acts on her, La Valette, and their friends. Marie and the others
were not shy about offering Corneille suggestions along with encouragement.

But Marie admired his talents enough that she got her uncle to invite him into a new group called Les Cinq Auteurs—five men whom Richelieu hoped would bring to life with their pens and imaginations plays whose basic plotlines he enjoyed dreaming up.[1]

Le Cid was Corneille's breakout play. It was an unconventional tragicomedy, and it is still today considered one of the finest plays ever written in French. Dramatizing the story of the eleventh-century Spanish folk hero Rodrigo "El Cid" Díaz de Vivar, *Le Cid* premiered in December 1636 at the Théatre du Marais in Paris, with Marie and other courtiers attending. Its plot developed around a love triangle—that of El Cid, who became a hero in a war against the Moors, and the two women who adored him, Princess Urraque and Lady Chimène. In the story, the princess selflessly throws her friend Chimène together with the soldier Rodrigo, because she knows that due to her exalted rank she would never be free to marry him as Chimène would be. Rodrigo and Chimène fall in love, just as the princess intends. However, although Chimène's father wishes for the two to marry quickly, and although the marriage would facilitate political stability at a time of crisis, Chimène's scruples about family honor get in the way after Rodrigo kills her father in a duel.

The play was immediately controversial. One reason was because of the way Chimène, despite her passionate feelings for Rodrigo, postponed marrying him for her own private reasons when public, political goods were at stake. Another was that the play's tragicomic form and some of its plot devices violated Greco-Roman norms to which the traditionalists and purists of the Académie clung almost religiously.[2]

Despite this, Marie confidently backed Corneille, defending *Le Cid* as an excellent play. She also encouraged Richelieu to support Corneille in the wake of the premiere. The Cardinal then facilitated additional performances at the Louvre, in the presence of members of the royal family and honored military leaders such as La Valette and Saxe-Weimar. He even invited Corneille's troupe to perform *Le Cid* not once but twice in his own home. And he secured letters of ennoblement for Corneille from the King.[3]

Corneille expressed his gratitude for Marie's patronage on many occasions, but he was most emphatic when dedicating the published version of the play, which appeared in bookstores in 1637. He confessed in his epistle to her at the front that he had doubted the quality of *Le Cid* when he first wrote it but that Marie's love for it helped him believe in its worth. "Fake things never have the power to dazzle you," he said to his patroness, so "one cannot rightly doubt the value of something which has the good fortune of pleasing you."[4]

The publication of *Le Cid* only fueled the controversy over it. Marie did not seem to mind this, as she went out of her way at this time to back yet another tragicomedy that was ruffling feathers. Jean de Rotrou, also from Normandy and a member of Richelieu's Cinq Auteurs group, had written a play called *Agésilan de Colchos* that had premiered in Paris two years before. It was one of several plays by which Rotrou hoped to introduce conservative French theatergoers to the new sort of romantic tragicomedies that had been entertaining Spanish and English audiences for some time.

Agésilan de Colchos, however, dared not only to mix the two classical forms of drama but also to feature a cross-dressing king among its characters. This was something not seen at the time in French comedy but tolerated in Spanish theaters.[5] Yet, after the controversy over it swirled together with that over *Le Cid*, Marie backed *Agésilan*'s publication, as well. It appeared in 1637 from Anthoine de Sommaville's established house in Paris. Rotrou's dedication to his bold patroness appeared at the front of it.[6]

While enjoying with La Valette and her other friends the hubbub she was helping to create in the French literary world, Marie was beset by two major sorrows later in the spring. First, on April 30, her longtime spiritual advisor and mother-figure, Madeleine de Saint-Joseph, died at Carmel de l'Incarnation. Second, on May 17, the King gave La Valette command of the French armies fighting in the Low Countries, ordering the cardinal-commander to depart from Paris to join his men.

La Valette left the next day for the Château-Porcien in the Ardennes, where 15,000 infantrymen and 6,770 cavaliers awaited him. This new command, coveted by other French officers, was a great honor for Marie's secret beau, and one that would have made her proud given the high value she placed on honorable, patriotic military service. But judging by the handful of surviving letters from Marie to La Valette, which all date from the latter half of 1637, his absence and exposure to danger in the war were sources of grief and anxiety.

"I will be very impatient until your enterprise is ended, both for the sake of your glory and because of the danger you are in," Marie wrote to La Valette on July 13. "You would not believe how much pain this gives to me," she added.[7] In another letter from two weeks later, the young, unmarried woman thanked a churchman and military leader who was busy with the countless preoccupations of his command yet still was making sure to communicate with her: "*Monseigneur,* there is not one day that I do not receive new assurances of the honor of your remembrance of me, for which I am so obliged to you that I wish for nothing so passionately as to testify to you, with my humble services, the obligations I have toward you."[8] In November, she was more emphatic: "I have more tenderness than you can imagine. . . . I await [your return] with impatience, as well as the ways in which I will testify to you that I am, with greater fidelity than anyone else in the world, your most humble and obedient servant."[9]

Marie's surviving letters to La Valette were carefully worded and indicate that each was doing various favors for the other's friends and family members. Marie's cousin La Meilleraye, for example, was serving as La Valette's *lieutenant-général,* and Marie sought assurances regarding his well-being and interests. But two factors make the letters difficult for a modern-day reader to decipher with confidence.

First, there was the wartime sensitivity of both La Valette's and Marie's correspondence, given their ranks and positions. Their letters would have been of interest to spies working for the enemies of Richelieu and of France. Cognizant of this, both parties wrote guardedly and with coded phrasings.

Second, it was also the convention among French aristocrats of the period to employ highly sentimental terms and stylized prose. What strikes a modern, Anglophone reader as impassioned language is not, in and of itself, evidence of exceptionally intense feelings or a romantic, sexual relationship behind the scenes.

And in fact, there are hints in the surviving sources that perhaps Marie's moral and spiritual scruples had been preventing La Valette, when he was with her in Paris, from getting everything he wanted.

In a letter from November 29, Marie was playful with the reluctant churchman after reporting to him that her uncle Richelieu had recently become "more devout than ever." Assuming La Valette might come home and stay with them before too long (as La Valette's room at Rueil awaited him), she wrote:

> I had no doubt that [my uncle] will work this winter at making
> you more devout, too. I take too much interest in everything that
> touches you not to rejoice in the hope of your sanctification. I desire
> extremely that you want this blessing, as much to begin working on
> this as for you to give me the joy of seeing your return. This is one
> of the things I desire most in the world, with so much passion.[10]

La Valette was only able to spend a short season in France, however, as Riche-lieu and the King required his military services in Luxembourg early in 1638 and then in Piedmont by March. He took over the command of the French armies in Italy after the previous commander, Charles I de Blanchefort, the Marquis de Créqui, was killed in a siege at Crema near Milan in March.[11] Although no letters between Marie and La Valette are known to have survived from after 1637, the most remarkable poem ever composed for Marie came to her in this period from Voiture, the pair's trusted go-between. The poet had, as it happens, ventured into Piedmont around this time to visit La Valette, who was a bit surprised to suddenly see the frilly fellow amid his hard-bitten soldiers.[12] The poem itself was a plea on behalf of a man who loved Marie but was increasingly frustrated by her chastity:

> Let this man enter unreservedly,
> Without a struggle, and without impediments,
> Into the place that is his home,
> A man who, if he does not see it soon,
> Will be enraged within the hour.
>
> You are too strict with him
> In your home, and he protests loudly,
> That by manifest larceny,
> You accept his soul and his heart,
> But you do not want the rest.
>
> The former are inside, the latter kept out,
> While all together are on fire.
> It is reasonable, Madame,
> That you either receive his body,
> Or you give him back his soul.[13]

Later in 1638, Richelieu himself wrote to La Valette about Marie:

> I saw yesterday a person who cares greatly about everything that touches you, including matters of conscience. She spoke to me about the latter with so many natural testimonies that you should,

out of consideration of this, redouble your devotion [to God], not only for your own sake, but also for her, to satisfy the desire that she has to be one day with you in Heaven to praise God's goodness jointly with you and without end. In truth, she is a very virtuous person, very devout and very affectionate toward your interests.[14]

In his reply from Turin, written almost a month later, La Valette said a bit curtly to Richelieu about his niece, "You have reason to believe that she is virtuous, because it is certain that she is extremely so."[15]

22

Chosen

B y the time La Valette was commanding troops in Italy, Marie had proven to her inner circle that she was rather more self-controlled—even amid her passionate feelings for a man who desired her in return—than moralists of the time expected a woman to be. She contrasted sharply with the image of her peddled in the streets by enemies of her uncle. She differed, too, it seems, from the version of her that La Valette was urging her to become. She held tightly to a Catholic moral code that demanded one of two things from her and La Valette, should they wish to share the blisses of Heaven together rather than fall into permanent states of sin and damnation. They were either to avoid sexual congress for the rest of their lives or until both were free to marry. A marriage could only take place, of course, if La Valette renounced his prestigious ecclesiastical positions with the permission of both the Pope and (as this mattered greatly then) the King.

While dealing for months on end with mostly hidden emotions over La Valette and the uncertainties of his future, Marie had also proven herself to her uncle Richelieu to be the most loyal and capable member of his family. In spite of prejudices that the Cardinal-Minister harbored about women, he made a decision in 1637 that shocked his relatives and countless others in and outside of France. Although it would not be official until 1638, he had determined with the King to make Marie a duchess-peeress of France in her own right—that is, a duchess with powers and privileges possessed only by an elite handful of dukes and princes of the realm.

This was something unheard of, to dignify a woman this way. Men who were selected to become duke-peers, who did not inherit the title from a father or uncle, generally were being rewarded for exceptional service, usually military, to the Crown, as well as for having estates vast enough, family lineages exalted enough, and wealth great enough to be deemed a "peer" of the monarch. The few other duchess-peeresses of France then, including the Princesse de Condé and La Grande Mademoiselle, derived their titles and powers secondarily from husbands or fathers who were duke-peers, usually by virtue of close blood ties to the King. Yet Richelieu went even further than this. He guaranteed, in a most unorthodox fashion, that Marie would have the right, at any point, to pass on the duchy and rights and emoluments connected to it to whomever she might choose—male or female. This was unprecedented in French inheritance law, which was based on the highly patriarchal Salic code dating back to the sixth century.[1]

Marie specifically would be made the Duchesse d'Aiguillon as well as a Peer of France. The Duchy of Aiguillon was a territory with feudal dependencies in Gascony, situated about 180 miles southeast of La Rochelle. It had recently been given by Richelieu to Antoine de l'Âge, who had wed one of Marie's cousins at the grand triple wedding celebrated at L'Arsenal in 1634. Temporarily called the Duchy of Puylaurens, it had been taken from L'Âge in 1635 after he had gotten on the wrong side of the Crown during a fraught time of preparations for the war with Spain. He was arrested and imprisoned at Vincennes, where he soon died from (it was officially reported . . .) natural causes. Richelieu in the meantime had purchased the duchy and gotten the King to hold it in reserve, vacant, until he knew which member of his inner circle would be invested as its lord.

Chosen for this instead of her brother or another male relative, Marie would now shoulder rights and obligations of overlordship over Aiguillon and its dependencies, including the right to appoint all local officers of the Crown.[2] She would also be considerably responsible for the spiritual well-being of the duchy and was expected to work on this with local ecclesiastical officials. There was a substantial Protestant population in the region, and the Catholic communities were suffering in many cases from poverty and a general lack of education and formation in the faith, so this would not be simple business for her.

Richelieu himself had been made a duke-peer only a few years earlier. Securing the same title for Marie put her in the most elite group of the already small upper echelon of French nobles. This cohort stood in a long line going back to the original twelve, half of them churchmen, raised to the peerage by the Capetian kings of the twelfth century. Among their privileges, which Marie now shared despite her sex, was a right to participate in deliberations of the Parlement de Paris. Another, which Richelieu had in truth already been letting her exercise unofficially, was to help the King select men for appointment as bishops of the Church.[3] Nicolas Pavillon, the new Bishop of Alet, for example, had been elevated after Marie told Richelieu that he was a wonderful preacher who spoke powerfully to the heart and was capable of moving even the least sensitive souls to do penance and amend their lives.[4]

Richelieu's enemies (and some friends, at this point) whispered various things about all this. The Cardinal had failed, some said, to marry off now middle-aged Marie to a duke or prince who would elevate her to a similar position in the normal way, so she could now enjoy a princely rank while remaining unmarried. Others believed that Richelieu was trying to raise Marie to a rank suitable enough for the likes of Gaston d'Orléans, Saxe-Weimar, or the still unmarried Comte de Soissons to take her seriously as a prospective consort. Still others wondered if the Cardinal was paving the way for Cardinal La Valette, once fully laicized, to marry his niece with minimal embarrassment given the eminent position of his own ducal family and the loss of princely status his renunciation of a cardinalate would entail.[5]

The first and last of these theories were more plausible than the middle one. In fact, the King's cousin Soissons had resurfaced as a prospective match for Marie in late 1636, when his mother, the dowager countess, raised the possibility again with Richelieu.[6] Word got out to some courtiers who believed that such an alliance might help reconcile the handsome count to the King after his rumored involvement with another plot against Richelieu. But Richelieu quelled such rumors by the following summer, insisting in writing that he had no interest in forcing such a marriage on Marie when "nothing [was] capable of disposing her toward it."[7]

Additionally, the continued rumors about Marie and the King's brother had been fueled in 1636 and 1637 by the cordial friendship—but nothing further—that the two had developed. Gaston had settled into the Palais de Luxembourg, his mother's former home, which made him Marie's neighbor when they were both in Paris. They also enjoyed some of the same theatricals and visited each other's country estates with their entourages as a matter of courtesy.

One such visit occurred in August 1637. That summer, Richelieu had asked Marie to return to his family's ancient seat in the Loire Valley where she had lived between the time of her mother's death and that of her marriage to the Marquis de Combalet. By this point, the old Château de Richelieu as Marie had known it was unrecognizable from the outside, as was its surrounding terrain. Like the Cardinal's new Château de Rueil close to Paris, the Château de Richelieu had been undergoing remodeling and expansion on a spectacular scale. Several years earlier, Richelieu had hired the architect Lemercier to transform the modest medieval manor home of his youth into one of the grandest palaces in Europe—partly to properly display his growing art collection. The Papal States had authorized the transport of sixty ancient statues to adorn the château's façades and interiors. Lemercier and his crew of some two thousand laborers were also bringing to life gorgeous outbuildings and pleasure gardens that would later inspire André Le Nôtre's more famous ones at Versailles. Nearby, they were building an innovative, planned "ideal city" that Richelieu had dreamed up. The Cardinal envisioned opening an academy for young nobles there.[8]

Marie and her entourage, including Catherine de Rambouillet and Anne du Vigean, traveled to Richelieu to check on the progress of all this for her uncle, who had little time to visit the place himself. She reported back to the Cardinal how beautiful everything was, but she also had to endure an unpleasant drama.[9]

In late August, Marie welcomed the King's brother and his daughter, now ten years old, to stay at the new château for several days, along with many of their attendants and friends. At this point, Gaston's wife, Marguerite de Lorraine, was still outside the country, given the standing annulment of his marriage under French law. So there was a growing expectation that the prince would repudiate her and choose a bride acceptable to the King and Richelieu.

La Grande Mademoiselle still feared this possibility, so she did her best to spoil the visit for Marie. To create awkwardness for her hostess and ruin any chance Marie might have had to become her stepmother, the little princess ensured, while playing the innocent, that tensions arose between her father and Marie over the presence at Richelieu of Anne du Vigean's estranged husband. The Baron du Vigean was then employed by one of Gaston's secretaries who had made the journey with the prince. Gaston's daughter later bragged about the enjoyment she took in exploiting the situation, looking for opportunities to increase everyone's embarrassment and frustration over the unexpected throwing together of the baron and his wife. The princess also, in subtle ways, made herself so unpleasant a companion that Marie feigned illness so that she could spend less time with the girl and her attendants.[10]

After this excruciating visit, Marie and Gaston made it absolutely clear to their intimates that a marriage between them would never happen. All the same, songs continued to be sung in the streets about Richelieu and his niece scheming together to entrap one or another of France's most eligible princes.[11]

By this point, Richelieu's plans to elevate Marie as the Duchesse d'Aiguillon and as a Peer of France were firmly in motion. And whether or not he was still hoping Marie would marry someone of princely status—including La Valette—he had many reasons now, having nothing to do with her marital prospects, to elevate her in status over and above other contenders in the family, especially her brother François and her uncle Maillé-Brézé.

The latter was a capable and accomplished military commander and ambassador and a brilliant figure in many ways. But he had also shown himself on many occasions to be intemperate, fractious, envious of others' success, and, perhaps worst of all in Richelieu's eyes, vindictive toward Marie.

François, for his part, had since his rapid elevation to high offices and prestigious knighthoods proven to be a disaster of a man and not at all a reliable heir to the Richelieu legacy.

While preoccupied with the war and countless matters of state, Richelieu was required to take time to scold François many times for his spendthrift ways and his increasing neglect of his wife, Marie-Françoise, and of their young children. He also asked Chavigny and other agents to monitor the young man's affairs. Among other things, François, when traveling to Marseilles in his capacity as Général des Galères, would take a large staff and leave his wife and children without the number of servants, ladies, and nursemaids appropriate to their station.

For a time, Richelieu indulgently had been paying down François's debts. By the summer of 1636, however, the Cardinal had had enough. In June he reminded the young man that part of the money he was given month to month, on top of his ordinary income, was intended for his wife and children and for covering the cost of mounting "lawsuits . . . accrued annuities and other debts and obligations." "If you do not set yourself up on that footing," Richelieu warned his nephew, "you can seek help wherever you wish, and we will find some other suitable way to preserve for your children what we can of your property and that of your wife, despite this mess of yours."[12]

Two follow-up letters from Richelieu dated July 10 reveal how damaged the relationship between uncle and nephew had become after François refused to reform his ways. In one, Richelieu expressed disbelief that François kept with him at all times "five ordinary gentlemen and six secretaries." "I confess," the prime minister of the largest kingdom in Western Europe added sarcastically, "you must have more business than I do, because I have only two." Additionally, François employed for himself "six chamber valets," while Richelieu "never had more than three." The Cardinal informed his nephew, who appeared to be on the path to "total ruin," that his young wife and youngest children had left their grand home in Paris, which François was financially neglecting, for a humbler but more secure situation in Poitou.[13]

Marie in the meantime took over the rearing of Francois's older boys, who remained in Paris. In the second letter, Richelieu insisted again that François reduce his personal expenses and urged him to consider his family's well-being before his own. He mentioned that he had seen young Armand-Jean and Jean-Baptiste at Marie's home and that they were well. But he warned François, "If you continue as you are, you will make them the heirs of very little. Put things in order, if you want me to love the father as well as the children."[14]

Clearly, François was not a man Richelieu could trust with the power and responsibilities that came with a dukedom and peerage. But apart from all the negative reasons why the Cardinal chose to elevate Marie above her male relatives, there were many positive ones, too, related to her proven character and capabilities, not just in comparison to her prodigal brother. The list included her constantly demonstrated loyalty, her discretion, her steadfastness in the face of ruthless and malicious opponents (including royal figures and family members), as well as her ever-expanding capacity to perform many different kinds of tasks efficiently and gracefully—even amid intensifying public scrutiny.

Furthermore, while she enjoyed herself (recently, at least) as a great lady of fashion, Marie seemed less tempted by power, wealth, and fame than others of her station. And she had a surprising ability to stand up to Richelieu when she disagreed with him but without seriously offending him. At times she even brought him around to her views.

An instance of this had occurred during her sojourn in the Loire Valley in the summer of 1637. Not far from the Richelieu estates was a town called Loudun that had become infamous as a place where Ursuline nuns were possessed by devils and where a too-handsome priest, Urbain Grandier, had reportedly led them into evil congress with the fallen angels. In 1634, Grandier had been locally tried, found guilty of sorcery, and burned at the stake after brutal rounds of torture.

Richelieu, who had been following the case, was glad to be rid of Grandier, who had been causing trouble by publicly opposing the Church's increasingly enforced discipline of clerical celibacy. He also vocally opposed Richelieu's administration and a local, royal project of dismantling the fortifications around Loudun, where there was a large Huguenot population that favored retaining them.

Even after Grandier's execution, however, reports of demonic possessions at Loudun continued to reach Richelieu's desk. Marie heard the stories, too. Like her uncle, she believed on hearsay that some of the Ursulines really were possessed. Nevertheless, she wished to see for herself and for Richelieu whether the situation was as bad as many said.

In a show of independence from her uncle, Marie sent on ahead of herself a known skeptic about the possessions: François Hédelin, the Abbé d'Aubignac, who later became famous for his plays, novels, and scholarly reflections on theater. His belief that the possessions were being faked was doing him no favor with Richelieu at the time. Marie appreciated his talents, though, and by involving him in her mission to Loudun, she managed to save him from an open break with her uncle that might have cut short his career, if not his life.[15]

Marie's own visit to the convent was an all-day affair on September 26, 1637. With her were Julie d'Angennes, Anne du Vigean, the poet Voiture, and her ever-obtruding uncle Maillé-Brézé. According to D'Aubignac, who recorded details about the visit in a *Relation* published soon afterward, the exorcists arranged Marie's schedule so that she might see, efficiently, every single woman and girl believed to be controlled by demons.

The *Relation* details interactions Marie had with nuns who seemed variously to her to be acting, not suffering from something authentically horrific, and demonstrating behaviors that the local exorcist was erroneously assessing as demonic. Much to this priest's surprise, the young woman challenged his assessments of the evidence before them both in front of the nuns, the other local officials, and her friends standing around them.[16]

In short, the soon-to-be Duchesse d'Aiguillon by the end of the day came closer to D'Aubignac's skepticism regarding the possessions. Communicating all of this quietly to Richelieu and then backing the publication of the *Relation*, Marie not only rescued D'Aubignac's career but subtly called into question the original execution of Grandier, which Richelieu had backed, without undermining the prime minister's authority.

23

The Investiture

O n New Year's Day 1638, Marie was welcomed by the King with special
ceremony to the Château de Saint-Germain-en-Laye. Louis had greeted
Marie many times before as "my cousin"—an honorific used for many nobles by
members of the royal family. This time was different, though, because he also
called her, for the first time, *Madame la Duchesse d'Aiguillon, la Comtesse d'Agenois
et de Condomois*, and *Pair de France*.

An investiture ceremony ensued, in which the King conferred on Marie not
just her new powers as a duchess-peeress in her own right, but also the regalia and
symbols of her new authority. The ceremony had a sacred aura about it, because
Louis himself had been sacrally anointed at his own coronation years before. The
French monarch was seen, indeed, as a kind of priest-king, in the line of David
of ancient Israel and Judah, and there was a sort of equivalency presumed—by at
least some of the onlookers at Saint-Germain—between what Louis was doing
to Marie and the action of consecrating new bishops of the Church.

During the ceremony, Louis solemnly placed a new coronet on Marie's head.
It was a small crown, but more elaborate than the bejeweled and pearl-encrusted
one she already possessed as the widowed Marquise de Combalet. This one surpassed even those given to ordinary dukes of the realm, which featured distinctive
circles of golden acanthus leaves. It was adorned further with a cap of blue velvet
that matched the new mantle the King also gave her, which was fringed with
gold, lined with ermine, and embroidered with her new coat of arms.

This heraldic mark of her status and lineage contained, in the shape of a shield
divided into four quarters, two fields of white on the bottom left and top right,
with three red chevrons on them, which represented her Du Plessis de Richelieu

forebears. The opposite two fields of gold had three black boars' heads on them and represented her paternal Vignerot du Pont Courlay line.

In honor of Marie's new rank, Richelieu gave her the Petit Luxembourg. He would now take up residence in his newly constructed Palais-Cardinal near the Louvre. Just a stone's throw now from the Palais de Luxembourg, Marie had readier access than ever to some of the finest gardens and groves in Paris, enabling her gardeners to cultivate in the middle of Paris the flowers and fruits, especially lemons and oranges, that she most loved. She also had a private garden.

One of Marie's newest friends from the Blue Room, the future famous writer Madeleine de Scudéry, said of the Petit Luxembourg, "It was a delicious house, with a garden terrace which was surrounded by windows and mirrors, which together doubled the extent of the salons and gardens around it. The trees and flowers were portable and constantly renewed. All the apartments opened on to this garden and communicated with a magnificent salon." The rooms were "splendidly furnished," and the house contained "a gallery and three great rooms filled with rare and precious things"—not only paintings by some of the finest artists in Europe, including Rubens, and statues that dated back to ancient times, in some cases, but also "mosaic tables, ebony cabinets, and gold and silver vessels studded with jewels of inestimable price."[1]

This grand Parisian home and everything inside it would belong to Marie for the rest of her life. Now the primary seat of her ducal court, the Petit Luxembourg also quickly became the scene of Marie's own literary *salon* and innumerable planning sessions for some of the most important and innovative religious and social charitable enterprises of early modern France.

Amid all this, Marie eagerly but quietly awaited news of her friend La Valette's whereabouts in war-torn Italy and his next journey home. What a joy it would be to welcome him into her new home. They had spent many hours together in the Petit Luxembourg already, when it was Richelieu's. It was easy, then, for Marie to imagine La Valette's presence there with her, and the conversations, meals, and entertainments they would enjoy.

But during wartime, as Marie knew only too well as the widow of Combalet, it was also impossible not to worry that a dedicated commander like La Valette might never return again alive or as the same man she had known.

24

Heartbreak

The years 1638 and 1639 were full of honors and celebrations for Marie because of her new status as a duchess-peeress. Some of these were in print form. Poems, engravings, and books appeared that were dedicated to the famous niece of Richelieu. These included a novel by Jean Desmarets, who was a founding member of the Académie Française, and a Latin textbook by a scholar named Pierre Bense-Dupuis that women—traditionally discouraged from learning the Church's official language—could study at home.[1]

There was fanfare not only over Marie but also, of course, a great deal over Richelieu. In 1638, his great Palais-Cardinal near the Louvre was ready for him to live in, and he began employing it, along with the Château de Rueil, as a visual reinforcement of his power and the trust the King had in him. It was full of treasures, such as the finest chandeliers money could buy, a relic of Saint Louis of France encased in a reliquary with 9,000 diamonds and 224 rubies, and artwork and furnishings rivaling anything seen in the royal palaces.[2] As the Cardinal began to host parties, theatricals, and other events there, Marie was regularly at his side and orchestrating a great deal behind the scenes.

Furthermore, the French and their mostly Protestant allies in the continental war won victory upon victory—in the Alsace region, in northeastern Germany, in Bohemia, in the Low Countries, at sea, and even overseas in the Americas and Africa on the fringes of the Spanish empire. This gained Richelieu much credit among the French people. A new kind of national pride swelled, politically girding the foreign policy Richelieu had pushed for so long. There was, to be sure, unrest over the cost of the war, which led to increased taxation, and—especially among older noble families that saw Richelieu and his "creatures" as dangerous arrivistes—over the power Richelieu personally wielded. (In this era, the term "creature" was used in French descriptively, not always in a derogatory way, to mean a client who owed his rise in the world to one major patron.[3]) But the pro-Habsburg position of the Dévot party looked increasingly treasonous, let alone untenable, as Richelieu stirred up patriotic displays that linked military gains abroad—despite all the Protestant allies involved—to the glory of Louis XIII's crown and the fidelity of France to God and His Church.

There were ordinary celebrations, too, over things such as births and baptisms. In March of 1639, for example, Marie joined her brother, sister-in-law, and other family members in welcoming into the world her youngest nephew, Emmanuel-Joseph.

But the greatest cause of rejoicing in this period for Marie and all of France occurred on September 5, 1638. Shortly after eleven in the morning that day, church bells began ringing first near the royal palace in Saint-Germain-en-Laye and then, with remarkable speed, all over Paris and into the remotest corners of the kingdom. They signaled what many regarded as a miracle. Queen Anne, who had been married to a sexually reluctant king for more than two decades without bearing him an heir, had just given birth to a healthy son. He was christened not only with the name *Louis*, after his father, but also the second name *Dieudonné*, or "God-given."[4]

Celebrations of the future King Louis XIV's arrival were all the more joyous and extended because of all the anxiety and political unrest that France had suffered over the long-fruitless royal marriage. The spotlight shifted away from the King's brother, Gaston, and from all the intrigues around him in a way that seemed, with the new patriotic feeling in the air, to promise healing and unity for the kingdom.

Marie took advantage of her new rank as a duchess-peeress to celebrate the birth of the *dauphin* in grand style. She orchestrated eight straight days of festivities in her neighborhood in Paris, the Faubourg Saint-Germain, where she now presided over a ducal court at the Petit Luxembourg. Beginning the evening of September 5, she ordered bonfires and other illuminations to light up the neighborhood every night, culminating in a great fireworks show with celebratory gunfire and cannon shots that lasted four hours, until one in the morning, on the octave of the baby's birth.[5]

The young duchess also that same week hosted a grand dinner in Louis Dieudonné's honor at her home. According to the *Gazette*, the distinguished guests at the Petit Luxembourg included one of Cardinal La Valette's sisters-in-law and the wives of both the King's chancellor Pierre Séguier and the military commander Henri de La Trémoille. Also attending were the Princesse de Condé and her beautiful nineteen-year-old daughter, Anne-Génévieve de Bourbon-Condé, whom Marie—along with La Valette, Anne du Vigean, and the others of their inner circle—had known since she was a little girl.[6] She had been educated, with Marie's encouragement, by the nuns at Carmel de l'Incarnation and was now one of the most sought-after young women in French high society.

Amid the celebrations of this long season, Marie was occupied not only with a growing list of responsibilities as Richelieu's right hand and as a duchess-peer, but also with an expanding portfolio of charitable endeavors and financial investments. Some of these, such as a hospital project across the Atlantic in New France that she had devised, were innovative for the time and went far beyond what was expected even from a woman in her exceptionally privileged position.

But then the autumn of 1639 broke into all of this as a terrible shock.

La Valette, Marie learned, had become gravely ill while with his troops in Rivoli, a town near Turin in northern Italy. He was suffering headaches, a fever, sweats, and an inability to speak. Richelieu was so upset by this news that he sent to Italy one of the best French physicians he knew, named Guillemin, whom he hoped would be able to save the younger cardinal's life.[7]

He was too late. By the time Guillemin arrived in Rivoli, La Valette's condition had worsened beyond remedy. Marie learned some days after the fact that on Monday, September 28, her beloved friend—whom she had always been required to address in front of others as *Monseigneur* and *Vôtre Éminence*—had died among his men. He had been without the consolation of any loved ones nearby during his final hours. He had a Jesuit confessor with him and, as Marie learned from Chavigny, the cardinal-commander had demonstrated "extraordinary feelings for God" in his last moments.[8]

Chavigny hoped this information might console Marie in some small way. But she was devastated by La Valette's death. She confided to Chavigny a month later that she had been "constantly sick" since learning the news. "There is no way for me to get over it," she went on. "This person is always present to me, and I cannot believe that we will be separated forever without extreme pain."

She hastened to add, "I implore you to burn this letter."[9]

For some reason, Chavigny did not. Chavigny was a friend but also politically ambitious and a realist about the sometimes deadly, shifting winds of French political life; such a letter could serve one day as an insurance policy. Or he may have saved the letter for sentimental reasons, as he was close to Marie just as he had been to La Valette. (Rumors eventually spread, in fact, that Chavigny was secretly Richelieu's son; these seem to be unfounded, but they were later exploited by the novelist Alexandre Dumas in the nineteenth century, and their existence is a testament, at least, to how close he was to both the Cardinal-Minister and to Marie.[10]) Either way, because Chavigny kept the letter rather than destroying it, something of the depths of Marie's feelings for La Valette was not buried in time, along with whatever hopes she had been harboring silently in her heart about their relationship before he died at the age of forty-six.

Given the scandal it would have caused had Marie displayed any serious attachment to the dead churchman, she grieved this death in secret. And she suffered the additional pain of watching how others responded to La Valette's demise. Pope Urban VIII refused to say a Mass for the repose of his soul, even though it was his custom to offer one personally for every cardinal who died. At the French court it was presumed that this was because La Valette had died in military service to France at a time when the Papal States were more favorably disposed to the Habsburgs and their allies. It had not been sufficient the year before when La Valette had attempted to assure the Pope of his concern for the unity of Christendom and his loyalty to the Holy See.[11]

Then there was the vulturous haste with which various nobles went after the monasteries, churches, and other benefices in the deceased cardinal's portfolio. Thirty such claims were successful, receiving royal approval.[12] Although La Valette's secretary had been in touch with Marie, having a sense of how important she had been to his late master, in the hope that she would be able to inherit at least one of his benefices, she was too late even though only a week and half had passed since her friend's death when she attempted to act on the prospect.[13]

As she had during happier times, Marie in her grief relied emotionally on Chavigny. She unburdened other things on him in this same period, such as her increasing contempt for her real brother, François, whose older sons she was now helping to raise because of his neglect. "He is worse than ever," she said in one letter. "His extravagances are unbearable." This was after Richelieu had reprimanded him in strong terms, earlier that year, for daring to seek more income from the King when he was doing a mediocre job in his public offices and making no effort to reform his life.[14] Among other embarrassments, François spoke "pitifully" about Richelieu to whomever would listen at parties. He also complained that he had not been given more lands and a title like his sister's. "I cannot begin to tell you what a cross my brother is to me," Marie exclaimed to Chavigny.[15]

Marie fell ill several times in the subsequent months, her condition exacerbated by severe sadness.[16] But her position in French society and political life, her religious devotions, and her energetic and sometimes restless personality prevented her from dwelling debilitatingly long on any one problem. This season of hope and rejoicing turned one of terrible grief and aggravation—this early season of her new identity as the Duchesse d'Aiguillon and as a Peer of France—was also the busiest of her life up to then.

What is more, Richelieu's assessments of his niece's actions and accomplishments in this period would prove most consequential once it became clear that the Cardinal-Minister, though he was still relatively young as well as feared by some as a godlike figure, was, too, only mortal.

25

A New Relationship

An unusual book appeared in 1639 that was dedicated to Marie. Its title translates as *Images of Foundresses, Female Reformers, and Leading Nuns of All the Orders of the Church*. It was full of portraits of numerous Catholic women from across the centuries. While it featured canonized saints such as Catherine of Siena, it also contained portraits of uncanonized women, including one who was still living: Jeanne de Chantal, the foundress of the Visitation order, who was known to Marie and her friends.[1]

Marie had commissioned a talented young artist from Antwerp, Michel Van Lochom, to bring this book to life. Several years earlier, he had done engravings for a mostly textual work by a Celestine monk, Louis Beurier, on well-known, saintly leaders of the Church's religious orders.[2] But that book overlooked women. With Van Lochom's help, Marie corrected the historical record.

The new book on women featured eighty-eight engravings with brief captions in simple Latin. It was designed to teach its audience that, contrary to what they might presume based on other books out there, there were numerous leaderly women in the Church's history who had simply not received sufficient attention yet.

Among them were figures who had a special place in Marie's regard, such as the nuns Ana de Jésus from Spain and Marie de l'Incarnation (Barbe d'Acarie), who had helped to establish the Discalced Carmelites in France. Also included was Madeleine d'Amboise, a fifteenth-century Benedictine abbess based in Thouars—a town close to Glénay in Poitou, where Marie had spent her childhood. D'Amboise had reformed several convents that she governed, well in advance of the Protestant Reformation.[3]

At the beginning of the book, Van Lochom likened Marie to the variety of women represented in it. Marie's life was "a copy of theirs," he claimed, because by 1639 she had already become active in charitable endeavors and founded a number of Catholic institutions herself.[4]

This was not hyperbole. In addition to donating to a wide array of charitable causes, she had by the early 1630s become a leader of a charitable confraternity at her parish of Saint-Sulpice in Paris. This enabled her to play a hands-on, organizational role in addressing poverty and other social ills in her neighborhood in Paris.[5] Also, in 1630, she had established her beloved Discalced Carmelites in Poitiers, setting them up with a new convent there.[6] Furthermore, in 1633, she had joined with her uncle's close friend, the Capuchin priest Père Joseph, to establish the second convent in Paris of the Benedictine Filles du Calvaire, a new, reform-minded community committed to living out the Rule of Saint Benedict in strict terms.[7] The first of these communities had been based just next to the Petit Luxembourg since 1622, and the second community was given a stately house and a newly built chapel in the Marais district.

Much of Marie's early charitable activity and patronage of religious institutions was in keeping with the kind expected of devout noblewomen of the era. As a child, she had seen her mother and grandmother take a financial and charitable interest in their parishes and surrounding communities, and later on at court she noted the supports given by Marie de' Medici, the Princesse de Condé, and other great ladies to religious orders, new and old parish churches, and hospitals for the poor.

But at Richelieu's side, with the unusual vantage point his position as prime minister allowed her, Marie began to understand more clearly the roles that both public and private funds, and negotiations with civil and ecclesiastical authorities at different levels, played in the foundation, upkeep, and success of different institutions. This broadened her view of what was possible for a woman of position to do for society and the Church.

Marie also became more ambitious for the good she could do for both the Church and the poor in France after she got to know a priest named Vincent de Paul—a man who, in time, would be remembered as one of the most famous canonized saints of the period. She had learned of him when she was a *dame d'atour* and was in contact with him by 1631, when he was fifty and she in her mid-thirties. She arranged for this priest to meet Richelieu.[8] This marked the beginning of De Paul's long and fruitful collaboration with the Cardinal and even more so with Marie, with whom the priest would be close until the end of his life in 1660.

De Paul had started life as a peasant. Born in 1581 in a place called Pouy in southwestern France, he was able despite his obscure origins to receive an excellent education at the University of Toulouse before pursuing an ecclesiastical career. For several years after his ordination to the priesthood, he was focused more on advancing that career than on seriously discerning God's will in his life. This led him, ironically, to encounter in Paris the likes of François de Sales (another future canonized saint) and Pierre de Bérulle, Marie's one-time spiritual guide. Under their influence, he experienced an awakening that deepened his sense of his priestly calling.

He also became troubled by the poverty of rural communities like the ones he had known in his youth. He saw a dynamic relationship between poverty and a lack of decent medical care on the one hand and moral and spiritual problems on the other. It troubled him, too, that poor, rural populations were vulnerable to Protestant preachers who often spoke more to the heart, with their Gospel emphases, than typical Catholic clergymen then did.

De Paul's eventually radical devotion to the poor and the sick would, in time, secure him not only canonization as a saint but also a legacy as one of the most beloved French saints in history. But when Marie and Richelieu began to work with him, he was the relatively obscure founder and superior of an odd new association of clergymen and brothers that he called *la Congrégation de la Mission*.

These men were eventually known as *Lazaristes* in French (and variously as *Lazarists* and *Vincentians* in English) because in 1632 they were given the ancient Priory of Saint-Lazare in northern Paris as a motherhouse. Their mission was to support one another in their priestly ministries and fidelity to the Church while serving the poor and sick in material and spiritual ways. They were focused on rural populations, in particular, which were often neglected even by charitable nobles and government officials, who increasingly were concentrated in Paris and other cities.

At this point, seven years after De Paul had formed them, the Lazarists were still negotiating and discerning their position in France as they had only just been approved by the Pope, and not as a religious order in a traditional sense. They had secured several important patrons, however, including Richelieu.

Richelieu's initial support of De Paul in 1631 was in the form of financial sponsorship of twelve seminarians affiliated with his congregation who were studying in Paris.[9] Within a few years, however, Marie would encourage her uncle to join her in supporting the congregation's infrastructural development.

In the meantime, Marie got to know an unusual woman who was De Paul's good friend and primary female collaborator. Her name was Louise de Marillac, and she would also eventually be canonized as a saint. De Marillac was the niece of Michel de Marillac, the leading Dévot and royal councilor who had been arrested after Richelieu's *coup d'état* of 1630 and who had died in prison less than two years later. The illegitimate daughter of Michel's brother Louis, Louise had been forced to grow up in a convent and then urged to marry a man she barely knew—one who left her widowed with a son in 1625, when she was in her early thirties. She then accepted De Paul as her spiritual director and got involved with charitable missions among the poor that several of his aristocratic female associates had been developing for several years, calling themselves the *Dâmes de la Charité* (Ladies of Charity).

De Marillac became exceptionally devoted to this kind of work, so in 1633 she cofounded with De Paul an innovative organization of women called the *Filles de la Charité* (Daughters of Charity). The Daughters were an organization of women of humbler social origins than were found among the Ladies of Charity or in traditional religious orders of women. Taking decades to be acknowledged by Church authorities because of their rejection of a strict, cloistered model of religious life, they combined an intensive regimen of prayer and contemplation with active service among the poor, the sick, and the socially marginalized.

Marie became involved with the Ladies of Charity by linking to them her confraternity at the parish church of Saint-Sulpice. Given this new affiliation, she expected that De Paul and De Marillac would assign at least one or two Daughters to work with her there.[10] In May 1636 she arranged for a young Daughter named Barbe Angeboust to reside in her home. Barbe was supposed to engage part-time in domestic service while devoting many hours a week to serving the poor of the parish. She ended up begging De Paul to release her from this work, because Marie's home was "a grand court," and serving such a "great lady" seemed inconsistent with what she believed God wanted from her. De Paul encouraged her to remain with Marie a bit longer, however, despite De Marillac's reservations.[11]

It was hardly unexpected that Marie, as a powerful laywoman of her time, would attempt to assert authority over some of De Marillac's sisters. Even apart from her active leadership among the Ladies, she presumed that her financial

generosity to De Paul's and De Marillac's projects, and the protection she offered
them at court when their status under French and ecclesiastical law was still in
doubt, came with privileges.[12] Lay patrons even of cloistered religious houses
were accustomed to such deference and favors in exchange for their support.

More surprising was the purposefulness with which Marie got involved as a
foundress of Lazarist institutions, as this required dealings with high-ranking
ecclesiastical officials. In time, she would be the only woman among De Paul's
patrons, and one of only a few members of the laity, to found Lazarist seminaries.[13] By the end of her life, she would establish and expand Lazarist institutions
not only across France but also in distant locations in Europe and Africa. Indeed,
she became the only major patron of De Paul's congregation to prioritize such
scale and internationalization.

Marie's first significant involvement with the Lazarists was tied to her new
role as the Duchesse d'Aiguillon. In the summer of 1637, several months before
she was crowned by the King, she established with De Paul a community house
that would be the home base for missions to the poor in her duchy. To do this,
she secured the support of the local bishop, Barthèlemy d'Elbène of Agen. Initially, she provided to the Lazarists a founding gift of 22,000 livres, paid all at
once at her home in Paris, and an income of 1,000 livres annually drawn from
a local tax farm that she controlled. (Tax farms were common in France then;
they were excise and customs operations, outsourced by the Crown usually to
powerful nobles, who in exchange for collecting royal taxes during contracted
terms took substantial cuts for themselves.) Her conditions were that at least four
of De Paul's priests would perform missions in the duchy, take care of a local
shrine, and offer masses daily for her intentions and her family.[14]

The Lazarists in Marie's duchy were originally supposed to be based in a
house in the town of Aiguillon. After a consultation with D'Elbène, however,
Marie established them at Notre-Dame de La Rose, a house with a chapel in
the nearby parish of Saint-Livrade in Agen. Agen was a feudal dependency of
Aiguillon, and Marie was now its reigning countess. Before the end of 1637, a
twenty-nine-year-old Lazarist priest named Robert de Sergis was leading missions from there into surrounding villages and hamlets. More priests would join
him in coming years.[15]

These beginnings of Marie's considerable, lifelong patronage of the Lazarists were part of a broader agenda. Both Marie and Richelieu determined that
De Paul's men were well suited to the work of alleviating poverty and misery

in rural France and, at the same time, making populations less susceptible to abandoning the Church for Protestant congregations.

It was with such a program in mind that the Cardinal, with Marie's encouragement, established the Lazarists in his ancestral seat of Richelieu in the Loire Valley. He signed a contract with De Paul in January 1638 for seven Lazarist priests to set up a house and missions, for which he would provide property and generous annual incomes, based in the center of his new "ideal city" close to the Château de Richelieu. Within a few months, the local bishop assented to the priests' staffing the new parish church, Notre-Dame de Richelieu, which was designed by Lemercier and which was one of the only Italian-style Baroque churches in France at the time.[16]

From this base in Richelieu, as from their new base in Marie's county of Agen, a growing number of priests trained in a new way began to engage the local populations as Catholic priests rarely had done since the medieval heyday of the itinerant Franciscan and Dominican friars. Although they were sent partly to counteract the influence of Protestants, they were instructed not to spend their resources on overt attempts to win Protestants back to the Church. Rather, they focused on catechizing the Catholic population, nourishing them with the sacraments, and meeting their corporal needs where they were beset by poverty and poor health. They also preached in plain terms, stressing core Gospel teachings and relating them to the ordinary lives of peasants, eschewing the rhetorical adornments and erudite sophistication of the fashionable urban preachers of the day.[17]

At a time when moral laxity, poor education, and careerism still predominated among French clergymen, due to long delays in implementing the reforms of Trent, the Lazarists made strong impressions on many ordinary laypeople. Observing this, Marie and her uncle determined to continue investing in their ministries. Richelieu would establish another Lazarist house in Luçon and convince the King to establish the congregation in additional locations. Marie in time would go on to establish the Lazarists in Marseilles, Rome, and more distant places. She would also support similar new associations of clergymen devoted to charity and reform that emerged in the years ahead.

26

Across the Atlantic

Published celebrations of Marie's new status as the Duchesse d'Aiguillon were not limited to ones penned in France. In 1638 and 1639, a Jesuit missionary living across the Atlantic in Québec gave a prominent place to Marie in several of his *Relations de la Nouvelle-France*. Published annually in Paris by Richelieu's favorite printer, Sébastien Cramoisy, these serial books had become bestsellers in France and would remain so for decades.

The Jesuit, a Protestant convert to Catholicism named Paul Le Jeune, reported at the beginning of his *Relation* of 1638 that "Madame the Duchesse d'Aiguillon" had successfully "laid the foundations of [a] great work" in Canada.[1]

He was referring to a charitable hospital Marie was establishing in the Saint Lawrence River Valley for Native Americans who were suffering from a relentless smallpox epidemic and other diseases. When Le Jeune and his confreres first arrived in Québec in 1632, they were shocked at the prevalence of sickness among various indigenous communities. They were unaware that the smallpox epidemic traced back to the arrival, decades earlier, of Europeans in New Spain. By the time it had traveled northward into the Eastern Woodlands, the French presumed that the sickly, impoverished state of some Native American communities had been the longtime norm among them. The early *Relations* were thus full of descriptions of sickness and poverty, and Le Jeune called upon French elites to help remedy the situation.[2]

Marie elected to lead this effort. The hospital she founded was the first in the continent north of Spanish Mexico. It was intended for sick, poor, and infirm Natives, not the colonial French. Named *L'Hôtel-Dieu du Précieux-Sang*

("Charitable Hospital of the Precious Blood") according to her wishes, it would
be operated not by the Jesuits or laypeople in the colony but by members of a
new women's religious congregation that Marie liked, the Canonesses of Saint
Augustine of the Mercy of Jesus.

Thanking Marie for this in the *Relation* of 1639, the rhetorically adept Le
Jeune took a different tack than others who praised the new duchess in print in
the period:

> Madame, all France honors you for that noble ducal coronet that
> encircles your brow. I assure you that all the diamonds which
> embellish it have no effect on either my heart or my eyes; their
> lustre is too weak to shine across the vast extent of the ocean. But I
> confess that your heart, which so deeply honors the Blood of Jesus
> Christ, touches me to the quick. You go to the source of life, and
> no one can love Jesus without loving those who cherish and honor
> His Blood.[3]

He then referred to Saint Teresa of Avila's similar devotion to the Blood of
Christ, knowing this would appeal to Marie, given the influence of Carmelite
spirituality on her soul, which had in fact been the inspiration behind her hospital's name.

The establishment of the Hôtel-Dieu in Québec was just the beginning of
the charitable efforts in North America and other parts of the world that would
come to preoccupy Marie in an unusual way for a wealthy aristocrat of the time.
It was also the initial fruit of plans Marie had been developing for Québec for
several years.

Marie's interest in New France stemmed from her privileged knowledge
of French activities there since the days she was a *dame d'atour* for the Queen
Mother. The Marquise de Guercheville, the Queen Mother's *dame d'honneur*
with whom Marie had worked closely in the palace, had been a primary investor
in early French mercantile and missionary activity in Acadie, a colony established in 1605 that included parts of present-day Maine and Canada's Maritime
provinces. And in 1627, Richelieu had established a merchant company for
North America, the Compagnie de la Nouvelle-France, which had a hundred
initial investors interested in the fur trade, agricultural prospects, and lumber
and other natural resources.

The Compagnie de la Nouvelle-France, from which Marie purchased the land for her hospital, claimed that "New France" included most of what is today Canada and the eastern half of the United States. But it concentrated its activity around Québec, a colony established by Samuel de Champlain in 1608. It also planned to work closely with missionaries, especially the Jesuits, who would spread the Catholic faith among diverse Native American populations and at the same time encourage intermarriage, trade, and military alliances.

Father Le Jeune was fully supportive of these simultaneously secular and religious French ambitions for New France, and he was chosen as the Jesuit mission's superior partly because of Richelieu's approval. He had spent many of his early years of Jesuit formation in Paris and was known to Marie, her brother François, and their uncle by the time of his departure for Canada in the spring of 1632.[4] Marie was not surprised, then, by the publication that same year of Le Jeune's first *Relation*, especially given Richelieu's longtime relationship with the publisher, Cramoisy, who had been assisting the Cardinal's ambitions for two decades.

Marie read Le Jeune's early *Relations* with interest, as they brought to life a whole new world for her. They detailed interactions among the missionaries, Native American nations such as the Hurons, Montagnais-Naskapis, and Iroquois, and French traders and settlers.

Marie's interest was not passive. She was corresponding with Le Jeune and others in New France by 1634, and she had wheels in motion for her colonial hospital project by early 1636. Le Jeune reported in the *Relation* published that year that the niece of Richelieu had resolved to send hospital nuns to Canada and "six workmen, to clear some land and to construct a lodging for these good sisters." She had also explained her vision for the project to a young Jesuit, Pierre Chastellain, charging him to communicate it to Le Jeune and others in Québec and to serve as her eyes and ears in the colony. Marie had come to know Chastellain while he was completing his Jesuit formation and preparing to join the mission. He set sail for North America with her instructions in the spring of 1636.[5]

After securing Richelieu's approval and supplementary financial support for her project, Marie's initial founding gifts for the hospital included, by the summer of 1637, the purchase and preparation of land for the hospital grounds and an initial sum of 22,400 livres. This was the first part of an endowment that she promised of 40,540 livres—the equivalent of a multimillion-dollar gift today.[6]

The women whom Marie had in mind to staff the hospital were based at a convent with a charitable hospital for the poor in Dieppe, a Norman city in which Le Jeune had spent time before becoming a missionary. They were capable nurses, informed about some of the latest medical practices and committed, too, to orderly and sanitary conditions for their patients—something not yet the norm in European hospitals. They were also deeply prayerful and serious about the transcendent purposes of their medical work among the poor: they were interested in communicating the love of Christ to their patients and interested in the health of souls as well as bodies. All of these things appealed strongly to Marie.[7]

These women belonged to a new, independent congregation of Augustinian nuns that had been established in France in 1625. The Canonesses of Saint Augustine of the Mercy of Jesus, known by the nickname *Hospitalières*, had found a way to get around the strict rule of claustration—or separation from the world, behind convent walls—that had been set down for female monastics in the Council of Trent. They had formed two classes of membership: the canonesses themselves, who lived inside the cloister, and lay sisters who were free to move about in ordinary society. But the canonesses were devoted in a special way to hospital work and assistance to the poor, even as they spent many hours in prayer and contemplation. This permitted them to engage with patients who were brought into the convent, as their hospitals were on-site.

The innovative approach of the Hospitalières and its adaptability to a mission setting far from the urban spaces of France also appealed to Marie. The staff of her hospital indeed would be some of the first female missionaries ever sent from Europe to another continent in the history of the Church. However, before this could happen, Marie had to convince the Archbishop of Rouen, François de Harlay, to release the Hospitalières volunteering for the assignment from their legal ties to the convent in Dieppe in which they were professed.

As Le Jeune put it in a *Relation*, Archbishop Harlay proved only too pleased to show the niece of Cardinal Richelieu "how willing he was to contribute, to the best of his ability, to the good works she had undertaken."[8] Three Hospitalières were then able to set sail for Canada late in the spring of 1639. They were young, all in their twenties, and their names were Anne Le Cointre de Saint-Bernard, Marie Forrestier de Saint-Bonaventure de Jésus, and Marie Guenet de Saint-Ignace.

Guenet was the superior of the new colonial community of Hospitalières. She carried a letter Marie had written to her across the ocean. A transcript was published in the *Relation* of 1639. It explained the duchess's vision for the hospital project:

> [My object] is to dedicate this hospital to the Blood of the Son of God, that was shed in order that mercy might be granted to all men—and to ask Him to apply it to our souls, and to those of these poor barbarous people. . . . I desire that all the nuns should know . . . my purpose in the foundation, and that they devote themselves to the service of the poor with that object.[9]

According to Marie's wishes, a sign was fixed on the hospital's entrance, announcing its consecration to Christ's sacred Blood and the hope that divine mercy would extend, through Christ, to "all." Even apart from what it signaled about Marie's understanding of the humanity that Native Americans shared with her fellow Europeans, this language was not uncontroversial in an era in which a growing number of French Catholics, not only many Protestants, believed that God did *not* offer a chance at Heaven to most, let alone all, human beings.

Le Jeune reported in the same *Relation* that the three women immediately set about assisting many sick Native men, women, and children and, indeed, that they were overwhelmed by the number in need of medical care.[10]

As soon as Marie learned that the initial support she had given for the hospital was insufficient, she ensured that the rest of the 40,540 livres she had promised was released by her bankers.[11] She also had Archbishop Harlay authorize the transfer of two more Hospitalières from Dieppe. However, she ran into a problem. The merchant ship *L'Espérance*, which was set to carry the cash, the nuns, and more medical supplies to Canada, was stopped off the coast by armed vessels serving the Habsburgs in the ongoing war.

A Jesuit on the scene named René Menard reported with some awe on what transpired next. The Duchesse d'Aiguillon, once she learned of the ambuscade, got Richelieu to order the entire French fleet parked at Le Havre to convoy *L'Espérance*. "We found fifty ships . . . awaiting us," Menard wrote. "I did not think that I was upon the sea . . . seeing myself encompassed by so much wood. As we floated along in this security, the ships of the King discovered eight hostile frigates, to which they gave chase." This naval escort accompanied *L'Espérance* into safe Atlantic waters, and the money, supplies, and new staff for the hospital made it in good time to Québec.[12]

On board the same ship was some artwork Marie had commissioned for the Hôtel-Dieu. In time she would send at least ten paintings across the Atlantic for the hospital alone. Two of these were large portraits of herself and Richelieu, each kneeling in prayer, which unfortunately were lost in a fire in 1755. But mediocre copies that were made around the same time give us an idea of what they looked like. One depicted Marie contemplating a vision of the pierced and bleeding heart of Jesus, and the other showed Richelieu in prayer, before a simple cross, in his study.[13]

Marie also sent to Québec a portrait of the recently deceased Carmelite nun Madeleine de Saint-Joseph, with the intention of spreading devotion to her. Marie believed that her former spiritual mentor and mother figure was a saint, so she was advocating her canonization. Furthermore, she commissioned devotional images for the hospital's chapel, including a tender portrayal of a youthful Saint Joseph with the infant Jesus and another of a pregnant Virgin Mary visiting her cousin Elizabeth.[14]

The most impressive painting Marie sent across the Atlantic was a large image of the crucified Christ, with the Blessed Mother, Saint John the Evangelist, several Native Americans, and Marie and Richelieu surrounding the cross. (It was a common practice, going back to medieval times, for donors to have their portraits added into scenes such as the Nativity of Christ or the Crucifixion in this fashion.) This painting was also lost in the eighteenth-century fire, but Le Jeune described it one of his *Relations*. In it, the Blessed Mother pointed to Marie, who was on her knees, and Saint John gestured toward the Cardinal, who was also devoutly kneeling before his dying Lord. Le Jeune may have been exaggerating to flatter Richelieu's niece, but he punctuated his description with an account of how some Native girls, when they regarded the painting, were drawn to the figure of Marie and attempted to imitate her posture.[15]

Although Marie would never cross the Atlantic to see New France for herself, she got to meet several Native Americans in Paris. At the start of 1637, before the planned hospital was off the ground, she welcomed several young Natives who had been sent to France by their families and the Jesuits to learn some French ways firsthand. After she became acquainted with two young Montagnais-Naskapi women, Marie arranged for them to be baptized as Catholics at the convent church at Carmel de l'Incarnation. A newly consecrated bishop, Bernard Despruets de Saint-Papoul, performed the sacred rites. The Princesse de Condé and the Chancellor of France, Séguier, were also present and they stood as godparents to one of the young women, who received *Marguerite-Thérèse* as her Christian name.

Marie became godmother to the other young woman, who was given the new name *Marie-Madeleine* in honor of this fact. The soon-to-be Duchesse d'Aiguillon stood alongside her Native American goddaughter at the baptismal font with François Sublet de Noyers, who agreed to serve as godfather. Sublet de Noyers was a devout Catholic nobleman who was also Richelieu's loyal new Secretary of State for War. Sadly, the young Native woman's given name has been lost to posterity. Furthermore, she and her companion from Canada caught sick and died inside the convent not long after this event.[16]

In this same period, Marie got to know another young Native American whom she invited into her home for a time. Baptized with the name *Anne-Thérèse*, she was an Iroquois by birth but had been taken captive by the Algonquins as a child before encountering the Jesuits. Once in Paris and living with Marie, she spent considerable time at the noblewoman's side. Marie taught her Christian doctrines, prayers, and French manners while learning from the young woman about life back in Canada.

Initially, Marie had agreed that Anne-Thérèse would return in a year to New France and then reside with the Hospitalières, working for the nuns as a gardener and in other servile ways. But Le Jeune was eventually annoyed to learn that Anne-Thérèse had settled in to stay in Paris and that Marie was acculturating her to her own aristocratic mode of life. The missionary went so far as to chide Marie in a *Relation* over this, arguing that the Native girl was intended for a simpler, humbler life and should "not long taste . . . the sweetness of repose and the abundance of a great house."[17]

But the new duchess was not one to take unsolicited instruction from a Jesuit priest—let alone one from an obscure family who owed his career as both a mission superior and bestselling author to her uncle and his network. She ignored Le Jeune in this instance and even permitted Anne-Thérèse to receive attentions from a young nobleman who frequented her home.

Then, when Anne-Thérèse showed an inclination toward a Carmelite vocation—a path generally reserved in that era for aristocratic women with dowries—Marie arranged for her to reside inside the cloister of Carmel de l'Incarnation, with the hope that she would be accepted as a novice. There, the young Iroquois woman learned to read, participated in the community's liturgical life, and was furthermore emboldened at times to critique the nuns' behaviors, as when she informed one who began reciting her rosary aloud just after receiving the Eucharist at Mass, "You must look at Jesus Christ in your heart, without speaking; He must be adored in silence."[18]

Tragically, Anne-Thérèse also died too young—inside the cloister, from a disease she had contracted in Paris, and before she had been able to decide, for sure, whether to become a Carmelite or return to Québec. This was not long before Cardinal La Valette died. Although there is no record of how Marie mourned her Iroquois charge or whether she experienced any sort of guilt over the girl's whole situation, Anne-Thérèse's premature death added to Marie's sorrows in this season of her life. And it is not a stretch to imagine that, as she increased her supports for charitable and religious endeavors across the Atlantic in the years ahead, her memories of Anne-Thérèse were a motivation.

27

Childlessness

A striking book published in honor of the new Duchesse d'Aiguillon was the first part of a novel entitled *Rosane*. It appeared in 1639 in Paris and featured Marie's name and a strange triple portrait of her on its cover page etched by Abraham Bosse, an artist favored by French courtly elites at the time. Its author, Jean Desmarets, was a cousin of Anne du Vigean, Marie's close friend and lady-in-waiting. He had been known to Marie and Richelieu for several years and was treated very well by them. Initially a commoner and employed as the last official court jester in France, he was ennobled as the Sieur de Saint-Sorlin and named as the first chancellor of the Académie Française.[1]

Desmarets was a man of many talents. He excelled at architecture and painting, as well as dancing, acting, and singing. But his plays and prose offerings were what interested his most powerful patrons at this time.

Rosane, in particular, told the story of a fictional daughter of a Persian king who lived during the third-century reign of the Roman emperor Valerian. It had two more major female characters: Zenobie, based on an historical Palmyrene queen, and her fictional sister Uranie. These were the women represented on Bosse's cover page—but each with Marie's face and figure. Rosane, the princess in the center, is buxom in her low-cut dress, wearing a crown atop her head, from which long curls flow to her shoulders. She is attended by three winged cherubs who hang about her skirts, suggesting fecundity. With her half smile at the viewer, her head turned slightly to the side, she is a bit reminiscent of Da Vinci's Mona Lisa.

To the left of the page is Zenobie—also a robust woman with prominent breasts, but dressed in armor and bearing a sword, her curly hair covered by a helmet. Staring outward with her mouth open, she almost distracts the viewer, with her questioning expression, from the man—an enemy in war—whom she is trampling with her sandaled foot at the bottom of the page.

Opposite Zenobie, at Rosane's other hand, is Uranie. She is modestly clad. Her free-flowing, dark curls are also graced with a crown, but with pearls around it. She has a serious expression, appearing more introspective than the other two, and she holds a distaff that is aimed downward—parallel with her sister's sword—at a fourth cupid, whom she tramples. The symbolism from head to toe is unmistakable. Uranie has chosen chastity and renounced her fecundity in favor of a contemplative existence.

Desmarets explained in *Rosane* that the three characters as he developed them in the novel were all modeled on Marie. But he suggested that Marie was most like Uranie in her day-to-day life, with her "wisdom, moderation, and contempt for grandeur, riches, and pleasures." This was because she appeared, by the path she had taken, to be opposed to the kinds of adventures of the heart that dominated Rosane's story after Rosane was forced, by her father, to marry a man she detested. Also, Marie did not fight in wars like a man as Zenobie did, even though she had been more than capable—should she have pursued the profession of arms—of "valor, generosity, martial enterprises, and worldly conquests."[2]

As Desmarets told the stories of the two sisters Zenobie and Uranie, especially, he included details that have an odd resonance with Marie's life, especially where her hidden relationship with Cardinal La Valette was concerned. Zenobie, the warrior queen, was deeply in love with a man named Odenat, whom she married but with whom she enjoyed only short, occasional moments of passion. Odenat was separated from her for long periods not only by military obligations that carried him far away, but also due to pressures by family members opposed to their union. Uranie, for one, counseled her sister to embrace chastity along with her, and to renounce Odenat.

Is it possible that Desmarets, who was close to Marie's inner circle, had the young duchess's blessing to tell a story that in some way dramatized what she had been going through with La Valette? Is it possible that Rosane represented young Marie, forced to marry Combalet, and Zenobie the Marie who had developed strong feelings for La Valette? Did Uranie represent that other part of herself—perhaps interiorly at war with her "sister"—who had attempted to become a Carmelite, who was influenced greatly by Madeleine de Saint-Joseph, and who held to strict beliefs about when and where both sex and marriage were acceptable in the eyes of God and His Church?

These questions cannot be answered with certainty. But it may not be a coincidence that the second part of the novel Desmarets was planning—one that would have tied together some of the loose threads in the stories of the two sisters and Odenat—was never written, and that the timing of the first part's publication and the decision not to produce the second was the same as that of La Valette's unexpected death in Italy.

Whatever was the case, it is clear that by beginning of 1640, at thirty-five, Marie had stopped being the object of significant public speculation, or pressure by family members or friends, with regard to a second marriage. By circumstances and choice, she had assumed the part of Uranie, renouncing marriage and motherhood while remaining "in the world" as a laywoman with extraordinary responsibilities.

Some of these responsibilities involved the mentorship of young people. Although Marie never had any children of her own, she was surrounded by young people in this season of her life and often went out of her way to direct their paths. There were, for example, her brother's three sons and two daughters—whom she took an active hand in rearing, because of François's behavior—and her friend and attendant Anne du Vigean's two girls and two boys, all of whom resided at various times with Marie in the Petit Luxembourg.

Marie's closeness to such young people at times occasioned great grief, as when Anne's eldest, François, the Marquis de Fors, died in late August 1640. Several weeks earlier, the French had won a great victory in the war at Arras in the Low Countries. But Marie and her friends could not fully celebrate this, because Anne's son was among the gravely wounded. Not yet twenty, the marquis was already a hardened veteran, having survived difficult battles and two stints as a prisoner of war.[3] Marie was with Anne on August 29 when they learned that the young man had died from his wounds while laid up in Amiens. They called in Father De Paul to offer words of consolation and to pray with them for the young man's soul. De Paul was so struck by the resigned, faithful state in which he found Anne at the Petit Luxembourg that he wrote just after to De Marillac, "Never have I seen the reflection of God's strength in affliction as in that virtuous lady."[4]

Among many other young people in Marie's life in this period were the children of her other friends, attendants, and servants, some of whom also at times were welcomed into her homes and whom she helped to educate, find employment, and make respectable marriages.[5] Marie took an interest in Julie d'Angennes's younger sister, Claire-Diane, who joined a community of Cistercian nuns at the Abbey of Pont-aux-Dames east of Paris, and who, due to Marie's influence, was later appointed as the abbess of a Benedictine community at Yerres.[6]

There were also young people of the parish of Saint-Sulpice for whom Marie intervened in various ways. One of them, Geneviève Dupuy, found herself pregnant out of wedlock in the spring of 1641. Her parents owned a cabaret close to the Petit Luxembourg. When Marie learned that the father of the unborn child was the musically talented young Michel Lambert, she exerted pressure on him to propose to Geneviève. She as well as Richelieu then attended the wedding to ensure it took place. Eventually, Lambert rose to become a famous court composer and singing master, and another child later born to him and Geneviève would herself grew up to marry Jean-Baptiste Lully, one of the great French composers of the century.[7]

Furthermore, there were young people of exceptional intellectual talent whom Marie patronized with enthusiasm. Among them were the teenaged children of a royal tax officer and widower named Étienne Pascal: a sickly boy named Blaise, who was a math and science prodigy, and his sisters, Gilberte and Jacqueline, who were exceptionally learned for girls of the era thanks to their father's unusual commitment to their education.

In 1639, the playwright Corneille informed Marie about these remarkable Pascal children. Marie initially took an interest in thirteen-year-old Jacqueline, as she was a gifted poet. Jacqueline had placed first in a poetry contest in Rouen after Corneille had encouraged her to submit a poem about the immaculate conception of the Blessed Virgin.[8]

Marie believed that Jacqueline and her siblings should have a chance to develop their knowledge and talents in Paris. But there was a problem. Their father had gotten on the wrong side of Richelieu's administration as a result of a financial dispute, and the family was suffering dishonor as he was working for the Crown in Rouen, exiled from Paris.

Marie decided to stage an elaborate intervention with Richelieu on the talented Pascals' behalf. While she could not have predicted it at the time, the success of her scheme, by changing the family's fortunes, would alter the course of French intellectual and religious history. Young Blaise Pascal, in particular, would eventually achieve prominence in his own lifetime. He is celebrated to this day as one of the leading French mathematicians and men of letters of his age. Also, his sisters would play central roles along with him in a movement called Jansenism—ironically one that Marie would oppose strongly in her later years.

It was many years before this when, late in the winter of 1639, the Pascal children were in Paris without their father. At the time, Richelieu had asked Marie to stage a new tragicomedy, George de Scudéry's *L'Amour Tyrannique*, in the theater of the new Palais-Cardinal. The play was to be performed in early April, and Scudéry would go on to dedicate the published version to Marie.[9] After Richelieu expressed openness to allowing young girls to do the acting, Marie recruited Jacqueline into the production.

Just as Marie hoped would be the case, Richelieu on the evening of April 4 was impressed with Jacqueline Pascal's performance before a large audience of friends and family members in his new theater. After the play ended, he encouraged the girl to approach him, and while she paid her respects, she also recited one of her poems to him, as Marie had earlier prepared her to do. The poem was a petition for her father Étienne. It included the line, "Recall from exile now my hapless sire," which Jacqueline recited with genuine sorrow and trepidation in her voice. She learned only later that Marie, her new patroness, had earlier spoken to Richelieu of her father's situation and communicated her opinion that he had been too harshly punished for his financial blunder.

This explains why the Cardinal, after greeting Jacqueline warmly—saying "Voilà, la petite Pascal!"—reacted not with surprise at her bold plea but with laughter and a kiss on her cheek. He told her he would grant everything she requested, and instructed her to write to her father, who could return to Paris. Marie then added, in front of all the guests and performers standing around her uncle, that she believed Richelieu was doing the right thing for this man, whom she had heard was honest and learned.[10]

Marie next informed Richelieu and the company about Étienne's son Blaise, describing him as exceptionally gifted in mathematics, despite being fifteen years old. Marie then took young Jacqueline and her sister Gilberte into a room where they enjoyed a dinner of "dried sweetmeats, fruits, lemonade, and such things," as Jacqueline later told her father. Marie stayed with them through the meal, chatting with them, and before they left the Palais-Cardinal, she asked if she could meet Blaise, who had not been well enough to attend that evening.

Afterward, Marie communicated more to others about the boy's mathematical and scientific interests and assisted his precocious rise to renown.[11]

Blaise Pascal was not the only young mathematician in whose career Marie took an interest in this period. Through a priest and polymath named Marin Mersenne, Marie became acquainted with a young René Descartes, whom it is believed she assisted privately when he sought to publish his controversial *Discourse on the Method of Rightly Conducting One's Reason and of Seeking Truth in the Sciences*.[12] The book was printed in the Netherlands in order to get around strict French censors working for Richelieu's administration.

A young woman named Marie Crous, one of the first female mathematicians in Europe whose name is remembered today, also owed her modest renown to the duchess. Marie helped her publish a book that laid out her original mathematical research, the most enduring contribution of which was her introduction of the modern decimal system into France.

That book, entitled *Abbregé Recherché de Marie Crous*, appeared from the presses of Jacques Auvray in Paris in 1641. Like Marie Le Jars de Gournay before her, Crous was able to see her own name—so rare for women writers and researchers then—on the cover of a book that shared her work with the public. In her dedicatory letter to Marie at the front, Crous thanked the duchess for support that she believed would shield her from slander—slander that she assumed she would suffer simply because she was a woman who dared to study and write about mathematics.

But she also went far beyond this. She announced that Marie's protection emboldened her to dedicate her research more broadly to women and girls who could benefit from her work. Shop girls, domestic servants, and other women who worked with numbers would find her decimal system useful in keeping accounts and budgeting. But they would also, she hoped, find in some of her demonstrations some "contentment of the eye" and "contentment of mind"—that is, pure intellectual pleasure of a kind usually reserved for the most privileged, educated members of her society.[13]

Not all of Marie's interventions in the lives of young people speak as well of her to twenty-first-century observers as these others. Her role in facilitating the marriage of her cousin Claire-Clémence, the elder daughter of Maillé-Brézé, is a case in point.

Claire-Clémence was a small child in 1635, the year her mother Nicole had died. Since then, she and her little sister Marie-Françoise had been living neither with their father nor their brother, Jean-Armand, but primarily in the countryside with Madame de Bouthillier, the mother of Secretary Chavigny, Marie's friend and confidant.

Unsurprisingly, Maillé-Brézé and Richelieu both were determined to see Claire-Clémence marry well. An opportunity neither could pass up arose early in 1640 when the King's eighteen-year-old cousin, Louis de Bourbon, the Duc d'Enghien, was put forward as a candidate for the girl's hand. In time, this young man, eventually called *Le Grand Condé*, would become one of the most famous Frenchmen of his generation as well as an enemy for a time to Marie. When young, though, he was known simply as the son of Marie's old friend the Princesse de Condé and of Henry II de Bourbon, the Prince de Condé.

The Condés were exceedingly high-ranking but also cash poor. An alliance with Richelieu's young niece would give both families things they desired: greater wealth on one side, and ties to the royal family on the other.

Almost twenty years after her fateful journey to Paris for her own wedding, Marie at the end of the winter chaperoned her cousin from the Bouthillier's country home to the capital. She then helped to arrange a meeting between her and the young duke.[14]

It was a relief to Marie that she was no longer the object of dynastic match-making. Nevertheless, this was unpleasant business. Claire-Clémence had only turned twelve in February. She still played with dolls and she was accustomed to a sheltered, provincial life. By contrast, Enghien had already bedded mistresses and had recently fallen in love with Marthe du Vigean, the beautiful fifteen-year-old daughter of Anne, Marie's friend and lady-in-waiting. Marthe, indeed, was one of the young people Marie knew best in this period, as she was often in the duchess's homes with her mother.

Whatever reservations Marie may have harbored about disappointing Marthe's hopes, especially in light of her own experience with an arranged marriage, she played the part that custom and Richelieu required of her in this situation. Marie saw Claire-Clémence's Parisian meeting with Enghien through to success.[15]

The families agreed that a wedding would take place the following year, to allow Claire-Clémence time to mature. The delay would also allow Richelieu to carefully work out, with his lawyers, a marriage contract that would not alienate too much of his family's wealth in the form of the girl's dowry and the Condé line's legal claims once the couple produced children.

Marie, in the meantime, welcomed the motherless Claire-Clémence to the Petit Luxembourg, hoping that a year would also be enough time for Enghien to get over Marthe. However, the lovestruck young man continued pining for Marthe even after going off to the war, throwing himself into his duties as an officer, and showing precocious leadership abilities on the battlefield. Richelieu lamented to Marie in late May that the young man was sending Marthe love letters from the front.[16]

The marriage went forward despite Enghien's feelings for Marthe. The festivities surrounding it were among the grandest Marie ever hosted with her uncle. These opened on January 14, 1641, more than a month before the small, dark-haired Claire-Clémence's thirteenth birthday. That evening, Richelieu and Marie fêted the engaged couple at the Palais-Cardinal while celebrating, too, the formal grand opening of the palace's finished great theater.

A tragicomedy entitled *Mirame* was chosen for this occasion. Richelieu had cowritten it with Desmarets. It was about a princess who fell in love with a king's envoy who was visiting to arrange a marriage for his master. Queen Anne and Prince Gaston were the most notable guests that evening in the theater, which could seat some two thousand spectators and which featured gold-encrusted Corinthian columns and sixteen of the finest chandeliers in Europe. The state-of-the-art stage setting included statues, depictions of grottos and a sea in the background, moving ships, and lighting effects mimicking sunrise, sunset, and hours in between.[17] A writer for the *Gazette* gushed later, "France . . . has never seen such magnificent theater."[18]

There was a ball later that evening, for which Marie's young cousin had been outfitted with a beautiful dress, jewels, and high-platformed shoes so that she would not look comically short next to her fiancé. At one point Claire-Clémence slipped and crashed to the floor, only to be laughed at by numerous, unsympathetic courtly witnesses.[19]

The events of February 7 surpassed the previous in grandeur. Richelieu and Marie hosted *La Prosperité des Armes de France*, a patriotic ballet at the same theater of the Palais-Cardinal, to honor Enghien's service in the war. A prototype of the opera-ballets that became popular in the eighteenth century, it included fine vocal performances and chamber music composed by Richelieu's *maître de musique*, François de Chancy.

In the audience this time were the King as well as the Queen, their toddler Louis, and his infant brother, Philippe, to whom Anne had given birth five months earlier. The presence of the royal family was so special to Richelieu that he had an artist stand behind them as the ballet proceeded. The sketch, which today is in the collection of the Musée des Arts Décoratifs in Paris, is the closest thing there is to a snapshot from Marie's life. Although it is unclear which of the four female figures in its foreground represents the duchess, it is probable that the woman with the fan seated in between the King and the dauphin is Marie.

Earlier that day, the King and Queen had welcomed Enghien, Claire-Clémence, and their close family members and friends to the Louvre, where the marriage contract was signed. The contract was the result of long and testy negotiations between lawyers working for Richelieu and the Prince de Condé. It was far more favorable to Richelieu's designs than the prince's. An unusual clause in it concerned both Marie and her brother's daughters, four-year-old Marie-Madeleine-Thérese and the infant Marie-Marthe. In the event of the couple's failure to produce a son, Marie and these nieces, not Claire-Clémence or any of her daughters, were to receive Claire-Clémence's share in Richelieu's estate when he died.[20]

Although the girl's father Maillé-Brézé and her future father-in-law were not pleased with these terms, they felt confident that Claire-Clémence would go on to give them grandsons. They and the rest of their families finally celebrated the nuptials with a courtly crowd of guests on February 11, inside the chapel of the Palais-Cardinal. A great banquet followed inside the palace.

Months later, in May, Enghien's feeling about his marriage and his child bride were on display when he threw a big party for himself, his sister, and their friends in Charonne just outside of Paris. His wife was not among the guests. Marthe du Vigean was.[21]

This was a bold move on the young duke's part, which angered Richelieu, who along with Marie had just seen Enghien and his wife several days earlier at the first Mass ever offered inside a stunning new Jesuit church in Paris, Église Saint-Louis in the Marais district. They had all received Holy Communion together, along with the King and Queen, and from Richelieu himself, who was the celebrant.[22] But the graces of the sacrament do not appear to have bent the young man's will toward fidelity to Claire-Clémence, who nevertheless would go on to bear him an heir when she was only fifteen.

28

Political Storms

Not long after Marie was elevated as a duchess-peeress, she sat for a formal portrait by Richelieu's favorite painter, Philippe de Champaigne. From a poor family in Brussels, Champaigne had been discovered quite young, and he moved to Paris before he was twenty to work under Nicolas Poussin, with whom he contributed to the décor of the Palais de Luxembourg during the heyday of the Queen Mother's time there.

Champaigne would receive many commissions from Richelieu over the years, but his portraits of the Cardinal-Minister that hang today in the Louvre and other world-class museums are among his most famous works. By contrast, his portrait of Marie, painted in the same period, fell into obscurity after Marie's lifetime, ending up in a succession of private galleries in Italy. It was misidentified as simply a "portrait of a lady" by a Dutch artist until 2005. That year, Xavier Salmon of the Louvre Museum and the Italian art historian Edoardo Pepino recognized it as Champaigne's work and as a portrait of Marie. Today, it hangs in Franco Maria Ricci's gallery in Parma.[1]

Among the portraits that Marie sat for over the years, this one is the most impressive. She faces the viewer straight on and is wearing a sumptuous red silk dress that is close in color to Richelieu's famous red robes. With her dark eyes, oval face, closed red lips, and curly hair—powdered or perhaps naturally graying already—she looks at us calmly, with a mixture of kindness and noble authority in her expression.

A striking feature of the painting is that in it, while Marie offers bread with her left hand to a spaniel at her knee, she lets a bouquet of white flowers slip out of her right hand, above which is a black widow's bracelet at the wrist. The action symbolizes perhaps the willingness she had, in her mid-thirties, to let go of her youth and of hopes she had once had—at one point to have become a nun, at another to have known happiness with La Valette.

It may also symbolize Marie's loss of innocence. As the closest relative and confidante of the ruthless, calculating, and widely hated Richelieu, Marie was acclimatized by this point to the darker side of political life. Richelieu had survived multiple attempts on his life and efforts to remove him from office, and Marie herself had been in the line of his enemies' fire in many ways for more than a decade. Furthermore, although the full extent of Richelieu's unofficial activity in punishing real and perceived enemies of the Crown remains unknown even today, Marie knew that her uncle had a large network of spies and unsavory henchmen at his disposal. She was also aware that many individuals languishing in prisons or exile, or who had died under suspicious circumstances, were believed by many to have been treated unjustly by Richelieu.

But powerful as the Cardinal-Minister had become by the time Champaigne painted Marie, several of the major conspiracies against him—led by prominent nobles Marie had known socially for many years—were still to come. For example, the Duc de Vendôme (Louis XIII's half brother by one of Henry IV's extramarital liaisons) in 1640 hired two elderly hermits to kill Richelieu. Communications about this were intercepted, and the duke escaped to England, avoiding trial.[2]

The political events that played out in 1640 and over the subsequent two years are crucial context for understanding Marie's position in France toward the end of Richelieu's life, which was nearer in time than anyone knew. By early 1640, it was becoming clearer that France was outperforming Spain in the war and that victory was on the horizon. Ironically, this posed a new problem for Richelieu: nobles who wanted him out of power stirred up new opposition on the premise that he was unnecessarily prolonging the war in order to remain in power.[3]

Among those advancing this view were the King's brother Gaston, his cousin the Comte de Soissons who had earlier attempted Richelieu's assassination, and two dukes from princely families who resented their political marginalization by the Cardinal's administration: Henri II de Lorraine, the Duc de Guise, and Frédéric de La Tour d'Auvergne, the Duc de Bouillon. Guise had gotten on the wrong side of Richelieu when staunchly supporting the Queen Mother years earlier. Boullion, while serving Louis XIII as a high-ranking military officer in the war, had been stripped of his offices in 1637 after attempting to negotiate with Spain without royal authorization.

Nicknamed *les Princes de la Paix* ("Princes of Peace"), these men joined into a conspiracy against Richelieu that they justified as an effort to end a needless war and bring relief to the overtaxed common people of France. Although Richelieu was liked among many of the common people because, in theory, he favored relieving them from taxes they could not afford and requiring noble families to pay more of a fair share, in practice the Third Estate was taxed at increasingly higher rates to cover the expenses of the ongoing war.[4] Rebellions had already broken out against war-related taxes in Normandy and in the southwest, especially. One in Normandy had become so large that Chancellor Séguier went there in January 1640 to mete out harsh punishments and suspend the local parlement. The months ahead saw a more general royal crackdown on the parlements throughout France, restricting their activities to the merely juridical and firing *parlementaires* who attempted to assert legislative power. Such heavy-handedness of course reflected back on Richelieu.[5]

By early 1641, Soissons and Boullion, with the tacit support of the other *Princes de la Paix*, were arranging a large-scale revolt against Richelieu's administration. They had Spanish backing. The plan was that Soissons, who was based in Sedan close to the Spanish Netherlands, would lead an army through the province of Champagne east of Paris while mostly Huguenot forces would rise up in the south and in western coastal areas of France.[6] Although the Habsburgs and the Huguenots had their own agendas in this action, the princely French conspirators believed they could control the outcome. They presumed that they could cast any defeat of fellow French officers, who were fighting for the Crown, as a defeat of Richelieu's administration by men with the best interests of France in mind, not as a defeat of France per se by Spain and rebels against royal authority.

Richelieu got wind of what was afoot when a letter was intercepted that implicated the Duc de La Valette—the deceased cardinal's brother—in the conspiracy. This was in April 1641. Richelieu presented the King with the evidence. Nevertheless, Soissons went forward with his plans, leading an army with Bouillon along the Meuse River that joined together with some seven thousand troops sent in by the Habsburgs. On July 6, they defeated a large force led by a Richelieu loyalist, Gaspard II de Coligny, the Maréchal de Châtillon, at a place called La Marfée near Sedan. But at the end of the battle, Soissons died. He was found hanging off his horse, his leg caught in his stirrup.[7]

La Marfée was just a momentary setback for the royal forces. The joint force of French rebels and imperial troops was roundly defeated later in July, at Aire north of Reims, by troops led by Marie's capable cousin La Meilleraye.

As all of this had been unfolding, Marie found herself at the center of a strange turn of events involving her former royal mistress, the exiled Queen Mother. Early in 1641, Marie de' Medici was residing not in Brussels but in England to be near her daughter Henriette-Marie, who had been the Queen of England since 1625. Although the Queen Mother had been receiving a pension in England, it dried up at this time as King Charles I was losing his grip on power and the Puritan-led Parliament was leading the country toward civil war.

Now near seventy, Marie de' Medici feared for her comfort and security as she never had before. She made overtures in France with the hope of securing financial assistance, if not a welcome back to the country, from her son. Curiously, she sent a Jesuit priest, Pierre Bonnefons, to speak to Marie in Paris, with the expectation that the duchess would advocate for her with Richelieu and the King.[8] Bonnefons had published several devotional works by this point and had been known to Marie for some time, so the Queen Mother was hopeful he would have influence with her.

Despite the Queen Mother's cruelty toward her in past years, Marie tried to assist the aging woman. After Marie made inquiries, however, the King sternly requested that she not interfere with anything concerning his mother.[9] The Queen Mother received no assistance and made her way to Cologne in Germany, where she lived in a small rental home that was humiliatingly shabby for a woman of royal rank and lineage. This would not go on for long, however, as she would die in Cologne the following summer, on July 3, 1642, having never returned to France since her departure more than a decade earlier.

The King's cold stance toward his mother is partly explained by his growing paranoia in the spring of 1641 regarding Soissons's and the others' plotting with Spanish agents and Huguenot rebels. Although Richelieu was the primary target of the conspirators, Louis took the actions of the *Princes de la Paix* as affronts to his own authority.

After the Battle of La Marfée, however, those who continued to plot against Richelieu attempted a new strategy: they began to confer secretively with the King's new favorite, a young man named Henri d'Effiat, the Marquis de Cinq-Mars. And they were able to shape events so that Richelieu, just as his health began to fail him, found himself by the spring of 1642 in the most precarious situation of his career.

Cinq-Mars had been placed near the King by Richelieu himself in 1639 when he was only nineteen years old. The young man's father, Antoine d'Effiat, had years earlier replaced Michel de Marillac as Keeper of the Seals and been a close friend of the Cardinal's. When this man had died, Richelieu had taken his orphaned boy under his wing, overseeing his education and eventually placing him in Louis's household as his *maître de la garde-robe*, the male counterpart to Marie's old *dame d'atour* position.

By late 1640, the King was extremely attached to Cinq-Mars. Although Louis was almost twenty years older, he treated the young man like his closest friend, confiding his inmost thoughts to him—including when he wished to vent privately about Richelieu. Understandably, the King often felt dominated by his remarkable prime minister. While he had no intention of firing him, he expressed frustrations about him to Cinq-Mars when in need of human sympathy and an outlet for anger that would have been politically dangerous if directed at Richelieu himself.[10]

Cinq-Mars learned to play Louis like a fiddle. As rumors began to swirl about the precise nature of the King's interest in the young man, Cinq-Mars grew tired of the King's constant conversation and serious, pious nature. Yet he was a good actor: he feigned interest in Louis's every word, stoked his frustrations with Richelieu, and even felt secure enough in the King's affections that he was able to enjoy a lavish lifestyle in Paris due to the gifts and freedoms Louis showered upon him.[11] He took up with a mistress—the famous courtesan Marion Delorme—and did nothing to stop the rumors (almost certainly false, despite their repetition even to this day) that Richelieu had at times shared her bed.

Richelieu's own relationship with Cinq-Mars broke down in early 1641. When the King permitted the young man to sit in on meetings of his privy council, Richelieu was unsparing: he berated Cinq-Mars as if he were a domestic servant, and he told Louis that "affairs of state" were not the business of "children."[12]

It was shortly after this that Cinq-Mars began meeting with the Duc de Bouillon and other conspirators against Richelieu, including a royal librarian named Auguste de Thou. He also communicated with the King's brother Gaston. By November 1641, in the wake of Soissons's failed action in July, Cinq-Mars and these men were plotting Richelieu's removal from the scene with Spanish support. Cinq-Mars also began to encourage Louis to dismiss Richelieu and to consider—for the sake of the French people and the reunification of Catholic Europe—opening up private talks with the courts of Spain and the Papal States. The young man named De Thou as a possible envoy.[13]

Early in 1642, the French court moved south because of planned military engagements near Roussillon and the Spanish borderlands. In the town of Narbonne, where the King stopped at the archbishop's residence for some days, Richelieu was lodged in a separate mansion while Cinq-Mars was constantly with the King. Louis barely spoke to Richelieu, who began to worry with his secretaries that something was seriously amiss.

Richelieu then fell terribly ill in late March. His right arm and other parts of his body broke out into painful sores—the result of tuberculous osteitis, or inflammation of the bones. When Marie learned of this in Paris, she told Chavigny that she was in a "pitiful state" while "being 200 leagues from His Eminence and knowing him to be sick."[14]

As the King, Cinq-Mars, and the rest of the court moved on to Perpignan in the Roussillon province, Richelieu remained bedridden in Narbonne. The state of his health alarmed him enough that he decided to prepare his last will and testament.

This was an arduous task, not only given the vastness of his fortune, lands, palaces, other real estate, and governmental offices that he owned, and ecclesiastical benefices and other preferments in his gift, but also given the political as well as dynastic considerations involved. Whatever he would choose to do with his monumental legacy, it was sure to have a major impact on the course of events in France for decades to come. It would also cause controversy and be contested in court by various disappointed, greedy, and vengeful parties. He made his decisions, however, and the document as he dictated it to his personal secretary Denis Charpentier was completed on May 23, 1641.[15]

By this point, Richelieu, Chavigny, and others in their inner circle—including Marie, who had remained in Paris—were convinced that a major plot against Richelieu was underway. Richelieu suspected that Boullion and Cinq-Mars were key players, but he had no idea of the extent of what was being planned. In some fear for his life, he left Narbonne several days after his will was drafted, and without the King's permission. For several weeks, even as he remained unwell, Richelieu moved about with his convoy throughout the south of France with no fixed destination.

Back in Paris, Marie was anxious for her uncle's health and safety. Richelieu had undergone surgery while moving from bed to bed, and he had confided to his secretaries and Marie that his courage and strength were failing him and that he greatly needed God's help.[16] Rumors swirled that his political demise was near. It did not help Richelieu's chances that France suffered an embarrassing military defeat at the end of May, at the Battle of Honnecourt in Picardy, and that as a result a large-scale enemy invasion of the region seemed imminent.[17]

Marie sent Richelieu warnings about what was being said of him during his long absence from Paris. She also passed on to Chavigny an anonymous warning she had received: that people close to the King were scheming to have Richelieu arrested as soon as his health improved. "Even though I am sure this is nothing," she noted optimistically, "you will make use of it with your customary prudence."[18]

The duchess was relieved when her uncle finally found a warm welcome in the home of a true loyalist, Jean de Pontevès de Carcès, the Governor of Provence. He welcomed the Cardinal and his men at Tarascon, not far from Avignon where Richelieu had long ago spent months of political exile with his brother Henry and Marie's father René. Nevertheless, Marie was concerned that if Richelieu did not return quickly to Paris and patch things up with the King, his career would be over.[19]

Then, in early June, something happened that caused Richelieu to exclaim to God in front of his secretary Charpentier, "Oh God! You must care deeply for this kingdom and for my person!"[20]

A document suddenly emerged—possibly with the assistance of Queen Anne—that shocked the King to his core. It was a secret treaty that his brother Gaston had signed with King Philip IV of Spain. Gaston had promised that French rebels, led by Bouillon and others, would support a Spanish army should it invade France. In exchange, Spain would promise to respect the royal rights of Louis, Anne, and their son the dauphin and assist Gaston and his associates with ruining Richelieu and replacing the Cardinal and his loyalists in the French government.[21]

The document also incriminated Cinq-Mars, whom the King was forced now to view as a traitor. Both Cinq-Mars and Bouillon were arrested. Cinq-Mars was accused of planning Richelieu's assassination. The twenty-two-year-old nobleman denied that his intentions went so far. De Thou was also arrested, and he refused to reveal what he knew of the conspiracy. An investigation unfolded, resulting in a trial that led to Cinq-Mars's and de Thou's beheading on September 12.

Bouillon and several others got off more lightly—including a young woman named Louise-Marie de Gonzague, who had become friendly with Marie and the Blue Room set. This future Queen of Poland and Grand Duchess of Lithuania had briefly hoped to marry Cinq-Mars and had spent time with him during the months of plotting. When she feared that her name would come up enough to possibly implicate her in the documents and interviews that Richelieu's agents were collecting, she asked Marie to intervene on her behalf. Marie obliged and this princess was not investigated.[22]

Gaston, differently, confessed many details regarding his own and others' involvements while insisting he had no wish to harm Richelieu. The King and Richelieu proceeded firmly but not violently against him. They saw him as weak but ultimately not malicious. Richelieu said of him at one point that "he entered into conspiracies from lack of will, and crept out of them for lack of courage."[23] He was forbidden from engaging in political activities of any kind, and when he formally inherited from his dead mother the Palais de Luxembourg in Paris that July, he faced the humiliation of having Marie appointed as its *capitaine concierge*.

This meant that Marie suddenly had the power, usually reserved for a high-ranking nobleman, to assess, and forcibly remove as necessary, various hangers-on of the prince who, as Richelieu put it, "lodged and ate everything" at the Luxembourg. Marie was thus at the heart of Richelieu's effort, while he was still away from Paris himself, to ensure that individuals in Gaston's orbit who were sympathetic to the conspirators, and others who were simply disreputable, were booted from positions of influence and no longer free-loaded off the public treasury.[24] It also gave Marie influence in decisions about both Gaston and his wife Marguerite's domestic staff and household officers.

As Richelieu remained away from Paris until October, Marie as well as his secretaries kept him informed of events and also on occasion represented him in audiences with the King.[25] Once he was back at the Palais-Cardinal, the mood among many of the upper nobility and even in the royal palace was subdued, as there was utter disbelief at how well events had played out in Richelieu's favor when it had seemed to many that he was finally about to be removed from office.

The King himself, whose own health was increasingly poor, was both glad that traitorous activity had been uncovered by Richelieu's agents but also resentful toward the Cardinal-Minister. Not only was Louis smarting over what had happed with Cinq-Mars, but, as his conditions for remaining in office, Richelieu had secured from the King, in a heavy-handed way, a signed declaration that he would never again raise up any royal favorites who were not well-vetted members of his royal council. Richelieu also appointed his creature Sublet de Noyers as *capitain concierge* at the Louvre, to oversee the personnel there as Marie was doing at the Luxembourg. The Cardinal was thus also able to pressure the King into firing a number of officers in the royal household whom he regarded as suspicious in various ways.[26]

29

Uncle Armand's Death

Richelieu was not able to enjoy or capitalize upon his greatest political triumph for very long. His health was rapidly deteriorating.

On November 29, the fifty-seven-year-old prime minister was overtaken by a sharp pain in his side and then by a high fever. Physicians were called into his bedchamber at the Palais-Cardinal, where they determined he was suffering from pleurisy. The next day, a Sunday, he showed little improvement and messages were sent out to Marie and others that things did not look promising.

Marie had her servants ready her things and prepare a carriage. She hastened to the Palais-Cardinal, where she would remain until the crisis was over, one way or another. Her cousin La Meilleraye and her uncle Maillé-Brézé showed up, too.[1]

Marie prayed fervently for Richelieu to recover. He was, after all, not that old. And there was still so much more he was planning to do for France, for the Church, for their family . . . And what shape would her life have if he left her alone now, before she felt ready to take on all the responsibilities and uncertainties his absence would thrust upon her?

On Monday, the first of December, Richelieu began coughing up blood. He also began to have great difficulty breathing. His doctors realized there was nothing they could do to prolong his life. Marie did what she could to make her uncle comfortable and she intensified her prayers.

The King came to visit Richelieu early in the afternoon on Tuesday. Although their relationship had become icy in the preceding months, the two had a fruitful conversation. Richelieu expressed his pride in the state of France as he was leaving it, and he asked the King both to protect his family members and to keep several trusted men at his side. Louis promised to retain Chavigny and Sublet de Noyers as secretaries of state and to accept Richelieu's recommendation to retain the services of the Italian-born Jules Mazarin, too. Mazarin had become a loyal deputy of Richelieu's after serving as the Pope's nuncio in France from 1634 to 1636. He had also been made a cardinal in 1641. He would indeed be appointed to the King's council and, ultimately, upon Louis's own death, maneuver his way into becoming the First Minister of State. It is unclear that Richelieu intended anything of the sort when he sung the younger churchman's praises to Louis when close to death.[2]

Not long after Louis departed the Palais-Cardinal with Maillé-Brézé close behind him, Richelieu called Marie to his bedside and whispered something to her. The first few words were audible to others in the room: "My niece, after my death, I want you to . . ." Onlookers wondered what it was he said next to her, especially since Marie, according to one account, quickly left the room while "completely melting into tears."[3]

A priest from Saint-Eustache, the nearby parish church, arrived later that evening to bring Richelieu the Eucharist. Before receiving the Body and Blood of Christ, the Cardinal gestured toward the holy bread and said, "Here is the judge who will soon decide my fate. . . . I pray with all my heart that He will convict me if I ever had any other intention than the good of religion and the state."[4] As Richelieu then faced long hours of pain and interrupted, restless sleep, another priest was called in at three in the morning to perform the sacrament of extreme unction. The rite was understood to be giving the dying man the graces he needed to persevere through his final agonies and his fears and to make a holy death. As the prayers were intoned to him in Latin, he demonstrated courage and piety, at various points praying intently and at others kissing a crucifix he held in his hands.

As Marie watched all this, she became so distressed that she had to depart her uncle's chambers to be checked herself by a physician. Before she left Richelieu's side that night, however, she spoke with him for a few more moments about what he expected from her after he was gone.[5]

At the end of this chat, the Cardinal took Marie's hands and kissed them. And he told her, loudly enough so that others in the room could hear, that she was the person he loved the most in all the world.[6]

As the sun rose on Wednesday, Richelieu's health seemed suddenly to rally. This was after a visiting physician gave him some medicine that eased some of his symptoms. The King came to see him again. Louis informed Richelieu that he had, that same day, ensured with the Parlement de Paris that his brother Gaston would be barred from any more involvement in the government.

Word soon got out to many nobles and into the streets that Richelieu was not dying, after all. Frustration over this among those who detested the Cardinal increased further on the morning of Thursday, December 4, when his condition seemed better still.[7]

But just before lunchtime, Richelieu was seized again with severe symptoms. Alongside clergymen, doctors, family members, and attendants, Marie watched helplessly as Richelieu, dizzy and soaked in sweat, tried to focus his thoughts, words, and small pious acts on the Lord—his stern but merciful judge—who awaited him.

Marie's sobs were extreme enough that they distracted Richelieu as he was trying to surrender himself fully to God. Knowing that it would pain her, but wishing to protect her from more pain and himself from further distraction, he asked her to leave the room. "My niece," he said tenderly, "I'm in a bad state. I'm about to die. Please, I beg you to leave. Your tenderness affects me too much. I don't want you to have the displeasure of seeing me die."[8]

Marie ran out of the room. Moments later, Richelieu's breath gave out.

30

The Will

On the afternoon of December 4, Marie suddenly faced a world in which no living man but the King was in any significant way master of her destiny. Richelieu had been like a father to her for almost twenty years. She had come to know him and love him, indeed, better than she had had the chance to know and care for her long-deceased, real father, René de Vignerot. She outranked her weak-willed brother François. She had no husband. And Maillé-Brézé, although he had hopes for what Richelieu might have left to him and his children in his will, had no special claim to assert himself as Marie's guardian or as the head of the Richelieu family.

Marie could not dwell on her feelings about any of this for very long, as she had to do her part now to help lead her family and the countless people who had worked for her uncle and depended upon him through some difficult hours and days. There was her uncle's grand funeral to oversee. There was also a terribly fraught political climate to navigate.

Indeed, it was rumored that the King himself, as well as many others in the upper nobility of France, could not contain their relief and joy that Richelieu was dead. Many expected that there would be major changes at court and throughout the government. Some hoped that they could counteract Mazarin's succession as prime minister by convincing the King to dismiss Richelieu loyalists from the royal council and other key posts. Some even hoped that, if they succeeded in this, the King might banish Richelieu's relatives from court, release from prison and recall from exile individuals Richelieu had ordered punished, and redistribute the Cardinal's vast cash reserves, lands, and properties to them and their friends.[1]

Of central importance to the political transition were the decisions Richelieu had made in his last will and testament, the contents of which were known to only a few trusted individuals.

Marie was one of them. Her brother François, her uncle Maillé-Brézé, and most of the others who gathered at the Palais-Cardinal on December 5 to hear the will read aloud were in the dark about what she knew.[2]

Richelieu had done what he could, in his final days, to prepare Marie for this moment, which was in a way the defining moment of her life. He had known that what he had chosen to do with his enormous and complex estate was unconventional, would put her in a difficult position, and would make her new enemies, including some powerful, titled men who had armies at their disposal.

While in anguish over her uncle's untimely death, Marie steeled herself as the contents of the will were read aloud:

> I wish and ordain that all the gold and silver money that I will leave when I die, in whatever place it may be, be put into the hands of Madame the Duchesse d'Aiguillon, my niece. . . .
>
> I give and bequeath to [her] all the rights that she would have and claim to all the goods of my succession; and besides this . . . I make her my heiress, namely, to . . . the Petit Luxembourg . . . my house and my lands in Rueil . . . my domain of Pontoise and other rights that I possess in that city . . . the incomes that I receive from the five largest tax farms in France, which amount to 60,000 livres a year or thereabouts.[3]

This was just the beginning of what Richelieu entrusted to Marie in the will. She was also given a considerable share, alongside the Crown, of his peerless collection of fine paintings, sculptures, crystals, jewels, rare *objets d'art*, and curiosities. And she was entrusted with most of his state papers and some of his private papers, as well—something that gave her the power to shape how the history of his administration would be told.[4]

She was, furthermore, made the administrator of everything the Cardinal left to his primary legal heir, her ten-year-old nephew, Armand-Jean. This little boy, already primarily in Marie's care, despite the fact that his parents were alive and healthy, was now the Duc de Richelieu. He—not his irresponsible, foolish father François—would eventually receive the Duchy of Richelieu with its magnificent château and all its dependencies, the Hôtel Richelieu in Paris next door to the Palais-Cardinal, which was given to the Crown, and diverse baronies, counties, and other domains with feudal rights throughout France. He was also to receive, one day, Richelieu's vast library and various incomes and offices in the gift of the Crown, soon to include the military governorship of Havre-de-Grâce in Normandy.[5]

But it was Marie, the Cardinal had stipulated, who would hold and manage all of these things in trust until that time her nephew was fit in her judgment to assert his rights over them.

By giving Marie this power while the boy's father and mother were both alive, Richelieu had flouted an ancient French legal principle known as *représentation successorale*.[6]

What is more, although the will formally empowered several men as executors—Bouthillier, Sublet de Noyers, and Séguier—the crafted terms of the document were such that everyone present on December 5 understood that Marie would be the de facto executrix of the will for as long as she lived.[7]

31

Burying the Prime Minister

Wearing all black from head to foot as she had done several times as a younger woman, Marie was reintroduced to her countrymen on December 11, 1642, as the head of her great, fractious family. That morning, she ordered the doors of the Palais-Cardinal thrown open to the public. The French people were invited to mourn with her for three full days.

Several days later, a writer for the *Gazette* expressed to all "good people" and "lovers of the glory of the state" that Cardinal Richelieu had regretted leaving them, but also that he had died satisfied in the knowledge that all the ways he had "ruined the health of his body" in his decades of public service had resulted in "many advantages" for France.[1]

Numerous French people agreed. Many thousands "of all conditions, sexes, and ages" streamed in and out of the Palais-Cardinal, sometimes in the presence of the grieving duchess, to pay respects to her uncle, whose corpse lay in state in an open casket.[2]

One of the greatest funeral processions in the history of France up to that time then took place on the evening of December 13, which was a Saturday. Beginning in the courtyard of the Palais-Cardinal, which was north of the Louvre on the Right Bank, it ended at the Chapel of the Sorbonne, which was almost a mile and half away on the Left Bank, south of Notre Dame Cathedral.

The procession took place after dusk. This allowed for ordinary shopkeepers and other laboring Parisians to attend. It also allowed for the maximum effect—a great, moving profusion of light—of the large white candles held by hundreds of relatives, friends, and servants of Richelieu in the solemn parade. Observers remarked that it seemed like the daytime, as a result, as the procession moved slowly from the neighborhood of the Louvre, across the Seine, and into the ancient Latin Quarter of the city.

The streets and the great Pont-Neuf were crowded with so many onlookers that the procession could hardly fit through them at times. Many in the crowd detested—but many also admired, as a hero who loved France—the man whose corpse was transported with the greatest reverence inside a magnificent carriage that was amply covered with black velvet, white satin crosses, and the heraldic symbols of the Richelieu family. The six horses that pulled the carriage were adorned in the same way.[3]

Marie and several other high-ranking relatives and dignitaries did not carry candles but sat in their own carriages that were part of the procession. Inside her vehicle, the young duchess would have been veiled in black lace. The procession was long enough, taking upward of an hour, that she surely experienced a great mix of emotions along the way as her thoughts moved between her uncle, prayers for his soul, and memories associated with each part of the city she passed through with the casket and the candle bearers.[4]

The faces of some in the crowd would have pressed closely to the window of her carriage in the narrower passes. Some of these faces must have been awestruck, some simply curious, and others perhaps smiling at her maliciously when they realized who she was, thinking of the lewd songs about her.

As the procession finally approached the Sorbonne, Marie could see only dimly, given the hour, the outlines of the grand dome of the chapel that Lemercier had designed for Richelieu. Richelieu had early on in his tenure as a royal minister become the *proviseur* (leading administrator) of the Collège de La Sorbonne, the prominent theological faculty of the University of Paris that dated back to the thirteenth century. Finding its buildings to be run down and architecturally unimpressive, he had commissioned Lemercier to transform them into a grand, Baroque-style masterpiece, crowned with the first dome of its kind in France.

Finished shortly before Richelieu's death, this chapel was where Richelieu had asked to be laid to rest—near the altar, where a sculpted tomb that did not yet exist would eventually be visible to congregants at every Mass to be offered there. The painter Champaigne had also just a few months before completed a strange, marvelous fresco for inside the dome and other parts of the ceiling, depicting numerous angels and images of the hierarchy of Heaven as envisioned by a sixth-century Neo-Platonic theologian, Pseudo-Dionysius the Areopagite.[5]

In a sense, the grand chapel itself was to be regarded as the Cardinal-Minister's shrine by future generations.

Richelieu's burial marked the end of an era for Marie and the beginning of a new one. And the newness of Marie's position as Richelieu's heiress and executrix, on top of her role as a duchess-peeress, was something she experienced intensively barely minutes after her uncle's funeral.

While exhausted from the days of mourning and overseeing the funeral procession and burial, Marie found herself inundated with letters and visits from people seeking preferments and other favors they had been expecting from her uncle. Others sought compensation for services they had rendered her, redress for various wrongs they attributed to Richelieu, or forgiveness of debts to his estate that they could not afford to repay. Many more newly wanted access to Marie given how much wealthier and more powerful she was now compared to when Richelieu was alive.

Still others refused to repay debts to Richelieu's estate that they could afford. This was the case, for example, with Henri de Sourdis, the Archbishop of Bordeaux, and Gédéon Tallemant des Réaux, a Huguenot writer and cousin of the Rambouillets whose biographical sketches of Marie and others of her era remain historically valuable. Both Sourdis and Tallemant owed 100,000 livres each but went to court over the matter rather than hand over the funds to Marie.[6]

Marie and the team of lawyers she assembled quickly faced additional legal challenges to the will. The first major contestations came from her uncle Maillé-Brézé and from the Prince de Condé, who were upset at how strictly Richelieu had held to the terms of Claire-Clémence's marriage contract with the prince's son, Enghien. Maillé-Brézé was also resentful at how he and his children were treated compared to Marie. They filed lawsuits within days of Richelieu's funeral.[7]

Not unrelated to these efforts, new dirty poems and songs began to circulate, alleging that Richelieu had favored Marie so much not simply because she had secretly been his mistress, but also because she was—at the same time—his secret daughter by means of an earlier incestuous relationship with her mother. "Are you astonished," one of these asked, "that the poor duchess is crying? Hasn't she just lost at the very same time a father, an uncle, *and* a spouse?"[8] Another suggested that her brother's children were actually her own and the fruit of unholy relations with Richelieu: "A husband left you a virgin, and an uncle made you a mother."[9]

Unsurprisingly, Marie's brother also began to consult with lawyers by January 1643. He was upset that he had been passed over in such an unorthodox way and received from Richelieu only forbearance regarding his debts, a cash gift of 200,000 livres, and annual pensions that amounted to 35,000 livres a year. These were great sums, considering what most French people survived on then. But they fell far short of what François believed he deserved as the Cardinal's closest and eldest male relative. His lawyers advised him to challenge the will in court, even though Richelieu had explicitly threatened in the will that if he did so and somehow were to succeed in obtaining the Duchy of Richelieu, everything Richelieu had left to his son Armand-Jean would go instead to Maillé-Brézé's line.[10]

Marie, her lawyers, and her loyal seconds such as Sublet de Noyers stood ready to fight these family members and others in the courts, just as Richelieu had planned. At the same time, Marie began almost immediately with her even greater wealth and power to build up a veritable empire of charitable, cultural, and religious enterprises that in time would reach across four continents. And she began to leverage her resources more intensively in a cause that was unexpected for a woman to get involved in: the reform and disciplining of the Catholic clergy.

Amid all this, Marie—as the late prime minister's most trusted protégée, his heiress, and as a duchess-peeress of France with unprecedented wealth and power for an unmarried and nonroyal Frenchwoman—was now firmly at the heart of her country's political, ecclesiastical, and cultural life. Resolutely keeping herself in that position well into the Golden Age of Louis XIV's reign, she would shape events, trends, and memories of the era and win many more admirers and friends—as well as new and dangerous enemies—in the process.

PART TWO

Pair de France

32

Uncle Armand's Papers

A mong the numerous things Cardinal Richelieu gave to Marie upon his death were most of his state papers and some of his personal papers. This was a highly unconventional decision in favor of a young female relative. These papers included sensitive communications with his secretaries, members of the royal family, and a range of political and ecclesiastical actors, domestic and foreign. Also among them were notes on matters ranging from theater to naval strategy and an unfinished draft of his planned *Testament Politique*—a treatise on his approach to French political life that he had been preparing for the King.[1]

Richelieu was confident that Marie would prevent these papers from getting into the wrong hands, such as those who might exploit state secrets or Richelieu family secrets for personal gain. Some of his own family members, such as Urbain de Maillé-Brézé, were among those whom Marie was to prevent from freely accessing the materials.

The late Cardinal-Minister also expected Marie, who had demonstrated time and again her love of scholarship and publishing, would ensure the papers' good order, preservation for posterity, and study by historians whom she deemed to be trustworthy. With respect to ordering and preserving the vast body of papers, the duchess shared the responsibility with one of her uncle's most loyal private secretaries, Michel Le Masle, who had himself been entrusted with most of Richelieu's personal papers, as opposed to his state papers. The former no doubt included some things that Richelieu had wished to hide even from Marie.[2]

The political papers' use to historians was something Richelieu had in mind before he died. He had been planning to sponsor a major writing project, with the expectation that scholars he trusted would consult his archive to tell the history of France in his time. Of course, he had wanted this history to put the policies he had pursued for Louis XIII and his vision of French political order in the best light possible.

Taking her uncle's unfulfilled wish to heart, Marie set about to identify a scholar who could produce a history of Louis XIII's reign. Her friend Catherine de Rambouillet recommended that she choose either Guy Patin, an up-and-coming man of letters who was also a physician and soon would be named the dean of the medical faculty at the University of Paris, or Nicolas Perrot d'Ablancourt, a young classicist who was a well-traveled member of the Académie Française. Marie favored Patin, as D'Ablancourt was a Protestant, but Patin was reticent to take on the responsibility, given the time it would require while he was ambitious for other things. Within a few years, D'Ablancourt was hired to do initial work on the history, but he produced nothing satisfactory, and the project stalled. It would not be for some years that Marie would identify the right person for the project—a Jesuit priest named Pierre Le Moyne.[3]

In the interim, Marie saw through to publication other works that were complimentary to her uncle's legacy. One was a French translation of a Spanish book about Richelieu's accomplishments and family history by Manoel Fernandes Villareal, *Epítome Genealógico del Duque de Richelieu y Discursos Políticos*. Villareal was a Portuguese merchant who had befriended Marie and her brother, François, in the late 1630s and became willingly entwined in Richelieu's machinations against the Habsburgs, which included support for the Portuguese war of independence from Spain in 1640.[4] Villareal was eventually tried by the Portuguese Inquisition and executed for the crime of secretly practicing the traditions of his Jewish ancestors. But when Marie first knew him, he was residing securely in France, assisting Richelieu's propaganda campaign. His book on the Cardinal-Minister, which first appeared in print in 1641, stressed the illustriousness of Richelieu's forebears and described Marie as a woman whose "rare beauty and excellent mind serve as marvelous ornaments to her illustrious nobility."[5] It also portrayed Richelieu's political policies as eminently Christian in motivation and in the fruit they were bearing—something that was stressed in the title for the French version that appeared some months after Richelieu died. It translates into English as *Very Christian Politics, or a Political Discourse on the Principle Acts of the Late Monsignor the Most Eminent Cardinal-Duc de Richelieu*.

The French translator of this work was a trusted young client of Marie's, François de Grenaille, a minor nobleman who had spent time in a monastery in Agen in Marie's duchy of Aiguillon. In 1640 he had dedicated a book on the moral and spiritual capacities of women to Marie, entitled *La Bibliothèque des Dames*, in which he complimented his patroness as one of the most impressive women on earth, just as her uncle Richelieu was one of the most impressive men.[6] In addition to making Villareal's flattering, detailed, and politically useful portrait widely available to French readers in 1643, Grenaille also that same year produced a work containing a eulogy for the deceased prime minister, more information on the Richelieu family, and a description of the Cardinal-Minister's funeral and burial at the Sorbonne.[7]

Not long after these works were disseminated to the French public, Marie sponsored the publication of a new edition of her uncle's *Instruction du Chrestien*, which had first been published in 1620. By 1646, the duchess secured authorization to republish the work under a new title, *Traitté de la Perfection du Chrestien par l'Eminentissime Cardinal Duc de Richelieu*. For this project, she recruited her steward Desmarets and the Archbishop of Chartres, Jacques Lescot, who together updated Richelieu's prose to match the French spelling and syntax that were fashionable at mid-century.[8] Readers of the book encountered, therefore, a deceased Richelieu who was reverent, scholarly, pastoral, even saintly—but not old-fashioned.

The frontispiece of this book was an engraved portrait of Richelieu that Marie had commissioned from an artist named Claude Mellan. From an obscure, bourgeois background, Mellan had studied in Rome and come into his own as an artist under the guidance of Simon Vouet, a painter who had been favored by Richelieu. Mellan's engraving depicted the deceased cardinal as already in Heaven and piously worshipping at the feet of the Virgin Mary and the infant Jesus.

As much as Marie hoped that Richelieu was safely in Heaven with the saints, this was, of course, a work of propaganda. The duchess understood the almost magical power such images had in her era, especially when paired with printed words in finely made books. Her purpose was to elicit pious feelings among ordinary French people toward the late Cardinal-Minister, and therefore various policies associated with him, even as she would devote many resources over the years to Catholic masses for his soul—something done from concern that his soul was suffering in Purgatory in reparation for untold sins.

Marie also had to look no further than all the papers Richelieu had left to her to see how preoccupied with worldly affairs her uncle had been, despite being a churchman. The extent to which he was absorbed in sometimes deadly political intrigues, political analysis and calculations, and the careful crafting of his own and the King's images was made clear from these papers. There was something astonishing about it, indicative of rare genius but also obsessiveness. There was also something educational in it for Marie. The mind of one of the great statesmen of the age was readily available to get to know, in the privacy of her study, in some ways better than had been possible while Richelieu was alive. Also accessible to her, as to no one else unless she permitted them access, was the full range of his political contacts, patronage network, and knowledge of French and international affairs—political, ecclesiastical, and cultural. Not even Richelieu's successors in high office had all of this as immediately and thoroughly available to them as Marie did.

Among the papers from her uncle that Marie guarded with special care were the unfinished manuscript and notes that would eventually be compiled, edited, and published as Richelieu's *Testament Politique*. It remains a mystery to this day who was responsible for the first effort, in 1646, when Marie entrusted an early manuscript to the Sorbonne, to turn the documents into a single, coherent work. Richelieu had intended to do this—for the King's eyes only, not for the general public—since 1640, when he began working on it in earnest.[9] The first published version would not appear in print (and then in the Netherlands, not in France) until 1688, thirteen years after Marie's death. During the duchess's lifetime, the text would be copied by a few trusted hands and read only by a select circle of people.[10] Remarkably, although Marie had access to Richelieu's nearly finished *Testament Politique* by the end of 1642, the Cardinal had not entrusted a copy either to the King or to Cardinal Jules Mazarin, his successor as prime minister, at the time of his death. The earliest Mazarin may have seen a copy of it would have been 1651, when his loyal aide, Jean-Baptiste Colbert, asked Marie if he could borrow some of her late uncle's manuscripts.[11]

Richelieu's *Testament Politique* treated a wide range of subjects. It offered considerations on the balance of powers that should be achieved in the French state: the King should ensure, for example, that the nobility, the Church, and the common people all be treated fairly and not permitted to become "heavy" or overstep their "limits." It urged the King to take more care that order, dignity, and a fitting degree of opulence prevail in the royal palaces: Richelieu had been dismayed over the years by the ease of access to the King's chambers that all sorts of people had enjoyed in the past and by the dirty and shabby quarters some foreign dignitaries had been offered during state visits. The French Crown needed to project more majesty outward to other princes of the world, and officials of the royal households needed to be more carefully chosen from among those who were both highborn and capable of acquitting their responsibilities with skill and decorum.[12]

The *Testament Politique* also offered wide-ranging advice on matters of statecraft, borne of Richelieu's long experience: how to balance diplomacy with decisiveness in foreign affairs, for the sake of the national interest; how to anticipate possible sequences of events; how to identify and keep at bay flatterers, gossipmongers, and intriguers at court; how and in what ways to press forward in the administration of affairs when beset by all sorts of political opponents and, at times, by one's own loneliness at the helm of the ship of state. Richelieu's thoughts on taxation, on the expansion and reform of the French armed forces, on how government officials did and should relate to both the King and the people, and on numerous other topics were presented throughout the work's eighteen chapters with a clarity and conciseness that revealed as much about the late prime minister's personality as about his ideas and time in office.

We cannot know how familiar Marie was at any given time with the content of the work. However, passages from it on a range of subjects help us to see to what extent the duchess was a student of her uncle's and which among his preoccupations and approaches to political life she most embraced as her own.

An early chapter of the *Testament Politique* concerns, for example, the reform of the Church and especially the French clergy. Richelieu had planned to urge the King "to take particular care to fill the bishoprics with persons of merit and exemplary life, to give abbeys and other simple benefices . . . only to persons of recognized integrity, to exclude from this favor those who lead too loose a life for a saintly profession that ties men particularly to God, and to make an example by punishing the scandalous."[13] Bucking a more general trend of the era, he also believed that it was beneficial to look beyond "persons from aristocratic families" and to consider men of lower birth as candidates for high office in the Church, because the former sometimes proved to be "less committed to their duty and less disciplined" than the latter. A capacity for "leadership," including care for administrative matters, was also to be valued in churchmen. At the same time, "learning" was also critical and best acquired in new, high-quality seminaries dedicated for forming clergymen intellectually as well as in the virtues of humility, piety, charity toward others, and courage and zeal on behalf of "the Church and . . . the salvation of souls."[14]

Whether or not Marie closely studied every word of the unpublished *Testament Politique* while safeguarding it, her actions over time would demonstrate how much she shared in her uncle's vision while developing it in her own ways, especially where ecclesiastical matters were concerned. Over the course of her life, although she was a laywoman and, due to her sex, excluded from political and ecclesiastical office, Marie would in some ways do more to achieve the reform, renewal, and expansion of the French Church than the Cardinal-Minister himself had had the opportunity to do during his decades in power.

33

Rueil

O n May 14, 1643, barely five months after Cardinal Richelieu had died, King Louis XIII breathed his last at only the age of forty-one. This was after a long bout with what was probably intestinal tuberculosis, and it meant that his four-year-old firstborn son, now King Louis XIV, was fully in the care of his Spanish-born mother, Queen Anne of Austria, and of others whom she favored. The late King had for a time forced a separation between his wife and the dauphin, from concern that little Louis would grow up as controlled by women as he had once been by his mother, Marie de' Medici.

Anne surrounded herself and the toddler king with powerful women who would shape events dramatically in France over the next decade. The period would see the realm riven by a civil war known as the Fronde—one that was seen by many as a belated response to the late Cardinal Richelieu's administration.[1] Surprisingly, given her frosty relations with Anne in the past, one of these women was Marie, who was now variously revered and detested as the great heiress of Richelieu as well as the Duchesse d'Aiguillon and a Peer of France. As Anne took on the new, challenging role of Queen Regent, ruling France in her son's stead as she would do until 1651, Marie and her vast network of clients and friends were as valuable to her as her gifts of royal favor and protection were to Marie.

The two great ladies shared the experience of being resented for their power *as* women and realized that they could accomplish more together than separately. Ironically, their friendship in time would come to be resented most of all by the man closest to Anne who initially had encouraged it: Cardinal Mazarin, Richelieu's protégé and eventual successor as prime minister. The role of First Minister of State was of course closed to Marie because of her sex. But there would come a period during the Fronde, at the height of Mazarin's unpopularity in France, when the new Cardinal-Minister would regard Richelieu's most beloved relative and protégée as his primary rival for power and influence at court.

Mazarin foresaw none of this in 1643 when he urged Anne, who trusted and liked the Italian churchman (too much, it was whispered . . .) to extend her hand to Marie. In the wake of Richelieu's death, Marie's inherited control of the governorship of Havre-de-Grâce in Normandy was at risk. Known for short as *Le Havre*, this well-fortified port city was home to a large fleet of royal warships and a cannon foundry and thus was deemed by many as too important to be left in the hands of a woman until her nephew, Armand-Jean, the new Duc de Richelieu, came of age.[2] Indeed, Queen Anne herself almost concluded this when a friend of hers from an old princely family, François VI de Marsillac, the future Duc de La Rochefoucauld, asked for the governorship partly with the aim of cutting the *arriviste* Richelieus down to size.[3]

Learning of this, Marie with Mazarin's support was given an audience with Anne in which she convinced the Queen Regent that Marsillac might have hidden political designs that could threaten her own and her son Louis's royal government. One of Anne's ladies-in-waiting, Françoise Bertaut de Motteville, was herself impressed enough by the duchess's arguments that she penned a dramatic account of the meeting in her memoirs. She noted that Marie shed some tears while making her case, and that these tears, shed as they were by one "who by her fine qualities surpassed ordinary women," moved Anne, who soon after decided against Marsillac.[4]

Mazarin had added his reasons to Marie's for maintaining the status quo, partly because he believed Le Havre would come more under his direct influence if a mere woman, rather than a prince with military experience, were its governor. It was presumed that Marie would govern in name only and leave real decisions for Le Havre to a lieutenant whom the Crown would vet. Regardless, Anne's decision in favor of Marie spoke powerfully to others at court that Richelieu's niece was still a player in French political life, despite the new central pieces on the chessboard.

Marie thanked both Anne and Mazarin by standing by them during a failed conspiracy against the latter that had arisen partly because he was seen as an extension of the late Cardinal-Minister. This was in the spring and summer of 1643. Among the prominent, conspiring nobles were the Duchesse de Chevreuse and the Vendômes, all of whom had plotted against Richelieu in the past.[5] The

Vendômes were aggrieved because Marie's cousin La Meilleraye was made the Governor of Brittany when they believed the post was rightfully their family's. Marie's former aunt-in-law, Chevreuse, had apart from all this been a close friend of the Queen's—including at the time in 1626 when she tried to have Richelieu assassinated by one of her lovers—so banishment by Mazarin and her escape to a stylish exile in Brussels was a sorrow for Anne, who suffered some loneliness and felt in need of a new companion.

Other marks of amicability between Marie and Anne soon grew into friend-ship. The two began spending long hours together, sharing confidences as well as leisurely enjoyments with their increasingly overlapping inner circles.[6]

Marie thus got to know Anne very well along with little King Louis, who was now among the children upon whom she exerted influence without being a mother herself. Anne would sometimes visit the Château de Rueil and bring both Louis (whom she both revered as her king and disciplined severely) and his little brother, Philippe (whom she dressed in girl's clothing, so that he would not become another Gaston d'Orléans, plotting to become King himself). Marie had inherited this great château from Richelieu. It held memories of happy times—with Cardinal La Valette, for example—and sad ones, as when a young man named Zaga Christos, a visiting prince from Ethiopia, died from pleurisy there in 1638.[7] The Queen Regent liked Rueil so much that she would occasionally stay there for weeks at a time with her sons and her retinue.[8] Marie herself had spent long periods there in the wake of La Valette's death and more recently her uncle's, usually in the company of Julie d'Angennes and other close friends whose company and conversation helped her to get through some difficult days.[9] By 1644, however, Marie was throwing open Rueil's doors to great parties of guests that rivaled those the French monarchs accommodated at their palaces.

Indeed, late that spring, Anne moved the entire court to Rueil.[10] The Queen's intention was partly political, to demonstrate her friendship with Marie and, relatedly, her disapproval of several powerful princes, especially the Prince de Condé. Just as he had done years earlier during Marie de' Medici's regency, Condé was at this time threatening the stability of Anne's government. He did this partly by challenging Marie's administration of Richelieu's will in court—and thereby stoking grievances against Richelieu's political legacy, as well—ostensibly in the name of his son the Duc d'Enghien and his daughter-in-law Claire-Clémence, Marie's cousin.[11]

But Rueil had attractions for Queen Anne quite apart from all this. The extensive, Tuscan-inspired gardens and waterworks there, the suites of rooms decorated with some of the finest art in Europe, and the kitchen kept by Marie's great staff rivaled those of the royal palaces. It was no wonder, either, given the 625,000 livres Richelieu had spent on the château's expansion and improvements after purchasing it in 1633 for only 147,000.[12] The artisans and laborers effecting these improvements, which included tennis courts, an *orangerie*, and many beautiful and whimsical fountains and grottoes (including a dragon statue atop a cascading fountain that occasionally spit jets of water at unsuspecting passers-by . . .), were still hard at work when Richelieu died. Marie authorized further renovations at Rueil while she was the mistress there.[13] Years later, after failing to persuade Marie to sell Rueil to him, Louis XIV would transform the Château de Versailles and its gardens in more dramatic ways, inspired in part by his childhood memories of all this busyness and beauty at Rueil.[14]

Invitations to Rueil were coveted, too, because of the company Marie kept. The Queen Regent and her courtiers mixed together at the château with some of the leading literary lights of the age and the wittiest, best-educated nobles and clergymen alike who were committed to a strong French kingdom and a reformed Catholic Church.

At Rueil that spring and early summer of 1644 were continual rounds of game playing, leisurely promenades, theatrical performances, and other entertainments. Rueil had a great theater, as did the other palaces built and remodeled by Richelieu, and Marie especially enjoyed producing comedies and ballets for her guests, some of which made use of then state-of-the-art staging effects.[15] Machinery imported from Italy in this vein reinforced a commitment at Rueil to what was new and fashionable in Europe—something quite different from what was seen at other great country homes frequented by the royal family, such as the Condé's beautiful Chantilly north of Paris, where a tranquil focus on the beauties of the natural world reigned.[16]

Marie loved music, as she had since childhood, so she arranged concerts and surprise serenades for Queen Anne and her numerous other guests featuring some of the latest compositions from French, Spanish, and Italian artists. Among those who performed at Rueil that season was Leonora Baroni, who had grown up at the Gonzaga court in Mantua and who had just come to France after many years in Rome. Her talents not just as a singer but also on the lute, on other instruments, and in composing her own music had been developed at the Palazzo

Barberini and other great houses. Marie appreciated not only Baroni's musical gifts but also her exceptional learning and social graces.[17]

Anne's lady-in-waiting Madame de Motteville underscored in her memoirs how delightful a time the Queen had at Marie's country palace, which was "very agreeable from the beauty of its gardens and the number of its streams." Anne especially loved "her evening walks" and chance encounters with the likes of Vincent Voiture, who made bold at one point to compose a poem for her on the spot that alluded to all the unhappiness she had endured in her marriage to Louis XIII.[18]

As the Queen Regent, her children, and numerous others soaked in countless pleasurable and refining experiences at Rueil, the governance of France, which was still at war with Spain, was securely in the hands of Cardinal Mazarin. The prime minister could not as a result be at the château for the full season but arrived some days later from Paris.[19] Marie thus found herself in the position that season of offering unofficial council to Anne on various matters in the absence of the Cardinal-Minister, and also of being busier in some respects with important affairs than the reigning queen. While playing the bountiful hostess at Rueil, Marie did not, as Anne did, have a single, trusted individual, or an institutionalized council that met regularly wherever she was, to whom she could delegate the supervision and management of her own growing empire of a sort.

Different from a kingdom, of course, Marie's was an entrepreneurial and increasingly international empire of charitable endeavors, properties and estates, cultural projects, governmental and ecclesiastical posts in her control, and religious institutions and ministries that she patronized. To maintain it and build it up further, Marie depended upon an expanding network of reliable people—lawyers and stewards, her lady-in-waiting and erstwhile secretary Anne du Vigean, many servants in her employ, friends and family members who assisted her informally, clients of her own and of her deceased uncle's patronage, and clergymen and religious with whom she collaborated.

Marie was busily in communication with all such people during her days at Rueil. She ensured that projects she favored progressed amid the promenades, plays, and other pleasurable distractions.

For example, Marie hosted unusual conferences at her château that season that were led by women, such as Charlotte de Lancy of an innovative institute called the Filles de la Croix that was devoted to charitable service to the poor in a more radical way than French aristocrats were accustomed to seeing.[20] These conferences drew in large, socially mixed crowds of courtly women and women of humbler origin who came from beyond the château grounds. They were designed not simply to win support for charitable endeavors among the wealthy and powerful but also to encourage all the women who came—including Queen Anne herself—to take a more active and personal interest in assisting the less fortunate in ways that were pleasing to God.

Such causes were especially close to the heart of one of Marie's most frequent guests at Rueil. Father Vincent de Paul, well into his sixties, was now the Queen Regent's spiritual director. At the château he worked diligently with Marie and the Queen to interest more wealthy and influential members of French society in the various charities, missions, and houses of formation under his supervision and spiritual care. These were multiplying dramatically and even now beginning to expand beyond the borders of France—due considerably to Marie's patronage and, occasionally where she deemed it necessary, her prodding of the sometimes slow-moving future canonized saint.[21]

34

Patroness of a Saint

F or Vincent de Paul and the Lazarists, Marie's succession to much of her uncle's legacy proved to be a major turning point. Marie encouraged the Queen Regent's newfound confidence in De Paul as a spiritual director. At the same time, she assured De Paul not only that she would continue to support the various projects she and her uncle had gotten off the ground with the Lazarists, but also that she had ambitions for the Lazarists to expand in new directions.

In his will, Richelieu had asked Marie to continue providing for the Lazarists in the town of Richelieu, as she would also be doing for the house she had established in Agen and for some of the priests' work in Paris. Indeed, the late churchman had asked his niece to increase support for the priests at Richelieu, to improve their facilities, and not to feel bound "to give an account of the expenses involved" to anyone, such as grasping relatives. [1]

Quickly following through with this, Marie also wasted little time in expanding the Lazarists at Notre-Dame de La Rose in Agen. De Paul was able to send three more priests there in the spring of 1643 who engaged in missionary work in the surrounding countryside and gave instruction to local young men who were training for the priesthood. [2]

But far more than this—and not without some resistance from De Paul, who was cautious by nature—Marie within five years of Richelieu's death employed her influence, connections, and wealth to establish the Lazarists in papal Rome, in the French Mediterranean port city of Marseilles, and in Ottoman-controlled North Africa.

Establishing the Lazarists permanently in Rome was a strategic move first envisioned while Richelieu was still alive. There was the obvious benefit to the

Lazarists, as a congregation only recently approved by the Pope, of having a base in the Church's capital city from which they could lobby curial officials to favor their ministries. There were, as well, advantages for France during wartime in sending more French churchmen to the Eternal City who could exert cultural and political influence there. As Richelieu's protégée, Marie was mindful of such secular considerations while hoping to see the Lazarists have a spiritual impact on the ecclesiastical hierarchy.

Although a handful of Lazarists were regularly in Rome by the late 1630s, plans for a permanent establishment were in motion by 1641. Marie financed the development of a Lazarist seminary in the city. Missions to the local poor would be overseen from this establishment in central Rome, which initially consisted of a house with a church attached to it close to today's Via della Missione (named for the Lazarists) and Bernini's Palazzo Montecitorio. In exchange for the duchess's initial endowment of 30,000 livres, the Lazarists promised to dedicate their church in Rome to "the most holy and adorable Trinity" and to offer a Mass every day for God's merciful protection of their patroness and her uncle Richelieu.[3]

Marie drew this gift from a tax farm that she held in the French royal postal service. (That is, in exchange for collecting taxes on mail for the Crown for contracted periods, Marie received a substantial cut—a common way state power functioned under the Ancien Régime.) The share in this tax farm was expected to produce at least 2,500 livres in interest per year for the Lazarists in Rome. However, after Richelieu died and left Marie five more tax farms that were among the most lucrative in the kingdom, Marie was able to donate another share worth 50,000 livres, which augmented the Lazarists' annual income in Rome by 5,000 livres per year.[4]

Marie stipulated that a plaque of black marble referring to her as the Roman house's foundress be placed in a prominent location inside its attached church. Furthermore, after making more demands on the priests in Rome with respect to the masses they would be offering for the repose of Richelieu's soul and eventually her own, the duchess clarified with De Paul that the house was perpetually "to honor the eternal priesthood of our Lord Jesus Christ and His love for the salvation of the poor." According to the contract agreed to by Marie and De Paul, clergymen from the house would go out among the poor in Rome, offering them spiritual and bodily assistance. But inside the priests and young men who were not yet ordained would be instructed in what was necessary for their own salvation. They would also be required to pray often, examine their lives, and make sure that they were not pursuing the priesthood for worldly reasons.[5]

In time, with Marie's further assistance and direction, the Lazarists would expand in Rome and influence a wide range of ecclesiastical officials as well as lay and religious men and women there. The same would be true of another Lazarist enterprise Marie established in the wake of Richelieu's death, in the southeastern French coastal city of Marseilles, which itself would become the launching point for Lazarist missions to North Africa.

De Paul had connections to Marseilles that predated his collaborative relationship with Marie. In 1619, when Marie was still a girl, De Paul had been named as a chaplain to the galley prisoners in the Mediterranean port city. This was the result of his first major patron's influence. Philippe-Emmanuel de Gondi was the Général des Galères, or commander of the French naval fleet based in Marseilles. In his chaplaincy role, De Paul occasionally visited the city and ministered to military deserters, common criminals, Muslim Turks, and other men who had been forced into penal servitude as oarsmen and dockworkers.

The priest's attention to Marseilles increased in 1635 when, with Marie's encouragement, Richelieu confirmed him in his chaplaincy role after purchasing the office of Général des Galères from the Gondis. This office was then given to Marie's brother, François, and eventually, when Richelieu died, to François's son Armand-Jean, who was too young to fulfill its obligations. Marie, as her nephew's guardian, thus took over some of the duties attached to this generalship. These included choosing ship captains and other personnel for the French Mediterranean fleet.[6]

She used this unusual opportunity for a noblewoman to ensure De Paul's permanent appointment as chaplain to the galley prisoners at Marseilles. She furthermore secured an ordinance from Louis XIII that permitted De Paul, who had long been based in Paris, to delegate the duties of the chaplaincy whenever he wished to another Lazarist priest. That deputy would reside in Marseilles with a community of confreres that Marie also worked to establish in the city.[7]

Marie was financially backing a fixed Lazarist presence in Marseilles by the summer of 1643. Her initial gift of 14,000 livres was for maintaining five men of the congregation who would minister to the galley prisoners and staff a new hospital in the city. This hospital was also intended to help the prisoners and was a joint effort: Marie was working with the newly appointed Bishop of Marseilles, Jean-Baptiste Gault, to get it up and running.[8] Gault had just been consecrated as a bishop in Paris in the fall of the previous year and had met with Marie and De Paul several times to map out plans for the Lazarists in his diocese.[9] Satisfied with these discussions, Marie promised an additional 9,000 livres that went toward the building chosen for the hospital.[10]

The mission that Marie established in Marseilles was innovatively collaborative as well as a model of the Lazarists' new approach to the poor and the marginalized. Gault assigned additional clergymen under his authority to assist the Lazarists' efforts, including several Oratorians and priests of a new order, the Congrégation du Saint-Sacrement, that was not yet recognized by the Pope. These men worked alongside Jesuits, too, who had already been working among the galley prisoners.[11]

Marie followed the progress of the mission through reports she received from Marseilles. The Lazarists and other clergy spent several months at a time aboard the galleys, teaching the basics of the Catholic faith, conversing with convicts about their troubles, hearing confessions, and encouraging the men who were prepared for Holy Communion and, in some cases, baptism, to receive sacraments. Some prisoners who made confessions had not done so for decades. Some who asked to be baptized had been raised as Muslims. The priests also attempted to ameliorate the poor treatment that the prisoners received from some of the wardens and ship captains. Eyewitnesses spoke with amazement about the newfound piety among some of the convicts after the first mission was over, seen for example in their joining the clergymen in evening prayers that included sung chants to the Blessed Virgin.[12]

Bishop Gault participated in this first mission. Although many French aristocrats were surprised that a bishop was exhibiting such genuinely apostolic behavior, Marie was not, as she had helped her uncle to evaluate Gault before his appointment. Sadly, however, although he was not yet fifty, he suffered a pulmonary hemorrhage and died in May 1643. This was before Marie's funding for the planned hospital had gone through, so he never saw that particular project come to life.

Marie in the wake of this untimely death assumed more leadership in developing the hospital. Working now especially with a layman involved with the project, a wealthy Parisian gentleman named Simiane de La Coste, she solidified the hospital's financial footing and saw to it that more Lazarists went to Marseilles to manage the hospital's day-to-day affairs. The hospital was operating by 1645 inside a building that had functioned as a naval arsenal up to then. La

Coste, who was in Marseilles at the time, was able to report back to Paris soon after this, "The hospital cures [the convicts] of half their sickness because they are relieved of the vermin with which they are covered; their feet are washed and they are then put in a bed somewhat softer than the wood on which they are accustomed to lie."[13]

Marie through her strengthening friendship with Queen Anne encouraged the Regent, as did De Paul, to give formal royal recognition to the hospital in Marseilles in the summer of 1646. Financial support from the Crown followed: an initial grant of 3,000 livres was followed by additional lump sums and an annual subsidy of 9,000 livres that would, in a few years, be raised to 12,000. The hospital thenceforth would be named L'Hôpital Royal des Forçats, and young Armand-Jean de Vignerot—so, in reality, his aunt Marie—was made the hospital's governing administrator alongside La Coste. The Crown also donated a garden and additional arsenal buildings that were close by, including one dedicated to quarantining patients with contagious diseases.[14]

Marie would devote more attention, money, and other resources to the Lazarists in Marseilles in the years to come, especially as a seminary project developed there during the tenure of the new bishop, Étienne de Puget. In the meantime, Marseilles became a launching point for new Lazarist ministries across the Mediterranean in Ottoman-ruled North Africa.

Sending Lazarists to Tunis, Algiers, and other areas near those cities was a priority for Marie, who urged the Lazarists to make more than the occasional visits across the sea that De Paul had been authorizing. In the contract she had signed with De Paul for Marseilles in July 1643, the duchess stipulated that one or more of the priests she would be maintaining financially should make regular journeys to the Barbary Coast. Initially, their instructions from Marie and De Paul were "to console and instruct the poor Christians captured and detained in [Barbary] in the faith, love, and fear of God and to carry out among them their customary missions, catechisms, instructions and exhortations, masses and prayers."[15]

Marie's ambitions for the Lazarists in North Africa would grow over the next several years. They would also cause tension between De Paul and his leading patroness. Disagreements with the strong-willed, influential, and by numerous accounts holy priest were not something Marie shied away from, and she would generally hold her ground and, on occasion, require De Paul to comply with her wishes when they arose. An early example of this was when, shortly after

Richelieu's death, Marie refused to release the full 60,000 livres the Cardinal had left to the Lazarists in Richelieu after learning that the priests there were already in debt. Instead, she made an initial payment of 13,600 livres and awaited evidence of more careful management of their funds. This frustrated De Paul.[16] Several years later, Marie and De Paul did not see eye to eye about merging two small women's congregations—the Filles de la Croix, whom De Paul spiritually advised, and the Filles de la Providence. Marie believed the women in both communities would be on better financial footing if they combined forces, but De Paul opposed the merger and had to forego Marie's conditional financial support as a result.[17]

Such dynamics in De Paul's relationship with Marie would later be ignored in published accounts of the priest's life, written after his canonization by the Church in 1737. In the Catholic hagiographical tradition that eventually developed around De Paul's memory, Marie by the revolutionary period came to be pigeonholed as just one of many aristocratic women who, moved emotionally by the churchman's charisma, underwrote projects that were characterized as the fruit of his creativity and zeal. One twentieth-century biographer indeed characterized Marie as a wealthy widow who felt a powerful "attraction" to the peasant priest and who therefore would do almost anything he instructed. De Paul, in turn, knew just how to use his appeal to this "certain type of woman" to promote selfless, holy ends.[18]

The real relationship between this formidable laywoman and priest was altogether different, however. They were collaborators, and on an array of matters De Paul deferred to Marie—and not simply because she controlled the purse strings. She often thought more innovatively and ambitiously than De Paul, who was cautious by nature. This was, to be sure, the dynamic at work in the story of the Lazarists' expansion into Ottoman domains.

35

Tunis and Algiers

N orth Africa was a region that had long been of concern to Cardinal Richelieu and his Capuchin advisor and friend, Père Joseph, who had died in 1638. As Marie had spent a great deal of time in the company of both men in her youth, she was familiar by the late 1620s with her uncle's hope to see the French become more commercially competitive in the Mediterranean and to put a stop to the Barbary slave trade. For many decades, pirates from North Africa had been capturing numerous Europeans—many of them French—and selling them in slave markets in Tunis, Algiers, and other locations across the Ottoman Empire.

Energetic and organized moral opposition to slavery as such would not emerge in Europe or anywhere in the world until a century after Marie's time. But in the duchess's day, alongside increasing European and early American exploitation of sub-Saharan slave markets, a tradition of fervent opposition to the enslavement of fellow baptized Christians was well in place. Père Joseph, for example, had hoped to see a new French-led crusade against the Ottomans in order to put a stop to it once and for all.[1]

There is no extant record of Marie's views on Black slavery or on race, per se, as the concept would emerge by the Enlightenment period after her time. Nor is there any evidence that she profited directly from the transatlantic slave trade or developing plantation system through her overseas investments (at least none discovered prior to this book's publication). The question should be raised, however, given that her uncle Richelieu had encouraged Louis XIII to transport enslaved people from Sub-Saharan Africa into France's new Caribbean colonies in the late 1620s and had also authorized the first French slave trade monopoly for Sénégal in 1633.[2]

Differently, there is abundant evidence of Marie's attitude toward the Barbary slave trade, which often but not exclusively involved baptized Christians of European extraction. Indeed, she became one of her era's energetic opponents of it.

By the time Marie was elevated as the Duchesse d'Aiguillon, the French under Richelieu's leadership had come to be the dominant trading power in the Mediterranean. Marie's brother, François, however, was living extravagantly in Paris and doing little in his capacity as Général des Galères in Marseilles to take advantage of this. This annoyed Richelieu, and it was one of the reasons the Cardinal deprived his nephew of his expected inheritance. In theory, the French Crown through agents such as François oversaw a range of actors who participated in the caravan trade in North Africa: merchants, consuls, missionaries, and others under the King's protection. In reality, François and other officials in Paris and Marseilles neglected obligations and opportunities in a region that they dismissed as a backwater.[3]

Several episodes late in Richelieu's tenure as prime minister illustrated to Marie the harm to some of her countrymen that this neglect was causing. As more French people were crisscrossing the Mediterranean to sell and purchase goods, more were getting captured by Barbary pirates and sold into slavery. Reports of French captives were commonplace by the late 1630s. In 1639, Richelieu attempted unsuccessfully to scare authorities in Tunis and Algiers into freeing more captives. He also offered to give 20,000 livres out of his own pocket to assist liberation efforts.

Soon after, a scandal arose when the French consul at Tunis, Lange Martin, refused to help French merchants and other royal agents to free any of his countrymen from slavery in the region. More than this, Martin stood accused of helping to sell his own people into slavery and turning a blind eye to the brutal labor conditions and sexual abuse that some French captives suffered at the hands of their masters. It was rumored, too, that he was satisfying his own lusts on an enslaved French pageboy. Some French captives, feeling abandoned by Martin and other French officials, chose to embrace Islam in the hope that it would at least soften their masters' attitudes toward them.[4]

This was the context in which the Lazarists, with Marie's encouragement, were planning by late 1642 to give a mission among slaves in Algiers. This mission, to be led by De Paul's associate Father François du Coudray, would be similar to the first one given to the convicts in Marseilles.[5] Marie and other Catholic lay elites in Paris tracked this activity, and in the spring of 1643 they encouraged Coudray and his confreres to make contact with the French consuls in both Algiers and Tunis. The priests were expected, in conjunction with the consuls, to facilitate communications between enslaved Christians and wealthy Parisians who were willing to pay ransoms for their liberation.[6] It was believed that the number of Christian slaves in and around Algiers was between ten and twenty thousand and that another five or six thousand people were held captive in Tunis. Those among them who had been born in France were of top priority to Marie and her friends.[7] (The racial makeup of all of these captives, in the sense that we discuss race in modern times, is not generally detectable from the existing records. We can presume that most were white, but this would not have been as conscious a concern—as it later would be to some eighteenth- and nineteenth-century French elites—to seventeenth-century Marie and her friends as the captives' status as baptized Church members and born subjects of Christian rulers.)

Marie's donations to the Lazarists in Marseilles facilitated the missionaries' early forays in North Africa. By 1645, however, plans were in motion to establish the Lazarists permanently in Tunis and Algiers. In November that year, a Lazarist priest named Julien Guérin was appointed as a chaplain to Martin, the scandalous consul in Tunis. Joining Guérin was a Lazarist lay brother, François Francillon. The two began to minister to Christian slaves and even to offer masses and public prayer services for the King of France. Some local Muslim elites permitted their slaves to attend these. This surprised Guérin and Francillon, who soon learned that the Muslims in Tunis were tolerant toward Frenchmen and even clergymen so long as they did not attempt to convert any of them to Christianity.[8]

Far more of a problem for the Lazarists than the Muslims were the French consuls and their staff in Tunis and Algiers. They simply would not assist their countrymen in their mission.

Once Marie was apprised of this, she determined upon a remarkable scheme.[9] The consulates in North Africa were, like so many other French offices in the gift of the Crown, proprietary in nature—offices owned by private persons who bought them and either served in them or gifted them to a family member or client.[10] Marie decided to acquire the consulates herself, as soon as each became available. This occurred in the spring of 1646 for Algiers, when Consul Balthazar de Vias retired and sold his office.[11] In the summer of 1648, Marie also gained control of the consulate in Tunis, shortly after Martin died while still in office, and purchased a caravanserai (a local style of inn with a wide courtyard) to serve as a new base for the French in the city.[12]

This most unusual acquisition of two consulates by a noblewoman transpired quickly. This was due both to the duchess's close relationship with Queen Anne and to the Crown's chronic financial indebtedness to Richelieu's estate in the period.[13]

The Crown authorized more than Marie's ownership of the overseas offices. The duchess got approval for the other part of her creative scheme: Lazarists would not simply serve as chaplains attached to these consulates but would be appointed as the consuls themselves. She and De Paul would choose the men who would staff them, with the understanding that French diplomatic activity in North Africa would thenceforth be united institutionally to their missionary and charitable goals, including the relief and redemption of Christian slaves.[14]

In mid-1646, Marie and De Paul persuaded a young man named Jean Barreau to travel to Algiers and serve as the new French consul there. Barreau, who was in his early thirties, was a Lazarist in minor orders who had formerly been a Cistercian monk and, before that, a parlementary lawyer. Accompanying him across the Mediterranean was the young priest Boniface Nouelly, who was not yet thirty, and who was given charge of the new mission to the Christian slaves of Algiers and its environs.[15]

Marie, more than De Paul, was the driving force behind the new Lazarist activity in North Africa. When Barreau and Nouelly set off for Algiers late in the summer of 1646, they did so with Marie's financial support and express encouragement, even though they had not yet received authorization for their Catholic mission from the papal curia in Rome. Officials at the new Congregation for the Propagation of the Faith—better known by its Latin name, *Propaganda Fide*—were charged by the Pope with authorizing new missionary activity around the world. And initially, Propaganda Fide refused to grant the Lazarists missionary faculties for any part of North Africa. This was due to the Capuchin order's claims to have a missionary monopoly in Ottoman imperial territories where there were French consuls.[16]

The ever-cautious De Paul was alarmed about this lack of support from Rome and did not want to alienate officials there. He preferred to wait, as long as necessary, to send his men to Algiers. But Marie's wishes prevailed. Authorization by the French Crown was enough, in her view, for moving forward. Officials at the Vatican would come around eventually, she presumed—and correctly.[17]

Only later was De Paul emboldened to express his dismay toward Propaganda Fide through Father Jean Dehorgny, the Lazarist superior at the house in Rome that Marie had established for the congregation. He furthermore suggested, in terms that would have resonated strongly with Marie, that anyone in the Church not eager to assist with the spread of the Catholic faith outside of Europe was thwarting one of the most necessary movements of the age: "In another hundred years we may lose the Church entirely in Europe. So, keeping this fear in mind, blessed are those who cooperate in extending the Church elsewhere."[18]

Marie's interests in North Africa were secular as well as evangelistic. Truly her uncle Richelieu's protégée in this regard, Marie was determined that the new Lazarist missions would facilitate French diplomacy and trade throughout the Mediterranean. She also shared her deceased uncle's view that ecclesiastical men, when they were morally and intellectually well formed, were better suited to public offices than many aristocratic laymen with children. This was because they were typically more oriented to the general good than they were to private gain.

In time Marie's range of goals for the consulates would be a source of frustration for De Paul and some of the men under his authority in North Africa. But in the early days after the duchess had acquired the posts for the Lazarists, the strongest emphasis was on the protection and spiritual nourishment of French subjects in the region, especially any French Christians captured into slavery. They were to help negotiate the release of French Catholics held by Muslim masters, usually by means of ransom payments from the consuls.[19]

The Lazarists made known to Marie and her friends the identities of particular French captives they might rescue. Among those upon whom Guérin reported were several "poor French women" who were "young and beautiful and in extreme peril" after they had been imprisoned by a "French renegade"—that is, by a Frenchman who had converted to Islam. Although in the end two of these women were rescued, one remained in captivity. She was pressured to "deny Christ" and, when she would not comply, was beaten with a stick and then stomped on at the shoulders in a way that split open her breasts.[20]

When Marie and other French elites sent funds to save captives from such fates, they did so primarily in Spanish silver dollars minted in Seville or Mexico. They worked with Jewish merchants in Paris who gave them bills of exchange that the Lazarists responsible for transferring the funds could take to Marseilles or to Livorno in Italy, from which they sometimes embarked for North Africa.[21] Friends who joined with Marie in making such ransom payments included women she knew from other charitable projects in France. Among them was Madeleine de Lamoignon, one of the leading Ladies of Charity in Paris, who sent some 18,000 livres to rescue a single French merchant in Algiers.[22]

In May 1647, Marie herself provided the staggering sum of 40,500 livres to demonstrate her "compassion for the poor slaves" not only in Tunis and Algiers, but also in "other places of the Barbary Coast" where the Lazarists might go. When making this gift, she encouraged the missionaries to venture beyond the two major cities and to minister however they could to the poor and the sick in smaller, more rural North African communities.[23] Some of this money was put quickly to use, as Consul Barreau in Algiers was able to report by midsummer of the rescue of a French surgeon named Gabriel Mirsane.[24] This pleased Marie, whose financial involvements in North Africa and direction of missionaries there, as elsewhere in the world, were still just beginning.

36

Reforming the Clergy

A story survives from the period of Marie's elevation as a duchess-peeress about a scolding she received from a priest named Adrien Bourdoise. While visiting Bourdoise's church of Saint-Nicolas du Chardonnet in Paris one day, Marie had an attendant prepare a seat for her within the sanctuary, or the area of the church around the altar generally reserved for the male-only choir and clergymen who assisted with the sacred liturgies. Noticing the duchess's cushion, Bourdoise moved it to a seat farther away in the church's nave. Indifferent to the fact that Marie was the niece of Cardinal Richelieu, Bourdoise explained that the sanctuary was not a place for members of the laity, especially not laywomen.

Richelieu was furious after he learned that a priest of Bourdoise's mediocre status had treated Marie in this way. He summoned Bourdoise, but the priest stood firm and reminded the Cardinal that he and other leading French churchmen had themselves insisted at different times that laypeople and espe-cially women should be forbidden entry into sanctuaries where the Church's most sacred rites were performed.

Marie, the story also goes, had taken no offense when reminded by Bourdoise of her proper place in the nave. Indeed, she visited his church regularly thereafter, and began to donate to a seminary he had founded next door.[1]

Although it may be apocryphal, the story symbolizes two things about Marie that seem contradictory. On the one hand, she often was and wanted to be unusually close to clergymen in the spaces where they prayed and labored. Being close, from her youth, to Cardinal Richelieu and then also to Cardinal La Valette and Vincent de Paul had much to do with this. On the other hand, she accepted that there were clear boundaries between the clergy and the laity, that priests represented Jesus Christ in ways no layperson did, and that there were contexts in which ordained men even of low birth could tell a duchess what to do.

But the latter did not mean that Marie had a low view of herself, as a layperson or as a woman, alongside clergymen. Rather the opposite, it stemmed considerably from the fact that she and other powerful laypeople had real positions of power within the Church of the time. Marie had not internalized from early childhood, in her deeply Catholic world, anything like what is referred to today as *clericalism*, or the belief that all clergymen by virtue of their consecration are superior in virtue to laypeople and should enjoy exclusive rights where Church governance and internal discipline are concerned. Indeed, Marie found it easy to obey clergymen in some prescribed contexts because, in most other times and places, priests and even bishops acknowledged her and numerous other princely laypeople as those who—also with a special charge from God—wielded considerable power within and for the Church, understood as the body of the baptized.

A better-documented story from Marie's earlier years illustrates how ready the young noblewoman was to employ her position to help discipline wayward priests. It concerns the strange case of the Abbé Jean-Baptiste de Croisilles, who was a regular attendee of the Blue Room gatherings and a cousin of Marie's friend and occasional singing partner Angélique Paulet, the morally reformed former mistress of many men.

Croisilles won favor early on in the Blue Room among Marie and her friends with a prose work, published in 1633, entitled (ironically, it would turn out) *Invincible Chastity*. Several years later, when well into his forties, he could not summon the willpower to love only from afar a fourteen-year-old girl with the surname Poque whom he had met and seduced. Instead, he married her in secret under a false identity, pretending he was not a priest vowed to celibacy but rather a minor government official. When Croisilles's new mother-in-law discovered, to her horror, that her daughter had unknowingly married a clergyman, she went straight to Marie with the news and a plea to bring the scoundrel to justice.

Marie recruited Vincent de Paul to help her confirm the woman's story. De Paul trailed Croisilles to a small town called Linas south of Paris. Croisilles was residing quietly there, dressed as a layman, with the former Mademoiselle Poque, but De Paul was able to identify him right away as the priest familiar to Marie and the Blue Room set. This was because Croisilles's red hair was similar to the flaming color of his cousin Angélique's, so it readily gave him away.[2]

Once it was clear that Croisilles was flagrantly violating his clerical obligations, Marie and Richelieu together swiftly tried to get him hanged as an example
to others. He might very well have been executed had not Angélique, of whom
Marie was fond, pleaded successfully on his behalf. Marie softened and ensured
instead that the priest was thrown into prison. Croisilles appealed this sentence
and penned from his cell a long defense of himself that was published in 1643.
But he would remain under lock and key for another six years.[3]

It is unclear what, fundamentally, drove Marie's intensifying interest in the
reform of the French clergy. But she cared about it in part because it was a
cause close to the hearts of the most important men in her life, beginning with
her mentors Richelieu and Bérulle. It had been important, too, to Cardinal La
Valette, who knew firsthand the problems that being forced into the clerical
estate as a child could engender and who had attempted, but failed, to reform
several monasteries temporarily in his possession. The promotion of higher
standards among clergymen was also one of the central purposes of De Paul's
Lazarist congregation.

In the period that Marie was advancing the Lazarists' ministries with
increasing energy, she became more cognizant of the power she had as a duchess-
peeress and as Richelieu's heiress to help De Paul and other reform-minded
clergymen improve the quality of men who entered the priesthood. Given the
moral laxity, spiritual unseriousness, and corruption that plagued the Catholic
clergy in France long after the reforming Council of Trent, this was a cause that
required lay elites to assert leadership over and against resistant bishops and other
clergymen for it to succeed.

Even before Richelieu left much of his fortune to her, Marie developed a keen
interest in developing new kinds of seminaries that would raise up clergymen
who were morally disciplined, prayerful, well-educated, unswervingly orthodox,
and articulate and sincere when preaching. Focused especially on improving
the ordinary parish clergy, Marie wished to see diocesan priests become more
outward-looking, like De Paul's Lazarists and the Jesuit missionaries she supported who were laboring in New France. That is, depending on their situation,
they were to be more concerned for the poor and the marginalized, ready to
share the teachings of the Church with those ignorant of them, and zealous
about saving all kinds of souls.[4]

Bourdoise's seminary at Saint-Nicolas-du-Chardonnet was among the first
of the new-style seminaries in France that demonstrated what was possible in

this vein. In operation by the 1620s, it enabled young men to complete their education in the classics while also studying theology and reflecting prayerfully on whether or not they truly had a calling from God to become priests—that is, apart from family pressures and other worldly motives. The seminarians at Saint-Nicolas also learned all of the parts of the Mass and the rationales for all of the Church's liturgies, and they made retreats to prepare for ordination first to the diaconate and then to the priesthood. Bearing fruit quickly in terms of the quality of young clergymen it was producing, Bourdoise's seminary became a model for the Oratorians (the congregation established by Bérulle) and for the Lazarists and other new associations of clergymen the duchess supported. In time it would be made into the official seminary of the Archdiocese of Paris.[5] Marie and other donors would contribute generously over the years to a merit-based scholarship fund that provided 300 livres apiece to clergymen from poorer backgrounds who were invited to train there.[6]

In her younger years, Marie also helped to finance Father Jean Eudes, a protégé of Bérulle and the founder of a refuge for repentant prostitutes in the city of Caen in Normandy. Eudes, a future canonized saint like De Paul, established a new kind of seminary in Caen that departed from the Council of Trent's program, which had emphasized training for preordained teenagers and young men. His seminary welcomed men who were already ordained, some of them far along into middle age, who had not had opportunities to complete studies and a program of spiritual formation when younger. Marie supported thirty clergymen under Eudes's direction who conducted a mission in the early months of 1642 out of the Abbey of Saint-Ouen, which Richelieu put in her control. This mission resulted in some Protestant conversions to Catholicism and impressed several local bishops with whom Eudes wished to establish more seminaries for the region.[7]

Once she inherited Richelieu's legacy, Marie took a greater part in a growing effort among French Catholic elites to transform seminary education for clergymen. Despite ways in which it departed from particular emphases and recommendations of Trent, it was broadly an attempt to achieve more of that council's ultimate goals in France. Trent had called for the systematic establishment of seminaries for teenagers and young men, and not for boys being pushed into the ecclesiastical estate by their families. The aim was to ensure a solid spiritual and intellectual formation for those to be ordained and to raise up new generations of priests who were maturely committed to the life and obligations of sacred ministry.

While it may seem unremarkable today that reform-minded Catholics of Marie's time were focused on seminary education, Trent's call for seminaries to be established throughout the Christian world was revolutionary in its era. Up to the time of the council, and in many places for decades after, it was the norm for those training for the priesthood to attend courses at universities—if they pursued higher learning at all, which a great number of clergymen, especially at the parish level, never did. Many priests attended grammar schools when they were children and then trained for the priesthood in unstandardized ways, depending upon what was on offer locally, expected by their bishop or religious superiors, or offered by aristocratic patrons, if they had any. The result was that a great many priests, especially in poorer, rural parishes, were ignorant of basic Catholic doctrines and of liturgical and moral norms, terrible at preaching if they gave homilies at all, and expected primarily to dispense sacraments to their flocks, who otherwise were accustomed to their priests' living like ordinary villagers. This not rarely included priests frequenting taverns and siring children by common law wives.[8]

While Trent had urged bishops to establish and supervise the envisioned new seminaries, in practice some seminaries sprung up without episcopal initiative or control. This was especially true in France, where the King and a mixture of lay and clerical elites had a lot of sway in ecclesiastical affairs. The irony was that the founders of these new institutions were at times more committed to the spirit of the Tridentine reform program than the bishops whom they worked around, and sometimes against.

This was the case with De Paul and Marie. By the time Marie established the Lazarists in Rome, her commitment to reforming the clergy was strong and rooted in a high conception of the priestly vocation. In 1643, her gift of more than 50,000 livres, which she added to an already generous founding donation, came with the stipulation that the Lazarist house in Rome "honor the eternal priesthood of Our Lord Jesus Christ" and "ensure that the clergy are instructed in the things necessary to their state before taking Holy Orders."[9]

The Lazarist houses in Rome and Marseilles were just two of a number of innovative seminaries Marie helped De Paul and his men get off the ground. In time, Marie would finance not only Lazarist houses in Richelieu, Agen, Marseilles, Rome, and other cities, but also a more extensive Lazarist seminary in Rennes, where she was able in 1646 to entrust De Paul with an entire parish, Romagné, which was in her gift.[10]

Marie's patronage was integral to the foundation and success of seminaries established by another famous figure in the story of the reform and renewal of the French Church. This was Father Jean-Jacques Olier, the founder of the Compagnie des Prêtres de Saint-Sulpice, a congregation of clergymen better known as the Sulpicians. The Sulpicians, whose name derives from the Parisian church where they were established—Saint-Sulpice, Marie's parish—remain to this day a society of apostolic life devoted to the intellectual and spiritual formation of priests engaged in pastoral ministry.

After his death, Olier would go on to be venerated by many French Catholics as a saint, even though efforts to open a cause for canonization would halt in Rome in modern times. But long before all that, Olier started out as a young clergyman whose profile resembled that of other talented churchmen of humbler backgrounds whose careers Marie advanced. Four years the duchess's junior, he was a native of the Marais district of Paris and the son of a parlementary lawyer and administrator. In his teen years, Olier studied at the Jesuits' celebrated Collège de Lyon. While there, he met the future canonized saint François de Sales, who was the Bishop of Geneva and the author of *L'Introduction à la Vie Dévote*, which is still one of the most widely read Catholic spiritual guides ever written.

Olier had been urged by his family to pursue an ecclesiastical career for largely social and professional reasons. Nevertheless, he was encouraged by De Sales to approach this path already chosen for him in a prayerful, intentional way. At seventeen, in 1625, Olier returned to the French capital to study philosophy and theology at the University of Paris. Although he would not be ordained a priest for several more years, he was already in possession of several benefices acquired by his father, who was now serving the King as a *conseiller d'État*. The young man's family thus was known by this point to Cardinal Richelieu.[11]

Marie was aware of Olier by the early 1630s, as he had become by then a close associate of De Paul's. De Paul mentored him through the period of his ordination to the priesthood in 1633.[12] Within a few years, Marie joined with a wealthy nobleman named Jérôme Le Royer de La Dauversière to assist a new missionary and charitable organization that Olier envisioned for colonial New France, the Société de Notre-Dame de Montréal.[13]

Olier's primary focus was in France, however. By 1641 he had hopes of establishing a seminary in Vaugirard, a village southwest of Paris. With this in mind, he formed a small community with several other clergymen, and he was encouraged by De Paul and another priest, Charles de Condren, who was Bérulle's successor as Superior General of the Oratorians.

Olier and his men had not long been established in Vaugirard when, in early 1642, Marie visited to offer them free use of the Château de Rueil as a more fitting environment for their new community. She was surprised and impressed by their response. While overwhelmed by the generosity of the offer, they preferred their humble home in Vaugirard to Cardinal Richelieu's famous country residence.[14]

Richelieu, too, was impressed with this response and, during the period he was suffering from very poor health, he continued to show favor to Olier. Indeed, before he died, the Cardinal approved a new scheme that Marie and some of her associates had in mind for Olier.

Although he resisted the idea initially, Olier accepted a challenging new position that was offered to him in June 1642: that of pastor of Saint-Sulpice. He furthermore agreed to spearhead the reform of the recalcitrant clergy in the parish—partly by relocating his new seminary to the parish grounds—together with the moral and spiritual renewal of the surrounding neighborhoods. In the process, he alienated his own family, who believed that taking on the role of a parish pastor, especially in such a neighborhood, was beneath a man of his birth and talents.[15]

Olier's willingness to take on Saint-Sulpice was a relief to Marie after she had had a difficult time, in 1641, convincing De Paul just to lead a one-time mission there.[16] The cautious and sober De Paul rightly feared what an uphill battle any reform-minded clergyman would be engaged in while assigned to that particular parish. This is because its territorial boundaries, which included the Faubourg Saint-Germain and the neighborhood of the Sorbonne, encompassed one of the most vicious and corrupt quarters of the French capital.

37

Saint-Sulpice

M arie's primary home, the Petit Luxembourg, had lovely, walled-in gardens and its own chapel, making it an island of decorum and Christian piety in a sector of Paris famous for its brothels, gambling houses, seedy cabarets and drinking dens, and filthy, overcrowded slums.[1] But unlike other aristocrats of the neighborhood who frequented churches elsewhere in the city to avoid all the riff-raff, Marie treated nearby Saint-Sulpice as her home parish. In doing so, she willingly mixed with all manner of people in the area—far more, indeed, than Cardinal Richelieu wished she would do while he was alive.[2]

The young duchess did not take merely a passive interest in charitable and religious projects in the parish, as would have been customary for a wealthy aristocrat seeking to demonstrate to her peers her fulfillment of the basic obligations of Christian nobility. Rather, Marie was determined to see Saint-Sulpice reformed from the inside out. The odds were against her, as the liturgical, financial, and moral life of the parish had long been in a disorderly state, and the church itself, which dated to the thirteenth century, was dilapidated from chronic neglect. Nevertheless, she went above and beyond all expectations for a laywoman of her rank to ensure that it happened.[3]

By 1642, the year Jean-Jacques Olier became pastor at Saint-Sulpice and relocated his seminary to the neighborhood, Marie had been serving for several years as the first president of the Ladies of Charity chapter at the parish.[4] Due in part to her financial contributions to the Daughters of Charity and their efforts for abandoned, homeless children in the city, she had gotten some of the Daughters to assist at Saint-Sulpice, as well.[5] But the women were often treated very poorly by the same impoverished and sick people they were trying to help.

One of the Daughters, called Sister Maurice, became so frustrated by this that she packed her things and left the Daughters altogether in 1641. This upset Marie greatly. "The duchess cried out in my presence when she learned of it," De Paul reported to Louise de Marillac. "She said that it was the bad treatment those sisters were receiving from their parish and she wanted to give up everything herself."[6] Marie did not give up, however. In fact, she began to strategize in new ways about how the Ladies and their associates could become more personally involved in the parish.[7]

The appointment of Olier as the pastor of Saint-Sulpice was, then, a coup for Marie. The duchess knew that once he and his associates set about their work, they would meet with a great deal of resistance and possibly some violence. But they would also bring new strength in numbers—and manful reinforcement to the reform that Marie, the Ladies, and the Daughters were already attempting.

Marie had flexibility as a patroness and lay leader at Saint-Sulpice to an extent she might not have had at most other churches in Paris. This is because Saint-Sulpice was not under the jurisdiction of the Archbishop of Paris, who governed a slow-moving, increasingly complex archdiocesan bureaucracy, but instead that of the Abbé de Saint-Germain-des-Prés, the superior of the Benedictine friars at the nearby abbey church of Saint-Germain that had stood since the era of the Viking raids in France. Dom Jean-Grégoire Tarrisse, the elderly abbot at that time, had already dedicated many years to the reform of his own order and of the Church broadly. He also had been nurturing new forms of critical scholarship among the Benedictines of his Congrégation de Saint-Maur, also known as the Maurists, that became foundational to the modern study of history. For such reasons, he had enjoyed a good working relationship with Cardinal Richelieu and his relationship with Marie was strong, too. He readily authorized Olier's appointment as pastor and the seminary project for the parish, along with the ongoing work of Marie and the Ladies.[8]

With Dom Tarrisse's approval and Marie's patronage, Olier's new seminary at Saint-Sulpice was free to be experimental—applying some norms for seminary education urged by the Council of Trent while circumventing others. Olier admitted men to the seminary who had completed their classical education and could therefore focus on theology, training in preaching, and the effective presentation of Church teachings to their future flocks.[9] At the same time, the Sulpicians formed at the seminary did not have to tie themselves in a canonically binding way to Olier's community by means of a vow. Instead, they would become subject to the authority of the local bishop or overseeing abbot of whichever parish they eventually agreed to serve.[10]

This arrangement allowed Olier, Dom Tarrisse, Marie, and De Paul to strategically place the seminarians, once they graduated, in ecclesiastical territories where they already had local allies. Some of these were bishops and abbots who owed their own appointments to the patronage of Marie and others in her network. The model was so successful that, within a decade, Olier was able to establish four more seminaries in France, in the dioceses of Nantes, Viviers, Le Puy, and Clermont. The bishops in these locations included, at Nantes, Gabriel de Beauvau de Rivarennes, whom Marie had known since their youth as Richelieu's one-time *maître de chambre* and loyal military administrator. And presiding at Le Puy was Henri Gachon de Maupas de Tour, an associate of De Paul's who was well-known to Marie and who authored, in 1644—to the applause of the duchess and other women who had known his subject—the first biography of Jeanne de Chantal, the foundress of the Visitation Sisters.[11] Due partly to Marie's transatlantic ties, plans would also be underway by 1657 to establish a Sulpician seminary in New France.[12]

Although Olier began serving at Saint-Sulpice in August 1642, his solemn installation as pastor took place several months later, on November 4—just a month before Richelieu died—with Marie and his other supporters in attendance. The date was chosen deliberately: November 4 was the feast day of the recently canonized Saint Charles Borromeo, a sixteenth-century reformer of the clergy in Milan who had faced fierce opposition during his lifetime. Olier himself was already by then facing a great deal of resistance in his parish as he engaged his flock, both from the pulpit and in the streets, in a veritable war on sin and ignorance.[13]

Olier preached against the sins of the great as well as the ordinary and the very poor. He alienated a number of nobles when he strongly opposed dueling.[14] But he did not upset Marie, as she was staunchly against the practice as her uncle Richelieu had been. The late prime minister had wanted justice for crimes, including those traditionally seen as private matters of aristocratic honor, to be meted out by the Crown and its agents and not by nobles—especially princely ones with large armies—acting independently of royal authority.[15]

As part of his multi-front spiritual and moral war in his resistant parish, Olier would send young men from his community into the streets to teach the basics of the Catholic faith to both children and adults. By 1650, they were armed with a published catechism by Olier that made it clear that the goal the Sulpicians had in mind for even the most wayward members of their flock was not simply obedience of God's commandments but rather a change within themselves—a sincere movement of the heart toward a God who loved them and wished to liberate them from sins that alienated them from His light and peacefulness.[16] Sinners would find healing as well as truer satisfaction of their deepest desires if they followed this way, and good priests were to help all Christians to experience this.

Such messages were fundamental to what Olier taught, although after his death some Sulpicians, when redacting his sermons and writings for publication, would underscore the moral reform of the clergy and even the superiority of the latter to the laity to degrees that he had not.[17] But Olier could hardly have gotten away with a low conception of the laity at Saint-Sulpice even if he had wished to, given the extent to which his pastorate was dependent on Marie's good graces during some of his most challenging moments in the role.

It was with the young duchess's encouragement and protection, for example, that Olier established a Benediction service that would take place in the church on the first Sunday and first Thursday of every month. In such services, which became more common in modern times and today take place in Catholic churches all over the world, a consecrated Eucharistic Host is carried in a solemn procession and then exposed for adoration by the faithful in a monstrance on the altar. This is because the blessed Host is believed by Catholics to be one and the same as the divine Christ, physically and spiritually present under the accidents of unleavened bread.

Benediction services were rare in France in Marie's time, but Olier and his patroness believed they should be held often, partly as acts of reparation to God for the countless offenses against the Holy Eucharist that had taken place in Europe over the previous century. Especially during the Wars of Religion, Protestant rioters would at times deliberately desecrate hosts, Communion wine, and the sacred vessels that contained them in order to demonstrate their equally strong belief that Catholics were offending God as idolators when they knelt down and worshipped the discs of bread.[18]

To underscore the importance of the new Benediction rite at Saint-Sulpice, at least thirty-eight ecclesiastics were to participate in it each time.[19] The drama of this, with its effects on several senses at once as some in the great procession would be chanting in Latin and others carrying lighted candles and swinging thurifers with incense, was intentional. And it was something that Marie, having been schooled by Richelieu in the importance of theater in religious as well as in political and social contexts, not only approved but made possible with her wealth and connections.

Marie's devotion to Christ in the Blessed Sacrament, enlivened years before at Carmel de l'Incarnation, was deep and sincere and it buttressed Olier's. But her money and position ensured not only that the new practice at Saint-Sulpice (which was expensive, given all the candles, vestments, and other liturgical paraphernalia involved) would take place regularly but also attract attention. Some of that attention would be negative, Marie knew full well. When the duchess decided to permanently endow the bimonthly service toward the end of 1644, the churchwardens at Saint-Sulpice tried to block the foundation. These churchwardens, laymen who according to longstanding custom were the primary custodians of any material offerings to the parish, opposed the service as newfangled and the duchess's efforts with Olier as undue trespassing on their domain.[20]

Objectionable, too, were the conditions Marie attached to her endowment. The Benediction services were to include organ music, the ringing of the church bells, and the singing of numerous Latin hymns and responses. As the duchess insisted, "To each of the greetings shall be sung, in order, the response *Homo quidam*, the hymn *Pange Lingua*, the verse *Panem de coelo*, the antiphon *O Sacrum*, and the canticle *Magnificat*, plus an antiphon of the Blessed Virgin according to the liturgical time, plus the verses *Domine salvum fac regem* ["God save the King"] and *Gloria Patri*." Marie's list went on from there. Furthermore, Marie also required as a condition of her initial endowment of 3,600 livres that all masses of the year said at Saint-Sulpice include a vocal prayer for the repose of the soul of the late Cardinal Richelieu.[21]

Richelieu was still hated, as well as loved, by many French people at this time, and tales about his unmarried niece's private relationship with him and possibly other men and even women were still being spread. The fact that she had never remarried did nothing to stop the wagging tongues. No doubt believing some of the dirty rumors, the churchwardens attempted to challenge Marie's foundation at Saint-Sulpice on legal grounds but made no headway in the courts.

Still, the drama over Olier and the duchess's projects had only just begun. On March 2, 1645, just as a Benediction service was concluding at the church, a band of disgruntled men, including four priests of the neighborhood, interrupted the service with loud denunciations.[22]

Matters came to a head two months later. On Thursday, June 8, Olier was assaulted by an armed mob inside his rectory. Stirred up by the former parish pastor, Julien de Fiesque, some of the attackers trashed the place and stole things while others went for the priest himself with the goal of removing him and his "missionaries," as they called the Sulpicians, from the premises. They dragged Olier out of the building and into the street, beating him to the sounds of curses and cheers from onlookers who encouraged the violence. De Paul was nearby and, risking his own safety although he was an old man, intervened and helped save the young priest from an even worse fate. De Paul also advocated for Olier with civil authorities who had been receiving conflicting reports about who was responsible for the unrest.[23]

Marie was at Rueil when she got word of the incident. She hastened to Paris to put a stop, once and for all, to the opposition to Olier. In the meantime, the Princesse de Condé together with De Paul had taken up Olier's cause with the Parlement de Paris even as the Prince de Condé—who had his own reasons for making things difficult for both Marie and his wife—attempted to influence the judges against the young priest. Once Marie was in Paris, however, she and Queen Anne together prevailed upon the *parlementaires* to formally recognize the Sulpicians under French law and to confirm Olier's position as pastor of the parish. Arrests were made and Olier returned to his rectory—now with an armed guard authorized by the Crown and the Parlement.[24]

This show of unity and force by Olier's patroness and other highly placed supporters inaugurated a new era at Saint-Sulpice. By February 20, 1646, when the Queen, Marie, and the Princesse de Condé visited to ceremonially place a cornerstone, construction had begun on a new and eventually magnificent church for the parish.[25] So many people had started coming to worship at the parish under Olier's confirmed leadership that the original, medieval church, a Romanesque structure, was deemed too small. The architect Christoph Gamard was spearheading the redesign. The new church's Chapel of the Holy Virgin would be finished by 1664. In the interim, the old church was still used for services. Although Marie contributed generously to the new church, she would not live to see its completion, as it took many decades.

Father Olier would live to see even less of the new church structure come into being. His pastorate at Saint-Sulpice and his direction of the Sulpician seminaries ended in 1652, when he suffered a stroke at the age of only forty-three. Succeeding him was a loyal and generous associate, Father Alexandre Le Ragois de Bretonvilliers, who had contributed considerable funds to the construction of a new building for the seminary next door to Saint-Sulpice. In 1653, another stroke left Olier paralyzed. After he died in 1657, his remains (later desecrated by French revolutionaries) were entombed in the chapel of the seminary at Saint-Sulpice, turning the building into a shrine, because many people, including Marie, regarded him as a saint who was interceding in Heaven for the parish and other good causes.

In the meantime, and despite all the trouble there, Saint-Sulpice became a true spiritual home to Marie. In addition to her activities with the Ladies of Charity in the parish, she frequently attended Mass there. At times she sought respite alone with God inside its walls. Father Jean du Ferrier, one of Olier's fellow priests at Saint-Sulpice, recorded in a journal his surprise one night when, while praying before the Blessed Sacrament after one o'clock in the morning, the exalted Duchesse d'Aiguillon entered the darkened church by herself. When Ferrier asked her what she was doing at such a late hour, Marie explained "that she had been engaged all day, and that, being on her way back from [Court], she wished to make her prayer, not having found time for it during the day; and that, as she would be more returned and collected in the church than at home, she had begged the ringer to open the door for her."[26]

Ferrier was amazed that a woman of Marie's rank should behave in this way, and he exited the church to allow Marie some privacy with the Lord.[27] But given how many responsibilities Marie shouldered day to day, it is no wonder she looked for a quiet, dark place—separate from the ordinary spaces of her busy life, including her home, where she held so many meetings—where she could pray, regather her energies for the next twenty-four hours, and think through various matters weighing on her.

In the mid-1640s, those worries included not only the challenges facing the parish and the increasing number of charitable and religious institutions Marie was developing, but also political affairs with which she was involved and battles with relatives and dangerous men, such as the Prince de Condé, who wanted the money and power that Richelieu had given her.

Philippe de Champaigne, *Marie-Madeleine de Vignerot, Duchesse d'Aiguillon*, c. 1639/1640. Oil on canvas, 151 x 114 cm. Collezione Franco Maria Ricci, Labirinto della Masone, Fontanellato, Parma, Italy.

LEFT: Pierre Mignard, *Portrait of a Lady, said to be the Duchess of Aiguillon (1604-1675)*, latter half of the 17th century. Oil on canvas, 119.2 x 94.5 cm. Bequest of Grenville L. Winthrop, object number: 1943.1349, Harvard Art Museums/Fogg Museum, Cambridge, Massachusetts, USA. If this is a portrait of Marie de Vignerot, the man depicted in the portrait within it would be the Marquis de Combalet, her long-deceased husband.

RIGHT: Anonymous, *Marie-Madeleine de Vignerot, Duchesse d'Aiguillon*, c. 1640–1660. Oil on canvas, 210 x 160 cm. Gift of Henri Flaud, Collection Ville de Dinan, Musée de Dinan, Dinan, France. This portrait may have been the work of either Charles Beaubrun or Henri Beaubrun. The text on the painting was added sometime after 1675.

RIGHT: Claude Mellan, *Portrait of Cardinal
Richelieu*, commissioned by Marie de Vignerot,
1651. Metropolitan Museum of Art, New York.
Public domain. BELOW: Philippe de Champaigne
and Studio, *Triple Portrait of Cardinal Richelieu*,
c. 1642. Oil on canvas, 58.7 x 72.8 cm.
The National Gallery, London. *Public domain.*

ABOVE: Michel Bourdin the Younger, funerary sculpture of Françoise du Plessis de Vignerot, Marie de Vignerot's mother and Cardinal Richelieu's sister, c. 1644. Marble. Château de Glénay, Deux-Sèvres, France. BELOW: Michel Bourdin the Younger, funerary sculpture of René de Vignerot du Pont Courlay, Marie de Vignerot's father, c. 1644. Marble. Château de Glénay, Deux-Sèvres, France. *Both photos by Bronwen McShea.*

LEFT: Anonymous, *Portrait of Suzanne de La Porte*, c. 1580–1590. Oil on canvas, 118 x 98 cm. Chancellerie des Universités de Paris, Paris. *Wikimedia Commons, public domain.* This is a portrait of Cardinal Richelieu's mother and Marie de Vigenrot's maternal grandmother, painted at least fourteen years before Marie was born. BELOW: Charles de La Fosse, *Equestrian Portrait of Armand-Jean de Vignerot, Duc de Richelieu, Général des Galères, Led by Victory*, c. 1670–1675. 276 x 194.5 cm. *Copyright © Musée des Beaux-Arts de Tours, France.* This is a portrait of Marie de Vigenrot's eldest nephew, for whom she attempted to keep intact his inheritance from Cardinal Richelieu.

LEFT: Philippe de Champaigne, *Louis XIII, King of France*, 1635. Oil on canvas, 108 x 86 cm. Museo del Prado, Madrid. *Wikimedia Commons, public domain.*

RIGHT: Anton Van Dyck, *Portrait of Gaston of France, Duke of Orleans*, c. 1628-1634. Oil on canvas, 193 x 119 cm. Musée Condé, Château de Chantilly, France. *Wikimedia Commons, public domain.*

RIGHT: Peter Paul Rubens, *Marie de' Medici, Queen of France*, 1622. Oil on canvas, 130 x 112 cm. Museo del Prado, Madrid. *Wikimedia Commons, public domain.*

LEFT: Peter Paul Rubens, *Portrait of Anne of Austria, Queen of France*, c. 1622–1625. Oil on canvas, 120 x 96.8 cm. The Norton Simon Foundation, Pasadena, California, USA. *Wikimedia Commons, public domain.*

RIGHT: Anonymous, after Claude Lefèbvre, *Portrait of Louis XIV of France*, c. 1670. Oil on canvas, 196 x 155 cm. Musée de l'Histoire de France, Château de Versailles, France. *Wikimedia Commons, public domain.*

ABOVE LEFT: Jacob Van der Heyden or Lazarus Van der Heyden, *Louis Cardinal de La Valette*, mid-17th century. Engraving. Bibliothèque nationale de France, Paris. ABOVE RIGHT: Peter Paul Rubens, *Portrait of Charlotte-Marguerite de Montmorency, Princess of Condé*, c. 1610. Oil on canvas, 109.2 x 86.4 cm. Accession number 1970.49, Frick Art & Historical Center, Pittsburgh, Pennsylvania, USA. BELOW: Abraham Bosse, *Wives at Table During the Absence of Their Husbands*, c. 1636. Etching, 26 x 34 cm. Metropolitan Museum of Art, New York. *Public domain.* This piece gives us an impression of what Catherine de Rambouillet's Blue Room gatherings were like.

LEFT: Anonymous, *Blaise Pascal*, 17th century. Oil on canvas. *Wikimedia Commons, public domain*. Marie de Vignerot patronized the celebrated mathematician and his talented sisters, and the first recognized female mathematician in France, Marie Crous, when they were young. She also invited Pascal to her salon after he had become sympathetic with the Jansenist movement, which she opposed.

RIGHT: Charles Le Brun, *Pierre Corneille*, 17th century. Detail of etching, 17 x 11.7 cm. Bibliothèque nationale de France, Paris. *Wikimedia Commons, public domain*. Marie de Vignerot's patronage of Corneille at the time he wrote and produced his controversial play *Le Cid* was critical to the playwright's success.

LEFT: Abraham Bosse, cover page of Jean Desmarets de Saint-Sorlin's novel *Rosane*, 1639. Etching on octavo-sized paper. Bibliothèque nationale de France, Paris. *Public domain*.

ABOVE: Abraham Bosse, *The Ball*, c. 1634. Etching, 29 x 37.7 cm. Metropolitan Museum of Art, New York. *Public domain*. This print gives us a sense of what courtly parties looked like during Marie de Vignerot's younger years. BELOW: Abraham Bosse, *Visiting Prisoners*, 1635. Etching, 25.4 x 32.4 cm. Metropolitan Museum of Art, New York. *Public domain*. This print illustrates the growing practice at the time, spearheaded by Marie de Vignerot and other Ladies of Charity, of elite, devout women getting more personally involved in social charitable work.

TOP: Anonymous after Simon François, *Saint Vincent de Paul*, c. 1660. Oil on wood, 38.2 x 28.5 cm. Musée Carnavalet, Paris. CENTER: Jean Marot, *Saint-Sulpice Church, the Sole Parish Church of the Neighborhood of Saint-Germain*, mid-17th century. Etching, 18.3 x 29.2 cm. This image shows how Marie de Vignerot's parish church in Paris looked before its grand renovation. BOTTOM: Claude Mellan, *Allegory Against the Pelagian Heresy and the Coat of Arms of the Duchesse d'Aiguillon*, c. 1675. Engraving, 24.2 x 33.5 cm. Metropolitan Museum of Art, New York. *Public domain.*

TOP: View of the Château de Glénay, Marie de Vignerot's childhood home, during recent renovation work. Château de Glénay, Deux-Sèvres, France. *Photo by Philippe Durand-Meyrier, 2022.* CENTER: View of the Château de Glénay prior to the current renovation. Château de Glénay, Deux-Sèvres, France. *Photo by Bronwen McShea, 2022.* BOTTOM: View of the entrance of the chapel at the Château de Glénay. Château de Glénay, Deux-Sèvres, France. *Photo by Bronwen McShea, 2022.*

ABOVE: Stéphane Berhault, architectural drawing of the Château de Glénay in its intact condition. Aedificio, Paris / Château de Glénay, Deux-Sèvres, France. This drawing is being employed as a guide for the current renovation of the château. BELOW: Justus Van Egmont, sketch of Cardinal Richelieu and Marie de Vignerot entertaining the royal family in the theater of the Palais Cardinal in Paris, 1641. Grisaille on panel, 30 x 39.5 cm. Musée des Arts Décoratifs, Paris. *Wikimedia Commons, public domain.*

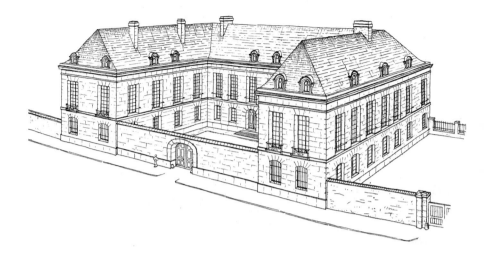

ABOVE: Arthur Hustin, rendering of the Petit Luxembourg's main building, Marie de Vignerot's primary residence in Paris, as it would have looked in the early 17th century, 1904. *Wikimedia Commons, public domain.* BELOW: View of the Petit Luxembourg in Paris today. Courtesy of the Office of the President of the Senate of France. *Photo by Bronwen McShea, 2022.* The section of the building in the foreground toward the right was not constructed until after Marie de Vignerot's time.

ABOVE: One of the larger rooms inside the oldest part of the Petit Luxembourg as it looks today. Courtesy of the Office of the President of the Senate of France. RIGHT: A view of the Palais de Luxembourg from inside the Petit Luxembourg, demonstrating how close Cardinal Richelieu and then Marie de Vignerot lived to the home of Queen Marie de' Medici and then her son Gaston d'Orléans. Courtesy of the Office of the President of the Senate of France. *Both photos by Bronwen McShea, 2022.*

Veuë du Chasteau de Ruel, du Costé du Jardin.

Israel silvestre fecit.   cum priuil Regis.

ABOVE: Adam Perelle after Israël Silvestre, *View of the Château de Rueil from the Garden*, late 17th century. Engraving. Dumbarton Oaks Library and Archives, Washington, D.C. *Public domain*. Perelle's engravings, after Silvestre's drawings, give a sense of the grandeur of Marie de Vignerot's country home outside of Paris that was the envy of King Louis XIV, who spent time there as a boy. BELOW: Adam Perelle after Israël Silvestre, *View of the Arch in the Garden of Rueil, Near the Orangerie*, late 17th century. Engraving. Dumbarton Oaks Library and Archives, Washington, D.C. *Public domain*.

Veuë de L'Arcque du Jardin de Ruel, ou est l'Orrangerie.

Israel silvestre delin.   Perelle sculp.

Claes Jans, map of Paris, 1618. 55 x 85 cm. Harold B. Lee Library, Provo, Utah, USA. *Wikimedia Commons, public domain.* This image gives us a sense of what Paris looked like around the time of Marie de Vignerot's journey there, at sixteen in 1620, to get married at the Louvre.

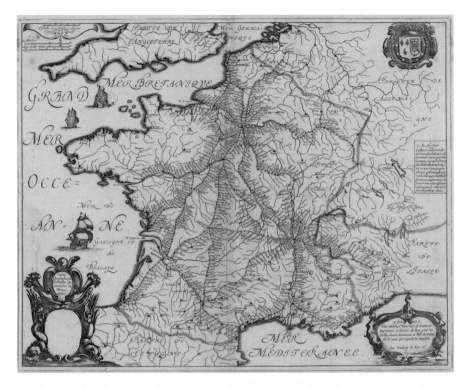

ABOVE: Melchior Tavernier, map showing the postal routes in France, 1632. Princeton University Library, Princeton, New Jersey, USA. *Wikimedia Commons, public domain.* This map was commissioned at the height of Cardinal Richelieu's control of the French state. BELOW: Anonymous, view of Havre-de-Grâce in Normandy, 17th century. Bibliothèque nationale de France, Paris. *Public domain.* Marie de Vignerot served for some years as the royal governor of this strategic port city, which was connected to the Atlantic trade routes and other important shipping routes.

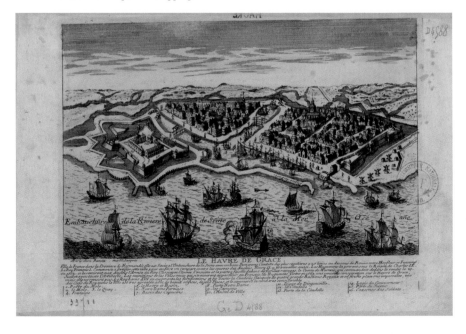

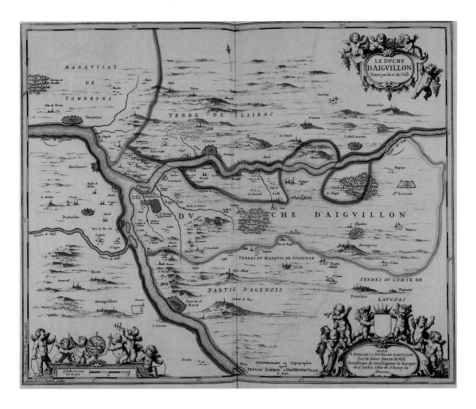

ABOVE: Pierre Duval, map of the Duchy of Aiguillon, after 1673. Biblioteca Comunale di Trento, Trento, Italy. *Wikimedia Commons, public domain.* BELOW: Samuel de Champlain, map of New France, 1632. New York Public Library, New York. *Wikimedia Commons, public domain.* French-colonial Canada was the first overseas location to which Marie de Vignerot devoted resources for the build-up of Catholic missions, charitable works, and a French cultural and commercial presence.

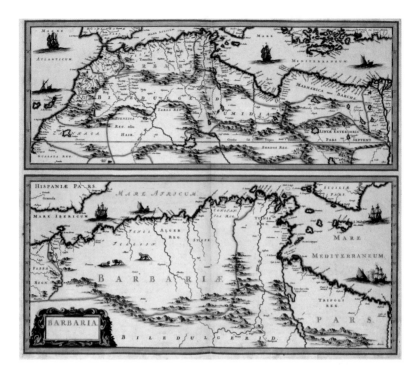

ABOVE: Jan Janssonius, map of North Africa with detail of the Barbary Coast, c. 1650. Copper engraving. Koninklijke Bibliotheek, The Hague, Netherlands. *Wikimedia Commons, public domain.* In the late 1640s, Marie de Vignerot purchased and controlled the consulates of Tunis and Algiers and staffed them with missionaries of Vincent de Paul's Congrégation de la Mission. BELOW: Carel Allard, map of the Indian Ocean region, 1697. *Wikimedia Commons, public domain.* Beginning in the 1650s, Marie de Vignerot supported a range of Catholic missionary endeavors and French trading ventures in various parts of the world represented on this map, including Indochina and Madagascar.

ABOVE: Nicolas Poussin, *The Abduction of the Sabine Women*, c. 1633–1634. Oil on canvas, 154.6 x 209.9 cm. Metropolitan Museum of Art, New York. *Public domain.* This is one of the many fine paintings, originally part of Cardinal Richelieu's collection, that Marie de Vignerot had on display at the Petit Luxembourg in Paris.

RIGHT: First page of Marie de Vignerot's last will and testament, 1675. MSRIC 151, f. 47, Salle de Réserve, Bibliothèque Interuniversitaire de la Sorbonne, Paris. *Photo by Bronwen McShea.*

François Girardon, funerary sculpture for the tomb of Cardinal Richelieu, completed in 1694. Chapelle de Sainte-Ursule de la Sorbonne, Paris. *Photo by Bronwen McShea, 2022.*

38

Inheritance Disputes

M arie's expansion of the Lazarists' and the Sulpicians' ministries did not endear her to everyone close to her. Neither did her support of other charitable and religious projects in France and abroad. In this period during which the duchess was employing her wealth on an increasingly grand scale for the sake of causes she favored, she also faced new rancor and resentment from some family members and from figures well known to her at court.

Much of this had to do with disputes over Richelieu's will. Almost from the moment the Cardinal had died, Marie began to face battles over her inheritance and that of her young nephew Armand-Jean. These battles would unfold inside and outside of courtrooms and would plague her for the rest of her life.

The first serious trouble in this vein came from her uncle-in-law Urbain de Maillé-Brézé. More came from the Prince de Condé. These men were the father and father-in-law, respectively, of Marie's cousin Claire-Clémence.

Richelieu had hoped before he died that Maillé-Brézé would be satisfied with what was bequeathed to him and his children. This included Maillé-Brézé's use of a château and its domains at Trèves in the Loire Valley and a substantial inheritance for his son Jean-Armand: the duchy-peerage of Fronsac, several estates in Normandy, the Loire Valley, and Savoy, a lucrative Norman tax farm, and a cash gift of 300,000 livres. But Maillé-Brézé resented what Marie and her Vignerot nephews inherited and the fact that Richelieu had stuck closely to the terms of Claire-Clémence's marriage contract with the Duc d'Enghien, the Prince de Condé's heir. In short, Claire-Clémence had received nothing from the Cardinal.[1]

Condé also objected to the will after learning from it the full extent of Richelieu's wealth. Suddenly, the dowry of 600,000 livres that he had accepted in 1641 when Enghien married Claire-Clémence seemed paltry in comparison.[2]

Almost as soon as Richelieu died, Marie began to meet at least once a week with three lawyers and with Sublet de Noyers, who was helping her to administer the will. Together they prepared for challenges to the will and for complications that would inevitably arise in executing it. They first acted to secure Richelieu's vast cash reserves, which were located in fortified places throughout France, such as Le Havre in Normandy, Richelieu in Poitou, and Brouage near La Rochelle. These reserves were just a part of the wealth entrusted to Marie, as much more was tied up in a range of investments. They also did not include the nearly two million livres stored at the Palais-Cardinal, which Marie already held safely.[3]

Maillé-Brézé's soldiers were, in the meantime, able to seize about 300,000 livres from the Cardinal's reserve at Saumur in the Loire Valley. This left Marie with a bit over four million livres of Richelieu's cash in her possession. It is difficult to say with any precision what the equivalent monetary value would be in today's economy. A very conservative estimate using the gold standard would be about 156 million U.S. dollars. However, Richelieu was one of the wealthiest men in all of Europe at the time and in the history of France, so Marie was bequeathed an exclusive status and purchasing power equivalent more to what today's billionaires enjoy.[4]

All this cash was in Marie's possession, that is, until the King's men stole more than a million livres on the last day of 1642. The Crown actually owed Richelieu's estate around 1,035,000 livres at the time of the Cardinal's death. Nevertheless, Louis XIII was unsatisfied with the 1.5 million Richelieu had bequeathed to the Crown and that Marie readily gave over to the public treasury.[5]

By the beginning of 1643, then, Marie, Sublet de Noyers, and their legal team were already on the defensive when both Maillé-Brézé and Condé mounted separate legal challenges to Richelieu's will. In the process, hoping it would advance their causes in public and therefore with the parlementary officials who would settle the matter, the prince and Marie's uncle-in-law exploited to a new and vicious degree the rumors that Richelieu's relationship with Marie had been perverse.[6]

Maillé-Brézé's challenge to the will was creative, if short-lived. His lawyers pointed out that his younger daughter, Marie-Françoise, was not mentioned at all by Richelieu. There was a principle in French customary law that such an unnamed person, should he or she have a reasonable claim to inherit anything from the deceased, could assert rights to two-thirds of the estate in question as an heir *ab intestat*. The existence of a true heir *ab intestat* in this case would have required Marie's nephew Armand-Jean to be downgraded to the legal status of a *légataire particulier*, which would have greatly diminished what Marie was holding in trust for him.

Marie-Françoise, however, had entered religious life while Richelieu was alive. Marie's lawyers were thus able to argue successfully in court that Richelieu had presumed, legitimately, that his youngest niece had renounced any worldly claims to part of his fortune.[7]

In the meantime, Marie's unreliable brother François was counseled by his own lawyers to challenge the validity of the will. François's lawyers underscored that Richelieu had been in too much pain to properly sign the will and that various items within it were questionable. The lawyers asserted François's claim to be considered the true heir *ab intestat*. To have a chance at convincing the judges of the Parlement de Paris who were reviewing the case, François had only to avoid stepping forward to claim the little bit that was specified for him in the will.[8]

It soon became clear that both Maillé-Brézé and François were fighting uphill battles, given the way their rival claims would put their lawyers at odds with each other as well as with Marie's excellent team. The latter got the other two teams to the table and a compromise was reached by the end of March 1643. Through a combination of diplomacy, legal maneuvering, and outright bribery, Marie and her team ensured the lasting, legal force of Richelieu's final wishes for his heirs—in general, if not in every particular. In exchange for an annual income of 60,000 livres from their eldest son's inheritance and some 20,000 livres worth of jewels, François and his wife promised never to question the will again.[9]

Beyond this, François fully accepted that Marie would be Armand-Jean's legal guardian—with full power over his inheritance—until he came of age. He consented to her control of the rest of his children's legacies, too.[10] In subsequent months, Marie and her brother reestablished amicable relations. Marie increased her brother's allowance in 1644 after François did a good turn by finalizing a commission he had ordered several years prior of beautiful funeral statuary for their parents' tombs in Glénay.[11] The recumbent marble statues of René de Vignerot and Françoise du Plessis, which are on display today inside the chapel of the renovated Château de Glénay, were sculpted by an artist named Michel Bourdin the Younger and cost François and his wife 5,000 livres. Before their defacement by revolutionaries late in the eighteenth century, they were some of the finest funerary statues of the era in existence.[12]

Maillé-Brézé, for his part, accepted several concessions from Marie in exchange for dropping his suit on his youngest daughter's behalf. Marie-Françoise was given 220,000 livres in cash, while her brother, the new Duc de Fronsac, was excused from having to pay various debts he had inherited as part of his share of Richelieu's legacy. Additionally, Marie bought out Trèves from her uncle-in-law, as he wanted money more than an old castle and its lands in the Loire Valley.[13]

The peace that Marie quickly achieved among her fractious relatives surprised and annoyed some of the great old families, such as the Condés, who were enjoying the prospect of Richelieu's family tearing itself apart over money and property. Within less than four months of Richelieu's death, that family was, instead, suddenly united—with Marie as its de facto head—as further challenges to the late cardinal's will and to his broader intentions for French political life were launched by powerful figures not related to them.

The Prince de Condé was initially the greatest threat. His own lawsuit on behalf of Claire-Clémence, his daughter-in-law, went forward in the Parlement de Paris. His and Marie's lawyers were at odds from the end of 1642 through the first half of 1644, with the former arguing on highly technical grounds that Richelieu's will was invalid under French law and that Richelieu had failed to obtain Maillé-Brézé's consent, in a proper way, in 1641, to the more disadvantageous terms of Claire-Clémence's marriage contract.[14]

Maillé-Brézé offered no public support of Condé's legal effort. Notably, neither did the prince's son, Enghien, whose claims by marriage to portions of Richelieu's estate were of course what were centrally in question. Indeed, after leading a great victory against the Spaniards at Rocroi in May 1643, the young man was openly paying court again to Marthe du Vigean—and scaring away serious suitors for her hand—despite the fact that his wife was pregnant by this point. The safe delivery of this child, a son and heir named Henri-Jules, guaranteed that what Richelieu *had* promised Claire-Clémence—and possibly much more, should the lawsuit succeed—would be secured by the Condés. Things looked more promising still for Condé after an initial judgment by Parlement came down, ordering Marie to relinquish 400,000 livres. Despite all of this, Enghien remained hopeful that, should his father's legal effort fail, his marriage to Claire-Clémence might be annulled and he might be free instead to marry the woman he preferred.[15]

Enghien would be disappointed in this, even though Condé's lawsuit ultimately failed with a judge's decision in Marie's favor. But this was not before the
prince raised his lawsuit's stakes by stirring up public doubt about the recently
deceased Louis XIII's decisions that made Richelieu and his family members
so wealthy and powerful. Marie, for example, would not have been raised up
as a Duchesse-Pair de France, and thus permitted such power over her family
members as Richelieu's heiress and executrix, had Richelieu not swayed Louis's
judgments to an excessive degree.[16]

It was suggestions like this that most offended Queen Anne at the time
she decided to visit Marie at Rueil with the whole court in 1644. She, the
prime minister Mazarin, and others in her government agreed that Condé's
arguments undermined the Crown itself, not just Richelieu's memory and the
position of his heirs.[17] As an additional mark of favor to Marie that spring,
the Queen's council acknowledged, belatedly, the debts the Crown still owed
to Richelieu's estate, issuing a formal decree that they should be paid. Marie
understood well enough at the time, given the Crown's chronic lack of ready
cash especially with the continental war still dragging on, that the actual
payment would not be made for some time. In fact, a similar decree would be
issued again in 1646, around the time Marie acquired the consulate in Algiers.
Although the money was still not forthcoming, royal favors were, especially in
terms of backing Marie's unconventional control of the North African consulates, the governorship of Le Havre, and other offices and patronal privileges
generally reserved to men.[18]

Despite the Queen Regent's support, various people well known to Marie
wanted Condé to succeed in his battle with Richelieu's heiress. Among
these was the author and former Blue Room attendee Jean-Louis Guez de
Balzac, whom Richelieu had, a decade before, elevated to the Académie
Française. When considering the legal proceedings with his friend Jean Chapelain, also of the Académie, Balzac referred meanly to Marie as "the greediest
of all creatures" and "our princess with the saffron complexion"—another slight
regarding her origins in rural, saffron-producing Poitou.[19]

Marie would have to contend with lasting impressions of her in this vein long
after Condé's legal efforts against her petered out in June 1644. Nevertheless, the
young duchess-peeress secured new respect and admiration from many observers,
too, as her lawyers succeeded beyond anyone's expectations in checking the
power of a prince of Condé's stature. More important to Marie, her team had

succeeded, for the second time in two years, in preserving Richelieu's estate from what would have been veritable dissolution had they lost in court.[20]

This double victory was bittersweet for Marie because of the political fall, in the interim, of her faithful associate Sublet de Noyers, who had been at her side for many months while contending with the inheritance disputes. He had initially caused offense, while Louis XIII was ill and close to dying, by inquiring with Queen Anne about who was likely to serve as Regent for her son when the time came. When the sick King then ordered an audit of Sublet de Noyers's expenditures as Secretary of State for War, the latter offered to resign, offended that his honesty was being questioned. Louis then shocked everyone by not simply accepting the resignation but ordering Sublet de Noyers's banishment to his estates in Normandy.

Although Sublet de Noyers was eventually welcomed back to court once Queen Anne was in power, he never got on well with Cardinal Mazarin, who regarded him as a rival for the Queen's trust. Louis XIII had originally chosen Sublet de Noyers, Mazarin, and Marie's longtime friend Léon Bouthillier, the Comte de Chavigny, as a triumvirate of first ministers of state, based on Richelieu's praise of all three. Mazarin and Chavigny both had maneuvered to cast Sublet de Noyers in a bad light at the time of the secretary's fall from favor. And after he returned to court, Sublet de Noyers found himself marginalized instead of consulted regularly on affairs of state, even though he had much to contribute.[21]

Awkwardly for Marie, Chavigny, who had long been like a brother to her, continued to side with Mazarin against Sublet de Noyers, so her respect and fondness for these fellow protégés of her uncle's were put into conflict. Marie grieved more acutely after Sublet de Noyers, feeling defeated, retired again to Normandy, only to die there less than a year later in October 1645. He had been a good friend to Marie, and his counsel with regard to the administration of Richelieu's will and many other matters, including some of her overseas projects such as the Canadian hospital, would be missed. Having been especially trusted by Richelieu, too, his death was yet another in the period that marked the end of an era for Marie.

39

A Wedding

The year 1645 marked the end of an era in another respect—but one that
brought Marie joy, not sorrow. Her dearest friend, Julie d'Angennes, was
finally, at thirty-eight, to marry her patient and loving suitor of fourteen years,
Charles de Sainte-Maure, the Marquis de Montausier. Charles was a fixture in
Marie's inner circle. He had long been deemed beyond worthy of Julie's hand
by Marie, by Julie's mother Catherine de Rambouillet, and by just about everyone
in that circle except Julie herself.

Marie and her friends had been encouraging Julie for years to accept Charles.
"I have an aversion for matrimony," Julie protested to Marie at one point, presuming she would receive sympathy from her long-widowed friend who had
herself refused many remarriage opportunities. But the duchess pressed Julie,
telling her, "There is no such thing possible before God as aversion to marriage,"
urging her friend to consider how marriage facilitated devotion to God through
the loving commitment it entailed.[1]

Charles, meanwhile, was creative as well as stubborn in expressing his devotion to Julie. An illustrative moment in their courtship occurred four years before
their marriage. On the morning of May 22, 1641, Julie found a remarkable
gift from Charles on her dressing table—one that is remembered to this day
by scholars of French poetry and culture. In honor of Julie's name day, but also
to declare love for her as emphatically as he could, Charles had put together a
manuscript of sixty-one madrigals composed by the greatest French poets of the
time. Its cover page featured a beautifully painted image of flowers, arranged in
a garland around the title, *La Guirlande de Julie*. It contained other illustrations,
and the poems inside were penned with such care as to appear almost like they

had been printed on a press. The manuscript of nearly a hundred numbered pages was bound in red morocco and presented inside a sweet-smelling wooden box.[2]

Charles had been in love with Julie for a decade by 1641, and he hoped that his *Guirlande* would soften her resistance. But even at thirty-four, in an era when aristocratic girls less than half her age were marrying and bearing children, Julie considered herself to be young enough to continue as she was for some time longer.

A veteran of the Thirty Years' War, Charles returned to the German front for a time after this latest disappointment. Even after he returned to France as a hero who had spent ten months in captivity as a prisoner of war, Julie still resisted. Remaining patient, Charles demonstrated his devotion further still by agreeing to become a Catholic after Julie began to cite his Protestant faith as the major obstacle to a union with him. This was not a decision he made in a fit of emotion over Julie, but one he made after Marie, Queen Anne, Cardinal Mazarin, and several other friends engaged him in rigorous conversations about his scruples over points of Catholic doctrine.[3]

Julie admitted defeat in the spring of 1645. As a gift to the couple, Marie offered to host the wedding festivities at Rueil early in the summer. But she was not simply being a good friend with this gesture. By this point, Charles had inherited from an uncle the militarily strategic royal governorship of Saintonge and Angoumois in western France. So Marie was shrewdly indebting the groom to her largesse just as he was becoming a more central player in national affairs.

It was a more intimate party than others Marie had hosted at Rueil. Close family and friends were invited, and the wedding took place on July 12 inside the chapel attached to the château. Officiating for the Church was Antoine Godeau, the Bishop of Grasse. Godeau was a capable poet who had contributed to the *Guirlande de Julie*, and he was a reform-minded churchman who had been favored by Richelieu while he was alive. He had also been a regular attendee of the Blue Room gatherings in Paris, earning there the nickname *Le Nain de Julie* ("Julie's dwarf") because of his small stature, cheerfulness, and fondness for the bride.[4]

Further tying Julie and the new Governor of Saintonge and Angoumois to her—not just as friends to a friend, but as clients to a patron—Marie gifted the newlyweds extra annual income, drawing from tax revenues she had been receiving since Richelieu's death from the coach services in Orléans.[5] She also facilitated gift-giving for the couple by others at her château. Most memorably, Queen Anne and young King Louis sent along their twenty-four-man, five-part royal string ensemble, Les Vingt-Quatre Violons du Roy. The musicians serenaded the couple, who joined in by dancing along in courtly fashion. The musicians chivalrously paid Julie the courtesy afterward of genuflecting and thanking her profusely for dancing so beautifully before them.[6]

Julie's wedding was one of the most talked-about events of the season in French high society, partly due to its magnificent and charming setting, which some had started to call Marie's *Maison Fée* ("Fairy House"). But some of the chatter concerned someone who was *not* on the guest list: the learned and philosophic Madeleine de Souvré, the Marquise de Sablé. Although Sablé had long been part of the Blue Room set and was among Marie's oldest friends, she deliberately had not been invited.

The wedding party was shocked, therefore, when Sablé showed up to the wedding anyway—in high dudgeon, dramatically expressing her disbelief that she had been overlooked. The awkwardness of this for Marie and the newlyweds was all the greater when gossip spread about the embarrassing scene, partly by means of an entire comedic poem penned about it by an eminent member of the Académie Française, Hippolyte-Jules Pilet de La Mesnardière.[7]

It may have been that a simple misunderstanding was behind the offense Sablé had taken. Sablé was showing her age a bit more than the other women in the set, graying and staying at home in Paris far more than the rest, and she had not been interested of late in leaving Paris for country houses when invited. So Marie, Julie, and Charles may have presumed she would not want to come out to Rueil.

But something else may have been behind Sablé's exclusion. Devout Catholic aristocrats in France were by this point dividing into two major camps, one increasingly known as *les Jansenistes*, and another united by their opposition to the same. By 1645, Sablé was associated with the former while Marie and most of her other closest friends, including Father De Paul, were staunchly opposed to beliefs the Jansenists were promoting. These included a highly pessimistic view, not unlike that of Calvinistic Protestants, of most people's chances at salvation. Jansenists also emphasized the unworthiness of sinners before God and believed, connected to this, that Catholics should approach the rail for Holy Communion only rarely, and with fear and trembling.

Marie was more optimistic than many in her devout circle about the chances of most people to reach Heaven—if given the means, such as the sacraments of the Church, the hearing of the Gospel, and the experience of Christ's love through acts of charity by His followers. She had been expressing this in different ways through the missions and charitable hospitals that she had been establishing, both in France and overseas. She also attended Mass and received the Eucharist frequently and had a special devotion to the Blessed Sacrament, especially in the form of the Blood of Christ in the sacred cup. The Benediction service at Saint-Sulpice expressed this devotion and Marie's desire to invite others into it.

Beyond all this, Marie was actively in conversation with leading Jansenists, attempting to win them to her side as they were attempting to do the same with her. In 1641, for example, she had agreed to meet with Jean du Vergier de Hauranne, the Abbé de Saint-Cyran, who had introduced into France the Augustinian teachings of Cornelius Jansen, the Flemish theologian and bishop after whom the Jansenists were named. Saint-Cyran, who had been close to Jansen, had gotten on the wrong side of Cardinal Richelieu with his teachings. He was a prisoner of two years already at the Château de Vincennes when Marie met with him on Ash Wednesday. He was hoping to convince her that his rigorous understanding of when it was appropriate for a repentant sinner to receive Holy Communion had deep roots in the Catholic tradition. Marie was unconvinced but attempted, albeit without success, to get Richelieu to show some mercy toward the churchman.[8]

Differently, Sablé was influenced by Saint-Cyran's teachings, which were reinforced by his disciple Antoine Arnauld's book *De la Fréquente Communion*, which was published in 1643 after Saint-Cyran's release from prison. Sablé began to associate with Saint-Cyran's disciples, some of whom were Cistercian nuns, led by Antoine's sister, Mother Angélique Arnauld, at the Abbey of Port-Royal in the Latin Quarter of Paris. As temperatures ran high over Antoine Arnauld's book, this abbey became the center of the Jansenist movement. Sablé's aversion to leaving Paris by 1645, and even to leaving her home where she had begun to live in a semi-monastic way, was due partly to the influence of these new friends, who vocally opposed the sort of entertainments that great courtly nobles and hostesses like Marie were famous for.

Despite their differences and the awkwardness of what happened at Julie's wedding, Marie and the marquise would remain good friends in the coming years. But they would also attempt to convert each other to their respective views.

The same could not be said for Marie and someone else who *was* invited to Rueil in the summer of 1645. This was one of the most prominent guests at Julie and Charles's wedding, Anne-Geneviève de Bourbon, the daughter of the Princesse de Condé, whom Marie had known for two decades, and the sister of the Duc d'Enghien, who was married to Marie's cousin Claire-Clémence.[9] Anne-Geneviève had grown up around Marie and the Blue Room set and attended school for several years at Carmel de l'Incarnation. But she was now the Duchesse de Longueville—and unhappily so.

In 1642, Anne-Geneviève at twenty-two had been required by her father, the Prince de Condé, to marry the old-looking, forty-seven-year-old widower Henri II d'Orléans, who was both the Duc de Longueville and the sovereign Prince of Neuchâtel in Switzerland. Descended from the Valois family, which had once been France's ruling dynasty, he was a capable military leader and often away from France, serving the Crown in the Thirty Years' War. Although uniting with this man made Anne-Geneviève a princess, the lovelessness of the marriage intensified the bitterness the young woman was already nursing toward Cardinal Richelieu and his heirs. Richelieu had not only pressured her father to favor this marriage, as he had in the case of her brother Enghien's marriage, but he had done so after having executed her uncle the Duc de Montmorency.

Richelieu's heirs and protégés as such increasingly represented to Anne-Geneviève an entire faction of upstarts who needed to be put in their place. Continuing to wield power and influence at Queen Anne's court and in the royal administration of Cardinal Mazarin, they were in her view usurping the rightful place of families like her own at the top of France's political and social order. It would not be long before Anne-Geneviève, as the Duchesse de Longueville, would assert herself in startling ways as a leader in an open, armed rebellion against all this.[10] All the same, she enjoyed Marie's hospitality at Rueil in 1645, all the more so as her husband was far away from her in Bavaria.[11]

Another man who missed Julie and Charles's wedding because of the war was the bride's brother, Léon-Pompée, the Marquis de Pisani. This hunchbacked apple of their mother's eye was also in Bavaria, serving militarily in the German front of the seemingly never-ending conflict. Sadly, the young man, who was only thirty at the time, never returned to France. Just a few weeks after Julie's great day, Léon-Pompée was killed in battle near the city of Nördlingen.

This event devastated his mother Catherine, who began to host her famous *salon* less frequently as she struggled under the weight of her grief. The Blue Room gatherings declined in influence as a result, just when they had reached their apogee. Some regarded the *salon* as "the court of the court," and the writer Tallemant called it "the rendezvous for all the most honorable gentlefolk [and] the most polished of the century's wits."[12] But attendees of the *salon* increasingly had to look elsewhere for anything like it—to gatherings hosted by the novelist Mademoiselle de Scudéry, the Marquise de Sablé and her Jansenists, the Grande Mademoiselle, and also Marie—as Catherine could not bear her son's absence in her once-happy *Chambre Bleue* after already losing her other son, Louis, back in 1631 when he was just eight.[13]

As Catherine, Julie, and their loved ones grieved that August, many others had reason to celebrate the end of the second Battle of Nördlingen. It was a great victory overall for France. Léon-Pompée had been one of the officers in an army of some twelve thousand men that included many Frenchmen as well as German Protestant allies who were under the command of the young Duc d'Enghien. Still in his early twenties, Enghien demonstrated great courage and daring, rejecting complex tactics and leading a frontal assault on the armies of the Holy Roman Empire and of the Bavarian Catholics that faced his men on an open field.

Like his sister Anne-Geneviève, Enghien would, within just a few years once he was the new Prince de Condé, turn his mettle and leadership skills against the regency government of Queen Anne and Cardinal Mazarin. But in the summer of 1645, he was welcomed home to Paris as the great young hero of Nördlingen—and one who had been wounded in the fight and was in need of care and attention from his loved ones.

Although Enghien was well into his marriage with Claire-Clémence—Marie's cousin who had given him a son at fifteen but would be mistreated by him for years, all the same—the young woman who wished most of all to care for him during his convalescence was Marthe du Vigean, the daughter of Marie's friend Anne. Marthe was still in love with Enghien and was pained, after all the letters and affection they had exchanged over the years, when he displayed cold indifference toward her upon his return from the front.[14]

Marthe spent a good deal of time in Marie's company, as her mother Anne was often in residence with the duchess. The young woman's tears and shifting moods with respect to Enghien would have weighed on Marie, especially given the way the duchess had facilitated Enghien's marriage to her cousin several years earlier.

More grief came to Marie's inner circle in this period. In June 1646, Marie's most impressive nephew, Jean-Armand de Maillé-Brézé who had succeeded Cardinal Richelieu as the Duc de Fronsac, was also much away because of the war and died during a siege at Orbetello in Italy. He was only twenty-five and, together with the general loss the French suffered at this battle, his death marked the tragic end of what had been a most promising military career. Despite his age, he had already led men several times, with great success, in the French assistance of the Portuguese in their war of independence from Spain. Young Fronsac had been the hope of his ambitious and ever-scheming father, Marie's uncle-in-law Maillé-Brézé, who now fell into a dark bitterness from which he would never recover.

The duke was hardly dead before the Prince de Condé and young Enghien—the father-in-law and husband of his sister Claire-Clémence—mounted a new challenge to Cardinal Richelieu's will. The two moved quickly to prevent Fronsac's legacy from reverting to his cousin, the young Duc de Richelieu, as the late prime minister had asked Marie to ensure in the event of such an untimely death. Condé claimed that his daughter-in-law Claire-Clémence should inherit her siblings' legacies from Richelieu now that both her brother and sister were dead (the latter, Marie-Françoise, had died the previous year).

Before Marie could mobilize her own men for a defense, the aging Prince de Condé took the Duchy of Fronsac in southwestern France by force with an army, along with several other domains and tax farms attached to them. He also demanded from the Crown that the deceased duke's office as Grand Maître (a senior admiralty) and his military governorships (Brouage, Aunis, and La Rochelle) go to his son, Enghien, as Claire-Clémence's spouse. Queen Anne, advised by Mazarin and Marie, refused this request, especially as Condé's family was regarded as too powerful already. Nevertheless, the admiralty and governorships were not given to any of Marie's other nephews. The Queen assumed the title of Grand Maître herself, and Mazarin took over the governorships. Despite her support of royal power over and above some of the resistance to it by families such as the Condés, this gave Marie new pause about Mazarin.[15]

While not getting everything he had wished for his son and his daughter-in-law, Condé, rather than Marie, would control the roughly 100,000 livres per year of income that came with the Duchy of Fronsac and its dependencies. This was a setback for Marie, who had presumed that the Queen, influenced by Mazarin, would honor what had been stipulated in Richelieu's will.[16]

Marie's relations remained frosty, then, with her cousin's in-laws by the time the Prince de Condé died, at fifty-eight, and bequeathed his own vast legacy to his son, Enghien. It was with some annoyance, then, as Marie watched, at close range, this young man—the same who had caused pain in Anne du Vigean's family—succeed his father on December 26, 1646, as the Prince de Condé. Her cousin Claire-Clémence, who had borne an heir three years earlier and who had many more child-bearing years ahead of her, became the new Princesse de Condé while commanding a greater fortune than Richelieu had ever intended for her.

Marie's irritation was matched by Marthe du Vigean's suffering, as it was finally clear that Enghien (henceforth Condé), however much he had loved her in the past, would never discard his wife for her. In her early twenties now, Marthe began to wonder if the only bearable path open to her was to become a cloistered bride of Christ.

The likeliest option was to take the veil with the Discalced Carmelites, with whom Marie and others in her mother's circle had familiarized her since childhood. But both her mother and her father opposed the idea—the latter very strongly, as he was a Protestant who believed that convent life and the idea of a spiritual marriage with the Son of God were perverse and wasteful.

Anne du Vigean and her husband, who had been elevated as the Marquis de Fors in 1640, had been estranged for some years by the time their daughter was considering the Carmelites in early 1647. Peace between them had already been difficult to maintain due to how devoutly Catholic Anne had raised their children to be. Marthe's desire to become a nun made matters worse.[17] From this point forward, while suffering financial setbacks, as well, Anne and her husband would make no pretense about sharing a home. Marie welcomed Anne into her own household permanently. Anne, who became a widow by 1657 and who would survive Marie by seven years, would go on to serve Marie as a lady-in-waiting and faithful companion for the rest of the duchess's days.

In the summer of 1647, in the weeks before Marthe entered her postulancy at Carmel de l'Incarnation, Marie attempted to mediate high, conflicting feelings among all the Vigeans at Rueil. The matter of Marthe's vocation was discussed for days at the château, and a truce seemed to have been reached when Marthe agreed to wait six months before taking the veil. The young woman changed her mind within a few days, however, and left for the convent without either of her parents' knowledge. According to her sister, their father "wished to kill everyone" after learning this, especially "all the missionaries and Carmelites in the world."[18]

Before the end of the decade, Marthe would go on to profess permanent vows at Carmel de l'Incarnation, espousing herself to Christ and taking the new name *Marthe de Jésus*. At that point, Marie and others who had known her in her sad years of unrequited love had reason to wonder whether, in the end, she had "chosen the better part," as Jesus says to the busy Mary of Bethany in the Gospel of Luke about her sister sitting contemplatively at His feet.[19] Because by then, France had plummeted into a civil war. And in it, Marie in her capacity as the Governor of Le Havre and as a close friend of the embattled Queen Regent would find herself on opposite sides of the conflict from the Duchesse de Longueville, others who had partied with her at Julie's wedding, and even some of her closest family members.

40

Civil War

The French civil war that broke out toward the end of 1648 was known as *La Fronde*—a name derived from the slang term for a rock-slinging imple- ment that poor boys wielded to break windows. Lasting more than four years, it was occasioned by both popular and elite unrest over fiscal measures taken by the Crown when Louis XIV was still a boy and his mother Anne ruled in his place. The prime minister, Cardinal Mazarin, took the brunt of the blame for a system of revenue collection, public borrowing, and government appointments that rewarded friends of the royal administration while burdening lower-level officials, provincial nobles, and the common people with the costs of both an endless war with Spain and the Crown's financial blunders.

The Fronde played out in two major phases. The first unfolded over 1648 and 1649. It was an uprising of the Parlement de Paris, urban magistrates in the capital and the provinces of Aix, Bordeaux, and Rouen, and high-ranking nobles who opposed Anne and Mazarin's government. The second lasted from 1650 to 1653. It was more widespread, violent, and confusing due to prominent figures switching sides sometimes more than once throughout. It was complexly tied to the initial urban and parlementary unrest but was driven along especially by young princes of the blood such as Marie's cousin-in-law, the new Prince de Condé who previously had been known as the Duc d'Enghien, and his brother Armand de Bourbon, the Prince de Conti. These princes resented royal limits on traditional privileges of the great old noble families, and they and other nobles who joined in with their rebellion were motivated, too, by aristocratic honor, vengeance for fallen friends and family members, and a desire to win glory on the battlefield. They also exploited popular resentments against Cardinal Mazarin and had support from urban magistrates, artisans, and peasants with different political grievances.

During the second phase of the Fronde, the rebelling princes made a show of championing the French people against the "tyranny" of the Queen Regent and Mazarin, who, they claimed, were holding the young King hostage. At the same time, their opponents who were aligned with the royal administration boasted of their own considerable support among lower-level and provincial political officeholders and populations who resented the "tyranny" of rapacious nobles. The Condés were foremost among the entitled nobility who seemed to believe that they were above the law, made war on their own countrymen, and did not pay anything close to a fair share of taxes. However, as the Fronde dragged on, it was often unclear who was on which side, and the armies of both sides engaged in pillage and rape. The common people who cheered on one or the other side faced soaring grain prices, dislocation, and eventually mass starvation as results of the violence, blockades, and neglect of their real interests. Incessant political intrigues and backbiting as well as political pamphleteering that stirred up popular anger also clouded the judgment of even those hoping to find political solutions to the kingdom's crises.[1]

Thus the war came to look like a senseless blood feud at a time when there was still an international war to win and pay for. Even some with high stakes and clear sympathies in the Fronde—such as Marie, who was at the Queen's side throughout—came to favor compromise with the rebels for the sake of national unity, getting a grip on the kingdom's finances, and securing relief for the common people.

Marie was destined to play a central role in the Fronde due to her exceptional wealth, closeness to Queen Anne, position as the acting royal governor of the militarily strategic port of Le Havre in Normandy, and identity as the heiress and most trusted protégée of the previous prime minister. Mazarin had been one of the most prominent of Richelieu's creatures, and the political storm that began to engulf the Italian cardinal's administration and devolve into armed conflict was something that Marie could hardly watch with detachment. Some of the governmental practices Mazarin's critics cited had been instituted by Richelieu, so Richelieu's legacy was at stake as Mazarin came increasingly under fire. Marie also commanded and wished to maintain a great deal of political influence herself—through friendships and patron-client ties stemming back to Richelieu's time—over an array of government officials, men of finance, and clergymen who advised the Queen. Father De Paul, for example, was a member of the Queen's four-member Council of Conscience, in which he and Mazarin had equal say about ecclesiastical appointments and royal financial decisions related to the same.[2]

Marie's network was extensive and tightly woven through the institutions and social relationships that were the beating heart of French political life—more tightly woven, in many ways, than Mazarin's. Despite his high position and his great favor with the Queen Regent, Mazarin had only lived in France regularly since 1634 while still spending time in Rome thereafter, and he had been naturalized as a French subject in 1639. Thus, as resentment toward the royal administration began to boil over in the spring of 1648, Marie at forty-three had her whole world at stake, in a manner of speaking, as Mazarin's captaincy of a ship of state he had not himself done a great deal to build came under serious scrutiny.

That May, a large group of Parisian officials formed a deliberative body, the Chambre Saint-Louis, that was not authorized by the Crown. They hoped to reverse several decisions that Queen Anne, Mazarin, and several finance ministers had recently made to raise revenues for the cash-strapped royal treasury and to address more broadly some of the fiscal and governmental challenges facing the kingdom. Fourteen of the thirty-two officials were members of the Parlement de Paris, which brought special notice to the extralegal nature of their proceedings. Courtly nobles around the Queen regarded the Chambre's meetings not simply as subversive but also as self-interested. They alleged that what aggrieved the officials was not the crisis facing the kingdom but the fact that the Queen's council had recently canceled several years' worth of their salaries as an austerity measure.[3]

Undeterred, the Chambre Saint-Louis demanded twenty-seven things from the Crown. These included the right of the Cours des Aides, or sovereign courts of the kingdom that traditionally had a say in such matters, to be consulted before any new taxes were levied, decisions about governmental salaries were made, or new royal offices were created. Because such offices were purchased from the Crown by the holders themselves or by their patrons, they were major investments and markers of status for a great many office holders who did not have great wealth otherwise. The multiplication of such offices by the Crown to bring in more revenue to the royal treasury deflated the market value of preexisting offices when resold or passed on to heirs.[4]

Additionally, the Chambre delegates insisted on abolishing the system of royal *intendants*, or bureaucratic officials posted all over France who had been appointed in increasing numbers by Richelieu and Mazarin. They further asserted that the courts should be involved in the execution of tax-related laws, making some around the Queen fear that they had revolutionary, republican designs. This anxiety was not so far-fetched in light of recent events across the English Channel, where Puritan members of the House of Commons led by Oliver Cromwell had imprisoned King Charles I after he had attempted to dissolve the Parliament against their wishes.[5]

Discontentment over royal policies persisted into the summer. The Crown's finances then collapsed. Mazarin and his finance ministers were forced to enter into high-interest borrowing arrangements with the kingdom's leading financiers—who included Marie—after having defaulted earlier on repayments to the same wealthy elites in order to satisfy the Chambre Saint-Louis's objections to such arrangements.[6]

In the meantime, violence had broken out in the Loire Valley, Provence, and other regions over complex local political matters. Riots, murders, and organized local resistance against landlords and magistrates were nothing new in France, but the increasing magnitude and frequency of such things alarmed many. Some of the violence stemmed from anger among poor populations, who were already facing rising bread prices and occasionally starvation due to bad harvests, when they were hit with tax increases by a Crown that was essentially bankrupt.[7]

This violence fueled and was in turn fanned by the growing unrest in Paris. Tensions everywhere were exacerbated by frustration among those most affected by royal taxes over the continuation of the war with Spain. Although a series of treaties signed in the German region of Westphalia brought an end to the Thirty Years' War that had resulted in at least 4.5 million deaths in many parts of Europe, France and Spain continued to fight. This was because the French, in the negotiations for the Treaty of Münster, gained territories in Lorraine and Alsace, and therefore advantage over the Habsburgs in the western Alps and northern Italy. More drawn-out war with Spain of course cost more money.

One of the first major political casualties of the spreading discord was an old Richelieu loyalist in Mazarin's administration, Michel Particelli d'Émery. D'Émery had been serving since Richelieu's time in the important position of Contrôleur-Général des Finances, with the expectation that he would reform the kingdom's taxation system. Over the next few years, he proved too effective

at this job. He invented the *taxe des aîses*, a tax on the wealthy to help pay for
the war, and he instituted the *octroi*, a tax on all items for consumption being
brought into Paris from everywhere else in France. He thus found himself hated
by commoners and nobles alike, including nobles in the Parlement de Paris who
were affected by the wealth tax.

On July 9, 1648, Mazarin dismissed D'Émery, hoping this would mollify
his critics. Marie's cousin, Charles de La Porte de La Meilleraye, a Marshal of
France, was chosen to replace the disgraced administrator, and Marie gifted
to the Crown a property she possessed, the small castle of Châteauneuf in the
Loire Valley, to provide D'Émery with a secure and dignified place of exile.[8]

Making D'Émery a sacrificial lamb did not work. Opposition to Mazarin
intensified, and it was similar to that which had often been stirred up against
Richelieu. Many of the nobles and officials who had once supported Marie
de' Medici against the previous cardinal-statesman had been scandalized by his
understanding of his own ministerial power. Richelieu had believed that the
monarch could truly hand over the reins of government to his prime minister
and that, as a result of royal fiat, the prime minister could then exercise power
like a king—even to the point of forcing decisions upon sovereign courts and
other traditional bodies in the name of the Crown and "reasons of state." Richelieu had even believed that, if the monarch did not wish to govern his kingdom
directly, God Himself was behind the transfer of governing power to the First
Minister of State.[9] Much of Richelieu's confidence in his own, sometimes ruthless decision-making had stemmed from this conviction that it was God-given.

Mazarin had the same high view of his own authority. However, he was less
effective an administrator and communicator than Richelieu had been. He also
courted even more suspicion and hatred than his predecessor—because he was
Richelieu's creature, for one thing, but even more because he was Italian and
rumored to be sleeping with Queen Anne. Indeed, his many nicknames during
the Fronde included "the Sicilian Monster" and "the Italian Sausage." Unsub-
stantiated stories circulated that Mazarin's sexual prowess was what kept him
in the Queen's favor and even that he was the real father of the "miracle baby"
Louis XIV, who had been born surprisingly late into his parents' long-fruitless
marriage.[10]

The rumors were plausible enough, as the blond, green-eyed queen and the
dark, mustached churchman were both in their mid-forties, attractive, and
fond of each other's company. Some speculated they had secretly married after

Louis XIII died, partly because Mazarin—like La Valette, Marie's deceased friend—was a cardinal who had somehow never been ordained to the priesthood. Indeed, he had been a layman studying law and engaged to be married when he was asked to serve as a papal legate and commence a career in the Church. Even after he was made a cardinal in late 1641, he was not present at the Vatican to receive his red hat. He was titularly and functionally a powerful churchman, but he never engaged in priestly ministries, and in most regards he was a statesman with a layman's outlook.[11]

Furthermore, the Queen and Cardinal-Minister's letters that survive today hint at strong feelings beneath the surface, especially on Anne's side.[12] However, what mattered politically in 1648 was not the veracity of the rumors but their effectiveness in agitating the French public against the regency. Powerful figures who had designs on the government, such as the young King's uncle, Gaston d'Orléans, fanned the gossip to undermine Mazarin's ministry. Horrified by the rumors as well as by the Crown's fiscal decisions, members of the Parlement de Paris began insisting that they, not the foreigner advising Queen Anne, were devoted to France's interests. They condemned particular royal policies and Mazarin himself as treasonous.[13]

The Queen and Mazarin decided to punish the *parlementaires* and other officials in Paris who, as they saw it, were agitating against legitimate royal authority. They did so at a strategic moment. In late August 1648, the young Prince de Condé, Marie's cousin by marriage, led the French to a decisive military victory at Lens near the northern French border with the Spanish Netherlands. As this win was being celebrated with great fanfare in the streets of Paris, the Crown arrested all the officials involved with the Chambre Saint-Louis, including a popular member of Parlement named Pierre Broussel.

The arrests elicited a much stronger response than Anne or Mazarin anticipated. The revolting magistrates and their mostly bourgeois supporters erected more than 1,200 barricades in the streets of Paris on the night of August 26. The next day, the Queen's chancellor, Pierre Séguier, attempted to visit the Palais de la Cité, where the Parlement held its sessions, in order to negotiate with the urban rebels, who were nicknamed *Frondeurs*. Séguier, appointed as chancellor during Richelieu's time, was a relative of Marie's by marriage and a friend to the duchess, too, as he was one of the official executors of her uncle's will. Marie had reason to be especially horrified when Séguier and members of his family were met near the Palais de la Cité by an angry mob and forced to flee to a nearby building. The crowd broke into the house, but Marie's cousin La Meilleraye and some royal cavalry officers rescued the Séguiers just in time. [14]

The Queen was at the Louvre. She now faced a crowd of more than 20,000 Parisians that was led by all 150 members of the Parlement. These Frondeurs demanded Broussel's release from prison, but Anne stood firm. She would only consider it if the political uprising stopped. But although the *parlementaires* were open to negotiating with the Queen, the crowd prevented them from heading back to the Palais de la Cité to meet with her representatives. [15]

Marie was regularly with the Queen during these challenging days and offered her château in Rueil as a haven for the royal family and the rest of the court. In mid-September, Anne decided indeed to leave for Rueil with the King, who had just turned ten, and with Mazarin and her other advisors.

In and of itself, a royal vacation from Paris was not unusual. However, given how tense the mood was in Paris, the decision was a dangerous one. It would appear to the people that the Queen Regent and the King were abandoning them and planning possibly to punish them militarily. [16]

This risk was taken. Early in the morning on September 13, Anne sent Mazarin, her son, and a small group of courtiers, servants, and guardsmen to Rueil. She would herself wait five days to join them, partly to give the impression that nothing was being done in haste or in a spirit of distrust toward the people. Nevertheless, groups of angry Parisians attempted to stop the initial train of royal carriages along the way to Rueil. [17]

As alarm spread through Paris about the departure of the King with the prime minister, Marie ensured that Louis and Mazarin were comfortable and well-protected at Rueil. At the same time, she was quietly troubled by the news on September 18, the day the Queen joined them, that a prominent officer of the Crown who was seen as too sympathetic to the Frondeurs was ordered to retire to his country estates. This was Léon Bouthillier, the Comte de Chavigny, who was serving as the governor of the Château de Vincennes prison after having been dismissed by Mazarin from a more prestigious office, that of one of the Queen's secretaries of state. This was, in other words, Marie's dear friend who had been like a brother to her when they were young and who had helped her through the difficult period after Cardinal La Valette's death. [18]

Mazarin had felt threatened by Chavigny as a rival for power since the time Louis XIII had appointed him, with Sublet de Noyers, as one of a triumvirate of ministers who succeeded Richelieu in late 1642. Even after achieving Chavigny's removal as a secretary of state, however, Mazarin believed his rival was stirring up resentment against his administration. Chavigny's friendship with the leading parlementary official Pierre Viole was a cause of particular suspicion. The governor of the Château de Vincennes thus found himself not simply ordered to retire from his post but to be under arrest, imprisoned in one of the château's cells, and forbidden visits from his wife.[19]

Marie cleverly stepped in to protect her friend—and create a line of access to him out of the range of Mazarin's control. She did this by offering her services as the acting Governor of Le Havre, as she was well-positioned in this new role to handle the valuable prisoner's removal from the capital region and his confinement from there. Indeed, an armed guard answerable to the duchess transported Chavigny from Paris to the remote citadel on the coast of Normandy. Although confined there for a number of weeks, he was treated well by Marie's lieutenant, Marc Pioche de La Vergne.[20] Marie also remained quietly in touch with Chavigny in the wake of his humiliating arrest, assuring him that no one had his interests more in mind than she did, partly because of their shared fondness for her uncle.[21]

After learning of what happened to Chavigny and to another official who was punished by the Crown (Charles de L'Aubespine, the Marquis de Châteauneuf), members of the Parlement de Paris decided to send a delegation to Rueil and to urge the Queen to bring the King back to the capital within twenty-four hours. The delegation departed for Marie's château on September 22 after the *parlementaires* sent messages, too, to the Prince de Condé and other princes of the blood, asking them to be present at the Palais de la Cité when, it was hoped, the Queen, back in Paris, would give her blessings to deliberations that would lead to real financial reforms and an end to the political unrest. However, Condé would not commit to meeting with the *parlementaires* until he received orders directly from Anne about what he should do. So he started out for Rueil, too.[22]

Informed by her own sources about these various machinations, Marie went forward with her ordinary schedule at Rueil that Tuesday, presiding over a generous, leisurely midday meal for whichever of her important guests wished to join in. Anne dined separately and prepared for her meetings with Condé and the parlementary delegates who were on their way. The latter arrived around three in the afternoon, and they were shown into a room to meet with the Queen, who—to their surprise—had Condé at her side as well as her brother-in-law, the Duc d'Orléans, who had been forgiven his past offenses against the Crown and who was in charge of the royal armies by this point. Flanked by these princes whom the *parlementaires* believed shared their grievances against Mazarin's administration, Anne informed the delegation that she would not be returning to Paris the next day with her son. Instead, she would go to the royal château at Saint-Germain-en-Laye, even farther from Paris. And through her son's authority she also forbade the Parlement de Paris from assembling the next day as they had been planning.[23]

Once the word spread through Paris about this unexpected response by the Queen, more aristocrats who had country homes removed to them, out of fear of violence. Within a few weeks, however, calm seemed to return when Anne agreed to terms with another parlementary delegation, at Saint-Germain-en-Laye, that gave the force of law to the demands the Chambre Saint-Louis had made of the Crown back in May. In exchange, the *parlementaires* agreed to accept the terms of the treaties French diplomats had been signing in Germany.[24]

The problem with this agreement is that Mazarin, and the Queen under his influence, saw it only as a stopgap measure until more royal troops were home from the war to help regain control of Paris. Furthermore, some nobles who had been publicly if not sincerely aligning with the *parlementaires* and the Frondeurs in the streets opposed a reconciliation with a royal administration still directed by Mazarin and indebted, too, to the deep pockets of Marie and other financiers. Among these nobles who favored more conflict was Anne-Geneviève, the Duchesse de Longueville, whom Marie had known since she was little and who had not so long ago attended Julie d'Angennes's wedding at Rueil. This young duchess tried to get her brother Condé to abandon the Queen and Mazarin.[25]

She failed. Civil war fully broke out in January 1649 when Condé, upon the Queen's orders, moved with an army to blockade and besiege Paris. His sister, in the meantime, set herself up in the Hôtel de Ville—Paris's city hall—and led the resistance effort. "She was like a queen of the Parisians," one historian has said of the Duchesse de Longueville. She was supported in her open war against one brother and the royal troops by her other brother, the nineteen-year-old Prince de Conti, by her husband the Duc de Longueville, who was the Governor of Normandy, and by her lover, the Duc de La Rochefoucauld. Joining the Frondeurs and this cozy group of noble leaders was, too, a Parisian bishop of Jansenist leanings, Jean-François-Paul de Gondi, better known later on as Cardinal de Retz.[26]

Privately, Marie and a number of her associates were increasingly convinced that Mazarin's continuation in office, especially if he punished the Frondeurs, would cost France more in blood and treasure than defending his ministry was worth. At this point, Father De Paul, under Marie's influence, became political in a way that was contrary to his instincts and asked Mazarin to resign and to leave the country for the good of France.[27] Marie nevertheless succeeded in keeping her own views on the matter secret from Mazarin and the Queen while continuing to support the royal forces militarily and financially—and thus appearing publicly like a firm ally of the prime minister. For example, she honored Mazarin's request toward the end of January, in her capacity as Governor of Le Havre, to raise companies of cavalry and infantry troops to support the royal forces.[28] She also helped to fund the Crown's effort during and after Condé's siege, too, including the forging of new cannons.[29] And even before Condé's siege had begun, she was the target of intense scrutiny by members of the Parlement de Paris. At issue, especially, was that she was among the powerful financiers receiving large sums of cash *from* the Crown, as repayments of longstanding loan debts, even while the Crown was still late in paying troops who had been serving in the Thirty Years' War.[30]

In the early days of the siege, with the Duchesse de Longueville and her associates urging them on, the leading *parlementaires* ordered a search for Marie's cash reserves. A myth was rampant that Marie had massive stockpiles of cash readily at hand. The reality was far more complicated than this: during periods when Marie gifted or lent large sums to the royal treasury, she sold valuable and sentimental items to obtain the money, such as fine furniture and art objects her uncle had left to her as well as a stunning pearl necklace she had famously worn at courtly functions during Richelieu's era.[31] All the same, armed men went into the Petit Luxembourg looking for the mounds of money that Marie was believed to have lying about her home. When they did not see any, they ripped up floorboards hoping to find them hidden away. Still finding nothing, they entered and searched the Carmelites' convents in Paris, believing Marie might be hiding all her money with the nuns. Several weeks later, the Frondeurs broke into the home of one of Marie's lawyers and stole various records. Similar searches were conducted in the homes of other financiers close to the Queen and Mazarin.[32]

The first phase of the Fronde resulted in a stalemate that brought representatives of the warring parties to the negotiating table. To the frustration of the Duchesse de Longueville and many *parlementaires*, Condé was in the end welcomed as a liberating hero by many ordinary, bourgeois and artisan-class Frondeurs. It was unclear, all the same, which side was victorious. Condé was now seen by Mazarin as a new threat to his administration while the *par-lementaires* and some of the princely leaders of the Parisian uprising had lost their popular base. And the latter, refusing to surrender, still hoped that the Crown—still facing financial woes, ongoing war with Spain, and unrest throughout the kingdom—would yet be amenable to recommitting to reforms that had momentarily become law a few months earlier.[33]

Since Paris was still a tinderbox, it was decided that the negotiations should take place outside the capital. Many presumed the talks would take several weeks and possibly devolve into renewed conflict. In a move that would have made her uncle Richelieu proud, Marie offered to take on the tremendous risk, and the expense, of accommodating the delegates at Rueil. By mid-February, then, the duchess was preparing to host at her charming *Maison de Fée*—where she and her staff knew every passageway, thin wall, and peephole—a political event that could sway the course of French history.

41

A Tenuous Peace

The Peace of Rueil, achieved by March 11, 1649, was hashed out over just one week by representatives of the Crown and the Parlement de Paris. Informal conversations, some of them secretive, began earlier, however. In late February, Marie personally welcomed to her château the two leaders of the parlementary delegation, Mathieu Molé and Jean-Jacques de Mesmes. With authorization from Chancellor Séguier, her cousin-in-law on the royal council, Marie ensured that these two officials were situated in style. It was important that these men of less exalted backgrounds were made to feel respected, partly by means of their accommodations, while negotiating with the highest-ranking Crown officials and nobles that soon joined them.[1]

The full parlementary delegation was welcomed to Rueil on March 4.[2] The Crown's delegation was present by then, too, but the talks initially broke down when the *parlementaires* realized that Cardinal Mazarin was representing the Queen Regent, who remained at Saint-Germain-en-Laye.[3] Président Molé refused to deal directly with the detested prime minister, so an arrangement was made that the two delegations would not meet in the same room but instead communicate with each other through messengers. Marie and other high-ranking nobles present, including the Prince de Condé, who was still on the Crown's side at this point while his army remained in Paris, made a show of being aloof about the talks.[4] But Marie remained informed about as much as possible through trusted staff members and friends at Rueil—friends who included Mazarin's Secretary of State for War, Michel Le Tellier, who had also first risen to prominence in Richelieu's time. Eventually Marie's friendship with Le Tellier would be noted with concern by Mazarin, but at this point the prime minister presumed the duchess was preoccupied with her hostessing responsibilities.

The Crown's delegation faced more formidable negotiators and calmer demeanors on the parlementary side than they expected at the outset of the talks. Molé, in particular, proved to be a skilled negotiator who was able to keep the radicals on his side from pushing him toward positions that would have jettisoned the peace process. Queen Anne was actually offended by this, as if by demonstrating intelligence, refinement, and impartiality Molé was acting above his station.[5]

The agreement that was reached was more favorable to the parlementary side than anyone had anticipated. Mazarin and the rest of the Crown's delegation accepted that various reforms favored by the Parlement de Paris would have the force of royal law. Judicial officials would be paid their salaries again by the Crown, and a limit would also be set on how much money the Crown could borrow through the year 1650.[6] Furthermore, King Louis and his reigning mother would return to Paris as soon as possible, the noble and bourgeois Frondeurs would be given amnesty so long as they committed themselves to the peace, and troops fighting for the Crown would return to the locations in which they had been garrisoned before the start of the civil war.

In exchange, the parlementary delegation agreed to disband the Parisian militias that had formed and to return buildings they had seized from the Crown, including L'Arsenal and the Bastille. All declarations by the Parlement issued that winter would be considered null and void, and the Chambre Saint-Louis would never again meet. On top of this, the Parlement would not receive an envoy from the Spanish Netherlands, as it had been planning to do, who was offering the Frondeurs assistance in the form of a possible Habsburg invasion from the north.

Signed on March 11, the Peace of Rueil was refined in the days following, as Molé and others spent additional time at Marie's château and further informal discussions ensued.[7] It was ratified in its final form by the Parlement de Paris on April 1, and it gave new force to the agreement that the Crown had accepted in bad faith in October 1648. More than this, it seemed to signal a new era of cooperation between the Crown and advocates of fiscal reform among the nobility and common people alike.[8] However, to the frustration of the *parlementaires* and some of the princely nobles in the kingdom, it also approved Mazarin's continued grip on the reins of government.

Mazarin's removal from office had been pushed unsuccessfully at Rueil. Marie quietly favored this alongside De Paul and others close to the Queen, but not yet openly. Anne insisted on retaining him, even after he had proven to be less formidable a negotiator at Rueil than many had expected.[9]

As the spring and summer of 1649 unfolded, the Peace of Rueil looked to be a success, despite ongoing unrest in several regions of France. Paris also remained volatile. Anonymous pamphlets kept appearing, attacking Mazarin especially but also at times the Queen, and these occasionally caused disturbances. The arrest and trial of an anti-government pamphleteer sparked a riot in July. A printer named Claude Morlot was caught printing an illegal pamphlet, the title of which translates as *The Queen's Bed Curtain Tells All*, that included the shocking verses: "People, don't doubt it any longer / It's true that he's fucked her / And through this hole Jules [Mazarin] shits on us." On the day officers of the law were ready to hang Morlot and his hapless assistant, a stone-throwing crowd that had been stirred up by several nobles intervened, dumping the platformed gallows into the Seine and forcing the executioner and a band of archers to flee the scene.[10]

The episode demonstrated how one-sided the political press had become during the Fronde. Mazarin was not giving nearly as much attention as he might have to a counter-campaign in print. Despite the Peace of Rueil, the public remained strongly opposed to retaining Mazarin as prime minister—and vulnerable to being stirred up by powerful opponents of Anne's regency who did devote resources to propaganda.

The Morlot incident also lent credence to the view of some advisors around the Queen that Paris was still too inhospitable for her to return there with the King, even several months after the Peace of Rueil had been signed. The court indeed remained away from the capital until mid-August. When the royal family finally returned, they settled into Richelieu's Palais-Cardinal rather than the Louvre.[11] Eventually called the Palais-Royal, this was another palace that Marie and some of her trusted friends and servants knew intimately—including its structural secrets. The duchess herself was based regularly again at the Petit Luxembourg but was also much at court with Queen Anne while engaged with numerous other affairs, including her charitable projects.

As Father De Paul was regularly in her company and receiving dispatches from Lazarists throughout France, Marie was continuously apprised of ways the war with Spain and the unrest of the Fronde were causing miseries and uncertainties for the kingdom's poor. The numbers of migrant and hungry poor were

increasing, and the Lazarists could not address the new level of need because
their own income sources were drying up. Their usually reliable patrons were
safeguarding their assets during the crises. Marie nevertheless ensured the sur-
vival of the range of Lazarist ministries she supported and facilitated De Paul's
efficient communications with Lazarists far and wide by having priests in his
network address letters for him to her and sent to the royal court.[12] This was not
a small thing at a time when mail deliveries were regularly being disrupted but
the correspondence of the most prominent courtiers prioritized.

Additionally, Marie assisted Louise de Marillac and the Daughters of Charity
with practical advice as well as funding. She identified ways they could more
effectively spend the funding available to them, which was stretched thin by the
economic pressures of the Fronde. She encouraged them, for example, to nourish
the growing number of abandoned children in their care with goat's milk instead
of milk from dairy cows.[13]

Marie took on new charitable commitments in this period, including some
that should have been Queen Anne's. In the lead-up to the civil war, the
royal family's hasty departure from Paris—and the drying up of funds from the royal
treasury—resulted in the neglect of some royal obligations in the capital. Anne
had promised, for instance, to support a group of nuns called the Filles de Notre-
Dame de la Miséricorde. This was a community that welcomed genteel women
who could not afford the dowry requirements of other religious orders and who,
in turn, provided free education to girls of humbler backgrounds. The Filles
had been struggling financially and Anne had promised to put them on a stable
footing in Paris. Marie stepped in, in the Queen's place, and initially welcomed
the community into the Petit Luxembourg. By 1651, the duchess and several of
her wealthy friends would provide the Filles with a large establishment of their
own in the neighborhood.[14]

A return to some normalcy for Marie after the Peace of Rueil unfortunately
also involved renewed headaches over the administration of Richelieu's will.
Although he had gotten sidetracked from it for a time, the Prince de Condé
had honored his dead father's wishes by commencing legal proceedings against
Marie and her nephews in November 1648. Although he was on the Crown's side
during the Fronde at this time, he calculated that members of Parlement would
sympathize with him during this period when Marie's financial arrangements
with the Crown were under scrutiny. Urged along by his sister the Duchesse de
Longueville, Condé took up this legal battle with energy in mid-1649, hoping

to obtain large portions of Richelieu's legacy in the name of his wife, Claire-Clémence, and their six-year-old son, Henri-Jules.[15] (This and their eventually having two more children did not stop Condé from mistreating his wife over the years, which would see the two estranged in different periods.)

With some assistance from Mazarin's agents, who brought influence to bear on some of the judges reviewing the case, Marie's lawyers fought tirelessly against Condé's, with little being resolved in the prince's favor. This added to Condé's growing resentment not against Marie per se but against the larger body of influential figures at court who advised Queen Anne. Condé, who had recently been given the preeminent seat on the royal council by Mazarin, had expected to be amply rewarded in other ways by the Crown for his services in helping to end the parlementary uprising. He expected, for one thing, that he and his family would—partly by means of a transfer of wealth and honors from the Richelieus—become, incontestably, the most powerful in the realm after the ruling Bourbons.[16]

It became clear to Condé by the autumn of 1649 that he was being hedged in more than rewarded by the royal administration. Mazarin's duplicity was considerably to blame. Presuming rightly that the young prince would not busy himself seriously with the workaday aspects of governing the kingdom, the Cardinal-Minister had made Condé the titular head of the royal council, agreed that he would serve someday as the grand master of the King's household once Louis came of age (a position that came with great financial benefits), and even promised that Condé could have the final say on the appointments of generals, governors, and even bishops and abbots. But he did all this with the ulterior motive of keeping Condé close and under surveillance, and he found ways not to honor their arrangement. Mazarin and others in the government regarded Condé and his family as too powerful and wealthy already and feared they might end up controlling the Crown itself before too long.[17]

Growing restless, Condé began to consider ways to collaborate with his sister and other Frondeurs who wished to see Mazarin ousted from office, an end to the regency, and themselves put into positions of power in the boy-king Louis XIV's government. This explains why, toward the end of the year, Marie's legal battle with the prince became the subject of an anti-administration pamphlet authored by a Frondeur and poet, Isaac de Laffemas, who held a minor office in Paris's municipal government. The pamphlet is classified by modern scholars as a *mazarinade*—one of thousands of pamphlets produced during the

Fronde that attacked the reputation of Mazarin and the financial elites and political "creatures" around the Queen Regent. This particular one satirized Marie's legal battle with Condé. The prince, his wife, Claire-Clémence, their lawyers, and those judges who appeared to favor their side came across as sympathetic figures in its thirty-five pages of verse. Differently, Marie, her lawyers and friends, and her deceased uncle Richelieu—especially because he was Mazarin's mentor—came across badly. In the very first lines, for example, Laffemas called Marie's Catholic piety into question and poked fun at the difficult period of her young widowhood when she had attempted to join the Carmelites. The author also referred to her skin tone as "vermilion"—a slight related to the "saffron" insult that implied her ancestors were obscure farmers, not proper nobles. [18]

It was inevitable that Marie would be attacked in the press by those favoring rebellion against the royal administration given the amount of time she spent in the Queen's company. Although a nonroyal woman could not sit on the royal council, Marie was informally one of Anne's leading advisers and her financial dealings with the Crown were considerable. Her status as a duchess-peeress and as the acting Governor of Le Havre justified this, as did her long experience of political life at the right hand of the last prime minister. There were periods during which Marie saw the Queen daily, and their long sessions in the morning were the cause of increasing suspicion. [19]

Just as the Peace of Rueil was being finalized, too, Marie had ensured the defense of Le Havre and nearby Harfleur, also under her jurisdiction, when these places she governed were under threat by the Duc de Longueville, who began stirring up trouble in Normandy, where he was also a regional governor. Marie secured military assistance from Charles de Sainte-Maure, the Marquis de Montausier, Julie d'Angennes's husband and the royal governor at Saintonge and Angoumois nearby in Brittany. With Montausier and his troops, Marie's able and loyal lieutenant, La Vergne, protected Harfleur and Le Havre decisively. [20]

La Vergne, who had also assisted Marie with her friend Chavigny's genteel imprisonment at Le Havre the previous year, sadly died before the year was out, on December 20, 1649. Marie had cared for him and his family, as she had known them for many years. La Vergne's widow, Isabella, had once been a lady-in-waiting to Marie, and his daughter, fifteen-year-old Marie-Madeleine, was Marie's goddaughter. Marie encouraged this bright girl's study of Italian and—still controversial for women at the time—Latin, while introducing her to men and women of intellect and quality. Within a year, Marie would secure the girl an appointment as a junior lady-in-waiting to Queen Anne—adding another pair of eyes and ears to those Marie had around the Regent. Marie-Madeleine herself would eventually become famous, once she was the Comtesse de Lafayette, as a great *salon* hostess in her own right and as the author of the first French historical novels, including *La Princesse de Montpensier*, which inspired a film in our own time.[21]

Marie in this period also had a range of responsibilities to deal with in her Duchy of Aiguillon. In addition to overseeing the work of the Lazarists at Agen, she had to confront some unpleasant business concerning the brother of her deceased friend Cardinal La Valette. Bernard de La Valette, the Duc d'Épernon, who had married one of Marie's cousins on the Richelieu side, had settled in the area with a mistress after years in political exile. Although he had taken part in a disastrous military venture in 1637 with the previous Prince de Condé, which had put him on the wrong side of Louis XIII and Richelieu, Mazarin had welcomed him back to France. Already disliked by many of the locals, Épernon and several other military officers in the region began to act like lords there, forcing inhabitants of the duchy to quarter their troops. This was something they believed they could do because of the state of unrest in France due to the Fronde, but in late 1649 Marie obtained a royal exemption for her duchy with respect to quartering troops. After Épernon ignored the Crown on this matter, Marie successfully intervened again several months later. This won her back favor among townspeople in the region who had previously complained to officials in Paris about the alienation of some traditionally royal, local domains to Marie—something she had worked out in exchange for the loans she had been providing to the Crown during the financial crisis.[22]

While busy with such things, Marie had reason to assume that her closest family members were politically aligned with her, despite the inheritance squabbles that divided some of them, as fears spread about renewed rebellion led by the Longuevilles and Condé. Her cousin La Meilleraye, a Marshal of France who was serving now as Mazarin's leading finance minister, had sided firmly with the Crown during the first phase of the Fronde and had his name dragged into the mud as a result. Rumors were going around, for example, not only that Marie had been part of a whole harem of women with whom her uncle Richelieu had engaged in lots of shameless sex in the last years of his life, but also that the late Cardinal-Minister shared some of those women with La Meilleraye.[23] Earlier in the year, her uncle Maillé-Brézé, also a Marshal of France and capable military officer, helped the Crown to put down a rebellion in Mirabeau, in the south of the kingdom. At Marie's request, he also commanded men newly attached to her inexperienced nephew, nineteen-year-old Armand-Jean, the Duc de Richelieu, who had taken up naval duties in Marseilles, to ensure they were quashing rebellions, too.[24]

In the latter half of 1649, the young duke was back at home with his aunt in Paris. He was often in her company and at court. He and his siblings fell prey to the anti-government rumormongers, too: a new slander being spread by the enemies of Queen Anne and Mazarin was that they were actually Cardinal Richelieu's children or grandchildren, by means of an incestuous relationship either with Marie or her long-dead mother, Françoise. *This*, the Fronde sympathizers whispered, was the reason Richelieu had left Marie and Armand-Jean so much of his vast fortune, and *this* was how Marie and her relatives had insinuated themselves into a corrupt royal administration.[25]

Given all that she had seen from her ambitious, sometimes greedy, and other times weak family members since she was very young, Marie was not naïve enough to trust only in appearances of peace within the Richelieu clan. It was possible, for example, that her uncle Maillé-Brézé—who was of course Condé's father-in-law, and who had engaged in such things before—was behind some of the ugliest rumors that were swirling. Still, at the close of 1649, Marie was entirely unprepared for news she would receive not about Maillé-Brézé but about her dear nephew Armand-Jean. This was just the time, too, that the Peace of Rueil began to break down and France entered into the much more violent second phase of the Fronde.

42

The Duc de Richelieu's Rebellion

Several years prior to the Fronde, Marie's wastrel brother, François de Vignerot, had died in Paris at the age of thirty-seven. This was on June 29, 1646. The reported cause was a sudden onset of pulmonary edema, which was known then as dropsy of the lung. Several days later, he was buried with solemnity close to Cardinal Richelieu at the Sorbonne chapel.[1]

François's demise was unexpected. One of the few portraits of him that survives, a black-and-white engraving, shows a robust man with a relatively dark complexion, long and thick dark hair, and a fashionable beard and moustache. The image shows what a dandy he was—dressed in an expensive-looking doublet with an elaborate lace collar. In his thirties, he no doubt had been looking forward to decades more of life in French high society, despite the humiliation that he had suffered over his uncle Richelieu's will and his continual dependence on Marie for everything, from finances to the proper rearing of his children.

But François's death was also, admittedly, a mercy to his family. His neglect of his wife and children, his endless extravagances, and his embarrassing comportment at social events were now things of the past. Marie and her widowed sister-in-law, Marie-Françoise, could look more fondly now on some of the more honorable moments of his life, such as his performances in battle. François had acquitted himself admirably, for example, during the invasion of Lorraine of 1633 and, five years later, in the naval battle of Vado off the coast of Genoa on September 1, 1638. Indeed, the young Lieutenant-Général of the French Mediterranean fleet had led his men to a crushing defeat of Spain, which lost four thousand men at Vado in what ended up being the last great battle between galley ships in European history.[2]

When François died, his eldest son, Armand-Jean, was sixteen. This maturing boy was already the heir to the Richelieu dukedom and peerage that the Cardinal-Minister had passed on to him four years earlier, in an unconventional way, while his father was still living. At the same time, he remained under his aunt Marie's governance—an arrangement that, as Marie understood the late prime minister's wishes, was to continue until Armand-Jean was mature enough to take on all the duties of his various titles, offices, and estates in a manner that served the interests of both France and the House of Richelieu.

Marie in the meantime controlled her nephew's cash legacies, incomes from a range of sources, and estates, including the magnificent Château de Richelieu and its domains in the Loire Valley. This gave Marie leverage over the boy when the two did not see eye to eye, as was first seriously the case when Armand-Jean was seventeen and decided to take up his inherited naval command at Marseilles. Although she was worried for his safety, Marie let him spend some months among his men but then withheld some of what he needed to maintain a proper equipage and crew for an officer of his status. This drew him back to her side in Paris.[3]

That was in the middle of 1649, several months after the Peace of Rueil had been signed. Without complaint, the young duke resided again with his aunt and his younger siblings at the Petit Luxembourg. He celebrated his twentieth birthday in October amid the excitement of courtly life as it had returned to some normalcy in the preceding months. Marie encouraged him to spend time with other high-ranking nobles. She also had him work on refining his manners and conversation skills while taking a break from naval life.

Marie was then blindsided by news about her nephew at Christmastime. Armand-Jean left Paris in secret and, on December 26, got married without her knowledge or permission. This was a violation of custom as well as trust: Marie was still the young man's legal guardian and had a right, under French norms, to be involved in his marriage plans. The duke's mother, too, was in the dark about the wedding. Differently, Marie's trusted steward, Jean Desmarets de Saint-Sorlin—the same man who had long ago written his novel *Rosane* for his patroness—had known of Armand-Jean's plans and assisted him in reaching the designated place for the nuptials, a village north of Paris called Trie.[4]

The bride was also someone Marie trusted and had known a long time. Anne-Françoise Poussard de Fors du Vigean was the daughter of Marie's friend and lady-in-waiting, Anne du Vigean. She had grown up in Marie's intimate circle—indeed, at times, in Marie's homes, along with her mother and her sister, Marthe, the nun who was brokenhearted over the young Prince de Condé.

But this was not a case of two childhood friends and sweethearts joining into matrimony. Anne-Françoise was almost a decade older than Armand-Jean and she was already an experienced widow. She had previously been married to a minor nobleman who had died the year before. Furthermore, Marie asked her to assist with her nephew's education in courtly manners—a task the widow had taken up readily, partly as an expression of thanks for the financial assistance Marie had long given to her mother and now offered to her.

Marie presumed that no serious attachment would develop between the two when throwing them together for these lessons. There was the obvious age gap, and Armand-Jean had already by then expressed interest in a young noblewoman of suitable rank and fortune whom Marie approved, and who descended from the princely houses of Lorraine and Rohan. But when the young duke developed a passion for his mature and lovely tutor, Anne-Françoise seduced him behind her patroness's back. Realizing she was potentially only steps away from becoming the first Duchesse de Richelieu, she quickly secured a marriage proposal. A courtier who knew her attributed this to the fact that, although Anne-Françoise was "without beauty," she was "kind, gentle," and "one of the cleverest of women . . . who knew how to triumph adroitly over a fresh heart."[5]

But there were other reasons why Anne-Françoise's scheme worked so well. She was friendly with the Duchesse de Longueville, the Fronde leader who secretly despised the Richelieu family. When that duchess and her brother, the Prince de Condé, learned of the budding romance, they encouraged it for their own ends. The prince—frustrated by his unsuccessful lawsuit against Marie and the ways Mazarin was not securing him all the power and honors he expected—hoped that in exchange for his protection, and for a promise to stop challenging Cardinal Richelieu's will in the courts, Armand-Jean would assert his claim to the governorship of Le Havre that Marie held. This would effectively give the Condés and Longuevilles control over all of Normandy and weaken Mazarin's grip on the government. Condé and his sister thus facilitated the secret marriage in Trie and were present as witnesses for it. Precisely according to their plan, the eager young groom departed for Le Havre with his new wife on the morning after the wedding, aiming to take possession of it as the rightful governor. And he was thrilled to suddenly be so favored by such an impressive prince and military hero who seemed to be taking him more seriously than his aunt Marie did.[6]

Naïve about the political stakes in the game he was being drawn into as a pawn, Armand-Jean appears to have presumed that his aunt and his mother would forgive his marrying in secret. He also thought they would approve of the match, given the great Condé's support and their familiarity with his bride.[7]

But Marie and her sister-in-law were furious once they received word of the nuptials. Marie initially raged at the bride's mother, Anne du Vigean, assuming she had been party to the whole business. But Anne had known nothing about it and was just as upset over the news. Regardless, as much as Marie loved Anne for her years of faithful friendship and service, she regarded Armand-Jean's union with her daughter as an embarrassing *mésalliance*.[8]

Worse, the marriage got in the way of the much more advantageous match she had been working on for her nephew—with his full awareness and interest. The young woman in question was twenty-three-year-old Charlotte-Marie de Lorraine, the daughter of the legendary, ever-scheming Marie-Aimée de Rohan, the Duchesse de Chevreuse, who had returned from a period of exile in Brussels. Chevreuse hated Mazarin for the way he seemed to control her once closest friend, Queen Anne, and she also had always been opposed to France's wars with Catholic Spain, which Mazarin had continued even after the Peace of Westphalia.[9] To be sure, Chevreuse had once plotted Cardinal Richelieu's assassination and had joined in with various other conspiracies that Marie knew all about. But Marie had, since the Peace of Rueil, become friendly with the older duchess, whom she had first known, many years before, as her beautiful, adventurous aunt-in-law through her own brief marriage to Antoine de Combalet. And Marie was calculating that a union between their powerful families would not only secure Chevreuse's fidelity to the Queen should a great princely revolt occur but also facilitate a new alignment between nobles tied to the Crown and nobles sympathetic to the Fronde who were united by a common goal: removing Mazarin from office.

In fact, toward the end of 1649, Marie had joined in with Chevreuse in an effort to reconcile her and other Fronde sympathizers with the royal administration, in the hopes, first of all, of neutering a feared, new rebellion by Condé and the Longuevilles. The matter of pushing out Mazarin would be worked on later. For now, Chevreuse's friends needed to be reconciled to Mazarin and not be tempted to join with Condé and his siblings. These Frondeurs close to Chevreuse included Charles de L'Aubespine, the Marquis de Châteauneuf, who was a former lover of Chevreuse's, and the Coadjutor Bishop of Paris, Jean-François-Paul de Gondi (later Cardinal de Retz), who himself was sleeping with Charlotte-Marie, the very young woman Marie hoped would marry her nephew.[10]

Chevreuse had encouraged her daughter's affair with Bishop Gondi. It is unclear whether Marie was aware of this or the affair itself. Regardless, with political and dynastic considerations in mind, Marie had regarded Charlotte-Marie as the best candidate to become the Duchesse de Richelieu. Charlotte-Marie was also considerably more beautiful than Anne-Françoise and had received indications from Armand-Jean that she appealed to him. But all of Marie's hopes—not just of making such a young woman part of her family, but also of making Armand-Jean a key player in the political realignment she was crafting—were dashed by the besotted stripling's rash undertaking at Trie.[11]

When she learned of the marriage, Marie ordered her new lieutenant, Guy de Bar, not to hand over Le Havre to her nephew. Queen Anne backed her up on this, sending troops to protect the city and counter any efforts by the Duc de Longueville to assert mastery over the region. This was just in time, as Condé had given a large sum of cash to the newlyweds, so that they could buy off some of the guardsmen at Le Havre. Armand-Jean soon left, unable to assert any command, as the soldiers remained loyal to Marie and her lieutenant.[12]

Marie and her sister-in-law attempted in the meantime to have the Queen order a bishop's annulment of the marriage. The annulment would have been on the grounds that Armand-Jean had not received permission from Marie to enter into the union. Although the Church since the Council of Trent had been formally opposed to such consent requirements for unions to be considered valid, powerful rulers and aristocratic families throughout Europe continued, in practice, to have sway over bishops with respect to approving and sometimes annulling marriages.

To Marie's consternation, the Queen did not back the annulment plan after Condé had hastened to Paris to speak with her. At this point, the nearly fifty-year-old Queen trusted and liked Condé, who was not yet thirty and whom she had known since he was a little boy. His help during the parlementary Fronde was fresh in her memory, and that combined with his status as a prince of the blood gave him leverage. In fact, he boldly said to the Regent, when she brought up the possibility that the Duc de Richelieu's marriage might be declared invalid, "Not when a person of my rank has signed as a witness!"[13] Anne appreciated such hauteur in princes.[14] She soon signaled to Armand-Jean and his wife that she would be willing to acknowledge the latter as the new Duchesse de Richelieu so long as they behaved loyally toward her.[15]

Armand-Jean and his wife also returned to Paris. When they arrived, Marie refused them entry to the Petit Luxembourg. Facing such opposition from his aunt, the young man put his pen to paper to make his case to her. "My unhappiness is extreme after having been reduced to displeasing you," he began, reminding her that she herself had put Anne-Françoise before him "as the most perfect person whom I was to make myself please" in order to become a more refined, courtly nobleman. He went on:

> While I did perhaps a bit more than you wished, you had not set
> any limit upon me. . . . Having fulfilled my duty toward you, I
> believed that I should satisfy my love. I found in a single person all
> that I could desire in terms of birth, beauty, and merit. And I found
> still more advantages of fortune that no other could bring me,
> among them . . . the benevolence of the most considerable prince in
> the world, who for her sake alone grants me his powerful protection
> and goods that I could have disputed about eternally.[16]

Writing of the Prince de Condé in an admiring and trusting way, Armand-Jean displayed his naïveté about all that was at stake politically and dynastically in becoming the client of his patronage. So his pleas to his aunt for approval and understanding did not budge her.

Armand-Jean realized more fully what he was up against after he learned with the rest of France on January 18 that his new protector, Condé, had suddenly been arrested by orders of the Queen and Mazarin, along with the Prince de Conti and the Duc de Longueville. Rumors went around, too, that his aunt Marie was behind these shocking arrests.

Marie's involvement, as far as it can be determined from historical records, had a Machiavellian quality about it. Despite the setback regarding a match between her nephew and Chevreuse's daughter, Marie had continued to confer with Chevreuse, Bishop Gondi, Châteauneuf, and another leading Frondeur, the dashing and blond young François de Vendôme, the Duc de Beaufort, who was the son of one of the late King Henry IV's out-of-wedlock children. At Chevreuse's instigation, this group was attempting to reconcile with

Mazarin—despite detesting him and secretly scheming, longer term, toward his dismissal as prime minister—in the hopes of reining in, for good, the troublesome young Prince de Condé, his siblings, and his brother-in-law. Several of them had mixed feelings about Condé's siblings, who had sided like they had done with the Parisian Fronde. But they all feared what more power and wealth in the hands of the young, politically untested, war-oriented Condés and Longuevilles would mean for their own positions and for France longer term once Queen Anne's regency gave way to her son's personal rule.[17]

Their challenge, however, was to convince Mazarin to drop any pretext of the friendship he had formalized with Condé the previous year. They needed to move the prime minister, and through him the Queen, to order the Condés' and Longuevilles' arrests—on the charge that their recent mobilizations of troops threatened royal authority.

It helped them to have Marie among their number, given her closeness to the Queen and her control of Le Havre. They were also supported in their goal by the Queen's brother-in-law, Gaston d'Orléans, Marie's next-door neighbor at the Palais de Luxembourg and the commander of the royal armies. Marie, who had been appointed *capitaine concierge* of the Luxembourg and knew many of the palace's secrets, helped to bring him round to their views. She did this by ruthlessly taking advantage of Gaston's romantic passion for one of his wife's ladies-in-waiting—a girl with the surname Saujeon who had fled to Carmel de l'Incarnation to avoid sinning with him. Anguished by this, Gaston asked Marie to help him pressure the Carmelites into sending the girl back to her duties at his palace. Marie agreed, using power she had over the girl's confessor, and Mademoiselle Saujeon was soon back at the Luxembourg. But then, with sleight of hand, Marie managed to convince Gaston, without evidence, that the girl had been urged to flee to the convent by a prominent churchman, the Abbé de La Rivière, who had designs on her himself. Marie's motive was to turn Gaston against La Rivière and therefore against the Prince de Condé, to whom the abbot was tied. Gaston, who always had favor with Queen Anne, thus pressed her and Mazarin for La Rivière's arrest and favored the arrest of Condé and the others.[18]

Condé was arrested during what he thought would be a routine visit to see the Queen and the rest of her council at the Palais-Royal, responding laconically in the moment, "Just take me somewhere warm."[19] His brother and brother-in-law were also imprisoned. His sister, however, escaped arrest, fleeing to Dieppe in Normandy and then to the Netherlands, after failing to convince her husband's men to join her in revolt against a royal army nearby. She had some support among her brothers' vassals, however, and by April she was joined in her rebellion against the Crown by Henri de La Tour d'Auvergne, the Vicomte de Turenne, one of France's best generals, who had shocked the royal administration by defecting that spring. The two negotiated with Spain, promising the Habsburgs control of any captured territories in France in exchange for mercenaries and money.[20]

In the same period, another powerful French nobleman threw his support behind the Duchesse de Longueville and her imprisoned brothers and husband. This was François IV, the Duc de Rochefoucauld and Prince de Marsillac. He had been the Duchesse de Longueville's lover for a time. He was the same prince whom Marie, with Mazarin's support, had prevented from being given the governorship of Le Havre by Queen Anne. Marie's suspicion years before, that he was capable of turning on the Queen Regent, had been prescient.[21]

In short, France by the spring of 1650 was wracked by renewed civil war. Frustratingly for Marie, she could not rely on her nephew Armand-Jean to remain loyal to her and the Crown in this fight. He was loyal now to Condé. And he resented that he was unable to take his place among the other young military leaders of the kingdom as the true Governor of Le Havre.

Partly as a warning to Armand-Jean, Marie showed no mercy toward her steward, Desmarets, after she learned about his role in facilitating the secret marriage. Desmarets, while a creature of both Cardinal Richelieu and Marie, was also a close cousin of the bride and her mother, Anne du Vigean. When he had decided to help Armand-Jean to marry Anne-Françoise, he was betting on his family's further rise in French society by means of the rewards the young duke and the Prince de Condé might bestow upon him. Desmarets knew that this was a betrayal of his protectress. Since the time of Cardinal Richelieu's death, he had been serving Marie as her *intendant des affaires*—a role that made him intimately familiar with all that the young duke stood to gain in possibly just a few years' time. Marie had also secured for Desmarets the office of royal secretary for naval activities in the eastern Mediterranean.[22] It is unsurprising, then—though it seems to have surprised Armand-Jean—that after Marie learned of Desmarets's role in the marriage scheme, she had him thrown into prison. This was on March 22, 1650. He remained under lock and key for several weeks while also being pressed to repay upward of 60,000 livres in debts that he owed to the duchess and the Richelieu estate. Marie would never again extend patronage to him.[23]

It was on the day of Desmarets's arrest that Marie arranged an "accidental" meeting with her nephew, whom she had continued to bar from the Petit Luxembourg. This was at the home of a painter she patronized. The painter, knowing Marie would be visiting, invited her nephew to visit that same day to consider having his portrait done. A contemporary account of the young man's surprise meeting with his aunt suggests that it was dramatic: "The Duchesse d'Aiguillon displayed her eloquence, which is very strong and persuasive, and drew tears from the eyes of her nephew, who, at least according to some among those present in the lady's large entourage . . . begged her for forgiveness." The young duke then asked to go home that day to the Petit Luxembourg, but Marie refused, suggesting that he visit another time soon.[24]

When the new Duchesse de Richelieu learned of this, she urged her husband to leave Paris altogether. She helped to persuade him that their future was tied to the Condés and Longuevilles, who were unjustly imprisoned and whom they should loyally support. The newlyweds left for Normandy, in the hopes that Armand-Jean could successfully this time assert himself as the Governor of Le Havre with the backing of the princes' rebelling troops, many of whom were very young and restless aristocrats from old sword-noble families. Motivated by honor more than awareness of the political fault lines and economic challenges plaguing the kingdom, they were eager to punish those responsible for the princes' ill-treatment and also to make their names and fortunes in a war to liberate their adolescent King from the clutches of his mother and the foreigner Mazarin.[25]

After siding with these rebels, the young Duc de Richelieu found himself beset by armed men in Marie's employ on June 11, 1650. This was after Marie learned her nephew was returning to Paris from Normandy. They brought him to the Petit Luxembourg, where he was put under house arrest. Queen Anne supported Marie in this detainment of Armand-Jean, because she agreed that it was necessary to prevent him from taking over at Le Havre and handing it over to the rebels. Marie also received a promise from Gaston d'Orléans's wife, Marguerite, next door that, in the event of any armed attacks on the Petit Luxembourg by the duke's friends, her guardsmen would help to defend it and prevent the young man's escape.[26]

Two days later, the Duchesse de Richelieu traveled into the capital to plead on her husband's behalf in the Grand Chambre of the Parlement de Paris. At her side were some of her relatives and friends, including her father, Anne du Vigean's estranged husband, who supported the marriage while his wife still opposed it. The judges took up her request and ordered that, in two days' time, a hearing would take place, to which Marie and her lawyers were invited.[27]

Marie, Anne du Vigean, and their lawyers succeeded in delaying the hearing. When it finally took place on June 18, a large crowd loyal mostly to the young duke and the imprisoned princes gathered at the doors of the Palais de la Cité. The *parlementaires* ended up split in their judgment, the majority favoring the young man's release but many taking Marie's side—a stronger showing for Marie than many expected. When the judges then ordered a search of the Petit Luxembourg to assist Armand-Jean's release, the officers sent there were surprised to be received by a calm Duchesse d'Aiguillon in a warm way, with her nephew nearby and protesting that he was already free to come and go as he pleased. The parlementary case died down amid the confusion this caused. It is unclear what Marie had done to effect this turn of events, which embarrassed her nephew's wife and her supporters—including not a few who were sympathetic with the imprisoned princes. But it appears to have involved Gaston d'Orléans and his wife, whose guards held Armand-Jean for several more days in their home.[28]

At the end of June, Armand-Jean left Paris—this time, however, under orders by the Queen not to return. He and his wife were supposed to go into genteel exile in a place called Sainte-Mesme toward the Atlantic, not far from La Rochelle. Instead, they found welcome close by in Brouage in the home of a sympathetic friend. In this setting, the young duke's resentment against his aunt—who had been like a second mother to him—only grew. He was now determined to claim what he believed was rightly owed to him by Marie—with violence if necessary.[29]

Observing the Richelieu family feud that season, Cardinal Mazarin expressed privately his growing disappointment in Marie to his Secretary of State for War, Michel Le Tellier. He wished Marie had handed over Le Havre to her nephew before all the recent troubles began. Marie, he suggested, was motivated by her feelings more than reason and was willing to divide the whole court over what should have been a privately settled family matter.[30] Later he would opine in relation to the same conflict to Hugues de Lionne, the Queen's secretary, "Madame d'Aiguillon has no limit to her passions, and as long as she can satisfy them, she does not pay attention to the evils that may happen to the State." Marie, he added with more than a touch of commonplace misogyny, was entirely motivated by self-interest.[31]

As others had done before him, Mazarin underestimated Marie. She was ambitious for far more than subduing her nephew and taking revenge on those who had gotten in the way of her plans for him. The Cardinal-Minister would learn soon enough, though, after finding himself in exile, what one of those goals was—and how capable Marie was, even while barred as a woman from high office, of quietly exercising political skills and raw power to achieve it.

43

Cardinal Mazarin's "Most Dangerous Enemy"

Y ears after the Fronde, a poet named Paul Scarron composed an ode to
Marie. In it, he devoted verses to Marie's feminine virtues, her beauty
that was the cause of heartbreak "to many a faithful Christian man," and her
always-admired voice, which was "an enchantment." Six lines of the poem,
though, portray someone different from a typical aristocratic patroness being
cast as a courtly artist's muse:

> Her eyes shine even more brightly
> Than that from which light itself comes,
> So that if they use their full power,
> They would make even the most
> Resolute eagles lower their eyelids,
> So intense are their glances.[1]

There was, in short, something fearsome about the Duchesse d'Aiguillon.

Among the "eagles" who came to fear Marie was Cardinal Mazarin. To a
young Jean-Baptiste Colbert, the man he would mentor to become his successor
as prime minister, Mazarin called Marie "the greatest and most dangerous enemy
that I have."[2] He also warned Queen Anne multiple times not to trust Marie,
who, to his frustration, was at the Regent's side far more than he was beginning in
February 1651. That was when he was forced to leave the French court for the first

of eventually two periods of exile during the confusing, violent second phase of the Fronde. Mazarin became convinced that Marie was behind his banishment.

Mazarin came to believe that Marie was the silent leader of a whole faction that was determined to drive him out of French politics—a "cabal," as he put it, that stretched like a thick web from the court through Paris and many parts of the kingdom.[3] This network, furthermore, included not just loyal servants of the Queen and his own administration and prominent *parlementaires* but also many repentant Frondeurs and friends of the princely rebels against royal authority.

Such things were far from Mazarin's suspicions in 1650 just after the arrests of Condé, Conti, and Longueville. At that point, even as he criticized Marie's handling of her nephew's affairs, the prime minister trusted and depended on the duchess as an ally. There was a public perception that they were close, too, something anti-Mazarin pamphleteers exploited.[4]

But behind the scenes, Marie was conferring with figures who nursed grievances against the Cardinal-Minister, believed Queen Anne was too dependent upon him, and regarded him as more of a threat to the peace and unity of France than the imprisoned princes and their supporters. Among them was her old friend Léon Bouthillier, the Comte de Chavigny. Fearing Chavigny as a rival for the position of prime minister, Mazarin had imprisoned him in 1648. Marie and her lieutenant at Le Havre assisted Mazarin with this, offering the citadel as the best place to keep the offending former secretary of state. But the duchess's men also protected Chavigny from a possibly worse fate, treating him well until his release. Later the following year, Chavigny penned a private memorandum on Mazarin's general incompetence as a prime minister. He cited the Cardinal's bad faith with Spain when overseeing the peace negotiations at the end of the Thirty Years' War and plunging France anew, unilaterally, into more conflict with that fellow Catholic power.[5]

In view of Marie's manner of dealing with Chavigny—publicly aiding his punishment while privately assuring him of her support—it is noteworthy that after the arrests of the three princes early in 1650, she offered to guard them at Le Havre, too. She had no special love for these princes and was glad to see her young cousin-in-law Condé punished, especially, given his lawsuit against her and his role in arranging her nephew's marriage. But she succeeded in urging the princes' transfer to Le Havre from a prison in Marcoussis south of Paris. This was something the Queen and Mazarin approved in the autumn of 1650 after Marie had entertained the entire French court again—this time at the Château de Richelieu. Marie had been perfecting this magnificent palace according to her late uncle's plans, as with his "ideal city" next door, where beautiful new townhouses were available for the overflow of courtiers.[6] Mazarin was charmed by the whole experience, and he and the Queen were able through that visit to stir up strong royalist feeling in the Loire Valley even while it was waning elsewhere, especially in Paris, where the people blamed Mazarin for the royal family's long absences.[7]

When the order was given to Marie and her lieutenant De Bar at Le Havre to move forward with the prisoner transfer, Marie commissioned her friend Julie's husband, Charles, who was the Governor of Saintonge and Angoumois, to lead the operation.[8] On November 15, the three offending princes were taken from Marcoussis to Le Havre by an escort of 1,400 men. Cleverly, Marie prior to this had arranged with Mazarin to cede back to the Crown her nephew's rights to the governorship of Le Havre and then to receive back the governorship in her own right, with the option to bequeath it to someone of her choice pending royal approval. She managed also to have Armand-Jean's freedom to reassert his Marseilles naval command curtailed by the Crown. In Marseilles, he would remain titularly the Général des Galères, but in actuality his aunt and her chosen lieutenants would be in control.[9]

Once at Le Havre, the Prince de Condé, the Duc de Longueville, and the young Prince de Conti submitted to royal authority while remaining imprisoned. Marie ensured that the closely guarded rooms they stayed in were fitted out as comfortably and elegantly as possible.[10] Reports circulated at court that Condé, in particular, was humiliated to be under Marie's authority. Queen Anne's lady-in-waiting, Madame de Motteville, recorded in her memoirs that Marie herself was not sorry to see the princes humiliated, but also that since they had arrived at Le Havre, "she had forgotten all the hatred she ought to feel for them; that it now seemed as if they had become her children, and that . . . she was resolved in her heart, as soon as the general peace was made, to serve them well."[11]

The forty-six-year-old duchess had reasons to soften a bit toward Condé and his brother Conti, at least. She had known them well when they were little boys, and she had been closely involved with Condé's marriage with her cousin Claire-Clémence. Beyond this, she had for years been dear friends with their mother, the dowager Princesse de Condé, Charlotte-Marguerite de Montmorency, who was, as it happened, only days away from dying in Paris at this time.

But Marie had ulterior motives in displaying kindness toward the princes. The younger two, especially, had become folk heroes. They were seen as some of the most promising noblemen of the kingdom who could do glorious things for France, but who were being grossly mistreated by the tyrant Mazarin. Some of Marie's own friends were caught up in the spirit of this. The Blue Room regular Madeleine de Scudéry, for one, made a pilgrimage to the prison cell in which the Prince de Condé was initially held and, on the spot, composed an ode to a pot of carnations that the young prince had cared to water while there.[12] Other women variously swooned at the very thought of the princes and joined into battle with the men who were rising up in arms in the name of young King Louis, whom they regarded as Mazarin's captive.[13] Handling the princes' imprisonment gave Marie the politically valuable ability to ensure, in her name more than Mazarin's, their decent treatment and to be involved with the timing and manner of their eventual release should royal clemency be extended. It also presented her with the potential opportunity of attaching at least one of the princes to a figure, such as Chavigny or the former Frondeur Châteauneuf, who could unite the court-centered, rebellious, and Fronde-sympathizing factions and then replace Mazarin as prime minister.

Reunification of the kingdom began to seem possible by the close of 1650—but with Mazarin presuming he would receive credit for it among those around the Queen. This was after a major victory for the royal forces against the rebel army of the Duchesse de Longueville, who had eluded the Crown's efforts to imprison her after her brothers' and husband's arrests. This army, led by Marshal Turenne, suffered a decisive defeat at Rethel in the Ardennes. By the start of 1651, the royal forces had retaken places that had fallen to the imprisoned princes' supporters. The outlook for the general restoration of royal authority was good, so much so that Mazarin believed the Fronde was ending. He did not realize that, in view of the same, Marie and other powerful figures believed they could soon drive him from power.[14]

With Marie and Chavigny's encouragement, the Duchesse de Chevreuse entered into a secret alliance with Gaston d'Orléans and discussions with representatives of the imprisoned Prince de Condé. New marriage alliances were considered in these talks, including a union between the Prince de Conti and Chevreuse's eldest daughter—the one Marie had hoped earlier would marry her nephew. Also, Condé's son Henri-Jules—Marie's young cousin, Claire-Clémence's firstborn—would, it was planned, one day marry one of Gaston's daughters, who were princesses of royal blood. Those party to these discussions also planned to propose to Queen Anne that she dismiss Mazarin, allow Gaston to have the major say in the choice of new members of her royal council, and appoint Châteauneuf as the new prime minister. Additionally, this group asked the Queen to give a cardinal's hat to Bishop Gondi, who would indeed soon be known as Cardinal de Retz. Both Châteauneuf and Gondi had been linked secretly to Marie, as well as to Chevreuse, since late 1649, when they were devising a way to set up the princes' imprisonment by Mazarin.[15]

To demonstrate how important Mazarin's dismissal, in particular, was to this group, Gaston on the first day of February issued an ultimatum: he would refuse to take his seat on the royal council until the Cardinal-Minister was banished.[16] He and the rest of the emboldened anti-Mazarin faction at court then joined together with members of the Parlement de Paris, led by Mathieu Molé. Molé had also been tied to Marie since she had hosted him at Rueil for the peace talks in early 1649.

On February 4, 1651, after Bishop Gondi affirmed Gaston d'Orléans's support for the action, the Parlement demanded Mazarin's dismissal by the Queen. Gaston furthermore ordered barricades erected in the streets of Paris—something he did without the Queen's permission in order to intimidate Mazarin and those loyal to him. At this point, the Queen began to receive advice to dismiss Mazarin from all around, even from normally apolitical actors, such as her lady-in-waiting Madame de Motteville. It became clear that not only former Frondeurs such as Châteauneuf and members of the Parlement wanted Mazarin gone, but so did many courtly elites who were impeccably royalist in their sympathies, self-consciously devout in their Catholic faith, and normally preoccupied with charitable projects such as those of Vincent de Paul.[17] Like De Paul, many of these courtly elites were linked to Marie, whom the Queen trusted and saw daily.

Mazarin was for a number of days ignorant of these machinations against him. He believed, initially, that Gaston, Gondi, and members of Parlement were behind the new unrest and united mainly by sympathy with the imprisoned princes. Indeed, Gaston seemed momentarily to be turning into an old-style princely rebel against royal authority, as in his younger days.

By mid-February, however, Mazarin understood that a large new "cabal" was united behind his more public critics and influencing the Queen. And he began to suspect that the strongest thread holding this cabal together was association with

Marie and Chavigny, either through current bonds of friendship and patronage or through past loyalties to Cardinal Richelieu.[18]

He began to suspect this too late—after Marie and Chevreuse, pretending to be loyal to him, convinced him to leave court by suggesting that, in a few weeks' time, things might be calm enough in France that he could return in complete triumph.[19]

With Marie's encouragement, Mazarin agreed to go to Le Havre for the Queen to personally order the release of the princes. This was not something he wished to do, but the Queen's hand had been forced by Gaston and the Parlement—and behind closed doors by many others who believed that the princes had been chastened over the previous year and, with the marriage alliances and concessions Anne might give them, would stop threatening royal authority. Mazarin was furthermore led to believe that the Queen was preparing to transfer the governorship of Le Havre to him, and that by the time he was ensconced in Le Havre, he would be able to order the release of the prisoners in his capacity as the new royal governor.[20]

But upon his arrival at Le Havre, the Cardinal-Minister waited . . . and waited. No royal authorization came for him to take over as governor before releasing the prisoners. Instead, Mazarin was humiliated after Marie's lieutenant De Bar made it clear that the prime minister had no special authority there.[21] Mazarin was thus put in the position of having to inform the princes as a mere royal messenger that they were free to leave. The princes were released, but without any ceremonial act of clemency from Mazarin from which the prime minister could benefit politically.

Mazarin now began to speculate in his communications with the Queen's secretary, Hugues de Lionne, that Marie was the leader of "the opposing cabal." He urged De Lionne to warn Anne not to trust Marie anymore.[22]

As Mazarin lingered in Le Havre and waited to be called back to court, Marie arranged with the Queen to have the young King confirm her authority as the Governor of Le Havre. Twelve-year-old Louis forbade the soldiers at Le Havre to take orders from anyone but Marie or her chosen lieutenant. Ostensibly this was done to prevent Marie's nephew from asserting rights to the governorship. But effectively this royal act prevented Mazarin from usurping authority there.[23]

Shocked and humiliated, Mazarin realized that he was exiled from court.[24] He traveled on to Brühl, a small German city in the Rheinland close to Cologne, where he would remain until late 1651. He learned, too, that on March 11 in

Paris, with both Gaston d'Orléans and the Prince de Condé present, the Parlement had called for his arrest and the interrogation of any of his servants or friends in France who remained in communication with him.[25] Six days later, Condé, Conti, and Longueville were publicly fêted in Paris. On March 17, crowds lined the streets as the princes made their way to the Palais-Royal to be greeted by the Queen. Gaston then hosted a banquet for them at the Palais de Luxembourg. The next day, the princes were received and applauded by the *parlementaires* inside the Palais de la Cité.[26]

Yet the Fronde continued. New *mazarinades* flooded the streets, including those with the most scurrilous suggestions about the Queen's private relationship with Mazarin. Street songs calling Anne a "whore" were sung. Anne still refused to dismiss Mazarin from office, even as she accepted his exile from court for a time. This raised eyebrows.[27]

Mazarin, in the meantime, was in regular, secretive communication with the Queen from Brühl, using a special numbered code as she kept him updated on everything going on at court. He advised her whom not to trust and how she might divide the faction that had been responsible for his exile. Marie, who was called "35" in their secret code, was too "subtle, artful, and self-interested." The Queen "should not open up to her." It was Marie, more than anyone else, who was doing her utmost to prevent his return to court. She was even using Father De Paul, "whom she rules," and other clergymen she controlled to make the Queen feel that she could not, in good conscience, call her Cardinal-Minister home.[28] Mazarin was dismayed that, despite such warnings, the Queen was starting to favor high-level appointees, such as new bishops for the French church, who were not only selected by Marie and De Paul but who were specifically not the candidates he himself had been recommending to her.[29]

By late spring, misunderstandings and personal affronts had frustrated any chance of peace among the partisans of the Crown, the original parlementary Fronde, and the princes of the blood. Conti's marriage with Chevreuse's daughter was called off, Gaston d'Orléans and the Prince de Condé were once again rivals, and the Duchesse de Longueville was able to goad her brothers into renewed rebellion against the Crown. This young duchess's hatred for the royal administration burned more coldly and steadily than her brothers'. She was motivated in part by the legacy of her father's rebellions against Marie de' Medici's regency and the memory of Cardinal Richelieu's execution of her uncle, the Duc de Montmorency, when she was thirteen. Her brothers, differently, were less confident that they could win in a renewed civil war, but they did not want to be accused of cowardice by their soldiers, who were already accusing Gaston and other princes of the older generation of timorous compromises with royal power.[30]

Marie's nephew Armand-Jean was among the young noblemen swept up in this resentment toward the Crown and its creatures. The latter, in his view, included his aunt Marie, who had been employing new royal legal mechanisms to sidestep traditional inheritance customs. Marie and others around the Queen were preventing noble male heirs such as himself and great princes such as his patron Condé from taking up rightful positions of honor and power. Now an avid partisan of the princely rebellion, the young duke in May 1651 departed with armed supporters from Brouage to attempt to take the Château de Richelieu and its domains in the Loire Valley. The palace guards and local knights in Richelieu were generally loyal to Marie and the Crown, however. Although the château and its domains were part of Armand-Jean's patrimony, Marie's royally backed rights of guardianship were still in force. The duke's effort failed.[31]

Not giving up, young Richelieu backed an effort to kidnap his aunt by his brother-in-law, François Poussard, the Marquis de Fors. By holding Marie captive, they hoped to force her to relinquish control of the duke's entire inheritance. But this stratagem also came to nothing. Marie was at Rueil again, entertaining the Queen and the King, and somehow her nephew's plot came to light there. At Marie's request, the Queen preempted the kidnapping by sending one of her own bodyguards to warn the duke not to travel again to Richelieu or any other city without royal permission.[32]

Marie's second-eldest nephew became a player in the drama at this point. Jean-Baptiste was eighteen, often in the company of the young King, and loyal to his aunt, who had recently agreed to unburden him of an ecclesiastical career that had been presumed for him by the Richelieu family from the moment of his birth. Not ordained but possessing several major benefices that Father De Paul was managing for him, he had arranged with Marie the year before to transfer his title of *Abbé* and all the ecclesiastical responsibilities that he had been planning to take on to the youngest of the Vignerot boys, thirteen-year-old Emmanuel-Joseph.[33]

Known now as the Marquis de Richelieu and wishing to assert himself as a sword-bearing noble, Jean-Baptiste expressed outrage on his aunt's behalf after the kidnapping plot was discovered. He challenged the Marquis de Fors to personal combat as a matter of honor. Both young men survived, but Marie's younger nephew believed he had restored some of his family's wounded honor—and made it clear that he was not a coward, as some of his peers who supported the rebellious princes had alleged. Indeed, the marquis was not at all sitting out the war. With financial assistance from both the Crown and Marie, he had been raising up, since the summer before, a whole cavalry regiment that he would lead for the Crown's side—that is, the side in the civil war that most highborn nobles his age were against.[34]

It is revealing that as Marie's relations with her nephews evolved in different directions—the eldest rebelling against the Crown and another loyally serving it—Mazarin became critical of the Richelieu heirs as a group, and especially of Marie as their head.[35] To a grandson of the late King Henry IV, the Duc de Mercoeur, the Cardinal-Minister warned that Marie had placed her nephew Jean-Baptiste too close to the young King in order to influence him indirectly.[36] To a trusted bishop friend in Italy, Horatius Onendei, Mazarin claimed that Marie and her nephews owed just about all they had in France to his interventions with the Queen since the time of Cardinal Richelieu's death. He saw her as an ungrateful woman who would be nothing in France without his protection, which he had been extending to her whole family out of loyalty to her deceased uncle. She was showing this ingratitude, he complained, by joining with Chavigny and others who wanted to oust him from office. Worse, he added, "She is the one who unites all the Dévotes who have access to the Queen, and she instructs them, with the dogmas of a new theology, about how they should speak to Her Majesty to convince her that she is obliged to abandon me."[37]

When Mazarin used the term *Dévotes*, he was not using it in the older sense of those who opposed France's anti-Habsburg foreign policy and alliances with Protestant powers. Although some of the individuals he was referring to, such as the Duchesse de Chevreuse, were also Dévots in this older sense, the term by the era of the Fronde had evolved to refer to a powerful network of influential Catholic elites who were focused on the moral and spiritual reform of French society and charitable projects such as the ministries of the Lazarists and the Daughters of Charity. Some of the most influential were women, such as Marie, who were close to Queen Anne, which is why Mazarin employed the feminine *Dévotes* rather than the masculine (and in French more inclusive) *Dévots*. But there were men in the movement, too—most of them members of a secretive, all-male organization, the Compagnie du Saint-Sacrement, whose meetings sometimes took place in Marie's homes.[38]

This organization had been active since 1630, had chapters all over France, and had been strongly approved by Richelieu even though it was never acknowledged under French law and was opposed by some powerful bishops, partly because its often lay-driven activities were difficult to put under episcopal control.[39] Marie's cousin La Meilleraye was a prominent member, and the organization had a patriotic as well as staunchly Catholic (and often anti-Protestant and increasingly anti-Jansenist) tone. When referring to their friends, Compagnie members sometimes employed phrases such as "truly French hearts."[40] Naturally, the Italian immigrant Mazarin had difficulty proving to everyone's satisfaction that he had one of those.

Mazarin, who would eventually work to suppress the Compagnie du Saint-Sacrement altogether, was suspicious of the Dévots given the unofficial but strong political influence they wielded during the Fronde. Some of the men closest to him in the government, such as his Secretary of State for War, Michel Le Tellier, were Dévots. Mazarin learned during his exile in Brühl that Le Tellier was among the government officials that his "enemy" Marie had in her "cabal." His concern about their friendship only grew after Le Tellier had been dismissed from the position of Secretary of State for War in July 1651, as part of a general purge of Mazarin's protégés from the royal council and household. Also dismissed was Abel Servien, a one-time creature of Richelieu who had been responsible for introducing Mazarin to the late Cardinal-Minister. Servien had risen to prominence in the royal council during Mazarin's absence together with his nephew, De Lionne, another Mazarin loyalist who had been serving as the Queen's secretary.[41]

After the Queen rebuffed an attempt by Chavigny to claim Servien's mantle as the de facto prime minister in Mazarin's absence, Mazarin began to warn the Queen in his letters about covert efforts by Marie and Chavigny to draw the newly disoriented Le Tellier, Servien, and De Lionne into the growing network that was pushing for Mazarin's full dismissal.[42] This was after he had attempted to turn De Lionne against Marie, writing to him, "That lady is very skillful at political intrigue, and unless you remain very alert, you run the risk of being surprised by her manner of acting and by her artifices."[43] Several weeks later, he suggested to De Lionne that Marie's efforts to have the Crown repay her for large loans she had made to the royal treasury were motivated by base self-interest and a lack of care about what "the State suffers."[44]

Mazarin was convinced, too, that Marie and Chavigny were quietly in league with one of the Queen's ladies-in-waiting, Catherine-Henriette de Bellier de

Beauvais, with a powerful finance minister named Jacques Tubeuf, and with
leading members of Parlement such as Pierre Viole and René de Longueil de
Maisons, the latter of whom had recently been appointed at the Surintendant
des Finances.[45] Because of this, Mazarin was all the more troubled, while stuck
in Brühl, that the Queen continued to meet with Marie every day. There is a
sense of the paranoia he was feeling in one of the coded warnings about Marie
that he sent to the Queen in the summer of 1651:

> I know from certain intelligence that there is no one in [Paris]
> who works with more effect against 46 [me] than 35 [Marie]. She
> is linked to most of the Dévots, whom she persuades toward what
> she wants, and then has them speak freely to 44 [you, the Queen].
> She has formed another large cabal with [Viole in the Parlement],
> whom she made fear [my] return on the last occasion. Since [Marie]
> meets with [you] every day at length, and since she is artful,
> skillful, speaks well, and is highly intelligent, it is to be feared that,
> under the pretext of the good and of service to [you] and [me], she
> will persuade [you] of something to [our] prejudice. This is why
> [you] must be more alert on that side than ever. [Chavigny] and
> [Maisons] are her greatest friends. It is important that [Le Tellier]
> does not form a connection with [Marie], because, upon my life,
> she does not love [me] and would like to see [my] total downfall.[46]

Mazarin was worried about Marie's political liaisons partly because several of
the figures involved, such as Chavigny and Maisons, had ties to the Prince de
Condé, as Marie herself did in several directions. There had been some movement
at court toward rearresting Condé, who was threatening—with substantial armed
support behind him in some parts of France—to renew his rebellion on a large
scale with assistance from Spain. He was not rearrested but instead rendezvoused
with supporters at Saint-Maur-des-Fossés, southeast of Paris, linking up with
his sister and her latest lover, Charles-Amédée de Savoie, the Duc de Nemours,
who had decided to join the princely rebellion with his men. Although Marie
opposed such activity as subversive to royal authority, Mazarin had reason to
be concerned, given the role she had played in Condé's release from Le Havre,
that the duchess and her friends would involve themselves in negotiations with
the princes in ways that could disadvantage him permanently.

Mazarin's urgent warnings to the Queen about Marie intensified in early September 1651. This was after he received an unexpected letter from the Secretary of State for Foreign Affairs, Henri-Auguste de Loménie, the Comte de Brienne, whose wife worked closely with Marie on charitable projects in Paris. Brienne informed the Cardinal-Minister that the Queen wished for him to leave Brühl for Rome to participate in an anticipated conclave to elect a new pope. Seventy-seven-year-old Innocent X was not well, and rumors were circulating that his time was near (incorrectly, it would turn out). Mazarin did not want to make this trip, which he feared would lead to his permanent exile from France, and he begged Anne not to send him.

The Cardinal-Minister soon learned that it was Marie and Chavigny who had persuaded Brienne, and through him the Queen, to order him to Rome. This convinced him that their secret hope was not only to put even more distance between him and the Queen, but also to expose him to jeering Roman crowds who would have been well-apprised of the dirty rumors that had been circulating far beyond the borders of France about his relationship with Anne.[47] This in turn would have embarrassed the Queen enough that she would have been unable to retain him in office. Although in the end he did not have to travel to Rome, as the plan was not pressed by the Queen, Mazarin by the end of the month was telling his confidants that Marie was his worst and most dangerous enemy in politics.[48]

This was around the same time that Mazarin received more unsettling news from Paris. Anne had stepped down as the Regent and permitted her son to take over as the reigning monarch—something that would allow her to continue influencing political affairs, as Louis was still only thirteen, but also something that would lay open the government to more direct influence by whomever became close to the King.

44

The Sun King Rising

O n September 7, 1651, in the middle of the second phase of the Fronde, Anne of Austria's regency ended and Louis XIV officially began to rule his kingdom. A solemn ceremony marked the transition of power. The bones of Saint Louis of France, the thirteenth-century monarch, were exposed for veneration at the Basilica of Saint-Denis north of Paris. Afterward, the adolescent King, in visibly high spirits, rode a majestic Arabian horse from the Palais-Royal on the Right Bank to the Palais de la Cité in the ancient heart of the capital. His coat was embroidered with so much gold that it shimmered blindingly in the sunlight.[1]

Conspicuously close to the King was Marie, who accompanied the Queen in her carriage. Anne had decided to give the duchess a place of honor in the procession and inside the Grand Chambre of the Parlement de Paris, where the ceremony, called a *lit de justice*, unfolded. Marie had one of the best views in the house as Louis and his mother exchanged words and embraced before all the ranking nobles and officials present. She was then close to the front of the procession of princes of the blood, peers of the realm, and officers of the Crown who paid homage to Louis before a speech was given in his honor by the Premier Président of the Parlement. At the end of the ceremony, the doors of the Palais de la Cité were opened to an ebullient crowd outside.[2]

Significantly, a new declaration of the Prince de Condé's innocence was read aloud at the ceremony, but one about Mazarin's banishment was not. Despite all the counsel against the Cardinal-Minister that Anne had received, the exiled Mazarin would be retained as the King's prime minister.[3]

Marie and others close to Anne, now referred to as the Queen Mother, blamed the continuing unrest in France on this fact. Condé renewed his rebellion that season, claiming opposition to Mazarin's continuation in office as his righteous *raison de guerre*. He mounted an armed takeover of Saintonge in the west, where Marie's friend and client Charles de Montausier was the royal governor. Marie's nephew Armand-Jean joined into this fight on the prince's side. After the duchess was momentarily scared by a false rumor that the young duke had been killed, she learned that, quite the contrary, he had become a hero to the local Frondeurs and partisans of the rebellious princes. Many local people around Saintonge, including not a few women, avidly supported him and Condé in the fight. Condé controlled Saintonge by the end of October, and the prince began expanding his rebellion far beyond this—this time, treasonously, with assistance from Spain, the country with which France was still at war.[4]

Once it was clear what Condé was up to, Marie's sister-in-law, Marie-Françoise, was persuaded to disinherit Armand-Jean, her eldest son.[5] Although she did not have much to add to what Marie was holding in trust for the young man, she had recently remarried with Charles de Gamache, the royal governor at Fougères in Brittany, which was not far from Saintonge. The disinheritance was an expression of loyalty to the Crown.

Gifts and promises were needed to ensure that more prominent figures who sympathized with the Frondeurs and opposed Mazarin's return to court did not join with Condé. Bishop Gondi was granted his red hat and was known thereafter as Cardinal de Retz. The King also promised to delay Mazarin's return to court, despite his mother's strong wish for the return to be immediate. Indeed, Mazarin's continued exile was the price paid to guarantee the continued loyalty of key members of Parlement, Gaston d'Orléans, and Cardinal de Retz.[6]

Learning of these developments, Mazarin was convinced that Marie and Chavigny had been the ones to influence Gaston and others close to the King to continue opposing his return to court as a condition of their loyalty.[7] He expressed concerns in this vein to young Jean-Baptiste Colbert, his future successor as prime minister, who was a low-level political minister in Paris at this time but whom Mazarin was trusting to assist him in various ways while he was in exile. Chiefly, Mazarin feared that should Condé meet with defeat in his rebellion, Marie and others "who will have the principal credit" for it with Queen Anne would then push for another reconciliation with the prince, who would demand Mazarin's dismissal from office as his primary condition. But Mazarin informed Colbert that he remained in touch with Marie and dissimulated with her about what he knew and suspected.[8]

In December, Mazarin was invited by the young King to return from Brühl, although it would not be until the end of January 1652 that he would be welcomed back to court, which was based in Poitou at that point. In the interim, Colbert assisted him in holding to account figures who appeared to have shifted their loyalties from Mazarin to Marie during the period of his exile. A letter from Colbert to Le Tellier is most revealing in this regard. Colbert informed the former Secretary of State for War, who hoped to be restored to a position of prominence in the government, that Mazarin remained concerned about the friendship he had "with Madame d'Aiguillon, whom he calls his most dangerous and most irreconcilable enemy." Colbert went on, revealing to Le Tellier that he and Mazarin had information about his dealings with Marie that they obtained by turning some of her own servants into spies:

> She makes war on him with arms more dangerous than the Parlement. . . . There is no invention on the world that she has not employed to make him lose credit with the Queen; all of this she has done with all imaginable presence of mind, never faltering from start to finish. She has apostated [from loyalty to Mazarin] Father Vincent, the curate of Saint-Sulpice [i.e. Father Olier], Madame de Polaillon [governess to the Duc d'Orléans's daughters], and the royal confessor. . . . She has gone on the attack in a clever but furious manner, in such a way that it is a marvel that the Queen's mind has resisted as it has. [Having] a great interest in knowing what springs move the mind of this lady, he has often detached from [loyalty to] her different people, even her domestic servants, having them enter into her thoughts by making her speak. By this means, they have discovered . . . that, even if you were not her peer [in the recent machinations against him], you at least provided useful material for her evil designs. On the basis of this apparent friendship that you have with Madame d'Aiguillon, and of the close connection she has with Monsieur de Chavigny, your enemies . . . have led people to believe that you were in league with them, and that you have had frequent, secret conversations with the said Sieur de Chavigny.[9]

While suspicious of Marie and her many associates at this time, Mazarin made a show of friendship toward the duchess while en route back to court. The Cardinal-Minister sent a letter to Marie paying his respects, because Marie was still so close to Queen Anne that it would seem discourteous not to do so.[10] He soon learned that Marie and Chavigny were encouraging Gaston to push for a reconciliation with Condé—something that, in mid-January, young Louis was not prepared to countenance, being advised to the contrary by Cardinal de Retz and others.[11]

It was just at this point, in mid-January, that Marie made the bold decision to advise Mazarin directly, in response to his courteous letter. She urged him to delay his return to court. If his return "were accompanied by a general approval" in France, as she claimed in her letter she "passionately wish[ed]," she would heartily welcome his return at that very minute. But given "the present state of the kingdom, agitated by divisions and troubles," his imminent arrival at court would be a dangerous "precipitation" contrary to "the service of Their Majesties." Marie asked Mazarin to remember, as well as she did, the example her uncle Richelieu had set as prime minister and in particular "the ardent desire that he had for the general peace."[12] In short, she was signaling that should the violence of the Fronde escalate again, the French people would regard it as his fault, not Condé's.

And escalate the Fronde did, almost as soon as King Louis greeted his prime minister ceremoniously on January 30. Gaston d'Orléans, in particular, was outraged that Louis greeted Mazarin two leagues from court and escorted him in the royal carriage—a courtesy normally reserved for other royalty. This was Gaston's excuse to join Condé's revolt. Some of the worst violence of the Fronde, including looting, rape, and other crimes against ordinary villagers by soldiers claiming to be opposed to tyranny, ensued in the months thereafter.

One of the most iconic moments of the Fronde was a furious fight on July 2, 1652, between the Crown and Condé's forces, now backed by Spain, near the gates of Paris close to the Bastille. Condé and his men were able to take over the city government after the royal troops defending Paris had almost trapped them near the walls outside the Porte de Saint-Antoine. This was after several hours of fighting in which Condé had been leading his men, risking his own life, and killing with a ferocity that shocked those who saw it. At one point, when there was a lull in the fighting, Condé threw off his armor and stripped naked to cool down in some grass. When the fighting resumed, he feared that loss was imminent after the royal forces, commanded by Marshal Turenne, gained the advantage outside the Saint-Antoine gate. It was shut and guarded by men under Gaston's command and sympathetic to Condé, but men who also feared Turenne's troops and possible arrest and execution for treason should they let the rebels in.

However, the tide turned when Gaston's blond, twenty-five-year-old, and still-unmarried eldest daughter—La Grande Mademoiselle, the same who had hated Marie and embarrassed her often when little—saw what was happening and shamed her father for his hours of inaction that day. She got him to order the commander of the Bastille to open the gate and allow Condé and his troops to enter the city and achieve victory. This princess was in talks at the time to marry King Louis but lost any chance at becoming Queen that day. But just as she wished to see in the moment, the young and fearsome Condé prevailed despite all odds and the Parlement de Paris welcomed him to take charge of the capital as the new Commander of France.[13]

But Condé and his allies quickly lost the support of the people of Paris once they began levying new taxes and permitting all sorts of abuses by their troops. This was after the King had ordered the Parlement to remove itself to Pontoise and some of the judges disobeyed, remaining in the capital and giving the appearance of forming a rival government in league with the rebels. Even those *parlementaires* who obeyed the royal order, however, demanded that Mazarin be dismissed as prime minister: this was so that Condé and the rebels could no longer claim, if they kept fighting, that they were doing so against Mazarin but not the Crown.[14]

Mazarin voluntarily exiled himself from court again after this, going this time to Bouillon in what is today southern Belgium. Remaining away from August 1652 until early February 1653, he effectively orchestrated a press campaign this time. This helped to sway public opinion especially in Paris against Condé and the rebels, who at this point began to fight for Spain.

During this second exile, Mazarin remained convinced that Marie was behind the opposition to his ministry that stubbornly persisted despite all that Condé had done.[15] He thus kept informed as much as possible about her dealings with a range of actors while guiding the King and Queen Mother as much as he could from abroad.

In the meantime, the royal family returned to Paris with much popular support in October 1652 as amnesty was granted to Gaston d'Orléans and other rebels who submitted to royal authority. Differently, Cardinal de Retz and Châteauneuf, who had once been part of Marie's "cabal," were arrested for their part in the Fronde. Chavigny, Marie's close associate, fell ill and died after attempting a *rapprochement* with Mazarin. When Mazarin finally returned to Paris on February 3, 1653, peace began to lastingly reign in the capital even as France remained at war with both Condé and Spain in various provinces.[16]

Several weeks later, on February 23, Marie and the rest of the court witnessed something extraordinary in the great hall of the Petit-Bourbon—the same room in which Cardinal Richelieu, when he was the young Bishop of Luçon, first impressed Queen Marie de' Medici before the Estates General more than forty years before. Young King Louis appeared in a thirteen-hour ballet, the *Ballet-Royal de la Nuict*, dressed from head to toe in a dazzlingly gold costume, playing the mythical sun god Apollo. The fourteen-year-old monarch's dance that night, which suggested to the gathered company that he was truly more than a mortal creature—and one whose God-given authority should never be challenged—symbolically inaugurated the new reign even more than the *lit de justice* before the Parlement de Paris had done a year and half earlier.

Ultimately unsuccessful in seeing Mazarin driven out of the government, Marie at the end of the Fronde nevertheless also remained firmly in a place as both the Governor of Le Havre and one of the nobles at court who was most often at the Queen Mother's side and had access to the King. Bitterness between these two most impressive protégés of Cardinal Richelieu lingered as France moved from the troubled era of the regency into the new, promising era of the Sun King's personal reign. Committed equally, however, to serving their young sovereign and to helping him make France the envy of Europe, the duchess and the Cardinal-Minister would, despite their differences and resentments, find ways to work together on matters of mutual and national interest. These included developments affecting Le Havre, which Mazarin would never manage to wrest from Marie.

45

Governor of Le Havre

I t was a rare occasion that required Marie to wear the blue-and-gold, ermine-lined mantel and bejeweled gold crown with its blue velvet cap that she had been given when Louis XIII invested her as the Duchesse d'Aiguillon and a Peer of France. One such occasion was fifteen-year-old Louis XIV's coronation at Reims Cathedral on June 7, 1654.

This was the only coronation of a French monarch that Marie would ever attend, as it was one of only two to occur during the whole of the seventeenth century. The event was regarded as sacred, similar in some respects to the consecration of new bishops and the investiture of new cardinals and popes. To be sure, new French kings were recognized as soon as their predecessors were dead and buried at the Basilica of Saint-Denis. But the coronations that had regularly taken place in the cathedral city of Reims since the late tenth century signified and achieved the sanctification of kings and their reigns by the Church. Once Louis was at Reims, he ceremonially was crowned by the archbishop of the city with the crown of the early medieval monarch Charlemagne. He also received his royal scepter while dressed with the royal blue robe of kingship, which was lined with ermine like Marie's mantel and embroidered with numerous fleurs-de-lis. Finally, the most important of the rituals at Reims was what was called the *sacre*—the archbishop's anointing of the king with a sacred oil that was kept in a special phial.

Marie had a place of honor at this ceremony not only as a duchess-peeress and close friend of the Queen Mother but also as the Governor of Le Havre in Normandy.[1] There were only twenty-five royal governors in France at this time, and Marie was the only woman among them—something that was resented by

Cardinal Mazarin and not a few French princes and military leaders who also had prominent places at the coronation that day.

It had not been a foregone conclusion that Marie would serve so long as the Governor of Le Havre. By 1654 she had withstood several attempts to have the office taken from her, the first in 1643 by the Prince de Marsillac and two more in 1650 by Mazarin and by her nephew and the Prince de Condé. Furthermore, Queen Anne in early 1652 had asked Marie to hand back the governorship of Le Havre to the Crown—with giving it to Mazarin in mind. Marie flatly refused. Anne did not press the matter, as Marie had too many important allies and clients of her patronage to risk alienating her.[2]

A few weeks later in April 1652, rumors had spread that the English were going to send a fleet of warships across the Channel to attack Le Havre and employ it as a base for a ground-troop invasion. This attack would never happen. A more serious problem at the time was piracy by English privateers who targeted French ships and also Dutch ships that carried French goods. But the fear of the English that spring had been real, and Marie had employed it to further strengthen her control of Le Havre. In preparation for the possible siege of many months, she had urged every citizen of Le Havre to stock up on six months' worth of wheat, for their own families and for the sake of the local garrison, under penalty of expulsion from the city. The leading alderman of the city, too, had been given the authority to prevent any exit of grain from the town. The duchess had ensured that other material and military preparations were made, setting precedents for subsequent years when her authorization would be sought for anything significant concerning the defense of the city.[3]

Young King Louis had fully reconfirmed Marie in her authority over Le Havre and its neighboring cities of Harfleur and Montivilliers on June 15, 1653. The royal lettres patentes for this decision were intended to "remove all doubts" that anyone might still have that Marie was fully to enjoy "the pledges, statements, salaries, rights, and emoluments" belonging to the office. The governorship was hers "for the rest of her life," should she wish to keep it. From the Crown's perspective, Marie's nephew Armand-Jean could not assert a hereditary right to take over the governorship unless both his aunt and the King authorized it.[4]

While securing this royal decision, Marie had also negotiated with the Crown to secure exemptions from certain taxes—including repayment of back taxes supposedly owed—for herself and several loyal officials at Le Havre. In exchange, Marie and other local leaders were to cover some of the upfront expenses for improvements to the city's defenses, as well as improvements of the conditions of the basin and quays where merchant ships docked, which the chronically delinquent royal treasury had been unable to cover.[5]

Controlling Le Havre was important for Marie for political reasons related to the Fronde but also for reasons that transcended the power games at court. To understand what was at stake when Marie secured her governorship several times over, it is necessary to look at the duchess's range of activities and interests connected to Le Havre.

An early modern English traveler described Le Havre in these terms: "This is one of the strongest towns in Europe, with an excellent port for men of war, which ride in great safety. It is situated at the mouth of the River Seine, in the county of Caen in Normandy. . . . It was built by Francis I in 1509, and has since been well fortified, and a fine citadel erected, with a large arsenal for naval stores."[6] Le Havre indeed was of utmost strategic importance for the naval defense of France at a time when battles on the high seas were common. Furthermore, from its position 125 miles to the northwest, it connected Paris by water to the port city of Caen—by way of the Seine and then by way of a short trip along the coast of Normandy. Caen was a great commercial hub, connected by trade to many other parts of France and to other lands, such as England, the Netherlands, and the Americas.

The governorship of Le Havre put Marie in the position to influence French mercantile affairs as well as matters of national defense. It gave her access to economic opportunities in the region, as when sea crystals were discovered near a local beach and Marie invested in their refinement as gemstones on a large scale.[7] It also connected her in a concrete way, despite never crossing the Atlantic herself, to projects and people that she had been funding for many years in New France. Money, supplies, and artwork for her charitable hospital in Québec; letters and donations for the Jesuits in Canada; merchants and mission personnel to whom Marie entrusted verbal messages for individuals in New France, including several godchildren there—all of these were sent up from Paris first to Le Havre and then onward to Dieppe and across the ocean.

Travelers, goods, and communications from various parts of the Americas came to Paris through the same route, in reverse. Among the former was a Carib native called Marabouis, who had survived a shipwreck that killed two Dominican friars who had brought him to France. He ended up staying with the Dominicans in Paris and was baptized in the presence of Marie, who had agreed to become his godmother.[8] Marie had been financially supporting the Dominican mission he was connected to on the island of Guadeloupe and had earlier helped select staff for it, including a priest and friar named Raymond Breton, who in time published a Carib catechism and a Carib-French dictionary.[9]

Individuals whom Marie got to know in France and then sent across the Atlantic by way of Le Havre did not always follow the paths she planned for them. One young woman whom she sent to join the Augustinian Hospitalières in Québec was deemed too pious and spirited by the nuns. The girl ended up marrying the son of the Governor of Québec but then, later on when widowed, she got to join the hospital nuns after all.[10]

A sad fate awaited a clergyman whom Marie had selected to help lead French colonial expansion in Guiana in South America. As the Governor of Le Havre and as one of the leading financiers in France, Marie (practically unheard of for a woman of the era) was a major shareholder in several merchant companies involved in overseas commerce and colonization, including the new Compagnie de la France Équinoxiale formed in 1651. The purpose of this company was to establish a new colony, and Marie chose as the leader of the expedition the Abbé de l'Isle de Marivault, a theology professor at the Sorbonne whom she believed would make a competent governor—and one who would ensure that the venture would be more humane than a previous French one in Guiana that had resulted in many deaths of local Galibí natives. Sadly, Marivault accidentally drowned in the Seine while en route to Le Havre.[11]

Despite such setbacks, Marie's ties to the Americas strengthened as the years of her governorship drew on. Her support for the Hospitalières in Québec was steady and included considerable sums for the labor and materials that went into the construction, by 1658, of new and larger facilities for the nuns and their mostly Native American patients.[12] She remained helpful to the Jesuits in New France and became involved eventually in the selection of the first French bishop for New France and early French efforts to build up the presence of diocesan clergymen in North America.

Le Havre was a vital link not only to the Americas but also to the British Isles. Affairs there had become challenging for the French at the time Cardinal Richelieu died and entrusted Le Havre to Marie. This was due above all to the outbreak of the English Civil War of 1642 to 1651.

When she was first serving as the acting Governor of Le Havre, Marie became responsible for the safe entry into France of exiles from England who were fleeing the violence that pitted Puritan revolutionaries led by Oliver Cromwell against the royalist supporters of King Charles I. Among them was the Queen of England and the aunt of King Louis XIV, Henriette-Marie, whose wedding by proxy to Charles I had been one of the first major courtly events Marie had attended as a young lady-in-waiting in 1625. In 1644, Marie ensured a warm welcome at Le Havre for Henriette-Marie and her newborn daughter, Princess Henrietta Anne. The devoutly Catholic Henriette-Marie had been forced to flee her husband's kingdom after she had been judged guilty of treason by the Puritan-dominated Parliament. She and her infant had endured a harrowing journey to the coast of Normandy, as her galley ship, motored by sixteen oarsmen, was chased the whole way by an English fleet.[13]

Once at Le Havre, however, Henriette-Marie and the little princess were received by the aldermen of the city, who conducted them to the Hôtel de Ville, where crowds of townspeople cheered their arrival. About fifty guardsmen in service to Marie greeted the royals ceremoniously and showed them and their small entourage to apartments that had been carefully prepared for them. From Le Havre, Henriette-Marie and her daughter would journey onward to the province of the Bourbonnais southeast of Paris.[14]

Thereafter, Henriette-Marie would spend a lot of time at court and in the company of Marie as well as Queen Anne. Marie got to know the English queen's young daughter and, in time, the eldest of her seven children, the future King Charles II of England, who joined his mother in exile in France in 1646 when he was sixteen. Henriette-Marie became involved in some of the charitable projects that preoccupied Marie, Queen Anne, and Vincent de Paul. From Henriette-Marie and other English exiles, Marie became more knowledgeable about the dire state of affairs across the English Channel as well as the suffering of Roman Catholics throughout the British Isles, who were bracing for severe persecution in the event of Cromwell's victory.

That victory of course came. The most important event, symbolically, toward the end of the English Civil War was Charles I's execution by beheading in London on January 30, 1649. The news reached the French court within hours, and Henriette-Marie was so stunned by it that observers noted she stood motionless, not responding to anyone around her, for almost an hour. She would never really recover. In the meantime, her son Charles was briefly recognized by the English Parliament as his father's successor, but then Cromwell, completing his *coup d'état*, abolished the monarchy and declared England to be a republic.

In spite of her strong sympathies with Henriette-Marie and with the royalist cause in England, Marie was cautious not to influence Queen Anne and others at court toward open conflict with the English revolutionaries across the Channel. The situation in France during the Fronde was too fragile to risk such a posture, and Marie did not wish to see Le Havre endangered by English naval attacks that potentially would ensue. The Crown's policy at the time, which Marie was supposed to enforce at Le Havre, was to treat both royalist exiles from England and English merchants and other travelers favorable to the revolutionaries as friends.[15] Furthermore, France's ongoing war with Spain, even after the conclusion of the Thirty Years' War, made robust support of restoring Charles II to the English throne untenable.

Indeed, it was partly to forestall a possible Anglo-French alliance even after Cromwell came to power that the Crown of Spain shocked Catholic Europe by leaping to recognize the Commonwealth government of England. This put the French in the challenging position of having to stand firm against Cromwell's regime, but not so firm as to push the English into active assistance of Spain in the ongoing war. The French Crown thus refused to recognize the Commonwealth for several years while insisting it was simply because the English were not reining in their privateers.

Marie and others at the French court supported a Stuart restoration indirectly, behind the scenes, and more as an ideal to hope for than something to be vigorously pursued. Marie herself was in communication with Pope Innocent X about the matter by early 1651. In March, when Mazarin was in exile, she attempted to persuade the Pope to back the young Charles Stuart's efforts to recapture his throne should Catholic armies around Europe unite to assist him. Innocent was reticent, however, because Charles was an Anglican and was offering to convert to the Church of Rome—or, short of that, to do his best to protect Catholics in the British Isles—only on the condition of such support.[16]

Marie had a realist's understanding of how bleak the Catholic cause was in the British Isles at this time through her work with Father De Paul and the Lazarists. The Lazarists had launched a mission to Ireland in the autumn of 1646. The group that traveled from France to Ireland at that time included two Irish-born priests, Edmund Barry and Dermot Duggan, who had both joined the Lazarists in France. Their mission was especially dangerous given the war that was then going on in Ireland—related to the English Civil War—that pitted Catholics of both Gaelic and Anglo-Norman descent against different groups of Protestants from within Ireland and from England and Scotland. The priests had to conceal their identities and were hunted down. Some of them escaped back to France in the summer of 1648, on the eve of both the Fronde and Cromwell's brutal conquest of Ireland. Father Barry remained in-country until the capture of Limerick by Cromwell's army in late 1651. Once back in France, he was sent to Richelieu for a time and then directed the Lazarists' seminary in Montauban in southern France for a number of years.[17]

The violence only grew worse in Ireland as the Cromwellian conquest advanced. After Limerick fell, the youngest Irish Lazarist, Thaddeus Lee, became the first martyr of De Paul's society of priests and brothers. Lee's own mother was forced by English soldiers to watch as the young cleric's feet and hands were cut off and his head was bashed into a pulp.

When news of this reached Marie, she was able through her contacts in Le Havre to arrange the escape of several Lazarists back to France. She paid for their voyage—a difficult one, as they traveled in disguise, fearing discovery by Cromwell's agents along the way.[18] Over time, she would donate funds to the upkeep and training of Irish clergymen and to some poor Irish refugees who resided in France. But her assistance beyond this to Catholic missions not only in Cromwellian Ireland but also in Scotland, where Lazarists disguised as merchants also became active, is not well documented.[19]

It was the politics of the Fronde, above all, that complicated Marie's desire to assist the cause of Catholicism in the British Isles. By the spring of 1652, the Prince de Condé was in touch with Cromwell's government, hoping to secure English support for his rebellion when he was already working with Spain.[20] He was hoping by this means to stir up French Protestant support—which politically necessitated an effort by the French Crown to appeal to Protestant subjects. Mazarin, although away from court, persuaded the King, Queen Mother, and royal council to issue the Declaration of Saint-Germain, which thanked Protestants throughout France for their loyalty up to that point during the Fronde. Mazarin achieved an unofficial *rapprochement* with the Commonwealth by December. Although a treaty of friendship would not be signed for another three years, the opening of amicable relations with the revolutionaries across the Channel made efforts by high-level French Catholics to assist the Stuart restoration politically perilous.[21]

Friendly relations with the English Commonwealth became more important to the French after the Spanish succeeded, in September 1652, in taking the important harbor city of Dunkirk close to Flanders. The French had previously taken Dunkirk from Spain in 1646. It would take several years for the French to be in a position to retake Dunkirk again, but when the attempt was finally mounted in 1658, the English were ready to assist and Marie, as the Governor of Le Havre, was closely involved. Prior to this, she was regularly in contact with Mazarin and other officials about matters of defense in the region, as when the French suffered a difficult loss to the Spanish at a fortress town called Valenciennes.[22]

In the spring of 1658, Marie traveled to Le Havre to act in person as its wartime governor rather than to communicate her wishes, as she usually did, through lieutenants. She inspected the city's defenses, as there was concern there could be a Spanish counterattack at Le Havre should the French succeed at Dunkirk, and she assessed the men and munitions that would be assisting not only with the local defense but also at Dunkirk itself. She chose new officers, for the garrison, including a new commander.[23] The King was grateful for the ammunition she was supplying, saying to her about Le Havre, "As long as you are there, we can have peace of mind here." With Le Havre secure in his rear, the King, Marshal Turenne and his army, and their English allies took Dunkirk. The Spanish surrendered on June 14.[24] Known as the Battle of the Dunes, this engagement was a key step toward the Treaty of the Pyrenees that would be signed by France and Spain the following year, finally ending a generation of conflict between the two powers.

Although Marie worked with Mazarin on a range of matters respecting Le Havre and the defense of the region during this period, her relationship with the prime minister remained icy. In the spring of 1654, just a few weeks before the King's coronation at Reims, Mazarin was still smarting over ways Marie had almost succeeded in driving him from power during the Fronde, saying to the duchess's cousin La Meilleraye, "I [am] unhappy that, while making a profession of honoring . . . the memory of the late Monsieur the Cardinal, she employed all her care to destroy someone whom His Eminence had loved so much and whom he had thought capable of filling his place." It is unclear that Richelieu had ever intended Mazarin to succeed him as the First Minister of State, but Mazarin claimed as much. He also suggested to La Meilleraye, as to others, that Marie and the rest of the Richelieu family would have fallen into hard times had it not been due to his effort, early during Queen Anne's regency, to secure their position in French society and defend their possession of offices such as the governorship at Le Havre.[25]

In 1657, fishermen, merchants, and other inhabitants of Le Havre were under new pressure from Mazarin's administration to pay taxes to the Crown that they could not afford without some hardship. They were also expected to lay out some of the expenses for the local garrison—at a time, too, when Marie's lieutenant-governor, without her authorization, began to infringe on some of the traditional rights and privileges of the city's aldermen. Marie intervened quickly and replaced the lieutenant-governor with another one she trusted. She visited Le Havre at this time to preside over the local assembly several times and smooth over relations between the garrison and the local citizens. She also provided for new charitable initiatives, especially the care and education of father-less and orphaned children in the city, and did her best in the months ahead to ensure that more funds would come into Le Havre than would be leaving it in the form of taxes.[26]

Mazarin often disapproved of Marie's activities in Le Havre, painting her mode of leadership as feminine weakness more than smart politics. Indeed, amid the preparations for the battle at Dunkirk, Mazarin attempted to instruct Marie several times on how to do her job at Le Havre, urging her for example to treat soldiers found guilty of certain offenses as harshly as possible rather than "to let [her]self be moved to pity" for them.[27]

In 1658, Marie ran into difficulties with Mazarin as he was late in securing her royal reimbursement for funds she had given to assist the retaking of Dunkirk. When she asked for 6,000 livres in December, Mazarin ordered the kingdom's Surintendant des Finances, Nicolas Fouquet, to take the money out of the ordinary annual fund budgeted by the Crown for Le Havre.[28] Marie was dissatisfied with this, as the expenses had been extraordinary ones related to the war. The following year, she demonstrated that her men at Le Havre lacked sufficient funds from the Crown now even for basic sustenance. By September 1659, Mazarin grudgingly instructed Fouquet to ensure that additional funds were, finally, sent along.[29] In the interim, Marie had done the King various favors, including entertaining him and six carriages full of young, fashionable friends over an extended royal stay at the Château de Rueil—a visit during which twenty-year-old Louis was pleased with a comedy that was presented in Rueil's great theater and with new, tasty dishes prepared by the duchess's chef that featured an array of exotic fruits.

Mazarin's political creature Fouquet would, within a few years, infamously be jailed by the King, partly for outshining the royal châteaus and their hospitality with the magnificence he had on display at his new Château de Vaux-le-Vicomte southeast of Paris. Marie's château was also envied by young Louis, who offered to buy it from her before he began planning in earnest for the great expansion of the Château de Versailles that would later become the primary seat of his government. But just as Marie had refused the Queen Mother's request years before to hand over the governorship of Le Havre, she refused the King's request for Rueil in a manner that it would be difficult to imagine anyone else in France doing so boldly at the time. Alluding to all that she had expended on Rueil's expansion and improvements over the years, she might as well have been silently reminding him, when explaining that she could not even imagine selling the château, of how much she and her late uncle Richelieu had expended from their personal wealth for the sake of the French monarchy, French commerce, and the national defense.

The duchess punctuated her unhesitant refusal of the Sun King with a reference, too, to what Richelieu had taught her countrymen, including members of the royal family, about the very authority of its consecrated sovereign with his once controversially high view of royal power: "The King is the master. And the one who bequeathed Rueil to me taught all of France so well the obedience that she owes to him, that His Majesty must not doubt my own."[30]

Louis did not bring up the subject again.

46

The Petit Luxembourg

At the time of Louis XIV's coronation, Marie was approaching fifty. She had seen many changes in the preceding years, in French political and cultural life and in her relationships with family members and friends. She had suffered the loss of her friend and ally of many years, the Comte de Chavigny, late in 1652. He was only forty-eight at the time. She had also seen more frustrating developments in the lives of her nephews. To her shock and dismay, just weeks after Chavigny's death, her second-eldest nephew Jean-Baptiste had, at the age of twenty, married in secret just as his older brother had done. The bride, who was fifteen, was a young and pretty courtier named Anne-Jeanne-Baptiste de Beauvais. Marie knew her well, as she was one of the Queen Mother's junior ladies-in-waiting and the daughter of Catherine-Henriette de Bellier de Beauvais, the King's first mistress (when the latter was thirty-eight and Louis only fourteen). Marie had had greater expectations for the Marquis de Richelieu's marriage, especially as it was possible that he might at some point inherit his elder brother's dukedom should Armand-Jean remain childless.[1]

In the meantime, Armand-Jean himself was showing signs of being too much like his late father. He was spending money too quickly and, worse, gambling some of his inheritance away, partly on the assumption that his legacy from Cardinal Richelieu, most of which Marie still held in trust for him, was even greater than it was.

Amid such changes and headaches, a comforting constant in Marie's life was the Petit Luxembourg. From the time Richelieu had gifted it to her when she was newly a duchess and through to her final years, Marie spent more time in her Parisian home than anywhere else.

It was full of treasures as well as memories. Among them was a marble portrait bust of Richelieu by the Italian master Bernini. Today it is a prized possession of the Louvre Museum. Richelieu, however, had hated it when Bernini completed it for him early in 1641, deeming it a bad likeness. He had banished it from sight, but Marie later displayed it lovingly in her home and ensured its preservation for posterity.[2]

Many works of art that Richelieu had liked much more were also on view at the Petit Luxembourg. There were sculptures of ancient Roman provenance, including a Bacchus and a faun. There was also a bronze copy of Michelangelo's *Moses*. Among the paintings Marie possessed in Paris were some that hang today in the Metropolitan Museum of Art in New York, such as Caravaggio's *The Musicians* and Poussin's *The Abduction of the Sabine Women*. There were also paintings and drawings by Perugino, Tintoretto, Bellini, Dürer, Rubens, Champaigne, and many other fine artists. Some works had been part of the Petit Luxembourg's collection for years; others, such as the Caravaggio and the Poussin, Marie brought together after Richelieu had died, as they had been hanging in other homes Richelieu had owned. She kept as much of his art collection together as she could, sometimes purchasing works that had once belonged to him for more than their market value.[3]

Beautiful tapestries also adorned some of the walls in the Petit Luxembourg, and Marie had magnificent collections of gemstones and crystals, globes, vases from different eras, and some of the finest-quality mirrors, candelabras, and furnishings available at the time. Some of the items had been imported from China and other distant lands.[4] Especially precious items of gold and silver graced Marie's private chapel and were employed liturgically by the many priests the duchess invited to say Mass there.

Visits by people of diverse ranks and circumstances were frequent at the Petit Luxembourg, especially as Marie often hosted *salon* gatherings as Catherine de Rambouillet had long done. Marie was too busy to build up anything quite like the Blue Room in its heyday, but the Petit Luxembourg was a place where men and women of intellectual curiosity, talent, and wit wished to be seen and make new contacts. One such memorable gathering in Marie's home, in the spring of 1652, featured a demonstration by Blaise Pascal, the young mathematician and man of letters. He had invented a mechanical computer and Marie gave him the chance to show it and to explain his theory of the vacuum.[5]

If the Petit Luxembourg did not develop a reputation for a *salon* quite like the Hôtel de Rambouillet's, this is partly because it was increasingly famous for something else. A young French clergyman whom Marie got to know,

Jacques-Charles de Brisacier, put it best. The duchess's home, he said, was "far less like the hall of a lady of quality than like a bishop's palace, given the continual flowing in and out of ecclesiastics and of religious of all orders, who came from all places to blend together there."[6] Marie was a laywoman. Clerical ordination was impossible by virtue of her sex. But as the heiress and protégée of Cardinal Richelieu, and by virtue of the patronage power she wielded even over the heads of bishops and clerical founders such as Fathers De Paul and Olier, she presided over a kind of unofficial curia of the French church. She was undeniably a great leader in that church.

In the early 1650s, the French church was increasingly divided into two new parties—the Jansenists and the anti-Jansenists. Marie was staunchly in the latter camp, even as many guests of her *salon*, including young Pascal, were in the former. She opposed the Jansenists' preferences for the infrequent reception of Holy Communion by sinners needing God's grace, and she had a distaste for Jansenist pessimism regarding the number of wretched souls God would allow into Heaven. She hoped that God would be generous with His mercy, however stern a judge He was regarding sin. The duchess's beliefs were such that she attempted to convert Jansenist friends and acquaintances to them—at a time when many Jansenists and anti-Jansensists stopped socializing with one another and were lobbing accusatory publications at their opponents.

A dinner gathering Marie hosted at the Petit Luxembourg in this period was memorable in this regard. Marie invited a leading light of the Jansenist movement along with other elegant guests, most of whom wished that their hostess would stop going to confession to one of the most ardent—and ugly—anti-Jansenist priests in Paris. That was Charles Picoté, a priest at Marie's parish of Saint-Sulpice who was intensely devoted to the poor and who had been deformed from birth. He had an unseemly large growth on his neck, bulbous and deadpan eyes ringed with red skin, and a cleft lip on top of what were disturbingly large lips to begin with. He also was hunched and unable to sit or stand up straight. Marie valued his counsel, however, and invited him to the same grand dinner, knowing that the Jansenist guest of honor would attempt to embarrass him. According to a source close to the scene, however, after the Jansenist asked Picoté to explain to the company an especially difficult passage from the writings of Saint Augustine, assuming he would respond in a bumbling way, Picoté "expounded on the passage with such clarity that the learned Jansenist became confused and did not dare to interrogate him any further."[7]

Marie tried to prick her elegant friends' consciences in other ways with this detested, anti-Jansenist Father Picoté. At another dinner, one of her servants placed a platter of six expensive ortolans near him; these delicacies were supposed to be divided among the company, but Picoté, who was not accustomed to *haute cuisine*, assumed they were sparrows and that everyone at the table would receive a similar plate. He ate them all, horrifying the company. Marie turned things around on his critics, announcing to him—knowing full well that it would scandalize him—that the ortolans had cost 60 livres. Picoté responded boldly to his hostess, "That money would have been better employed in helping the poor." To the shock and confusion of some of Marie's friends, Picoté after this was allowed even more, not less, coveted access to the great Duchesse d'Aiguillon.[8]

In addition to allowing grand dinners at the Petit Luxembourg to become arenas for Jansenist encounters with anti-Jansenists, Marie often met privately with Jansenists whom she hoped to win over to her views. She did so for many years with one stubborn churchman named Amable de Bourzeis, who was an author of several Jansenist tracts. She employed both humor and theological acumen in their conversations, sometimes drawing effectively from the teachings of Saint Thomas Aquinas in them. Eventually, Bourzeis surrendered to his persistent and winsome interlocutor, publicly disavowing his Jansenism.[9]

The duchess had less success with her old friend from the Blue Room days, the Marquise de Sablé, whose *salon* from 1648 onward was a bit of a rival to her own. Sablé by the mid-1650s aligned herself so completely with the Jansenists that she had an apartment constructed on the grounds of the Port-Royal convent in Paris, the spiritual center of the movement. In 1655 she moved her *salon* there, and leading Jansenists such as Pascal and the theologian Antoine Arnauld regularly attended it.[10] She and Marie engaged in friendly disagreements over the different understandings of God that were at stake, both in person and in their frequent letters—letters, though, that were also full of personal news, including about food they loved and gifts they received from each other.

Marie countered the influence of Jansenism above all by supporting religious and charitable institutions that were staffed by men and women whose theological outlook she trusted, and whose approach to the Christian life embodied her own cherished beliefs about God's mercy as well as justice. She remained a pillar of financial support for the Discalced Carmelites, for example, who by late in her life had scores of convents throughout France.[11]

She also played a leading role in promoting the cause of sainthood for her former Carmelite spiritual adviser and mother-figure, Madeleine de Saint-Joseph, who had died in 1637. Partly due to Marie's influence, a process was opened in France in 1645 and then formally was opened in Rome in 1650 in order to consider the evidence of Mother Madeleine's holiness.[12] In the same period, Marie and her friends circulated a biography of Mother Madeleine that was endorsed by many French bishops and theology professors and openly referred to the nun as a "saint."[13]

Marie established, protected, and nurtured a range of other consecrated women's communities in France. Some were based in her Duchy of Aiguillon and near the Château de Rueil.[14] In Paris alone, Marie patronized not only the Carmelite convents on the Rue Saint-Jacques and the Rue Chapon, but also the Filles du Calvaire, the Bernardines Réformées du Précieux Sang, the Filles de la Croix, the Filles de Saint-Joseph, the Madelonnites, and the Religieuses de Notre-Dame de la Miséricorde.[15]

That last congregation had appealed to Marie in a particular way during the Fronde, when so many French people fell into dire poverty. At that point, Marie enabled a nun called Mère Marie-Madeleine de La Trinité to establish the Religieuses de Notre-Dame in order to house and educate girls of genteel but poor backgrounds, partly to prevent them from falling into unrespectable circumstances. Marie served as the community's primary donor in its early years, providing the women with a house in Paris and supplying funds for their food and other needs. Aristocratic friends of Marie's soon became patronesses of the community, too, including Louise de Béon, the Comtesse de Brienne, who was the wife of the same Comte de Brienne who conspired with Marie to have Cardinal Mazarin exiled from France.[16]

Marie's support of Vincent de Paul and the Lazarists also remained strong during the Fronde and the years in which the French church became divided over Jansenism. De Paul was one of the staunchest opponents of Jansenism in France. Along with Mazarin, he favored imposing a religious test called the *formulaire* on French clergymen and religious whereby they had to publicly disavow five Jansenist teachings that had been condemned by the Pope in 1653 and 1656.[17] De Paul lost friends in this period, as a result, but Marie's efforts to sustain and expand his ministries only multiplied.

The duchess and the peasant-priest continued to work together, for example, on the Lazarists' North African missions. One matter the two often disagreed about was whether or not Lazarist priests should continue to hold the consular offices in Tunis and Algiers. De Paul was greatly relieved, therefore, when Marie approved the appointment of a layman as the consul of Tunis. This was Martin Husson, who took up the post in July 1653. He had previously been serving as an advocate in the Parlement de Paris, and De Paul regarded him as "not only wise, accommodating, vigilant, and pious," but also as "an astute businessman."[18] Within a few years, however, Husson would end up on the wrong side of the Bey of Tunis, who expelled him from the region. In return for his consular service, Marie entrusted him with the most important position in her household, that of her personal attorney and *intendant des affaires*, which gave him responsibility over all of her wide-ranging legal and business affairs. He would serve the duchess loyally the rest of her days.[19]

Husson's departure from Tunis was indicative of a more general problem the North African missions were facing since Marie began to fund and develop them: a chronic shortage of manpower. Only ten Lazarists were sent to Tunis and Algiers combined up to the mid-1650s, and half were either banished by local authorities or died in-country after contracting the plague.[20] A considerable portion of the business Marie conducted with De Paul related to North Africa concerned, thus, selecting replacements for missionaries who died all too young, such as Father Julien Guérin, who contracted the plague at forty-three after tending to slaves in Tunis who were sick with it.[21]

Given the Lazarists' often weak position on the ground in Algiers and Tunis in the years after Marie purchased the French consulates, it is all the more remarkable that, by means of interventions with the funds Marie and her network sent across the Mediterranean, the missionaries paid more than 1 million livres as ransom money between the mid-1640s and early 1660s. Roughly equivalent to at least 39 million U.S. dollars today, these gathered funds resulted in the redemption of as many as 1,200 Christian slaves in the region. Marie was the most generous among the individuals who contributed to these ransoms, in addition to funding a charitable hospital in Algiers for both rescued and abandoned slaves.[22]

Marie's association with Vincent de Paul and with the peasant-priest's other great collaborator, Louise de Marillac, became more formalized in 1653. This was because Marie agreed to serve as the President of the Ladies of Charity. Advised by De Paul, loosely affiliated with De Marillac's Daughters of Charity, but also independent, structurally, from the Lazarists and the Daughters, the Ladies of Charity was the largest and most innovative Catholic laywomen's organization of its time. Marie had been friends with the organization's first president, Marie Deslandes de Lamoignon, who had died while in office. Marie would end up serving in this position until her own death more than two decades later.[23]

At the time that Marie became the President of the Ladies of Charity, she had a growing reputation for doing things noblewomen were not supposed to do when involved with charitable work: she visited prisons, she sometimes served the poor directly with her own hands at Saint-Sulpice, and she spent time occasionally with repentant prostitutes and unwed mothers at refuges set up for them.[24] This duchess whom a contemporary poet called a "severe beauty" also had a reputation for toughness where the administration of charitable services was concerned.[25] She had recently required, for example, that Daughters of Charity with whom she was working in a prison ministry draw up a list of prisoners who mistreated any of the women serving them, so that further charity might be denied to them in punishment. Even Louise de Marillac found this to be a harsh policy.[26]

One of Marie's first priorities as the President of the Ladies of Charity was to assist communities in the French regions of Picardy and Champagne, which had been hit especially hard during the Fronde. Marie held an emergency meeting with De Paul early in 1653 and learned of the suffering in many communities resulting from the brutality and pillaging of the Prince de Condé's army and his allies throughout northeastern France. The Ladies were unable to send in as much aid as they wished, so strict conditions were applied to the Lazarists' distribution of alms. In Champagne, the Lazarists were ordered by Marie to find out, through discreet interviews, which poor villagers were truly in need of gifts of clothing in the colder months and which were hoarding alms.[27]

Marie's most significant endeavor as the President of the Ladies of Charity was to lead an effort, in collaboration with officials in the Parlement de Paris, to establish a state-sponsored general hospital for the poor in Paris. The famous institution that would emerge from this effort was the Hôpital-Général de Paris, which not only provided medical assistance to the impoverished but also employed enforced residency as a solution to the problems of increased mendicancy and slum conditions in Paris that had reached alarming levels during the Fronde. In modern times, the French philosopher Michel Foucault would analyze this confinement of the poor in his book *Madness and Civilization*.

Marie oversaw from the Petit Luxembourg a massive fundraising campaign for this planned Hôpital-Général. She brought in almost 250,000 livres—a staggering sum for the era. She had also already gifted, in addition, 50,000 livres out of her own pocket and an arsenal building called La Salpêtrière, which Queen Anne had earlier given to her. This building, which had formerly been employed as a munitions factory, would become the main building of the new hospital.[28]

By the middle of 1653, Marie and the Ladies of Charity hoped to involve De Paul in the planned hospital. However, De Paul was ambivalent about the idea.[29] The duchess pressed him on the matter, as she wished not only that he would play a leading role in the administration of the hospital, but also that both the Lazarists and the Daughters of Charity would staff the institution. In spite of the priest's reservations, Marie went ahead and had conversations with members of Parlement and Crown officials in which she urged that De Paul be given an official directorship. This would require that he take a seat on its founding board of directors.[30]

De Paul was concerned, however, that the Hôpital-Général would distract the Lazarists, Daughters, and their patrons too much from the needs of the rural poor. The latter were chronically underserved compared to the urban poor, as so many charitable French elites were concentrated in cities. While De Paul had allowed the Lazarists to assist many urban ventures over the years, especially in Paris, a formal relationship with the Hôpital-Général was for him a bridge too far.[31]

De Paul was not the only important person who was ambivalent about the project. Some members of Parlement were hesitant until more men in official positions joined Marie and the Ladies of Charity in driving it forward. Marie's masons were even forbidden for a time by a Crown official from completing their work at La Salpêtrière. Such complications only magnified De Paul's reticence, which he made clear to Marie in late 1653.[32] Months later, after De Paul urged the Ladies to distance themselves from the project, Marie made it clear to the priest that she was unsure he was accurately discerning God's wishes: "I respect your ideas, but allow me to tell you mine. . . . The Ladies [who] have control of the funds . . . will be accused perhaps before God and most certainly before men of having ruined the whole affair. . . . [We] wish to see that it is established under proper management, with a permanent system of government."[33]

In spite of many hurdles, the Hôpital-Général came to life in April 1656 by means of a royal edict that would be affirmed soon after by the Parlement de Paris. This marked the beginning of an eventually kingdom-wide effort—urged along in many cases by the Ladies of Charity and Marie's friends in the govern-ment and in high society—to establish general hospitals in every French city, something that would be ordered by the King in 1662. The original edict of 1656 expressed the wishes of Marie, other Ladies of Charity, and political officials with whom they had collaborated that the hospital "save the poor who were living together out of wedlock" and "living always in ignorance of religion, disdain for the sacraments, and in continuous habits of all sorts of vices." By encouraging Christian piety and moral practice among the hospital's inmates, Marie and the other founders hoped not only to facilitate their salvation but also to attract more French elites as prospective donors, who tended to be reticent about extending alms to poor people they too often presumed were irredeemable.[34]

Demonstrating Marie's and the Ladies' influence, the Crown charged the Lazarists with the spiritual affairs of the Hôpital-Général. De Paul protested by refusing to sit on the hospital's board and putting restrictions on what roles his men could and could not play in the enterprise. This displeased Marie greatly. The priest and the duchess argued over the matter on several occasions.[35]

One of the reasons the Hôpital-Général project moved forward despite De Paul's opposition was that, as influential as the priest was as a member of the royal Council of Conscience, Marie and the Ladies had effective working relationships with a larger coterie of wealthy and highly placed men, both lay and clerical, who belonged to the Compagnie du Saint-Sacrement, which had rallied behind the project. Although the group primarily was a pious confraternity devoted to charitable works, it became militant and politically powerful, committed to the renewal and strengthening of the Church within and beyond the borders of France. This sometimes took the form of anti-Protestant and anti-Jansenist activity. By the early 1650s, it had chapters throughout the kingdom that brought numerous charitable and religious enterprises to life despite the opposition of some French bishops and also Cardinal Mazarin, who tried to suppress it.[36]

Never formally recognized under French law, the Compagnie over time included a range of churchmen well known to Marie, including De Paul and Jean-Jacques Olier of Saint-Sulpice. Many lay nobles well known to Marie belonged, too, including her cousin La Meilleraye. Additionally, the Compagnie was composed of laymen and clergymen of diverse social backgrounds, geographical origins, and institutional affiliations within the Church—not a few of them in, or just a degree away from, Marie's extensive network of friends and patronage clients.[37]

The Compagnie was closed to women. This was less due to misogyny, as some modern scholars have presumed, than to the inefficient redundancy of a sister organization, given the emergence and expansion of the Ladies of Charity in the same period, and given the strong collaborative relationship the Compagnie had with Marie, in particular, who sometimes hosted its meetings at the Petit Luxembourg.[38] Over the years, members of the Compagnie du Saint-Sacrement worked with Marie on a number of projects in addition to the Hôpital-Général. These included the Lazarists' operations in Marseilles and North Africa, the development of new seminaries, and the ongoing reform of the parish of Saint-Sulpice.

Members of the Compagnie also worked with other pious and wealthy women in Marie's circle. Some of the prominent Ladies of Charity were married to members of the Compagnie or related to them in some other way. Some of these women became important friends to Marie in this period. One was Marie Bonneau de Rubelles, known better by her married name, Madame de Miramion. She was a young widow who worked closely both with the Ladies and the Compagnie. She had been considered one of the most beautiful young ladies in French aristocratic society at the time of her marriage to a royal councilor in 1645. Like Marie, Madame de Miramion had been motherless from a young age and was brought up by a cultured uncle. She also became a widow very soon into her marriage. Unlike Marie, however, Madame de Miramion was left pregnant by her husband, and she gave birth to a daughter, Marguerite, in March 1646. Not long after this, she was abducted by a lascivious count, Roger de Rabutin de Bussy, cousin to the famous woman of letters Madame de Sévigné. But she frightened him, once he had her in his clutches, by proclaiming her fidelity to Jesus Christ and daring him, in the sight of the God of Justice, to do his worst with her. The count set her free without violating her body.[39]

It is easy to see why Marie liked this young woman and extended friendship to her. In the midst of the Fronde, Madame de Miramion started a retreat house for the Daughters of Charity and experienced a call to dedicate her life to God and the poor. She made a vow of chastity in 1649, encouraged in this by Marie, De Paul, and other friends. With assistance from Marie and the Ladies of Charity, she established within a few years an orphanage, a group of sisters called the Filles de Sainte-Geneviève who offered schooling and nursing care to the poor in Paris, and a House of Refuge for unwed mothers and other young women in morally and socially perilous situations. In time, Marie and the Ladies were able to incorporate the latter into the Hôpital-Général. Marie would visit this House of Refuge with regularity to wait upon its residents.[40]

Additionally, as Madame de Miramion was not without some means, she would join in with some of Marie's projects as a donor. These would include a new French mission to the Far East that Marie helped to launch in the 1650s—although not until after the duchess encountered an extraordinary man among her numerous guests at the Petit Luxembourg.

47

A Jesuit Visitor

O ne of the most unusual Catholic clergymen to visit Marie several times in Paris came first toward the beginning of 1653. His name was Alexandre de Rhodes. He was a Jesuit priest who had spent many years in Southeast Asia, attempting to conduct a mission to the kingdoms of what we know today as Vietnam.

Rhodes's encounters with Marie were fateful for both figures, as they would lead to a great dream of the Jesuit's coming to life and to a set of new projects to which the duchess devoted special energy. These would include the creation of new, French-sponsored missionary dioceses around the world, the selection of bishops to lead them, and the establishment of a lay-directed Catholic missionary society and seminary in Paris that would staff these dioceses with clergymen prepared for the rigors of missionary assignments. The seminary, called Le Séminaire des Missions Étrangères de Paris, still operates today. And the dioceses were the beginnings of institutionalized Catholicism in lands across Asia that today are home to many millions of Roman Catholics.

It took more than a decade for these projects to launch. And while many hands were involved and orchestrated at key moments by Marie, their story begins with Rhodes, whose path to Marie's *salon* was an unlikely one.

Born in 1593 to parents of Jewish heritage in the city of Avignon, which was not part of the French kingdom at the time, Rhodes as a young man joined the Society of Jesus in Rome, not in France. He wished to follow in the footsteps of Jesuit missionaries to the Far East such as Francis Xavier, Alessandro Valignano, and Matteo Ricci, who were sent by the Society's Roman province. By 1618, after six years of formation at the Roman College (today's Gregorian University), he was on his way to Goa in India, where he completed his Jesuit training.[1]

In 1622, the same year young Marie became a widow far away in France, Rhodes began cutting his teeth as a missionary in Malacca and then in Macao, where he would teach theology to other aspiring missionaries. But he spent most of his time as an active missionary up through the 1640s in the two major regions of what is today Vietnam. The northern region, Dong Ngoai, was known to Europeans as Tonkin, although Tonkin was actually one of several kingdoms within it. The southern region, Dang Trong, was known to Europeans as Cochinchina. Working alongside Portuguese clergymen, Rhodes saw success especially in the north, where he opened a church in Hanoi in 1627 and within a few years baptized some six thousand people.[2] He was forced to leave, however, in 1645—barely escaping with his life—after the King of Annam and other Vietnamese lords began cracking down on missionaries, who they regarded as tools of Portuguese merchants and soldiers who were, indeed, looking to make imperial inroads in the country.[3]

Rhodes journeyed back to Europe and was ensconced again in Rome in 1649. Hoping to recommence missionary labors in Vietnam, but in a way that made it clear to the indigenous authorities that he had nothing to do with the Portuguese, he presented an innovative idea to officials at the papal court of Innocent X.

The Pope, he urged, should appoint missionary bishops for Southeast Asia, technically referred to as *vicarii apostolici* ("apostolic vicars"). They would answer to Rome alone and not to the Portuguese Crown, therefore bypassing an old right the Portuguese had enjoyed since 1493, thanks to a prior pope's affirmation, to sponsor all new missions in Africa and most of Asia. (This was the so-called *padroado*; the Spanish, with their *patronato*, enjoyed similar privileges in the Americas and the area around the Philippines.) These new bishops could then, according to Rhodes's scheme, raise up an indigenous clergy in Vietnam so that the Church would become more acceptable to the country's leaders.[4] The Christian population was large enough in Tonkin, he claimed, that at least three hundred priests were needed. But he also believed firmly that most of these should be indigenous men, not Europeans, for the Church to truly take root among the Vietnamese.[5]

While waiting for a papal response to his idea, Rhodes proactively sought support from prospective donors in and outside of Rome who could help finance the new dioceses and their missions. He wrote a book, published in 1650 in

Rome, about his experiences in Vietnam and his hopes for the country.[6] The Pope then proposed that Rhodes himself become the new Apostolic Vicar for Tonkin. However, Rhodes felt this would be inconsistent with his Jesuit charism and his religious superiors' wishes for him. He was also certain that the Portuguese—who had gotten wind of what he was up to—would attempt to prevent his return to Southeast Asia and even declare war on the Papal States if he dared to take up episcopal duties in the region.[7]

This Portuguese opposition slowed the already glacial pace of the Vatican discussions Rhodes had initiated. Nevertheless, the Jesuit by the summer of 1652 was permitted by the Pope to travel through Europe and identify other possible candidates for the post of missionary bishop. He was also determined to secure major backing from a Catholic kingdom other than Portugal for an expanded mission to Southeast Asia, knowing that ready power and money would quicken officials' steps at the Vatican. However, he risked the ire of Innocent X, who preferred Spain to France, when he drew up an itinerary that would take him to Avignon, Lyon, and finally Paris.[8]

Rhodes was being pragmatic in his choice of France. The French, due to their maverick role in the Thirty Years' War, were relatively friendly with the Dutch and the English, who were active commercially alongside the Portuguese in South and East Asia. Those powers might not interfere aggressively with French efforts to establish footholds in the region. Additionally, Rhodes had connections in France through his brother, who was a Jesuit professor in Lyon. Georges de Rhodes and his faculty colleagues enjoyed the protection of Lyon's cardinal-archbishop, Alphonse-Louis du Plessis de Richelieu, brother of the deceased, more famous Cardinal Richelieu, and uncle to the great Duchesse d'Aiguillon, whose reputation for generous support of missionaries preceded her. Georges was also connected with lay and clerical elites in Paris who were affiliated with the Compagnie du Saint-Sacrement—also just a degree away from Marie.[9]

Rhodes secured access to Marie and other leading French figures by the spring of 1653—the period when the Fronde was subsiding and Marie and her wealthy friends were taking up new, ambitious projects again. He did this initially with his brother's help, by putting his name and ideas out in print in French. First he published in Lyon a French history of Vietnam, dedicating it to young Louis XIV and claiming that the peoples of Southeast Asia wished to be taken to the bosom of France, "the eldest daughter of the Church," and to be called "her children."[10] Then, after meeting Marie and securing assistance from her and the prestigious publisher Sébastien Cramoisy, he was able to put forward five more books in Paris.

These publications sounded a strongly French and patriotic note—something unnatural for their author, as he spoke and wrote French only with difficulty and was not a proper Frenchman by any conventional definition of the time. In his book *Divers Voyages et Missions*, which he dedicated to Anne of Austria, he insisted that France was his "chère patrie" and that he was dedicated to "announcing the Gospel on behalf of the greatest king among all Christians," by which he meant Louis XIV.[11] He also depicted himself as a Frenchman who formed bonds quickly with French nationals and French speakers during his travels. He claimed even that one Frenchman he befriended in Persia—the travel writer François Le Gouz de La Boulaye, who blended in with the locals with his clothing and beard—embodied the truth that "a good Frenchman can circle the globe without making an enemy."[12]

Such rhetoric facilitated Rhodes's introduction to Queen Anne and King Louis.[13] Rhodes also began to collaborate with a Parisian Jesuit, Jean Bagot, who led a group of young priests and theology students called the Société des Bons Amis that was tied to the Compagnie du Saint-Sacrement. Members of the Compagnie were interested in the possibility that Frenchmen might be appointed as missionary bishops for Southeast Asia, and they favored Bons Amis clergymen as possible candidates.[14]

Marie's patronage was most critical to Rhodes's success in Paris. She gathered in her *salon* some of the wealthiest members of the Compagnie du Saint-Sacrement and urged them to join her in financially backing the prospective missionary dioceses. She offered what influence she had, too, to try to convince the Pope not only to authorize the new dioceses but also to accept French clergymen whom she and her friends favored to staff them.[15]

Rhodes publicly thanked Marie at the front of his book *Sommaire des Diverses Voyages et Missions Apostoliques*. He displayed his self-consciousness, however, that he was different from other clergymen who enjoyed Marie's patronage, insofar as he was not a natural subject of the King of France but Avignonnais (Avignon was still at this time tied to the Papal States). He admitted that he had spent very little time in France throughout his sixty years of life. "Behold a poor pilgrim," he declared to the Duchesse d'Aiguillon, "who after having begun to criss-cross the world for close to forty-two years . . . finds shelter no more secure than that of your favor." He praised her for both her own merits and her blood relationship to two great cardinals who had served the Church and France, at once, in glorious ways. And he went so far as to depict France as ready with her standing armies, as Louis XIV matured in "courage . . . and piety," to "give law to all her neighbors, after having rendered obedient all subjects to the King."[16] Such rhetoric reveals as much about Marie—about what sort of language she found appealing and useful—as it reveals about Rhodes.

Rhodes helped to cultivate Marie's public image as a pioneering leader of Paris-centered Catholic expansion across several continents at once:

> Even as you reside in Paris, you traverse the most dangerous seas and bring knowledge of Jesus Christ to barbarous countries. . . . You think up ways to convert infidels. . . . You make apostolic people go from one pole to the other, and contrary to the order of the visible world, you bring daylight at one and the same time to the East of China and the West of Canada.[17]

Elsewhere, with Marie and her associates in mind, Rhodes painted a picture of high-ranking French persons who, while supporting his project, were bonded by their piety and commitment to a spiritual venture that was about to become "the most glorious France has seen in several centuries."[18]

When he wrote this, Rhodes believed that Rome would quickly appoint several French apostolic vicars and that he would be able to join a group of mostly French Jesuits who would labor under the new bishops' authority in Vietnam. However, discussions stalled in Rome, and Rhodes's relative lack of formal French ties dashed his hopes. Just as he was coming to identify keenly with his new Parisian friends, he received orders from his Jesuit superior in Rome to leave France and lead a new Jesuit mission to the Persian Empire. Rhodes would end up dying in Isfahan in 1660, at the age of sixty-seven, while struggling to master the local language in any way close to how he had succeeded, beautifully, with Vietnamese.

All the same, Rhodes had stirred up definitive interest in Marie's circle in that part of the world that had always been foremost in his thoughts and prayers. Had he not spent a year and a half in their midst, some of the most innovative actions Marie took on behalf of the French church's global expansion might never have come to pass.

48

Negotiating with the Pope

Convincing Rome to authorize the creation of four French missionary dioceses would prove to be Marie's most impressive accomplishment as a Catholic laywoman, as well as a major coup in the ongoing French effort to undercut Spanish and Portuguese influence abroad. By the early 1660s, three such dioceses were set up for Asia and a fourth for North America. According to a plan similar to Rhodes's original idea, several Frenchmen were consecrated as bishops of long-vacant, ancient episcopal sees in what had centuries before become part of the Muslim world—bishops *in partibus infidelium*, they were called—while in actuality serving as bishops, each with the title Apostolic Vicar, for mission lands recently accessed by European Christians.

This was no easy feat considering that since the 1490s, nearly all prospective mission lands around the world had been deemed by the Vatican, and under Europe's developing international law, to fall under either the Spanish *patronato* or the Portuguese *padroado*. Furthermore, the two popes to whom Marie and her associates successively advocated the project, Innocent X and Alexander VII, had been disinclined to support French expansionist ambitions per se, given friction over various matters between the papal curia and Cardinal Mazarin's political administration.

However, Marie saw that there was an opportunity for France despite all this, given that Vatican officials had already been working toward subordinating far-flung, Spanish- and Portuguese-sponsored missions to Roman oversight. This was especially true of the cardinals at Propaganda Fide, the department of the curia founded in 1622 expressly for such oversight. As negotiations with Marie and other French leaders proceeded, new French-sponsored missions came to be seen favorably by these cardinals, as they could facilitate the goal of breaking up what had effectively become Iberian royal monopolies on missionary activity across parts of Asia, Africa, and the Americas.[1]

These negotiations commenced in March 1653 during the Jesuit Rhodes's stay in Paris. Marie and several members of the Compagnie du Saint-Sacrement contacted Rome, expressing their willingness to finance a new mission centered in Tonkin, which they first imagined would be staffed by twenty French Jesuits. They pledged initially to provide at least 20,000 livres in cash and material supports valued at 6,000 livres. Among the laymen in this group was Bertrand Drouart, a churchwarden and ally of Marie's at Saint-Sulpice who assisted with other charitable works the duchess favored.[2]

The group petitioned for French sponsorship of at least two new missionary dioceses that would be formally answerable to Rome but staffed by French churchmen. They offered to provide 600 livres a year in income to each bishop.[3] They did this by employing Rhodes and the papal nuncio in Paris, Nicolò Bagni, as their intermediaries. Rhodes was sure to express to Rome that the highly qualified young clergymen whom Marie and her associates had in mind for the posts would conform to directives from Propaganda Fide.[4] Bagni, for his part, underscored to Innocent X that it was the great heiress of Cardinal Richelieu who was leading the French group that was petitioning for the apostolic vicariates.[5]

In the summer of 1653, Marie and her friends amplified their requests in Rome through more prominent clergymen. The Pope was presented with letters of support for the hoped-for French missionary dioceses from Vincent de Paul, the bishops of Senlis, Puy, Amiens, and Condom, and the newly selected Archbishop of Rheims, Henry de Savoie-Nemours.[6]

While awaiting a response from Rome, Marie and her friends selected a preferred candidate for the not-yet-existent post of Apostolic Vicar of Tonkin. This was François Pallu, a diocesan priest and cathedral canon from Tours who was not yet thirty. The son of a lawyer and minor provincial nobleman, he was a member of the Jesuit Bagot's Société des Bons Amis.[7]

Pallu was the kind of talented, serious, and devout clergyman from respectable but non-noble origins whom Marie preferred to patronize and raise up to positions of influence in the French Church. It is significant that she had him in mind for the episcopate, as French bishops were increasingly drawn at this time from the upper nobility.[8] He was, instead, the product of an excellent education given him by disciplined, reform-minded clergymen. He had great facility with Latin and Scriptural interpretation and, before and after his ordination as a diocesan priest, he had studied theology at the Jesuits' Collège de Clermont in Paris. His time among the Jesuits proved fateful, as his intelligence, sincere piety, good morals, and growing interest in overseas missions were soon recognized by members of the Compagnie du Saint-Sacrement. Pallu was therefore invited into discussions with Marie and leading French churchmen as they strategized about overseas missionary dioceses.[9]

However, toward the end of Innocent X's pontificate, the Portuguese, with carrot-and-stick diplomacy, offered to fund seventy new missionary posts in Asia while threatening war with Rome after learning of the French scheme. They made it clear that they would break peace with the Papal States if any French priests traveled to Vietnam, let alone French bishops, with any claims of authority. Cowed by this, the Holy See signaled that the plan for the French apostolic vicariates was off the table.[10] This was frustrating to Marie and her associates as they had already made arrangements by mid-1654, based on a green light they had received from Propaganda Fide, to advance to the Holy See's bankers some of the funds for the planned dioceses.[11]

As the project stalled, the clergymen with the most at stake drew strength from Marie's unflagging commitment to it. Young Pallu told a confidant in late July 1654 that the duchess was not losing heart and was going to press officials in Rome.[12] She recruited De Paul to do the same. De Paul raised the issue of the apostolic vicariates in a letter to Propaganda Fide that concerned another mission with which Marie was increasingly involved behind the scenes—a Lazarist mission to Madagascar.[13]

Nevertheless, prospects for a French mission in Southeast Asia remained bleak for a time, even more so following the death of Innocent X and the election of Fabio Chigi as his successor in April 1655. Taking the name Alexander VII, the new pope was seen as hostile to France, just as his predecessor had been.[14]

Not giving up, Marie and her lay and clerical friends in Paris devised a new plan whereby Pallu would simply show up in Rome, making a pilgrimage there with Vincent de Meur, another impressive young priest of the Bons Amis group. The two would attempt to win over officials in the curia while expressing their hopes to serve Christ in the Far East and reiterating how much cash was already available from Marie and her associates for this purpose. In the meantime, Marie sent along additional letters to Rome, urging Alexander VII to take Pallu under his wing and establish French missionary dioceses that had been under discussion for years.[15]

Pallu was ensconced in Rome by mid-June 1657. He kept Marie and other contacts in France regularly informed about his activities, movements in his prayers, and hunches about where the negotiations for the apostolic vicariates were heading. Marie encouraged him to persevere through the setbacks he would inevitably face.[16]

Negotiations moved forward that summer as young Pallu did credit to his Parisian backers while in Rome. Officials at Propaganda Fide prodded Pallu to obtain Marie's confirmation of four things before the missionary dioceses would be formally approved by the Pope. These included her commitment to recommending candidates for all of the proposed apostolic vicariates, not just for Tonkin, and to providing reliable information about their morals and habits of life. The Vatican officials also wanted assurance from the duchess that she would guarantee financial support for the bishops and that security for this purpose would be deposited with the Holy See's bankers in Avignon. They also wanted Marie to obtain, through her international contacts, a promise of safe passage from Portugal for the French bishops.[17]

Marie confirmed to Rome her intentions on all four counts before the end of September.[18] Her word—rather than that of Queen Anne, Mazarin, or any high-ranking ecclesiastical official in France—was sufficient for the Vatican to take the unprecedented step of appointing Frenchmen to not one or two but *four* new missionary dioceses. These churchmen would have formal jurisdiction over vast American as well as Asian mission territories that had been claimed by the Iberian monarchs for almost two centuries.

The inclusion of New France among the new French missionary dioceses solved a problem that had been preoccupying Marie and members of the Compagnie du Saint-Sacrement for some years. When they had first begun envisioning French-sponsored missions in South and East Asia, plans had already been underway at the French court to turn New France into a suffragan diocese of one of the French archdioceses. This would have meant that a bishop chosen for the colonial territory would not have had independent jurisdiction there but would be answerable to a particular archbishop back home in France. This also would have meant, potentially, that Marie and her friends would have lost some of the ability to directly influence missionary affairs in North America as they had been doing for years.

Marie and the Compagnie du Saint-Sacrement gained some time when disagreements arose among the churchmen with the most at stake in the matter, including the superiors of the Jesuit missionaries who were laboring in the colony. Rival candidates were put forward for the prospective post, and the Archbishop of Paris and the Archbishop of Reims argued over who would be in charge of the chosen clergyman.

Well informed about all of this, Marie and her friends devised a way forward from this stalemate. The new bishop could be chosen from the Bons Amis group and also be appointed as an apostolic vicar formally answerable to Propaganda Fide, rather than to either of the squabbling archbishops. But just like the bishops proposed for Southeast Asia, the bishop for New France could operate de facto under the direct influence of Marie, her friends in Paris, and the Crown of France.

The young churchman chosen for the role was a future canonized saint, François-Xavier de Montmorency-Laval, who hailed from the French province of Perche. He was the scion of one of the oldest, most distinguished families of the kingdom. At the same time, he was the pious and intellectually brilliant fruit of both a Jesuit education and the spiritual influences of the circle around Bagot.

Montmorency-Laval was among the French churchmen to be appointed by Alexander VII as a bishop *in partibus infidelium*—specifically to the long-vacant see of Petraea in Arabia. This was in the summer of 1658, when he was made Apostolic Vicar of Québec. Like several of his compatriots who would soon venture off to the Far East, Montmorency-Laval was formally appointed in Rome but consecrated as a bishop in Paris, in the presence of his patroness Marie and her powerful friends. The Mass of Consecration took place at the ancient abbey church of Saint-Germain-des-Prés on December 8. The papal nuncio presided. Montmorency-Laval also took an oath of loyalty to the French monarch before sailing to Canada, which he reached in mid-June 1659.

Montmorency-Laval's appointment would be highlighted decades later by the preacher Jacques-Charles de Brisacier as one of Marie's major accomplishments:

> She advanced by her negotiations in the courts of France and Rome the sending of an . . . apostolic vicar [to Canada] who . . . had no more powerful support than that given by our duchess. This worthy prelate had the joy to see the secular and regular clergy of his diocese . . . holily united. But all those who agreeably enjoy those two fruits perhaps do not know that Madame d'Aiguillon was in

part the tree which bore them, by the role she played in this episcopal mission.[19]

Of Marie's persistence more generally in pushing forward the project of the
apostolic vicariates for Asia as well as North America, Brisacier was even more
laudatory: "She rose like an eagle above all obstacles."[20]

It was especially satisfying to Marie that Pope Alexander nominated young
Pallu for episcopal consecration in August 1658. Formally, Pallu was to be
consecrated as the new Bishop of Heliopolis, an ancient and long vacant see in
Islamic Egypt. But soon after his nomination, the Prefect of Propaganda Fide
named him Apostolic Vicar of Tonkin. His new diocese would include not only
Tonkin itself, but also Laos and several Chinese provinces: Hukuang (today's
Hunan and Hubei), Jiangxi, Guizhou, Sichuan, and Yunnan.

Another young priest favored by Marie and her associates, Pierre Lambert
de La Motte, was nominated by the Pope at the same time to become the
Bishop of Beirut, another defunct see in the Middle East. He was then named
Apostolic Vicar for Cochinchina and informed that his diocese would include
part of Vietnam and the Chinese provinces of Fujian, Guangxi, Guangdong,
Zhejiang, and Hainan.[21]

In his mid-thirties at the time, Lambert hailed from Lisieux in Normandy,
where his family were wealthy but not high-ranking members of the local
nobility. Educated by the Jesuits, he had also studied law and gained experience
in the Cours des Aides—dealing with taxation and public finance—before
training for the priesthood. He had the additional practical experience, after his
ordination, of serving as director of the Hôpital-Général de Rouen. He had been
appointed to this position by members of the Compagnie du Saint-Sacrament.
This brought him to Marie's attention in Paris. After she took an interest in his
future, Lambert communicated to her his desires to become a missionary.[22]

Eventually another Frenchman, Ignace Cotolendi, who had some Italian
ancestry, was named Bishop of Metellopolis, yet another ancient, vacant episcopal
see located in the heart of the Ottoman Empire. His missionary diocese as Apostolic Vicar of Nanjing would include not only that Chinese city but also Beijing
and the provinces of Shaanxi, Shanxi, and Shandong. In theory, they also would
include Korea as well as Manchuria and the rest of the vast areas of Central Asia
that Europeans called Tartary. Even younger than Pallu and Lambert, Cotolendi
came from a humble, bourgeois family in Brignoles, close to the Mediterranean

port city of Toulon. He had spent much of his youth in Aix-en-Provence, where he attended the Jesuit college in the city. He was serving as a parish priest in Aix at the time he was chosen for one of the new missionary dioceses.

Once formalities were underway in Rome to turn these young Frenchmen into missionary bishops, Alexander VII recognized Marie as the French leader most responsible for the project's success. The duchess received an extraordinary brief from the Pope in late 1658:

> Our dear daughter in Jesus Christ and noble lady, our greetings and apostolic blessings to you. Among the illustrious acts of charity to which Your Excellency, to the edification of the faithful, applies your whole heart, it may justly be believed that the most upright and preferable among them is the ardent and continual care you give to favoring and assisting apostolic missionaries—with all kinds of help, and with as much piety as generosity. These missionaries labor for the propagation of the faith among infidels in the most remote countries, in which their zeal exposes them to the gravity and heat of the day, and in which they suffer great inconveniences. . . . And certainly, what can you practice in this life that is more advantageous for the salvation of your soul, or even for acquiring public esteem, than to consecrate your cares and your riches to making the truth and the Christian faith known throughout the whole world, to associate with those who perform the functions of apostolic men, and to cooperate in some way in their labors? And because, as Christians we are obliged to seek the Kingdom of God in all things, and even to suffer in our reputation and expose ourselves to all kinds of disgraces and afflictions, it seems that they are more favorably treated who have received this particular grace from Heaven: to make themselves worthy of it even amid flourishing prosperity and a great increase in praise and esteem. This is why our most beloved daughter in Jesus Christ should continue to walk constantly in this same way, which will lead you so happily to your eternal salvation, and which will carry the brilliance of your name down through all the centuries.[23]

As this papal message was making its way to Paris, young Pallu "wrote amply to Madame d'Aiguillon about the happy state of [his] affairs" in Rome, as he told another friend in France.[24] Prior to this, Marie had set up a fund to pay Pallu, out of her own pocket, 600 livres annually to support his planned mission. She also arranged to have her nephew Emmanuel-Joseph support Bishop Lambert in the same way. Emmanuel-Joseph had inherited the clerical career and the Abbeys of Marmoutiers and Saint-Ouen renounced by Jean-Baptiste-Amador.[25] Tying up some of his inheritance in one of the missionary bishoprics effectively gave Marie controlling interest in all the planned missionary dioceses in Asia set aside by the Pope for "outstanding Frenchmen," as a Vatican official put it.[26] Marie secured additional funds for the bishops from friends and clients of her patronage.[27]

Upon his return from Rome to Paris, Bishop Pallu met privately with Marie and her associates to report on all he had seen and heard at the Vatican. During a gathering on April 17, 1659, he was fêted by members of the Compagnie du Saint-Sacrement, with whom he shared his aspirations for his planned mission along with news items he had picked up during his travels.[28]

Although Pallu had been consecrated as a bishop in Rome as a courtesy from his patrons in Paris, Lambert and Cotolendi, like Montmorency-Laval, were consecrated in their own country, as was traditional for Frenchmen elevated to the episcopate. Lambert's Mass of Consecration was celebrated by the papal nuncio on June 11, 1660, at Sainte-Marie de la Visitation, the beautiful, new domed church in the fashionable Marais district. Marie and other prominent French elites attended. For the occasion, Bishop Lambert donned vestments that Marie and some of her ladies had embroidered.[29]

Cotolendi was consecrated several months later with similar fanfare at the stunning Church of Saint-Louis on the Rue Saint-Antoine. This church was the Jesuits' Baroque masterpiece in the Marais district and featured on its façade—as can be seen today—the Bourbon coat of arms and a large statue of the sainted King Louis IX.[30] These prominent symbols of the Parisian Jesuits' ties to the Crown of France had been strongly approved years before by Cardinal Richelieu when the church was constructed and consecrated during his tenure as prime minister.

Due in no small measure to Marie's leadership, the royal ties to the new missionary dioceses in the Far East and in North America were more than symbolic. There was a tacit acknowledgment from Rome that the bishops would be answerable to the King of France and their patrons in Paris while formally being under the direction of Propaganda Fide. In reality, the Vatican still had few mechanisms in place to exert much control, and the success of the new apostolic vicariates would depend on investments and guidance from outside of Rome, as Marie had known full well while pressing her case for them with two popes. The bishops' ties to the French monarchy were soon reinforced with public funds. In addition to the incomes guaranteed by Marie, her nephew, and her friends, lifetime pensions of 1,000 livres a year were guaranteed to each apostolic vicar by the Crown. This amount would increase to 3,000 each per year by 1674.[31]

Despite the excitement in Paris surrounding the consecration of the four French apostolic vicars, none but Montmorency-Laval in Canada was able to commence his missionary labors immediately. This was due first to the unwillingness of the Portuguese to guarantee safe passage to the Far East through regions they controlled.[32]

Furthermore, the new bishops were not, in the end, welcomed aboard Dutch or English ships departing French ports out of concern—justified, it would turn out—that the clergymen would use their influence in Asia to cultivate competing trading relationships for the French.[33] Marie and her fellow investors in the new dioceses appear to have overestimated the goodwill of these Protestant powers, especially when it came to welcoming their maverick Catholic ally in Europe to the Far East as a commercial competitor.

It was thus decided that the new bishops and additional missionaries should travel to Southeast Asia by way of the Mediterranean and overland through Persia and India. Lambert and the priests Jacques de Bourges and François Deydier would depart France in the autumn of 1660. Marie's protégé Pallu, Cotolendi, four other priests, and a layman working with them would follow later.[34] Marie would await with interest the letters that Pallu, especially, would send along the way to keep her informed about their progress and the challenges they encountered.

49

Saint Vincent

As the new overseas missions were being planned, Marie suffered a sad but expected loss. Early in the morning on September 27, 1660, Father De Paul died while sitting in a chair, preparing to offer his daily prayers with other members of his priestly community at Saint-Lazare. He was seventy-nine.

Although the canonization process would take some time, De Paul was destined to become one of the most well-known and beloved French Catholic saints in history. Given the nickname *Apostle of Charity*, he would be venerated as a humble priest of peasant origins who had inspired generations of clergymen and laypeople to live with more fidelity to God and the Church, especially by means of moral and spiritual self-discipline and intensive service to the poor, the sick, and the socially marginalized. Catholic pilgrims today still visit his tomb in Paris, at the Chapelle Saint-Vincent-de-Paul on the Rue de Sèvres, where his bones are encased in a wax figure of his body that is displayed above the altar. They venerate his heart, too, which is enclosed in a reliquary safeguarded by the Daughters of Charity at their motherhouse on the Rue du Bac. De Paul would come to be honored as a saint within the Anglican Communion, not just among Catholics, and in the nineteenth century would inspire a French layman, Frédéric Ozanam, to create the Société de Saint-Vincent-de-Paul, a voluntary organization of laypeople serving the poor that is active today in some 140 countries.

Without the role Marie played in De Paul's life, first as his major patroness for over thirty years and then in promoting his legacy after his death, he would not be known as the beloved, sainted peasant-priest in the way that he is in modern times. It had been Marie, even more than his mentor Pierre de Bérulle, who had drawn De Paul into the power centers of France and enabled him to

build up the Lazarists as a congregation and other projects with the assistance
of her uncle, bishops of the Church, and other lay elites like herself.[1] Marie,
too, did a great deal upon De Paul's death, such as gifting the original reliquary
that encased his heart, to promote the cult of sainthood that emerged around
his corpse and memory.

In addition to leading the Ladies of Charity for many years and working
regularly with De Paul on their projects and on others of the Daughters of
Charity, Marie had also been a driving force behind the Lazarists' expansion in Paris as well as in Poitou, the Loire Valley, and Marseilles.[2] This had
been early on in the Lazarists' institutional buildup, during the period when
De Paul was still discerning the scope and scale of the priestly congregation
he had founded. More than any other patron, Marie was behind the Lazarists'
expansion into Rome and North Africa and was involved, too, in the congregation's first missions in the British Isles and, eventually, Madagascar.[3] In short,
the duchess had opened wide for De Paul and the Lazarists not only national
and European stages for their ministries, but also a global stage beyond the
priest's initial imaginings.

Marie's establishment of the Lazarists in Rome proved especially beneficial to
the congregation's longevity in the Church. The year before De Paul died, Pope
Alexander VII ordered that all young clergymen in Rome do ten-day retreats
at the Lazarists' house in Rome prior to their ordinations to the priesthood.
Whether these young men were from obscure origins or close relatives of the
Pope himself, they were all to go through the same program the Lazarists had
developed in Rome at both De Paul and Marie's behest. They were led in spiritual exercises, meditations, and lectures by French priests. Some cardinals and
bishops sat in on the lectures, and at times the understanding of the Catholic
priesthood expressed in them was so elevated that it caused some young men to
question their calling to ordained ministry in new ways.[4] This was something
Marie approved, as she believed the reform of the Catholic clergy across Europe
depended upon weeding out men who pursued clerical careers for primarily
worldly reasons, rarely reflecting with maturity on their motives, or simply
because they were pushed into it by their families.

To help the Lazarists' further growth in Rome, Marie provided resources
in 1659 for them to expand into a larger area near the artist Bernini's new and
unfinished palazzo, today's Palazzo Montecitorio where the Italian Chamber of
Deputies meets. This was where the Lazarists' new church, Santissima Trinità

della Missione, already stood and where a street, Via della Missione, would be named for the congregation.

Marie was behind some of De Paul's influence on the life of the Church more broadly in France, not simply as the superior general of the Lazarists. She had been responsible for De Paul's elevation as Vicar General of several Benedictine abbeys—those of Marmoutiers in Tours and Saint-Ouen in Rouen. She had also entrusted him with the priory of Saint-Martin-des-Champs in Paris. This had occurred in the wake of Cardinal Richelieu's death, when Marie's nephew Jean-Baptiste became the commendatory abbot of all of these institutions. Some years later, when Jean-Baptiste passed on these ecclesiastical benefices to his brother Emmanuel-Joseph, De Paul at Marie's behest was reconfirmed as Vicar General.

To modern ears, the title of Vicar General or Prior of such institutions does not sound like it would have involved a great deal of power over others. In pre-Revolutionary France, however, taking over an abbey such as Saint-Ouen was similar to being given, simultaneously, a diocese in the Church and lordship over a territory and its population. Many abbeys in the Ancien Régime came with extensive lands and tenantries as well as a range of ecclesiastical dependencies, including various local churches whose pastors answered to the abbot (or his vicar) in the way that parish pastors answered to bishops and cathedral chapters. The vicar generalship of Saint-Ouen alone put De Paul in command of about eighty parish churches and other chapels, that of Martin-des-Champs about fifty, and Marmoutiers another thirty. De Paul was thus charged by Marie not only with supervising the monks who dwelt in the abbeys themselves, but also with overseeing ecclesiastical affairs on a large scale. He also selected candidates for subordinate positions within the abbeys and far beyond them in a range of other institutions.[5]

These appointees were typically men whom Marie favored and who already were, or by their appointments became, clients in her patronage network. De Paul consulted with Marie, and waited for her approval, before making major decisions regarding these benefices. This was true even after he had been elevated—also partly due to Marie's influence—to the royal Council of Conscience and was advising Queen Anne of Austria, during her regency, on a range of matters.[6]

As in the case of the Hôpital-Général de Paris, Marie and De Paul did not always see eye to eye on things and sometimes engaged in battles of will with each other. The Lazarist missions in North Africa were regularly a cause of disagreement between Marie and De Paul. This was partly because Marie wanted the Lazarist consuls she supported to be as energetically engaged with their secular functions as with their missionary ones. The consuls in Tunis and Algiers were charged with protecting not only French subjects who traveled in the region, but also Jews, Greeks, Armenians, and others without consuls of their own in either city. The French consuls were supposed to safeguard their rights and interests, facilitate their business activities in the region, and ensure that they adhered to treaties with local governors and the Ottoman imperial state in Istanbul. The consuls were also authorized to collect taxes on products carried into the port cities by French merchants and other merchants under their protection. Furthermore, none of these merchants could enter or depart Tunis or Algiers without the consuls' permission. Consuls also occasionally served as judges in cases involving French nationals in the region.[7]

Given how much attention the consuls had to pay to such matters, it is unsurprising that, over time, the generally apolitical De Paul wished to free his men from responsibility for the consulates in Tunis and Algiers. In 1655, he complained that his priests in North Africa, under Marie's influence, were preoccupied more than he believed they should be with "temporal affairs . . . far removed from their [normal priestly] functions."[8] The Lazarist consuls were involved with the transport of cotton and even contraband goods into North Africa at the time.[9] De Paul attempted to convince Marie to release the Lazarists from commercial, diplomatic, and other worldly responsibilities. But she refused. The priest accepted the duchess's position, which he articulated to another Lazarist in 1657: "She thinks that our priests would have no certainty of being able to assist the poor slaves if they were living under [lay rather than Lazarist] consuls who had private interests to look after, who would be governed by other principles than those of charity and the public good."[10]

The Lazarists faced difficulties stemming from this entanglement with the consulates that caused De Paul anguish in his final years. For example, in 1657, the Lazarist consul at Algiers, Jean Barreau, was beaten with canes by soldiers working for Ibrahim II, the local Ottoman pasha, after he refused to pay the debts of a French merchant who had gone bankrupt. One of the pasha's men then drove sharply pointed awls beneath the consul's fingernails. Even after the consul scrounged up enough cash to satisfy the pasha's men, he endured similar maltreatment and was thrown into prison the following year. De Paul urged Marie to at least replace Barreau with a Lazarist more up to the difficulties of the post.[11] His replacement, Jean Le Vacher, did prove more effective in the dual role of missionary and consul in Tunis, and he would later be appointed to the consulate at Algiers. Both Marie and De Paul were long dead when, in 1683, Le Vacher would be killed by being strapped to an Ottoman cannon that was loaded up with shrapnel and then fired at the French fleet during the French-Algerian War of that era.

Over the years, the duchess and the future canonized saint butted heads over more personal matters. For instance, De Paul on several occasions refused Marie's requests to have him sit for a formal portrait, reportedly because he did not wish to be represented in any way that seemed affected. The only portraits done of him during his lifetime had to be done in secret, by an artist who, with the help of other Lazarists who were in on the conspiracy, observed him in different settings and then sketched and painted from memory until he achieved a satisfying likeness.[12]

Marie had begun to take an interest in De Paul's physical well-being early on during their decades of collaboration, as he was already in his fifties and declining in his health when they first began to work together in the 1630s. By the 1640s, he suffered painful swelling in his legs which made it difficult for him to move around. Travel was essential to his handling properly the many responsibilities he shouldered—many of them ones Marie urged him to take on. So the duchess wished to facilitate it by gifting him a modest carriage and a team of horses that he could use any time, both within Paris and throughout France.

De Paul found it a bit challenging to get up and down from the carriage and preferred to stay in Paris whenever he could—something Marie believed was inconducive to the priest's effective leadership over all the institutions and personnel under his care. De Paul also seems to have suffered some sort of self-consciousness about having a better-than-average carriage and well-bred horses at his disposal, as if he were a gentleman rather than a peasant. He stubbornly refused to use the rig for a long time and, when travel was unavoidable, would choose instead to walk, ride on horseback, or use the coach services that other commoners used. Marie put her foot down, however, in mid-1649 when she learned that De Paul was sick in the town of Richelieu, where he was conducting some administrative business for the Lazarists. After De Paul had refused to use the carriage to get there, Marie sent on a driver with it after him to Richelieu—a journey of almost two hundred miles from Paris—to bring him home both comfortably and speedily. De Paul returned the carriage to Marie once he got to Paris and insisted that he wished to stop traveling altogether.[13]

The two squabbled over the carriage and horses for several more years until finally Marie had the Queen Mother and the Archbishop of Paris order De Paul to make use of it even for short journeys. This was in the mid-1650s, when De Paul was around seventy-five years old. Cornered in this way, De Paul complied but also began to refer to the rig as his "shame," characterizing it as something too grand for a peasant like himself, even though the carriage was quite small and lacking in stylish adornments. The real problem, however, was that it enabled him to travel more often and farther than he wished to. To express his annoyance, the future canonized saint sometimes treated the horses like common pack animals, hitching them to carts and even ploughs in villages he visited.[14]

Serious as some of Marie's disagreements with De Paul were, respect and love for the priest were at the heart of them. Even in the period when she was at odds with De Paul over the Hôpital-Général, Marie was anxious about De Paul in the way a daughter might be for her elderly father. De Paul was in his seventies by this point, and Marie, solicitous for his health, reprimanded other Lazarists for allowing their superior to exert himself as if he were a younger man. "I cannot help being astonished," she wrote to Father Portail at a time when the Paris region was suffering unseasonably high temperatures, "that . . . good priests of St. Lazare should allow M. Vincent to go and work in country places in this heat, considering his age and the long hours he will have to spend out of doors." De Paul's life was "too precious," she insisted, and "too valuable to the Church for him to squander it in this way."[15]

De Paul's health seriously began to falter in 1658, when he suffered from ulcers, eye pain, fevers, and increased pain in his legs. At that point, Marie and several other friends convinced him to agree to a diet that included a lot of broth and poultry, even though he found himself periodically not wishing to eat anything.[16] Eventually Marie failed to have De Paul transferred to her home in Paris during his final months, when she was urgently concerned that he would be much better nursed there than he was being at Saint-Lazare.[17]

When De Paul died in late September 1660, Marie lost yet another father figure. At the same time, she lost one of her most faithful and diligent collaborators of many years and one of the few prominent champions of the independence and public leadership she asserted as a woman in their highly patriarchal culture. De Paul had once encouraged the Ladies of Charity, when some among them were demurring from public duties on behalf of the poor, by telling them that God throughout history "used persons of your sex to do the greatest things ever done in this world." The founder of the Lazarists and cofounder of the Daughters of Charity urged women—as Marie also did, with his encouragement—to see themselves as part of a great line of brave, faithful, and daring female servants of God above man, a line that included the biblical Judith and Esther, the medieval savior of Paris, Saint Geneviève, and the then-uncanonized Maid of Orléans, Jeanne d'Arc.[18]

It would have been with gratitude and love for De Paul, as well as sorrow over his death, that Marie sat in a prominent place at his funeral on the day after he died. On September 28, 1660, she had a seat of honor at the church of Saint-Lazare, next to the Prince de Conti (the same who had rebelled against the Crown during the Fronde), the papal nuncio to France, and six French bishops and abbots. The church was filled to capacity that day. After the funeral Mass, De Paul's body was placed in a stone vault in the church's choir. Before the ceremonies had begun, however, De Paul's heart, intestines, and liver had been removed from the corpse to be preserved separately. (This was not unusual in Catholic cultures then when the deceased was deemed to be an important, holy figure; it was customary, too, in the cases of some deceased members of royal families.) The priest's heart would be encased in its own silver reliquary that Marie commissioned. She personally determined the reliquary's size and decorative elements. It was shaped like a heart with flames rising from it, and it stood on four small feet, also of silver, and was over a foot tall.[19]

Doing this for De Paul's heart was Marie's signal to Catholics far and wide that she believed De Paul should be venerated as a saint whose soul had gone straight to Heaven when he died. Marie took a leading role in promoting his cult and his cause for formal canonization by the Church—something she would not live to see, however, as it would not happen in Rome until 1737, sixty-two years after her own death.

Within four years of De Paul's death, Marie and others promoting the priest's cult welcomed the publication of the first book on his life. Published by Florentin Lambert in Paris in 1664, *La Vie du Vénérable Serviteur de Dieu Vincent de Paul* was authored by Louis Abelly, the newly appointed Bishop of Rodez and a longtime friend of the Lazarists. It was dedicated to Queen Anne of Austria, who was in her mid-sixties by this point and not far from death herself. A second edition, testifying to its popularity, appeared four years later. More than a thousand pages long, it referred to De Paul as a "holy man" and was intended to make him and all he had done more well known to the public as well as to lay ground for his canonization.[20]

Abelly credited Marie in his biography for her major role in the development of Lazarist ministries and other projects upon which she and De Paul worked. He included Marie's contributions to the Lazarists' work among galley prisoners in Marseilles and in war-torn regions throughout France, her being the power and the money behind the congregation's work in Rome and its hospital in Algiers and other ministries in North Africa, and her leadership of the Ladies of Charity.[21] Unlike modern biographers who would relegate Marie to the backdrop of a story in which De Paul was always the active protagonist, Abelly portrayed Marie as a woman with whom the peasant-priest collaborated and to whom he deferred on a number of occasions. Just as Marie "had extraordinary feelings of esteem and confidence in Monsieur Vincent," Abelly wrote, "Monsieur Vincent had reciprocally for her a respect, a deference, and a very particular recognition."[22] Contemporaries who were familiar with both the priest and the duchess understood that, should De Paul go on to be canonized and revered by the Church as a great patron saint of charity toward the poor, the Duchesse d'Aiguillon should be remembered with him as the great patroness of that saint who had shaped his life and legacy.

50

Missions for France

W hen she was an infant in rural Poitou, the future Duchesse d'Aiguillon had been christened with the name *Marie-Madeleine* after a saint best known in the Christian tradition for having left behind a life of sin after befriending Jesus of Nazareth. But this saint had also by Marie's time been honored in the Catholic Church for her unique role as *Apostolorum Apostola*—the apostle to Christ's leading male apostles who had run away scared at the time of the Lord's passion, death, and resurrection. The first to see the risen Christ on the first Easter morning, Mary Magdalene, not Peter "the rock" nor even the beloved apostle John, testified to the Twelve about the greatest miracle of all time and spurred them on to greater faith and courage in announcing the Gospel among people who did not always warm to it.

From the time she began collaborating with the Jesuits of New France and Vincent de Paul in the 1630s up until the final years of her life, Marie engaged in a most unusual amount of activity on behalf of the missionary expansion of the Church. Over time the portfolio of mission projects she helped to launch and sustain included not only the Canadian, rural French, and North African ministries she had supported since her younger years, but also the early activities of French missionary bishops and affiliated priests and laypeople in South and East Asia, a Lazarist mission to Madagascar, and a range of other Catholic efforts in the Middle East, the Americas, and parts of Europe including the British Isles and Poland. By the end of her life, Cardinal Richelieu's unlikely protégée had, with her power, privileges, and sheer determination, apostolically spurred on the first generation of French Catholic missionaries to fan out across the globe—to places as far afield as Québec, Tunis, and Ayutthaya.

Marie's commitment to the growth of the Church became legendary among clergymen during her lifetime. One Parisian preacher described the duchess's apostolic zeal as so great that it could not be confined to France or even to all of Christendom. "One world was not enough for her," Father Jacques-Charles de Brisacier proclaimed from a pulpit. So it became "necessary that she join the Christian world" to a whole new world beyond it. Brisacier then went on to liken the duchess to Saint Mary Magdalene, the "Apostle of Apostles," because she had acted as "the mother and the support of all those who . . . devoted themselves to oriental missions."[1]

Yet, in some ways, Marie's efforts in expanding the French church into many lands at once had no clear parallel in ecclesiastical history. Unlike Mary Magdalene, who had been called very personally by Jesus of Nazareth to join Him in gathering up adopted sons and daughters of God, Marie gathered up many churchmen, religious, and other laypeople for apostolic labors while receiving little apparent inspiration from any one priest or spiritual guide to devote herself to it. Furthermore, although she was uniquely positioned as Cardinal Richelieu's niece and heiress and as a duchess-peeress of France, she did not have the royal powers of an Isabella of Castile or an Elizabeth of England to authorize overseas ventures or order apostolic churchmen toward particular lines of work. What she was able to achieve, rather, through persuasion, diplomatic maneuvering, the leveraging of patronage powers, and targeted donations and investments makes the diversified character and global scope of her achievements all the more impressive.

To be sure, other European noblewomen of the early modern era made marks in support of overseas missions. These included Antoinette de Pons-Ribérac, the Marquise de Guercheville, who had helped to launch the first Catholic missions to Canada, and María de Guadalupe de Lencastre, the Duchess of Aveiro in Portugal, who was beloved by the Jesuits. These women tended, however, to devote resources either to one major geographical context or to one religious order they favored for conducting missions.

Marie's achievements in spurring on and aiding apostolic labors throughout the world appear, on the whole, less like those of a mother figure and more like those of a pioneering, prudent executive of a growing empire of enterprises. The duchess over the years marshaled whatever human resources, capital, and political supports that were at her disposal to bring them into being and to sustain them.

Churchmen who knew Marie appear to have grasped something of this while praising her in the rhetorical terms available to them at the time. Pierre Oudin, an Augustinian canon who recognized how significant it was that the duchess enabled women of his order to serve as hospital nuns overseas, dedicated to her his book, *Zeal for the Salvation of Souls*, which was a manual for pastors and missionaries. He said to Marie, "You imitate . . . the great Cardinal-Duc de Richelieu, your uncle, whose vast and untiring spirit . . . not content to give itself wholly to urgent necessities of the State, also acted very profitably throughout Europe and other parts of the world."[2] William Lesley, an expatriated Scottish priest who advocated in Rome for the new French missionary bishops sent to the Far East, urged other clergymen to appreciate not only the zeal Marie devoted to extending the Christian faith to many nations, but also the wise and practical measures she devised to support missionaries and their work over the long term.[3] Even Pope Alexander VII acknowledged Marie's growing and international reputation for "the ardent and continual care" she devoted "to favoring and assisting apostolic missionaries."[4] And Brisacier likened the duchess not only to Saint Mary Magdalene but also, more daringly still, to busy prelates of the Church and even to the Apostle Paul.[5]

However, none of these churchmen acknowledged a key difference between their beloved duchess and other figures in the Church's history whom they praised. Marie was motivated in her sponsorship of missions not just by her devotion to the Catholic faith but also by her French patriotism. Marie directed resources to missions that were not only to be responsive to indigenous cultures and synchronized with her vision of reformed Catholicism but also favorable, at every turn, to French interests, including commercial and social-charitable ones. This had been the case from the earliest years of her involvements with New France, where she was in communication with military men as well as missionaries in the colony. In 1642, for example, she had secured funding from her uncle for the buildup of French fortifications needed to protect a valuable French-Huron trading partnership from increasingly aggressive Iroquois efforts to disrupt that alliance.[6]

Marie's simultaneously secular, French-national and spiritual, universally Catholic preoccupations were continually a source of frustration for Vincent de Paul especially in the context of the Lazarist missions in North Africa. In the years after De Paul's death, it was something that raised eyebrows in Rome, too. In 1663, Propaganda Fide began to scrutinize the Lazarist consul at Tunis, Jean

Le Vacher, after some clergymen in the region complained about his preoccupa-
tion with trade.[7] This was at a time when the French were attempting aggressive
expansion into North Africa for the first time. An invasion of Algiers was on the
table among French officials by 1661 and was launched in July 1664 after
the French had broken with the Ottoman Empire in order to protect Hungary
from absorption into it. It was only a momentary success, as the French captured
the port city of Jijel but were unable to keep it after an outbreak of plague and
a lack of reinforcements prevented them from turning it into a base for further
operations. Marie had supported such an invasion as early as 1658. De Paul had
favored it, too, but he had wished for a clearer separation in function and identity
between French clergymen serving in North Africa and the French who were
there on political, commercial, and military business.[8]

Commitment both to the spread of the Catholic faith and to French commercial and political success internationally also motivated Marie in developing the
projects and organizational infrastructure of the Société des Missions Étrangères
de Paris. This was an association of Catholic laypeople and secular clergymen
who came to be known for short by the acronym MEP.

Among the three MEP-affiliated French missionary bishops intended for
Asian posts whose appointments Marie had helped to secure from Alexander VII,
Pierre Lambert de La Motte was the first to depart France, in November 1660,
along with two other MEP priests, Jacques de Bourges and François Deydier.
They arrived in Alexandretta in Turkey a month and a half later. They then traveled through Aleppo, Baghdad, Surat, and eventually around the Bay of Bengal,
arriving at Mergui in Siam on April 28, 1662. Although they had intended to
travel onward to the Mekong Delta, the band of missionaries decided to stay in
Siam and commenced their apostolic labors there due partly to unrest among
the rival ruling families of southern Vietnam and Cambodia. But another
reason was because the Kingdom of Ayutthaya in Siam proved to be hospitable
to French merchants as well as missionaries. It was partly for this reason that
Bishop François Pallu, four other priests, and an MEP-affiliated layman joined
Lambert and his band there by late January 1664.

The MEP clergymen in Siam had to engage in diplomacy with local Portuguese merchants and both Jesuit and Dominican missionaries, most of whom
were of Iberian origin. Portuguese merchants and their often half-Siamese
offspring had enjoyed trading privileges in the region since the early sixteenth
century, and the Portuguese Dominicans and Jesuits had been active there, too,

since 1567 and 1607, respectively.[9] Fortunately for the French missionaries, the local Portuguese merchants and Dominicans, if not the Jesuit missionaries in the region, were generally accommodating in the mid-1660s, partly because the Portuguese priests in the region were stretched thin in ministering to the growing local Catholic population. The French were thus able to gain a solid commercial as well as ecclesiastical foothold in Siam.

Marie's communications with the MEP missionaries over the years referred often to French commerce as well as spiritual and ecclesiastical matters.[10] Such matters were not of secondary importance to the duchess. In 1660, at the same time that the MEP missions were being planned, Marie was the first member of the French nobility to invest in a new merchant company, the Compagnie de Chine, devoted to trade in and around China. She put forward 3,000 livres at the time and was one of only three women among the original thirty-eight shareholders in the company. (The other two were Elisabeth Dournel de Jolly, the widow of a royal councillor, and Suzanne de Bruc de Plessis-Bellière, a widowed marquise.)[11] Many of the other investors were members of the Compagnie du Saint-Sacrement. This merchant company would, by 1664, merge with the larger Compagnie des Indes Orientales that was established by the French prime minister Jean-Baptiste Colbert and funded quite handsomely by the Crown, several princes of the blood, and the leading nobles of France.[12]

It is not surprising, then, that when eventually several MEP missionaries made it as far as Tonkin in Vietnam, they described their purposes as commercial to the local authorities and announced their hope to establish a French trading company in the country. They did not even dress in clerical garb but rather in the fashion of French merchants. The King of Annam provided them with a home close to his palace with the understanding that they would facilitate trade between his people and the Europeans.[13]

While such developments were occurring overseas, Marie was helping to staff the new missions with talented, faithful clergymen well trained for apostolic work abroad and loyal both to the reformed, post-Tridentine Catholic Church and to the Crown of France. Specifically, she helped to establish a new seminary in Paris that was devoted to the formation of priests for overseas mission work, the Séminaire des Missions Étrangères de Paris. Still active today, this MEP seminary is most famously associated with nineteenth-century missions in Vietnam and Korea that were aligned with the imperial activity of the French Third Republic. First recognized by Louis XIV in 1663 and by the Holy See a year later, it was and remains a project of the dually lay and clerically led MEP society.

The MEP society and its seminary announced to the world by their names that they were French and specifically Parisian. The seminary itself was housed in a complex of buildings along the Rue du Bac and what became known as the Rue de Babylone, an area that was about ten minutes by foot from Marie's home.[14] Due to enterprising developers such as Louis Le Barbier, this district that had for a long time been dominated by monastic communities was by the mid-seventeenth century becoming a fashionable area into which moneyed nobles and prominent bourgeois alike were relocating.[15] The seminary over time would benefit from this strategic proximity to pious and generous French Catholic elites in the Faubourg Saint-Germain.

Already by 1658 Marie had had young Pallu, before he was nominated as a bishop, advocate in Rome for an innovative French seminary that would be based on the Rue du Bac.[16] By this point, a number of French clergymen were committed to the seminary project, some of them affiliates of the Bons Amis group and all of them approved by Marie and high-ranking members of the Compagnie du Saint-Sacrement who gathered regularly in the duchess's *salon* at the Petit Luxembourg. Among these clergymen was Vincent de Meur, a priest of strong anti-Jansenist leanings who had actually renounced a position as a royal chaplain in order to spend time with the Bons Amis group and to obtain his doctorate in theology at the Sorbonne. There was also Michel Gazil of the Diocese of Évreau, who also held a doctorate in theology and was especially vigilant about Catholic doctrinal orthodoxy.[17]

Many other clergymen helped with the MEP seminary's establishment. Marie took a lead, however, by galvanizing others' commitment to the project. She organized and moderated early planning meetings and fundraising efforts. The preacher Brisacier, who eventually served as the seminary's superior, even credited her with the institution's founding vision. "We must send an apostolic army to the East," he claimed she said to a group of churchmen and laymen sometime in the late 1650s. "If we were to establish a house in Paris in which missionaries might be formed, and where pious people can direct their alms so that they can then travel to foreign lands, then I would die contented," she also reportedly declared. Marie furthermore leveraged her rank and influence at court to obtain not only Louis XIV's approval of the seminary in early 1663 but also the Parlement de Paris's swift registration of its *lettres patentes* in July.[18]

These developments constituted the seminary's official birth under French law.[19] It would not be for another year that Alexander VII's nephew Flavio Chigi, in his capacity as papal legate, would formally confirm the seminary's existence in the eyes of the Holy See. He did so faster than expected, however, in August 1664. This was no accident. His approval followed a state visit to France in which Marie hosted him and a very large party of guests at Rueil. The duchess impressed Chigi to no end as a hostess while talking favorably to him of the seminary project.[20]

Even before Chigi's visit, the clergymen involved in the MEP project were celebrating its success. The expatriated Scotsman Lesley rejoiced over Marie's effective leadership, in particular: "I praise Madame d'Aiguillon's . . . conduct. . . . She has very wisely weighed the matter of establishing solid and durable means of sustaining ministers who propagate the faith. [N]othing may contribute so much to this purpose as a great seminary that will serve as a kind of nursery for raising up missionaries."[21]

Indeed, Marie and her associates had determined long before obtaining a Vatican stamp of approval which priests, including De Meur and Gazil, would hold leadership positions in the seminary. So, by the middle of the decade, the institution was already training young clergymen who would labor overseas under the direction of Pallu and the other new French apostolic vicars.[22]

Marie's financial contributions to the seminary included an initial donation of 300 livres in June 1663.[23] By 1664, her annual contribution of 600 livres to Bishop Pallu was legally contracted to be dispensed through Gazil's hands at the seminary. In 1667, she offered another lump sum to the seminary's directors.[24] She assisted the seminary's development far beyond this, too, by convincing various women and men of her acquaintance to donate money as well as material supports, such as books for the library, sacred artwork for the chapel, and furniture and other necessities for the classrooms and dormitories.

The MEP seminary in the French capital was only the first of several seminaries Marie and the Société des Missions Étrangères de Paris got off the ground in this period. At the same time that the primary MEP seminary was formally recognized by Louis XIV, royal *lettres patentes* were also registered in Paris for a new seminary in colonial Québec that would be directed by Bishop Montmorency-Laval.[25] This first seminary in Québec would be directed by the MEP society, and the society was also authorized by the colonial bishop to establish missions throughout the extent of New France.

Furthermore, MEP clergymen established a seminary on the other side of the world, in the Siamese Kingdom of Ayutthaya. King Narai offered the French priests a plot of land for this purpose in 1665 in Ba Plah Het, the Cochinchinese quarter of Ayutthaya. Dedicated to Saint Joseph, the seminary was constructed over the next two years. Ten indigenous Siamese students enrolled, and over time more students came from elsewhere in the region, including Vietnam. Within a few years, several Tonkinese men were ordained as priests. Other men from indigenous populations were welcomed into minor orders and served the MEP mission as catechists. By 1669, the French had established a hospital next door to the seminary and its church building.[26]

However, while all of this was beginning to unfold, the Portuguese Archbishop of Goa in India got wind of the MEP missionaries' activities, which included dispensing the sacrament of confirmation to Siamese Christian neophytes. He condemned Bishop Pallu, in particular, in a formal rite of excommunication at the cathedral at Goa, claiming that the Frenchman was trespassing on his ecclesiastical jurisdiction, which he believed stretched across all of the East.[27]

Marie stepped in on behalf of her protégé Pallu in this dispute. In late 1664, she pressed Cardinal Chigi on the matter, knowing that he would take an interest in her concerns given the exceptional visit he had recently enjoyed at her château west of Paris. By January 1665 she was assured that Chigi would seek a judgment from Rome that would clarify new limits on the Archbishop of Goa's authority.[28]

This clarification was not obtained until the next pontificate, however. Clement IX, elected in June of 1667, was exceptionally friendly to the French for a pope. In 1669, he decreed that the French apostolic vicars should exercise the functions of episcopal office in those parts of the world that were not otherwise acknowledged by the Pope as falling under the purview of the Iberian monarchs.[29] This was after Pallu had returned to France and worked with the directors of the Société des Missions Étrangères de Paris to publish a *Relation* he had authored. Shared with officials in Rome, this *Relation* portrayed the French church as exceptionally vital, reformed, and prepared to set good examples to the rest of the world in mission settings. It also made the case to the Holy See for the French missionary bishops to enjoy complete and independent jurisdiction in Siam and other places formerly seen as part of the Archbishop of Goa's extensive ecclesiastical territory.[30]

The Archbishop of Goa refused to accept this papal decision for four years. Nevertheless, Pallu was armed with the Pope's decree when he returned to

Siam after an extended period away from his mission. But this only exacerbated what were now very tense relations with the Jesuits in the region—including two Frenchmen, Fathers Pierre Albier and Joseph Tissanier, who voluntarily transferred from the French Assistancy of the Society of Jesus to the Portuguese Assistancy. Tissanier was especially hostile to Pallu, claiming in 1669 that he intended to "exterminate" the Jesuits in the region and that he showed signs of being a heretic.[31]

Pallu's difficulties with the Jesuits had less to do with the earlier jurisdictional dispute than it did with the growing commercial rivalry between the French and the Portuguese in Southeast Asia. The MEP missionaries were tied to French merchants in the region and unapologetically undermined Portuguese commerce even while promoting the Catholic faith. This was part of the simultaneously religious and secular vision for French Catholic influence in Southeast Asia that had motivated Marie and her friends in Paris to press for missions in the region in the first place. However, additional strain was caused by Pallu's efforts from 1673 onward to get all Jesuits in the region to submit to either his own or Lambert's episcopal authority.[32]

The MEP missionaries whom Marie and her friends funded became a thorn in the side of Spanish authorities in the region, too, who did not acknowledge Pallu's episcopal jurisdiction and resented the commercial inroads the French were making. In 1674, when Pallu had to make an unplanned stop in the Philippines while en route to Tonkin, he was arrested in Manila and then sent in chains to Mexico and onward to Spain to be put on trial.[33] He was held in Madrid until both the Pope and Louis XIV intervened and secured his release.[34] In the meantime, the other MEP missionaries in eastern and southern Asia remained under scrutiny by Iberian authorities and clergymen in the region. The Portuguese Jesuits accused them not only of dressing as merchants but also of keeping a veritable warehouse, and directly selling commodities into local markets, including ivory, porcelain, and pepper.[35]

Not coincidentally, Marie set up a trust in this period for the MEP seminary in Paris and for Bishop Pallu and his successors with the strict condition that, should Rome ever appoint a man who was not French as the Bishop of Tonkin, all income payments would cease.[36] This was done in concert with King Louis XIV, who agreed at this same time to supplement all the MEP-affiliated missionary bishops' incomes with an additional 1,000 livres on top of the 2,000 that the Crown had already been giving annually in the preceding years.[37]

Marie would go on to support the MEP seminaries and missions until her last days. In her will she would provide 3,000 livres to the Parisian seminary's directors, to be used at their discretion, and an extra 8,000 for Pallu and Lambert's missions.[38] All of these supports were intended to ensure both that the MEP clergymen carried the Gospel and the Church's sacraments to more people across Asia and that the MEP projects remained bound up with French commercial and diplomatic interests.

51

Madagascar

As Marie and the other French backers of the MEP missionary dioceses understood it, the ecclesiastical jurisdiction that Rome had granted to Bishop Pallu stretched far across the Indian Ocean to places in its southern reaches where the French had also become active as merchants. These included the large island of Madagascar off the southeastern coast of Africa. In modern times, Madagascar would become part of the French Third Republic's large global empire. At the time of the French invasion in 1894, apologists for French imperialism would cite precedents of French activity on the island that went back to the era of Marie's entrepreneurial activity for the French church.

French involvement in Madagascar commenced during the reign of Louis XIII. Cardinal Richelieu formed a merchant company for the region, the Compagnie de l'Orient, whose investors quickly identified Madagascar as the potential heart of a new French trading empire in that part of the world. By 1643 the company men had established a French settlement called Fort Dauphin on the southeastern coast of the island where today's city of Tôlanaro is located.

Catholic priests accompanied the first French merchants in Madagascar. But Marie's support of missionary activity there was tentative at first. She was involved in early discussions with investors in the merchant company and with Vincent de Paul about a Lazarist mission to the island that was launched in 1646. However, there is no record of her funding the Lazarist mission to the island at the time of its establishment. This had to do in part with the scrutiny her finances came under once the Fronde had broken open. She also may have been concerned about offending her favorite religious order, the Discalced Carmelites, who at the time held exclusive missionary faculties for Madagascar from Propaganda Fide.

As was the case when Marie urged the Lazarists to commence their work in Tunis and Algiers, the Lazarists whom De Paul sent to Madagascar in 1648 had no authorization from Rome to engage in missionary activity there. Indeed, that summer, the cardinals at Propaganda Fide attempted to prevent two Lazarists en route to the island, Charles Nacquart and Nicolas Gondrée, from commencing their work.[1]

After Gondrée died in 1649, Nacquart was the only Lazarist in Madagascar and his relationship with the French merchants was uneasy. He preached against working on Sundays and feast days and, as he explained to De Paul, this led many annoyed French laymen at Fort Dauphin to regard him "as someone who wants to lay down the law and to infringe upon the temporal through ambition." There was little love lost, furthermore, between the priest and the company-appointed governor at Fort Dauphin, Étienne de Flacourt, whom the Lazarist condemned as "pious in appearance only" and as too tolerant of immoral behavior among the French and the local "men and women who service[d]" them sexually at Fort Dauphin.[2]

Marie learned of this situation through De Paul and took to heart Nacquart's hopes that wealthy Catholic elites in Paris would take an interest in his work in Madagascar. He hoped that they might raise the funds to send several Lazarist brothers to the island, including a skilled tailor, who could make uniforms for young indigenous students if the Lazarists were able to open a school, and others skilled in pharmacy, surgery, and nursing. There was a need for medicines, too, along with capable teachers who could instruct indigenous, Arabic-speaking catechumens how to read and write in French. Pious laymen skilled at carpentry, joining, other trades, and agriculture were also needed to "build churches and wooden houses," to supply furnishings and other basic household necessities, and to cultivate "wheat, vines, grains, seeds and kernels." Finally, Nacquart asked for armed laymen who could protect the mission from other Frenchmen prone to thievery and drunken brawling.[3]

Marie began to openly support the Lazarist mission to the island after she had successfully pressed Rome to create the new French missionary dioceses for Asia and North America. By that point, the French had more ground to stand on, in the eyes of Vatican officials, as sponsors of missions in an Indian Ocean region that traditionally had been reserved for the Portuguese. And by that point, too, Marie's cousin Charles de La Porte, the Marquis de La Meilleraye, had formed a new merchant company, the Compagnie de Madagascar, with the intention of squeezing out the older, failing company that had been established in Richelieu's time.[4]

A turning point for the mission came with the arrival of La Meilleraye's fleet at Fort Dauphin on May 29, 1656. A Lazarist priest named Claude Dufour was on board the flagship *Le Grand Armand*, which was named for Cardinal Richelieu. La Meilleraye had wished to bring Capuchin friars to the island to serve his men as chaplains and to instruct the local people in the truths of Christianity. But Marie and her friend Anne Pétau de Traversay, who was the wife of a prominent member of the Parlement de Paris, had ensured instead that the Lazarists would be able to build upon what they had already begun in Madagascar. La Meilleraye had promised Marie before departing France that he and his men would protect the Lazarist mission as best they could.[5]

By 1659, the Lazarists came under pressure to swear an oath of allegiance to La Meilleraye's company. De Paul urged his men in Madagascar to resist them but at the same time to work with La Meilleraye and demonstrate loyalty to the company in other ways.[6] Also by this point, both La Meilleraye and Marie were presuming—despite doubts De Paul himself had about sending more of his men to the island—that the French could expand the mission to Madagascar under the authority of a new French bishop.[7]

Madagascar was a challenging mission field for the Lazarists. The sixteen French-born members of De Paul's apostolic society who eventually traveled to the island up to the year 1663 served both as chaplains to the French and as evangelists, schoolteachers, and providers of medical care among the locals, a mixed population that included some Muslims and Jews as well as the many who practiced indigenous Malagasy rituals. In the process, however, many of the missionaries died from malaria. Like its North African counterparts, the Madagascar mission was continuously frustrated by insufficient manpower.

Yet it bore some fruit. By 1661 the Lazarists claimed to have baptized some five thousand men, women, and children on the island. This was an exaggeration, but the Vatican officials to whom this number was specifically communicated knew how to read between the lines where such claims were concerned. There were enough Christians on the island, the Lazarists were really saying, to justify the appointment of a bishop for them. At this time, at Marie's encouragement, La Meilleraye was offering to finance the establishment of yet another French missionary diocese in addition to the four that had been erected. But this request fell on deaf ears in Rome.[8]

La Meilleraye did not press his case in Rome. He was preoccupied with his business affairs and, by 1663, with his responsibilities as the newly created Duc de La Meilleraye, thanks to Louis XIV. Furthermore, within a year, he was dead. Significantly, Marie did not take the opportunity to press for the new diocese herself. She was focused instead on the difficulties Pallu was facing as a result of Portuguese opposition to his episcopal authority and hoping that, in the event Rome defined his ecclesiastical jurisdiction broadly, as it eventually did, the battle for Madagascar could be included among the lands encompassed by it.

By this point, Marie was a primary contact in France for the mission in Madagascar. The Lazarist leading the mission then was Father Nicolas Étienne. In 1663, he had sent Marie a long memorandum explaining to her what was most needed in the colony in order to ensure a future for the Church and a stable French settlement there. He hoped Marie would endow a Lazarist house and seminary there, as she had in other places. The mission also needed at least sixteen priests, in his view—some of them skilled in medical work and others in practical trades such as carpentry and masonry. He asked her to send along basic amenities that were still greatly needed, such as mattresses, furniture, and French wine and wheat. Étienne also hoped the duchess and her contacts in Paris would support the construction of a proper church building nearby the proposed seminary. Étienne wished, too, that more French settlers would soon arrive in Madagascar, including a number of French women, who would be skilled in various trades and assist the mission's development in a range of ways. He imagined that a functioning hospital, a school for French and indigenous children, and European-style homes would soon make Fort Dauphin a proper satellite of his Catholic homeland.[9]

Despite Étienne's efforts, Marie's gifts to the Madagascar mission were irregular compared to those she bestowed on other overseas Catholic ventures. The Lazarist enterprise in Madagascar was often short on basic supplies, and several missionaries themselves, who came from moneyed families, donated significant sums to help keep it afloat.[10] Occasionally, Marie's contributions to the mission were unintentional: an MEP missionary priest whom she financially supported, a Father Flachier, began collaborating with the Lazarists in 1663, but this was because a ship that was supposed to take him to Cochinchina ran aground at the Cape of Good Hope, so he ended up attaching himself to the French at Madagascar instead.[11]

The mission's fate was inextricably linked to that of the Compagnie de Madagascar, which itself was largely a failure in the years following La Meilleraye's death in 1664. By 1667 the company was almost 2 million livres in debt, and the French government and financial elites in Paris were disinclined to save it, especially as the prime minister, Colbert, was hopeful by this point that the Compagnie des Indes Orientales would take over French trade and colonization in the region. Colbert was too optimistic. By 1670 it looked doubtful that the colony at Fort Dauphin would survive. Within four years, it would collapse.[12]

Although Marie may have contributed to it by some inaction, the instability of French activity in Madagascar explains why the duchess devoted less of her time and resources to a Catholic mission there compared to other overseas contexts. All the same, she was, after her cousin La Meilleraye, the major French donor to the mission over the course of its existence. And even as she was pessimistic by the late 1660s about the future of French colonization in Madagascar, Marie arranged for a formal assessment of the mission's future to see if it might be saved. Toward the close of 1670, she communicated with Pallu about the island, urging him to travel to Madagascar for this purpose.[13] The bishop was able to reach Fort Dauphin early in 1671. While there he performed various episcopal duties, such as sacramentally confirming in the faith many indigenous neophytes of the Lazarists' mission. By August, however, he was compelled to report frankly to Marie that conditions were unhealthy in Madagascar. Yet another Lazarist priest had died from an illness and another seemed likely to die soon despite the best efforts of the bishop's personal surgeon.[14]

Furthermore, Marie by the 1660s had been attempting to gather support for more French activity on additional islands in the Indian Ocean and also farther east toward rumored new lands that a handful of well-informed French were then calling *les Terres Australes*. In other words, Marie hoped to sponsor French commercial and missionary activity in what later generations of Europeans would know to be the continent of Oceania but which, in Marie's time, did not yet appear on maps of the known world. As early as 1663, the duchess was holding meetings at the Petit Luxembourg in which such plans were discussed, in conjunction with the publication of a book on the subject. She also got behind a renewed but failed attempt, endorsed by Louis XIV, to convince the Pope and Propaganda Fide to create a new French diocese, headquartered at Fort Dauphin, for that part of the world. As she had done with Pallu, Marie offered to cover the new bishop's expenses and secure additional support from her Parisian associates. But the Pope was understandably reticent about appointing a bishop for a territory that included lands and peoples his fellow Europeans were not actually certain existed.[15]

In any event, the Lazarist mission to Madagascar was dissolved in 1671. This discouraged Marie and her associates from taking any more energetic interest in the region, which would not see a significant French presence again for another two centuries.

52

Ventures in the Near East

A s Marie's missionary projects in Africa, the Americas, and the Far East were in turns developing and stalling, there was one other part of the world to which the duchess looked for similar opportunities. This was the region that had long ago been the cradle of Christianity: Ottoman-controlled Syria and neighboring lands that had become heartlands of Islam.

Marie's interest in the Levant was focused on the figure of another young protégé, François Picquet. He served France and the Church initially in a lay capacity in Syria but eventually in a priestly and episcopal one. The course of his career was such that we can easily imagine that Marie hoped her uncle Richelieu would have approved of him and the way she shaped his path.

Picquet was welcomed into Marie's circle in 1650, when he was twenty-four and she in her mid-forties. Wavering between a career in the Church or in royal service, the young man required noble patronage either way, as he was merely the son of a Lyonnais banker who had lost some of his fortune after some early business successes. Although Picquet had an inclination toward the priesthood, his father required him to engage in trade in different French cities and abroad in Italy and England.

It was in this period of his developing international business career that young Picquet first met Marie.[1] Due in part to Marie's intercessions at court, Picquet was within two years of that initial encounter appointed as the French consul to Aleppo. In Syria for the next eight years, he would energetically serve French interests and promote the unification of the local Jacobite church (an Eastern Orthodox church that rejected papal authority) with the Maronite church that was in communion with Rome.

Marie would not live long enough to see her political and clerical protégé Picquet formally elevated to the episcopate as the Apostolic Vicar of Babylon. She would also never see the beginnings of MEP missionary activity in the Levant under Bishop Picquet's leadership. But it would be in part in honor of his patroness's memory that Picquet, in his newly formalized apostolic role, would—like so many of the churchmen, religious, and lay Catholics whom Marie had supported in mission contexts—go on to serve the interests of both France and the Church quite diligently. He would do so in the additional role of Louis XIV's ambassador to Persia.[11] This is something his patroness, as well as the late Cardinal Richelieu, would have applauded and seen as the natural fruit of their always dynamically linked ecclesiastical and political efforts.

53

"Précieuse Ridicule"

A s Marie aged, she spent more of her time, on balance, on her missionary and charitable projects than on courtly politics. Her cultural engagements, too, moved toward more patronage of works on sacred themes. This was at a time when the young King Louis XIV, his bride Marie-Thérèse of Spain and his mistresses, and a whole new generation of courtly nobles and officials were coming more fully into power. By this point, too, French high society was moving in directions that ran counter at times to the duchess's increasingly tradition-minded and devoutly Catholic outlook.

Especially fashionable was a new, up-and-coming playwright of the time, a Parisian named Jean-Baptiste Poquelin who was known better by his stage name, *Molière*. In the past, Marie had championed bold playwrights. But she had little love for this one, who was patronized by the King's cross-dressing and promiscuously homosexual brother, Philippe d'Orléans. In late 1659, Molière put out a one-act play at the Petit-Bourbon entitled *Les Précieuses Ridicules* that many French courtiers and wealthy Parisians found greatly entertaining but which seemed to make gratuitous sport of the kinds of women Marie had long counted among her closest friends.

Les Précieuses Ridicules, which is still performed today for appreciative audiences, mocked well-read, witty, and well-mannered women who were highly attentive to language and sometimes puristic about it—women, in short, such as those who had gathered for years in the Blue Room and the other first literary *salons* of Paris. The play was also a humorous attack on the Académie Française—one of the late Cardinal Richelieu's proudest achievements—and its efforts to standardize and elevate the French language. Ironically, Molière's own crisp and elegant French had been molded by, and further advanced, the very standardization of the language at issue.[1]

With the support of the King and of many influential nobles, Moliére went on to write and perform more daring plays that, thanks to a royal gift of the space in 1660, were regularly performed in the theater of what had once been Richelieu's Palais-Cardinal. One of them was *The School for Wives*, which was full of double entendres and undermined the moral influence of the King's preacher, Jacques-Bénigne Bossuet, who had been mentored by Vincent de Paul. Another was entitled *Tartuffe* and is known sometimes in English as *The Hypocrite*. In this play, which was first staged in 1664, Moliére caricatured the Dévots as sticks-in-the-mud who were publicly hostile to theater, especially comedies, and to other worldly enjoyments, but who were also privately immoral. The word *tartuffe* still today is used by the French and some English speakers to mean someone who is showy about Christian virtue but also leads a secretly sinful life.[2]

In 1664, Marie and her wide network of friends and clients at court, in the Compagnie du Saint-Sacrement, and throughout French society wielded a great deal of cultural power, even if they were not setting trends as they once did. *Tartuffe* was received by many prominent elites as an attack on Christian society itself.[3] The negative response was so strong that the King, despite his fondness for Molière, felt obliged to ban the play. He nevertheless threw a bone to Molière by agreeing to serve as godfather to the playwright's son.

Marie for many years had associated with women who fell into both categories targeted by the fashionable Molière, the *précieuses* and the Dévots. On the one hand, she had longstanding friendships with Catherine de Rambouillet, Julie d'Angennes, the writer Madeleine de Scudéry, and the Jansenist *salonnière* Madame de Sablé. On the other, she was energetically involved in charitable projects with noble-women who had abandoned the norms of high society for lives focused on pious devotion and assisting the poor and the marginalized. Among them were Louise de Marillac, who had famously abandoned her elevated life as a noble-woman to found the controversially uncloistered Daughters of Charity, who dressed in plain gray dresses and not in conventional religious habits, and Madame de Miramion, who had recently started a new community of women who were devoted to educating poor girls and had a special devotion to the Holy Family.

But Marie left herself open to charges of hypocrisy because, unlike these devout women who pursued more radical forms of life and took vows of chastity while doing so, she remained a worldly widow, never abandoning her palatial homes or eschewing the theater, balls, and banquets. She genuinely loved fine silks, satins, lace, jewels, and other adornments, just as she loved the best food money could buy and fine music, ballets, and artwork depicting profane as well as sacred subjects. Furthermore, while Anne of Austria remained alive (the Queen Mother would die in 1666), Marie regularly attended court and dressed the part, remaining attentive to fashionable cuts and designs in her attire.

Marie served as a bridge at court, however, between the *beau monde* and the more behaviorally extreme devout and learned women who were on the edge of respectability in the age of Molière. A telling incident was when her devout friend Charlotte de Ligny, who was a cousin of Jean-Jacques Olier, was stopped in Marie's presence by a young palace guard at the Louvre who treated her like an intruder because of her severe, unfashionable mode of dress. Marie intervened. She reprimanded the guard and ordered him to let her eccentric friend pass, reportedly saying, "This lady is far more highly thought of by the Queen just as she is than we with all our foolish fripperies."[4]

At other times, Marie provided a different, consoling point of view to younger women at court who were feeling pressured by their families and the conventions of the time. She was able to do this because of her simultaneously high position at court and her having survived, with style and triumph, decades of gossip about the unconventional path she had taken—that is, remaining independent rather than remarrying or becoming a nun after being widowed so young and then inheriting so much from Richelieu. In April 1660, the King's fifteen-year-old cousin, Marguerite-Louise, who was the daughter of the late Gaston d'Orléans, sought comfort and advice from Marie after escaping the room at the Louvre where her planned marriage to the overweight Cosimo III de' Medici, the future Grand Duke of Tuscany, was being negotiated. The young princess was in love with another young man at the time and had embarrassed her older sister (La Grande Mademoiselle) as well as other members of the royal family and the visiting Italian dignitaries when she had fled the marriage talks in tears. After Marie chatted with her privately, Marguerite-Louise dared to call King Louis a "tyrant" for his part in encouraging the marriage, even though, the next day, after thinking through the Grand Duke's marriage proposal a bit more on her own, she offered her free consent to the plan and apologized to the King.[5]

In Marie's day, the word *feminism* did not yet exist, nor did phrases such as *the empowerment of women*. The tradition-minded, devoutly Catholic duchess was nevertheless a pioneering figure where it came to expanding women's options in

French society and securing women greater respect for their talents and their moral and spiritual worth. In addition to her other charitable interests in this vein, she was a proponent of schooling for girls of all backgrounds, not just privileged ones.

The period during which Marie lived was one in which formal schooling for most boys was still not the norm, even though the Jesuit order, in particular, had been doing much to change that since the 1540s. Schooling for girls of any social background lagged far behind: it was in its infancy in Europe and controversial among many who believed girls should not be free to come and go from their homes with regularity. Carefully monitored convent settings were thus the first normalized spaces outside the home in which girls of more ordinary circumstances were offered opportunities to engage in formal studies and acquire marketable skills such as sewing and basic accounting. The Order of Saint Ursula, known better as the Ursulines, had been founded in Italy in 1535 and by Marie's time was leading the way in promoting girls' education in this form. After observing the success of several new Ursuline convent schools in France as well as in colonial Canada, where Ursuline mothers were active alongside the Augustinian hospital nuns whom Marie patronized, Marie helped to establish the Ursulines in a rural town called Sainte-Livrade in Poitou that was feudally dependent upon her dukedom of Aiguillon.[6]

Marie was generous toward the Daughters of Charity, too, partly because they opened many schools for girls, in rural areas as well as urban ones, as well as took over the running of hospitals and staffing of a range of charitable centers for the poor and the sick.[7] And Marie was a primary supporter of Madame de Miramion's community, which eventually merged with a congregation called the Filles de Sainte-Geneviève, which focused its efforts on teaching the Catholic faith and various other subjects to hundreds of poor Parisian girls and young women whom it helped to keep off the streets.[8]

In addition to supporting more education for girls, Marie was among the first major patronesses of women who wished to engage in hospital work. She was such an early supporter of it, indeed, that by the time the French were becoming more accustomed to lay and religious women serving as nurses, dispensing medicines, and even administering hospitals, the hospital nuns whom she supported in New France occasionally feared that she might forget them, given how many other projects preoccupied her.[9]

They were assured to the contrary in the spring of 1664, when the duchess intervened with political authorities in Paris and Québec to ensure that the

Hospitalières maintained full control over the administration of their finances and over the goods supplied to them for the Native Americans they served. That control was under threat as changes were being made to the governing structures of New France by Louis XIV and his prime minister, Colbert. Colbert had appointed a royal *intendant* for New France, Jean Talon, who was pressing the nuns to quarter French troops on their hospital grounds and even to build new barracks for them, at their own expense.[10] Marie put a stop to this, ensuring that the nuns' independence was preserved according to the terms originally affirmed by the previous French monarch at the time she founded the hospital.[11] In the same period, Marie sent additional funds to the nuns in Québec to save them from having to spend from their ordinary budget after Colbert increased French emigration to the colony, something that put new pressure on the hospital as a result of an influx of sick French-colonial patients.[12]

Marie had also, as we have seen, worked hard against political pressures of the time to have the Daughters of Charity staff the Hôpital-Général de Paris that was established in 1656. In time, Marie as the President of the Ladies of Charity oversaw the expansion of the Hôpital-Général by means of a merger, in 1670, with a home for foundlings that the Daughters had run for many years. That home became known as the Hôpital des Enfants-Trouvés, and it would have its own building by 1672 on the Rue Neuve-Notre-Dame, close to the city's famous cathedral.

Marie's contributions to women as such had also, for decades, included shaping public perceptions through book projects she patronized. Most of the books that Marie helped to bring to publication in her later years were on themes such as Christian missions and charitable service to the poor. They included unusual ones, however, that underscored women's capabilities for more forms of Christian witness than were traditionally open to their sex, such as educational and hospital work, including overseas in mission settings. An Augustinian priest, Pierre Oudin, published a work in this vein in 1669 that he dedicated to Marie. Oudin credited Marie and other women of the time with zeal as well as capability for apostolic as well as charitable action—something that was not yet mainstream in the Catholic culture of the time.[13]

Another book, appearing in 1671 and authored by Paul Ragueneau, a veteran of the Jesuit mission to New France, was a biography of Mother Catherine de Saint-Augustin, a nun who had dedicated more than twenty years of her life to the hospital project Marie had founded years before in Québec. In his dedicatory letter to Marie, Ragueneau was sure to point out some of the unusual ways she, too, had spent her life on behalf of the Church: "We know well enough, Madame, that your charity extends not only throughout this whole kingdom, in which no province has not experienced its extraordinary effects, but that it penetrates even to the furthest countries of infidels." The Jesuit referred also to the duchess's "greatness of soul and zeal to establish and support the interests of God and religion even in the New World" before going into detail about the remarkable life and Christian heroism of Mother Catherine, who had died in Canada at only thirty-six after two decades of hard work there, helping to build up and run the first charitable hospital in North America intended primarily for indigenous patients.[14]

If Marie used the power that she had to help other women of her time in unconventional ways, she also went out of her way to employ her position and wealth in ways that strike a modern viewer, looking back, as illiberal. This is the case with some of her efforts against Jansenism. It is also the case with her increasingly visible, staunch opposition to Protestantism in her later years. As usual, the duchess generally did not follow the lead of others in this area but attempted to draw and push others toward her position. This was one reason she was out of step in the early 1660s with Molière and his fashionable friends, who increasingly saw faith as a matter of private conscience. She was not out of step with royal policy, however, which under Louis XIV moved toward more repression of la réligion prétendue réformée ("the so-called reformed religion"), as French Catholic officials called it, than had been seen since the era of the religious wars.

In her younger years, Marie was tolerant of Protestantism in the way that Cardinal Richelieu had been, both for pragmatic reasons related to the war against Spain and from a commitment to civilité in a French society that had been torn apart by too much by religious conflict. She never presumed, though, that departures from Catholic orthodoxy were acceptable in the eyes of God. She had several Protestant friends, including for a long time Charles de Sainte-Maure de Montausier before he converted in order to marry Julie d'Angennes. Marie had urged this conversion, however, and prior to that she had also assisted the playwright Jean Puget de La Serre with the production and publication of a French play that dramatized the story of Sir Thomas More, the English chancellor who had been put to death by King Henry VIII after refusing to accept his break with Rome.[15] From early on in her life, in short, the duchess's distaste for the disharmony among Christians since the Reformation era was well known.

In her work with Vincent de Paul, the Lazarists, and the Daughters of Charity, Marie had been alarmed at the impoverished state of many rural Catholic parishes around France in areas where local elites were often members of thriving Reformed congregations that elected their pastors and rejected Catholic teachings about the sacraments, grace and good works, and the hierarchical nature of the Church. These elites variously ignored the Catholic poor—whose poverty they sometimes saw as God's just punishment of them for their "superstitions" and "idolatrous" posture toward saints, popes, and bishops—and, just as bad in Marie's view, attracted struggling Catholics to their Protestant ways.[16] Marie's support of Lazarist missions and other charitable ministries in central and southwestern French communities was intended to address this problem. The duchess also made donations over the years to Protestant converts to the Catholic Church in rural areas who were cut off financially by their disappointed families. In Loudun, near Richelieu, she sponsored a refuge specifically for girls who converted called the Maison de Nouvelles-Catholiques. She donated to similar institutions in La Rochelle and in Paris.[17]

Early in the 1650s, Marie was supportive of efforts by the secretive Compagnie du Saint-Sacrement to suppress several Protestant schools that had been established. Among them was a secondary school in Pavilly, which was close to Le Havre in Normandy where Marie was the royal governor at the time. In 1653, after learning that a Protestant-run hospital was quietly being developed in Paris, the Compagnie had it shut down and its beds and other supplies were taken to the Hôtel-Dieu de Paris, the hospital at which the Ladies of Charity, then directed by Marie, were headquartered. This was just the time when Marie and the Ladies were springing into action to bring their hoped-for and thoroughly Catholic Hôpital-Général de Paris to life.[18]

After the long war with Spain ended in 1659, French Catholic authorities newly directed their energies to bringing Protestants in the kingdom back into the Church. Lazarist priests and other clergymen and religious ventured into Protestant areas as if they were mission territories, preaching and offering catechism classes to children as well as assistance to the poor.[19] At this time, young King Louis began to exhibit more public anti-Protestant sentiments. He was not fond of Protestantism to begin with, seeing it as an inherent threat to the unity and order of the body politic, which he closely identified with the Church itself and believed that he shepherded in France as God's anointed one. He identified the Huguenots in France with the English Puritans who had been responsible for executing his uncle, Charles I of England. Still, it came as a surprise to a delegation of Protestant French leaders who came to court to pay their respects when Louis received them with noticeable froideur.[20]

For several years, Louis's approach to Protestants in his kingdom was passive.[21] But famously, after the French went to war with the Dutch over the years 1672 to 1678, Louis's government shifted toward repression, billeting troops among Huguenot communities and favoring coercive measures to achieve conversions to the Church. By 1685—ten years after Marie's death—Louis revoked his grandfather's Edict of Nantes, which had granted basic forms of toleration to French Protestants, such as freedom to worship and to hold public offices. Numerous Huguenots fled France at the time.

Notably, Marie quietly counseled the King on occasion to favor anti-Protestant measures even before the Franco-Dutch War broke out. In the spring of 1671, for example, she was foremost among a group of French nobles who urged Louis to purge Protestants from governmental offices. Her activity in this regard was alarming enough to English Protestant agents working in France that it was discussed in dispatches to London. William Perwich, for example, reported to the Parliament minister Joseph Williamson that Marie had given orders to fire all known Protestants serving in posts throughout her domains, especially in the Duchy of Aiguillon. She favored, too, a religious test that was being given to parish clergymen, consisting of 160 articles of faith to which they had to subscribe in order to keep their posts.[22]

It is unclear what Marie's more specific motives were in all this. Was she, at some level of her consciousness—and in a penitential way—attempting to make reparations for all that her uncle, as prime minister, had done to favor Protestant powers in Europe, ending any realistic Catholic dreams of restoring confessional unity to Christendom? Whatever was the case, it is certain that her Catholic faith, which had been strong since her youth, grew more fervent over time. We can see this in the kinds of artwork she patronized later in life. Although she continued to patronize experimental artists, such as the troubled but wonderfully talented Flemish painter Michiel Sweerts, whom she sent to the Far East with Bishop Pallu, most of the artistic works she commissioned in her later years treated sacred themes.[23] She ordered a number of large paintings for chapels and churches overseas in the missions she funded. Many of these works have been lost or were destroyed, but descriptions survive. A missionary in Madagascar wrote in 1660 of a very large painting, about seven feet high, of the crucified

Christ with a repentant Mary Magdalene at His feet. The missionary failed to record the artist's name but did report that Marguerite Rousseau, the wife of the French colonial governor in Madagascar, had declared she had never seen a more beautiful or moving painting in her life.[24]

An engraving of the crucified Christ made for Marie by the artist Louis Testelin survives and gives us a sense of how the duchess envisioned Christ, to whom she prayed daily and whose Body and Blood she believed fervently she consumed when at Mass. In this engraving, the dying Christ is robust and manly, and his arms are stretched out widely. This was symbolic of His merciful embrace of sinners, which was contrary to what Jansenists and some Protestants preferred, as their crucifixes at times had Christ's arms positioned vertically (something that was condemned by Rome). A poem below the image addresses the ordinary sinner—the Catholic everyman, so to speak—urging contemplation of Christ's suffering and self-sacrifice as well as the reality of human mortality and, in view of all that, repentance and acceptance of Christ's gifts. A snake near a skull at the bottom of the cross appears to be dying, crushed under the wood of the cross and a stone that foreshadows the Resurrection from the tomb on Easter morning. There is something subtly triumphant in this image of the dying Christ.

Whatever it was that Marie experienced before such sacred images, that kept bringing her back to Mass and her rounds of devotions, and that encouraged her to patronize Catholic institutions of all kinds beyond anything any other laywoman of her time was doing, it was clearly something that she wanted others to experience. She wished that other women would come to know and love God and the Church as she had done, partly through more access to education and opportunities to serve God in ways traditionally not open to them. She also seems to have become almost painfully aware of, and convinced it was her special burden to do something about, how many poor, sick, and uninstructed men and women—many of whom had never had a chance to learn the rudiments of Christianity—lived in her own country and across the whole world. And she wished that Jansenists and Protestants throughout France would come to share in the faith as she and her dearest friends understood and practiced it.

It is no wonder that she had so little time, let alone affection, for figures such as Molière, who ridiculed erudite and pious women and sniffed out hypocrisy in high society less for the sake of reform than for mere sport. Such people clearly did not see what she was seeing. Besides, there was still so much to get done for God and for France.

54

Uncle Armand's Legacy

There was something else, beyond increasingly fervent Catholicism, that set Marie apart from others in French courtly society in the early years of Louis XIV's personal reign. Her devotion to Cardinal Richelieu's memory, and her determination that her uncle would be remembered with more gratitude than hate by his countrymen, had been thorns in Cardinal Mazarin's side for a number of years. After Mazarin fell ill and died in early 1661 and young Louis decided to take the reins of government himself rather than delegate most duties to his First Minister of State, celebrations of a deceased prime minister were becoming passé, at best, and were in truth a bit of an inconvenience for the young sovereign. Louis's decision to rule France directly the way his great-grandfather Philip II had ruled Spain was concerning to many, who doubted his capacity to govern effectively, especially given his mere twenty-two years of age.[1] Louis had to prove himself, and publicly honoring the late Cardinal-Minister who had been the real power behind his father's throne was not an effective way to do that.

Given that Marie's efforts to preserve Richelieu's memory and legacy were incongruous with the new ways of doing things at the court of the Sun King, it is all the more impressive how she pressed forward with them. She had at least one admirer for it at the time, the poet Paul Scarron who included this verse in his "Ode to Madame the Duchesse d'Aiguillon":

> With what generosity
> Has she conserved [Richelieu's] glory,
> And revived his memory
> Despite so many injuries?

And who more than she
Will instruct posterity in history?[2]

For a long time, Marie had intended to produce a history of Louis XIII's reign, employing Richelieu's unpublished memoirs and various state papers, and highlighting her uncle's policies and approach as prime minister. Initially, she hired a member of the Académie Française named Nicolas Perrot d'Ablancourt to work on this project. He was respected by other members of the Académie for both the elegance and humanistic rigor of his writing. However, their arrangement proved unsatisfying to Marie, and for a number of years the project stalled. D'Ablancourt was well known to be a Protestant. Given her own uneasiness about Protestantism and the controversial legacy of her uncle's alliances with Protestant powers during the Thirty Years' War, the duchess was loathe to risk any identification of the planned work with the international Protestant cause.

As she was approaching her sixtieth birthday, Marie was eager to get the project underway after having put it aside for so long. She finally found a scholar whom she trusted, a Jesuit priest named Pierre Le Moyne, whom she hired in 1663, providing him with an income of 1,500 livres per year for his labor.[3]

Two years older than Marie, Le Moyne had come of age, like her, in the era of Richelieu's rise to power. He shared her general outlook with regard to French political life as well as religion and society. Marie's selection of him was enough to prompt Guy Patin, a respected man of letters and professor of medicine, to complain, "Of course only a Jesuit could be chosen to publicize the life, the achievements, and the deeds of such a red tyrant as that cardinal. Good God, what credit that money, flattery, lies, and deception have in this world!"[4] Patin had actually once been offered the job himself but had turned it down. By the 1660s, after having sympathized with some of the more radical Frondeurs in years past, his political outlook was strongly anti-royalist.

Marie was well aware that her choice of Le Moyne would ruffle feathers. The Jesuit already had a wide-ranging oeuvre, having published since the 1620s works of poetry, history, spirituality, and anti-Jansenist polemics. He had been well-liked by Richelieu himself in his younger years, having produced, also, propagandistic celebrations of the Siege of La Rochelle of 1628 and of the early French victories in Italy that Richelieu had masterminded.[5]

Beyond this—and this was one reason Marie liked him—Le Moyne in 1647 had produced, with the excellent French printmaker Abraham Bosse, a monumental, illustrated book on great women in history, beginning with a number of "strong Jewish women" of the Biblical era and "strong Barbarian women" of pre-Christian Europe alongside better known heroines of the Greco-Roman world.[6] At the time that Marie hired him to work on a history based on Richelieu's papers, this book, *Galerie des Femmes Fortes*, was heading toward its sixth reprinting in Paris. Marie had reason to be confident that Le Moyne would not downplay the important roles played by some women in French political life while her uncle had been alive, just as she could be assured the Jesuit would present Richelieu in as favorable a light as possible for posterity.

Marie was confident, too, that Le Moyne would not make a mistake another historian and his publishers had made in 1649 when an earlier history of her uncle's administration had appeared in print. This was the *Histoire du Ministère d'Armand Jean du Plessis, Cardinal duc de Richelieu* by the churchman Charles de Vialart de Saint-Paul, the one-time Bishop of Avranches. Marie had given Vialart privileged access to Richelieu's papers, resulting in a work that was highly favorable, overall, to the late prime minister. However, a decision was made just before publication to include at the back of the volume many transcriptions of sensitive wartime communications between the Cardinal and other individuals who had been consulted.[7]

Marie had not been informed of this plan, let alone offered a chance to authorize the letters to be included. After the hefty book went on sale in Parisian bookstores in the middle of the Fronde, Marie used her influence with the Parlement de Paris to have an injunction issued against the further sale and dissemination of the work. Those in violation would potentially face the death penalty, and all existing copies of the work were to be confiscated and burned, although a number of copies survived and the book was even reprinted amid the disorder of the period. The justification for this censorship was twofold: Marie denied that many of the published words were actually her uncle's, and various statements in the history of what had transpired during Richelieu's administration were "scandalous, injurious, impertinent . . . and prejudicial to the State." The Parlement furthermore ordered that in the future, any publication of the late Cardinal's papers required the express permission of both the King and the Duchesse d'Aiguillon.[8]

Many of the printed missives were, as it happens, ones that had passed between Richelieu and the late Cardinal La Valette in the final months of the latter's life, when he was stationed in northern Italy with his troops. It would have caused Marie pain to see these letters in print. They contained details about military matters but also clarified for the French public what it was that La Valette and his troops were primarily doing in the Piedmont in early 1639. They were assisting the recently widowed sister of Louis XIII—Christine de France, the Regent of Savoy—in her effort to maintain control of the independent Duchy of Savoy while her brothers-in-law, the uncles of the new, young Duke of Savoy, were hoping with Spanish backing to take her place. La Valette was regularly in the company of this princess, who was two years younger than Marie and whose love affairs with various men were known at the French court. In a sense, La Valette had died for Christine—when, in the end, the princess had not even allowed France, in recompense, to dominate decision-making in Savoy once peace had been restored.

Whatever the parlementary injunction claimed about the book's inaccuracies, it was surely *this* that most upset Marie, having to relive in silence one of the most painful periods of her life, thanks to a leak of page after page of La Valette's and her uncle's conversational correspondence. These pages revealed with accuracy and precision—not with misrepresentations of Richelieu's words—much of what Marie's secret beau and his men were up to in northern Italy for the sake of a formidable and captivating princess.[9]

In the same period that she stopped the publication and sale of this unauthorized history, Marie permitted other papers of her uncle to be printed, including a collection of his notes on various happenings at court during the crucial years of 1630 and 1631, when Marie de' Medici had gone into exile.[10] She also saw through to publication a work that her uncle had written while he was in office on the subject of the best means of winning Protestants back to the Catholic Church. Just as she had earlier supervised the revision as well as publication of Richelieu's *Traitté de la Perfection du Chrestien*, she had a team of scholars and writers, including Desmarets (just before he betrayed her by helping her nephew marry in secret), review the work and update Richelieu's sometimes old-fashioned language. It was then printed in 1651 by the eminent printer Sébastien Cramoisy, whose publishing house was famous in Europe for the quality of its volumes. The work featured at the front a fine engraved portrait of Richelieu at work at his desk by Claude Mellan, one of Marie's favorite artists.[11]

Marie commissioned other portraits of her uncle in different media and spent time, too, ensuring that her uncle's great art collection, some of which had already been gifted to the Crown upon his death, remained intact and preserved for posterity. At times this involved buying works from Richelieu's estate to prevent her relatives from selling them for cash. Among these were Caravaggio's *Musicians* and Poussin's *The Abduction of the Sabine Women*, which today hang in the Metropolitan Museum of Art in New York.

The most significant art commission Marie pursued for the sake of memorializing Richelieu was also one she hesitated to see through to completion until the end of her life. This was the late prime minister's planned funerary monument at the Sorbonne's Chapelle de Sainte-Ursule, which in modern times has attracted visitors from all over the world.

Richelieu had asked Marie before he died to commission a grand tomb with a funerary sculpture for him, leaving its form up to her. It took her several decades to determine the nature and scale of the monument. In 1665, she surprised the leadership at the Sorbonne with a demand that the tomb be placed right in front of the altar of the chapel. This was a most unusual request, as this would put the sculpted figure of Richelieu that Marie had in mind directly in the line of sight of worshippers as they viewed priests performing the sacred rites of the Mass up on the high altar. She countered objections to the idea with the fact that the entire chapel was Richelieu's creation.[12]

At that point, Marie had the great Bernini in mind as the sculptor who would bring the monument she envisioned to life. This was after working with several other sculptors (and paying them a lot of money) who variously disappointed her with their designs or died before they had a chance to work on the monument. Marie had also personally inspected and selected the marbles that would be used for the tomb, dealing directly with the marble merchant in a manner that was unconventional for a noblewoman of her rank. She had a definite idea in mind for the funerary sculpture and was concerned that the artists and artisans she consulted on the matter could not successfully execute it. So the monument remained just a vision in her mind for many more years as both she and Bernini, who was six years her senior, aged. Her vision remained controversial at the Sorbonne, as the plan was to have the figure of Richelieu leaning forward as if sitting up in his deathbed, offering himself to God, rather than lying in a recumbent position with his hands folded in prayer, which was the traditional mode for such monuments.[13]

Marie's negotiations with the Sorbonne leadership over the matter of her uncle's tomb were made difficult from an unexpected quarter. Her nephew Armand-Jean, the Duc de Richelieu, had been entrusted by Cardinal Richelieu with a project that had been close to his heart before he died: transferring many of his books and papers to the Sorbonne and helping the university build up what would become a great research library. However, once Armand-Jean was old enough to take this responsibility seriously, he did the opposite. He neglected the project, putting Marie in an embarrassing position as the Sorbonne would end up taking him to court over the matter and be locked in conflict with his lawyers for three decades.[14]

This drama was part of a larger one that would enshadow the final decade and a half of Marie's life. It was one, too, that would prevent her from achieving what she had solemnly promised her uncle when he was dying: holding together the House of Richelieu as a great patrimony and passing it on securely to future generations of their family.

Within a few years of his marriage to Anne du Vigean's daughter, Armand-Jean began to show signs of being as improvident as his late father had been—and also to engage in too much gambling, to which he developed an addiction. Because his aunt Marie was one of the wealthiest nobles in France and had been safeguarding much of his vast inheritance since he was a boy, he somehow came to believe that there would be bottomless wells of cash eventually at his disposal. His growing resentment toward Marie stemmed partly from this. He accused her at various points of hiding money that by right was his. Once his debts began to add up, however, Armand-Jean began selling off important parts of his inheritance. This started in the late 1650s and continued unabated long past his aunt Marie's death in 1675.[15]

Marie attempted to stop these sales through interventions by her own lawyers both inside and outside of court, but in the end she watched, in agony, as Armand-Jean began to dismantle what she had been holding together in trust for him over two decades. He sold off several Paris townhouses and other buildings, the great woods at Bois-le-Vicomte north of Rouen, the Îles d'Hyères off the Mediterranean coast, and the domain of Mortagne in Normandy. After being delinquent for more than a decade in meeting his financial obligations toward the Sorbonne, he also sold the site of the planned university library while under orders by the courts to pay fines to the Sorbonne. For these properties, the spendthrift duke received a total of 896,000 livres from various buyers, much of which quickly passed from his hands to debtors or was targeted by the courts for the payment of various fines. He sold another 200,000 livres' worth of furniture, paintings, and other objects in 1660.[16]

The worst blow of all to Marie was that, to cover some of her nephew's debts, the governorship of Le Havre had to be sold in 1660 for 300,000 livres, as did the Général de Galères position for 850,000.[17] These were positions that would have further increased in value and gone to the Duc de Richelieu's heir, who at that time was his still-living younger brother Jean-Baptiste. Instead they and the political patronage powers attached to them passed into the hands of noblemen outside of the family.

There were moments when aunt and nephew worked together. Armand-Jean dutifully helped to fund various Lazarist ministries based in his inherited domains as well as some of Marie's overseas mission projects, such as the Augustinian nuns' hospital in Québec, that Cardinal Richelieu had earlier established precedents of funding when he was also the reigning Duc de Richelieu. The duke also stood up with Marie at courtly functions and other special events in which their show of unity was valuable.[18]

Armand-Jean also at times was a codefendant with his aunt in legal challenges still being made against the late Cardinal-Minister's estate by members of other powerful families. This was the case, most notably, when a suit was brought against Richelieu's heirs in the late 1650s by the King's cousin Anne-Marie-Louise d'Orléans, the Duchesse de Montpensier, better known as La Grande Mademoiselle.

La Grande Mademoiselle's father, Gaston d'Orléans, wished in his later years to maintain peace with Marie and the other members of the Richelieu family, partly due to their alliance and shared interests in the period of the Fronde. Although in the past Gaston had been at odds with Richelieu's heirs over damages done by Richelieu, with the Crown's backing, to a property called Champigny in the Loire Valley, he was determined by the mid-1650s to let the matter languish in the courts.[19]

The property had belonged to Gaston's late first wife, however, and La Grande Mademoiselle—who had no desire to maintain peace with the Richelieus and who was still angry with her father for not opposing the Crown more energetically during the Fronde—was strongly attached to Champigny. It had been in the possession of her maternal, Montpensier ancestors for several generations, and it symbolized to her the power that those ancestors had once had but which had been violated by a grasping, bureaucratizing monarchical state and its creatures, especially the Richelieus. She had been nursing outrage most of her life since King Louis XIII's decision, when she was a toddler, to merge Champigny with the Duchy of Richelieu. Due to some high-handed maneuvering by Cardinal Richelieu, her father had even been bullied into paying for the demolition of a major part of the Montpensiers' family château at Champigny in 1635, to clear the way for Richelieu's Château de Richelieu and its neighboring planned city.[20]

Against her father's wishes, La Grande Mademoiselle pressed her family's case regarding Champigny with the Parlement of Paris. In the spring of 1657, the Parlement declared that Champigny belonged to the young woman as the reigning Duchesse de Montpensier and that the Richelieus did indeed owe her extensive damages for what had occurred. Toward the end of the year, La Grande Mademoiselle proudly took up residence in the Château de Champigny, which was mostly in ruins, but which had one standing wing as well as a family chapel with ancestral tombs still intact. And she worked out precisely how much she believed she was owed from the heirs of the late Cardinal-Minister who, in her eyes, had engendered most of the political crises France had faced throughout her life. That amount was 550,000 livres. In the coming years, she did battle with Marie and the Duc de Richelieu, who countered in court with an appeal, refusing to pay any such amount.[21]

Marie's lawyers, led by Jacques Pousset de Montauban, who was a talented speechwriter and playwright as well as a successful lawyer, made a dramatic public case, to try to win some popular support if not ultimately a favorable judgment in their appeal to the Parlement. Ultimately the duchess and her lawyers were unsuccessful, and the Duc de Richelieu, especially, would be burdened with the payment of the damages and interest that accrued while he remained delinquent. He would only pay the final balance of what he owed La Grande Mademoiselle in 1694.[22] But in 1660, Marie's lawyers nevertheless, by means of the Champigny case, communicated to the public and to the governing authorities of France Marie's view of her late uncle's devotion to the Crown and something of Richelieu's own vision of royal authority and the ways the high nobility should relate to it.

Central to the argument that Marie's lawyers put forward was that the King's elevation of her uncle as both a duke and as a Peer of France conferred upon Richelieu special powers over others. (As Marie herself had also been elevated in the same way, it can be assumed she regarded her own powers over others in the same terms.) According to a *Plaidoyé pour Madame la Duchesse d'Aiguillon* that was published in Paris early in 1660 and was more or less a transcript of what Pousset de Montauban pleaded to the Parlement, duke-peers and duchess-peeresses

were consecrated by the King to exercise "a species of priesthood," one devoted
to preserving the King's laws as well as safeguarding his royal majesty. Indeed,
duke-peers and duchess-peeresses served alongside the monarch within his
royal "temple" in a way set apart from other members of the nobility. The same
thing could be said of the duke-peers and duchess-peeresses that Saint Paul the
Apostle had said of his own and the other disciples' personal callings by Christ:
"we are a royal priesthood and a noble race."[23]

In the published *Plaidoyé*, Marie's team put forward a lengthy, detailed expla-
nation and justification of various royal acts, including *lettres patentes* issued both
in 1631 and 1637, that they believed should be respected as contracts that should
enjoy "the authority of the public faith" and should be deemed "inviolable" by the
Parlement. La Grande Mademoiselle, the lawyers agreed, was in essence attacking
royal authority itself by "disturb[ing] the late Cardinal Richelieu even in his tomb."
The Parlement needed to tread carefully, because "the Cardinal de Richelieu was
the work of the late King's hand; he was his creature," and it would be difficult
to blame his conduct without undermining "the glory of the master who chose
him." La Grande Mademoiselle was seeking for her family a position higher than
the King's law and needed to be ordered by Parlement, instead, to "confirm the
authority of kings in their ministers."[24] Marie's lawyers added further that when
Louis XIII called Richelieu to "ascend to the foot of the throne" as his prime
minister, he "purge[d him] of all the weaknesses of the earth." Indeed:

> Those who are thus called [by the King] are no longer what they
> were. They are reformed by the grace of the Prince, as by another
> nature. They no longer have enemies except those of the *patrie*.
> They have no other passions but the interests of the State. They
> have no other ambitions than the greatness of their Master. The
> movements of hatred, revenge, force, and violence, which agitate
> the souls of the vulgar, cannot touch them. They are in a state of
> greatness. . . . The late King cast his eyes on the late Cardinal
> Richelieu. . . . [He] found a great minister; he found . . . the gold of
> which Plato speaks, that of a great soul, a heroic soul worthy of his
> age, his Prince, and his *patrie*.[25]

The Parlement, which sided with La Grande Mademoiselle, was insufficiently
moved by these words. Furthermore, the political moment had passed for this

kind of rhetoric. As we know, after Cardinal Mazarin died in March 1661, the King surprised just about everyone in France and beyond who paid attention to politics by eschewing the assistance of another great minister at his side. He began to work long days, as no French king had done in recent historical memory, alongside the lowborn Colbert and a number of other secretaries and advisors, and he took a direct hand in a wide variety of affairs, domestic and foreign, economic, ecclesiastical, and military.[26]

Ironically, this enabled Marie to occasionally offer counsel to the King more directly at times than she might have been able to had Louis chosen a new cardinal-minister. It is not a coincidence that some of her most important achievements, such as the establishment of the missionary bishoprics around the world, occurred early on during Louis's personal reign. At the same time, moments of access to a king she had known since he was a toddler did not always imply influence over him. Where her efforts to hold intact the great inheritance Richelieu had entrusted to her was concerned, the king and his council were generally indifferent. At times they were even sympathetic with her nephew Armand-Jean and those who nursed grievances against the Richelieu family.

55

Family Tragedies

As Marie approached sixty in 1664, she was blessed with good health, unlike many of her family members over the years. Many of the projects toward which she had directed time, money, and energies were going strong, and the duchess remained an influential and respected figure at the court of Louis XIV and in the Church and wider French society.

Despite all this, a sense of defeat began to settle in as Marie watched her nephew Armand-Jean fritter away much of the fortune and position among the ruling elites of the kingdom that she had labored to preserve and grow for him since 1642. Indeed, between 1655 and 1665, the duke sold off some 2.3 million livres' worth of his estates and other property bequeathed to him by Cardinal Richelieu. Remarkably, despite the influx of funds from these sales, Armand-Jean still found himself plagued by creditors and government officials who were after him for fines and past-due taxes. His spendthrift ways became so notorious that the famous memoirist Louis de Rouvroy, the Duc de Saint-Simon, later referred to him as "a pierced basket."[1]

As it was becoming painfully clear to Marie what sort of man Armand-Jean would likely remain, the duchess pinned more hopes on his brother Jean-Baptiste, the Marquis de Richelieu. Jean-Baptiste had been positioned well at court in the early days of Louis XIV's personal reign. He was also an experienced and loyal military officer, having participated in a number of important battles since his teen years, including the retaking of Dunkirk from the Spanish in 1658.[2] But he also gave his aunt headaches. Just as his elder brother had done, he married without Marie's permission. Toward the end of the Fronde, he wed a fellow young courtier, Anne-Jeanne-Baptiste de Beauvais. She was the daughter of

Queen Anne's lady-in-waiting Catherine-Henriette de Bellier, the Baronne de Beauvais, who at thirty-eight—and while her husband was alive—had deflowered the fifteen-year-old Louis XIV at his own mother's request. Although Marie knew and liked Anne-Jeanne-Baptiste, she had expected that her nephew would marry someone of greater status, wealth, and substance—and safer distance, at least publicly, from the extramarital *galanteries* (to use the euphemism of the time) of the royal court.

Jean-Baptiste himself proved to be an unfaithful spouse, having an affair with, among others, Anne-Madeleine de Conty d'Argencourt, a junior lady-in-waiting in the Queen Mother's household who had also had an affair with the King.[3] He exhibited spendthrift ways, too. At the same time, the marquis and his wife produced four healthy children—a son and heir named Louis-Armand, who was born in 1654, and daughters Marie-Françoise, Elisabeth, and Marie-Marthe. By contrast, the Duc de Richelieu's marriage with Anne du Vigean's eldest daughter remained fruitless. Marie therefore had hoped to transfer the office of Général des Galères at Marseilles to Jean-Baptiste, but by 1661 that office was sold to cover some of Armand-Jean's debts.[4]

Marie was at least able to work out that Jean-Baptiste would take up duties as the *capitain concièrge* of the royal châteaus of Versailles and Saint-Germain-en-Laye, a position that came with 20,000 livres a year and the repayment of 100,000 livres of debt that the marquis had outstanding.[5] This was an important position, as the King had begun to signal that the court would spend a great deal of time at Versailles in the coming years. The *capitain concièrge* would have power over—and collect intelligence on—whomever entered, exited, and resided in the château.

It came as a terrible blow to Marie, then, when Jean-Baptiste died suddenly in early April 1662 at the age of only twenty-nine. It is unclear from the historical record how or why he died so young. But he was mourned in *La Muze Historique* as a man of great honor and valor who had been "worthy of his noble lineage."[6] His young widow would die just over a year later, which required Marie to take a more direct role in the upbringing of her orphaned grandnieces and grandnephew, the latter of whom, though just a child, was now the Marquis de Richelieu and the heir-presumptive, as well, to his uncle Armand-Jean.

In view of Jean-Baptiste's untimely death and of the childlessness of her eldest nephew, Marie opened up to the possibility of her youngest nephew Emmanuel-Joseph's abandoning the ecclesiastical estate. Having taken on several benefices as a child—those of Marmoutiers and Saint-Ouen in Normandy, and the Parisian abbey of Saint-Martin-des-Champs—the young Abbé de Richelieu, now in his early twenties, was proving to have more of a taste for women and other worldly pleasures than a churchman should. He may even have had an affair with the teenaged Armande-Grésinde Béjart not long before her marriage to a forty-year-old Molière.[7] This was at a time when the young abbot was displaying promise in his theological studies at the Sorbonne, if not in moral matters.[8] But it was also after a difficult period, in 1659, when he had to spend six months imprisoned in Amiens, as a detainee of the Crown, for crimes he had not been aware he was committing.

At that time, the King was still under Mazarin's influence and was attempting to transfer priories and monasteries deemed to be deserted, and local taxation rights associated with them, into the hands of the superior generals of the major religious orders. This was despite various legal rights to them that commendatory abbots such as Emmanuel-Joseph, and their aristocratic families generally, had been enjoying up to that point. Several smaller dependencies of the Abbé de Richelieu's benefices were marked for such a transferal, but the young abbot, while still a teenager and taking advice then from Marie and Father De Paul, did not readily comply. Having already been thrust as a mere boy into this confused, always evolving French ecclesiastical and political system, Emmanuel-Joseph was blindsided by the mercilessly swift royal legal action taken against him.

Marie was anxiously in communication with Mazarin about her imprisoned youngest nephew. The Cardinal-Minister was considering taking away the young man's ecclesiastical benefices altogether as a punishment for this state-invented delinquency. Mazarin relented in the end, and Marie was able to reconfirm a reluctant, elderly De Paul as the young abbot's vicar in his ecclesiastical posts as added security.[9] The young man was released from the citadel at Amiens but was also named as a defendant in a solemn judgment, handed down by the King's council early in 1660, about the ecclesiastical properties to be transferred to religious orders by the Crown.[10]

It is not surprising, then, that the young abbot wished to abandon his ecclesiastical career as he matured. With Marie's blessing, Emmanuel-Joseph took up arms and gained some experience of military life and leadership. By mid-1664 he was part of an international campaign in Eastern Europe as a French officer. There, he participated in the Battle of Saint Gotthard of August 1, a great land engagement along the Rába River in what is today western Hungary.

His troops, others fighting for France, and forces of the Holy Roman Empire, Bavaria, Sweden, and other states prevented the armies of the Ottoman Empire from advancing into Hungary.

Emmanuel-Joseph delayed his return to France after this successful wartime experience, enjoying the sights and other pleasures that southern Europe had to offer. While Marie was awaiting his return, she received the devastating news in January 1665 that he had died while en route to Venice. He was only twenty-five. It is unclear from the known sources what happened.[11]

As if the loss of a second nephew who was like a son was not enough, Marie lost one of her nieces, who was like a daughter to her, the following year. Marie-Marthe suffered a stroke late in mid-1665 when she was only about fifteen. She was severely debilitated and died within a few months. In the interim, Marie spent many hours at the girl's bedside, nursing her with experimental medicines. One of the doctors whom Marie brought in to see the girl was Antoine Vallot, the King's leading personal physician. Vallot gave the duchess hope that the girl might regain her consciousness and some of her functions. But this was not to be. Marie tended to her niece at the Petit Luxembourg until her final hours in late summer.[12]

Marie was joined in her mourning by her longtime friend and lady-in-waiting Anne du Vigean. Anne lost two of her own children in this period after already losing a son years before in the Thirty Years' War. Marthe, who had years before joined the Carmelites after suffering a broken heart over the young Prince de Condé, died inside Carmel de l'Incarnation in Paris in 1665. She was only thirty but had served as the sub-prioress of the community there for several years.[13] Two years earlier, Anne had lost her son, François du Vigean, the Marquis de Fors, who was in his late thirties. He had been murdered. A group of masked men had attacked him on the road, cutting off his ears and nose and tearing out his eyeballs before killing him. His steward, a page, and another servant were killed in the same incident. Officials at the time concluded that the marquis and his attendants were the victims of a resentful tenant who felt dishonored: De Fors, representing the Crown, had recently demanded that the chief assassin, a minor nobleman, pay a poll tax that only commoners had been paying up to that time.[14]

A year later, however, something more sinister was suspected. Partly due to Marie's clout with Crown officials, Anne du Vigean was able to see her son's widow and the young woman's new husband, Charles Achille de Battefort, imprisoned at the Bastille, on the charge that they had been behind the marquis's assassination.[15] The young marquis's death had cleared the way for these two lovers to join together as man and wife. By 1666, thirteen individuals had been arrested, and one of them executed, in connection to the murders.[16]

It was in the wake of such tragedies that deeply affected Marie and her most intimate friend that, in 1666, a cash-greedy Armand-Jean initiated a lawsuit against his aunt. His lawyers alleged that she still owed him a great deal of money connected to her former stewardship of the Général des Galères position that had been sold off. They based this claim on the fact that she had overseen sales of galley ships and other transactions during the years when she had held the generalship in trust for her nephew.[17] The lawsuit stalled, but the duke would continue to press Marie for money in a resentful way, year in and year out, for the rest of her life.

Given her continued alienation from Armand-Jean and the tragic loss of her other nephew and niece, Marie in her sixties increasingly looked to her eldest niece, and to the late Marquis de Richelieu's young, orphaned children, for some consolation and reasons to hope for the Richelieu family's prospects once she was gone. Marie-Madeleine, who had been named after her back in 1636 when she was born, was the duchess's closest family member in her later years. The memoirist Saint-Simon, who knew her when she was older, described her as a most extraordinary person of great intelligence, and one who was a strange mix of "vanity and humility" and who both loved high society and wanted to escape from it.[18] Her aunt Marie decided that she would pass along her Duchy of Aiguillon to her rather than to a male relative, as Cardinal Richelieu had enabled her to do when he set up the unusual terms of her own investiture as a duchess-peeress years before.

Known in this period as La Demoiselle d'Agenois and, less formally, Mademoiselle de Richelieu, Marie-Madeleine had spent some of her teen years in a Carmelite convent on the Rue Chapon. Although she had considered becoming a Carmelite at the time, her aunt disapproved of some of the rules the prioress was enforcing among the resident girls who were not professed sisters, such as restricting their time for physical exercise and time outdoors and time away from the convent with family members.[19] Discouraged from pursuing a Carmelite vocation by Marie (ironically, given how Marie had once been discouraged by her uncle), Marie-Madeleine had been living at the Petit Luxembourg since she was eighteen.[20] There, she was regularly in the company of the many visitors and guests who frequented her aunt's residence. She befriended Bishop Pallu, for example, prior to his departure to East Asia. The two corresponded, and one of their letters suggests that she grew dependent upon the young bishop's counsel.[21]

Marie-Madeleine was welcomed at the court of Louis XIV in this period. She attended a great feast with the King at the Château de Versailles in July 1668—one at which most of the upper nobility of France were presented and wished to be seen.[22] She would never marry, however. It is unclear whether this was for lack of effort by her aunt Marie to help her find a suitable match. Partly due to her older brother's gambling away of his inheritance, her prospects were, in any case, more limited than they ought to have been. The Duc de Richelieu was responsible for part of her annual income and a portion of the dowry she might bring into her marriage. But in the late 1660s, Armand-Jean was only providing Marie-Madeleine with 4,000 livres a year—a rather modest sum compared to the amounts he was demanding from his aunt and spending irresponsibly in the same period.[23]

As she advanced through her childbearing years at her aging aunt's side, never experiencing married life or motherhood, the future second Duchesse d'Aiguillon struggled to find a satisfying place in high society. She was caught between the grandeur of her aunt's lifestyle and position and the reality of her own humbler, more obscure future. Later in life, Marie-Madeleine would live in an odd sort of genteel poverty, as she had considerable property but at times no proper carriage and horses as suited her exalted rank. She would several times consider joining a religious community she funded, the Filles du Saint-Sacrement in Paris, among whom she would eventually die as a non-professed resident of their convent.[24]

Not much can be determined about Marie's relationships with her young grandnephew, Louis-Armand, the Marquis de Richelieu, and his three sisters, Marie-Françoise, Elisabeth, and Marie-Marthe. Saint-Simon would later describe the marquis as "an obscure, ruined, and debauched man" who was unwelcome at court and "who for a long time lived outside the kingdom after having abducted a daughter of the Duc de Mazarin" from a convent before marrying her.[25] That girl, Marie-Charlotte de La Porte Mazarin, was Louis-Armand's third cousin. Her father was a La Meilleraye who had married a niece of Cardinal Mazarin's and been made a duke in exchange. The more respectable paths that Louis-Armand's three sisters eventually took suggest that Marie influenced them with her connections but that brilliant marriages were not possible for them, either. They grew up to become, respectively, a religious

sister and prioress at Crécy-en-Brie east of Paris, the wife of Nicolas Quélin of
the Parlement de Paris, and the Abbess of Saint-Rémy-des-Landes southwest
of Paris and close to Rambouillets' country seat.[26]

Marie's familial relationships mattered a great deal to her in her later years but
brought her little joy. This may partly explain why she continued to involve herself
with new missionary and charitable projects even in her last years, despite all she
had achieved in this vein already, and at a time of her life when it was socially
expected that she would retire into a quieter, more domestic life. In the late
1660s, for example, she helped to arrange for the return of Franciscan Récollet
missionaries to New France—which Bishop Montmorency-Laval invited them
to do in 1670—four decades after her uncle Richelieu, favoring the Jesuits at the
time, had asked their order to abandon a small mission they had been building
up near Québec.[27]

Also, in 1669, Marie and several French bishops directed an effort to care
for wounded and sick soldiers at the time of a disastrous French effort to aid
the Venetians, who had been locked in conflict for decades with the Ottoman
Empire over the city of Candia (today's Heraklion) on the island of Crete.
Although the French Mediterranean fleet that was involved in this fight
was no longer in the hands of one of her relatives, Marie remained attentive
both to naval affairs and charitable needs in this theater due to her projects
in Marseilles, North Africa, and the Levant. At the same time, in the wake
of her nephew Emmanuel-Joseph's death near Venice just a few years earlier
after fighting the Ottomans, Marie surely felt strong emotions after hearing
sad stories about young French soldiers and sailors during this failed campaign.
She and the bishops with whom she collaborated obtained approval to establish
a hospital for these men. Several Jesuits and Capuchins were put in charge of
the hospital's operations and Marie and her friends went door to door in Paris,
collecting donations of linens, medicines, clothing, and other supplies to send
along to Candia.[28]

After Pope Clement IX learned of Marie's leadership in this effort, he had his
nuncio in France pass along his special thanks to her.[29] It is telling that among
the sources that survive from the period, we find more enthusiastic and grateful
messages to Marie from such figures on the world stage than from any of her
close, younger relatives and dependents.

56

Breast Cancer

M arie decided to draw up her last will and testament in the spring of 1674, several months before her seventieth birthday. The long document, written in her clear and still steady hand, is preserved today at the Sorbonne. It begins with a small cross that the duchess drew and a prayerful salutation, "In the name of the Father, Son, and Holy Spirit—the very holy and adorable Trinity." It goes on with instructions for Marie's burial: the duchess asked to be laid to rest inside the convent of Carmel de l'Incarnation, the same in which she had attempted to stay permanently as a nun half a century earlier. Furthermore, her body was to be enrobed in one of the simple brown habits of the Discalced sisters.[1]

In the spring of 1674, that body—once the object of admiration by artists, desire by disappointed suitors, and dirty speculation by loose-lipped political enemies—was not just old and tired but also under attack by breast cancer.[2] By Marie's era, the best-informed European physicians knew a lot already about the causes and possible treatments of breast cancer. As one of the richest and most well-informed women of the time, Marie would have known from the time of her diagnosis that she had a handful of years left to live, at most. She would have known, too, that surgery—including a full mastectomy, of the kind performed decades earlier by Johannes Stultetus in Germany—would be terribly painful and unlikely to excise the cancer entirely or extend her life any further.[3]

Marie at least had the benefit of some time to put her affairs in order while having a sense of when, and in what manner, she would depart from this life. And while making various preparations, she was able to count on several loyal and caring family members and friends. Chief among them were her niece and heiress, Marie-Madeleine, and her friend of many decades, Anne du Vigean, both of whom resided with her at the Petit Luxembourg.[4]

The Petit Luxembourg remained a bustling scene even as Marie no longer hosted as many dinners, *salons*, and meetings as in the past. Her steward Martin Husson, the former consul to Tunis, was continuously present, as were several clergymen who regularly said Mass for her in her private chapel. Other domestic officers, servants, and guards were busy inside and outside her home. Her will mentions more than twenty by name, such as a secretary named Chaboüylle, her coachman Jacques, and a valet named Dardelle. It gives evidence, too, that some of her staff members had spouses and other family members regularly around the premises. She would provide monetary gifts to all of them upon her death, and she made provisions for additional servants, gardeners, and officers who resided at Rueil and other properties she possessed.[5]

While surrounded by people in the closing chapter of her life, Marie also knew loneliness, too, as many of her dearest companions had preceded her in death. She missed Catherine de Rambouillet, for example—her beloved mentor, mother-figure, and then friend of many years. Catherine had died in December 1665 at the age of seventy-seven. She had lived a very full life and had hosted gatherings in her Blue Room, however infrequently compared to earlier years, until her final days. As the first great literary *salon* hostess of Paris, she had made an indelible mark on French history and culture. France, not only Marie and her other protégées, owed much to her.

The Queen Mother, Anne of Austria, died less than two months after Catherine, on January 20, 1666. Marie and this one-time Regent of France had spent many of their younger years disliking each other, but they had more in common over the years than not, including their commitments to poverty relief and curtailing Jansenist and Protestant influences in the kingdom. Even though they never saw eye to eye about Cardinal Mazarin, they spent considerable time in each other's company in their mature years and became genuine friends.

Several years later, in September 1669, another friend of Marie's later years, Henriette-Marie, the King's pious aunt and the Queen Mother of England, was laid to rest at the Basilica of Saint-Denis. She had spent most of her final years in Paris, including considerable time at the Chaillot convent that she had founded back in 1651 during her first period of exile from her adopted country.

A death that Marie mourned especially keenly in this period was that of her dear friend Julie d'Angennes. Titled the Duchesse de Montausier since

1664, when her husband's marquisate had been elevated by the King as a duchy-peerage, Julie died on November 15, 1671. She was only sixty-four and left behind her grieving husband Charles and a twenty-five-year-old daughter, Marie-Julie, who was one of Marie's many godchildren.

Before she died, Julie asked to be entombed inside Carmel de l'Incarnation, where her mother had also been interred. It is impossible to know what thoughts and emotions ran through Marie's mind as she watched Julie's casket lowered into the ground in this familiar, quiet place that had been so important to them over the years. But the hope surely surfaced that her friend had finally found some peace after some difficult years at the court of the Sun King.

In her later years, Julie had been linked to scandalous courtly business related to young Louis's chronic marital infidelities. Serving at court as Queen Marie-Thérèse's *première dame d'honneur*, she became friendly with another lady-in-waiting, Françoise-Athénaïs de Rochechouart, the Marquise de Montespan. The King became infatuated with Montespan while enjoying the favors of his mistress Louise de La Vallière, who would bear five of his numerous bastards before repenting and becoming a Discalced Carmelite nun.[6] Julie sometimes shared quarters with Montespan even after the King started sleeping with her, so it is unlikely she did not know about the affair as it intensified. The Queen trusted both Montespan and Julie, however, so Julie lived in a continual state of discomfort, suspended between the Queen's fragile goodwill toward her and the King's infidelities. Julie decided to exit the scene, retiring from court altogether in 1669. She suffered from poor nerves until her final days.

Given how well-informed Marie always was through her still considerable network of clients and spies, she may have known more about her friend Julie's part in the courtly dramas of the day than Julie was aware. In the memoirs of Antoine Blache, a priest at Saint-Sulpice with whom Marie spoke often in this period, there are suggestions that the duchess was keeping abreast of various rumors at court about the King's mistresses and about others, including Jesuit confessors, seeking to sway the royal conscience on various matters. She was no longer regularly attending court, but affairs of state as well as ecclesiastical business remained central preoccupations.[7] She followed closely, for example, the slow and at times tense process as King Louis's government, which was increasingly at odds with the papacy, negotiated the possible elevation of the missionary diocese of Québec into an ordinary diocese of the Church. Although it took a number of years to achieve, Marie before she died got to see Bishop

Montmorency-Laval formally become the Bishop of Québec after his years of service as an apostolic vicar.

When Marie wrote her will in early 1674, she had the full range of mission lands that had concerned her over the years on her mind. She wished for various gifts of cash to be sent along to the missionaries she funded there. These bequests in some cases supplemented larger gifts of income she had set up in past years, in the form of endowments that provided interest payments each year. The cash gifts for the missions included 8,000 livres for Bishop Lambert in Southeast Asia, 2,000 for the Lazarists in Algiers and Tunis, another 2,000 for the Augustinian hospital nuns in Québec, 1,000 for the French Jesuits serving in and around Istanbul, and a small gift for the Lazarists in Ireland. She also gifted 3,000 livres to the MEP seminary that was training men to be sent on overseas missions in the future, and she provided generously again for the Lazarists in Rome, setting aside 7,000 livres for them.[8]

The duchess's final gifts for domestic French hospitals, charitable missions to the poor, houses of refuge, seminaries, other schools, and religious congregations were even more extensive. The Lazarists throughout France topped this list, as Marie left 18,000 livres to them in total. She was also generous toward the Daughters of Charity, her parish of Saint-Sulpice, the scholarship program for young clergymen at Saint-Nicolas du Chardonnet, the Discalced Carmelites, and the Hôpital-Général de Paris. Numerous other institutions, communities, and ministries would receive charitable gifts from Marie, some on the condition that masses for the repose of her soul regularly be offered in the chapels of those that had them.[9]

In total, Marie would direct nearly 124,000 livres to charitable ends when she died and another 747,100 livres to family members other than her eldest niece, to close friends, and to various servants, officers, and clients. The rest of her cash that was not tied up already in endowments, investments made in previous years, and Richelieu's legacies for other heirs was supposed to go to Marie-Madeleine. It is unclear how much was left for her niece, but the amount was less than it might have been had Marie's relationship with Armand-Jean been stronger over the years. Marie had known other financial setbacks later in life, too: she lost some of the wealth she had hoped to pass on to new taxes imposed on the nobility by Louis XIV, to various lawsuits against her uncle's estate over the years, and to failed projects such as the Madagascar mission and merchant company.

Another disappointment Marie faced in her last years was that she never got to see the publication of the history of her uncle's political administration that she had been funding. The Jesuit Pierre Le Moyne, whom she had hired some years before to write a history based on her uncle's state papers, died in August 1671. The manuscript was close to being finished at the time Le Moyne died and was supposed to be published under the title *Histoire du Regne de Louis XIII.* But although Le Moyne had asked his superior to give it to Marie, the Jesuit leadership in Paris for some reason confiscated it. Marie was unable to liberate it and it was kept under lock and key by the leading Jesuits of Paris until the time of the Jesuit order's suppression by the French Crown in 1763, at which time it was stolen by the state. It disappeared thereafter. Its contents, still lost, would have provided most valuable insights into what Marie most wanted the world to think about Richelieu's political legacy and the times generally through which she had lived.[10]

When Marie decided to draft her will, she had to determine what to do with all the valuable papers of her uncle's that she still kept secure in her home. Some of Richelieu's papers were by then in the Sorbonne's library. But Marie made the unorthodox decision—like Richelieu's choice decades earlier—to entrust her niece Marie-Madeleine with those still in her possession, including the manuscript of his still unpublished *Testament Politique.* Those papers would not be handed over to French royal archivists until 1704, the year Marie-Madeleine died.[11]

The duchess made Marie-Madeleine her heiress and the executrix of her will. The young woman and her lawyers would have the power to distribute various bequests to other legatees from Marie's cash reserves, which were still ample, however depleted compared to what they had been earlier in her life. Marie-Madeleine also stood to inherit the Duchy of Aiguillon and its dependencies and all other properties and goods that Marie owned that were not specified in the will or that were not previously entailed to others by Richelieu at the time of his death.[12] The Petit Luxembourg and the Château de Rueil were among the latter. They were to go to Armand-Jean, so the young woman would be dependent upon her brother's good graces for continued use of the homes she had shared with her aunt for many years.

Apart from honoring certain requests of Cardinal Richelieu such as the aforementioned one, Marie planned to leave next to nothing to Armand-Jean. She stipulated that once her niece died, the Duchy of Aiguillon would go to her grandnephew Louis, the Marquis de Richelieu, or to his male heirs, and only transfer back to Armand-Jean or any descendants of his should the cadet line die out prematurely. Demonstrating her disappointment and some bitterness toward Armand-Jean, Marie summarized in her will all the expenses she had already laid out for him over the years and many things she had done for his sake respecting the governorship at Le Havre and other positions he had sold off for cash to pay for his lavish lifestyle. The only items in her possession that she offered to him in the first draft of her will were six paintings of his choice.[13]

Just a few weeks before Marie made these decisions, a lawsuit the Prince de Condé had brought against Marie and her nephew years before had been settled in Armand-Jean's favor. The duke received back from the prince the Duchy-Peerage of Fronsac and Beaufort, which the prince's father had seized from the Richelieu family back in 1646. However, Condé was permitted to keep the small domain of Graville in Normandy and rights to some tax revenues from several small Norman towns that should, by right, have gone to the Duc de Richelieu in the era of Anne of Austria's regency.[14] Following a strategy that Cardinal Richelieu had used, Marie did not wish to concentrate too many titles in the family's gift into one male line: it was strategically better for the House of Richelieu in the long run for the Duchy-Peerage of Aiguillon to be passed down through a cadet line and the primary titles and domains of Richelieu, Fronsac, and Beaufort to be passed down through the senior line. Interestingly, however, in a codicil she added to the will in June 1674, Marie stipulated that should all the lines descending from her brother François die out, the Duchy of Aiguillon and its dependencies would not go to any cousins but rather to the directors of a new Hôpital-Général in the region, for use by the local poor.[15]

After setting such plans in motion with her will, Marie's last months were spent mostly in three rooms at the Petit Luxembourg: her bedchamber, a sitting room where she occasionally received visitors, and her private chapel. She always had a priest available to offer Mass and to hear her confessions. It had been her custom for many years by then to have priests residing in her homes and to have at least one on call at all times. But now she depended on this more than ever, as it became difficult for her to attend Mass or confess outside of her home, which had become a kind of cloister for her. She also wanted a priest ready at a moment's notice once it seemed the right time for the sacrament of extreme unction to be administered to her.

Whatever peace the duchess found in her hours of prayer, solitude with her books, and meals and conversations with her remaining close family members and friends, it was continually disrupted by meetings with Armand-Jean and his lawyers. In early September 1674, those lawyers secured an injunction for Marie to hand over to her nephew any furniture she still owed him from an inventory that was made of Cardinal Richelieu's possessions more than three decades earlier. When the duke did not receive the fine furnishings that he was expecting in response to this, he hounded his aunt and her lawyers for them until a binding agreement was made on March 3, 1675. That same day, Marie also agreed to hand over to Armand-Jean some lands and feudal rights she possessed at a place called Cosnac in central France.[16]

The duke in this period also pressed his exhausted and ailing old aunt for advances on incomes he was supposed to inherit, once she died, connected to her proprietorship of the château and domains at Rueil, as well as for large sums of money he believed he was still owed by her related to transactions she had made in her capacity, years before, as the Governor of Le Havre. Marie and her lawyers agreed to the former by March 1675 while working out some minimally satisfying compensation connected to the Le Havre governorship. They made some other concessions to the duke, handing over some funds from the estate of his late mother, who had disinherited him, that would otherwise have gone to his sister, nieces, and nephew.[17]

Some of the funds Armand-Jean secured from Marie, about 26,000 livres, were to cover all the expenses he claimed to have laid out over the prior decade for the education and military training of his nephew Louis-Armand.[18] But, as usual, the duke, now in his mid-forties, needed most of the 370,100 livres he acquired from his aunt in March 1675 to pay various creditors and support expensive habits. He kept mistresses in this period, for example. One of them, Françoise de Dreux, would attempt but fail to murder his wife, Anne-Françoise, during the famous Affair of the Poisons—a scandal involving allegations of black masses, blood sacrifices of infants, and multiple other murders that rocked French high society for years and resulted eventually in more than two hundred arrests and thirty-six executions.[19]

On April 9, 1675, Marie called in three notaries and amended her will one last time. The notaries recorded that they went to her bedside in a room with a view of the inner courtyard and garden of the Petit Luxembourg and found her to be sick in body but completely sound in mind, memory, and understanding. She wished to alter certain lines in her original will respecting her nephew and show him some "marks of affection." So she formally made the Duc de Richelieu the heir of the land and *comté* of Cosnac in Saintonge, together with its appurtenances and dependencies. She left to him, as well, the domain of Hiers in Brouage with its dependencies. These, she added, should go to his wife, Anne-Françoise, should she outlive him.[20]

The duchess made additional gifts to servants and other members of her domestic staff, including a pension for life to a chambermaid named Marie Gaunon and an increase in the pension she had left to a senior maid named Sebastienne Mulois. She also donated more money to the Filles de la Croix on the Rue Saint-Antoine and Madame de Miramion's community, the Filles de Sainte-Geneviève, which was devoted to educating poor and mistreated girls.[21]

The last provision on Marie's mind that day was for a sculptor named François Girardon.[22] Girardon would be the sculptor who would complete the great funerary statue for Uncle Armand at the Sorbonne that Marie had been envisioning for three decades. The duchess signed a contract with Girardon three days later, on April 12, guaranteeing him a modest initial sum of 14,500 livres for the project.[23] She hoped that her niece Marie-Madeleine would provide whatever else he might need after she was gone. The second Duchesse d'Aiguillon—who was thirty-eight as her aunt approached death, just as Marie herself had been when Cardinal Richelieu was dying—would honor this request.

57

Carmel Once More

M arie-Madeleine de Vignerot du Pont Courlay, briefly known as the Marquise de Combalet but known best as the Duchesse d'Aiguillon, died at the Petit Luxembourg on April 17, 1675. The precise time of day, the manner in which she died, and the details regarding who, if anyone, was with her in her final minutes are lost to history. The difference could not be starker between what is known about her death and what was recorded, in granular detail, about her uncle Richelieu's passing more than three decades earlier.

Given the way Marie had conducted herself throughout her life, her death was probably a prayerful one. The deeply Catholic duchess would have faced death with the hope that—once her soul was cleansed painfully in Purgatory of any lingering sinfulness—death would reunite her joyfully with many people whom she had loved and lost over the years, including her parents and brother, dear Uncle Armand of course, good Father Vincent, and her beloved Cardinal La Valette.

Some of Marie's last prayers were surely for her nephew Armand-Jean. Incredibly, the duke believed until his aunt's final hours that he was still owed large sums of money. He also could not be trusted to provide sufficiently for his sister or his brother's children. Indeed, not long after his aunt's death, he would have around forty servants and armed loyalists forcibly dispossess Marie-Madeleine of the Petit Luxembourg, even as she lay sick in bed in late January 1676, guarded in her room by several eventually overpowered Swiss guards. He would then sell the Petit Luxembourg to the Prince de Condé and his cousin Claire-Clémence for 100,000 livres. Marie-Madeleine, who failed to get sufficient support from Parlement to rectify her situation in accordance with what her aunt had intended, would be dependent on the goodwill of the Condés and others in order to maintain any semblance of the elevated noblewoman's lifestyle that was her birthright.[1]

Marie-Madeleine, as the executrix of her aunt's will, was responsible for ensuring that the late duchess's wishes regarding her own burial were honored.[2] Marie had given orders that her corpse be dressed in a brown Carmelite habit and laid to rest not near any members of her family but instead inside the crypt of Carmel de l'Incarnation on the Rue Saint-Jacques in Paris. She wanted her tomb to be close to that of her former spiritual advisor Mother Madeleine de Saint-Joseph, whom she believed to be a saint, and to those of her friends from the Blue Room days: Julie d'Angennes, Catherine de Rambouillet, and the elder Princesse de Condé. Also inside this convent was the heart of the long-deceased Cardinal Pierre de Bérulle, who had been an early spiritual mentor to Marie. That heart was encased in a silver reliquary Marie herself had gifted upon his death in 1629.

Even up to the present day, scholars familiar with Marie's story have presumed that she had asked to be buried at Carmel de l'Incarnation because she had never gotten over being forced to leave the convent as a young widow. The historical record gives no clear indication that this was true. It was not extraordinary for a wealthy aristocrat's corpse to be clothed in a religious habit before burial, and it seems more likely that Marie simply wished to return one last time, and for good, to a place that had been spiritually nourishing to her and her friends during many periods of her life, including those in which she was enthusiastically engaged with worldly matters. It is also probable that it was just as important to her to be interred near Julie and her other friends as to be close to the Carmelite nuns' tombs. Carmel de l'Incarnation was also a place that held some memories other than those of a spiritual nature. It was where she was when she learned that her uncle Richelieu would be stepping in as her guardian after her father died—surely the pivotal moment of her life. It was also the place where Cardinal La Valette found her, after the frightening Day of the Dupes in 1630, and shared the news that Louis XIII would not dismiss her uncle from office but that the Queen Mother, Marie de' Medici, would be banished from court. That was also a turning point for young Marie.

The duchess's intentions for the forms her funeral and burial were to take are clearer than her motivations for the location. Marie had stipulated in her will that both be simple, inexpensive affairs. She was not to have anything like what she had arranged decades earlier for her uncle Richelieu.

On April 18, Marie's body was transported from the Petit Luxembourg to the convent in a small, solemn procession that would have taken about twenty or thirty minutes at a slow, pedestrian pace. The next day, a short obituary appeared in the *Gazette de France*, mentioning how the procession and the reception of Marie's coffin by the papal nuncio at Carmel de l'Incarnation had occurred "without any pomp." The writer of the obituary also described the deceased duchess in these terms:

> She was the niece of the Cardinal-Duc de Richelieu, who, when he died, adjudged her worthy—due to her merit and virtue—to sustain the greatness of his dynasty, the leadership of which he left to her. Just as she spent her entire life on charitable works, spreading her wealth even into the New World, for the propagation of the faith, her death has been an example of true piety.[3]

Marie had tried to define herself at death in a different way than this. She had asked for one simple line, in Latin, to be inscribed on her modest lias tombstone: *Domine, miserere super ista peccatrice.* But the stonemason that was hired carved nine more lines, in French, above it, so that the full inscription translates this way:

HERE LIES

THE HIGH AND MIGHTY LADY

MARIE DE VIGNEROT, DUCHESSE D'AIGUILLON, COMTESSE D'AGENOIS

WHO ASKED AND WAS PERMITTED TO BE BURIED

WITH THE HABIT OF A CARMELITE, IN THIS MONASTERY OF

THE ORDER OF MOUNT CARMEL IN FRANCE.

THIS ILLUSTRIOUS AND PIOUS DUCHESS ACCORDING TO HER HUMBLE

FEELING ABOUT HERSELF HAS ALLOWED NO OTHER EPITAPH

EXCEPT THIS ONE:

LORD, HAVE MERCY ON THIS SINFUL WOMAN.[4]

Elsewhere in Paris, not far from the convent, a much more elaborate monument finally began to come to life to mark Cardinal Richelieu's place of rest at the Sorbonne. The sculptor Girardon would, in the coming years, complete the great funerary statue Marie had envisioned for decades. The fine marble sculpture, which for more than three centuries has attracted visitors from all over the world, sits atop Richelieu's tomb and depicts the Cardinal upon his deathbed, facing the altar of the Sorbonne chapel and appearing to see a heavenly scene into which he is about to enter. Richelieu is held up by a female figure who has a calm, almost smiling countenance, and who represents Piety. Another female figure is at Richelieu's feet, bent over, weeping, and covering her face with her hand. This figure represents Knowledge.

It has long been believed that Girardon employed Richelieu's late, renowned niece as his model for the agonized figure of Knowledge, not the serene figure of Piety.

58

A Forgotten "Femme Forte"

Many people regarded Marie de Vignerot in her own time as a *femme forte*—a developing ideal in French culture of the "strong woman" who, while exhibiting properly feminine traits such as beauty, chastity, and compassion, excelled, too, in virtues traditionally associated with men, especially patriotism, valor, resolute action, and heroic degrees of Christian faith and devotion.[1] The poet Scarron, who said that the duchess had the ability to intimidate "the most resolute eagles," was among these admirers:

> Her spirit is solid and strong,
> Nothing is purer than her language,
> She was wise before her time,
> She is holy before her death;
> And her conduct and her courage
> Make her the mistress of her destiny.[2]

Prominent figures of Marie's era believed she would be remembered and honored through time. Pope Alexander VII thought that her work for the Church's expansion across the world would be enough "to carry the brilliance of [her] name down through all the centuries."[3]

They were wrong. Cardinal Richelieu's heiress and protégée, the woman who in a real sense made Saint Vincent de Paul, the woman whom Cardinal Mazarin regarded as his "most dangerous enemy," the woman whom the Enlightenment-era *philosophe* Voltaire credited with saving the career of the great dramatist Pierre Corneille, the woman who was involved in numerous central episodes in Golden

Age France's political, cultural, and religious history—this woman was all but forgotten by modern times.

Richelieu's name is familiar to every French schoolchild. Marie de Vignerot's name up until now has been known among a small minority of the French and her story has been preserved in diffuse, scattered, and often highly distorted forms primarily in specialized scholarly works inaccessible to most people. Even where she has been acknowledged in passing or in footnotes, whether in biographies of great men of her era or in academic works on social charity or Catholic missions in the seventeenth century, she has tended to appear as a pious, rich widow who had wished all her life to be a nun and who lived retiringly at the Petit Luxembourg, treating it like a cloister while possibly having been subjected for years to inappropriate advances by her uncle. She has appeared, too, as someone who simply inherited a fortune in which she took little interest and who passively underwrote with it various projects driven by the creative zeal of others, especially priests and religious she knew.

How far all of this is from the truth. The most powerful men and women of her time, including Louis XIV, whom she first knew as a toddler scampering around her gardens at Rueil, knew that Marie de Vignerot was a leaderly and politically engaged woman. She was a force of nature, even. She prodded and pushed clergymen—including De Paul, one of the best-known saints in the history of Catholicism—into things they were skeptical about at first. She made marks in French literary and artistic life. She was one of the first prominent female financiers and investors, with a portfolio of projects that stretched across five continents. And she built up an innovative, diversified French and Catholic empire of hospitals, seminaries and other schools, ministries to the poor and marginalized, and evangelistic missions that has few parallels before or after her time. All the while, she was a prominent courtly figure mixed up with espionage and intrigues, helping her uncle Richelieu to build one of the most effective political and cultural clientage networks ever seen in Europe, developing that network for her own ends after Richelieu's death, serving as a wartime royal governor, and retiring from an active life only when she had no more energy for it. It was breast cancer, in the end, not a frustrated desire to have been a Carmelite nun, that made her retreat into her home, and only in the final months of a long life.

The story of how such a woman's life could become so distorted and forgotten over time is complex and tragic. It is unsurprising, however, in view of how many other remarkable women were buried by the grand historical narratives of the past several centuries. That story begins with a lack of agreement about Marie's significance even among those who loved and honored her at the time she died.

Conflicting interpretations of Marie's life were broadcast almost as soon as the duchess had been buried. Her own friends and admirers disagreed about what was remarkable and praiseworthy about her. In the wake of her death, two major memorial masses took place in Paris at which extended funeral orations were given. The first occurred on May 13, 1675, inside the chapel at the MEP seminary that Marie had helped to establish. The preacher was Jacques-Charles de Brisacier, a young MEP priest. The second occurred on August 12 at the Carmelites' convent church on the Rue Chapon, and the preacher there was the older and more established Esprit Fléchier, who had a ceremonial position at court. Brisacier preached in some of the boldest terms possible that a clergyman could in that time about an accomplished, independent-minded, and formidable Catholic laywoman. Fléchier spoke differently—and with more consequence for how Marie would be remembered—about the pious, docile niece of Cardinal Richelieu who, had God and her powerful male protector required something different from her, would have spent most of her life hidden away as a nun.

Both funeral orations were published quickly and widely circulated. Both, too, shied away from crediting Marie with achievements of a political, social, and cultural nature distinct from her labors for the Church and for the poor. But Brisacier's at least captured something about how exceptionally leaderly Marie was. The Duchesse d'Aiguillon was, according to the younger priest, "one of the people in the world who merits the most to be immortal." She was "one of the richest and most abundant sources of charity in Europe" and "one of the principal columns" holding up the Church in France. Brisacier struggled a bit to find the right words for Marie, given some prejudices and rhetorical norms of the time regarding both women versus men and members of the laity versus the clergy. What he did say therefore spoke volumes: "O woman, who have surpassed many people of your own sex"; "we can say of her what Christ said at Cana [to His mother], *O Mulier magna est Fides tua*"; her heart was too great to be enclosed by one country, so "the whole of the Christian world had to become the theater of her zeal." She was a person of magnanimity, courage, and great negotiating skills. She was "a hero of Christianity," "another Saint Paul," an "angel of the Apocalypse," and a true example of "La Femme Forte."[4] Brisacier said, too:

She surpassed even the limits of her sex and of her estate. . . . Her
sex placed her among the ranks of women, and her estate among the
laity. But grace elevated her above these two obstacles, inspiring in
her a male zeal and—dare I say it—a priestly zeal.

You may even say that the Holy Spirit had given her some stewardship over the Church. Her home seemed far less like that of a
lady of quality than like a bishop's palace, with the continual coming
and going of all sorts of ecclesiastics and religious of all orders, who
came from all places to blend together there. . . . The ardor of her
faith gave to her . . . the part of a leader, which made her supervise
unceasingly the preservation of the spiritual kingdom that the Son
of God had conquered by the outpouring of His Blood.

In politics there are three means of safeguarding one's conquests. One must arm oneself to defend them against enemy
attacks. One must choose good governors and wise magistrates for
cities and provinces. And ultimately one must soften, even while
making it feared, the yoke of domination through a gentle mode
of governance.

Madame d'Aigulllon worked with all her might to support
[God's] empire in these three ways. She helped to defend it against
heretics, who are its enemies. She provided it with worthy pastors
and holy priests, who are its governors and magistrates. And she
softened the suffering of peoples, helping the afflicted and the poor
everywhere to bear the yoke of the justice of God.[5]

Brisacier went on to credit Marie with many things for which, in time, others
would be praised in history as if she had not been at their side or directing them.
She worked "in concert with" the Jesuits of New France, and "she advanced
by her negotiations in the courts of France and Rome" the sending of French
missionary bishops to North America and parts of Asia. She directed some of
Vincent de Paul's and the Lazarists' projects as well as founded some of their
missions and seminaries. She was thinking like Christ Himself, who sent Saint
Peter to Rome, when she established the Lazarists in the Eternal City, as her
design was to ensure that the Lazarists would quickly start to influence the entire
Church, from the head down to all parts of the ecclesiastical body. She was also
responsible for the career of Jean-Jacques Olier and the reform at the parish of

Saint-Sulpice. She played such a leading role in the establishment of missions, hospitals, schools, and ministries to the poor in so many places across France, Europe, and the rest of the world that "without exaggerating, one would have to make a map simply in order to note in a simple way the names and situations of all the places into which her zeal extended," and one would have to go on at length to put into words "all the different kinds of assistance that she gave to meet diverse needs."[6]

Brisacier went on to enumerate all sorts of things that Marie did for the poor and for the Church and, by the end of his oration, seemed ready to declare her a saint. He did not forget, however, to underscore her relationship to Cardinal Richelieu. After praising the Cardinal-Minister's greatness and genius and his plans for France and other parts of the world, the preacher lamented that his early death almost prevented the execution of his many unfinished plans. Marie stepped up, however, and was bestowed "the honor of continuing with his work" while being animated by a similar zeal. She did more than anyone else to make Richelieu live on even in death.[7]

At the Carmelite chapel several months later, the more established preacher Fléchier spoke far more conservatively about his subject. He went on at length about Marie but said little on balance about her leaderly and enterprising qualities or any achievements that could be considered hers in any real way. He wove a narrative of her life that, altogether, has more the characteristics of a caricature and an apology than an accurate likeness. As a child she was pure in her morals and exceptionally wise. She had only good desires and grew up wishing to do only good works. She grew up to be a woman of exceptional "modesty" and even "austere virtue." She would have remained among the Carmelites after her brief marriage to the Marquis de Combalet except that "power and authority opposed her design." She left Carmel de l'Incarnation in a spirit of "obedience" and in subsequent years she suffered the sorrow of wishing to be a nun while accepting God's, her uncle's, and her spiritual counselors' determinations that she was not called to be a nun.[8]

Fléchier went on to interpret the rest of Marie's life as the fruit of a frustrated religious vocation. She assisted the poor and the miserable of the world because of how disabused she was of the vanities of worldly life. She was "a heroic woman," he was sure to say, but her heroism had to do with her spiritual detachment from her riches, palaces, and the world of theater, dinner parties, and the royal court. She "retired from court" as soon as she was able, due to the "fervor of her charity."

Fléchier also believed Marie was a saint, that she had gone straight to Heaven, but for very different reasons than those offered by Brisacier.[9]

Over the long term, Fléchier's portrait prevailed over Brisacier's where Marie was remembered in positive terms. Unsurprisingly, her memory was kept alive most appreciatively by the Catholic institutions and communities she had sponsored throughout her life. Her influence on projects in New France made it into some of the first works of history on French Canada.[10] Her leading role in the establishment of the MEP seminary and affiliated French missionary dioceses was noted in nineteenth-century and twentieth-century narratives about them.[11] For many years, priests, brothers, nuns, and not a few ordinary laypeople remembered and learned about the late Duchesse d'Aiguillon through the thousands of masses for the repose of her soul that she had endowed in churches all over France, in Rome, and in mission lands. The Augustinian hospital nuns in Québec would at their annual Mass for Marie drape black cloth throughout their convent church and light candles around images of the duchess's coat of arms. By the eighteenth century, Marie was regarded as a saint by the hospital nuns, who prayed *to* her, not only for her.[12]

The Lazarists, too, would remember Marie as one of their great founding-era patrons. Over time, however, while pressing for Vincent de Paul's sainthood and while spreading devotion to his cult after his canonization in 1737, the congregation's histories de-emphasized ways Marie had collaborated with De Paul and often directed him in his work. Hagiographies of De Paul made it appear that Marie was just one of a number of rich women who were swayed by the saint's charisma to engage in charitable works.

Marie was remembered for a time in France in negative ways, too. It could hardly have been otherwise, given her association with Cardinal Richelieu—a polarizing figure in French historiography and national mythmaking long after his time. Defamatory stories about her private relationship with her uncle long survived her and were even exaggerated in the wake of her death, sometimes simply to entertain the growing reading public in France that had a growing appetite for tawdry tales from history. Tales circulated, for example, about ways in which Richelieu had attempted to use his niece to trap princely men into a marriage alliance with his family. A well-traveled French merchant named Robert Challes, who had been born long after the time in question and who penned memoirs in the eighteenth century, recycled one about how the "cunning" Richelieu, after failing to get Gaston d'Orléans to discard his wife in favor of

Marie, arranged for the Comte de Soissons to accidentally see Marie emerge "quite naked" from a bath, hoping that the young nobleman would lunge lustfully toward "so beautiful a Diana" and then have to marry her as a matter of honor.[13]

An early French novel, by Gatien Courtilz de Sandras, was published thirteen years after Marie's death and told the story of a fictional page in Richelieu's household. The page at one point mentions in it that, while the late prime minister may very well have been in love with his niece, who was "handsome enough to tempt as great a man as he," the secretive meetings Richelieu often held with Marie had to do with political intrigues and espionage. The same novel also exploited and perpetuated the rumors that did abound, even while Richelieu was alive, that Marie's nephew Armand-Jean was really her son. De Sandras pointed out in his novel, correctly, that this rumor was "more publicly spoken about after [Richelieu's] death, until at last it was so widespread that not only the common people but also persons of the first quality believed it."[14]

Not much of an effort was made by Marie's admirers to counter such stories. They were divided enough among themselves about how to speak about her accomplishments, and about the nature of her unconventional life as a widow who never remarried or became a nun. Members of the Richelieu family in the late seventeenth and eighteenth centuries also did not work effectively together to preserve Marie's historical legacy. They were often at odds with one another, including over things Marie had done in her will to favor her niece Marie-Madeleine and the heirs of her younger nephew Jean-Baptiste over the elder Armand-Jean. Marie-Madeleine and Armand-Jean fought each other in court in the wake of their aunt's death, especially after the latter finally sired an heir in 1696 after marrying for a second time. That heir, Louis-François-Armand, the third Duc de Richelieu, would go on to live until 1788. Inheritance disputes among the heirs of Jean-Baptiste, those of Armand-Jean, and descendants, too, of Marie's cousin Claire-Clémence and her husband the Prince de Condé would plague the Richelieu family throughout the eighteenth century. Painting Marie and her intentions in a bad light was as useful to some of the lawyers in these court battles as the opposite was to others.[15]

Once the French Revolution became a factor, there were parties interested in tarnishing the legacies of noble families that were loyal to the overthrown and guillotined monarch, Louis XVI. Direct descendants of Marie's brother, François, reigned up to the Revolution as the dukes of Richelieu and Aiguillon. One of them, Armand-Desiré de Vignerot, the Duc d'Aiguillon, was as a young man one of the first high-ranking French nobles to join with the Third Estate revolutionaries in 1789 but fled France several years later during the Reign of Terror. The ongoing defamation of prominent families of the Ancien Régime for contemporary political reasons explains why, in 1808, a slanderous publication about Marie—who had been dead for 133 years—appeared in France entitled *Histoire Secrète du Cardinal Richelieu, ou Ses Amours avec Marie de Médicis et Madame de Combalet, depuis Duchesse d'Aiguillon*. Its author was the bibliographer Simon Chardon de La Rochette, a bureaucrat in Napoleon Bonaparte's imperial government. Pretending to have discovered documents in the French archives, La Rochette spun the tale of a sordid love triangle: Marie de' Medici was in love with Richelieu, but Richelieu was in love with his niece, who acquiesced to his advances out of fear of losing her place and his protection; thus the Queen Mother's rage over the latter was the real reason for the drama of the Day of the Dupes in 1630 and its aftermath.[16]

Later in the century, the novelist Alexandre Dumas plausibly pilloried Marie in *The Red Sphinx*, which is known better in French as *Le Comte de Moret*. Dumas depicted Marie as a pious drip in public, covered from head to toe like a nun and shielding her eyes from anything morally questionable in high society, but also as a minimally clad, sighing sexpot in private, especially when her uncle was anywhere near.[17]

There were efforts in the nineteenth century to counter these portrayals. When editing funeral orations by Fléchier and other great preachers of the seventeenth century, the French journalist and literary critic Jean-Joseph Dussault penned a biographical essay on Marie. He accepted uncritically, however, Fléchier's portrayal of a woman who, "after her uncle's death . . . renounced the world and its affairs, which never had any appeal for her." Dussault also gave Saint Vincent de Paul most of the credit for Marie's charitable works: she pursued them "under the direction of that great man." She willingly and meekly became De Paul's "disciple" after her many years of having dutifully "served" her uncle Richelieu.[18] In 1854, an Anglo-Irish aristocrat, poet, and critic named Aubrey Thomas de Vere, after converting to the Catholic Church, put forward a book on great Catholic women from history who had been neglected. But in this book, *Heroines of Charity*, he described the Duchesse d'Aiguillon as just one of "many other illustrious ladies who were won by the pleadings of St. Vincent [de Paul]" and as a woman who found "her chief happiness in devoting her immense fortune to carrying out the various schemes of benevolence which that apostle of charity conceived."[19]

The most thorough attempt to tell Marie's story properly up until now was the full-length French-language biography published in 1879 and authored by the pious Catholic aristocrat and amateur historian, Alfred Bonneau-Avenant. Bonneau-Avenant lived from 1823 to 1889 and was a relative of Marie's friend Madame de Miramion, whose story led him to Marie's. Bonneau-Avenant did a great deal of research and had access to many of the archival sources consulted for the present book. But he also did not have at his disposal anything like the quantity of primary and secondary sources readily available today to scholars trained in the age of air travel and digital technology. Nor was he adequately trained in historical methods.

Bonneau-Avenant tried once and for all to rescue Marie's reputation from her long line of detractors—especially his contemporary Dumas, but also going all the way back to the propagandists working for Marie de' Medici, Urbain de Maillé-Brézé, and the Frondeurs. Bonneau-Avenant also recognized that the Great Man tradition of historical scholarship that was then in its heyday was obscuring the stories of some truly great women. Daringly for a man of his day, he devoted himself to the histories of important women of the seventeenth century. The problem was, he was by turns hamstrung and motivated in his work by three things: his desire to see causes for his subjects' canonizations opened up by the Catholic Church, his projection backward in time onto his subjects of nineteenth-century ideals of femininity, emphasizing domesticity and meekness, and his penchant for discarding and sometimes revising complicated details from the historical record to complete predetermined story lines.

In Marie's case, two of these complicating facts were her relationships—one secretively romantic, and the other overtly political and rivalrous—with Cardinal La Valette and Cardinal Mazarin. La Valette's presence in Marie's life and his untimely death in 1639 help to explain why Marie never remarried when she had opportunities, and why she also suffered a dark period of depression in late 1639 but then threw herself more fully into many of the projects that became her life's work. Bonneau-Avenant, looking at the archival sources that hint at this, cited only the most innocent-sounding lines from Marie's letters to La Valette and averred that the two friends' relationship was like that of a father and a daughter, despite the churchman's mere eleven-year seniority in age and his known attractiveness to all the women in Marie's inner circle.

Bonneau-Avenant also failed to account for Marie's tense relationship with Cardinal Mazarin during the Fronde and indeed downplayed altogether the duchess's political activities. The formidable aspects of Marie's personality—including her occasional ruthlessness and her capacity to dominate in the dangerous games of courtly intrigue of the mid-seventeenth century—are nowhere to be found in Bonneau-Avenant's portrait. Furthermore, Bonneau-Avenant appears to have made up from whole cloth a number of stories about Marie, including that her nephew Jean-Baptiste died in her arms, not in Italy, in 1665, and that in her youth Cardinal Richelieu acquired a papal bull forbidding her from becoming a nun. Presumably this was to assuage concerns, which would have been strong among devout Catholic readers in the late nineteenth century, about why Marie never remarried after the age of eighteen but also never took the veil as a religious—as many of her friends and relatives did—even when she had the freedom to do so in her mature years.

Thus Bonneau-Avenant got too much in his own way while trying to ensure that Marie became widely known and honored again. While pursuing his goals, he ended up passing down a kind of verbal plaster-of-Paris portrait of Marie. Unsurprisingly, that portrait was far less compelling to later generations of French Catholics, history readers, and researchers than a more naturalistic portrait—one honest about the duchess's complexities and flaws and about gaps in the historical record—would have been.

Thus, up to the present day, information about Marie's full, remarkable life has remained scattered mostly in dusty old books, archives, research libraries, and occasional pages and footnotes in academic studies of various themes and subjects that intersect with the duchess's legacy: women and charitable action in the seventeenth century, early colonial-era French Catholic missions, the first literary *salons* in Europe, early modern French literature and the arts, and of course the lives and relationships of Cardinal Richelieu, Vincent de Paul, and other figures who were never forgotten as Marie was. The seeds for this biography, indeed, were only accidentally sown amid the author's doctoral research on a highly specialized theme, that of lay Catholic elites' historiographically neglected contributions to the storied missions of the Jesuits in New France.

Just as Marie has remained mostly invisible in historiographical terms up to now, she has also not been well remembered by means of artwork and architectural monuments that have survived since the seventeenth century. Although many portraits of her were done during her lifetime, not that many still exist. Several that have long been believed to depict her were misattributed long ago. This is true of two small enamel portraits owned by the Louvre, one depicting a very young woman with brown eyes and light brown hair, the other a more overweight young woman with blue eyes and even lighter hair. Both have been presumed to be portraits of Marie when she was very young—the sort that might have been employed to show suitors what she looked like when she was put on the marriage market. The problem is, the artist, Jean Petitot, was not active when Marie was very young, and the hairstyles have a mid-century quality about them. They are almost certainly, instead, a pair of portraits of Marie's two nieces, Marie-Madeleine and Marie-Marthe, done by Petitot at the height of his career. Marie is known to have commissioned such miniatures of family members in this period.[20] Furthermore, the face of the brown-eyed girl resembles that of a later portrait believed to depict Marie-Madeleine, and we can presume that the overweight, blue-eyed young woman was Marie-Marthe, who we know tragically died after suffering a stroke while just a teenager.

The rather beautiful portrait used for this book's cover is believed to be of Marie and is in the Fogg Art Museum's collection at Harvard University. Painted by Pierre Mignard, it depicts a dark-haired woman of uncertain age with dark eyes and a longer nose who holds up for the viewer a portrait within the portrait—presumably a deceased husband. Mignard was active as a court painter only in Marie's later years and in subsequent decades, and the hairstyle and dress in this portrait suggest it was painted sometime in the last four decades of the seventeenth century. If it is indeed a portrait of Marie and her long-deceased husband Combalet, as the French family that sold it to the Winthrops in America in the nineteenth century believed it was, it must have been an idealized portrait intending to depict her much younger than she was—possibly one done at the time of her death for her niece or nephew.[21]

Other works of art that are known for certain to depict Marie are strangely wide-ranging in what they show. The engraving for the frontispiece of Desmarets's novel *Rosane* depicts a more beautiful woman than others done by the engravers Jean Le Blond and Balthasar Moncornet. Copies of several portraits of the duchess that were sent to Québec in the seventeenth century differ considerably, too, from a painting in France that is most likely to have been done from life sometime in the middle of the seventeenth century. It hangs in the city hall of Dinan, a small town in Brittany. It depicts a woman with dark hair, dark eyes, a longer nose, and rich attire including ducal robes, but in the style that Marie would have worn in the late 1630s or early 1640s. A textual description of the subject was painted sometime after she died. This painting was gifted to the town by one of its nineteenth-century mayors, Henri Flaud, and is believed to have been painted by Charles Beaubrun or his cousin Henri Beaubrun, both of whom were Marie's contemporaries and both of whom painted numerous portraits of high-ranking courtiers of the time.[22]

Ironically, the painted portrait that is most reliably a representation of Marie as she appeared as a subject seated before the artist was misattributed for several centuries. This is the one by Philippe de Champaigne that hangs in the gallery of the Labirinto della Masone of Franco Maria Ricci in Parma. It was in private hands in Italy for many centuries and not known to be a portrait of Richelieu's niece until it was examined in the early twenty-first century by art historians at the Louvre in collaboration with Edoardo Pepino in Italy. Although the woman in this portrait has hair on the lighter side, Marie's hair may have had some grays in it by the time this was painted around 1639 or 1640, and her darker brown hair may have looked lighter when reflecting sunlight or the light of a bright chandelier. The subject in this portrait, with her dark eyes, long nose, and formidable expression, also bears a subtle resemblance to Cardinal Richelieu. She furthermore wears a red dress of the finest make and latest style of the period that harkens in color to the robes Richelieu famously wore, and she dons a magnificent string of pearls, similar to one Marie was known to have worn to many courtly functions.

The places that the duchess called home also have a checkered history. Her childhood home, the Château de Glénay, lay in ruins for several centuries in a rural area of France remote from Paris or other major cities. It is only over the past few years that the château is being restored, and its history properly reintroduced to the French people as part of their patrimony, by its new owners, Philippe and Michel Durand-Meyrier, in partnership with the French Republic.

A far worse fate awaited Marie's beloved Château de Rueil. It was confiscated and sold during the French Revolution and then, early in the nineteenth century, bought at a bargain price by a speculative syndicate, part of the Bande Noire that purchased various great properties of the Ancien Régime to make quick profits from them. The Bande Noire syndicate had the château destroyed in pieces, profiting from the sale of its stones, sculptures, and other physical materials, and then sold the land it sat on in smaller lots. Some of the artwork that had belonged to Cardinal Richelieu and Marie from this château and from other properties they had owned over the years ended up either destroyed or scattered in various museums and private collections across France and in various other countries.[23]

Likewise, the Château de Richelieu in the Loire Valley was confiscated during the Revolution. It was destroyed more quickly, in acts of political vandalism against the symbols of the Ancien Régime, but not before most of the artwork inside was variously sold and seized by agents of the new regime. Once Napoleon was in power, however, the young Armand-Emmanuel de Vignerot, the Duc de Richelieu, returned to France after some time in exile fighting for the Czar of Russia. He took possession of his ancestral domain but sold it to a Bande Noire syndicate on the condition that it be demolished. Napoleon attempted but failed to save the château in 1807, and over the next several decades it, too, was turned into a quarry where marble, stone, cobblestones, and other building materials were sold at very low prices. Some of the remaining paintings of the château, however, were donated to the Musée d'Orléans. Others ended up in Tours, Versailles, and many other places.[24]

Marie's primary home still stands, of course, and is well maintained by the French government. This is because the Petit Luxembourg has been utilized, since 1958, as the official residence of the President of the French Senate. For this very reason, however, it is not generally open to the public for visits, and its history—not just from Marie's era but also from Napoleon's—has therefore not been pressed upon a great many French people or foreign visitors over the years.

Finally, Marie's burial place is unmarked and cannot be properly visited in the way that her famous uncle's at the Sorbonne can be. This is because the convent of Carmel de l'Incarnation was destroyed by real estate developers in the twentieth century and its crypt was sealed off from view. Passersby today where the Rue Saint-Jacques intersects with the Place Alphonse Laveran have no idea about the storied Carmelite community that once stood there, let alone about Marie de Vignerot, the Duchesse d'Aiguillon and Peer of France, whose bones and dust rest silently somewhere near their feet.

Author's Afterword

During one of my research trips to Europe for this book, I was disappointed when I learned that I could not visit Marie de Vignerot's tomb in Paris. The convent that the duchess loved on the Rue Saint-Jacques had been vacated by the Carmelites long ago, at a time of violent suppression of Catholic religious orders by French revolutionaries. The convent buildings and grounds were then gradually destroyed, definitively by the 1960s, to make way for new streets and apartment buildings.

Marie was one of the most high-achieving and fascinating women of the early modern period. Yet her remains, together with those of Catherine de Rambouillet, Julie d'Angennes, the Princesse de Condé, and some remarkable nuns she had known, rest somewhere unmarked beneath the buildings that stand today at 284 Rue Saint-Jacques and 25 Rue Henri-Barbusse.

I decided to make a pilgrimage, at least, to the sidewalk at these addresses. That was in the summer of 2016. My plan was to buy a white rose at a flower shop, leave it on the pavement in front of one of the apartment buildings that stood where Carmel de l'Incarnation once did, and offer some silent prayers.

I kept delaying my visit because 284 Rue Saint-Jacques was farther away by foot from places I had to be most days that summer. However, a friend from New York unexpectedly joined me in France for a few days and insisted we make the pilgrimage together.

The day we chose proved to be a rainy one. Starting out in the district of Saint-Germain, we bided time in a few historic churches, a chocolate shop, a café, and the Bon Marché, where we lingered through the afternoon. By the time the rain stopped, I wondered whether it was getting too late and whether we should head back to the Marais district, where I was staying that summer, for an apéritif and dinner.

My friend encouraged me to stick to our plan, reminding me I had only a few days left in France before heading home to the U.S.

So we looked for a flower shop, only to find that the one I had in mind, and another along the way, were closed for the August *vacances*.

"I don't think this will work," I said. "If I can't bring a white rose, I'd rather wait to do this the next time I am in Paris." It was also beginning to drizzle again, so it was unclear whether the rain was done for the day.

"We can't back out of this now," my friend insisted. "It doesn't matter what kind of flower we bring to the duchess. Let's just take one from the Luxembourg Gardens along the way! It would be like we were bringing her a flower from her own yard, wouldn't it?"

I admitted that this was a great idea. I also enjoyed our little act of subversion: we surreptitiously plucked a pink flower from one of the beautiful beds in the Jardin de Luxembourg, hoping no park attendants had noticed.

The walk from there to 284 Rue Saint-Jacques was more challenging than expected because of the weather and because a pain in one of my feet was worsening. Although we considered turning around, we pressed on.

As we neared our destination, we stopped dead in our tracks, each of us noticing the same thing. A florist was in her shop, and on the sidewalk near her open door was a sign that said, in French, "Final day before summer closing." My friend and I looked at each other, eyes widened, and walked in.

We stopped again in disbelief. A large bouquet of white roses, shaped into a cross, was displayed in the center of the shop. Numerous loose white roses were on sale all around it. I purchased one of them, just as I had originally planned.

The stretch of sidewalk we were looking for was only steps away from the flower shop. When we arrived, my friend and I could not believe, again, what we were seeing. The building at 284 Rue Saint-Jacques was home, it turned out, to an Eastern Christian media company with religious literature for sale. Open books with old icons of Christ and the Blessed Mother were displayed in one of its ground floor windows, just above the place on the sidewalk where we thought we should leave the rose.

Once the rose was on the concrete, my friend and I stood at a slight distance from each other, facing opposite directions as if we did not know each other. Suddenly self-conscious about what we were doing, we did not want to draw attention to ourselves or to the rose from any of the chic Parisians passing by us.

It was rush hour, and the area was busy with pedestrians and with commuters in cars and on bicycles and mopeds.

As horns blared, we silently offered our prayers for the Duchesse d'Aiguillon and other forgotten people buried in the Carmelite crypt that we could not see but knew was somewhere close to us in the ground.

As I was praying, my hand over my mouth and chin in my embarrassment, I was startled by a man's voice.

"Excuse me, may I help you with something?" The man spoke kindly in accented English.

I looked up and was surprised to see a clergyman, perhaps in his fifties. He was at the door of the building, fishing out a key.

Unprepared for the interaction, I blurted out, "Oh, no, thank you! I'm fine! It's just that, uh, someone who, well, means something to me is buried somewhere near this building—there used to be a church here with tombs—and my friend and I just wanted to leave a flower and say some prayers."

The man was an Eastern Orthodox priest, it turned out, so he found nothing at all strange in what I had said. My embarrassment melted away.

"Oh, you must mean the crypt of the old Carmelite convent," the priest said. He pointed and added, "If you look through the window here, you can see that part of the portal of the convent is still here, incorporated into this building. I run this center here. I can let you in so you can see it better, if you like. And perhaps you'd like to bring the rose inside, too, and place it a bit closer to the person you are praying for."

We followed him inside. He stood back as we admired the old stonework of the partially intact portal and the way it was artfully joined to an otherwise modern interior. He then sat us down for a few minutes as he looked up the name of a local historian whom he thought might have more information for me about the Carmelite convent and its crypt. He also asked me about what I was up to in Paris and seemed delighted to learn that an American was taking the time to research the life of an accomplished Catholic Frenchwoman of the distant past.

My friend sat silently, watching my face and the priest's, and then looked at me again wide-eyed after our unexpected host offered next to take us down to the basement of the building, where there was an office with computers, so that we could leave Marie's rose there.

"You won't be able to see any tombs, I'm sorry to say," he added, "just our whitewashed walls. But it's the closest I can get you to your duchess."

We followed him down the stairs and I stopped in front of a blank, arching wall of stone and concrete. I laid the rose on the floor and this time, when I offered more prayers in silence, I pressed my hands to the wall. It was surely my imagination, but as I prayed, I felt a gentle vibration, as if there were some stirring of recognition and joy concentrated somewhere just beyond that interface between the living and the dead.

My friend and I both left the Rue Saint-Jacques that evening in awe at what had happened.

I also left with new conviction—at a time when my career as a scholar was in doubt, and before I had finished my first book, on the Jesuits of New France, let alone begun writing this one—that I was supposed to keep researching and then write about Marie's story, come what may. That conviction ended up taking me to amazing places, including the remote hamlet of Glénay, where Marie was born, and the frozen-in-time town of Richelieu that her uncle had dreamed up in the Loire Valley.

My hope, now that this book is done and out in the world, is twofold. First, I hope simply that Marie would recognize herself in this portrait, give or take some errors I have unintentionally made while interpreting the existing sources, and the gaps in them, to the best of my ability. Second, I hope that this book puts a strong, high-achieving, faithful, but also flawed and real woman of the Catholic Church and of France's Golden Age back onto history's center stage where she belongs—standing alongside Cardinal Richelieu, Saint Vincent de Paul, and great princes in some parts of the drama, and standing tall and alone in others.

Acknowledgments

A mong the many individuals and institutions who had a hand in this book, I thank first and foremost Jessica Case, Maria Fernandez, and everyone at Pegasus Books and Simon & Schuster who made my dreams for this book become reality.

I first learned of Marie de Vignerot when I was a graduate student in History at Yale University. Although I did not begin work on the project that became this book for some time thereafter, *La Duchesse* bears many imprints of the training I received from my advisor, Carlos M.N. Eire, and a range of other historians who mentored me early in my career, including Charles Walton, Stuart Schwartz, Ronald Rittgers, Brad S. Gregory, the late John Merriman, and the late Father John O'Malley, S.J. I am grateful for their support over many years, without which this book would not have germinated successfully.

I was a postdoctoral fellow at the Leibniz-Institut für Europäische Geschichte in Mainz, Germany, when I first began envisioning a book about Vignerot. I thank Irene Dingel, Judith Becker, and all who welcomed me to IEG for a full year of uninterrupted research, writing, and fellowship with scholars from many different countries.

It was at Columbia University, where I taught for several years, that I began working on this book. I am grateful to the Department of History and the ACLS/Mellon New Faculty Fellow program for the research and travel support I was given from 2013 to 2015. The archives and libraries I visited at that time include the Archives des Missions Étrangères de Paris, where Brigitte Appavou was helpful, and the Archivio Storico Propaganda Fide in Rome, where the staff was gracious and of great assistance. In Rome, Betta Povoledo was a generous hostess.

The project took further shape while I was a member of the History faculty at the University of Nebraska Omaha from 2016 to 2018. Colleagues including John

Grigg, Martina Saltamacchia, and Mark Celinscak were supportive, and some of
my overseas research was funded by UNO's Department of History. Additional
research funding at the time came from the Western Society for French History
and the University of Notre Dame's Cushwa Center, the latter of which enabled
me to visit the Archives Départementales de la Drôme in Valence, France, where
Françoise Martinez-Pujante and her colleagues were both kind and helpful.

Robert P. George and Bradford P. Wilson deserve warm thanks for the
two full years they and the James Madison Program provided me at Princeton
University from 2018 to 2020. Much of the research and writing for this book
occurred there as I benefited, too, from the advice and convivial company of
other excellent scholars, including Matthew Franck, William Hay, Nathan
Pinkoski, Rabbi Mitchell Rocklin, and Aaron Zubia who all offered feedback
on my manuscript.

I finished writing this book in New York City during the period of the global
COVID-19 pandemic. R.R. Reno and the Institute on Religion and Public Life
welcomed me as a Writer-in-Residence for a year at the offices of *First Things*,
and I am grateful for the support I received there from the whole magazine staff.
Likewise, Colin T. Moran and his congenial team at Abdiel Capital Advisors
was generous with office space and encouragement during critical final stages for
the book. Also greatly supportive since this same period have been Tim Gray,
Christopher O. Blum, and so many at the Augustine Institute Graduate School
in Denver, for which I have been teaching since 2020.

I am grateful for the hospitality I received from my friends Florence Lotz and
Eric de Bettignies while doing research in France for this book. And I cannot
express enough thanks to those who arranged and assisted with my private
visits to the Palais de Luxembourg, the Petit Luxembourg, and the Chapelle
de Sainte-Ursule at the Sorbonne, including Senator Philippe Mouiller and his
aide Christelle Geay, Director Jean-Marc Ticchi and Cordelia Jouishomme of the
Bibliothèque du Sénat, and Fabrice Tenret of the Division de l'Administration de la
Chancellerie Rectorat de l'Académie de Paris. Furthermore, Philippe and Michel
Durand-Meyrier, co-owners of the Château de Glénay in Poitou-Charentes,
offered invaluable insights into Marie de Vignerot's origins, as well as a wonderful
tour of her childhood home and several images for this book.

More colleagues, contacts, and friends than I can mention here were supportive in so many ways as this book was coming into being. Among them are
Gwendolyn Adams, Philip Byers, Vivian Choi Milton, Muriel Clair, Elbridge A.

Colby, Susan Dinan, Michael B. Kelly and his colleagues at Christendom College, Thomas D. Lehrman and the staff of Sacred Heart Greenwich, Francis X. Maier, Casey Kane Monahan of the Harvard Art Museums, Melissa Moschella, Father Peter Nguyen, S.J., Andrew and Caroline Pillsbury Oliver, Lorenzo Polvani and his family, Juliana Miller Reno, the late Father Christopher Roberts, Father Ross Romero, S.J., Adina Ruiu, John and Eileen Safranek, Stephen and Helena McCarthy Schmalhofer, Patricia Schramm and other friends affiliated with the American-Swiss Foundation, Patricia Snow, Ping-Yuan Wang, Daniel I. Wasserman-Soler, Kristin Williams, Father Stephen Wolfe, S.J., Sarah Yellin, Clifford Zink, the Catholic Classics reading group in Omaha, my students at the Augustine Institute and the University of Nebraska Omaha, and the staff of all the libraries, archives, museums, and historic sites I visited for the book.

This book would not exist without the love and encouragement I have always received from my parents, Kevin and Maureen McShea, from my siblings, Brendan, Colleen, and Thomas, and from other members of my family. My thanks to and for all of them is boundless.

Finally, I must give special mention to several individuals whose imprint on this book is especially palpable to me, and for whose support, feedback, and sheer time and attention I am most grateful. Alice Martell, my agent, not only connected me to Pegasus Books but helped me to discover and then discipline a much stronger narrative voice than I was initially brave enough to employ in telling Marie de Vignerot's story. Father Sam Zeno Conedera, S.J., a faithful interlocutor of many years, read through large portions of the manuscript and offered critiques, moral support, and humorous perspectives that were beneficial beyond measure. Urs Staub shared some of his extensive private research on the Richelieu family that proved critical in several chapters. Louis W. Miller, my former Harvard professor and now friend of many years, as well as Daniel Zinsser, a friend in Princeton, both read through the entire manuscript and offered careful, useful feedback on every chapter.

Daniel's wife, Patricia Siedlecki Zinsser, did the same. Far beyond this, however, she took such a serious, sustained interest in my subject beginning in 2019—enthusiastically and capably discussing countless aspects of my research and writing process over long coffees, walks, and then pandemic-time phone conversations, following up with ideas, comments, and questions at every turn—that I cannot imagine what this book would be without her friendship. There is no one else to whom I can more fittingly or joyfully dedicate *La Duchesse* than to her.

Sources

MANUSCRIPT COLLECTIONS AND UNPUBLISHED SOURCES

Ader Auction House, Paris, www.ader-paris.fr/en/home: Digitized records of sold items in private collections, Lots 127, 182.

Archives Départementales des Deux-Sèvres (AD Deux-Sèvres), Niort: E 1274, 3 E 15210.

Archives Départementales de la Drôme (AD Drôme), Valence: Fonds d'Aiguillon, 100 Mi 126, 134, 150, 157 (R1), 157 (R2), 180.

Archives of the Jesuits in Canada (AJC), Montreal: Fonds du Collège Sainte-Marie.

Archives des Missions Étrangères de Paris (AMEP), Paris: Volumes 2, 23, 101, 107, 200, 350, 650, 858.

Archives Diplomatiques du Ministère des Affaires Étrangères (AMAE), La Courneuve and Nantes: Correspondance Politique, Lorraine 27; Mémoires et Documents (La Courneuve), Afrique 8, France 53MD/834.

Archives du Monastère des Augustines, Québec: HDQ-F1-A1/2:2.

Archivio Segreto Vaticano (ASV), Vatican City: Segretaria di Stato, Vescovi e Prelati, 36.

Archivio Storico de Propaganda Fide (ASPF), Vatican City: Acta congregationis, Volume 26; Scritture originali riferite nelle congregazioni generali (SOCG), Volume 252; Scritture riferite nei Congressi (SC), Indie orientali, Volume 193.

Bibliothèque Interuniversitaire de la Sorbonne (BIU Sorbonne), Paris: Manuscrits Richelieu (MSRIC), 17, 18, 20, 151; Fonds Victor Cousin (MSVC), 2.

Bibliothèque Nationale de France, Site Arsenal (BnF Arsenal), Paris: Français 4213, 6314.

Bibliothèque Nationale de France, Site Mitterand (BnF Mitterand), Paris: 340; Fol-FM-14283; Morel de Thoisy, 54.

Bibliothèque Nationale de France, Site Richelieu (BnF Richelieu), Paris: Clairambault, 1135, 1140; Dupuy, 640; Français, 4584, 5843, 6314, 6644, 17333, 25058; Italien, 1271; NAF 19735.

Centre de Recherches des Archives Nationales (CARAN), Paris: Série E, Conseil du Roi, 1688, 1690; Série MC, Minutier Central des Notaires de Paris, Études (ET) XXIV, XLVI, LXXXVI; Microfilms de la Réserve du Minutier (MI/RI), 1063, 1064; Série S, Biens des Établissements Religieux Supprimés, 6707, 6715, 1716; Série Y, Châtelet de Paris et Prévôte d'Île de France, 178, 180, 181, 188, 204, 210; Série Z, Juridictions Spéciales et Ordinaires, 1J; Chambre et Greffiers des Bâtiments, 258.

Harvard Art Museums, Cambridge, Massachusetts: Curatorial files.

Library and Archives Canada (LAC), Ottawa: C11A, Fonds des colonies; MG3-III, Étude XLIII; MG8-A23, Fonds de greffes de notaires du Québec; MG17-A10, Correspondance; Série B, Ordres du roi.

PRINTED PRIMARY SOURCES

Abelly, Louis, C.M. *La vie du venerable serviteur de Dieu Vincent de Paul, Instituteur et premier Supérieur General de la Congrégation de la Mission.* 3 volumes. Paris: Florentin Lambert, 1664.

Acarie, Marguerite. *Lettres spirituelles.* Edited by Pierre Sérouet. Paris: Les Éditions du Cerf, 1993.

Advis aux Parisiens, servant de Response aux impostures du Cardinal Mazarin. Paris: 1650.

Allier, Raoul, ed. *La Compagnie du Très-Saint-Sacrement de l'autel à Marseille.* Paris: Honoré Champion, 1909.

Anselme, Père, O.A.D., ed. *Histoire des Grands Officiers de la Couronne de France, avec l'Origine et le progrez de leurs families.* Volume 2. Paris: Estienne Loyson, 1674.

Arnauld, Antoine. *Oeuvres de Messire Antoine Arnauld.* Volume 26. Edited by Gabriel du Pac de Bellegarde and Jean Hautefage. Paris: Sigismond d'Arnay, 1779.

Arrest de la cour de Parlement, contre un livre intitulé Histoire du Ministère d'Armand Jean du Plessis, Cardinal Duc de Richelieu . . . *prononcé et executé l'unzième May 1650.* Paris: Imprimeurs et Libraires ordinaires du Roy, 1650.

Arrest solomnel du Conseil privé du Roy, du deuxième Mars 1660, donné en faveur des Generaux d'Ordres. Paris: 1660.

Aubery, Antoine. *L'histoire du Cardinal-Duc de Richelieu.* Volume 2. Cologne: Pierre du Marteau, 1666.

Aubineau, Léon, ed. *Mémoires du P. René Rapin de la Compagnie de Jésus sur l'église et la société, la cour, la ville et le Jansénisme, 1644–1669.* Volume 2. Paris: Gaume Frères and J. Duprey, 1865.

Avenel, Denis-Louis-Martial, ed. *Lettres, instructions diplomatiques et papiers d'État du cardinal de Richelieu.* 8 volumes. Paris: Imprimérie Impériale, 1853–1877.

Barrière, F., ed. *Mémoires inédits de Louis-Henri de Loménie, Comte de Brienne, Sécrétaire d'État sous Louis XIV.* Volume 1. Paris: Ponthieu et Compagnie, 1828.

Barthélemy, Édouard de, ed. *Les amis de la marquise de Sablé: Receuil de lettres des principaux habitués de son salon.* Paris: E. Dentu, 1865.

Bassompierre, François de. *Mémoires du Mareschal de Bassompierre.* Cologne: Pierre de Marteau, 1665.

Baudier, Michel. *Histoire du mareschal de Toiras.* Paris: Sébastien Cramoisy, 1644.

Baudiment, Louis, ed. *Un mémoire anonyme sur François Pallu, principal fondateur des Missions Étrangères.* Tours: René et Paul Deslis, 1934.

Bense-Dupuis, Pierre. *La clef de la langue romaine dedié à Mme de Combalet, duchesse d'Esguillon.* Paris: Pierre Bense-Dupuis, 1638.

Blache, Antoine. "Mémoires de l'Abbé Blache, docteur en théologie." *Revue rétrospective, ou Bibliothèque historique.* Volume 1. Paris: H. Fournier Ainé, 1833.

Boisrobert, François Le Métel de, ed. *Le sacrifice des Muses au grand cardinal de Richelieu.* Paris: Sébastien Cramoisy, 1635.

Bourges, Jacques de. *Relation du voyage de Monseigneur l'Évêque de Beryte, vicaire apostolique du royaume de la Cochinchine, par la Turquie, la Perse, les Indes, etc. jusqu'au Royaume de Siam et autres lieux.* Paris: Denys Bechet, 1666.

Brisacier, Jacques-Charles de. *Discours funebre pour Madame la duchesse d'Aiguillon, prononcé a Paris dans la Chapelle du Seminaire des Missions Estrangeres.* Paris: Charles Angot, 1675.

Capron, Loïc, ed. *Correspondance complète et autres écrites de Guy Patin.* Paris: Bibliothèque Interuniversitaire de Santé, 2018: www.biusante.parisdescartes.fr/patin/.

Challes, Robert. *Mémoires de Robert Challes, écrivain du Roi: Un colonial au temps de Colbert.* Paris: Plon, 1931.

Champollion-Figeac, Aimé, ed. *Mémoires de Mathieu Molé, Procureur Général, Premier Président du Parlement de Paris et Garde des Sceaux de France*. Volume 3. Paris: Jules Renouard, 1856.

Chéruel, Adolphe, ed. *Lettres du Cardinal Mazarin pendant son Ministère*. 9 volumes. Paris: Imprimérie Nationale, 1872–1906.

Chroniques de l'ordre des Carmélites de la réforme de Sainte-Thérèse depuis leur introduction en France. 5 volumes. Troyes: Imprimérie d'Anner-Andre, 1846–1865.

Clément, Pierre, ed. *Lettres, instructions et mémoires de Colbert*. 8 volumes. Paris: Imprimerie Impériale, 1861–1873.

Colletet, Guillaume. *Les couches sacrées de la Vierge, poème héroique de Sannazar*. Paris: Jean Camusat, 1634.

Constant, Charles, ed. *Mémoires de Nicolas Goulas, gentilhomme ordinaire de la chamber du duc d'Orléans*. Paris: Librarie Renouard, 1879.

Contassot, Félix, ed. "Les Lazaristes à Notre-Dame de La Rose avant la Révolution: Études documentaires." Unpublished manuscript, Paris, 1961.

Corblet, Jules, ed. *Origines royennes de l'institut des Filles-de-la-Croix d'après des documents inédits*. Paris: J.-B. Dumoulin, 1869.

Corneille, Pierre. *Le Cid: Tragi-comédie*. Paris: Augustin Courbé, 1637.

Coste, Pierre C. M., ed. *Vincent de Paul: Correspondence, Conferences, and Documents*. 14 volumes. Translated by Marie Poole, D.C., et al. Brooklyn: New City Press, 1985–2014.

Croisilles, Jean-Baptiste de. *Apologie de l'abbé de Croisilles*. Paris: Toussainct Quinet, 1643.

Crous, Marie. *Abbregé recherché de Marie Crous, Pour tirer la solution de toutes propositions d'Aritmetique*. Paris: Jacques Auvray, 1641.

D'Anthelmy, Charles-Léonce. *La cie de messire François Picquet, consul de France et de Hollande, a Alep, ensuite Evêque de Cesarople, puis de Babylone, Vicaire Apostolique de Perse, avec titre d'Ambassadeur du Roy auprès du Roy de Perse*. Paris: La Veuve Mergé, 1732.

D'Argenson, René II de Paulmy de Voyer. *Les annales de la Compagnie du Saint-Sacrement*. Edited by Henri Beauchet-Filleau. Marseilles: Saint-Léon, 1900.

Desmarets de Saint-Sorlin, Jean. *Rosane: Histoire tirée de celles de Romaines et des Perses*. Paris: Henry Le Gras, 1639.

Dessein des Assemblées de la bourse clericale, Establie à Sainct Nicolas du Chardonnet. Paris: Jean Dincourt, 1655.

Du Bosc, Jacques. *L'honnête femme: The Respectable Woman in Society and the New Collection of Letters and Responses by Contemporary Women*. Edited and translated by Sharon Diane Nell and Aurora Wolfgang. Toronto: Centre for Reformation and Renaissance Studies, 2014.

Dubuisson-Aubenay, François-Nicolas Baudot de. *Journal des guerres civiles, 1648–1652*. Edited by Gustave Saige. 2 volumes. Paris: Champion, 1883–1885.

Dumas, Alexandre. *The Red Sphinx*. Translated by Lawrence Ellsworth. New York: Pegasus Books, 2017.

Dussault, Jean-Joseph, ed. *Oraisons funèbres de Bossuet, Fléchier, et autres orateurs*. Paris: Louis Janet, 1820.

El-Mudarris, Hussein I., and Olivier Salmon, eds. *Le Consulat de France à Alep au XVIIe siècle: Journal de Louis Gédoyn, vie de François Picquet, mémoires de Laurent d'Arvieux*. Aleppo: El-Mudarris, 2009.

La Feste de Versailles. 1668.

Fléchier, Esprit. *Oraisons funèbres de Fléchier, Évèque de Nîmes*. Angers: Fourier-Mame, 1821.

Fontrailles, Louis d'Astarac de. *Relation des choses particulières de la Cour pendant la faveur de Monsieur le Grand*. Cologne: Jean Sameix, 1723.

La Gazette de France. Paris: 1631–1915.

Gournay, Marie de. *Oeuvres Complètes*. 2 volumes. Edited by Jean-Claude Arnould. Paris: Honoré Champion Éditeur, 2002.

Grenaille, François de. *La Bibliothèque des Dames*. Paris: Toussainct Quinet, 1640.

———. *Le mausolée cardinal, ou Éloge funèbre de feu Mgr le cardinal duc de Richelieu, contenant sa naissance, sa vie, sa mort et sa sépulture*. Paris: J. Paslé, 1643.

Grillon, Pierre, ed. *Les papiers de Richelieu*. 6 volumes. Paris: Pedone, 1975–1997.

Grosez, Jean-Étienne, S.J. *La vie de la Mère Marie-Madeleine de La Trinité, fondatrice des Religieuses de N. Dame de Misericorde*. Lyon: Jean Thioly, 1696.

Hertz, Solange, trans. *Rhodes of Viet Nam: The Travels and Missions of Father Alexander de Rhodes in China and Other Kingdoms of the Orient*. Westminister, MD: Newman Press, 1966.

Hill, Henry Bertram, ed. and trans. *The Political Testament of Cardinal Richelieu*. Madison: University of Wisconsin Press, 1961.

Hillman, Richard, and Colette Quesnel, eds. *Marie Le Jars de Gournay: Apology for the Woman Writing and Other Works*. Chicago: University of Chicago Press, 2002.

Histoire de l'ordre de Sainte Ursule, depuis sa Fondation jusqu'à nos jours. Volume 2. Paris: Noyon, 1787.

Horric de Beaucaire, Charles-Prosper-Maurice, ed. *Mémoires de Du Plessis-Besançon*. Paris: Renouard, 1892.

Juchereau de La Ferté de Saint-Ignace, Jeanne-Françoise, O.S.A. *Histoire de l'Hôtel-Dieu de Quebec*. Montauban: Jerosme Legier, 1751.

Laffemas, Isaac de. *Procez burlesque entre Mr le Prince et Madame la duchesse d'Esguillon, avec les plaidoyers*. Paris: La Veuve Théodore Pépingué, 1649.

La Houssaie, Amelot de. *Mémoires historiques, politiques, critiques et littéraires*. Volume 2. Amsterdam: Zacharie Chatelain, 1722.

La Rochette, Simon Chardon de, ed. *Histoire secrète du Cardinal de Richelieu, ou ses amours avec Marie de Médicis et Madame de Combalet, depuis Duchesse d'Aiguillon*. Paris: Simon Chardon de La Rochette, 1808.

La Serre, Jean Puget. *Thomas Morus, ou Le triomphe de la foy, et de la constance: Tragédie en prose, dediée à Madame la Duchesse d'Esguillon*. Paris: Augustin Courbé, 1642.

Launay, Adrien, ed. *Documents historiques relatifs à la Société des Missions-Étrangères*. Volume 1. Paris: Lafoyle, 1904.

———. *Lettres de Monseigneur Pallu: Écrites de 1654 à 1684*. Paris: Les Indes Savantes, 2008.

Leclercq, Chrestien, O.F.M. *Premier établissement de la foy dans la Nouvelle-France*. Volume 2. Paris: Amable Auroy, 1691.

L'Estoile, Pierre de. *Journal d'Henri III, roy de France et de Pologne*. Volume 4. The Hague: Pierre Gosse, 1646.

Le Moyne, Pierre, S.J. *La galerie des femmes fortes* (Paris: Antoine de Sommaville, 1647).

———. *Le portrait du roy passant les Alpes*. Paris: Sébastien Cramoisy, 1629.

———. *Les triomphes de Louys Le Juste en la réduction des Rochelois et des autres rebelles de son royaume*. Reims: N. Constant, 1629.

Le Vassor, Michel. *Histoire du règne de Louis XIII, roi de France et de Navarre*. 10 volumes. Amsterdam: Zacharie Chatelain et Fils, 1750–1753.

Livet, Charles-Louis, ed. *La muze historique, ou Receuil des lettres en vers contenant les nouvelles du temps, écrites à Son Altesse Mademoizelle de Longueville, depuis Duchesse de Nemours (1650–1665)*. 4 volumes. Paris: P. Daffis, 1858–1891.

Louis XIV. *Édit du Roy, portant etablissement de l'Hôpital General, pour le renfermement de pauvres mendians de la ville & fauxbourgs de Paris, donné à Paris au mois d'Avril 1656*. Paris: Prault, 1765.

Mancini, Hortense, and Marie Mancini. *Memoirs*. Edited and translated by Sarah Nelson. Chicago: University of Chicago Press, 2008.

Mandrou, Robert, ed. *Possession et sorcellerie au XVIIe siècle: textes inédits*. Paris: Fayard, 1979.

Marchetti, François. *La vie de Messire Jean-Baptiste Gault, evesque de Marseille*. Paris: Sébastien Huré, 1649.

Mémoire concernant les prétentions élevées par la duchesse d'Aiguillon sur l'hôtel du Petit-Luxembourg, qui lui est contesté par le duc d'Enghien en vertu d'une substitution du cardinal de Richelieu. 1676.

Mémoires de la Congrégation de la Mission. 9 volumes. Paris: Congregation de la Mission, 1863–1866.

Mercure François. 24 Volumes. Paris: Estienne Richer, 1605–1643.

Le Mercure Hollandois, contenant les choses les plus remarquables de toute la Terre, arrivées en l'an 1675 jusqu'à l'an 1676. Amsterdam: Henry and Theodore Boom, 1678.

Meulenbroek, B. L., ed. *Briefwisseling van Hugo Grotius*. Volume 7. The Hague: Martinus Nijhof, 1969.

Michaud, Joseph-François, and Jean-Joseph Poujoulat, eds. *Nouvelle collection des mémoires pour servir à l'histoire de France, depuis le XIIIe siècle jusqu'à la fin du XVIIIe*. Volume 9. Lyon: Guyot Frères, 1853.

La Miliade, or *Le gouvernement présent, ou Éloge de Son Éminence*. 1635.

Montresor, Claude de Bourdeille de. *Mémoires de Monsieur de Montresor*. Volume 2. Leiden: Jean Sameix, 1665.

Morgues, Mathieu de. *La verité défendue: ensemble quelques observations sur la conduicte du Cardinal de Richelieu*. N.p., 1635.

The Nature and Utility of Expeditions to the Coast of France. London: G. Burnet, 1758.

Oudin, Pierre, O.S.A. *Le zèle du salut des âmes et la manière de s'y employer avec fruit*. Paris: Claude Josse, 1669.

Pallu, François. *Relation abbrégée des missions et des voyages des Evesques Francois, envoyez aux Royaumes de la Chine, Cochinchine, Tonquin, et Siam*. Paris: Denys Bechet, 1668.

Paulmier, Jean. *Mémoires touchant l'établissement d'une mission chrestienne dans le Troisième Monde: Autrement appelé, La Terre Australe, Meridionale, Antarctique, & Inconnue*. Edited by Margaret Sankey. Paris: Champion, 2006.

Petitot, Claude-Bernard, ed. *Mémoires du cardinal de Richelieu*. 10 volumes. Paris: Foucault, 1823.

"Plaidoyé pour Madame la Duchesse d'Aiguillon, intervenante & defenderesse, contre Monsieur le Duc d'Orleans, & Mademoiselle d'Orleans sa Fille." *Arrest de la cour de Parlement intervenu dans la cause des Daubriots de Courfraut . . . et quelques autres plaidoyez*. Paris: Pierre Lamy, 1660. 36–65.

Plantet, Eugène, ed. *Correspondance des beys de Tunis et des consuls de France avec la cour, 1577–1830*. Volume 1. Paris: F. Alcan, 1893.

Pommereuse, Marie-Augustine de Saint-Paul de., O.S.U. *Les chroniques de l'ordre des Ursulines*. Volume 1. Paris: Jean Henault, 1673.

Provost, Honorius, ed. *Le séminaire de Québec: Documents et biographies*. Quebec: Archives du Séminaire de Québec, 1964.

Rabbath, Antoine, S.J., ed. *Documents inédits pour servir a l'histoire du Christianisme en Orient*. Volume 1. Paris: Picard et Fils, 1907.

Ragueneau, Paul, S.J. *La vie de a Mère Catherine de Saint Augustin, réligieuse hospitalière de la miséricorde de Québec en la Nouvelle-France*. Paris: Florentin Lambert, 1671.

Ravenel, Jules Amédée Desiré, ed. *Lettres du Cardinal Mazarin a la Reine, a la Princesse Palatine, etc, écrites pendant sa retraite hors de France, en 1651 et 1652*. Paris: Jules Renouard, 1836.

Rébelliau, Alfred, ed. *La compagnie secrète du Saint-Sacrament: Lettres du groupe parisien au groupe marseillais, 1639–1662.* Paris: Honoré Champion, 1908.

Recherches historiques de l'ordre du Saint-Esprit. Volume 1. Paris: Claude Jombert, 1710.

Récit véritable de tout ce qui s'est passé au Chasteau de S. Germain en Laye, au retour de Monseigneur Frère Unique du Roy prés da sa Majesté. Paris: Pierre Targa, 1634.

Rennard, Joseph, ed. *Les Caraïbes, La Guadeloupe, 1635–1656: Histoire des vingt premières années de la colonisation de la Guadeloupe d'après les relations du R. P. Breton.* Paris: G. Ficker, 1929.

Rhodes, Alexandre de, S.J. *Divers voyages et missions du P. Alexandre de Rhodes en la Chine et autres royaumes de l'Orient.* Paris: Sébastien Cramoisy, 1653.

———. *Histoire du Royaume de Tunquin, et des grands progrez que la prédication de l'évangile y a faits.* Lyon: Jean Baptiste Devenet, 1651.

———. *Relazione de' felici successi della santa fede predicata da' padri della Compagnia di Gesù nel regno di Tunchino.* Rome: G. Luna, 1650.

———. *Sommaire des diverses voyages et missions apostoliques.* Paris: Florentin Lambert, 1653.

Richelieu, Armand-Jean du Plessis de. *Harangue prononcée en la salle du petite Bourbon le XXIII Fevrier 1615.* Paris: Sébastien Cramoisy, 1615.

———. *Instruction du chrestien.* Paris: N. de la Vigne, 1626.

———. *Traitté de la perfection du chrestien par l'eminentissime Cardinal Duc de Richelieu.* Paris: Antoine Vitré, 1646.

———. *Traitté qui contient la méthode la plus facile et la plus asseurée pour convertir ceux qui se sont séparez de l'Église.* Paris: Sébastien Cramoisy, 1651.

Rollin, Sophie, ed. *Vincent Voiture: Lettres (1625–1648).* Paris: Honoré Champion Éditeur, 2013.

Rotrou, Jean de. *Agésilan de Colchos: Tragi-comédie.* Paris: Anthoine de Sommaville, 1637.

Roux, Amédée, ed. *Les oeuvres de monsieur de Voiture.* Paris: Librairie de Firmin Didot, Frères, 1856.

Ruffi, Antoine de. *La vie de M. le chevalier de la Coste.* Aix: Charles David, 1659.

Rybolt, John, C.M., ed. "Unpublished Correspondence." Vincentian Studies Institute, Chicago, 2020.

Le sacre et couronnement de Louys XIV, Roy de France et de Navarre, dans l'Église de Reims, le septième Juin 1654. Reims: La Veuve François Bernard, 1654.

Saige, Gustave, ed. *Journal des Guerres civiles de Dubuisson-Aubenay, 1648–1652.* 2 volumes. Paris: H. Champion, 1883–1885.

Saint-Joseph, Madeleine de. *Lettres spirituelles de Madeleine de Saint-Joseph.* Edited by Pierre Sérouet. Bruges: Desclée de Brouwer, 1965.

———. *La vie de Soeur Catherine de Jésus, religieuse de l'ordre de Notre-Dame du Mont Carmel établi en France, selon la réformation de sainte Térèse de Jésus.* Paris: F. Dehors, 1626.

Saint-Simon, Louis de Rouvroy. *Mémoires de Saint-Simon.* Volume 12. Edited by André de Boislisle. Paris: Librairie Hachette, 1896.

———. *The Memoirs of the Duke of Saint-Simon on the Reign of Louis XIV and the Regency.* Volume 1. Translated by Bayle St. John. London: Swan Sonnenschein and Co., 1900.

Scarron, Paul. "Ode à Madame la duchesse d'Aiguillon." *Les oeuvres de monsieur Scarron.* Rouen: Guillaume de Luyne, 1663.

Senault, Jean-François, O.S.A. *La vie de la Mere Magdeleine de S. Joseph, religieuse carmelite déchaussée.* Paris: Veuve Jean Camusat, 1645.

Sonnino, Paul, ed. *The Political Testament of Cardinal Richelieu.* Lanham: Rowman and Littlefield, 2020.

Souleyreau, Marie-Catherine Vignal, ed. *La correspondance du cardinal de Richelieu: Au faîte du pouvoir, l'année 1632*. Paris: Harmattan, 2007.

――――. *Le cardinal de Richelieu à la conquète de la Lorraine: Correspondance, 1633*. Paris: Harmattan, 2010.

――――. *Correspondance du cardinal de Richelieu, Année 1634*. 2 volumes. Paris: Harmattan, 2013.

Sue, Eugène, ed. *Correspondance de Henri d'Escubleau de Sourdis, archevêque de Bordeaux*. Volume 2. Paris: Crapelet, 1839.

Sullivan, Louise, D.C., ed. *Spiritual Writings of Louise de Marillac*. Brooklyn: New City Press, 1991.

Table ou abrégé des cent trente-cinq volumes de la Gazette de France. Volume 3. Paris: Galeries du Louvre, 1768.

Le Tableau de la vie & du gouvernement de Messieurs les Cardinaux Richelieu & Mazarin. Paris: Pierre Marteau, 1693.

Tallemant des Réaux, Gédéon. *Les Historiettes*. 6 volumes. Edited by Louis Monmerqué. Paris: Alphonse Levasseur, 1834-1835.

Tamizey de Larroque, Philippe. *Lettres de Jean Chapelain, de l'Académie Française*. Volume 1. Paris: Imprimerie Nationale, 1880.

――――. *Lettres de Peiresc aux Frères Dupuy*. Volume 3. Paris: Imprimerie Nationale, 1892.

Thompson, William M., ed. *Bérulle and the French School: Selected Writings*. New York: Paulist Press, 1989.

Thwaites, Reuben Gold, ed. *The Jesuit Relations and Allied Documents: Travels and Explorations of the Jesuit Missionaries in New France, 1610–1791*. 73 volumes. Cleveland: Burrows Brothers, 1896–1901.

Van Lochom, Michel. *Images des fondatrices, reformatrices, ou principales religieuses de tous les ordres de l'Église*. Paris: Michel Van Lochom, 1639.

Vialart de Saint-Paul, Charles de. *Histoire du ministère d'Armand-Jean du Plessis, Cardinal duc de Richelieu, sous le règne de Louys le Juste, XIII du nom*. Paris: Gervais Alliott, Antoine de Sommaville, Toussainct Quinet, Jean Gugnard, Edmé Pepingué, and Michel Bobin, 1649.

Vigneul-Marville, M. de. *Mélanges d'histoire et de littérature*. Volume 2. Paris: Claude Prudhomme, 1713.

Villareal, Manoel Fernandes. *Le politique tres chrestienm ou Discours politiques sur les actions principals de la vie de feu Monseigneur l'Eminentissime Cardinal Duc de Richelieu*. Translated by François de Grenaille. Paris: Toussainct Quinet, 1643.

Le vray journal des assemblées du Parlement; contenant ce qui s'y est fait depuis la Saint Martin mil six cens quarante-neuf, jusques à Pasques 1651. Paris: Gervais Alliot, 1651.

Wormeley, Katharine Prescott, trans. *Memoirs of Madame de Motteville on Anne of Austria and Her Court*. 3 volumes. Boston: Hardy, Pratt and Company, 1902.

SECONDARY SOURCES

Alberts, Tara. *Conflict and Conversion: Catholicism in Southeast Asia, 1500–1700*. Oxford: Oxford University Press, 2013.

Allain, Mathé. "Colbert and the Colonies." *The French Experience in Louisiana*. Edited by Glenn R. Conrad. Lafayette: Center for Louisiana Studies, 1995.

Antoine, Michel. *Le coeur de l'État: Surintendance, contrôle general et intendances des finances, 1552–1791*. Paris: Fayard, 2003.

Aronson, Nicole. *Madame de Rambouillet ou La Magicienne de la chambre bleue*. Paris: Fayard, 1988.

Avenel, Denis-Louis-Martial, ed. *Le dernier épisode de la vie du Cardinal de Richelieu: Louis XIII, Cinq-Mars, Aug. de Thou.* Paris: Bureaux de la Revue, 1868.

Avezou, Laurent. "Autour du 'Testament politique' de Richelieu: À la recherche de l'auteur perdu (1688–1778)." *Bibliothèque de l'École des chartes* 162/2 (2004): 421–453.

Barine, Arvede. *Louis XIV and La Grande Mademoiselle, 1652–1693.* New York: G. P. Putnam's Sons, 1905.

Barnouin, Michel. "La parenté vauclusienne d'Alexandre de Rhodes." *Mémoires de l'Académie de Vaucluse* 4 (1995). 9–40.

Battifol, Louis. "Richelieu a-t-il persécuté Corneille?" *Revue des deux mondes* 14/3 (1923): 626–657.

Beaumont, Keith. "Pierre de Bérulle (1575–1629) and the Renewal of Catholic Spiritual Life in France." *International Journal for the Study of the Christian Church* 12/2 (2017): 73–92.

Beik, William. *A Social and Cultural History of Early Modern France.* Cambridge: Cambridge University Press, 2009.

Benoist, Pierre. *Le Père Joseph: L'Éminence grise de Richelieu.* Paris: Perrin, 2007.

Bergin, Joseph. *Cardinal Richelieu: Power and the Pursuit of Wealth.* New Haven: Yale University Press, 1990.

———. *Church, Society and Religious Change in France, 1580–1730.* New Haven: Yale University Press, 2009.

———. *The Politics of Religion in Early Modern France.* New Haven: Yale University Press, 2014.

Bingham, D. *The Bastille.* New York: James Pott & Company, 1901.

Blanchard, Jean-Vincent. *Éminence: Cardinal Richelieu and the Rise of France.* New York: Walker & Company, 2011.

Blet, Pierre, S.J. *Richelieu et l'Église.* Versailles: Via Romana, 2007.

Bluche, François. *Louis XIV.* Translated by Mark Greengrass. Oxford: Blackwell, 1990.

———. *Richelieu.* Paris: Perrin, 2003.

Bonnaffé, Edmond. *Recherches sur les collections des Richelieu.* Paris: E. Plon, 1883.

Bonnassieux, Pierre. *Les grandes compagnies de commerce: Étude pour servir a l'histoire de la colonisation.* Paris: Plon, 1892.

Bonneau-Avenant, Alfred. *La Duchesse d'Aiguillon, nièce du cardinal de Richelieu: Sa vie et ses oeuvres charitables, 1604–1675.* Paris: Didier, 1879.

Borély, A. E. *Histoire de la Ville du Havre et de son ancien gouvernement.* Volume 2. Le Havre: Lepelletier, 1881.

Bosseboeuf, L. A. *Histoire de Richelieu et des environs, au pont de vue civil, religieux et artistique.* Tours: L. Péricat, 1890.

Boucher, Philip P. *France and the American Tropics to 1700: Tropics of Discontent?* Baltimore: Johns Hopkins University Press, 2007.

———. *Les Nouvelles-Frances: France in America, 1500–1815.* Providence: The John Carter Brown Library, 1989.

Bourque, Bernard. *All the Abbé's Women: Power and Misogyny in Seventeenth-Century France, Through the Writings of Abbé d'Aubignac.* Tübingen: Narr Verlag, 2015.

Brémond, Henri. *Histoire littéraire du sentiment religieux en France depuis la fin des guerres de religion jusqu'à nos jours.* Volume 3. Grenoble: Éditions Jérôme Millon, 2006.

Bresc-Bautier, Geneviève, et al. *La Sorbonne: Un musée, ses chefs-d'oeuvre.* Paris: Éditions Chancellerie des Universités de Paris, 2007.

Briggs, Robin. "Dubious Messengers: Bodin's Daemon, the Spirit World and the Sadducees." *Angels in the Early Modern World.* Edited by Peter Marshall and Alexandra Walsham. Cambridge: Cambridge University Press, 2006: 168–190.

Britland, Karen. "Exile or Homecoming? Henrietta Maria in France, 1644–1669." *Monarchy and Exile: The Politics of Legitimacy from Marie de Médicis to Wilhelm II.* Edited by Philip Mansel and Torsten Riotte. Basingstoke: Palgrave Macmillan, 2011: 120–143

Brunelle, Gayle K. "Ambassadors and Administrators: The Role of Clerics in Early French Colonies in Guiana." *Itinerario* 40/2 (2016): 257–277.

Calmet, Dom Augustin. *Histoire généalogique de la maison du Châtelet, branche puînée de la maison de Lorraine.* Nancy: Veuve de Jean-Baptiste Cusson, 1741.

Campeau, Lucien, S.J. "Le Voyage du Père Alexandre de Rhodes en France, 1653–1654." *Archivum Historicum Societatis Iesu* 48 (1979): 65–86.

Carrier, Hubert. "Women's Political and Military Action during the Fronde." *Political and Historical Encyclopedia of Women.* Edited by Christine Fauré. New York: Routledge, 2003.

Chappoulie, Henri. *Aux origines d'une église: Rome et les missions d'Indochine au XVIIe siècle.* Paris: Bloud et Gay, 1943.

Châtellier, Louis. *The Religion of the Poor: Rural Missions in Europe and the Formation of Modern Catholicism, c. 1500–c. 1800.* Translated by Brian Pearce. Cambridge: Cambridge University Press, 1997.

Church, William F. *Richelieu and Reason of State.* Princeton: Princeton University Press, 1972.

Cid, Jesús Antonio. "'Centauro a lo pícaro' y voz de su amo: interpretaciones y textos nuevos sobre *La vida y hechos de Estabanillo González.*" *Criticón* 47 (1989): 29–76.

Coleman, Francis X.J. *Neither Angel nor Beast: The Life and Work of Blaise Pascal.* New York: Routledge & Kegan Paul, 1986.

Collins, James B. *The State in Early Modern France.* Cambridge: Cambridge University Press, 1995.

Colombière, H.-M., S.J. "A Propos du livre de M. Bonneau-Avenant sur la duchesse d'Aiguillon." *Revue de Gascogne* 20 (1879): 437–459.

Compère, M.-M., and D. Julia. "L'éducation en France du XVIe au XVIIIe siècle." *Annales* 32/3 (1977): 549–553.

Conley, John J., S.J. "Madame de Sablé's Salon of Reconciliation." *Early Modern Women* 9/1 (2014): 115–126

———. *The Other Pascals: The Philosophy of Jacqueline Pascal, Gilberte Pascal Périer, and Marguerite Périer.* Notre Dame, IN: University of Notre Dame Press, 2019.

Cook, Harold J. *The Young Descartes: Nobilty, Rumor, and War.* Chicago: University of Chicago Press, 2018.

Coste, Pierre, C.M. *The Life and Works of Saint Vincent de Paul.* 3 volumes. Translated by Joseph Leonard, C.M. Brooklyn: New City Press, 1987.

Courajod, Louis. *Jean Warin: Ses oeuvres de sculpture et le buste de Louis XIV du musée du Louvre.* Paris: Honoré Champion, 1881.

Cousin, Victor. *Jacqueline Pascal; or, Convent Life at Port Royal.* Translated by H. N. London: J. Nisbet, 1854.

———. *Madame de Longueville.* Second edition. Paris: Didier, 1853.

Couyba, Louis. *Études sur la Fronde en Agenais et ses origines: Le duc d'Épernon et le Parlement de Bordeaux (1648–1651).* Villeneuve-sur-Lot: Reynaud Leygues, 1899.

Cramail, Alfred. *Le Château de Rueil et ses jardins sous le cardinal de Richelieu et sous la duchesse d'Aiguillon.* Fontainebleau: E. Bourges, 1888.

Craveri, Benedetta. *The Age of Conversation.* Translated by Teresa Waugh. New York: New York Review Books, 2005.

Crouch, Christian Ayne. *Nobility Lost: French and Canadian Martial Cultures, Indians, and the End of New France.* Ithaca: Cornell University Press, 2014.

Dandelet, Thomas James. *The Renaissance of Empire in Early Modern Europe*. Cambridge: Cambridge University Press, 2014.

Davis, Natalie Zemon. "The Rites of Violence: Religious Riot in Sixteenth-Century France." *Past and Present* 59 (1973): 51–91.

Davis, Natalie Zemon, and Arlette Farge, eds. *A History of Women: Renaissance and Enlightenment Paradoxes*. Cambridge: Belknap Press, 1993.

De Broglie, Emmanuel. *Saint Vincent de Paul*. London: Duckworth, 1906.

Deloche, Maximin. *Le Cardinal de Richelieu et les femmes*. Paris: Émile-Paul Frères, 1931.

Delumeau, Jean. *Catholicism between Luther and Voltaire*. Translated by Jeremy Moisier. London: Burnes and Oates, 1977.

Depping, G. B. "Un banquier protestant en France au xviie siècle, Barthélemy Herwarth." *Revue Historique* 10 (1879): 285–338.

Deschamps, Léon. *Histoire de la question coloniale en France*. Paris: Librairie Plon, 1891.

De Sousa, Ivo Carneiro. "The First French in Macao: The Jesuit Alexandre de Rhodes (1591/3–1660)." *Revista de Cultura* 44 (2013): 122–144.

De Vere, Aubrey. *Heroines of Charity*. London: Burns and Lambert, 1854.

Diefendorf, Barbara. *From Penitence to Charity: Pious Women and the Catholic Reformation in Paris*. Oxford: Oxford University Press, 2004.

Dinan, Susan E. *Women and Poor Relief in Seventeenth-Century France: The Early History of the Daughters of Charity*. Aldershot: Ashgate, 2006.

Dubost, Jean-François. *Marie de Médicis: La reine dévoilée*. Paris: Éditions Payot, 2009.

Duffy, Eamonn. *Saints and Sinners: A History of the Popes*. New Haven: Yale University Press, 2006.

Dussieux, Louis. *Le Cardinal de Richelieu: Étude biographique*. Paris: Victor Lecoffre, 1886.

Edwards, Peter J. "An Aspect of the French Counter-Reform Movement: la Compagnie du Saint-Sacrement." *Dalhousie Review* 56/3 (1976): 479–492.

Eire, Carlos. *The Life of Saint Teresa of Avila: A Biography*. Princeton, NJ: Princeton University Press, 2019.

———. *Reformations: The Early Modern World, 1450–1650*. New Haven: Yale University Press, 2016.

Elliott, J. H. *Richelieu and Olivares*. Cambridge: Cambridge University Press, 1989.

Elmore, Richard F. "The Origins of the Paris Hôpital Général." PhD dissertation, University of Michigan, 1975.

Evans, Jean Neva. "The Mystical Writings of Madeleine de Saint-Joseph du Bois de Fontaines (1578–1637)." PhD dissertation, University of South Africa, 2002.

Ferrer, Véronique. "Réforme et poésie en Europe aux XVIe et XVIIe siécles: Avant-propos." *Revue de l'histoire des religions* 226/1 (Jan.–Mar. 2009): 5–8.

Filleau, Henri. *Dictionnaire des familles de l'Ancien Poitou*. 2 volumes. Poitiers: Imprimerie de A. Dupré, 1840–1854.

Fisquet, M. H. *La France Pontificale (Gallia Christiana): Histoire chronologique et biographique des archevêques et évêques de tous les diocèses de France, depuis l'établissement du Christianisme jusqu'à nos jours*. Volume 2. Paris: E. Repos, 1864.

Forest, Alain. *Les missionnaires Françaises au Tonkin et au Siam, XVIIe–XVIIIe siècles*. Paris: L'Harmattan, 1998.

Forrestal, Alison. *Vincent de Paul, the Lazarist Mission, and French Catholic Reform*. New York: Oxford University Press, 2017.

Forrestal, Alison, and Felicia Rosu. "Slavery on the Frontier: The Report of a French Missionary on Mid-Seventeenth-Century Tunis." *Vincentian Heritage Journal* 34/1 (Summer 2017): via.library.depaul.edu/vhj/vol34/iss1/2.

François, Antoine. *Histoire générale des voyages, ou nouvelle collection de toutes les relations de voyages par mer et par terre*. Volume 11. The Hague: Pierre de Hondt, 1755.

Frazee, Charles A. *Catholics and Sultans: The Church and the Ottoman Empire, 1453–1923*. Cambridge: Cambridge University Press, 1983.

Freer, Martha Walker. *The Regency of Anne of Austria, Queen Regent of France, Mother of Louis XIV*. Volume 1. London: Tinsley Brothers, 1866.

Froidevaux, Henri. *Les Lazaristes à Madagascar au XVIIe siècle*. Paris: Poussielgue, 1903.

Gallais, Henri. *Glénay: Son vieux château, son église fortifié, depuis les temps le plus reculés jusqu'à la Révolution*. Niort: Imprimérie Saint-Denis, 1936.

Gardner, Rawson. *History of the Commonwealth and Protectorate, 1649–1660*. Volume 2. London: Longmans, Green, and Co., 1897.

Gil, Vincent, and Philippe Luçon. "Le Château de Glénay." *Congrés Archéologique de France, 159e session, 2001: Deux Sèvres*. Paris: Société Française d'Archéologie, 2004: 159–170.

Grammont, H. D. "Les consuls et les envoyés de la cour de France à Alger." *Revue d'histoire diplomatique publiée par les soins de la Société d'histoire diplomatique* 2 (1888): 100–108.

Greenberg, Mitchell. *Subjectivity and Subjugation in Seventeenth-Century Drama and Prose: The Family Romance of French Classicism*. Cambridge: Cambridge University Press, 1992.

Gude, Marie Louise, C.S.C. "Madame de Miramion and the Friends of Vincent de Paul." *Vincentian Heritage Journal* 20/2 (1999): 239–250.

Haag, Eugène, and Émile Haag, eds. *La France Protestante, ou Vies des Protestants français*. Volume 8. Paris: Joël Cherbuliez, 1858.

Hall, Hugh Gaston. *Richelieu's Desmarets and the Century of Louis XIV*. Oxford: Clarendon Press, 1990.

Haynes, Henrietta. *Henrietta Maria*. New York: G. P. Putnam's Sons, 1912.

Hennessy, Kathryn, ed., *Fashion: The Definitive History of Costume and Style*. New York: Dorling Kindersley, 2012.

Horric de Beaucaire, Charles-Prosper-Maurice. "Un collaborateur de Richelieu et de Mazarin: Bernard du Plessis-Besançon (1600–1670)." *Revue d'histoire diplomatique* 9 (1895): 77–123, 225–243, 404–416.

Horst, Louis. *Pre-Classic Dance Forms*. Princeton: Princeton Book Company, 1987.

Huc, L'Abbé Évariste Régis. *Christianity in China, Tartary, and Thibet*. Volume 3. London: Longman, Brown, Green, Longmans, & Roberts, 1858.

Hutchinson, E. W. "The French Foreign Mission in Siam during the XVIIth Century." *Journal of the Siam Society* 26/1 (1933): 1–71.

Ibbett, Katherine. *Compassion's Edge: Fellow-Feeling and Its Limits in Early Modern France*. Philadelphia: University of Pennsylvania Press, 2018.

Inventaire-Sommaire des Archives départementales antérieures à 1790: Lot-et-Garonne. Agen: Prosper Nouvel, 1878.

Israel, Jonathan I. *Conflicts of Empires: Spain, the Low Countries, and the Struggle for World Supremacy, 1585–1713*. London: Hambledon Press, 1997.

Jacquin, Jules, and Joseph Duesberg. *Rueil: Le Château de Richelieu, la Malmaison, avec pièces justificatives*. Paris: Dauvin et Fontaine, 1845.

James, Alan. *Navy and Government in Early Modern France, 1572–1661*. Woodbridge: The Boydell Press, 2004.

Jones, Colin. *Paris: The Biography of a City*. New York: Penguin Books, 2004.

Joseph, John. *Muslim-Christian Relations and Inter-Christian Rivalries in the Middle East: The Case of the Jacobites in an Age of Transition*. Albany: SUNY Press, 1983.

Kettering, Sharon. "The Household Service of Early Modern French Noblewomen." *French Historical Studies* 20/1 (1997): 55–85.

———. "Patronage, Language, and Political Culture: Patronage in Early Modern France," *French Historical Studies* 17/4 (1992): 839–862.

———. "Strategies of Power: Favorites and Women Household Clients at Louis XIII's Court." *French Historical Studies* 33/2 (2010): 177–200.

Kleinman, Ruth. *Anne of Austria, Queen of France*. Columbus: Ohio State University Press, 1985.

Knecht, Robert J. *Richelieu*. New York: Routledge, 2013.

L., T. de. Review. *Revue critique d'histoire et de littérature*. Volume 7. Edited by M. Bréal et al. Paris: Ernest Leroux, 1879: 461–466.

Labatut, Jean-Pierre. *Les Ducs et pairs au XVIIe siècle*. Paris: Presses Universitaires de France, 1972.

Lacroix, Laurier, ed. *Les arts en Nouvelle-France*. Québec: Publications de Québec, 2012.

Lair, Jules, and Alphonse Chodron de Courcel, eds. *Rapports et notices sur l'édition des Mémoires du Cardinal de Richelieu, préparée pour la Société de l'Histoire de France*. Booklet 4. Paris: Renouard, 1907.

Launay, Adrien. *Histoire de la mission de Cochinchine, 1658–1823*. Paris: Anciennes Maisons Charles Dauriol et Retaux, 1923.

Ledain, Bélisaire. *La gatine historique et monumentale*. Paris: Jules Claye, 1876.

———. *Histoire de la ville de Bressuire*. Bressuire: E. Landreau, 1888.

Levi, Anthony. *Cardinal Richelieu and the Making of France*. New York: Carroll & Graf Publishers, 2001.

Livet, Charles-Louis. *Les intrigues de Molière et celles de sa femme*. Paris: Isidore Lisieux, 1877.

Lynch, Katherine A. *Individuals, Families, and Communities in Europe, 1200–1800: The Urban Foundations of Western Society*. Cambridge: Cambridge University Press, 2003.

Madrolle, Claudius. *Les premiers voyages Français à la Chine*. Paris: Challamel, 1901.

Maillet-Rao, Caroline. "Mathieu de Morgues and Michel de Marillac: The *Dévots* and Absolutism." *French History* 25/3 (2011): 279–297.

Maître, Myriam. *Les précieuses: Naissance des femmes de lettres en France au XVIIe siècle*. Paris: Honoré Champion, 1999.

Mallick, Oliver. "Clients and Friends: The Ladies-in-Waiting at the Court of Anne of Austria (1615–66)." *The Politics of Female Households: Ladies-in-Waiting across Early Modern Europe*. Edited by Nadine Akkerman and Birgit Houben. Leiden: Brill, 2014: 241–264.

Maloney, Robert P., C.M. "Vincent de Paul and Jean-Jacques Olier: Unlikely Friends." *Vincentian Heritage Journal* 28/1 (2008): 7–19.

Mazel, Claire. "Un tombeau d'exception: Comparaison des monuments funéraires de Richelieu à la Sorbonne et de Mazarin au collège des Quatre-Nations." *Richelieu patron des arts*. Edited by Jean-Claude Boyer et al. Paris: Maison des sciences de l'homme, 2009: 175–202.

McLeod, Jane. *Licensing Loyalty: Printers, Patrons, and the State in Early Modern France*. University Park: Pennsylvania State University Press, 2011.

McShea, Bronwen. *Apostles of Empire: The Jesuits and New France*. Lincoln: University of Nebraska Press, 2019.

Merrick, Jeffrey. *Order and Disorder Under the Ancien Régime*. Newcastle: Cambridge Scholars Publishing, 2007.

Miller, Christopher L. *The French Atlantic Triangle: Literature and Culture of the Slave Trade*. Durham: Duke University Press, 2008.

Misermont, Lucien, C.M. *Le plus grand des premiers missionnaires de Saint Vincent de Paul: Jean Le Vacher, prêtre de la Mission*. Paris: Librairie Lecoffre, 1935.

Montzey, Charles de. *Father Eudes, Apostolic Missionary, and His Foundations, 1601–1874.* London: Thomas Richardson and Son, 1874.

Nadeau, Jean-Benoît, and Julie Barlow. *The Story of French.* New York: St. Martin's Press, 2006.

Newman, Karen. *Cultural Capitals: Early Modern London and Paris.* Princeton: Princeton University Press, 2007.

Noailles, Le Vicomte de. *Le Cardinal de La Valette, Lieutenant Général des armées du Roi, 1635 à 1639.* Paris: Librairie Académique Didier, 1906.

Pacifique, R. P. *Études historiques et geographiques.* Restigouche: R. P. Pacifique, 1935.

Pavy, A. *Histoire de la Tunisie.* Tours: Alfred Cattier, 1894.

Peeters, Thérèse. "Trust and Mission: Seventeenth-Century Lazarist Missionaries in North Africa." *Trajecta* 26/1 (2017): 107–132.

Petitfils, Jean-Christian. *Louis XIII.* Paris: Perrin, 2008.

Petto, Christine M. "Mapping Forbidden Places and Places of the Forbidden in Early Modern London and Paris." *Environment, Space, Place* 2/1 (2010): 33–58.

Phan, Peter C. *Mission and Catechesis: Alexandre de Rhodes and Inculturation in Seventeenth-Century Vietnam.* Maryknoll, NY: Orbis Books, 1998.

Pierre, Benoist. *Le Père Joseph; l'Éminence grise de Richelieu.* Paris: Perrin, 2007.

Pinard, M., ed. *Chronologie historique-militaire.* Volume 6. Paris: Claude Herissant, 1763.

Pinkard, Susan. *A Revolution in Taste: The Rise of French Cuisine, 1650–1800.* New York: Cambridge University Press, 2009.

Pitts, Vincent J. *Embezzlement and High Treason in Louis XIV's France.* Baltimore: Johns Hopkins University Press, 2015.

———. *La Grande Mademoiselle at the Court of France, 1627–1693.* Baltimore: Johns Hopkins University Press, 2000.

Pizzorusso, Giovanni. *Rome nei Caraibi: L'Organizzazione delle missioni cattoliche nelle Antille e in Guyana (1635–1675).* Rome: École Française, 1995.

Pond, Shepard. "The Louis d'Or." *Bulletin of the Business Historical Society* 14/5 (1940): 77–80.

Poumarède, Géraud. "Naissance d'une institution royale: Les Consuls de la nation Française en Levant et en Barbarie aux XVIe et XVIIe siècles." *Annuaire-bulletin de la Société de l'histoire de France* (2001): 65–128.

Prawdin, Michael. *Marie de Rohan, duchesse de Chevreuse.* London: Allen & Unwin, 1971.

Price, Eleanor C. *Cardinal de Richelieu.* New York: McBride, Nast & Company, 1912.

Ranum, Orest A. *Paris in the Age of Absolutism: An Essay.* University Park: Pennsylvania State University Press, 2002.

Rapley, Elizabeth. *The Dévotes: Women and Church in Seventeenth-Century France.* Montreal: McGill-Queen's University Press, 1990.

Rea, Lilian. *The Life and Times of Marie Madeleine, Countess of La Fayette.* London: Methuen and Co., 1908.

Resbecq, Eugène de Fontaine de. *Les Tombeaux des Richelieu à la Sorbonne.* Paris: Ernest Thorin, 1867.

Richefort, Isabella. "L'iconographie religieuse de Richelieu." *Richelieu, patron des arts.* Edited by Jean-Claude Boyer et al. Paris: Maison des Sciences de l'Homme, 2009: 315–336.

Roche, Daniel. *The Culture of Clothing: Dress and Fashion in the Ancien Régime.* Cambridge: Cambridge University Press, 1996.

Rodway, James, and Thomas Watt. *Chronological History of the Discovery and Settlement of Guiana, 1493–1668.* Georgetown: *Royal Gazette* Office, 1888.

Román, José María. *St Vincent de Paul: A Biography.* Translated by Joyce Howard. Herts: Melisende, 1999.

Rosa, Mario. "The Catholic Clergy in Europe." *The Cambridge History of Christianity*. Volume 7. Edited by Stewart J. Brown and Timothy Tacket. Cambridge: Cambridge University Press, 2008: 87–108.

Saint-Allas, Nicolas Viton de. *Nobiliaire universel de France*. 21 volumes. Paris: Bachelin-Deflorenne, 1872–1877.

Schatz, Klaus. *"Dass diese Mission eine der blühendsten des Ostens werde": P. Alexander de Rhodes (1693–1660) und die frühe Jesuitenmission in Vietnam*. Münster: Aschendorff, 2015.

Scott, Mary Maxwell. "Marie de Vignerod, Duchesse d'Aiguillon (1604–1675)." *The Dublin Review* (1905): 358–374.

Smith, Séan Alexander. *Fealty and Fidelity: The Lazarists of Bourbon France, 1660–1736*. London: Routledge, 2016.

Société Archéologique de Rambouillet. *Mémoires de la Société Archéologique de Rambouillet*. Volume 9. Rambouillet: Alfred Douchin, 1891.

Société d'Émulation des Cotes-du-Nord. *Bulletins et Mémoires*. Volume 30. Saint-Brieuc: Imprimérie Francisque Guyon, 1892.

Somerset, Anne. *The Affair of the Poisons: Murder, Infanticide, and Satanism at the Court of Louis XIV*. New York: St. Martin's Press, 2014.

Sonnino, Paul. "The Dating of Richelieu's *Testament politique*." *French History* 12/2 (2005): 262–272.

Spagnolo, Tabitha. "'Mars respire ici sous l'habit de Venus': Transvestism and Transformation in Jean Rotrou's 'Agésilan de Colchos' (1635)." *Rocky Montain Review* 70/1 (Spring 2016): 71–80.

"Sur la revue rétrospective, et sur l'histoire de l'Abbé Blache." *L'ami de la religion: Journal ecclésiastique, politique et littéraire* 90 (1836): 225–230.

Tabacchi, Stefano. *Marie de' Medici*. Rome: Salerno Editrice, 2012.

Tamizey de Larroque, Philippe, ed. *Lettres de Peiresc aux Frères Dupuy*. Volume 3. Paris: Imprimerie Nationale, 1892.

Tamizey de Larroque, Philippe. "Un Languedocien oublié: L'Abbé Croisilles." *Annales du Midi: Revue archéologique, historique et philologique de la France méridionale* 5/18 (1893): 145–169.

———. "Lettre du Duc de Richelieu à la duchesse d'Aiguillon." *Revue d'Aquitaine et des Pyrénées* 12/11 (1867): 137–140.

Tapié, Victor-L. *La France de Louis XIII et de Richelieu*. Paris: Flammarion, 1967.

Terrien, Marie-Pierre. *The Ideal City and the Château of Richelieu*. Translated by Howard Leigh Copping. Cholet, France: Éditions Pays et Terroirs, 2017.

———. *Vincent de Paul à Richelieu*. Cholet: Éditions Pays et Terroirs, 2017.

Terrien, Marie-Pierre, et al. *Le Château de Richelieu, XVIIe–XVIIIe siècles*. Rennes: Presses Universitaires de Rennes, 2009.

Thieffry, Marc. *Saint Vincent de Paul et la mission Lazariste à Madagascar au XVIIe siècle*. Paris: Harmattan, 2017.

Thompson, Edward Healy. *The Life of Jean-Jacques Olier, Founder of the Seminary of St. Sulpice*. London: Burns and Oates, 1886.

Toulier, Christine. "Richelieu: La Ville du cardinal." *Bulletin de la Société des amis du vieux Chinon* 9 (1993): 785–816.

Treasure, Geoffrey. *Mazarin: The Crisis of Absolutism in France*. London: Routledge, 1995.

———. *Richelieu and Mazarin*. London: Routledge, 1998.

Trévédy, J. *Le Couvent de Saint-François de Quimper: Quelques épisodes de son histoire*. Quimper: M. Salaun, 1894.

Tulloch, John. *Pascal*. Edinburgh: William Blackwood and Sons, 1878.

Van der Cruysse, Dirk. *Louis XIV et le Siam*. Paris: Fayard, 1991.

Van Grasdorff, Gilles. *La belle histoire des missions étrangères, 1658–2008*. Paris: Perrin, 2007.

Vaumas, G. de. *L'éveil missionnaire de la France au XVIIe siècle*. Tournai: Bloud & Gay, 1949.

Vergé-Franceschi, Michel. *Guerre et commerce en Méditerranée, IXe–XXe siècles*. Paris: Éditions Veyrier, 1991.

Weiss, Gillian. *Captives and Corsairs: France and Slavery in the Early Modern Mediterranean*. Stanford: Stanford University Press, 2011.

Wilkie, Carsten L. "Manuel Fernandes Villa Real at the Portuguese Embassy in Paris, 1644–1649: New Documents and Insights." *Journal of Levantine Studies* 6 (2016): 153–176.

Wilkinson, Richard. *Louis XIV*. London: Routledge, 2007.

Williams, H. Noel. *The Love Affairs of the Condés (1530–1740)*. New York: Charles Scribner's Sons, 1912.

Wilson, Peter H. *The Thirty Years War: Europe's Tragedy*. Cambridge: Belknap Press, 2009.

Wiltgen, Ralph M. *The Founding of the Roman Catholic Church in Oceania, 1825 to 1850*. Eugene, OR: Pickwick Publications, 2010.

Windler, Christian. *Missionare in Persien: Kulturelle Diversität und Normenkonkurrenz im globalen Katholicizimus (17.–18. Jahrhundert)*. Cologne: Böhlau Verlag, 2018.

Wolfgang, Aurora, and Sharon Diane Nell. "Reclaiming the Works of Early Modern Women: Authorship, Gender, and Interpretation in the *Nouveau recueil de lettres des dames de ce temps* (1635)." *Intertexts* 13/1-2 (2009): 1–16.

Wygant, Amy. *Medea, Magic, and Modernity in France: Stages and Histories, 1553–1797*. Aldershot: Ashgate, 2007.

Yalom, Marilyn. *A History of the Breast*. New York: HarperCollins, 1997.

Notes

PART ONE—PRINCESSE NIÈCE

1. A Long Journey

1   Richelieu to Béthune, early 1620, in Denis-Louis-Martial Avenel, ed., *Lettres, Instructions diplomatiques et papiers d'État du Cardinal-Duc de Richelieu*, 8 vols. (Paris: Imprimerie Impériale, 1853–1877), 1:647–648.

2. Glénay

1   Alfred Bonneau-Avenant, *La Duchesse d'Aiguillon, nièce du cardinal de Richelieu: sa vie et ses oeuvres charitables, 1604–1675* (Paris: Didier, 1879), 7.

2   *La Miliade*, or *Le gouvernement présent, ou Éloge de Son Éminence* (1635), 61–62; Gédéon Tallemant des Réaux, *Les Historiettes*, 6 vols., ed. Louis Monmerqué (Paris: Alphonse Levasseur, 1834–1835), 1:344; Pierre de L'Estoile, *Journal d'Henri III, roy de France et de Pologne*, vol. 4 (The Hague: Pierre Gosse, 1646), 32n; William Beik, *A Social and Cultural History of Early Modern France* (Cambridge: Cambridge University Press, 2009), 77–82.

3   Vincent Gil and Philippe Luçon, "Le Château de Glénay," *Congrès Archéologique de France, 159e session, 2001, Deux-Sèvres* (Paris: Société française d'archéologie, 2003), 160.

4   Beik, *Social and Cultural History*, 73, 82–85.

5   Henri Filleau, *Dictionnaire des familles de l'ancien Poitou*, 2 vols. (Poitiers: Imprimerie de A. Dupré, 1840–1854), 2:798; Dom Augustin Calmet, *Histoire généalogique de la maison Du Châtelet, branche puînée de la maison de Lorraine* (Nancy: Veuve de Jean-Baptiste Cusson, 1741), 129; Bonneau-Avenant, *Duchesse d'Aiguillon*, 1, 5–6, 9.

6   Bonneau-Avenant, *Duchesse d'Aiguillon*, 6.

7   Gil and Luçon, "Château de Glénay," 160.

8   Register of acts of homage rendered to Thouars in the Barony of Bressuire, 1605, AD Deux Sèvres, E 1274; Bonneau-Avenant, *Duchesse d'Aiguillon*, 7; Filleau, *Dictionnaire*, 2:798.

9   R. P. Pacifique, *Études historiques et geographiques* (Restigouche: R. P. Pacifique, 1935), 71.

10   Beik, *Social and Cultural History*, 77–85.

11   Bonneau-Avenant, *Duchesse d'Aiguillon*, 7.

12   Pacifique, *Études*, 69.

13   Register of acts of homage rendered to Thouars in the Barony of Bressuire, 1605, AD Deux-Sèvres, E 1274; Purchase of a third of the *seigneurie* of Glénay made by

Gilbert Joubert for the benefit of René de Vignerot, 4 Aug. 1606, and purchase from François de Hautclere of another third of the *seigneurie* of Glénay by René de Vignerot, 19 May 1607, AD Deux-Sèvres, 3 E 15210; Filleau, *Dictionnaire*, 2:798.

14   Bonneau-Avenant, *Duchesse d'Aiguillon*, 9; Henri Gallais, *Glénay: Son vieux château, son église fortifié, depuis les temps les plus reculés jusqu'à la Révolution* (Niort: Imprimérie Saint-Denis, 1936), 36, 139.

15   Richelieu to Françoise de Vignerot, c. 1607 or 1608, in Avenel, *Lettres*, 1:46.

16   Bonneau-Avenant, *Duchesse d'Aiguillon*, 11.

17   J. H. Elliott, *Richelieu and Olivares* (Cambridge: Cambridge University Press), 10; Maximin Deloche, *Le Cardinal de Richelieu et les femmes* (Paris: Émile-Paul Frères, 1931), 196; Pierre Blet, S.J., *Richelieu et l'Église* (Versailles: Via Romana, 2007), 17.

18   Blet, *Richelieu*, 17; Anthony Levi, *Cardinal Richelieu and the Making of France* (New York: Carroll & Graf Publishers, 2001), 22–23; Jean-Vincent Blanchard, *Éminence: Cardinal Richelieu and the Rise of France* (New York: Walker & Company, 2011), 12–14.

19   Bonneau-Avenant, *Duchesse d'Aiguillon*, 16–17.

20   See for example Procuration, 10 Dec. 1614, CARAN, MC ET XXIV 125.

21   Françoise du Plessis de Vignerot to Richelieu, before 1616, BIU Sorbonne, MSRIC 18, ff. 123–126.

22   Gallais, *Glénay*, 35–36; Bonneau-Avenant, *Duchesse d'Aiguillon*, 8.

3. Richelieu

1   Bonneau-Avenant, *Duchesse d'Aiguillon*, 480.

2   Bélisaire Ledain, *Histoire de la ville de Bressuire* (Bressuire: E. Landreau, 1888), 198.

3   Blanchard, *Éminence*, 12.

4   Ibid., 12; Bonneau-Avenant, *Duchesse d'Aiguillon*, 27; Joseph Bergin, *Cardinal Richelieu: Power and the Pursuit of Wealth* (New Haven: Yale University Press, 1990), 15–20, 33–34; Elliott, *Richelieu*, 9–10.

5   Blanchard, *Éminence*, 11–12; Elliott, *Richelieu*, 9; Bergin, *Cardinal Richelieu*, 16.

6   Bergin, *Cardinal Richelieu*, 32–33; Tallemant, *Historiettes*, 2:29–30; Deloche, *Richelieu*, 186.

7   Bonneau-Avenant, *Duchesse d'Aiguillon*, 11–13, 36.

8   Ibid., 9, 25.

9   Beik, *Social and Cultural History*, 289–291.

10   Bonneau-Avenant, *Duchesse d'Aiguillon*, 27; Blanchard, *Éminence*, 12; Elliott, *Richelieu*, 9.

11   Bergin, *Cardinal Richelieu*, 24–26.

12   Ibid., 24–27, 31.

4. Uncle Armand's Fortunes

1   James B. Collins, *The State in Early Modern France* (Cambridge: Cambridge University Press, 1995), 26.

2   Lévi, *Richelieu*, 1.

3   Armand-Jean du Plessis de Richelieu, *Harangue prononcée en la sale du petit Bourbon le XIII Fevrier 1615* (Paris: Sébastien Cramoisy, 1615), 17–18, 21–22, 59–62.

4   Richelieu, *Harangue*, 51–55; Blanchard, *Éminence*, 15.

5   Blanchard, *Éminence*, 32, 35.

6   Ibid., 10, 32.

7   L. A. Bosseboeuf, *Histoire de Richelieu et des environs, au pont de vue civil, religieux et artistique* (Tours: L. Péricat, 1890), 151.

8   Blanchard, *Éminence*, 27, 35.
9   Elliott, *Richelieu*, 15–16.
10   Bergin, *Cardinal Richelieu*, 34–35.
11   Bonneau-Avenant, *Duchesse d'Aiguillon*, 54–55, 66.

5. A Political Marriage

1   Bergin, *Cardinal Richelieu*, 29.
2   Ibid., 36; Blanchard, *Éminence*, 42.
3   Nicolas Viton de Saint-Allas, *Nobiliaire universel de France*, 21 vols. (Paris: Bachelin-Deflorenne, 1872–1877), 10:223–234.
4   Bonneau-Avenant, *Duchesse d'Aiguillon*, 81.
5   Claude-Bernard Petitot, ed., *Mémoires du cardinal de Richelieu*, 10 vols. (Paris: Foucault, 1823), 2:130.
6   Richelieu to Béthune, early 1620, in Avenel, *Lettres*, 1:647–648.
7   Blanchard, *Éminence*, 49.

6. Paris

1   Karen Newman, *Cultural Capitals: Early Modern London and Paris* (Princeton: Princeton University Press, 2007), 78; Susan Pinkard, *A Revolution in Taste: The Rise of French Cuisine, 1650–1800* (New York: Cambridge University Press, 2009), 57–58.
2   Orest A. Ranum, *Paris in the Age of Absolutism: An Essay* (University Park: Pennsylvania State University Press, 2002), 8.
3   Marriage contract, 26 Nov. 1620, CARAN, MI/RS/1063, f. 6; Bergin, *Cardinal Richelieu*, 39.
4   François Boucher, *20,000 Years of Fashion: The History of Costume and Personal Adornment* (New York: Harry N. Abrams, 1987), 252–255; Kathryn Hennessy, ed., *Fashion: The Definitive History of Costume and Style* (New York: Dorling Kindersley, 2012), 118–121.
5   Bonneau-Avenant, *Duchesse d'Aiguillon*, 88.
6   Tallemant, *Historiettes*, 2:25, 27.

7. Antoine

1   *Mercure François*, 24 vols. (Paris: Estienne Richier, 1605–1643), 8:618–619, 815; Bonneau-Avenant, *Duchesse d'Aiguillon*, 89–92.
2   Ruth Kleinman, *Anne of Austria: Queen of France* (Columbus: Ohio State University Press, 1985), 51.
3   Esprit Fléchier, *Oraisons funèbres de Fléchier, Évèque de Nimes* (Angers: Fourier-Mame, 1821), 53–54.
4   *Mercure François*, 8:815–816; Michel Baudier, *Histoire du mareschal de Toiras* (Paris: Sébastien Cramoisy, 1644), 20; François de Bassompierre, *Mémoires du Mareschal de Bassompierre* (Cologne: Pierre de Marteau, 1665), 253.
5   BnF Richelieu, *Clairambault 1140*, f. 195; Tallemant, *Historiettes*, 2:25, 27.
6   Marriage contract, 26 Nov. 1620, CARAN, MI/RS/1063, ff. 2–5; AD Drôme, Fonds d'Aiguillon, 100 Mi 134; Jean-François Dubost, *Marie de Médicis: La reine dévoilée* (Paris: Éditions Payot, 2009), 613; Bergin, *Cardinal Richelieu*, 39. The estimate is based on a rough calculation based on the livre's weight in gold around 1640, the year Louis XIII standardized currency with the 10-livre Louis d'Or. One livre was worth about 0.67 grams in gold; early in 2022, a gram of gold

was worth 58.2 U.S. dollars. Cf. Shepard Pond, "The Louis d'Or," *Bulletin of the Business Historical Society* 14/5 (1940): 77–80.

8. Carmel de l'Incarnation

1   Carlos Eire, *The Life of Saint Teresa of Avila: A Biography* (Princeton: Princeton University Press, 2019), 37–47.

2   Barbara Diefendorf, *From Penitence to Charity: Pious Women and the Catholic Reformation in Paris* (Oxford: Oxford University Press, 2004), 101–116.

3   H.-M. Colombier, S.J., "A Propos du livre de M. Bonneau-Avenant sur la duchesse d'Aiguillon," *Revue de Gascogne* 20 (1879): 452–453; Diefendorf, *Penitence to Charity*, 113–114.

4   Keith Beaumont, "Pierre de Bérulle (1575–1629) and the Renewal of Catholic Spiritual Life in France," *International Journal for the Study of the Christian Church* 12/2 (2017): 78, 84; Henri Brémond, *Histoire littéraire du Sentiment Religieux en France depuis la fin des guerres de religion jusqu'à nos jours*, vol. 3 (Grenoble: Éditions Jérôme Millon, 2006), 26–141.

5   Diefendorf, *Penitence to Charity*, 157–158.

6   Avenel, *Lettres*, 2:15n; Bonneau-Avenant, *Duchesse d'Aiguillon*, 109, 480.

7   Bonneau-Avenant, *Duchesse d'Aiguillon*, 110–112.

9. The Young Cardinal's Ward

1   Vincent Voiture, "Trois rondeaux à Madame de Combalet, sur ses beaux yeux," BnF Arsenal, Français 4123, ff. 1057–1059; Voiture to Marie de Vignerot, 5 Jan. 1635, in Sophie Rollin, ed., *Vincent Voiture: Lettres (1625–1648)* (Paris: Honoré Champion Éditeur, 2013), 250–251.

2   Tallemant, *Historiettes*, 2:25–26; Fléchier, *Oraisons funèbres*, 56.

3   Daniel Roche, *The Culture of Clothing: Dress and Fashion in the Ancien Régime* (Cambridge: Cambridge University Press, 1996), 285.

4   Avenel, *Lettres*, 2:15n. Cf. Richelieu to the electors of Thouars, 8 Jan. 1627, in Avenel, *Lettres*, 2:340.

5   Edmond Bonnaffé, *Recherches sur les Collections des Richelieu* (Paris: E. Plon, 1883), 1–4.

6   R. J. Knecht, *Richelieu* (New York: Routledge, 2013), 205.

7   Victor-L. Tapié, *France in the Age of Louis XIII and Richelieu* (Paris: Flammarion, 1967), 135.

8   Benoist Pierre, *Le Père Joseph: l'Éminence grise de Richelieu* (Paris: Perrin, 2007).

9   Tapié, *France*, 138.

10   Quoted in Blanchard, *Éminence*, 2.

11   William F. Church, *Richelieu and Reason of State* (Princeton: Princeton University Press, 1972), 90.

12   Bergin, *Cardinal Richelieu*, 45.

13   Joseph Bergin, *The Politics of Religion in Early Modern France* (New Haven: Yale University Press, 2014), 121.

14   Church, *Richelieu*, 93; Blanchard, *Éminence*, 65.

15   Tapié, *France*, 129–130.

16   Ibid., 133.

17   Bergin, *Cardinal Richelieu*, 70.

18   Peter H. Wilson, *The Thirty Years War: Europe's Tragedy* (Cambridge: Belknap Press, 2009), 382–383.

19   Tallemant, *Historiettes*, 2:151–53.
20   Dubost, *Marie de Médicis*, 686.
21   Bonneau-Avenant, *Duchesse d'Aiguillon*, 116.

10. Serving Marie de' Medici
1   Tallemant, *Historiettes*, 2:25; Elizabeth Rapley, *The Dévotes: Women and Church in Seventeenth-Century France* (Montreal: McGill-Queen's University Press, 1990).
2   Blanchard, *Éminence*, 63; Oliver Mallick, "Clients and Friends: The Ladies-in-Waiting at the Court of Anne of Austria (1615–66)," in *The Politics of Female Households: Ladies-in-Waiting across Early Modern Europe*, eds. Nadine Akkerman and Birgit Houben (Leiden: Brill, 2014), 235.
3   Tallemant, *Historiettes*, 2:25–26.
4   Louis Horst, *Pre-Classic Dance Forms* (Princeton: Princeton Book Company, 1987), 9; Bonneau-Avenant, *Duchesse d'Aiguillon*, 120.
5   Mallick, "Clients," 234–237.
6   Dubost, *Marie de Médicis*, 613.
7   Michael Prawdin, *Marie de Rohan, Duchesse de Chevreuse* (London: Allen & Unwin, 1971), 15.
8   Stefano Tabacchi, *Maria de Médici* (Rome: Salerno Editrice, 2012), 40–53.
9   Tallemant, *Historiettes*, 1:350–351; Sharon Kettering, "Strategies of Power: Favorites and Women Household Clients at Louis XIII's Court," *French Historical Studies* 33/2 (2010): 193.
10   Mallick, "Clients," 231–232.
11   Sharon Kettering, "Patronage, Language, and Political Culture: Patronage in Early Modern France," *French Historical Studies* 17/4 (1992): 855.
12   Dubost, *Marie de Médicis*, 748.
13   Benedetta Craveri, *The Age of Conversation*, trans. Teresa Waugh (New York: New York Review Books, 2005), 35–38; Nicole Aronson, *Madame de Rambouillet ou la Magicienne de la chamber bleue* (Paris: Fayard, 1988), 115, 209; Le Vicomte de Noailles, *Le Cardinal de La Valette, Lieutenant Général des armées du Roi, 1635 à 1639* (Paris: Didier, 1906), 95, 104.
14   Richelieu to Marie de Vignerot, 27 Jan. 1630, in Pierre Grillon, ed., *Les Papiers de Richelieu*, 6 vols. (Paris: Pedone, 1975–1997), 5:50.
15   Bonneau-Avenant, *Duchesse d'Aiguillon*, 134–135.
16   Marie de Vignerot's last will and testament, 17 Apr. 1675, BIU Sorbonne, MSRIC 151, f. 47; Tallemant, *Historiettes*, 2:25–26; Bonneau-Avenant, *Duchesse d'Aiguillon*, 135.

11. A Pivotal Year
1   Colombier, "A propos du livre," 453.
2   Extract from prepared manifestos shown to the King, 1626, in Grillon, *Papiers*, 1:574.
3   Mercure François, 4:332–333; J. Trévédy, *Le Couvent de Saint-François de Quimper: Quelques épisodes de son histoire* (Quimper: M. Salaun, 1894), 33.
4   *Chroniques de l'ordre des Carmélites de la Réforme de Sainte-Thérèse*, vol. 3 (Troyes: Imprimérie d'Anner-André, 1856), 212.
5   Duc de Brissac to Richelieu, 2 Jun. 1626, and Bouthillier to Richelieu, 6 Sep. 1626, in Grillon, *Papiers*, 1:355, 456; *Mercure François*, 12:416; Société de Émulation des Cotes-du-Nord, *Bulletins et mémoires*, vol. 30 (Saint-Brieuc: Imprimérie Francisque Guyon, 1892), 101–102; *Recherches historiques de l'ordre du Saint-Esprit*, 1:309, 341; Trévédy, *Couvent de Saint-François*, 34.

6   Marguerite du Saint-Sacrement to Richellieu, 8 Jul. 1626, in Colombier, "A propos du livre," 453–454.
7   Blanchard, *Éminence*, 79.
8   Ibid., 80.
9   Quoted in Prawdin, *Marie de Rohan*, 8.
10   Blanchard, *Éminence*, 80.
11   Ibid., 80–81.
12   Tapié, *France*, 156.
13   Blanchard, *Éminence*, 82.
14   Ibid., 82–83.
15   Ibid., 88; Prawdin, *Marie de Rohan*, 42–44.
16   Ibid., 18.
17   Marguerite du Saint-Sacrement to Richelieu, 8 Jul. 1626, in Colombier, "A propos du livre," 453–454.
18   Richelieu to Béthune, 22 Oct. 1626, in Avenel, *Lettres*, 2:276–277.
19   Bonneau-Avenant, *Duchesse d'Aiguillon*, 138–139. Bonneau-Avenant claimed that Marie de' Medici seconded Richelieu's request for a papal brief and that Urban sent one in the end. Although Bonneau-Avenant claimed to have seen a brief in the Richelieu family archives, such a document has not surfaced in my own research. I suspect Bonneau-Avenant of fabrication, as the date he listed for the brief was February 15, 1626, which would be a year too early given other documented information about Marie's retreat at the convent on the Rue Chapon and of Richelieu's efforts to secure a brief from Rome.
20   Richelieu to Bouthillier, 24 Dec. 1629, in Grillon, *Papiers*, 4:726.

12. The Blue Room

1   Natalie Zemon Davis and Arlette Farge, eds., *A History of Women: Renaissance and Enlightenment Paradoxes* (Cambridge: Belknap Press, 1993), 400.
2   Craveri, *Age of Conversation*, 27.
3   Ibid., 3.
4   Ibid., 29; Wiesner-Hanks, *Women and Gender*, 165.
5   Quoted in Ranum, *Paris*, 144.
6   Craveri, *Age of Conversation*, 29, 32.
7   Ibid., 107; Édouard de Barthélemy, *Les Amis de la marquise de Sablé: Receüil de lettres des principaux habitués de son salon* (Paris: E. Dentu, 1865), 97–101.
8   Tallemant, *Historiettes*, 1:106, 2:33; *Miliade*, 61–62; Bonneau-Avenant, *Duchesse d'Aiguillon*, 365; Aurora Wolfgang and Sharon Diane Nell, "Reclaiming the Works of Early Modern Women: Authorship, Gender, and Interpretation in the *Nouveau receuil de lettres des dames de ce temps* (1635)," *Intertexts* 13/1–2 (2009): 11.
9   Craveri, *Age of Conversation*, 35–36.
10   Ibid., 35–36, 38; Eleanor C. Price, *Cardinal de Richelieu* (New York: McBride, Nast & Company, 1912), 214; Aronson, *Madame de Rambouillet*, 115.
11   Aronson, *Madame de Rambouillet*, 209; Noailles, *Cardinal de La Valette*, 71–74, 94–95; Craveri, *Age of Conversation*, 35–36.
12   Craveri, *Age of Conversation*, 37.
13   Ibid., 69–70.
14   Ibid., 1.
15   Ibid., 38.

13. Uncle Armand's Triumph
1   Craveri, *Age of Conversation*, 27.
2   Bergin, *Cardinal Richelieu*, 53.
3   Tapié, *France*, 175–209.
4   Blanchard, *Éminence*, 95–96.
5   Ibid., 108.
6   Tapié, *France*, 190–191.
7   Blanchard, *Éminence*, 109.

14. The Cardinal-Minister's Reluctant Aide
1   Ibid., 129.
2   Ibid., 110–111.
3   Ibid., 113–115; Dubost, *Marie de Médicis*, 768.
4   Richelieu to Bouthillier, 24 Dec. 1629, in Grillon, *Papiers*, 4:726.
5   Blanchard, *Éminence*, 118.
6   Jean Neva Evans, "The Mystical Writings of Madeleine de Saint-Joseph du Bois de Fontaines (1578–1637)," Ph.D. diss. (University of South Africa, 2002), 2.
7   Madeleine de Saint-Joseph, *La vie de Soeur Catherine de Jésus, religieuse de l'ordre de Notre-Dame du Mont Carmel établi en France, selon la réformation de sainte Térèse de Jésus* (Paris: F. Dehors, 1626); Pierre Sérouet, ed., *Lettres spirituelles de Madeleine de Saint-Joseph* (Bruges: Desclée de Brouwer, 1965).
8   Quoted in Evans, "Mystical Writings," 137.
9   Madeleine de Saint Joseph to Marie de Vignerot, s.d., in Sérouet, *Lettres spirituelles*, 66.
10   Blanchard, *Éminence*, 118.
11   Richelieu to Marie de Vignerot, 27 Jan. 1630, in Grillon, *Papiers*, 5:50.
12   Richelieu to Marie de Vignerot, 27 Jan. 1630, in Ibid., 50.
13   Tapié, *France*, 203.
14   Richelieu to Madame Bouthillier, 20 Sep. 1630, in Grillon, *Papiers*, 5:577.
15   Bouthillier to Richelieu, 30 Jul. 1630, in Ibid., 456.
16   Bouthillier to Richelieu, 30 Jul. 1630, in Ibid., 456–457.

15. The Coup d'État
1   Tabacchi, *Maria de Médici*, 327.
2   Grillon, *Papiers*, 4:294–295; 5:49.
3   Marie-Catherine Vignal Souleyreau, ed., *Correspondance du cardinal de Richelieu, Année 1634*, 2 vols. (Paris: Harmattan, 2013), 1:520; Tapié, *France*, 155.
4   Tallemant, *Historiettes*, 2:26.
5   Petitot, *Mémoires*, 5:451–452.
6   Collins, *The State*, 58.
7   Katharine Prescott Wormeley, trans., *Memoirs of Madame de Motteville on Anne of Austria and Her Court*, 3 vols. (Boston: Hardy, Pratt and Company, 1902), 1:48–49.
8   Dubost, *Marie de Médicis*, 776.
9   Tabacchi, *Maria de Médici*, 335.
10   Blanchard, *Éminence*, 128.
11   Bonneau-Avenant, *Duchesse d'Aiguillon*, 174; Aronson, *Madame de Rambouillet*, 106.
12   Blanchard, *Éminence*, 141.
13   Kettering, "Strategies," 194; Tapié, *France*, 236–239.

14 Madeleine de Saint-Joseph to Marie de Vignerot, 21 Dec. 1630, in Sérouet, *Lettres spirituelles*, 64–65.
15 Madeleine de Saint-Joseph to Marie de Vignerot, early 1631, in Ibid., 66–67.
16 Richelieu to Marie de Vignerot, 21 Feb. 1631, in Grillon, *Papiers*, 6:97–98.

16. An Abduction Plot
1 Bonneau-Avenant, *Duchesse d'Aiguillon*, 178-179.
2 Duchesse de Vendôme to Richelieu, Nov. 1630, in Grillon, *Papiers*, 5:690.
3 Madame de Marillac to Richelieu, 21 Jul. 1631, in Ibid., 6:460–461.
4 Mallick, "Clients," 248–249; Kettering, "Strategies," 193.
5 Armand-Jean du Plessis de Richelieu, *Journal de Monsieur le cardinal duc de Richelieu qu'il a fait Durant le grand Orage de la Cour és années 1630 & 1631*, vol. 1 (Lyon: André Olyer, 1666), 6.
6 Blanchard, *Éminence*, 139–140.
7 Testu to Richelieu, 5 Sep. 1632, in Marie-Catherine Vignal Souleyreau, ed., *La Correspondance du cardinal de Richelieu: Au faite du pouvoir, l'année 1632* (Paris: Harmattan, 2007), 424.
8 Testu to Richelieu, 5 Sep. 1632, in Ibid., 427.
9 Tabacchi, *Maria de Médici*, 364.
10 Dussault, *Oraisons funèbres*, 104.
11 Church, *Richelieu*, 231–232; Guron to Richelieu, 25 Oct. 1632, in Souleyreau, *Correspondance . . . 1632*, 466.
12 Testu to Richelieu, 25 Oct. 1632, in Ibid., 466.
13 Testu to Richelieu, 11 Nov. 1632, in Ibid., 471.
14 Bouthillier to Richelieu, 4 Dec. 1632, in Ibid., 484.
15 La Rivière to Louis XIII, c. 6 Sep. 1633, in Marie-Catherine Vignal Souleyreau, *Le cardinal de Richelieu à la conquète de la Lorraine: Correspondance, 1633* (Paris: Harmattan, 2010), 427–431; Charles-Prosper-Maurice Horric de Beaucaire, ed., *Mémoires de Du Plessis-Besançon* (Paris: Renouard, 1892), xxiii–xxiv; Charles-Prosper-Maurice Horric de Beaucaire, "Un Collaboreateur de Richelieu et de Mazarin: Bernard du Plessis-Besançon (1600–1670)," *Revue d'histoire diplomatique* 9 (1895): 105–106.
16 Mathieu de Morgues, *La Vérité défendue: ensemble quelques observations sur la conduicte du Cardinal de Richelieu* (n.p., 1635), 32, 50.

17. "Demi-Vierge"
1 This recipe for *une tourte à la Combalet* was included in the first-ever French cookbook: "Take three egg yolks without mixing in any of the whites, half a pound of lemon peel, some orange blossom water, and musk. Beat the lemon peel, mix everything together, and dry it with a handful of sugar, beating it all again. Then pour the mixture into a saucepan and give it three or four turns on the fire. Form a large pie crust and put the heated mixture into the crust with some powdered sugar above and below the mixture. Then close it and surround it with fire. When it is half cooked, raise it, and place it in the oven to dry." François Pierre de La Varenne, *Le Cuisinier françois* (Paris: Pierre David, 1655), 412–413.
2 Bonneau-Avenant, *Duchesse d'Aiguillon*, 180.
3 François Bluche, *Richelieu* (Paris: Perrin, 2003), 106.
4 Morgues, *Vérité défendue*, 32, 50, 57–59.
5 Ibid., 57–59.

6   Bergin, *Politics of Religion*, 120.
7   Morgues, *Vérité défendue*, 58–59.
8   Craveri, *Age of Conversation*, 29–30.
9   Tabacchi, *Maria de Médici*, 327.

18. A Budding Friendship
1   Noailles, *Cardinal de La Valette*, 71, 107.
2   Ibid., 71–74, 95.
3   Ibid., 107.
4   Ibid., 163.
5   Craveri, *Age of Conversation*, 65.
6   Ibid., 56–57.
7   Dussault, *Oraisons funèbre*, 107.
8   Memo, Oct. 1933, in Souleyreau, *Cardinal de Richelieu . . . 1633*, 531–532.
9   Souleyreau, *Cardinal de Richelieu . . . 1634*, 1:24, 524.
10   Tallemant, *Historiettes*, 2:26.
11   Ibid.
12   *Miliade*, 61–62.
13   Kleinman, *Anne of Austria*, 80.
14   Tallemant, *Historiettes*, 2:32; Wolfgang and Nell, "Reclaiming," 11–14n.
15   Sharon Kettering, "The Household Service of Early Modern French Noblewomen," *French Historical Studies* 20/1 (1997): 55–85.

19. A New Kind of Literary Patroness
1   Jacques du Bosc, O.F.M., *L'honnête femme*, eds. Sharon Dianne Nell and Aurora Wolfgang (Toronto: Centre for Reformation and Renaissance Studies, 2014), 41.
2   Ibid., 44.
3   Hugh Gaston Hall, *Richelieu's Desmarets and the Century of Louis XIV* (Oxford: Clarendon Press, 1990), 280–281.
4   Guillaume Colletet, *Les couches sacrées de la Vierge, poème héroique de Sannazar* (Paris: Jean Camusat, 1634), n.p.
5   Bonneau-Avenant, *Duchesse d'Aiguillon*, 224–225.
6   Gournay to Richelieu, 16 Jun. 1634, in Marie de Gournay, *Oeuvres Complètes*, 2 vols., ed. Jean-Claude Arnould (Paris: Honoré Champion Éditeur, 2002), 2:1943.
7   Richard Hillman and Colette Quesnel, eds., *Marie Le Jars de Gournay: Apology for the Woman Writing and Other Works* (Chicago: University of Chicago Press, 2002), 10.
8   See for example Gournay, *Oeuvres complètes*, 2:1795–1796. Cf. François Le Métel de Boisrobert, ed., *Le Parnasse Royal, où les immortelles actions du tres-chrestien et tres-victoriex monarque Louis XIII* (Paris: Sébastien Cramoisy, 1635); François Le Métel de Boisrobert, ed., *Le sacrifice des Muses au grand cardinal de Richelieu* (Paris: Sébastien Cramoisy, 1635).
9   Morgues, *Vérité défendue*, 58–59.
10   Tallemant, *Historiettes*, 1:108.
11   Richelieu to Bouthillier, 5 May 1633, in Avenel, *Lettres*, 4:461; Kleinman, *Anne of Austria*, 83–84.
12   Transaction signed by Gondi and Richelieu, 31 Jan. 1635, BIU Sorbonne, MSRIC 151, ff. 7–8.
13   Notice on François de Vignerot taken from the armorial of the Ordre du Saint-Esprit, BIU Sorbonne, MSRIC 151, f. 31; Bluche, *Richelieu*, 389.

14 Bélisaire Ledain, *La Gatine historique et monumentale* (Paris: Jules Claye, 1876), 306-307.
15 Bluche, *Richelieu*, 389.
16 Tallemant, *Historiettes*, 2:29-30; Lilian Rea, *The Life and Times of Marie Madeleine, Countess of La Fayette* (London: Methuen and Company, 1908), 6-7.
17 Tallemant, quoted in H. Noel Williams, *The Love Affairs of the Condés (1530-1740)* (New York: Charles Scribner's Sons, 1912), 188.
18 *La Gazette de France* (Paris: 1634), 376.
19 Kettering, "Household Service," 63-64.
20 Tallemant, *Historiettes*, 2:29-30; Rea, *Life and Times*, 6-7; Bergin, *Cardinal Richelieu*, 61.

20. Falling in Love

1 Memo delivered to Richelieu, 7 Jun. 1634, in Souleyreau, *Correspondance... 1634*, 1:523-524.
2 Thomas James Dandelet, *The Renaissance of Empire in Early Modern Europe* (Cambridge: Cambridge University Press, 2014), 226; Blanchard, *Éminence*, 150-152.
3 Jesús Antonio Cid, "'Centauro a lo pícaro' y voz de su amo: interpretaciones y textos nuevos sobre *La vida y hechos de Estabanillo González*," *Criticón* 47 (1989): 47n.
4 *Récit véritable de tout ce qui s'est passé au Chasteau de S. Germain en Laye, au retour de Monseigneur Frère Unique du Roy prés da sa Majesté* (Paris: Pierre Targa, 1634), 15.
5 Vincent J. Pitts, *La Grande Mademoiselle at the Court of France, 1627-1693* (Baltimore: Johns Hopkins University Press, 2000), 12.
6 *La Gazette de France* (Paris: 1634), 526.
7 Ibid.
8 Mazarin to Beringhen, 15 Mar. 1644, in Adolphe Chéruel, ed., *Lettres du Cardinal Mazarin pendant son Ministère*, 9 vols. (Paris: Imprimérie Nationale, 1872-1906), 1:622-623.
9 Deloche, *Richelieu*, 179-180; Kleinman, *Anne of Austria*, 80.
10 *La Gazette de France* (Paris: 1634), 526-527.
11 Ibid., 527-528.
12 Ibid., 528.
13 Richelieu to Cardinal La Valette, 15 May 1635, quoted in Noailles, *Cardinal de La Valette*, 132.
14 Ibid., 132-135.
15 Voiture to Cardinal La Valette, c. Jul. 1635, in Voiture, *Lettres*, 257-259.
16 Voiture to Cardinal La Valette, 12 Oct. 1635, in Ibid., 254-255.
17 Cardinal La Valette to Chavigny, 11 Dec. 1635, AMAE, Correspondance Politique, Lorraine 27, ff. 241-242.
18 Vincent Voiture, "Trois rondeaux à Madame de Combalet, sur ses beaux yeux," BnF Arsenal, Français 4213, f. 1057.
19 Ibid., f. 1059.
20 Amédée Roux, ed., *Les oeuvres de monsieur de Voiture* (Paris: Librairie de Firmin Didot, Frères, 1856), 513.
21 Voiture to Marie de Vignerot, 5 Jan. 1635, in Voiture, *Lettres*, 250-251.
22 Roger Lathuillère, *La préciosité: Étude historique et linguistique*, vol. 1 (Geneva: Droz, 1969), 401.

23 Voiture to Cardinal La Valette, c. August 1636, in Voiture, *Lettres*, 259–261. The dating is based on my own judgment, as the letter refers elsewhere to recent ambushes near Paris by Croatian cavalrymen under a Spanish command. These occurred in August 1636. On the rumors about Gaston and Marie, see Louis d'Astarac de Fontrailles, *Relation des choses particulières de la Cour oendant la faveur de Monsieur le Grand* (Cologne: Jean Sameix, 1723); Michel Le Vassor, *Histoire du règne de Louis XIII, roi de France et de Navarre*, 10 vols. (Amsterdam: Zacharie Chatelain et Fils, 1750-1753), 8(I):489.

24 Noailles, *Cardinal de La Valette*, 237–244.

25 Ibid., 244.

26 Le Vassor, *Histoire*, 8(II):144–146.

27 G. B. Depping, "Un banquier protestant en France au xviiie siècle: Barthélemy Herwarth," *Revue Historique* 10 (1879): 296. Cf. Le Vassor, *Histoire*, 8(II):169–170.

28 *La Gazette de France* (Paris: 1636), 220.

29 Chavigny to Cardinal La Valette, 28 Nov. 1637, in Noailles, *Cardinal de La Valette*, 372n. Cf. Charles Constant, ed., *Mémoires de Nicolas Goulas, gentilhomme ordinaire de la chamber du duc d'Orléans* (Paris: Librarie Renouard, 1879), 461.

30 Grotius to Oxenstierna, 22 Aug. and 5 Dec. 1636, and Grotius to Van Reigersberch, 5 Dec. 1636, in B. L. Meulenbroek, ed., *Briefwisseling van Hugo Grotius*, vol. 7 (The Hague: Martinus Nijhof, 1969), 336, 552, 554.

31 Cardinal La Valette to Pope Urban VIII, 8 Apr. 1638, BnF Arsenal, Français 6314; Noailles, *Cardinal de La Valette*, 387–390.

32 Le Vassor, *Histoire*, 9(I):42–43.

33 Philippe Tamizey de Larroque, ed., *Lettres de Peiresc aux Frères Dupuy*, vol. 3 (Paris: Imprimerie Nationale, 1892), 633.

21. La Valette

1 Blanchard, *Éminence*, 154, 156.

2 Mitchell Greenberg, *Subjectivity and Subjugation in Seventeenth-Century Drama and Prose: The Family Romance of French Classicism* (Cambridge: Cambridge University Press, 1992), 58.

3 Bonneau-Avenant, *Duchesse d'Aiguillon*, 222–223; Louis Battifol, "Richelieu a-t-il persecute Corneille?" *Revue des deux mondes* 14/2 (1923): 633–634.

4 Pierre Corneille, *Le Cid: Tragi-comédie* (Paris: Augustin Courbé, 1637), ii–iv.

5 Tabitha Spagnolo, "'Mars respire ici sous l'habit de venus': Transvestitism and Transformation in Jean Rotrou's 'Agésilan de Colchos' (1635)," *Rocky Mountain Review* 70/1 (Spring 2016): 79.

6 Jean de Rotrou, *Agésilan de Colchos: Tragi-comédie* (Paris: Anthoine de Sommaville, 1637), ii–iii.

7 Marie de Vignerot to Cardinal La Valette, 13 Jul. 1637, BnF Richelieu, Français 6644, ff. 221-222.

8 Marie de Vignerot to Cardinal La Valette, 27 Jul. 1637, Ibid., ff. 240–241.

9 Marie de Vignerot to Cardinal La Valette, 9 Nov. 1637, Sorbonne BIU, MSRIC 18, ff. 94–97.

10 Marie de Vignerot to Cardinal La Valette, 29 Nov. 1637, BnF Richelieu, Français 6644, 236-237. Cf. Chavigny to Cardinal La Valette, 28 Nov. 1637, in Noailles, *Cardinal de La Valette*, 372n.

11 Noailles, *Cardinal de La Valette*, 372, 377.

12 Roux, *Oeuvres de monsieur de Voiture*, 48.

13   Bonneau-Avenant, *Duchesse d'Aiguillon*, 252.
14   Richelieu to Cardinal La Valette, 4 Nov. 1638, in Avenel, *Lettres*, 6:232–233.
15   Cardinal La Valette to Richelieu, 11 Dec. 1638, in Ibid., 6:233n.

22. Chosen
1   Erection of Aiguillon as a duchy-peerage in favor of Marie de Vignerot, widow of the
      Sieur de Combalet, 1 Jan. 1638, BnF Richelieu, Français 4584, ff. 23-26; Jean-Pierre
      Labatut, *Les Ducs et pairs au XVIIe siècle* (Paris: Presses Universitaires de France, 1972);
      Beik, *Social and Cultural History*, 87. Cf. BnF Richelieu, Dupuy 640, ff. 83–86v.
2   *Inventaire-Sommaire des Archives départementales antérieures à 1790: Lot-et-Garonne*
      (Agen: Prosper Nouvel, 1878), 12.
3   Le Vassor, *Histoire*, 8(II):183. Cf. Jean-Pierre Labatut, *Les Ducs et pairs au XVIIe
      siècle* (Paris: Presses Universitaires de France, 1972).
4   Antoine Aubery, *L'Histoire du Cardinal-Duc de Richelieu*, vol. 2 (Cologne: Pierre du
      Marteau, 1666), 412.
5   Le Vassor, *Histoire*, 9(I):42–43.
6   Ibid., 41.
7   Memoirs of the Cardinal-Duc de Richelieu, in Joseph-François Michaud and
      Jean-Joseph Poujoulat, eds., *Nouvelle collection des mémoires pour servir a l'histoire
      de France depuis le XIIIe siècle jusqu'à la fin du XVIIIe*, vol. 9 (Paris: Éditeur du
      Commentaire Analytique du Code Civil, 1838), 118–119.
8   Marie-Perrier Terrien, *The Ideal City and the Château of Richelieu*, trans. Howard
      Leigh Copping (Cholet: Editions Pays et Terroirs, 2017); Christine Toulier,
      "Richelieu: La ville du cardinal," *Bulletin de la Société des amis du vieux Chinon* 9
      (1993); 785–816; Bonnaffé, *Recherches*, 24–26.
9   Marie de Vignerot to Richelieu, 1 Sep. 1637, BIU Sorbonne, MSRIC 17, ff. 55–56.
10   Pitts, *La Grande Mademoiselle*, 19–21.
11   Ibid.; Bonneau-Avenant, *Duchesse d'Aiguillon*, 221.
12   Richelieu to François de Vignerot, 6 Jun. 1636, in Avenel, *Lettres*, 5:481–482;
      Memoir regarding the train that Madame the Générale des Galères should have
      during her husband's absence, c. Jun. 1636, in Avenel, *Lettres*, 5:483–484.
13   Richelieu to François de Vignerot, 10 Jul. 1636 (1), in Ibid., 502–503.
14   Richelieu to François de Vignerot, 10 Jul. 1636 (2), in Ibid., 504.
15   Amy Wygant, *Medea, Magic, and Modernity in France: Stages and Histories,
      1553–1797* (Aldershot: Ashgate, 2011), 152–153; Bernard Bourque, *All the Abbé's
      Women: Power and Misogyny in Seventeenth-Century France, Through the Writings
      of Abbé d'Aubignac* (Tübingen: Narr Verlag, 2015), 13; Robin Briggs, "Dubious
      Messengers: Bodin's Daemon, the Spirit World and the Sadducees," *Angels in the
      Early Modern World*, eds. Peter Marshall and Alexandra Walsham (Cambridge:
      Cambridge University Press, 2006), 183.
16   Robert Mandrou, ed., *Possession et sorcellerie au XVIIe siècle: textes inédites* (Paris:
      Fayard, 1979), 144, 165–174, 187–193.

23. The Investiture
1   Quoted in Mary Maxwell Scott, "Marie de Vignerod, Duchesse d'Aiguillon
      (1604–1675)," *The Dublin Review* (1905), 367–368.

24. Heartbreak
1   Jean Desmarets de Saint-Sorlin, *Rosane: Histoire tirée de celle des Romains et des*

Perses (Paris: Henry Le Gras, 1639); Pierre Bense-Dupuis, *La Clef de la langue romaine dedié à Mme de Combalet, duchesse d'Esguillon* (Paris: Pierre Bense-Dupuis, 1638).

2 Bonnaffé, *Recherches*, 24–25.
3 Kettering, "Patronage, Language," 848.
4 Kleinman, *Anne of Austria*, 43–51, 88–89, 109–110.
5 *La Gazette de France* (Paris: 1639), 325.
6 Ibid.
7 Noailles, *Cardinal de La Valette*, 532–533.
8 Chavigny to Marie de Vignerot, 8 Oct. 1639, in Avenel, *Lettres*, 6:233n.
9 Marie de Vignerot to Chavigny, 24 Oct. 1639, in Ibid.
10 Amelot de La Houssaie, *Mémoires historiques, politiques, critiques et littéraires*, vol. 2 (Amsterdam: Zacharie Chatelain, 1722), 76–77; F. Barrière, ed., *Mémoires inédits de Louis-Henri de Loménie, Comte de Brienne, Sécrétaire d'État sous Louis XIV*, vol. 1 (Paris: Ponthieu et Compagnie, 1828), 277–279.
11 La Valette to Urban VIII, 15 Apr. 1638, BnF Richelieu, Français 6314, f. 220; Noailles, *Cardinal de La Valette*, 535.
12 List of thirty of La Valette's royally approved beneficiaries, BnF Richelieu, Français 5843, ff. 404–406.
13 Memorandum to Marie de Vignerot, 8 Oct. 1639, AMAE, Mémoires et documents, *France 53MD/834*; Noailles, *Cardinal de La Valette*, 535.
14 Richelieu to François de Vignerot, c. Mar. 1639, in Avenel, *Lettres*, 8:798–800.
15 Marie de Vignerot to Chavigny, 21 Oct. 1639, and Richelieu to Bouthillier, 2 Nov. 1639, in Ibid., 6:606–608.
16 Philippe Tamizey de Larroque, ed., *Lettres de Jean Chapelain, de l'Académie Française*, vol. 1 (Paris: Imprimerie Nationale, 1880), 588n, 640.

25. A New Relationship

1 Michel van Lochom, *Images des Fondatrices, Réformatrices, ou principales réligieuses de tous les orders de l'église, dédiée à Madame la duchesse d'Aiguillon* (Paris: Michel van Lochom, 1639), 55, 86.
2 Louis Beurier, *Sommaire des vies des fondateurs et réformateurs des ordres réligieuses* (Paris: Widow of G. Le Noir, 1635).
3 Van Lochom, *Images*, 68, 82.
4 Ibid., 5–6.
5 Alison Forrestal, *Vincent de Paul, the Lazarist Mission, and French Catholic Reform* (New York: Oxford University Press, 2017), 140.
6 *Chroniques de l'ordre des Carmélites*, 1:205.
7 M. H. Fisquet, *La France Pontificale (Gallia Christiana): Histoire chronologique et biographique des archevêques et évêques de tous les diocèses de France, depuis l'établissement du Christianisme jusqu'à nos jours*, vol. 2 (Paris: E. Repos, 1864), 408.
8 Forrestal, *Vincent de Paul*, 130.
9 Ibid., 119.
10 Ibid., 140.
11 De Paul to De Marillac, 27 May 1636, in Pierre Coste, C.M., ed., *Vincent de Paul: Correspondence, Conferences, and Documents*, 14 vols., trans. Marie Poole, D.C., et al. (Brooklyn: New City Press, 1985–2014), 1:321–323. This source collection is hereafter cited with the abbreviation *CCD*.
12 De Marillac to De Paul, 1638, in Louise Sullivan, D.C., ed., *Spiritual Writings of Louise de Marillac* (Brooklyn: New City Press, 1991), 16.

13   Forrestal, *Vincent de Paul*, 196.
14   Ibid., 275; Chronological list of minutes concerning the Duchesse d'Aiguillon, 1637–1647, recorded by notary Nicolas Charles, CARAN, MC ET XLVI 1, f. 460. See additional documents on the Lazarists' work in Agen in AD Drôme, Fonds d'Aiguillon, 100 Mi 180.
15   Forrestal, *Vincent de Paul*, 141.
16   Ibid., 275; Marie-Pierre Terrien, *Vincent de Paul à Richelieu* (Cholet: Éditions Pays et Terroirs, 2017).
17   Forrestal, *Vincent de Paul*, 140–142.

26. Across the Atlantic

1   Reuben Gold Thwaites, ed., *The Jesuit Relations and Allied Documents: Travels and Explorations of the Jesuit Missionaries in New France, 1610–1791*, 73 vols. (Cleveland: Burrows Brothers, 1896–1901), 14:123–125. This source collection is hereafter cited with the abbreviation *JR*.
2   Sheldon J. Watts, *Epidemics and History: Disease, Power, and Imperialism* (New Haven: Yale University Press, 1997), 92; Bronwen McShea, *Apostles of Empire: The Jesuits and New France* (Lincoln: University of Nebraska Press, 2019), 95–96.
3   JR, 16:29.
4   McShea, *Apostles*, 4–11.
5   JR, 8:233.
6   Donation by Marie de Vignerot entrusted to Cramoisy, *procureur* for Hospitalières of Québec, 16 Aug. 1637, CARAN, Y 178, f. 206v; McShea, *Apostles*, 100.
7   McShea, *Apostles*, 100.
8   JR, 16:21–23.
9   Ibid., 25–27.
10   Ibid., 23–25.
11   Donation by Marie de Vignerot to the Hospitalières of Québec, 31 Jan. 1640, LAC, MG17-A10, 216-219, 228-236; Transfer of funds by Marie Vignerot to Cramoisy, *procureur* for the Hospitalières of Québec, 21 Jan. 1640, CARAN, Y 180, f. 203.
12   JR, 18:71–73.
13   Laurier Lacroix, ed., *Les Arts en Nouvelle-France* (Québec: Publications de Québec, 2012), 50–51.
14   Ibid., 47–49, 53; Victor Cousin, *Madame de Longueville*, 2nd ed. (Paris: Didier, 1853), 461.
15   JR, 20:247–249; Katherine Ibbett, *Compassion's Edge: Fellow-Feeling and Its Limits in Early Modern France* (Philadelphia: University of Pennsylvania Press, 2018), 204.
16   JR, 11:97–99.
17   Ibid., 93–95.
18   Ibid., 29.

27. Childlessness

1   Hall, *Richelieu's Desmarets*, 3–4, 46–47.
2   Desmarets, *Rosane*, 3–4, 40–41, 105–107.
3   *Table ou abrégé des cent trente-cinq volumes de la Gazette de France*, vol. 3 (Paris: Galeries du Louvre, 1768), 169.
4   De Paul to De Marillac, 30 Aug. 1640, CCD, 2:126.
5   See for example the marriage contract of Catherine Collet and François Thoue, Jun. 1641, CARAN, Y 181, f. 575.

6   Aronson, *Madame de Rambouillet*, 131.
7   Hall, *Richelieu's Desmarets*, 70–71.
8   John J. Conley, S.J., *The Other Pascals: The Philosophy of Jacqueline Pascal, Gilberte Pascal Périer, and Marguerite Périer* (South Bend: University of Notre Dame Press, 2019), 2–3.
9   Georges de Scudéry, *L'Amour tyrannique* (Paris: Augustin Courbé, 1640).
10   Victor Cousin, *Jacqueline Pascal; or, Convent Life at Port Royal*, trans. HN (London: J. Nisbet, 1854), 24–26; John Tulloch, *Pascal* (Edinburgh: William Blackwood and Sons, 1878), 12–13.
11   Tulloch, *Pascal*, 13–14.
12   Harold J. Cook, *The Young Descartes: Nobilty, Rumor, and War* (Chicago: University of Chicago Press, 2018), 158, 230.
13   Marie Crous, *Abbregé recherché de Marie Crous, pour tirer a solution de toutes propositions d'Aritmetique* (Paris: Jacques Auvray, 1641), i–vi, viii.
14   Williams, *Love Affairs*, 190; Avenel, *Lettres*, 6:509.
15   Avenel, *Lettres*, 7:788n.
16   Richelieu to Marie de Vignerot, 29 May 1640, in Ibid., 6:697n.
17   Blanchard, *Éminence*, 197; Kleinman, *Anne of Austria*, 116.
18   Quoted in Louis Dussieux, *Le Cardinal de Richelieu: Étude biographique* (Paris: Victor Lecoffre, 1886), 255.
19   Williams, *Love Affairs*, 183, 194.
20   Ibid., 195; Richelieu to Bouthillier, 30 Jan. 1641, in Avenel, *Lettres*, 6:751.
21   Williams, *Love Affairs*, 196–197.
22   Blet, *Richelieu*, 247.

28. Political Storms

1   I am grateful for my correspondence with Edoardo Pepino of March 2017 that informed me about this painting's history.
2   Levi, *Cardinal Richelieu*, 239.
3   Elliott, *Richelieu*, 146.
4   Colin Jones, *Paris: The Biography of a City* (New York: Penguin, 2004), 248.
5   Collins, *The State*, 63; Levi, *Cardinal Richelieu*, 238.
6   Levi, *Cardinal Richelieu*, 239.
7   Ibid., 241; Blanchard, *Éminence*, 200.
8   Philippe Delorme, *Histoire des Reines de France: Marie de Médicis* (Paris: Pygmalion, 1998), 307.
9   Richelieu to Chavigny, 19 Apr. 1641, Avenel, *Lettres*, 6:778.
10   Kleinman, *Anne of Austria*, 115.
11   Ibid.
12   Blanchard, *Éminence*, 203.
13   Ibid.; Levi, *Cardinal Richelieu*, 242.
14   Marie de Vignerot to Chavigny, 29 Mar. 1642, AD Drôme, Fonds d'Aiguillon, 100 Mi 134.
15   Richelieu's last will and testament, 23 May 1641, BIU Sorbonne, MSRIC 20, ff. 66–105; Bergin, *Cardinal Richelieu*, 256.
16   Blanchard, *Éminence*, 206.
17   Ibid., 207.
18   Marie de Vignerot to Chavigny, 31 May 1642, quoted in Denis-Louis-Martial Avenel, ed., *Le dernier épisode de la vie du Cardinal de Richelieu: Louis XIII,*

Cinq-Mars, Aug. de Thou (Paris: Bureaux de la Revue, 1868), 50–51.
19 Blanchard, *Éminence*, 207.
20 Ibid., 208.
21 Levi, *Cardinal Richelieu*, 243.
22 Ibid., 246.
23 Quoted in Richard Wilkinson, *Louis XIV* (London: Routledge, 2007), 11.
24 Richelieu to Chavigny and Sublet de Noyers, 22 Jul. 1642, in Avenel, *Lettres*, 7:47–48.
25 Chavigny to Richelieu, 28 Jul. 1642, and Richelieu to Chavigny, 10 Aug. 1642, in Ibid., 88.
26 Tapié, *France*, 423.

29. Uncle Armand's Death
1 Blanchard, *Éminence*, 219.
2 Ibid., 219–220; Kleinman, *Anne of Austria*, 135.
3 Claude de Bourdeille de Montresor, *Mémoires de Monsieur de Montresor*, vol. 2 (Leiden: Jean Sameix, 1665), 175.
4 Blanchard, *Éminence*, 220.
5 Montresor, *Mémoires*, vol. 2, 177.
6 Ibid., 178.
7 Blanchard, *Éminence*, 220.
8 Montresor, *Mémoires*, vol. 2, 181.

30. The Will
1 Bergin, *Cardinal Richelieu*, 264.
2 Ibid., 265.
3 Richelieu's last will and testament, 23 May 1642, in Michaud and Poujoulat, *Nouvelle collection*, vol. 9, 355–356.
4 Bergin, Cardinal Richelieu, 7; Souleyreau, *Correspondance . . . 1632*, 8.
5 Richelieu's last will and testament, 23 May 1642, in Michaud and Poujoulat, *Nouvelle collection*, vol. 9, 357–358.
6 Bergin, *Cardinal Richelieu*, 261.
7 Ibid., 262.

31. Burying the Prime Minister
1 *La Gazette de France* (Paris: 1642), 1155.
2 Ibid., 1168.
3 Ibid., 1196; Blanchard, *Éminence*, 222.
4 *La Gazette de France* (Paris: 1642), 1196.
5 Isabella Richefort, "L'iconographie religieuse de Richelieu," *Richelieu, patron des arts*, eds. Jean-Claude Boyer et al. (Paris: Maison des Sciences de l'Homme, 2009), 328–329.
6 Bergin, *Cardinal Richelieu*, 273.
7 Ibid., 265–268; Williams, *Love Affairs*, 198–200.
8 Bluche, *Richelieu*, 365–366.
9 *Le tableau de la vie & du gouvernement de Messieurs les Cardinaux Richelieu et Mazarin* (Cologne: Pierre Marteau, 1693), 75.
10 Bergin, *Cardinal Richelieu*, 258, 266.

PART TWO—PAIR DE FRANCE

32. Uncle Armand's Papers

1   Paul Sonnino, "The Dating of Richelieu's Testament Politique," French History 19/2 (2005): 271; Jules Lair and Alphonse Chodron de Courcel, eds., *Rapports et notices sur l'édition des Mémoires du Cardinal de Richelieu, préparée pour la Société de l'Histoire de France*, booklet 4 (Paris: Renouard, 1907), 269.

2   Bergin, *Cardinal Richelieu*, 7; Souleyreau, *Correspondance . . . 1632*, 8.

3   Lair and de Courcel, *Rapports*, 270; Henri Chérot, S.J., *Étude sur la vie et les oeuvres du Père Le Moyne (1602–1671)* (Paris: Alphonse Picard, 1887), 398–400.

4   Carsten L. Wilkie, "Manuel Fernandes Villa Real at the Portugues Embassy in Paris, 1644–1649: New Documents and Insights," *Journal of Levantine Studies* 6 (2016): 153–176.

5   Manoel Fernandes Villareal, *Le Politique tres chrestien, ou Discours politiques sur les actions principals de la vie de feu Monseigneur l'Eminentissime Cardinal Duc de Richelieu*, trans. François de Grenaille (Paris: Toussainct Quinet, 1643), 26.

6   François de Grenaille, *La Bibliothèque des Dames* (Paris: Toussainct Quinet, 1640), n.p.

7   François de Grenaille, *La Mausolée cardinal, ou Éloge funèbre de feu Mgr le cardinal duc de Richelieu, contenant sa naissance, sa vie, sa mort et sa sépulture* (Paris: J. Paslé, 1643).

8   Hall, *Richelieu's Desmarets*, 262.

9   Sonnino, "Dating," 263–266.

10   Laurent Avezou, "Autour du 'Testament politique' de Richelieu: À la recherche de l'auteur perdu (1688–1778)," *Bibliothèque de l'École des chartes* 162/2 (2004): 426; Henry Bertram Hill, ed. and trans., *The Political Testament of Cardinal Richelieu: The Significant Chapters and Supporting Selections* (Madison: University of Wisconsin Press, 1961), xi–xii.

11   Colbert to Mazarin, 10 Nov. 1651, in Pierre Clément, ed., *Lettres, instructions et mémoires de Colbert*, 8 vols. (Paris: Imprimerie Impériale, 1861–1873), 1:163–169; Sonnino, "Dating," 271–272.

12   Paul Sonnino, ed., *The Political Testament of Cardinal Richelieu* (Lanham: Rowman and Littlefield, 2020), 100, 112–113.

13   Ibid., 45.

14   Ibid., 46.

33. Rueil

1   Wilkinson, *Louis XIV*, 17–18.

2   Alan James, *Navy and Government in Early Modern France, 1572–1661* (Woodbridge: The Boydell Press, 2004), 113–114.

3   Kleinman, *Anne of Austria*, 153–154; A. E. Borély, *Histoire de la Ville du Havre et de son ancien gouvernement*, vol. 2 (Le Havre: Lepelletier, 1881), 468.

4   Wormeley, *Memoirs*, 1:74.

5   Ibid., 75.

6   Bergin, *Cardinal Richelieu*, 269.

7   Dussieux, *Cardinal de Richelieu*, 274.

8   Wilkinson, *Louis XIV*, 15.

9   Chapelain to Montausier, 15 Jun. 1640, in De Larroque, *Lettres*, 1:640.

10   Dussieux, *Cardinal de Richelieu*, 273.

11   Adolphe Chéruel, ed., *Lettres du Cardinal Mazarin pendant son Ministère*, 9 vols. (Paris: Imprimérie Nationale, 1872–1906), 1:736–737n; Bergin, *Cardinal Richelieu*, 268–270.

12   Bonnaffé, *Recherches*, 23; Dussieux, *Cardinal de Richelieu*, 270–271.
13   Dussieux, *Cardinal de Richelieu*, 272–272; Order for masonry work at Rueil, 15 Jun.
      1642, CARAN, MC ET LXXXVI 311.
14   Letter 27, 12 Jul. 1664, in Charles-Louis Livet, ed., *La Muze Historique, ou Receuil
      des lettres en vers contenant les nouvelles du temps, écrites à Son Altesse Mademoizelle de
      Longueville, depuis Duchesse de Nemours (1650–1665)*, 4 vols. (Paris: P. Daffis, 1858–
      1891), 4:220; Jules Jacquin and Joseph Duesberg, *Rueil: Le Château de Richelieu, la
      Malmaison, avec pièces justificatives* (Paris: Dauvin et Fontaine, 1845), 34.
15   Rea, *Life and Times*, 48.
16   Cousin, *Madame de Longueville*, 475–476.
17   Rea, *Life and Times*, 49.
18   Wormeley, *Memoirs*, 1:113–115.
19   Chéruel, *Lettres*, 1:735–737.
20   Diefendorf, *Penitence to Charity*, 221–222.
21   Wormeley, *Memoirs*, 1:115.

34. Patroness of a Saint
1   Richelieu's last will and testament, 23 May 1642, in Michaud and Poujoulat,
      Nouvelle collection, vol. 9, 360.
2   Contract for three additional priests at Notre-Dame de La Rose, 27 Mar. 1643,
      in Félix Contassot, ed., "Les Lazaristes à Notre-Dame de La Rose avant la
      Révolution: Études documetaires," unpublished manuscript, Paris, 1961, 13–17.
3   Foundation of the Congrégation de la Mission in Rome, 4 Jul. 1642, BIU
      Sorbonne, MSRIC 20, ff. 56–59.
4   Chronological list of minutes concerning the Duchesse d'Aiguillon, 1637–1647,
      CARAN, MC ET XLVI 1, f. 464; Foundation, 2 May 1643, CARAN, MC ET
      XLVI 30, Pierre Coste, C.M., *The Life and Works of Saint Vincent de Paul*, 3 vols., trans.
      Joseph Leonard, C.M. (Brooklyn: New City Press, 1987), 2:3; José María Román,
      Vincent de Paul: A Biography, trans. Joyce Howard (Herts: Melisende, 1999), 380.
5   Foundation by Marie de Vignerot, 2 May 1643, CARAN, MC ET XLVI 30;
      Coste, *Life and Works*, 2:3.
6   See for example Mazarin to Marie de Vignerot, 16 and 19 Aug. 1646, in Chéruel,
      Lettres, 2:795–796.
7   Forrestal, *Vincent de Paul*, 204.
8   Foundation by Marie de Vignerot, 25 Jul. 1643, CARAN, S 6707; Coste, *Life and
      Works*, 2:330–332.
9   Coste, *Life and Works*, 2:324.
10   Larcher and Brandon to the Gentlemen of the Compagnie du Saint-Sacrement in
      Marseilles, 18 Apr. 1643, in Raoul Allier, *La Compagnie du Très-Saint-Sacrement de
      l'autel à Marseille* (Paris: Honoré Champion, 1909), 155.
11   Marie de Vignerot to Gault, 29 May 1643 in François Marchetti, *La vie de Messire
      Jean-Baptiste Gault, evesque de Marseille* (Paris: Sébastien Huré, 1649), 209;
      Forrestal, *Vincent de Paul*, 204.
12   Coste, *Life and Works*, 2:325–326.
13   La Coste to De Paul, c. 1645, quoted in Ibid., 328–329.
14   Forrestal, *Vincent de Paul*, 205; Royal *lettres patentes* for the hospital for galley
      convicts in Marseilles, 16 Aug. 1646, CARAN, S 6707.
15   Foundation by Marie de Vignerot, 25 Jul. 1643, Ibid.
16   Forrestal, *Vincent de Paul*, 143.

17   Jules Corblet, ed., *Origines royennes de l'institut des Filles-de-la-Croix d'après des documents inédits* (Paris: J.-B. Dumoulin, 1869), 28–29.

18   Román, *Vincent de Paul*, 78.

35. Tunis and Algiers

1   Tapié, *France*, 141.

2   Philip P. Boucher, *France and the American Tropics to 1700: Tropics of Discontent?* (Baltimore: Johns Hopkins University Press, 2008), 154–155; Christopher L. Miller, *The French Atlantic Triangle: Literature and Culture of the Slave Trade* (Durham: Duke University Press, 2008), 19–20.

3   Alison Forrestal and Felicia Rosu, "Slavery on the Frontier: The Report of a French Missionary on Mid-Seventeenth-Century Tunis," *Vincentian Heritage Journal* 34/1 (2017): https://via.library.depaul/vhj/vol34/iss1/2.

4   Procedure against Lange Martin, consul in Tunis (1635–1641), AMAE, Mémoires et Documents, Afrique 8; Eugène Sue, ed., *Correspondance de Henri d'Escubleau de Sourdis, archevêque de Bordeaux*, vol. 2 (Paris: Crapelet, 1839), 414–436; Gillian Weiss, *Captives and Corsairs: France and Slavery in the Early Modern Mediterranean* (Stanford: Stanford University Press, 2011), 45–46.

5   De Paul to Dufestel, 28 Nov. 1642, in John Rybolt, C.M., ed., "Unpublished Correspondence," Vincentian Studies Institute, Chicago, 2020, 73; Lucien Misermont, C.M., *Le plus grand des premiers missionnaires de Saint Vincent de Paul: Jean Le Vacher, prêtre de la Mission* (Paris: Librairie Lecoffre, 1935), 31.

6   Larcher and Brandon to the gentlemen of the Compagnie du Saint-Sacrement in Marseilles, 18 Apr. 1643, in Allier, *Compagnie*, 153–155.

7   Coste, *Life and Works*, 2:340.

8   Ibid., 341.

9   Antoine de Ruffi, *La vie de M. le chevalier de la Coste* (Aix: Charles David, 1659), 167.

10   Géraud Poumarède, "Naissance d'une institution royale: Les consuls de la nation Française en Levant et en Barbarie aux XVIe et XVIIe siècles," *Annuaire-bulletin de la Société de l'histoire de France* (2001): 65–128.

11   CCD, 2:678n; H. D. de Grammont, "Les consuls et les envoyés de la cour de France à Alger," *Revue d'histoire diplomatique publiée par les soins de la Société d'histoire diplomatique* 2 (1888): 102.

12   A. Pavy, *Histoire de la Tunisie* (Tours: Alfred Cattier, 1894), 343.

13   Bergin, *Cardinal Richelieu*, 272.

14   De Paul to La Haye-Ventelay, 25 Feb. 1654, CCD, 5:90; Coste, *Life and Works*, 2:343.

15   Coste, *Life and Works*, 350; CCD, 3:6n.

16   De Paul to Dehorgny, 31 Aug. 1646, CCD, 3:40.

17   Barreau to De Paul, 27 Jul. 1647, Ibid., 223.

18   De Paul to Dehorgny, 31 Aug. 1646, Ibid., 40–41.

19   Forrestal and Rosu, "Slavery."

20   Guérin to De Paul, c. 1646, CCD, 2:638–639.

21   Memorandum for Lazarist missionaries going from France to Barbary, 1647, in *Mémoires de la Congrégation de la Mission*, 9 vols. (Paris: Congrégation de la Mission, 1863–1888), 2:149–150.

22   Forrestal, *Vincent de Paul*, 202.

23   Quoted in Eugène Plantet, ed., *Correspondance des beys de Tunis et des consuls de France avec la cour, 1577–1830*, vol. 1 (Paris: F. Alcan, 1893), 148. Cf. Donation by Marie de Vignerot, 20 May 1647, in *Mémoires de la Congrégation*, 2:147–149.

24   Barreau to De Paul, 27 Jul. 1647, CCD, 3:223.

36. Reforming the Clergy

1   Jacques-Charles de Brisacier, *Discours funebre pour Madame la duchesse d'Aiguillon, prononcé a Paris dans la Chapelle du Seminaire des Missions Estrangeres* (Paris: Charles Angot, 1675), 18; Edward Healy Thompson, *The Life of Jean-Jacques Olier, Founder of the Seminary of St. Sulpice* (London: Burns and Oates, 1886), 100–101.

2   Philippe Tamizey de Larroque, "Un Languedocien oublié: L'Abbé de Croisilles," *Annales du Midi: Revue archéologique et philologique de la France méridionale* 5/18 (1893): 151n.

3   Jean-Baptiste de Croisilles, *Apologie de l'abbé de Croisilles* (Paris: Toussainct Quinet, 1643); Tamizey, "Languedocean," 152–153.

4   Jean Delumeau, *Catholicism Between Luther and Voltaire*, trans. Jeremy Moisier (London: Burnes and Oates, 1977), 179–181.

5   William M. Thompson, ed., *Bérulle and the French School: Selected Writings* (New York: Paulist Press, 1989), 12; Coste, *Life and Works*, 176–178.

6   *Dessein des Assemblées de la bourse clericale, Establie à Sainct Nicolas du Chardonnet* (Paris: Jean Dincourt, 1655), 7–8; Louis Abelly, *La vie du vénérable serviteur de Dieu Vincent de Paul, Instituteur et premier Supéreiur Général de la Congrégation de la Mission*, 3 vols. (Paris: Florentin Lambert, 1664), 1:129.

7   Thompson, *Bérulle*, 20; Charles de Montzey, *Father Eudes, Apostolic Missionary, and His Foundations, 1601–1874* (London: Thomas Richardson and Son, 1874), 81, 88.

8   Delumeau, *Catholicism*, 181.

9   Foundation by Marie de Vignerot, CARAN, MC ET XLVI 30, 2 May 1643.

10   De Paul to Portail, 15 Jul. 1646, CCD, 2:666.

11   Fisquet, *France Pontificale*, vol. 2, 620–621.

12   Alison Forrestal, "Venues for Clerical Formation in Catholic Reformation Paris: Vincent de Paul and the Tuesday Conferences and Company," *Journal of the Western Society for French History* 38 (2010): 44–60; Fisquet, *France Pontificale*, vol. 2, 620–621.

13   Bonneau-Avenant, *Duchesse d'Aiguillon*, 290–291; Léon Deschamps, *Histoire de la question colonial en France* (Paris: Librairie Plon, 1891), 127.

14   Thompson, *Life*, 141.

15   Fisquet, *France Pontificale*, vol. 2, 621.

16   Coste, *Life and Works*, 2:128.

37. Saint-Sulpice

1   Carlos M. N. Eire, *Reformations: The Early Modern World, 1450–1650* (New Haven: Yale University Press, 2016), 439.

2   Bonneau-Avenant, *Duchesse d'Aiguillon*, 446–447.

3   Forrestal, *Vincent de Paul*, 186.

4   CCD, 2:9n.

5   Coste, *Life and Works*, 2:350, 360.

6   De Paul to De Marillac, Feb. or Mar. 1641, CCD, 2:187–188.

7   Responses of De Paul to some questions of De Marillac, c. Jun. 1642, and Olier to De Paul, c. Nov. 1643, Ibid., 291, 474–475.

8   Joseph Bergin, *Church, Society and Religious Change in France, 1580–1730* (New Haven: Yale University Press, 2009), 95–97, 102–103.

9   Coste, *Life and Works*, 179.

10   Eire, *Reformations*, 439–440.

11   Séan Alexander Smith, *Fealty and Fidelity: The Lazarists of Bourbon France, 1660–1736* (London: Routledge, 2016), 27.

12   Fisquet, *France Pontificale*, vol. 2, 623.
13   Eire, *Reformations*, 439.
14   Ibid.
15   Blanchard, *Éminence*, 88; Beik, *Social and Cultural History*, 275–276.
16   Fisquet, *France Pontificale*, vol. 2, 623.
17   Beaumont, "Pierre de Bérulle," 75, 90.
18   Natalie Zemon Davis, "The Rites of Violence: Religious Riot in Sixteenth-Century France," *Past and Present* 59 (1973): 51–91.
19   Agreement between Marie de Vignerot and Guillaume Chehon and Laurent Gadoulleau, 1 Sep. 1644, CARAN, MC ET XLVI 34.
20   Thompson, *Life*, 241.
21   Agreement between Marie de Vignerot and Chehon and Gadoulleau, 1 Sep. 1644, CARAN, MC ET XLVI 34.
22   Thompson, *Life*, 242.
23   Robert P. Maloney, C.M., "Vincent de Paul and Jean-Jacques Olier: Unlikely Friends," *Vincentian Heritage Journal* 28/1 (2008): 12.
24   Bonneau-Avenant, *Duchesse d'Aiguillon*, 345; Thompson, *Life*, 248.
25   *La Gazette de France* (Paris: 1646), 136.
26   Quoted in Thompson, *Life*, 298.
27   Ibid.

38. Inheritance Disputes
1   Bergin, *Cardinal Richelieu*, 258, 261.
2   Ibid., 268–270.
3   Ibid., 271.
4   Ibid.
5   Ibid., 272.
6   Deloche, *Richelieu*, 186; Williams, *Love Affairs*, 198–200.
7   Bergin, *Cardinal Richelieu*, 265–266.
8   Ibid., 266. Notice signed by François de Vignerot's lawyers, early 1643, BnF Mitterand, Morel de Thoisy 54, ff. 162–166.
9   Bergin, *Cardinal Richelieu*, 267.
10   Transaction, 31 Mar. 1643, AD Drôme, Fonds d'Aiguillon, 100 Mi 134, ff. 2–3; Bergin, *Cardinal Richelieu*, 267.
11   Bergin, *Cardinal Richelieu*, 267.
12   Quittance, 14 May 1644, CARAN, MC ET XLVI 32; Gil and Luçon, "The Château de Glénay," 160–162.
13   Bergin, *Cardinal Richelieu*, 268.
14   Ibid.
15   Williams, *Love Affairs*, 198–202.
16   "Receuil des plaidoyers touchant la cause de Monseigneur le Prince contre Madame la Duchesse d'Aiguillon pour la succession de Monsieur le Cardinal de Richelieu," BnF Richelieu, Français 17333, ff. 72–86; Bergin, *Cardinal Richelieu*, 268–269.
17   Mazarin to the Maréchal de Guiche, 7 Jun. 1644, in Chéruel, *Lettres*, 1:735.
18   Decrees of the royal council, 6 Apr. 1644, CARAN, E 1688, ff. 41–42, and 7 May 1646, CARAN, E 1690, ff. 57–58; Bergin, *Cardinal Richelieu*, 272.
19   Quoted in T. de L., Review, *Revue critique d'histoire et de littérature*, vol. 7, ed. M. Bréal et al. (Paris: Ernest Leroux, 1879), 464–465n.
20   Bergin, *Cardinal Richelieu*, 268.

21   Geoffrey Treasure, *Richelieu and Mazarin* (London: Routledge, 1998), 9;
      Kleinman, *Anne of Austria*, 135–136.

39. A Wedding

1   Rea, *Life and Times*, 128–129; Aronson, *Madame de Rambouillet*, 195.
2   "La guirlande de Julie," BnF Richelieu, NAF 19735. The bound manuscript,
      acquired by the Bibliothèque Nationale de France, can be viewed digitally:
      https://gallica.bnf.fr/ark:/12148/btv1b8451620k/f1.item.
3   Craveri, *Age of Conversation*, 65–66; Myriam Maître, *Les précieuses: Naissance des
      femmes des lettres en France au XVIIe siècle* (Paris: Honoré Champion, 1999).
4   Aronson, *Madame de Rambouillet*, 195–196.
5   Ibid., 201.
6   Alfred Cramail, *Le Château de Rueil et ses jardins sous le cardinal de Richelieu
      et sous la duchesse d'Aiguillon* (Fontainebleau: E. Bourges, 1888), 24; Société
      Archéologique de Rambouillet, *Mémoires de la Société Archéologique de Rambouillet*,
      vol. 9 (Rambouillet: Alfred Douchin, 1891), 379.
7   Ibid., 380–382.
8   Antoine Arnauld, *Oeuvres de Messire Antoine Arnauld*, vol. 26, eds. Gabriel du Pac
      de Bellegarde and Jean Hautefage (Paris: Sigismond d'Arnay, 1779), xxiii.
9   Société Archéologique de Rambouillet, *Mémoires*, vol. 9, 379.
10   Hubert Carrier, "Women's Political and Military Action During the Fronde,"
      Political and Historical Encyclopedia of Women, ed. Christine Fauré (New York:
      Routledge, 2003), 40.
11   Jonathan I. Israel, *Conflicts of Empires: Spain, the Low Countries, and the Struggle for
      World Supremacy, 1585–1713* (London: Hambledon Press, 1997), 94.
12   Pierre Le Moyne, S.J., *Galerie des femmes fortes* (Paris: Antoine de Sommaville,
      1647), 252–253; Craveri, *Age of Conversation*, 35.
13   Ibid., 70.
14   Williams, *Love Affairs*, 203.
15   Bergin, *Cardinal Richelieu*, 270.
16   Ibid.; Wormeley, *Memoirs*, 1:152.
17   Eugène and Émile Haag, eds., *La France Protestante, ou Vies des Protestants
      françaises*, vol. 8 (Paris: Joël Cherbuliez, 1858), 313–314.
18   Quoted in Williams, *Love Affairs*, 205.
19   Luke 10:38–42.

40. Civil War

1   Ranum, *Paris*, 292–296.
2   Forrestal, *Vincent de Paul*, 223.
3   Kleinman, *Anne of Austria*, 204.
4   Vincent J. Pitts, *Embezzlement and High Treason in Louis XIV's France* (Baltimore:
      Johns Hopkins University Press, 2015), 17.
5   Collins, *The State*, 71.
6   Gustave Saige, ed., *Journal des Guerres civiles de Dubuisson-Aubenay, 1648-1652*,
      2 vols. (Paris: H. Champion, 1883-1885), 1:95; Pitts, *Embezzlement*, 20.
7   Ranum, *Paris*, 273–275.
8   Saige, *Journal*, 1:34–35.
9   Caroline Maillet-Rao, "Mathieu de Morgues and Michel de Marillac: The *Dévots*
      and Absolutism," *French History* 25/3 (2011): 283.

10   Jeffrey Merrick, *Order and Disorder Under the Ancien Régime* (Newcastle: Cambridge Scholars Publishing, 2007), 31–36; Wilkinson, *Louis XIV*, 18; Kleinman, *Anne of Austria*, 224–225.
11   Kleinman, *Anne of Austria*, 230–231.
12   Ibid., 232.
13   Ranum, *Paris*, 278.
14   Collins, *The State*, 70.
15   Ibid., 70–71.
16   Wormeley, *Memoirs*, 1:343.
17   Ibid., 344.
18   Wormeley, *Memoirs*, 1:348–349; Bonneau-Avenant, *Duchesse d'Aiguillon*, 373.
19   Martha Walker Freer, *The Regency of Anne of Austria, Queen Regent of France, Mother of Louis XIV*, vol. 1 (London: Tinsley Brothers, 1866), 346–347.
20   Wormeley, *Memoirs*, 1:348–349; Saige, *Journal*, 1:66.
21   Marie de Vignerot to Chavigny, 13 Nov. 1648, private collection; Digital record of sold item in Lot 182, consulted on Ader Auction House website: www.ader-paris.fr/en/lot/91644/8838058?npp=50&offset=150&.
22   Wormeley, *Memoirs*, 1:355.
23   Ibid., 357–358, 361.
24   Collins, *The State*, 71.
25   Ibid., 71.
26   Carrier, "Women's Political and Military Action," 40.
27   Emmanuel de Broglie, *Saint Vincent de Paul*, trans. Mildred Partridge (London: Duckworth, 1906), 203–204.
28   Vrillière to the Comte d'Harcourt, 22 Jan. 1649, in Chéruel, *Lettres*, 3:274.
29   Mazarin to the Comte de Harcourt, 1 Mar. 1649, in Ibid., 303.
30   Saige, *Journal*, 1:95.
31   Mazarin to Beringhen, 15 Mar. 1644, in Chéruel, *Lettres*, 1:622-623; Bergin, *Cardinal Richelieu*, 277.
32   Saige, *Journal*, 1:132, 146; Patin to Spon, 20 Mar. 1649, in Loïc Capron, ed., *Correspondance complète et autres écrites de Guy Patin* (Paris: Bibliothèque Interuniversitaire de Sainté, 2018), https://www.buisante.parisdescartes.fr/patin/.
33   Ranum, *Paris*, 290–291.

41. A Tenuous Peace
1   Aimé Champollion-Figeac, ed., *Mémoires de Mathieu Molé, Procureur Général, Premier Président du Parlement de Paris et Garde des Sceaux de France*, vol. 3 (Paris: Jules Renouard, 1856), 350–351n; Geoffrey Treasure, *Mazarin: The Crisis of Absolutism in France* (London: Routledge, 1995), 145.
2   Champollion-Figeac, *Mémoires*, vol. 3, 363n.
3   Ibid., 364n.
4   Treasure, *Mazarin*, 146.
5   Ibid., 146.
6   Collins, *The State*, 76.
7   Champollion-Figeac, *Mémoires*, vol. 3, 409, 443n.
8   Collins, *The State*, 71.
9   Kleinman, *Anne of Austria*, 212.
10   Jane McLeod, *Licensing Loyalty: Printers, Patrons, and the State in Early Modern France* (University Park: Pennsylvania State University Press, 2011), 16; Kleinman, *Anne of Austria*, 224–225.

11   Ibid., 212; Bonnaffé, *Recherches*, 22.
12   De Paul to Portail, 4 Mar. 1649, CCD, 3:413–414.
13   De Marillac to De Paul, Dec. 1648, in Sullivan, *Spiritual Writings*, 272, 295.
14   Diefendorf, *Penitence to Charity*, 190; Thompson, *Life*, 383–384.
15   Saige, *Journal*, 1:89.
16   Collins, *The State*, 72.
17   Kleinman, *Anne of Austria*, 212–213.
18   Isaac de Laffemas, *Procez burlesque entre Mr le Prince et Madame la duchesse d'Esguillon, avec les plaidoyers* (Paris: La Veuve Théodore Pépingué, 1649), 5–6, 12, 24–28.
19   Constant, *Mémoires*, vol. 2, 363.
20   Borély, *Histoire*, 477.
21   Rea, *Life and Times*, 94–95; Maître, *Précieuses*, 156.
22   Louis Couyba, *Études sur la Fronde en Agenais et ses origines: Le duc d'Épernon et le Parlement de Bordeaux (1648–1651)* (Villeneuve-sur-Lot: Reynaud Leygues, 1899), 7–8, 77–78, 152–153.
23   Patin to Spon, 5 Nov. 1649, in Capron, *Correspondance*.
24   Marie de Vignerot to Maillé-Brézé, 14 May 1649, private collection; Digital record of sold item in Lot 127, consulted on Ader Auction House website: www.ader -paris.fr/en/lot/20569/4386081?npp=100&offset=100&.
25   Patin to Vander Linden, 3 Jun. 1657, in Capron, *Correspondance*.

42. The Duc de Richelieu's Rebellion
1   *Recherches historiques de l'ordre du Saint-Esprit*, vol. 1 (Paris: Claude Jombert, 1710), 342.
2   Michel Vergé-Franceschi, *Guerre et commerce en Méditerranée, Ixe-Xxe siècles* (Paris: Éditions Veyrier, 1991), 165.
3   "Defense du Duc de Richelieu contre les violences de Madame la Duchesse d'Aiguillon," 1650, BnF Mitterand, 340, Fol-FM-14283, 1.
4   Hall, *Richelieu's Desmarets*, 47–48.
5   Wormeley, *Memoirs*, 2:198–199.
6   Ibid., 199–200; *Le Vray journal des assemblées du Parlement; contenant ce qui s'y est fait depuis la Saint Martin mil six cens quarante-neuf, jusques à Pasques 1651* (Paris: Gervais Alliot, 1651), 51.
7   "Defense du Duc de Richelieu," 1650, BnF Mitterand, 340, Fol-FM-14283, 1.
8   Prawdin, *Marie de Rohan*, 150.
9   Carrier, "Women's Political and Military Action," 46.
10   Kleinman, *Anne of Austria*, 213–214.
11   Wormeley, *Memoirs*, 2:200.
12   Ibid., 201; Borély, *Histoire*, 474–478.
13   Quoted in Prawdin, *Marie de Rohan*, 151. Cf. Wormeley, *Memoirs*, 2:201–203.
14   Treasure, *Mazarin*, 146.
15   Wormeley, *Memoirs*, 2:243–244; Saige, *Journal*, 1:225.
16   Armand-Jean de Vignerot du Plessis, early 1650, in Philippe de Tamizey de Larroque, ed., "Lettre du Duc de Richelieu à la duchesse d'Aiguillon," *Revue d'Aquitaine et des Pyrénées* 12/11 (1867): 138–140.
17   Kleinman, *Anne of Austria*, 213–214; Carrier, "Women's Political and Military Action," 41; Borély, *Histoire*, 478.
18   Wormeley, *Memoirs*, 2:208–209.
19   Kleinman, *Anne of Austria*, 214.

20   Ibid.; Carrier, "Women's Political and Military Action," 41; Collins, *The State*, 72;
      Wormeley, *Memoirs*, 2:241.
21   Ibid., 74.
22   Hall, *Richelieu's Desmarets*, 48.
23   Ibid., 4–5, 47, 243; Saige, *Journal*, 1:236–237.
24   Ibid., 237.
25   Wormeley, *Memoirs*, 2:202; Ranum, *Paris*, 295.
26   Saige, *Journal*, 1:273.
27   Ibid., 273–274.
28   Ibid., 274–279; Letter 6, 18 Jun. 1650, in Livet, *Muze Historique*, 1:19; "Defense
      du Duc de Richelieu," 1650, BnF Mitterand, 340, Fol-FM-14283.
29   Hall, *Richelieu's Desmarets*, 243.
30   Mazarin to Le Tellier, 18 Jun. 1650, in Chéruel, *Lettres*, 3:563.
31   Mazarin to de Lionne, 12 May 1651, in Ibid., 4:179.

43. Cardinal Mazarin's "Most Dangerous Enemy"

1   Paul Sacrron, "Ode a Madame la duchesse d'Aiguillon," *Les ouevres de monsieur
      Scarron* (Rouen: Guillaume de Luyne, 1663).
2   Mazarin to Colbert, 30 Sep. 1651, in Chéruel, *Lettres*, 4:455.
3   Mazarin to de Lionne, 15 Feb. 1651, Mazarin to Colbert, 30 Sep. 1651, and
      Mazarin to Le Tellier, 5 Oct. 1652, in Ibid., 27, 455, 5:246.
4   See for example *Advis aux Parisiens, servant de Response aux impostures du Cardinal
      Mazarin* (Paris: 1650), 25.
5   Kleinman, *Anne of Austria*, 220.
6   Marie-Pierre Terrien et al., *Le Château de Richelieu, XVIIe–XVIIIe siècles* (Rennes:
      Presses Universitaires de Rennes, 2009), 12; Mazarin to Le Tellier, 17 Jul. 1650, in
      Chéruel, *Lettres*, 3:607.
7   Mazarin to Le Tellier, 21 Jul. 1650, in Ibid., 615.
8   Mazarin to Le Tellier, 17 Jul. 1650, in Ibid., 609.
9   Patin to Spon, 18 Nov. 1650, Capron, *Correspondance*.
10   Borély, *Histoire*, 483–484.
11   Wormeley, *Memoirs*, 2:302.
12   Ibid., 302–303.
13   Carrier, "Women's Political and Military Action," 38.
14   Kleinman, *Anne of Austria*, 215.
15   Ibid., 216; Mazarin to Narmoutiers, 22 Sep. 1651, in Chéruel, *Lettres*, 4:436–437.
16   Kleinman, *Anne of Austria*, 216.
17   Ibid., 218; Collins, *The State*, 75.
18   Mazarin to De Lionne, 15 Feb. 1651, Mazarin to Le Tellier, 18 Feb. 1651, and
      Mazarin to De Lionne, 20 May 1651, in Chéruel, *Lettres*, 4:27, 31, 240–241.
19   Mazarin to De Lionne, 1 Apr. 1651, in Ibid., 114.
20   Ibid.
21   Wormeley, *Memoirs*, 2:330, 349–350.
22   Mazarin to de Lionne, 15 Feb. 1651, in Chéruel, *Lettres*, 4:27.
23   Patin to Spon, 1 Mar. 1650, in Capron, *Correspondance*; Borély, *Histoire*, 583.
24   Wormeley, *Memoirs*, 2:330, 349–350.
25   Kleinman, *Anne of Austria*, 218.
26   Wormeley, *Memoirs*, 2:353.
27   Kleinman, *Anne of Austria*, 218.

NOTES
437

28   Memorandum for Queen Anne, 12 May, in Jules Amédée Desiré Ravenel, ed.,
       *Lettres du Cardinal Mazarin a la Reine, a la Princesse Palatine, etc, écrites pendant sa
       retraite hors de France, en 1651 et 1652* (Paris: Jules Renouard, 1836), 61–62.
29   Mazarin to de Lionne, 23 May 1651, in Chéruel, *Lettres*, 4:208–209.
30   Kleinman, *Anne of Austria*, 235; Carrier, "Women's Political and Military Action,"
       42; Ranum, *Paris*, 295.
31   Alan James, *The Navy and Government in Early Modern France, 1572–1661*
       (Woodbridge: Boydell Press, 2004), 152.
32   Hall, *Richelieu's Desmarets*, 243–244; Saige, *Journal*, 2:74.
33   Saige, *Journal*, 1:248.
34   Ibid., 2:74; Mazarin to Le Tellier, 26 Jul. 1650, in Chéruel, *Lettres*, 3:628–629.
35   Mazarin to Onendei, 26 Nov. 1652, in Chéruel, *Lettres*, 5:475.
36   Mazarin to Mercoeur, 25 Sep. 1651, in Ibid., 4:444–445.
37   Mazarin to Onendei, 11 Aug. 1651, in Ibid., 384–385.
38   Alfred Rébelliau, ed., *La Compagnie secrète du Saint-Sacrement: Lettres du groupe parisien
       au groupe marseillais, 1639–1662*, vol. 2 (Paris: Honoré Champion, 1908), 55–56; Susan
       E. Dinan, *Women and Poor Relief in Seventeenth-Century France: The Early History of the
       Daughters of Charity* (Aldershot: Ashgate, 2006); Diefendorf, *Penitence to Charity*, 236.
39   Peter J. Edwards, "An Aspect of the French Counter-Reform Movement: La
       Compagnie du Saint-Sacrement," *Dalhousie Review* 56/3 (1976): 481, 485; René
       II de Paulmy de Voyer d'Argenson, *Les annales de la Compagnie du Saint-Sacrement*,
       ed. Henri Beauchet-Filleau (Marseilles: Saint-Léon, 1900), 196, 480.
40   Rébelliau, *Compagnie secrète*, 34.
41   Kleinman, *Anne of Austria*, 238.
42   Mazarin to Queen Anne, 18 Jul. 1651, in Chéruel, *Lettres*, 4:198.
43   Mazarin to De Lionne, 12 May 1651, in Ibid., 180.
44   Mazarin to De Lionne, 30 May 1651, in Ibid., 240–241.
45   Mazarin to De Lionne, 26 May 1651, in Ibid., 216; Mazarin to Queen Anne, 16
       Jul. 1651 in Ravenel, *Lettres*, 191–192.
46   Mazarin to Queen Anne, 3 Aug. 1651, in Ravenel, *Lettres*, 217–218.
47   Mazarin to Onendei, 19 Sep. 1651, in Chéruel, *Lettres,* 4:432.
48   Mazarin to Mercoeur, 25 Sep. 1651, and Mazarin to Colbert, 30 Sep. 1651, in
       Ibid., 443, 455.

44. The Sun King Rising
1   Kleinman, *Anne of Austria*, 241.
2   Ibid., 242; Coste, *Life and Works*, 1:326.
3   Kleinman, *Anne of Austria*, 242.
4   Hall, *Richelieu's Desmarets*, 244; Carrier, "Women's Political and Military Action,"
       38; Borély, *Histoire*, 490.
5   Insinuation, 21 Dec. 1651, CARAN, Y 188, f. 429.
6   Collins, *The State*, 75.
7   Mazarin to Onendei, 27 Sep. 1651, and Mazarin to D'Estrades, 8 Oct. 1651, in
       Chéruel, *Lettres*, 4:450, 460.
8   Mazarin to Colbert, 30 Sep. 1651, in Ibid., 455.
9   Colbert to Le Tellier, 16 Jan. 1652, in Pierre Clément, ed., *Lettres, instructions et
       mémoires de Colbert* (Paris: Imprimerie Impériale, 1861), 183.
10   Mazarin to the Abbé Fouquet, 26 Dec. 1651, in Chéruel, *Lettres*, 4:582.
11   Mazarin to the Abbé Fouquet, 11 Jan. 1652, in Ibid., 5:5.

12   Marie de Vignerot to Mazarin, 12 Jan. 1652, BIU Sorbonne, MSVC 2, ff. 30–30v.
13   Ranum, *Paris*, 292–299; Kleinman, *Anne of Austria*, 246.
14   Kleinman, *Anne of Austria*, 247.
15   Mazarin to Le Tellier, 7 Sep. 1652, and Mazarin to Servien, 7 Oct. 1652, in Chéruel, *Lettres*, 5:213, 358.
16   Pitts, *Embezzlement*, 25.

45. Governor of Le Havre

1   *Le Sacre et couronnement de Louys XIV, Roy de France et de Navarre, dans l'Église de Reims, le septième Juin 1654* (Reims: La Veuve François Bernard, 1654).
2   Patin to Spon, 5 Mar. 1652, in Capron, *Correspondance*.
3   Borély, *Histoire*, 494–496.
4   Louis XIV, *Lettres-patentes* confirming Marie de Vignerot in her charge as Governor of Le Havre, 15 Jun. 1653, quoted in Borély, *Histoire*, 501, 585–586.
5   Ibid., 501, 507–508.
6   *The Nature and Utility of Expeditions to the Coast of France* (London: G. Burnet, 1758), 6.
7   M. de Vigneul-Marville, *Mélanges d'histoire et de littérature*, vol. 2 (Paris: Claude Prudhomme, 1713), 14–15.
8   G. de Vaumas, *L'Éveil missionnaire de la France au XVIIe siècle* (Tournai: Bloud & Gay, 1949), 211n.
9   Joseph Rennard, ed., *Les Caraïbes, La Guadeloupe, 1635–1656: Histoire des vingt premières années de la Colonisation de la Guadeloupe après les Relations du R. P. Breton* (Paris: G. Ficker, 1929), 9–10; Giovanni Pizzorusso, *Rome nei Caraibi: L'Organizzazione delle missioni cattoliche nelle Antille e in Guyana (1635–1675)* (Rome: École Française, 1995), 203–204.
10   Jeanne-Françoise Juchereau de La Ferté de Saint-Ignace, O.S.A., *Histoire de l'Hôtel-Dieu de Québec* (Montauban: Jerosme Legier, 1751), 46–47, 92–93.
11   Gayle K. Brunelle, "Ambassadors and Administrators: The Role of Clerics in Early French Colonies in Guiana," *Itinerario* 40/2 (2016): 257–259; Philip P. Boucher, *Les Nouvelles-Frances: France in America, 1500–1815* (Providence: The John Carter Brown Library, 1989), 54; James Rodway and Thomas Watt, *Chronological History of the Discovery and Settlement of Guiana, 1493–1668* (Georgetown: Royal Gazette Office, 1888), 128–129.
12   LAC, MG17-A10, 216–219, 237–239; Juchereau, *Histoire*, 111–112.
13   Wormeley, *Memoirs*, 1:116.
14   Karen Britland, "Exile or Homecoming? Henrietta Maria in France, 1644–1669," in *Monarchy and Exile: The Politics of Legitimacy from Marie de Médicis to Wilhelm II*, ed. Philip Mansel and Torsten Riotte (Basingstoke: Palgrave Macmillan, 2011), 120–143; Borély, *Histoire*, 2:470.
15   Louis XIV to Dumé, 7 Dec. 1646, in Borély, *Histoire*, 2:607.
16   Marie de Vignerot to Innocent X, Mar. 1651, cited in Rawson Gardner, *History of the Commonwealth and Protectorate, 1649–1660*, vol. 2 (London: Longmans, Green, and Company, 1897), 95; Henrietta Haynes, *Henrietta Maria* (New York: G. P. Putnam's Sons, 1912), 267–269.
17   De Paul to Portail, 18 Oct. 1646, CCD, 3:93; Coste, *Life and Works*, 2:32.
18   Coste, *Life and Works*, 2:35.
19   Ibid., 36; Marie de Vignerot's last will and testament, BIU Sorbonne, MSRIC 151, f. 9.
20   Kleinman, *Anne of Austria*, 244.

21 Ibid.; Bergin, *Politics of Religion*, 230.
22 Mazarin to Marie de Vignerot, 26 Jul. 1656 and 5 Oct. 1656, in Chéruel, *Lettres*, 7:653, 691.
23 Mazarin to Marie de Vignerot, 25 May 1658, in Ibid., 8:371–372.
24 Mazarin to Marie de Vignerot, 3 Jun. 1658, in Ibid., 392–393; Louis XIV to Marie de Vignerot, 4 Jun. 1658, in Bonneau-Avenant, *Duchesse d'Aiguillon*, 421.
25 Mazarin to La Meilleraye, 21 May 1654, in Chéruel, *Lettres*, 6:166–168.
26 Borély, *Histoire*, 504–505, 509–512.
27 Mazarin to Marie de Vignerot, 25 May 1658, and Mazarin to the Abbé Fouquet, 25 May 1658, in Chéruel, *Lettres*, 8:371–373.
28 Mazarin to Nicolas Fouquet, 23 Dec. 1658, in Ibid., 9:122.
29 Mazarin to Nicolas Fouquet, 10 Sep. 1659, in Ibid., 296.
30 Marie de Vignerot to Colbert, 1666, in Jacquin and Duesberg, *Rueil*, 34.

46. The Petit Luxembourg
1 Eugène de Fontaine de Resbecq, *Les tombeaux des Richelieu à la Sorbonne* (Paris: Ernest Thorin, 1867), 30.
2 Louis Courajod, *Jean Warin: Ses oeuvres de sculpture et le buste de Louis XIV du musée du Louvre* (Paris: Honoré Champion, 1881), 37.
3 Bonnaffé, *Recherches*, 46–47. Information about various pieces owned by Marie de Vignerot may be found in the online databases of the Louvre Museum and the Metropolitan Museum of Art, among other institutions.
4 Ibid.
5 Francis X. J. Coleman, *Neither Angel nor Beast: The Life and Work of Blaise Pascal* (New York: Routledge and Kegan Paul, 1986), 210.
6 Brisacier, *Discours funèbre*, 10–11.
7 Léon Aubineau, ed., *Mémoires du P. René Rapin de la Compagnie de Jésus sur l'église et la société, la cour, la ville et le Jansénisme, 1644–1669*, vol. 2 (Paris: Gaume Frères and J. Duprey, 1865), 510.
8 Ibid., 510–511.
9 Ibid., 1:441–442, 2:133; Thompson, *Life*, 358.
10 Conley, "Madame de Sablé's Salon," 115–126.
11 Delumeau, *Catholicism*, 36.
12 Cousin, *Madame de Longueville*, 460–463.
13 Jean-François Senault, O.S.A., *La cie de la Mère Magdelaine de S. Joseph, religieuse carmélite deschaussée* (Paris: Veuve Jean Camusat, 1645). A second edition was published by Pierre Le Petit in Paris.
14 Abelly, *Vie du vénérable serviteur*, 176–178; Jacquin and Duesberg, *Rueil*, 115.
15 Diefendorf, *Penitence to Charity*, 254.
16 Jean-Étienne Grosez, S.J., *La vie de la Mère Marie-Madeleine de La Trinité, fondatrice des Religieuses de N. Dame de Miséricorde* (Lyon: Jean Thioly, 1696), 243, 247–249.
17 Forrestal, *Vincent de Paul*, 2:346–247, 265.
18 De Paul to Le Vacher, 15 Jul. 1653, CCD, 4:596–597.
19 Ibid., 549n.
20 Thérèse Peeters, "Trust and Mission: Seventeenth-Century Lazarist Missionaries in North Africa," *Trajecta* 26/1 (2017): 107–108.
21 Coste, *Life and Works*, 2:343, 351–354.
22 Ibid., 364–365.
23 Ibid., 35.

24 Brisacier, *Discours funèbre*, 22-23, 44-45.

25 Letter 18, 12 May 1652, *Muze Historique*, 1:241.

26 De Marillac to De Paul, 11 Jul. 1652, in Sullivan, *Spiritual Writings*, 400.

27 Coste, *Life and Works*, 2:428–434.

28 Christine M. Petto, "Mapping Forbidden Places and Places of the Forbidden in Early Modern London and Paris," *Environment, Space, Place* 2/1 (2010): 43.

29 Forrestal, *Vincent de Paul*, 212–214.

30 Ibid., 215.

31 Ibid., 216–219.

32 De Paul to Marie de Vignerot, 9 Nov. 1653, in Coste, *Life and Works*, 2:296.

33 Marie de Vignerot to De Paul, 17 Oct. 1654, in Ibid., 297.

34 Katherine A. Lynch, *Individuals, Families, and Communities in Europe, 1200–1800: The Urban Foundations of Western Society* (Cambridge: Cambridge University Press, 2003), 157.

35 Louis XIV, *Édit du Roy, portant Établissement de l'Hôpital-Général, pour la Renfermement de Pauvres Mendians de la Ville & Fauxbourgs de Paris, donné à Paris au mois d'Avril 1656* (Paris: L'Imprimérie Royale, 1658), 4, 10–11; Coste, *Life and Works*, 297–299, 301–302.

36 Edwards, "An Aspect," 481, 485, 491; Rébelliau, *Compagnie secrète*, 34; D'Argenson, *Annales*, 196, 480; Bergin, *Politics of Religion*, 110.

37 Edwards, "An Aspect," 480.

38 Diefendorf, *Penitence to Charity*, 236.

39 Louis de Rouvroy de Saint-Simon, *The Memoirs of the Duke of Saint-Simon on the Reign of Louis XIV and the Regency*, vol. 1, trans. Bayle St. John (London: Swan Sonnenschein and Co., 1900), 85.

40 Marie Louise Gude, C.S.C., "Madame de Miramion and the Friends of Saint Vincent de Paul," *Vincentian Heritage Journal* 20/2 (1999): 247; Coste, *Life and Works*, 1:327.

47. A Jesuit Visitor

1 Peter C. Phan, *Mission and Catechesis: Alexandre de Rhodes and Inculturation in Seventeenth-Century Vietnam* (Maryknoll: Orbis Books, 1998), 35; Klaus Schatz, *"Dass diese Mission eine der blühendsten des Ostens werde": P. Alexander de Rhodes (1693–1600) und die frühe Jesuitenmission in Vietnam* (Münster: Aschendorff, 2015), 31–32; Michel Barnouin, "La parenté vauclusienne d'Alexandre de Rhodes," *Mémoires de l'Académie de Vaucluse* 4 (1995): 9–40.

2 Delumeau, *Catholicism*, 66.

3 Gilles van Grasdorff, *La belle histoire des Missions étrangères, 1658–2008* (Paris: Perrin, 2007), 21; Ivo Carneiro de Sousa, "The First French in Macao: The Jesuit Alexandre de Rhodes (1591/3–1660)," *Revista de Cultura* 44 (2013): 127; Phan, *Mission*, 6–7.

4 Phan, *Mission*, 66–67; De Sousa, "First French," 128.

5 Delumeau, *Catholicism*, 66.

6 Alexandre de Rhodes, S.J., *Relazione de' felici succesi della santa fede predicate da' padre della Compagnie di Gesù nel regno de Tunchino* (Rome: G. Luna, 1650).

7 Phan, *Mission*, 67.

8 Eamonn Duffy, *Saints and Sinners: A History of the Popes* (New Haven: Yale University Press, 2006), 236; Van Grasdorff, *La belle histoire des Missions étrangères*, 24–25.

9 Barnouin, "Parenté vauclusienne"; Solange Hertz, trans., *Rhodes of Viet Nam: The Travels and Missions of Father Alexander de Rhodes in China and Other Kingdoms of the*

Orient (Westminster: Newman Press, 1966), 191–205; M.-M. Compère and D. Julia, "L'education en France du XVIe au XVIIIe siècle," *Annales* 32/3 (1977): 549–553.

10 Alexandre de Rhodes, S.J., *Histoire du Royaume de Tunquin, et des grands progrez que la predication de l'évangile y a faits* (Lyon: Jean Baptiste Devenet, 1651), n.p.

11 Alexandre de Rhodes, *Divers voyages et missions du P. Alexandre de Rhodes en la Chine et autres royaumes de l'Orient* (Paris: Sébastien Cramoisy, 1653), n.p.

12 Hertz, *Rhodes*, 220–221.

13 Lucien Campeau, S.J., "Le voyage du Père Alexandre de Rhodes en France, 1653–1654," *Archivum Historicum Societatis Iesu* 48 (1979): 69.

14 Phan, Mission, 67; Schatz, "*Dass diese Mission*," 191.

15 Van Grasdorff, *Belle histoire*, 32–34.

16 Alexandre de Rhodes, S.J., *Sommaire des diverses voyages et missions apostoliques* (Paris: Florentin Lambert, 1653), n.p.

17 Ibid.

18 Hertz, *Rhodes*, 238–239.

48. Negotiating with the Pope

1 Dirk van der Cruysse, *Louis XIV et le Siam* (Paris: Fayard, 1991), 145; Christian Windler, *Missionare in Persien: Kulturelle Diversität und Normenkonkurrenz im globalen Katholicizmus (17.–18. Jahrhundert)* (Cologne: Böhlau Verlag, 2018), 57.

2 Henri Chappoulie, *Aux origines d'une église: Rome et les missions d'Indochine au XVIIe siècle* (Paris: Bloud et Gay, 1943), 108; Michel Antoine, *Le coeur de l'état: Surintendance, contrôle general et intendances des finances, 1552–1791* (Paris: Fayard, 2003), 235; Richard F. Elmore, "The Origins of the Hôpital-Général of Paris" (Ph.D. diss., University of Michigan, 1975), 142; Campeau, "Voyage," 70.

3 Ibid., 74.

4 Rhodes to Propaganda Fide, 7 Mar. 1653, in Adrien Launay, ed., *Documents historiques relatifs à la Société des Missions-Étrangères*, vol. 1 (Paris: Lafoyle, 1904), 515–516.

5 Bagni to Pamphili, 7 Mar. 1653, in Ibid., 514–515.

6 Bagni to Innocent X, Jul. 1653, and Savoie-Nemours et al. to Propaganda Fide, 17 Sep. 1653, in Ibid., 1–3.

7 Phan, *Mission*, 67.

8 Mario Rosa, "The Catholic Clergy in Europe," in *The Cambridge History of Christianity*, vol. 7, eds. Stewart J. Brown and Timothy Tackett (Cambridge: Cambridge University Press, 2008), 91.

9 Alain Forest, *Les missionnaires françaises au Tonkin et Siam, XVIIe–XVIIIe siècles* (Paris: L'Harmattan, 1998), 55.

10 Phan, *Mission*, 67.

11 Louis Baudiment, ed., *Un mémoire anonyme sur François Pallu, principle fondateur des Missions Étrangères* (Tours: René et Paul Deslis, 1934), 23n; ASPF, SC, Indie orientali 193, ff. 399-400.

12 Pallu to M. X., 24 Jul. 1654, in Adrien Launay, ed., *Lettres de Monseigneur Pallu: Écrites de 1654 à 1684* (Paris: Les Indes Savantes, 2008), 711.

13 De Paul to Propaganda Fide, 1654, in Launay, *Documents*, vol. 1, 519; ASPF, SC, Indie orientali 193, f. 400.

14 Duffy, *Saints*, 236.

15 Brisacier, *Discours funèbre*, 37; Adrien Launay, *Histoire de la Mission de Cochinchine, 1658–1823* (Paris: Anciennes Maisons Charles Dauriol et Retaux, 1923), 3; L'Abbé

Évariste Régis Huc, *Christianity in China, Tartary, and Thibet*, vol. 3 (London: Longman, Brown, Green, Longmans, & Roberts, 1858), 99.

16   Pallu to Madame X, 18 Jun. 1657, in Launay, *Lettres*, 713–714; Forest, *Missionnaires*, 53.

17   Blouin to an unidentified recipient, 19 Aug. 1657, in Launay, *Lettres*, 714n; Audience of 11 Jul. 1657 and Resolution of 4 Aug. 1657, ASPF, Acta Congregationis, vol. 26, ff. 202, 256.

18   Response from France regarding the Duchesse d'Aiguillon's assignment of three bishops and apostolic to be sent to China, Tonkin, and Cochinchina, 26 Sep. 1657, Ibid., f. 449.

19   Brisacier, *Discourse funèbre*, 34.

20   Ibid., 37.

21   Alexander VII, bulls of episcopal nomination, Aug. 1658, and Barberini, decrees on the apostolic vicariates of Tonkin and Cochinchina, 17 Aug. 1658, in Launay, *Documents*, vol. 1, 24–27.

22   Forest, *Missionnaires*, 57–58.

23   Alexander VII to Marie de Vignerot, 30 Sep. 1658, in Brisacier, *Discours funèbre*, appendix.

24   Pallu to Madame X, 14 Oct. 1658, in Launay, *Lettres*, 716.

25   Foundation of annuity by the Duchesse d'Aiguillon, 18 Nov. 1658, AMEP, vol. 2, ff. 41, 421; Launay, *Documents*, vol. 1, 14–18.

26   Launay, *Documents*, vol. 1, 14–18.

27   See for example the gift of annuity from Miramion to Pallu, 29 Dec. 1664, AMEP, vol. 2, f. 445; Jacques de Bourges, *Relation du voyage de Monseigneur l'Évêque de Beryte, vicaire apostolique du royaume de la Cochinchine, par la Turquie, la Perse, les Indes, etc. jusqu'au Royaume de Siam et autres lieux* (Paris: Denys Bechet, 1666), 18.

28   D'Argenson, *Annales*, 185.

29   Van der Cruysse, *Louis XIV*, 155.

30   Van Grasdorff, *Belle histoire*, 46.

31   Forest, *Missionnaires françaises*, 64.

32   E. W. Hutchinson, "The French Foreign Mission to Siam during the XVIIth Century," *Journal of the Siam Society* 26/1 (1933): 9.

33   Huc, *Christianity*, vol. 3, 100–102.

34   Hutchinson, "French Foreign Mission," 9–12.

49. Saint Vincent

1   Forrestal, *Vincent de Paul*, 140.

2   Ibid., 192.

3   Abelly, *Vie du vénérable serviteur*, 2:358.

4   Coste, *Life and Works*, 2:164–165.

5   Forrestal, *Vincent de Paul*, 223, 228–230.

6   De Paul to Saveuses, 12 Jul. 1659, in Coste, *Life and Works*, 2:433; De Paul to Marie de Vignerot, 21 Nov. 1652, CCD, 4:507–508.

7   CCD, 2:677–678n.

8   De Paul to Ozenne, 21 May 1655, Ibid., 5:385.

9   De Paul to Get, 12 Mar. 1655 and 6 Aug. 1655, Ibid., 333, 412.

10   Quoted in Coste, *Life and Works*, 2:348.

11   Ibid., 355.

12   Ibid., 3:377–378.

13   Abelly, *Vie du vénérable serviteur*, 1:186.

14 Ibid.; Coste, *Life and Works*, 2:454–456.
15 Marie de Vignerot to Portail, quoted in Román, *Saint Vincent de Paul*, 343.
16 Abelly, *Vie du vénérable serviteur*, 1:145-147; Coste, *Life and Works*, 3:389.
17 Marie de Vignerot to Ducourneau, 1660, cited in Coste, *Life and Works*, 3:393.
18 Forrestal, *Vincent de Paul*, 194.
19 Coste, *Life and Works*, 3:398–399; Abelly, *Vie du vénérable serviteur*, 1:258–259.
20 Abelly, *Vie du vénérable serviteur*, 1:n.p.
21 Ibid., 129, 2:358.
22 Ibid., 221.

50. Missions for France

1 Brisacier, *Discours funèbre*, 8.
2 Pierre Oudin, O.S.A., *Le zèle du salut des âmes et la manière de s'y employer avec fruit* (Paris: Claude Josse, 1669).
3 Lesley to Gazil, 12 May 1664, in Launay, *Documents*, vol. 1, 272–273.
4 Alexander VII to Marie de Vignerot, 30 Sep. 1658, in Brisacier, *Discours funèbre*, appendix.
5 Ibid., 35–36.
6 JR, 11:133, 18:245–247, 21:269–273, 22:31–33; McShea, *Apostles*, 69.
7 Peeters, "Trust and Mission," 107.
8 Coste, *Life and Works*, 2:364–365.
9 Van der Cruysse, *Louis XIV et le Siam*, 141.
10 See for example Pallu to Marie de Vignerot, 23 Mar. 1663 and 1 Sep. 1663, AMEP, vol. 101, ff. 157–158, 189–192; Lambert de La Motte to Marie de Vignerot, 27 Mar. and 10 Oct. 1663, Ibid., vol. 858, ff. 9–14, 19–22; Pallu to Marie de Vignerot, 4 Aug. 1671, Ibid., vol. 107, ff. 206–208.
11 Pierre Bonnassieux, *Les grandes companies de commerce: Étude pour server a l'histoire de la colonisation* (Paris: Plon, 1892), 340; Claudius Madrolle, *Les premiers voyages Français à la Chine* (Paris: Challamel, 1901), xx–xxi.
12 Mathé Allain, "Colbert and the Colonies," *The French Experience in Louisiana*, ed. Glenn R. Conrad (Lafayette: Center for Louisiana Studies, 1995), 10.
13 Tara Alberts, *Conflict and Conversion: Catholicism in Southeast Asia, 1500–1700* (Oxford: Oxford University Press, 2013), 100. Cf. Bourges to his brother, 19 Feb. 1670, AMEP, vol. 650, f. 195.
14 Huc, *Christianity*, vol. 3, 101–110; Windler, *Missionare*, 59.
15 Ranum, *Paris*, 110–112.
16 Pallu et al. to Propaganda Fide, 1 Jul. 1658, in Launay, *Documents*, vol. 1, 292–295.
17 Fisquet, *France Pontificale*, vol. 2, 733–735.
18 Brisacier, *Discours funèbre*, 39–40.
19 *Lettres patentes* given by Louis XIV for the establishment of the Séminaire des Missions-Étrangères, in Launay, *Documents*, vol. 1, 324–327.
20 Cardinal-Nephew Chigi, official diary entry for 8 Jul. 1664, BnF Richelieu, Italien 1271, ff. 93–97; Letter 27, 12 Jul. 1664, in Livet, *Muze Historique*, 4:220.
21 Lesley to Gazil, 15 Apr. 1664, AMEP, vol. 200, ff. 248–262. Cf. Launay, *Documents*, vol. 1, 272–273.
22 Brisacier, *Discours funèbre*, 39–40.
23 Donation by Marie de Vignerot to Gazil and Poitevin, 5 Jun. 1663, CARAN, Y 204, f. 15v.
24 Donation by Marie de Vignerot to the MEP seminary, c. 1667, AMEP, vol. 2, f. 55.
25 Honorius Provost, ed., *Le Séminaire de Québec: Documents et biographies* (Quebec: Archives du Séminaire de Québec, 1964), 8–14, 18–25.

26   Alberts, *Conflict and Conversion*, 46, 85; Delumeau, *Catholicism Between Luther and Voltaire*, 67.

27   Hutchinson, "French Foreign Mission," 12–13.

28   Bourges to Marie de Vignerot, 20 Jan. 1665, AMEP, vol. 200, ff. 367–369.

29   Hutchinson, "French Foreign Mission," 13.

30   François Pallu, *Relation abbrégée des missions et des voyages des Evesques François, envoyez aux Royaumes de la Chine, Cochinchine, Tonquin, et Siam* (Paris: Denys Bechet, 1668), n.p., 6, 46.

31   Alberts, *Conflict and Conversion*, 40.

32   Campeau, "Voyage," 84; Hutchinson, "French Foreign Mission," 1–2.

33   Hutchinson, "French Foreign Mission," 13.

34   Alberts, *Conflict and Conversion*, 39.

35   Ibid., 100.

36   Donation by Marie de Vignerot in favor of apostolic vicars, 12 Feb. 1674, in Launay, *Documents historiques rélatifs à la Société des Missions-Étrangères*, 1:446-448.

37   Donation by Marie de Vignerot in favor of apostolic vicars, 12 Feb. 1674, AMEP, vol. 2, ff. 457–460; Memo in the French bishops, AMEP, vol. 23, f. 113; Forest, *Les missionnaires françaises au Tonkin et au Siam*, 64.

38   Marie de Vignerot's last will and testament, BIU Sorbonne, MSRIC 151, f. 11.

51. Madagascar

1   Smith, *Fealty and Fidelity*, 52–53, 57.

2   Nacquart to De Paul, 9 Feb. 1650, CCD, 3:570–572.

3   Ibid., 575–576.

4   Smith, *Fealty and Fidelity*, 59.

5   Mounier to De Paul, 5 Feb. and 6 Feb. 1655, in *Mémoires de la Congrégation*, 9:180–181, 185, 206; Henri Froidevaux, *Les Lazaristes à Madagascar au XVIIe siècle* (Paris: Poussielgue, 1903), 141, 173.

6   De Paul to Étienne, 22 Nov. 1659, CCD, 8:201.

7   De Paul to Jolly, 16 May 1659, in *Mémoires de la Congrégation*, 9:380–382.

8   Unidentified author to Propaganda Fide, 12 Jul. 1661, ASPF, SOCG, vol. 252, ff. 13–13v, 23.

9   Memorandom from Étienne to Marie de Vignerot, 1663 or 1664, in Marc Thieffry, *Saint Vincent de Paul et la mission Lazariste à Madagascar au XVIIe siècle* (Paris: Harmattan, 2017), 320–323.

10   Smith, *Fealty and Fidelity*, 74.

11   Antoine François, *Histoire générale des voyages, ou nouvelle collection de toutes les relations de voyages par mer et par terre*, vol. 11 (The Hague: Pierre de Hondt, 1755), 197.

12   Smith, *Fealty and Fidelity*, 74–75; Allain, "Colbert," 10.

13   Pallu to Marie de Vignerot, 28 Dec. 1670, in Launay, *Lettres*, 739.

14   Pallu to Marie de Vignerot, 4 Aug. 1671, Ibid., 741–742; Smith, *Fealty and Fidelity*, 74.

15   Brisacier, *Discours funèbre*, 3–31; Ralph M. Wiltgen, *The Founding of the Roman Catholic Church in Oceania, 1825 to 1850* (Eugene: Pickwick Publications, 2010), 167; Vaumas, *Éveil missionnaire*, 298; Jean Paulmier, *Mémoires touchant l'établissement d'une mission chrestienne dans le Troisième Monde: Autrement appelé, La Terre Australe, Meridionale, Antarctique, & Inconnue*, ed. Margaret Sankey (Paris: Champion, 2006). The last is a modern, critical edition of the work by the same title published by Cramoisy in 1663.

52. Ventures in the Near East

1   Charles-Léonce D'Anthelmy, *La vie de messire François Picquet, consul de France et de Hollande, a Alep, ensuite Evêque de Cesarople, puis de Babylone, Vicaire Apostoique de Perse, avec titre d'Ambassadeur du Roy auprès du Roy de Perse* (Paris: La Veuve Mergé, 1732), 9–10.

2   Picquet to Pope Alexander VII, 27 Feb. 1657, ASV, Segretaria di Stato, Vescovi e Prelati, vol. 36, ff. 330–331; Charles A. Frazee, *Catholics and Sultans: The Church and the Ottoman Empire, 1453–1923* (Cambridge: Cambridge University Press, 1983), 132–135.

3   Frazee, *Catholics and Sultans*, 134; John Joseph, *Muslim-Christian Relations and Inter-Christian Rivalries in the Middle East: The Case of the Jacobites in an Age of Transition* (Albany: SUNY Press, 1983), 40; Hussein I. El-Mudarris and Olivier Salmon, eds., *Le Consulat de France à Alep au XVIIe siècle: Journal de Louis Gédoyn, vie de François Picquet, mémoires de Laurent d'Arvieux* (Aleppo: El-Mudarris, 2009), 25.

4   Pallu to Marie de Vignerot, 14 Apr. 1662, AMEP, vol. 350, ff. 25–26.

5   D'Anthelmy, *Vie*, 224–225.

6   Ibid., 274; Fisquet, *France Pontificale*, vol. 2, 725.

7   Saint-Agnan to Marie de Vignerot, 4 Aug. 1662, BnF Richelieu, Français 25058, f. 1291; Superiors of the Missions of the Capuchin, Carmelite, and Jesuit Fathers, "Briève Relation de la Mission d'Alep en 1662," in Antoine Rabbath, S.J., ed., *Documents inédits pour servir l'histoire du Christianisme en Orient*, vol. 1 (Paris: Picard et Fils, 1907), 450–470.

8   Joseph, *Muslim-Christian Relations*, 44–45.

9   Brisacier, *Discours funèbre*, 19–20; Frazee, *Catholics and Sultans*, 135.

10   Marie de Vignerot's last will and testament, BIU Sorbonne, MSRIC 151, f. 10–11.

11   Windler, *Missionare*, 59, 208–209.

53. "Précieuse Ridicule"

1   Jean-Benoît Nadeau and Julie Barlow, *The Story of French* (New York: St. Martin's Press, 2006), 67.

2   Bergin, *Politics of Religion*, 88.

3   Edwards, "An Aspect," 479.

4   Quoted in Coste, *Life and Works*, 1:324.

5   Pitts, *La Grande Mademoiselle*, 160.

6   Marie-Augustine de Saint-Paul de Pommereuse, O.S.U., *Les chroniques de l'ordre des Ursulines*, vol. 1 (Paris: Jean Henault, 1673), 436–437; *Histoire de l'ordre de Sainte Ursule, depuis sa Fondation jusqu'à nos jours*, vol. 2 (Paris: Noyon, 1787), 212–213.

7   Diefendorf, *Penitence to Charity*, 214; Delumeau, *Catholicism*, 38.

8   Gude, "Madame de Miramion," 247.

9   Vimont to Saint-Bonaventure de Jésus, 3 Feb. 1660, AJC, Fonds du Collège Sainte-Marie, doc. 243.

10   Mother Duplessis de l'Enfant-Jésus to Marie de Vignerot and Armand-Jean de Vignerot du Plessis, c. 1664, LAC, MG17-A10, 237–239.

11   Juchereau, *Histoire*, 168.

12   Marie de Vignerot to Marie de Saint-Bonaventure, 29 Mar. 1664, Archives du Monastère des Augustines, HDQ-F1-A1/2:2, ff. 1–4.

13   Oudin, *Zèle du salut*.

14   Paul Ragueneau, S.J., *La vie de la Mère Catherine de Saint-Augustin, réligieuse hospitalière de la Miséricorde de Québec en la Nouvelle-France* (Paris: Florentin Lambert, 1671), iii.

15 Jean Puget de La Serre, *Thomas Morus, ou Le triomphe de la foy, et de la constance: Tragédie en prose, dediée à Madame la Duchesse d'Esguillon* (Paris: Augustine Courbé, 1642).
16 François Bluche, *Louix XIV*, trans. Mark Greengrass (Oxford: Blackwell, 1990), 401–402.
17 Marie de Vignerot's last will and testament, BIU Sorbonne, MSRIC 151, f. 9–11, 13.
18 Edwards, "An Aspect," 485; Forrestal, *Vincent de Paul*, 186, 211–219.
19 Louis Châtellier, *The Religion of the Poor: Rural Missions in Europe and the Formation of Modern Catholicism, c. 1500–c. 1800*, trans. Brian Pearce (Cambridge: Cambridge University Press, 1997), 37.
20 Bluche, *Louis XIV*, 401; Wilkinson, *Louis XIV*, 150.
21 Wilkinson, *Louis XIV*, 150.
22 Perwich to Williamson, 1 Apr. 1671, in William Perwich, *The Despatches of William Perwich, English Agent in Paris, 1669–1677*, ed. M. Beryl Curran (London: Offices of the Royal Historical Society, 1903), 141.
23 Pallu to MEP seminary directors, 6 Jul. 1662, in Launay, *Lettres*, 36.
24 *Mémoires de la Congrégation*, 9:423.

54. Uncle Armand's Legacy

1 Dandelet, *Renaissance*, 229–230.
2 Paul Scarron, "Ode à Madame la duchesse d'Aiguillon," *Les oeuvres de monsieur Scarron* (Rouen: Guillaume de Luyne, 1663).
3 Patin to Falconet, 21 Feb. 1667, in Capron, *Correspondance*; Chérot, *Étude*, 400.
4 Quoted in Ibid., 398.
5 Pierre Le Moyne, S.J., *Les triomphes de Louys Le Juste en la réduction des Rochelois et des autres rebelles de son royaume* (Reims: N. Constant, 1629); *Le portrait du roy passant les Alpes* (Paris: Sébastien Cramoisy, 1629).
6 Pierre Le Moyne, S.J., *La galerie des femmes fortes* (Paris: Antoine de Sommaville, 1647).
7 Charles de Vialart de Saint-Paul, *Histoire du ministère d'Armand-Jean du Plessis, Cardinal duc de Richelieu, sous le règne de Louys le Juste, XIII du nom* (Paris: Gervais Alliott, Antoine de Sommaville, Toussainct Quinet, Jean Gugnard, Edmé Pepingué, and Michel Bobin, 1649).
8 *Arrest de la cour de Parlement, contre un livre intitulé* Histoire du Ministère d'Armand Jean du Plessis, Cardinal Duc de Richelieu . . . *prononcé et executé l'unzième May 1650* (Paris: Imprimeurs et Libraires ordinaires du Roy, 1650), 4–5; Lair and de Courcel, *Rapports*, 271–272.
9 The letters appear in a separate, appended seventy-page section of the history entitled *Affaires d'Italie de l'Année MDCXXXIX, passées entre Madame la Duchesse et princes de la Maison de Savoye, contenant plusieurs lettres et Negotiations pour les Affaires du Piedmont et du Montferrat.*
10 This *Journal de M. le cardinal duc de Richelieu* would be published many times during Marie's lifetime, beginning with the first edition in 1648. Lair and De Courcel, *Rapports*, 276–277.
11 Ibid., 61; Armand-Jean du Plessis de Richelieu, *Traitté qui contient la méthode la plus facile et la plus asseurée pour convertir ceux qui se sont séparez de l'Église* (Paris: Sébastien Cramoisy, 1651).
12 Quoted in Claire Mazel, "Un tombeau d'exception: Comparaison des monuments funéraires de Richelieu à la Sorbonne et de Mazarin au collège des Quatre-Nations," in *Richelieu patron des arts*, edited by Jean-Claude Boyer et al. (Paris: Maison des sciences de l'homme, 2009), 178. See also Geneviève Bresc-Bautier et al., *La Sorbonne: Un musée, ses chefs-d'oeuvre* (Paris: Éditions Chancellerie des Universités de Paris, 2007), 53–57.

13   Bresc-Bautier et al., *La Sorbonne*, 57–58; Mazel, "Un tombeau d'exception," 178–179, 184–189.
14   Bergin, *Cardinal Richelieu*, 283.
15   Ibid., 282–283.
16   Ibid., 282, 284; Administration account for the Duchesse d'Aiguillon, AD Drôme, Fonds d'Aiguillon, 100 Mi 150.
17   Bergin, *Cardinal Richelieu*, 284; Patin to Falconet, 19 Jun. 1661, in Capron, *Correspondance*.
18   Letter 14, 4 Apr. 1657, *Muze Historique*, 2:320.
19   Pitts, *Grande Mademoiselle*, 122–123.
20   Ibid., 17.
21   Ibid., 135–136; Arvede Barine, *Louis XIV and La Grande Mademoiselle, 1652–1693* (New York: G. P. Putnam's Sons, 1905), 50-51; Bergin, *Cardinal Richelieu*, 282.
22   Bergin, *Cardinal Richelieu*, 283.
23   "Plaidoyé pour Madame la Duchesse d'Aiguillon, intervenante & defenderesse, contre Monsieur le Duc d'Orléans, & Mademoiselle d'Orléans sa Fille," *Arrest de la cour de Parlement intervenu dans la cause des Daubriots de Courfraut . . . et quelques autres plaidoyez* (Paris: Pierre Lamy, 1660), 44.
24   Ibid., 38–43, 63–64.
25   Ibid., 51–52.
26   Dandelet, *Renaissance*, 229–230.

55. Family Tragedies
1   Bergin, *Cardinal Richelieu*, 282–283.
2   M. Pinard, ed., *Chronologie historique-militaire*, vol. 6 (Paris: Claude Herissant, 1763), 353–354.
3   Hortense Mancini and Marie Mancini, *Memoirs*, ed. and trans. Sarah Nelson (Chicago: University of Chicago Press, 2008), 94–95.
4   Bonneau-Avenant, *Duchesse d'Aiguillon*, 431–434.
5   Ibid., 434–435.
6   Letter 14, 8 Apr. 1662, *Muze historique*, 3:490.
7   Charles-Louis Livet, *Les intrigues de Molière et celles de sa femme* (Paris: Isidore Lisieux, 1877), 146.
8   Letter 9, 20 Feb. 1660, *Muze historique*, 3:324–325.
9   Mazarin to Marie de Vignerot, 10 Sep. 1659, in Chéruel, *Lettres*, 9:847.
10   Mazarin to Marie de Vignerot, 15 Dec. 1659, in Ibid., 896; *Arrest solomnel du Conseil privé du Roy, du deuxième Mars 1660, donné en faveur des Generaux d'Ordres* (Paris: 1660).
11   Père Anselme, O.A.D., ed., *Histoire des Grands Officiers de la Couronne de France, avec l'Origine et le progrez de leurs families*, vol. 2 (Paris: Estienne Loyson, 1674), 376.
12   Ibid.; Marie de Vignerot to Sablé, 1665, in Bonneau-Avenant, *Duchesse d'Aiguillon*, 451.
13   Williams, *Love Affairs*, 206.
14   Ambassador Sagredo to the Doge of Venice, 10 Apr. 1663, in D. Bingham, *The Bastille* (New York: James Pott and Company, 1901), 317.
15   Petit to Bennet, 28 Mar. 1664, in Ibid., 317–318.
16   M. Chantelon to Dom Chantelon, 27 Apr. 1666, in Ibid., 319.
17   "Réqueste presentée à nosseigneurs de Parlement par le Duc de Richelieu, contre

Madame la Duchesse d'Aiguillon," c. 1666, BnF Richelieu, Clairambault 1135, ff. 24–48.

18   Louis de Rouvroy de Saint-Simon, *Mémoires de Saint-Simon*, vol. 12, ed. André de Boislisle (Paris: Librairie Hachette, 1896), 340–341.

19   Acarie to De Cabriès, 3 Jul. 1654, in Marguerite Acarie, *Lettres spirituelles*, ed. Pierre Sérouet (Paris: Les Éditions du Cerf, 1993), 79–80.

20   Letter 44, 7 Nov. 1654, in Livet, *Muze Historique*, 1:563.

21   Pallu to Mademoiselle de Richelieu [Marie-Madeleine de Vignerot du Plessis], 23 Jan. 1662, in Launay, *Lettres*, 723.

22   *La Feste de Versailles* (1668), 29.

23   Insinuation, 10 Aug. 1666, CARAN, Y 210, f. 355v.

24   Saint-Simon, *Mémoires*, vol. 12, 341–343.

25   Ibid., 343–344.

26   Resbecq, *Tombeaux*, 30.

27   Chrestien Leclercq, O.F.M., *Premier établissement de la foy dans la Nouvelle-France*. vol. 2 (Paris: Amable Auroy, 1691), 34.

28   Brisacier, *Discours funèbre*, 25–26.

29   Charles Terlinden, *Le Pape Clément IX et la Guerre de Candie (1667–1669)* (Louvain: Charles Peeters, 1904), 161.

56. Breast Cancer

1   Marie de Vignerot's last will and testament, BIU Sorbonne, MSRIC 151, f. 47.

2   *Le Mercure Hollandois, contenant les choses le plus remarquables de toute la Terre, arrivées en l'an 1675 jusqu'à l'an 1676* (Amsterdam: Henry and Theodore Boom, 1678), 215.

3   Marilyn Yalom, *A History of the Breast* (New York: Harper Collins, 1997), 205–240.

4   Aubineau, *Mémoires*, 2.

5   Marie de Vignerot's last will and testament, BIU Sorbonne, MSRIC 151, ff. 14, 31–32.

6   Maître, *Précieuses*, 161.

7   Antoine Blache, "Mémoires de l'Abbé Blache, docteur en théologie," *Revue rétrospective ou Bibliothèque historique*, vol. 1 (Paris: H. Fourneir Ainé, 1833), 36–41; "Sur la Revue rétrospective, et sur l'Histoire de l'Abbé Blache," *L'ami de la religion: Journal ecclésiastique, politique et littéraire* 90 (1836): 225.

8   Marie de Vignerot's last will and testament, BIU Sorbonne, MSRIC 151, ff. 5, 9–11.

9   Ibid., ff. 3–12.

10   Chérot, *Étude*, 401.

11   Bergin, *Cardinal Richelieu*, 7; Souleyreau, *Correspondance . . . 1632*, 8.

12   Marie de Vignerot's last will and testament, BIU Sorbonne, MSRIC 151, ff. 20–22.

13   Ibid., ff. 14–19.

14   Bergin, *Cardinal Richelieu*, 270; Williams, *Love Affairs*, 199.

15   Marie de Vignerot's last will and testament, BIU Sorbonne, MSRIC 151, ff. 24–26.

16   Transaction, 3 Mar. 1675, AD Drôme, Fonds d'Aiguillon, 100 Mi 134, ff. 1–2.

17   Ibid., ff. 3–4.

18   Ibid., f. 5.

19   Anne Somerset, *The Affair of the Poisons: Murder, Infanticide, and Satanism at the Court of Louis XIV* (New York: Saint Martin's Press).

20   Marie de Vignerot's last will and testament, 17 Apr. 1675, AD Drôme, Fonds d'Aiguillon, 100 Mi 157 (R1), ff. 16–18.

21   Gude, "Madame de Miramion and the Friends of Vincent de Paul," 247.

22   Marie de Vignerot's last will and testament, AD Drôme, Fonds d'Aiguillon, 100
      Mi 157 (R1), f. 18.
23   Mazel, "Tombeau," 186–187.

57. Carmel Once More

1   Mémoire concernant les prétentions élevées par la duchesse d'Aiguillon sur l'hôtel du
      Petit-Luxembourg, qui lui est contesté par le duc d'Enghien en vertu d'une substitution
      du cardinal de Richelieu (1676); Bergin, Cardinal Richelieu, 284.
2   Marie de Vignerot's last will and testament, BIU Sorbonne, MSRIC 151, ff. 20–22.
3   La Gazette de France (Paris: 1675), 284.
4   Bonneau-Avenant, Duchesse d'Aiguillon, 471.

58. A Forgotten "Femme Forte"

1   Ian MacLean, Woman Triumphant: Feminism in French Literature, 1610–1652
      (Oxford: Clarendon Press, 1977), 64–87.
2   Scarron, "Ode."
3   Alexander VII to Marie de Vignerot, 30 Sep. 1658, in Brisacier, Discours funèbre,
      appendix.
4   Ibid., 4–5, 7–8, 14, 30, 35–36.
5   Ibid., 10–11.
6   Ibid., 17, 22, 33–34.
7   Ibid., 12–13.
8   Fléchier, Oraisons funèbres, 52–56.
9   Ibid., 58–78.
10   Leclercq, Premier Établissement, vol. 2, 46–47, 92–93, 111–112, 223–225.
11   See for example Huc, Christianity, vol. 3, 99; Van Grasdorff, Belle histoire, 32–34.
12   Juchereau, Histoire, 223–225, 388.
13   Robert Challes, Un colonial au temps de Colbert: Mémoires de Robert Challes (Paris:
      Librairie Plon, 1931), 52–54.
14   I am quoting from the English translation that was published a few years later.
      Gatien Courtilz de Sandras, The Memoirs of the Comte de Rochefort, Containing an
      Account of What Past Most Memorable, under the Ministry of Cardinal Richelieu and
      Cardinal Mazarin (London: James Napton, 1696), 26–30, 325.
15   Sources related to these disputes may be found in AD Drôme, Fonds d'Aiguillon,
      100 Mi 126, 157 (R1), 157 (R2).
16   Simon Chardon de La Rochette, Histoire secrète du Cardinal de Richelieu, ou ses
      amours avec Marie de Médicis et Madame de Combalet, depuis Duchesse d'Aiguillon
      (Paris: Simon Chardon de La Rochette, 1808).
17   Alexandre Dumas, The Red Sphinx, or, The Comte de Moret, trans. Lawrence
      Ellsworth (New York: Pegasus Books, 2017), 45–47, 103–113, 378–379.
18   Jean-Joseph Dussault, ed., Oraisons funèbres de Bossuet, Fléchier, et autres orateurs
      (Paris: Louis Janet, 1820), 109–111.
19   Aubrey Thomas de Vere, Heroines of Charity (London: Burns and Lambert, 1854),
      109–110.
20   Saige, Journal, 1:237.
21   Curatorial file for object 1943.1349, Harvard Art Museums.
22   This is the view of Frédéric Bonnor, a director of the museums in Dinan.
23   Dussieux, Cardinal de Richelieu, 276, 289.
24   Ibid.

Index

125–127, 143, 181; Lazarists and, 199, 280,
311–313, 380; Louis XIV and, 268; Marie-Aimée
de Chevreuse and, 50; as Marquise de Combalet,
29–40; marriage of, 3–4, 23–26, 27–29, 30–32;
marriage proposals to, 71–72, 88–89; Mazarin
and, 179–181, 238, 239, 254–272, 275, 281,
282, 383–384; mentorship of young people by,
144–150; moral code of, 114; Native Americans
and, 276–277; patronage by, 44, 92–98, 108–110,
132–133, 147, 199–202, 298–299, 337, 344–345;
physical appearance of, 36, 101–102, 104; potential marriages of, 71, 81, 83, 87, 88–90, 98, 100,
104, 105, 106, 116–118, 144; power and influence
of, xii–xiii, 4, 78, 82–83, 129–130, 169, 215, 228,
356; as President of the Ladies of Charity, 204;
Queen Anne and, 179–184, 189, 242, 256, 260,
261, 266, 273, 339, 364; Queen Mother and, 53,
60–63, 65–66, 68–70, 71, 73, 79, 80, 81, 84, 154;
as Richelieu's heiress, 164–165; rumors about, 71,
79, 81–85, 89–91, 95, 98, 106, 168, 208, 212, 243,
244, 380–381; tomb and burial of, 372, 387, 389,
391–392; wardrobe of, 41; wealth of, 32; wedding
of, 27–29
Vignerot du Pont Courlay, René (father of Marie),
5–7, 11, 13, 21, 25, 32, 35, 163, 213
Vignerot family, 5–6

Villareal, Manoel Fernandes, 174, 175
Les Vingt-Quatre Violons du Roy, 219
Viole, Pierre (parlementary official), 233, 266
virginity, 12, 31, 58, 83, 88, 93–94, 95, 139, 168
Virgin Mary. *See* Mary of Nazareth
Visitation Sisters (Order of the Visitation of the
Virgin Mary), 128, 206
Viviers (city), 206
Vivonne, Catherine de. *See* Rambouillet, Catherine
Voiture, Vincent (poet), 58, 88, 103–104, 106, 112,
120, 183
Voltaire (François-Marie Arouet), 375
Vouet, Simon (artist), 175

W
warfare, 8, 18. *See also specific wars*
War of the Mantuan Succession, 65
Wars of Religion (French), 7, 10, 13, 18, 49, 62, 97,
207
Westphalia. *See* Peace of Westphalia

X
Xavier, Francis (saint), 295

Z
Zaga Christos of Ethiopia, 181

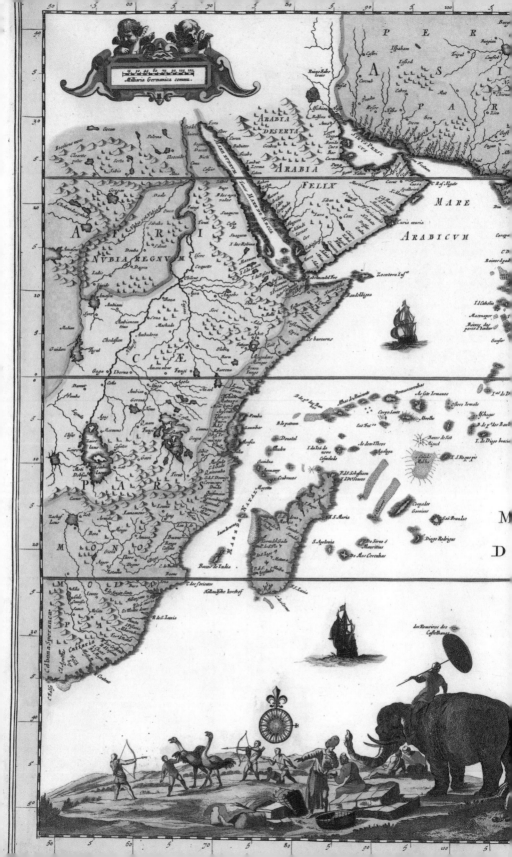